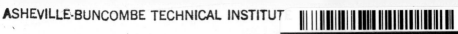

Fruit and Vegetable Juice Processing Technology

Second Edition

other AVI books on food processing

Amerine, Berg and Cruess	Technology of Wine Making, Second Edition
Arbuckle	Ice Cream
Brody	Fishery By-Products Technology
Desrosier	The Technology of Food Preservation, Third Edition
Goldblith, Joslyn and Nickerson	Thermal Processing of Foods
Hall and Hedrick	Drying of Milk and Milk Products
Hall and Trout	Milk Pasteurization
Heid and Joslyn	Fundamentals of Food Processing Operations
Joslyn and Heid	Food Processing Operations, Vols. 1, 2, and 3
Kramer and Twigg	Quality Control for the Food Industry, Third Edition, Vol. 1
Levie	Meat Handbook, Third Edition
Matz	Bakery Technology and Engineering
Matz	Cookie and Cracker Technology
Merory	Food Flavorings, Second Edition
National Canners Association	Laboratory Manual for Food Canners and Processors, Vols. 1 and 2
Peterson and Tressler	Food Technology the World Over, Vols. 1 and 2
Potter	Food Science
Sacharow and Griffin	Food Packaging
Sivetz and Foote	Coffee Processing Technology, Vols. 1 and 2
Smith	Potatoes: Production, Storing, Processing
Stansby	Fish Oils
Talburt and Smith	Potato Processing, Second Edition
Tressler, Van Arsdel and Copley	Freezing Preservation of Foods, Fourth Edition, Vols. 1, 2, 3, and 4
Van Arsdel	Food Dehydration, Vol. 1, Principles
Van Arsdel and Copley	Food Dehydration, Vol. 2, Products and Technology
Wall and Ross	Sorghum Production and Utilization
Weiser	Practical Food Microbiology and Technology, Second Edition
Woodroof	Peanuts: Production, Processing, Products
Woodroof	Tree Nuts, Vols. 1 and 2

Fruit and Vegetable Juice
Processing Technology

Second Edition

Edited by DONALD K. TRESSLER, Ph.D.
President, Avi Publishing Company
Westport, Connecticut

and MAYNARD A. JOSLYN, Ph.D.
Professor, Food Technology
Nutritional Sciences Department
University of California, Berkeley, California

in collaboration with a group of specialists

WESTPORT, CONNECTICUT
THE AVI PUBLISHING COMPANY, INC.
1971

THE AVI PUBLISHING COMPANY, INC.
Westport, Connecticut

REGISTERED AT STATIONERS' HALL
LONDON, ENGLAND 1961, 1971

Library of Congress Catalog Card Number: 75-138801
ISBN-0-87055-098-5

Printed in the United States of America
BY MACK PRINTING COMPANY, EASTON, PENNSYLVANIA

Contributors to Second Edition

DR. GEORGE E. FELTON, Vice President, Technical Division, Dole Company, Honolulu, Hawaii

DR. SHERMAN LEONARD, Lecturer in Food Technology, Department of Food Science, University of California, Davis, Calif.

DR. B. S. LUH, Food Technologist, Department of Food Science, University of California, Davis, Calif.

DR. HANS LÜTHI, Federal Experimental Station for Fruit, Wine, and Garden Crops, Wadenswil, Switzerland

DR. JAMES C. MOYER, Professor of Food Science and Technology, New York State Agricultural Experiment Station, Cornell University, Geneva, N.Y.

DR. CARL S. PEDERSON, Professor Emeritus, Food Science and Technology, New York State Agricultural Experiment Station, Cornell University, Geneva, N.Y.

MR. G. FRANK PHILLIPS, Manager, Research and Quality Control, Dr. Pepper Company, Dallas, Tex.

DR. HORTON E. SWISHER, Director of Research and Development Division and (Mrs.) L. H. Swisher, formerly Research Librarian, Sunkist Growers, Inc., Ontario, Calif.

DR. MATTHEW K. VELDHUIS, Chief, U.S. Fruit and Vegetable Products Laboratory, Southern Research and Development Division, Agricultural Research Service, U.S. Department of Agriculture, Winter Haven, Fla.

Preface to the Second Edition

In preparing the Second Edition of *Fruit and Vegetable Juice Processing Technology,* the book has been completely rewritten. With the exception of Dr. Hans Lüthi, Dr. Carl S. Pederson, Mr. G. Frank Phillips, Dr. Horton E. Swisher and Dr. Matthew K. Veldhuis, the collaborators who prepared the several chapters were not those who aided in writing the 1961 Edition.

The book contains few references to work carried out prior to 1940; in fact in order to save space, most of the references to studies carried out before 1960 have been dropped. Those who want a complete picture of the early development of the fruit and vegetable juice industry should consult the 1938 Edition of *Fruit and Vegetable Juices* by Tressler, Joslyn and Marsh, *The Chemistry and Technology of Fruit and Vegetable Juice Production* written by Tressler and Joslyn in 1954, and the First Edition (1961) of *Fruit and Vegetable Juice Processing Technology.* In order to save space, the general considerations of microbiology, plant location and design, plant sanitation, waste disposal, "syrup algebra," and preservation by addition of chemical preservatives, by freezing and dehydration, have been omitted. If these had been included, the price of the book would be beyond the reach of most students. However, the common methods of preserving the various fruit juices are considered in the discussion of each juice.

All of the presentations have been rewritten and brought up-to-date, giving details of the methods now used for the manufacture, preservation, concentration, and packaging of all important fruit and vegetable juices. Important additions to the literature on fruit juices are the chapters on "tropical fruit beverages" and "imitation fruit juice beverages."

In addition to the collaborators who have written the several chapters, the Editors wish to thank the following for their invaluable aid.

Mr. Herbert Aitken, Cooksville, Ontario, Canada

Mrs. Margaret N. Albury, N.Y.S. Agricultural Experiment Station, Geneva, N.Y.

Mr. Bertram Brink, Lemon Products Div., Sunkist Growers, Corona, Calif.

Dr. Joseph H. Bruemmer, U.S. Fruit and Vegetable Products Laboratory, Winter Haven, Fla.

Miss Ming Chang, Food Processing Institute, Hsin Chu, Taiwan

Miss Tai En Chang, Food Processing Institute, Hsin Chu, Taiwan

Mr. I. E. Friedman, Welch Grape Juice Co., Westfield, N.Y.
Mr. Howard Hall, Rietz Mfg. Co., Santa Rosa, Calif.
Mr. George C. C. Jang, Ma Ling Canned Goods Co., Taipei, Taiwan
Mr. Harvey Leslie, Brown International Corp., Covina, Calif.
Miss Rose L. Lin, Food Processing Institute, Hsin Chu, Taiwan
Mr. Y. T. Lin, Food Processing Institute, Hsin Chu, Taiwan
Miss Man Mei Lu, Food Processing Institute, Hsin Chu, Taiwan
Miss Sylvia Chang Lu, Food Processing Institute, Hsin Chu, Taiwan
Mr. J. E. McDaniel, Lemon Products Div., Sunkist Growers, Corona, Calif.
Mr. Karl Manke, Technical Agricultural Co-ordinator, Dole Company, Honolulu, Hawaii
Dr. Ferdinand P. Mehrlich, Food Laboratories, U.S. Army, Natick, Mass.
Mr. Sylvester D. Phillippi, Economic and Statistical Analysis Division, U.S. Dept. Agr., Washington, D.C.
Mrs. Jean Stevens, Librarian, Dole Company, Honolulu, Hawaii
Dr. J. T. Tseng, Food Processing Institute, Hsin Chu, Taiwan
Mr. James Walker, Lemon Products Div., Sunkist Growers, Corona, Calif.
Dr. J. G. Woodroof, Griffin, Ga.

DONALD K. TRESSLER
MAYNARD A. JOSLYN

August 1970

Preface to the First Edition

The world's fruit and vegetable juice industry has made great strides in the past decade. Preserved fruit and vegetable juices, formerly consumed principally by Americans, have become staple articles of the diet of the British, Canadians, Australians, South Africans, and most of the peoples of Western Europe. Notable advances have been made in the technology of the production and preservations of grape, apple, and black currant juices, and passion fruit and various other fruit juices. Concentration by freezing and freeze drying and puff and foam-mat drying procedures have been greatly improved and are being applied in the commercial production of dehydrated tomato, orange and other citrus juices. Extraction and processing equipment has been modified and improved both in Europe and in the United States. Continuous production of apple and grape juices has been introduced leading to improved quality and lower production costs. Many new fruit juice beverages, unknown a decade ago, are now being produced and distributed. Fruit juices are being produced and shipped in bulk for retail distribution as chilled juices. The distribution of chilled citrus juices, first marketed in the early 1930's has been revived and greatly expanded. New methods for the production of sterile concentrates and aseptic filling into tank trucks, tank cars, and drums and lined shipping containers have been developed and applied to the shipment of tomato concentrates from centers of production to centers of processing and distribution.

The marketing of juices such as grapefruit and pineapple, which in the past have had limited sales, has been greatly expanded by the introduction of grapefruit pineapple drinks. These are beverages prepared by blending grapefruit juice or concentrate with pineapple juice or concentrate and adjustment to a fixed Balling acid ratio by addition of sugar, citric acid and water. The grapefruit pineapple drink was successfully marketed and today large quantities of pineapple concentrate are being imported from Hawaii and the Philippines for the production of this and other pineapple drinks. Comminuted whole orange and lemon juices have been developed in Europe and Israel and are being used widely in the formulation of improved citrus beverage bases. While the consumption of carbonated beverages, usually artificially colored and flavored, still surpasses that of fruit and vegetable juices, interest in the preparation of beverage bases and syrups with pure fruit juices for color and flavor has revived. More stringent regulation and restriction on the use of artificial colors and flavors both in Europe and United States has resulted in the introduction and marketing of real fruit flavored and colored beverages. The recently introduced fruit flavored lemon juice products have had an excellent market reception.

Vitamin and mineral fortified food and beverage products have long been marketed in the United States and elsewhere and interest in this field has been revived by the successful introduction and marketing of diet controlling products. Powdered beverage bases compounded of carotene, ascorbic acid, citric acid, sugar and coloring and flavoring additives have been marketed recently. There is interest now in supplanting these products with pure fruit and vegetable products fortified with added vitamins. Fruit juices standardized as to vitamin C content by blending with natural fruit products high in vitamin C content, such as acerola or guava, or with ascorbic acid have been produced and these are finding more favor in the United States and in Europe.

Because of these great advances in the science and technology of the production and preservation of fruit and vegetable juices, the writing of a new book *Fruit and Vegetable Juice Processing Technology* was undertaken instead of the easier task of revising our 1954 book, *The Chemistry and Technology of Fruit and Vegetable Juice Production.*

New chapters and sections presented in Fruit and Vegetable Juice Processing Technology which were not included in either of the earlier books on the subject, include the following:

The Microbiology of Fruit Juices
Continuous Fruit Juice Production
Concentration by Freezing
The Manufacture and Preservation of Black Currant Juice
Analytical Methods for Routine and Research Use

Only the references actually cited in the text are included in the bibliographies given at the end of each chapter. The references cited do not include all of the technical papers on fruit and vegetable juices. For papers published before 1938, the reader is referred to Fruit and Vegetable Juices, and, for the many published between 1938 and 1954, to the Chemistry and Technology of Fruit and Vegetable Juice Production, both published by the Avi Publishing Co.

Twenty-five fruit and vegetable juice experts collaborated with us in the preparation of this, the most comprehensive treatise on the technology of fruit and vegetable juice production ever undertaken. Six of these twenty-five collaborators are foreign technologists. Their assistance has made possible the presentation of much detailed information concerning the Canadian, British, French, German and Australian juice industries.

In addition to the collaborators contributing one or more chapters or sections to this book, the authors wish to thank the many others who aided in various ways in the preparation of the manuscript. It is impossible to list all of those who helped in the work, but the assistance of the following has been noteworthy: W. E. Baier, P. V. Foster, H. H. Holton, H. P. Milleville, G. Stanley, and J. W. Stevens.

Further, the authors wish to thank the hundred companies and individuals who furnished illustrative materials. Credit is given to the donor directly under each figure.

DONALD K. TRESSLER
MAYNARD A. JOSLYN

September 1961

Contents

CHAPTER 1

D. K. Tressler

Historical and Economic Aspects Of the Juice Industry

PART 1. INTRODUCTION

Fresh apple juice has been an article of commerce since colonial times, but until the late 1920's no effort was made to preserve it by canning or bottling, although in some instances it was kept from fermenting by the addition of sodium benzoate (see p. 18).

Concord grape juice was the first fruit juice to be preserved by pasteurization. The procedure, invented by Welch, involved hot pressing the crushed grapes (see Chap. 7), filling the hot juice into carboys, which were then closed with paraffined corks. The carboys were stored in a cool cellar for three months or longer. During this period all of the pulp and other suspended matter settled. The clear juice was siphoned off, and filled into bottles, taking care to leave at least two inches headspace. The bottles were crowned and then placed in racks. Pasteurization was effected by holding the racks of bottles in water at 180° to 190°F.

It was not until the 1930's that flash pasteurization of fruit juices was perfected (Tressler 1938) and applied commercially to many different fruit juices. Flash-pasteurized juices retain the true fruit flavor and aroma much better than those preserved by holding pasteurization or sterilization; further, because all of the air in the containers is eliminated and the cans or bottles are filled completely full with hot juice, the flash pasteurized juice changes little in flavor during storage. Because of the much better quality of the flash pasteurized juice, and the simple procedure required to preserve it, the industry progressed rapidly during the 1930's and 1940's. The rapid rise in popularity of canned and bottled fruit juices has been "one of the most significant and colorful developments of the food business in the Twentieth Century" (Western Canner and Packer 1936).

GENERAL TRENDS

The meteoric rise of canned fruit and tomato juices from 1930 to 1968 is shown in Tables 1,9,10,12–14. The rapid rise in the canning of juices during the 1930 to 1940 to 1950 decades is particularly noteworthy.

In less than 35 years, the commercial output of fruit and vegetable juices in this country soared from almost nothing to approximately 900,000,000 gal, including juice in drinks but excluding home-prepared juices, and accounts for 75% of world production.

By 1945, the national commercial juice pack had jumped to 370,000,000 gal and a per capita consumption of 21 lb in 1946. Practically all of this was canned pasteurized single-strength juice, very largely tomato, citrus and pineapple juice. Since 1945, the trend in the pasteurized juice pack has been only slightly upward, ranging from 90,000,000 cases in 1949 to a peak of 121,000,000 in 1956. It has averaged only slightly above the 1945 figure because of the rising flood of frozen concentrated orange juice, which, because of its "fresh" flavor, has replaced much of the pasteurized citrus juice. The total hot pack of all juices has been maintained by further expansion of the pack of tomato and deciduous fruit juices during 1945–1960. The continued increase in citrus juice consumption after 1945 has been nearly all frozen concentrated juice, mostly Florida concentrated orange juice.

FRUIT JUICE DRINKS

Since 1950, consumption of noncarbonated fruit juice drinks has become increasingly important in the United States; both canned and pasteurized ready-to-serve drinks and concentrates, frozen or pasteurized, are of great importance. The fruit drinks are diluted fruit juices containing added water, sugar and sometimes citric acid, gum arabic, artificial color and flavors. No national standards have been established for the composition of fruit drinks but canners have proposed a minimum juice content of 40% and the more important ones probably contain at least 50% fruit juice. However, a few may contain less than 40%. A few of these fruit drinks contain only one kind of juice such as grape, lemon or orange, the largest seller of the unblended fruit drinks.

Imitation orange juice drinks, especially those fortified with vitamin C, have become very popular in recent years. Many persons prefer them to those prepared by diluting frozen orange concentrate, probably because of the deterioration of orange juice during vacuum concentration.

A number of other fruit drinks manufactured from fruit juice and other natural ingredients are popular and are sold nationally. These include grape, apple, cherry, wild berry and certain fruit blends such as Florida punch, pineapple-grapefruit, orange-pineapple, and citrus blends.

ORANGE JUICE

Figures 1 and 2 show the rapid upward trend in per capita consumption of processed citrus, compared with fresh sales in the United States and the tendency to level off in recent years at an average of about 36 lb or about 60% of total consumption of oranges in terms of the fresh fruit equivalent. Since 1953, changes in *total* per capita consumption of all oranges have

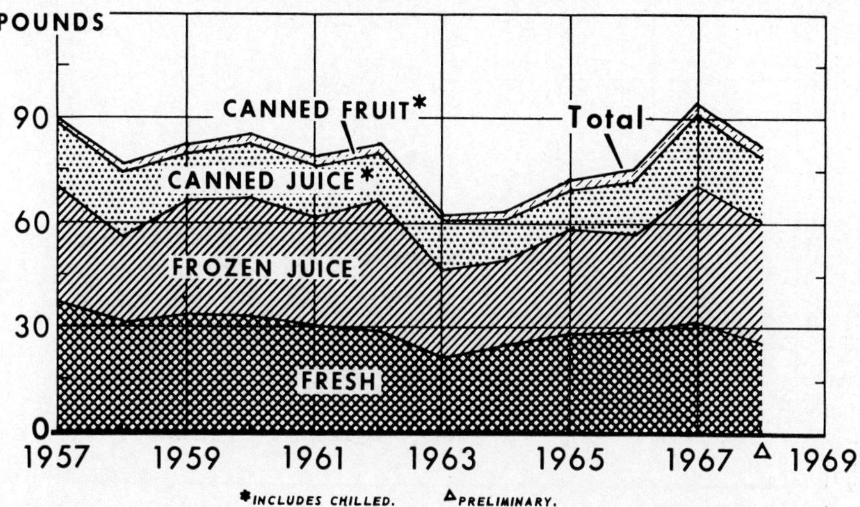

Courtesy of Economic Research Service, U.S. Dept. Agr.

FIG. 1. UNITED STATES CITRUS CONSUMPTION PER PERSON

Fresh; frozen juice; canned juice; canned fruit.

paralleled *processed* consumption rather closely. United States total production and processed utilization of oranges roughly paralleled, at a somewhat higher level, the per capita consumption lines shown in this figure, making allowance for a marked increase in United States population and some increase in exports.

Approximately 99% of all the oranges *processed* in the United States is used for making some form of juice product or marmalade and probably less than 1% for canned *segments.* Hence the quantity reported by the United States Crop Reporting Service as used for *processing* may be considered as a fair measure of the approximate quantity of fruit utilized for orange *juice* in all forms. Before canned orange juice was introduced commercially in 1929 only about 1% of the national orange crop was processed. As a result of the phenomenal growth of pasteurized canned juice, by 1945–1947 an average of over 1,400,000 tons of oranges and tangerines were processed, almost all for juice products, or at least 30% of a national crop of 4,600,000 tons. By 1959, about 3,500,000 tons were processed or 64% of a crop of over 5,600,000 tons.

Until 1940, all processed orange juice was *single-strength* canned pasteurized juice. By 1945, about 65% was single-strength and 35% hot

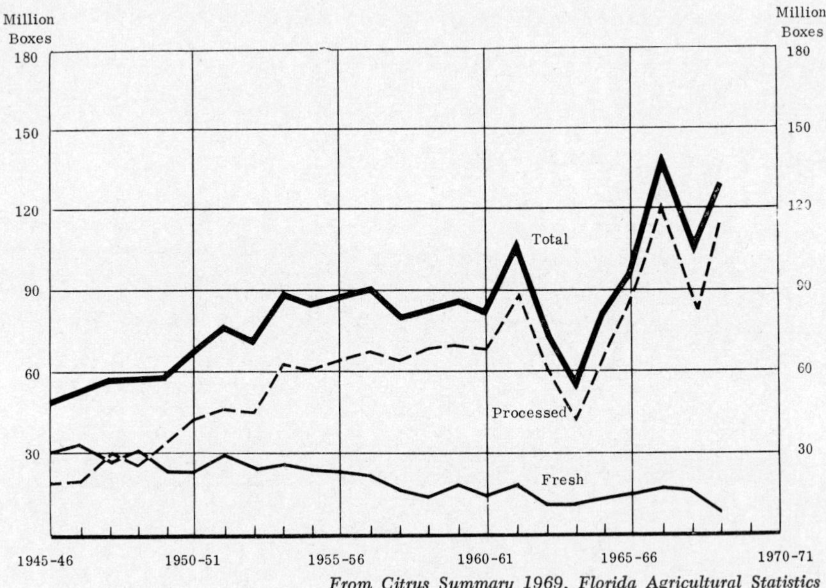

From Citrus Summary 1969, Florida Agricultural Statistics

FIG. 2. FLORIDA ORANGES: PRODUCTION AND UTILIZATION

Crop years 1945–1946 through 1968–1969.

pack concentrate. Consumption of all pasteurized orange juice reached a per capita peak of about 20 lb equivalent fresh weight in 1947, with a pack of over 34,000,000 cases. About 20% of this pack was concentrate and 80% single-strength juice. Since then the single-strength hot pack has decreased greatly chiefly because of competition from the great increase in frozen concentrate first introduced in 1945. By 1967–1968, per capita consumption of pasteurized juice had declined to 2.5 lb and the pack to only a little over 12,500,000 cases or less than 10% of the total pack of all forms of orange juice.

Frozen orange juice, practically all in concentrated form, rose very rapidly after World War II reaching a consumption of about 30 lb fresh weight in 1958–1959 with a pack of over 98,000,000 cases utilizing over 75% of the total pack of all forms of orange juice.

Chilled fresh orange juice has become commercially important since 1953 and by 1967–1968 production was nearly 25% of all orange juice produced.

Prior to 1946, Florida and California produced approximately equal quantities of oranges. Since then, the production of oranges in Florida has increased greatly, until now Florida produces approximately double

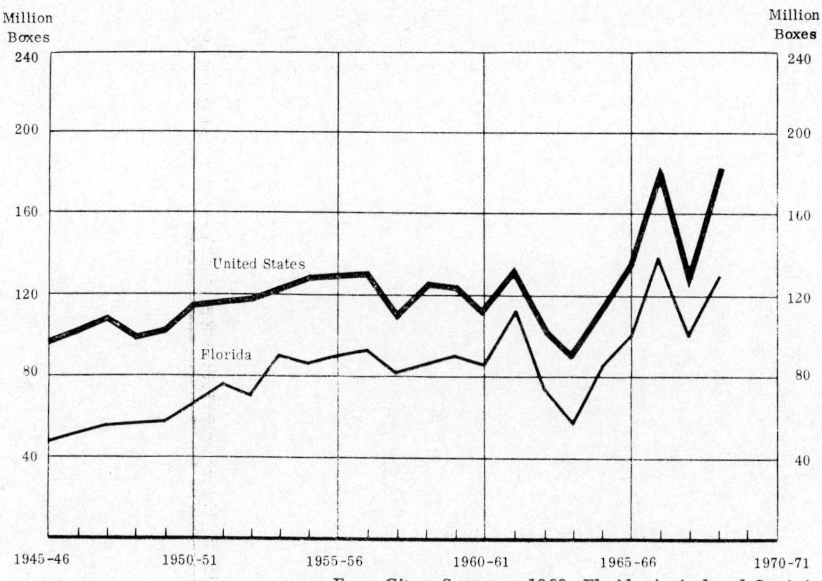

From Citrus Summary 1969, Florida Agricultural Statistics

FIG. 3. ORANGES: PRODUCTION FOR UNITED STATES AND FLORIDA

Crop years 1945–1946 through 1968–1969.

as many oranges as California (see Fig. 3). California and Florida contributed about equal proportions of all oranges processed in the United States for juice before the Second World War. However, the orange juice pack grew very slowly in California while it increased spectacularly in Florida, utilizing even more for orange juice than the great increase in the state's total production, resulting in a significant decrease in sales to the fresh market. By 1945–1947, Florida contributed about 75% of the United States pack of all kinds of orange juices and California less than 20%. By 1959, Florida's total production of oranges and the quantity processed had both risen so greatly that the state accounted for almost 90% of the national total utilized for juice while California's contribution had fallen to only about 10%.

The relative proportion of orange juice made in California, compared to that produced in Florida, has continued to fall; in 1967, only 320,000 cases of canned orange juice were packed in California and Arizona combined. The production of juice from Florida citrus is indicated in Table 1.

Over 95% of Florida's orange crop is Valencia and early mid-season varieties other than the Temple and over 80% of these have been processed in recent years as compared with only about one-third of the Temple

TABLE 1

YEARLY PRODUCTION OF CANNED GRAPEFRUIT JUICE, ORANGE JUICE, BLENDED JUICE, TANGERINE JUICE, BLENDED TANGERINE AND ORANGE JUICE, IN CASES

Seasons	Grapefruit	Orange	Combination	Tangerine
1930–31	412,066	61,119		
1931–32	247,652	36,362		
1932–33	725,967	64,319		
1933–34	610,115	57,678		
1934–35	2,236,726	240,967		
1935–36	1,758,497	161,952	84,958	
1936–37	3,918,604	498,206	271,599	
1937–38	3,370,002	806,183	547,329	
1938–39	6,190,290	926,278	699,295	
1939–40	4,682,057	2,851,373	1,402,662	
1940–41	10,646,985	3,078,043	2,537,437	
1941–42	6,179,780	3,466,302	2,305,309	
1942–43	15,192,952	2,429,251	3,675,919	
1943–44	16,778,124	7,075,467	6,176,168	
1944–45	12,025,099	13,935,381	7,744,505	
1945–46	15,089,056	18,420,825	12,267,484	523,499
1946–47	8,583,317	17,294,334	10,033,898	1,260,607
1947–48	7,986,515	25,593,134	11,893,735	591,964
1948–49	8,842,615	16,757,028	10,252,131	985,137
1949–50	7,894,334	17,419,271	6,768,370	1,788,057
1950–51	12,741,553	20,021,348	8,711,255	1,158,311
1951–52	8,735,247	19,321,032	6,401,978	456,084
1952–53	10,853,520	16,906,938	5,706,980	747,898
1953–54	14,882,282	17,790,137	6,401,720	800,120
1954–55	10,784,135	16,517,861	4,993,758	427,562
1955–56	12,805,164	15,499,755	5,264,874	555,213
1956–57	12,463,852	16,827,801	5,188,076	714,889
1957–58	9,483,915	17,845,767	4,885,049	302,515
1958–59	10,093,349	13,258,882	4,216,943	772,484
1959–60	9,323,417	15,128,446	4,382,212	231,700
1960–61	9,130,870	10,797,688	3,100,678	552,706
1961–62	10,190,156	13,762,433	3,862,507	262,102
1962–63	8,863,978	11,212,083	3,117,341	316,907
1963–64	5,142,936	7,682,293	2,416,174	220,909
1964–65	9,769,891	10,333,801	2,434,848	187,254
1965–66	12,089,959	11,363,420	2,683,633	62,115
1966–67	17,844,385	14,411,891	3,310,548	155,698
1967–68	13,299,686	9,817,125	2,042,831	49,349
1968–69	15,444,928	11,385,610	2,295,086	92,491

Source: Florida Canners Association, Winter Haven, Fla.

crop. Over 35% of California Valencias are usually processed as compared with only about 12% of its Navel and miscellaneous varieties. California production of Valencias has declined faster than of Navels and other varieties in recent years. In 1958–1959, Valencias accounted for about 58% of the State's total orange crop.

Florida started commercial packing of canned pasteurized single-strength juice in 1929 and of frozen concentrated orange juice in 1945. This state has accounted for nearly all of both of these packs ever since 1945 (Tables 2 and 3). California and Arizona combined contributed all

TABLE 2

PROCESSED AND FROZEN CONCENTRATED ORANGE JUICE—ANNUAL PACKS IN THE STATE OF FLORIDA, IN GALLONS

Year	Processed, 65°Brix	Frozen, 42°Brix
1945–46	244,000	226,000
1946–47	1,447,000	559,000
1947–48	1,739,000	1,935,000
1948–49	1,897,000	10,232,000
1949–50	1,529,422	21,647,447
1950–51	2,529,671	30,757,656
1951–52	1,897,848	44,030,633
1952–53	536,660	46,553,695
1953–54	1,339,222	65,531,204
1954–55	1,531,449	65,480,673
1955–56	1,085,697	69,592,264
1956–57	1,801,283	72,455,342
1957–58	1,149,081	56,763,752
1958–59	547,280	79,981,041
1959–60	377,877	77,998,819
1960–61	154,991	84,373,616
1961–62	277,501	115,866,452
1962–63	54,360	51,647,737
1963–64	41,108	53,674,426
1964–65	69,763	88,868,804
1965–66	48,506	70,831,316(45°)
1966–67	119,027	127,610,559(45°)
1967–68	22,374	85,697,047(45°)
1968–69	31,126	103,731,616(45°)

Source: Florida Canners Association, Winter Haven, Fla.

TABLE 3

FLORIDA PRODUCTION OF CONCENTRATED FROZEN GRAPEFRUIT, PROCESSED GRAPEFRUIT, AND FROZEN BLENDED CONCENTRATE

Year	Frozen Grapefruit, gal	Processed Grapefruit, gal	Frozen Blend, gal	Frozen Tangerine, gal	Processed Tangerine, gal
1951–52	1,097,564	16,112	535,703	349,161	
1952–53	1,226,485	50,563	479,745	551,397	
1953–54	1,656,469	55,372	965,430	443,105	
1954–55	1,155,314	31,860	560,545	877,011	
1955–56	2,511,831	30,719	954,142	618,986	25,055
1956–57	2,949,072	59,105	596,731	792,516	32,431
1957–58	3,330,301	107,896	506,915	146,576	
1958–59	4,952,488	165,115	689,521	1,151,782	23,039
1959–60	1,613,462	27,390	284,276	319,671	
1960–61	3,841,462	19,947	255,584	1,406,694	21,285
1961–62	3,162,798	116,171	266,594	1,370,187	3,989
1962–63	2,323,381	36,340	53,242	204,458	
1963–64	2,572,655	21,375	130,431	1,145,495	
1964–65	3,999,657	54,946	69,599	1,153,569	
1965–66	3,970,546	30,539	50,487	715,490	
1966–67	5,484,816	29,099	20,099	1,119,869	
1967–68	1,813,964	...	10,349	581,966	
1968–69	5,917,390	38,742	36,310	1,050,946	

Source: Florida Canners Association, Winter Haven, Fla.

TABLE 4

YEARLY FLORIDA PRODUCTION OF CHILLED CITRUS JUICES AND CHILLED CITRUS PRODUCTS

Year	Orange Juice, gal	Grapefruit Juice, gal	Grapefruit Salad, gal	Grapefruit Sections, gal	Orange Sections, gal
1956–57	30,902,976	911,983	N.A.	N.A.	N.A.
1957–58	33,244,277	780,395	2,745,807	560,120	474,352
1958–59	33,709,736	638,302	3,506,988	726,456	514,073
1959–60	38,990,259	548,572	2,651,806	876,841	354,618
1960–61	36,752,460	814,497	4,128,550	1,133,634	655,582
1961–62	41,762,938	1,516,305	5,264,991	1,197,726	868,481
1962–63	27,251,090	942,499	4,146,393	1,130,965	755,064
1963–64	28,163,661	1,431,162	6,349,582	1,915,269	999,511
1964–65	41,856,890	1,179,830	4,609,379	1,700,059	929,984
1965–66	67,643,125	3,073,505	6,408,726	2,570,785	1,275,202
1966–67	93,347,668	5,123,577	6,365,096	2,179,545	1,215,017
1967–68	90,012,623	5,432,263	5,600,793	2,294,337	1,289,395
1968–69	88,111,397	6,760,058	5,579,056	1,983,229	798,087

Source: Florida Canners Association, Winter Haven, Fla.

TABLE 5

CITRUS FRUIT—CONSUMPTION PER PERSON, IN POUNDS, 1950–1968[1]

		Processed						
		Canned		Chilled, lb				
Year	Fresh	Fruit	Juice	Fruit	Juice	Frozen Juice	Total Processed	Total
1950	41.7	1.5	19.8	...	...	10.8	32.1	73.8
1951	45.8	1.7	20.8	...	...	15.2	37.7	83.5
1952	45.1	1.5	17.0	...	...	21.5	40.0	85.1
1953	44.1	1.8	16.0	...	...	24.4	42.2	86.3
1954	42.0	1.9	15.8	...	...	27.1	44.8	86.8
1955	41.8	2.2	14.9	...	1.7	30.9	49.7	91.5
1956	39.1	2.0	14.3	0.4	2.0	30.3	49.0	88.1
1957	37.1	1.5	14.1	0.5	3.1	33.0	52.2	89.3
1958	31.0	2.1	14.3	0.5	3.3	25.8	46.0	77.0
1959	34.0	1.6	10.9	0.6	3.2	32.6	48.9	82.9
1960	33.7	2.0	11.6	0.8	3.6	34.2	52.2	85.9
1961	30.8	1.8	10.7	0.8	2.9	32.1	48.3	79.1
1962	29.5	1.9	10.5	0.8	3.7	37.2	54.1	83.6
1963	22.1	1.3	10.7	0.7	2.8	25.1	40.6	62.7
1964	26.1	1.7	8.7	0.9	2.6	23.5	37.4	63.5
1965	29.0	1.8	8.1	0.7	3.7	29.6	43.9	72.9
1966	29.0	2.0	9.5	1.0	6.1	28.0	46.6	75.6
1967	31.5	2.2	11.1	0.9	8.4	40.0	62.6	94.1
1968[2]	26.1	2.2	10.5	0.9	8.0	34.3	55.9	82.0

Data published currently in the Fruit Situation (ERS).
[1] Fresh-equivalent basis. 50 states beginning 1960.
[2] Preliminary.

of the remainder of the frozen concentrate and less than 4% of the single-strength hot pack of which Texas accounted for about 1%. The production of chilled orange juice, first made in California about 1947 has grown rather slowly in that State compared with Florida's output first reported

TABLE 6

CITRUS JUICE EXPORTS[1] ON SINGLE-STRENGTH BASIS IN 1,000 GAL, CALENDAR YEARS 1964–1968

	1964	1965	1966	1967	1968
		Canned—Not Frozen			
Orange	3,648	4,821	6,493	11,698	12,448
Grapefruit	2,484	4,105	3,247	5,607	4,390
		Concentrated, Frozen			
Orange	2,436	2,880	3,039	4,634	4,330
Grapefruit	197	198	242	321	373
		Concentrated, Hot Pack			
Orange	940	892	819	956	727
Grapefruit	173	210	159	158	182

[1] Anon. (1970).

in 1954–1955. By 1956–1958, however, the Florida pack has jumped to about 33,000,000 gal or close to 86% of a national total of 38,300,000 gal (Table 4). By 1967–1968, the quantity of oranges used in making chilled juice had risen to approximately 16 million cases (Table 5). The small pack of pasteurized concentrate is the only kind of orange juice of which Florida has not contributed nearly all of the national total.

In 1967, the latest year in which statistics are available, the United States exported nearly four million cases of canned orange juice, 724,000 gal of hot pack concentrated orange juice and over four million gallons of frozen orange juice concentrate. The amounts of the various citrus juices exported are given in Table 6.

GRAPEFRUIT JUICE

Commercial processing of grapefruit, first as segments, and then as juice started in the late 1920's as a means of expanding market outlets for the rapidly increasing production in Florida and Texas where well over 90% of the total world crop of grapefruit was produced until disastrous freezes in 1949 and 1951 destroyed most of Texas' citrus groves. Figure 4 shows U.S. and Florida production of grapefruit in Florida since 1935. Figure 5 indicates how Florida grapefruit is utilized. Florida has very largely determined the statistical trends and variations for the national grapefruit industry since 1949, as it has produced well over 75% of the total crop (Table 7). Until 1940, processed grapefruit juice was all pasteurized single-strength and this pack has continued to account for most of the grapefruit juice. The quantity of hot pack grapefruit juice packed dropped to only 5,662,202 cases in 1963–1964 because of the disastrous freeze in Florida that winter, but the pack has approximately tripled since then. In 1966–1967, over 18 million cases were packed. This is the peak

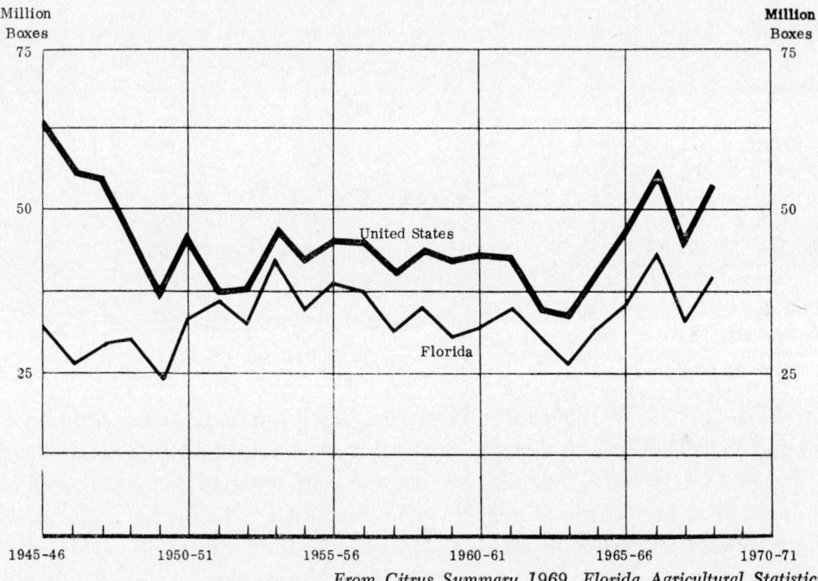

From Citrus Summary 1969, Florida Agricultural Statistics

FIG. 4. GRAPEFRUIT: PRODUCTION FOR UNITED STATES AND FLORIDA

Crop years 1945–1946 through 1968–1969.

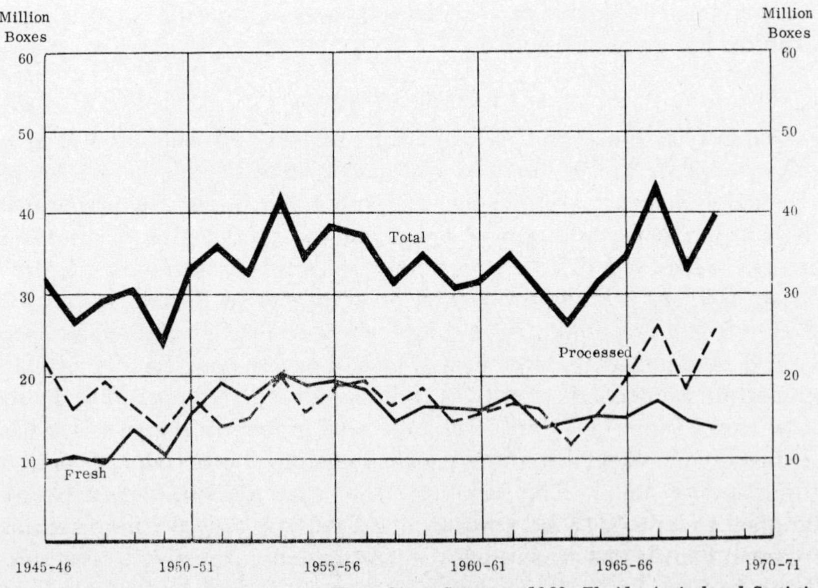

From Citrus Summary 1969, Florida Agricultural Statistics

FIG. 5. FLORIDA GRAPEFRUIT: PRODUCTION AND UTILIZATION

Crop years 1945–1946 through 1968–1969.

TABLE 7

GRAPEFRUIT—BEARING ACREAGE AND PRODUCTION, BY STATES

	Florida		Texas		California		Arizona		United States	
Crop Year	Bearing Acreage[1]	Production of Value[2]	Bearing Acreage	Production of Value	Bearing Acreage	Production of Value	Bearing Acreage	Production of Value	Bearing Acreage	Production of Value
1951–52	98.6	33,000	17.9	200	9.7	2,160	8.9	2,140	135,1	37,500
1952–53	102.2	32,500	20.9	400	9.4	2,458	8.5	3,000	141.0	38,358
1953–54	105.5	40,700	22.0	1,200	9.1	2,500	7.0	2,670	143.6	47,070
1954–55	111.2	34,800	24.1	2,500	8.2	2,414	6.0	2,470	149.5	42,184
1955–56	111.8	38,300	26.0	2,200	8.3	2,507	6.0	2,370	152.1	45,377
1956–57	112.4	37,400	29.7	2,800	7.2	2,407	5.5	2,180	154.8	44,787
1957–58	95.0	31,100	30.1	3,500	7.5	2,397	5.4	2,780	138.0	39,777
1958–59	94.0	35,200	34.1	4,200	7.4	2,527	5.6	1,870	141.1	43,797
1959–60	92.3	30,500	38.1	5,200	7.6	2,671	5.6	3,220	143.6	41,591
1960–61	92.5	31,600	[3]	6,800	8.1	2,630	5.7	2,340	[3]	43,370
1961–62	94.0	34,800	[3]	2,700	9.5	2,820	5.8	2,170	[3]	42,490
1962–63	88.0	30,000	[3]	70	10.9	2,498	6.0	2,170	[3]	34,738
1963–64	83.0	26,300	[3]	500	11.9	4,197	6.0	3,210	[3]	34,207
1964–65	84.0	31,900	[3]	2,000	11.9	4,227	6.1	2,900	[3]	41,027
1965–66	86.0	34,900	[3]	3,800	12.0	4,945	6.2	3,050	[3]	46,695
1966–67	87.0	43,600	[3]	5,400	12.8	4,996	6.6	1,680	[3]	55,676
1967–68	87.5	32,900	[3]	2,800	12.8	4,618	6.7	3,740	[3]	44,058
1968–69	91.2	39,900	27.5	6,700	12.8	4,960	5.1	2,510	135.6	54,070

Source: Citrus Summary 1969, Florida Agr. Statistics.
[1] 1,000 acres.
[2] 1,000 boxes.
[3] Not available.

of the canned juice pack; since then the pack dropped to about 14 million cases in 1968–1969.

Since the introduction of the hot concentrate pack in 1940 and frozen concentrate in 1948 both have been relatively unimportant in marked contrast to frozen orange concentrate. The pasteurized concentrate has grown slowly and in recent years accounted for only 3 to 4% of the total grapefruit juice pack while the frozen concentrate has grown more rapidly attaining an average of nearly four million gallons for the period 1964 to 1967 or about 25% of a total grapefruit juice pack (Table 8).

BLENDED CITRUS JUICES

Blended citrus juice, about equal parts of orange and grapefruit, was first packed in Florida in 1935–1936. Since 1946, tangerine-grapefruit and orange-tangerine blends have been packed in some years but in very small quantities. Aside from orange-grapefruit blends of juice, other blends of undiluted citrus juices and other fruit juices, blended juices have not been popular. However, in recent years numerous blended diluted fruit juice *drinks* have been introduced and several have proved

TABLE 8

U.S. PACKS OF FROZEN CONCENTRATED CITRUS JUICES, BY STATES[1]

	Orange and Tangerine Juice 42°Brix				Blended Juice			Grapefruit Juice			Concentrate		
Year Nov.–Oct.	Calif.-Ariz. Orange	Florida Orange	Florida Tan-gerine	Total U.S.	Calif.-Ariz.	Florida	Total U.S.	Calif.-Ariz.	Florida	Total U.S.	Lemon Juice Calif.-Ariz.	For Lemon-ade Calif.-Ariz.	For Lime-ade Calif.-Ariz.
1959–60	3,000[2]	78,149	320	81,469	...	284	284	[4]	1,613	[4]	1,150	14,750[5]	[4]
1960–61	2,400[3]	84,298	1,407	88,105	...	256	256	[4]	3,841	[4]	93	8,450[5]	[4]
1961–62	[4]	116,082	1,370	[4]	...	267	267	[4]	3,163	[4]	[4]	[4]	[4]
1962–63	[4]	51,648	204	[4]	...	53	53	[4]	2,323	[4]	[4]	[4]	[4]
1963–64	[4]	53,674	1,145	[4]	...	130	130	[4]	2,573	[4]	[4]	[4]	[4]
1964–65	[4]	88,869	1,154	[4]	...	70	70	[4]	4,000	[4]	[4]	[4]	[4]
1965–66	[4]	70,831[6]	715	[4]	...	50	50	[4]	3,971	[4]	[4]	[4]	[4]
1966–67	[4]	127,611[6]	1,120	[4]	...	29	29	[4]	5,485	[4]	[4]	[4]	[4]
1967–68	[4]	83,697[6]	582	[4]	...	10	10	[4]	1,814	[4]	[4]	[4]	[4]

[1] 1959–1960 to 1967–1968 (1,000 gal).
[2] Source: U.S. Dept. Agr., ERS., The Fruit Situation, June 1961.
[3] Source: Annual Statistical Report, Florida Citrus Mutual, 1960–1961 Season.
[4] Data not available.
[5] Source: U.S. Dept. Agr., ERS., The Fruit Situation, Aug. 1962.
[6] Basis 45°Brix.

quite popular and utilized a large quantity of citrus juices in their manufacture (see chap. 11).

The orange-grapefruit blend was developed in Florida in an effort to expand the demand for increasingly large crops of these citrus fruits. Normally 95% or more is packed in Florida where the pack grew slowly until World War II. It reached a peak of 12,400,000 cases in 1947–1948 when it accounted for 21% of the hot pack of all canned single-strength citrus juice. Since then it has shown a steady downward trend, dropping to a low of 1,808,881 cases during 1967–1968 accounting for only 14% of the total hot pack of single-strength citrus juices.

LEMON JUICE

The United States and Italy have for many years produced a large proportion of the world's lemons and since World War II have been the only significant commercial manufacturers of lemon juice products. Just before the War, each of these countries produced about 40% of the world crop of 23,300,000 boxes of lemons. Since the war, production in California-Arizona has increased so much more than in Italy that the United States accounted for about 45% of the total world crops averaging 38,600,000 boxes during 1956–1959 and Italy about 28%. Since then the quantity of lemons produced in the United States has dropped to about 16 million boxes. The balance of 27% is produced in small amounts in about 16 countries. Chief of these in order of importance are Argentina, Spain, Greece and Chile which have gradually increased their output since the war and now each usually produces from 3 to 5% of the world total. Italy has used about one-third of its lemon crop for juice products (C.E.C. 1960), and California and Arizona a little more than one-third of theirs. Italy contributed about one-fifth of total world lemon juice products and the United States four-fifths. However, Italy has exported more pasteurized lemon concentrate than the United States in recent years and the United States has been one of the chief markets for it. California accounted for the total national production of lemons reported by the Crop Reporting Service until the small but increasing crop of Arizona was first included in 1958 when it accounted for about 2% of the United States crop; in 1959, about 6%.

During 1956–1958, the hot pack of single-strength lemon juice averaged almost 2,600,000 gal or 14% of the total lemon juice pack and *frozen* single-strength juice 1,400,000 gal or only 5% of the total. *Hot pack* concentrated lemon juice, introduced in 1945, nearly doubled from 1951–1955 to 1956–1958 when it accounted for 21% of all lemon juice. The pack of frozen concentrate, introduced in 1949, during 1956–1958 was more than

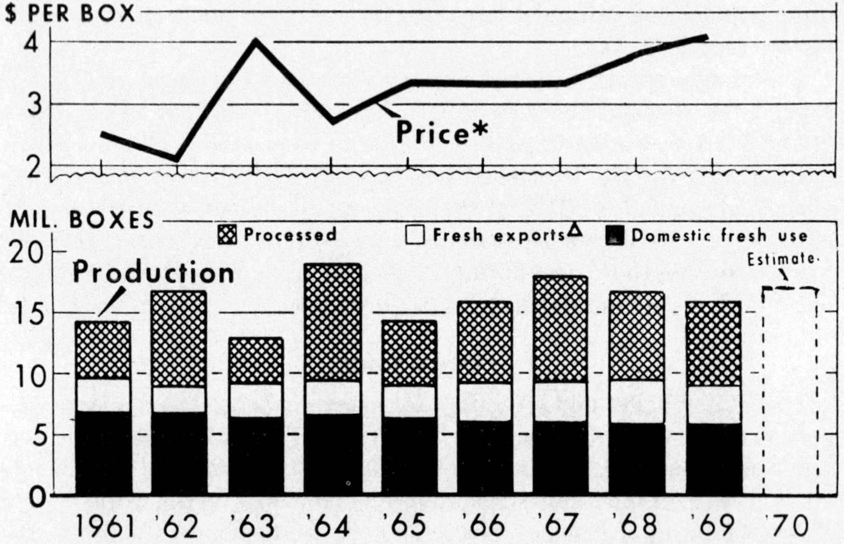

Courtesy of Economic Research Service, U.S. Dept. Agr.

FIG. 6. U.S. LEMON PRODUCTION USE AND PRICES

double the average of the preceding five years and accounted for 37% of the lemon juice total. Lemonade base, which is about two-thirds pure juice, was introduced in 1949. The pack increased less rapidly than concentrated juice averaging nearly 8,000,000 gal of pure juice by 1956–1958 and accounting for 28% of the total lemon juice pack. Nearly all of the lemonade base is frozen. *Frozen* juice in some form actually has accounted for an average of 69% of the total pack of lemon juice since 1951. About one-third of the concentrate has been pasteurized and two-thirds frozen.

United States consumption of commercially processed lemon juice on a per capita basis has increased from an average of only 0.03 lb processed weight before the last war to 0.21 lb during 1945–1949, to about 1.20 lb in 1959. Production and consumption data since then are not available.

It must be remembered, however, that, unlike oranges and grapefruit, most of the lemons marketed fresh are also finally used for juice purposes and these fresh shipments accounted for about 64% of the national production of lemons during 1956–1958. Sales for consumption are now very largely in the form of frozen lemonade base and frozen concentrate. Single-strength juice, mostly hot pack, accounted for about 15% of total consumption in 1958–1959, frozen lemonade base about 30%, frozen

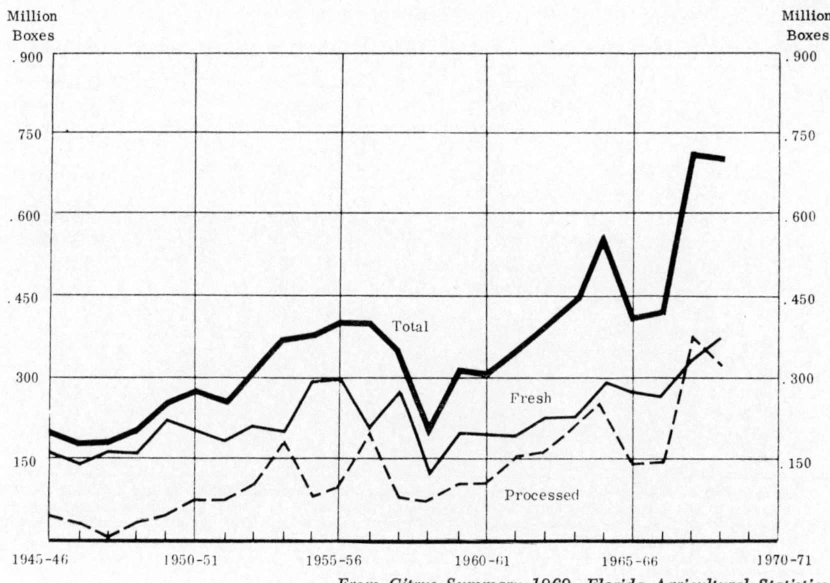

From Citrus Summary 1969, Florida Agricultural Statistics

FIG. 7. FLORIDA LIMES: PRODUCTION AND UTILIZATION

Crop years 1945–1946 through 1968–1969.

concentrate over 40%, and hot pack concentrate only about 15% (Pubols 1960). Figure 6 indicates the annual production of lemons in the United States from 1961 to 1969 and the quantity processed for juice.

LIME JUICE

The production and consumption of limes are the smallest of any kind of citrus for which United States production statistics are available. National consumption of both fresh and juice products, however, is relatively larger than that of other kinds of citrus juices because a significant amount of both fresh limes and of juice is imported. Imports of fresh limes, nearly all from Mexico, have amounted to about one-fourth of Florida fresh sales of limes in recent years. Some of these fresh imports were used for commercial manufacture of lime juice in this country. Figure 7 indicates the quantity of limes and the lime juice produced in Florida during the period 1945–1967.

GRAPE JUICE

Commercial bottling and canning of heat-sterilized, unfermented fruit juice in the United States started in 1869 when Welch began bottling un-

TABLE 9

GRAPE JUICE—U.S. PRODUCTION, IMPORTS FOR CONSUMPTION AND APPARENT CONSUMPTION

Year	Production Quantity[1]	Imports[2]	Apparent Consumption
	Quantity in 1,000 Gal		
1963	45,534	25	45,559
1964	46,000	120	46,120
1965	46,800	1,237	48,037
1966	47,300	95	47,395
1967	53,000	22	53,022
1968	40,800	100	40,900
	Value, $1,000		
1963	49,912	38	[3]
1964	52,400	94	[3]
1965	52,900	490	[3]
1966	51,600	80	[3]
1967	58,300	51	[3]
1968	44,700	63	[3]

Source: Production based on 1963 Census of Manufactures, U.S. Dept. of Commerce, and partial trade data in noncensus years; import data compiled from official statistics of the U.S. Dept. of Commerce, presented in U.S. Tariff Commission, Summaries of Trade and Tariff Information, Schedule 1 Animal and Vegetable Products, Volume 10 Beverages.

[1] Partially estimated.
[2] Single-strength basis.
[3] Not available.

fermented Concord grape juice in Vineland, New Jersey. In this country, the grape juice industry has been built around the Concord grape, the most important variety of the native American *Labrusca* species of grapes which is grown mostly in the cooler parts of the United States and Canada. Consumption has grown slowly and is limited almost entirely to those North Americans who have acquired a taste for the distinctive flavor of Concord grape juice, which is quite unlike the comparatively neutral flavor of *Vinifera* varieties of European grapes grown in California.

The Concord grape juice industry grew so slowly that consumption was only about one-third of a pint per capita during 1910–1914. By 1934–1938, production had risen to about 4,000,000 gal a year (1,800,000 cases, equivalent 24 No. 2 cans) still only about one-third of a pint per capita, accounting for approximately four per cent of national consumption of all fruit and vegetable juices.

Exports and imports of grape juice are so small that national production and consumption are approximately the same (Table 9). Only small amounts of grape juice have been imported into the United States, mostly Concord juice from the Great Lakes Region of Canada. Exports of grape juice, grape syrup, and concentrate are not separately reported but are known to be very small. In 1960, the industry produced about 50,000,000 gal, almost all Concord juice. Nearly all of the unfermented grape juice consumed in the United States is made from Concord grapes grown

TABLE 10

APPLE JUICE—TOTAL UNITED STATES PACK[1]—ACTUAL CASES

1939	393,211	1949	2,760,792	1959	6,769,247
1940	505,782	1950	3,469,946	1960	6,288,541
1941	1,726,131	1951	3,174,417	1961	6,973,649
1942	1,645,282	1952	3,199,427	1962	7,483,008
1943	1,739,815	1953	3,080,844	1963	8,558,066
1944	2,851,394	1954	4,219,890	1964	9,784,293
1945	1,315,547	1955	3,507,894	1965	9,670,271
1946	3,524,282	1956	4,265,583	1966	8,953,054
1947	1,180,769	1957	4,652,718	1967	9,028,856
1948	1,181,130	1958	5,346,198	1968	9,640,877

Pack of Recent Years by States

	1964–65	1965–66	1966–67	1967–68	1968–69
Pennsylvania, Virginia, and West Virginia	2,575,836	2,512,245	2,034,162	2,545,887	[2]5,214,193
Michigan	1,113,148	1,699,888	939,551	910,239	[3]1,791,023
California	1,932,997	933,930	1,379,202	982,179	1,629,485
Other states	4,162,312	4,524,208	4,600,139	4,590,551	[4]1,006,176
Total	9,784,293	9,670,271	8,953,054	9,028,856	9,640,877

Pack by Size of Container

	1964–65	1965–66	1966–67	1967–68	1968–69
Indiv. 5–6Z[5]	716,593	477,408	436,461	589,730	695,078
No. 211 cyl. (48 per case)	21,057	24,330	18,393	34,538	29,298
29 and 32 ounce	231,224	159,388	139,452	42,090	11,967
No. 3 cyl	3,116,892	3,176,616	2,827,447	2,462,280	2,537,844
24–26Z glass	123,527	48,831	48,314	49,647	62,769
32Z glass	3,829,966	3,889,023	3,485,797	3,909,260	3,735,286
64Z glass	408,635	537,367	544,453	646,379	683,793
1 gallon jug	599,135	811,112	828,969	631,063	852,046
Misc. tin and glass	737,234	546,196	623,768	663,869	1,032,796
Total	9,784,293	9,670,271	8,953,054	9,028,856	9,640,877

[1] From Canned Food Pack Statistics 1968, National Canners Assoc., Washington, D.C.
[2] East.
[3] Michigan and other midwest.
[4] Other west.
[5] Includes some 3½-4-oz glass through 1967–68, in misc. for 1968–69.

outside of California, chiefly in the five states of New York, Michigan, Washington, Pennsylvania, and Ohio. With yields per acre about double the average of eastern states and, hence, relatively low unit production costs, the acreage and production of grapes and grape products in Washington have increased relatively much more than in the other four leading Concord producing states. It now vies with Michigan as the state second to New York in normal output.

APPLE JUICE AND CIDER

As indicated on p.1, fresh apple juice or cider has been made by many farmers and in large numbers of small cider mills since colonial times. In fact, until 1869, it was the only available fruit juice, and even so its availability was seasonal, being marketed only in the late summer, autumn and early winter. Until the 1920's, the only attempt to preserve it was by the addition of sodium benzoate and refrigeration at temperatures above freezing.

Farm production of cider decreased greatly from 1899 to 1919, according to the U.S. Census of Agriculture,[1] dropping from 55,280,000 gal in 1899 to 32,584,000 in 1909, to only 13,366,000 in 1919. In 1909, almost 333,000 farms reported making cider and only about 217,600 in 1919. Farm production of vinegar was reported separately. How much of the reported farm production of cider was actually consumed as sweet cider and how much as hard cider is not known. These census data are probably incomplete even for production on farms, and they definitely do not include the large amounts of cider made by local custom presses for farmers or for sale to outlets for which no estimates are available.

Small commercial packs of pasteurized apple juice under vacuum in sealed containers were first reported about 1939 for both the United States and Canada. Table 10 shows the fairly rapid rate of growth of the hot pack of single-strength apple juice in the United States in tin and glass containers of one gallon or less in cases equivalent to 24 No. 2 cans. The 1956–1958 average pack of nearly 4,600,000 cases a year was about the same as the pack of unfermented grape juice and accounted for about 4% of the national hot pack of all single strength fruit and vegetable juices. Peak production of apple juice of 9,784,000 cases in 1964 plus a slightly larger additional quantity of sweet cider utilized about 5% of the commercial apple crop.

Production of apple juice and of cider varies greatly from year to year depending chiefly on the size of the apple crop. Since cider is more of a by-product than canned apple juice, its production varies even more from season to season than the hot pack of juice. The proportion of the commercial apple crop used for juice during 1952 to 1957 varied from 3.5 to 4.5%; that for cider, from 2.5 to 5.5%.

The number of apple juice packers is relatively small, probably not much over 100. On the other hand, there are thousands of cider mills in the United States scattered through all apple-producing areas but probably most thickly concentrated in the Northeast. The National Canners Association reported 72 canned juice packers in 1959; 35% in both the East and Midwest; and 30% in the West. Pack statistics are not segregated on a comparable geographical basis. In 1959, California accounted for 18% of the hot pack, gaining a few points relatively in recent years; Michigan with 15% in 1959 and Maryland, Virginia, and Pennsylvania, com-

[1] U.S. Bureau of the Census, *Fourteenth Census of the United States:* 1922. Agriculture 5, 870.

bined, with 27% just about maintained their relative position; whereas all other unspecified states as a group totaled 39%, showing a slight decline in relative importance.

The pack of canned apple juice (Nat'l. Canners Assoc. 1969) is characterized by the large proportion packed in glass and in large containers, both glass and tin. Glass accounted for about 60% of the pack in 1968. Approximately 90% was packed in glass and tin containers of 24 oz or larger in size. Quart containers (nearly all glass until 1959) and the 46 oz, No. 3 cylinder tin can account for about half of the total pack. Gallon jugs were once much more important than in recent years. Less than 10% of the 1968 pack was in containers less than 16 oz in size, all tin.

PRUNE JUICE

No statistics are available on the output of fresh prune and plum juice nectar, although small amounts are produced commercially. However, prune juice made from California dried prunes has been produced commercially since 1934 and consumed in recent years in substantial quantities in the United States. Very little, if any juice is manufactured abroad from prunes produced in foreign countries. No official statistics on U.S. exports of prune juice to foreign countries are available, but trade information indicates that the total is very small and that mostly to Canada.

Commercial production of dried prune juice began about 1934 in California with an estimated pack of only about 40,000 cases and national consumption only 0.01 lb per capita. The pack increased erratically before the war, averaging less than 400,000 cases a year during 1934–1941 or less than 1% of the total national hot pack of all single-strength fruit and vegetable juices. In 1942, it jumped to 1,700,000 cases and then rose to 5,000,000 by 1949. During 1947 to 1951, it averaged over 4% of the national hot pack of all single-strength juices.

The trend in production of prune juice continued upward until 1956, as the supply of California prunes diverted to juice and concentrate rose to a peak of nearly 49,000 tons.

Concentrate is usually packed at 72°Brix or nearly a 4 to 1 ratio. Single-strength juice is packed at about 20°Brix with a minimum standard of 18.5°Brix. About a dozen firms have manufactured prune juice or the concentrated juice made from California dried prunes in recent years.

During the decade 1959 to 1968, the annual production of "single-strength" prune juice has increased only slightly from about eight million to nine million cases, nearly all of which has been packed in California. A large proportion of the pack is put in quart bottles.

TABLE 11

CANNED AND CHILLED FRUIT JUICES (EXCLUDING FROZEN)—PER CAPITA CONSUMPTION, 1960–1968[1] LB.

	Canned Citrus						
Year	Orange	Grapefruit	Blended Orange, Grapefruit	Lemon and Lime	Tangerine	Citrus Concentrate	Total
1960	2.12	1.51	0.51	0.13	0.07	1.45	5.79
1961	1.70	1.39	0.45	0.13	0.06	1.52	5.25
1962	1.92	1.48	0.47	0.13	0.06	1.05	5.11
1963	1.69	1.30	0.42	0.13	0.04	1.70	5.28
1964	1.17	1.09	0.30	0.11	0.04	1.61	4.32
1965	1.24	1.39	0.30	0.10	0.02	0.97	4.02
1966	1.53	1.73	0.34	0.10	0.02	0.99	4.71
1967	1.57	2.33	0.39	0.10	0.02	1.08	5.49
1968[2]	1.19	2.22	0.32	0.10	0.01	1.35	5.19

	Canned Noncitrus								
					Pineapple[3]				
	Berry	Apple	Fruit Nectars	Grape	Single-strength Juice	Concentrate[4]	Prune	Total[3]	Total Canned
1960	[5]	0.89	1.06	0.76	2.15	1.25	1.06	7.17	12.96
1961	[5]	0.95	0.52	0.71	2.07	1.19	1.05	6.49	11.74
1962	[5]	1.05	0.52	0.65	2.09	1.18	1.06	6.55	11.66
1963	[5]	1.21	0.36	0.63	2.61	1.74	1.11	7.66	12.94
1964	[5]	1.49	0.28	0.65	1.97	1.64	1.11	7.14	11.46
1965	[5]	1.53	0.38	0.74	1.84	1.20	1.16	6.84	10.86
1966	[5]	1.17	0.40	0.63	1.92	1.73	1.10	6.95	11.66
1967	[5]	1.35	0.39	0.67	1.76	0.96	1.09	6.22	11.71
1968[2]	[5]	1.70	0.41	0.60	2.14	1.51	1.08	7.44	12.63

	Chilled[6]		
	Orange	Grapefruit	Total Chilled
1960	2.10	0.02	2.12
1961	1.65	0.03	1.68
1962	2.19	0.08	2.27
1963	1.14	0.03	1.17
1964	1.29	0.07	1.36
1965	1.90	0.05	1.95
1966	3.04	0.14	3.18
1967	4.15	0.23	4.38
1968	3.96	0.24	4.20

Source: Food Consumption, Prices, Expenditures Supplement to Agricultural Economic Report No. 138. Economic Research Service, U.S. Dept. Agr.

[1] Civilian consumption. Includes major portion of frozen pineapple juice.

Calendar-year basis except for citrus juices and grape juice which are on a pack-year basis beginning in November of year prior to that indicated.

[2] Preliminary.

[3] Includes frozen pineapple juice.

[4] Single-strength equivalent.

[5] Not available.

[6] Chilled fruit juices produced commercially in Florida; does not include reconstituted frozen juice or fresh juice produced for local sale.

TABLE 12

U.S. PACKS OF FRUIT JUICE AND U.S. IMPORTS OF PINEAPPLE JUICE

Crop Year	Pack Million Cases 24/2's	Total Fruit and Tomato Juice, %	Canned Single-Strength Fruit and Tomato Juices, Million Cases 24/2's						Frozen Fruit Juices Million Pounds[2]
			U.S. Imports of Pineapple Juice[1]	Grape	Fruit Nectars Apple, Prune and Other Fruit Juice	Total Fruit Juice	Tomato	Total Fruit and Tomato Juices	
1959–60	32.4	30.6	13.4	7.8	21.2	74.8	31.1	105.9	1,084
1960–61	26.7	25.6	14.4	8.2	22.0	71.3	33.0	104.3	960
1961–62	30.4	28.1	15.3	8.1	22.7	76.5	31.6	108.1	1,036
1962–63	24.7	21.9	15.3	9.3	23.4	72.7	40.2	112.9	1,369
1963–64	17.3	17.4	14.8	8.3	24.6	65.0	34.5	99.5	614
1964–65	24.4	[3]	13.8	[3]	[3]	[3]	35.3	[3]	[3]
1965–66	29.0	[3]	15.4	[3]	[3]	[3]	32.8	[3]	[3]
1966–67	41.2	[3]	15.0	[3]	[3]	[3]	31.9	[3]	[3]
1967–68	29.6	[3]	15.1	[3]	[3]	[3]	35.1	[3]	[3]

Data provided by Sunkist Growers.
[1] Figures represent packs including Hawaiian and foreign operations. Prior seasons represent U.S. imports of pineapple juice.
[2] Processed weight.
[3] Data not available.

NECTARS

Approximate estimates of the total pack of canned hot pack single strength nectars are given in Table 11. The so-called nectar pack includes several pulpy fruit juices for which no data are available separately, chiefly apricot, peach and pear. The 1956–1958 packs are estimated at an average of nearly 8,500,000 cases or 85% above the 1951–1955 average. Per capita consumption of 1.36 lb during 1956–1958 was more than double the average for the preceding five years and accounted for 8% of the total consumption of all canned hot pack single-strength juices in the United States.

The U.S. production of nectars has declined sharply since 1960 (from approximately eight million to four million cases in 1968), probably because of the marked loss in the export market.

PINEAPPLE JUICE

Pineapples had been canned in Hawaii for about 30 years before commercial production of the juice became economically feasible with the introduction of the process for extracting it from the pulp, perfected in 1932. The methods developed in Hawaii have been applied elsewhere. The history and development of the production and merchandising of Hawaiian canned pineapple, the second largest canned fruit industry in the United States, has been presented by Havighorst (1948, 1949). Havighorst describes the remarkable growth from 1903 to 1948 in the production and sales of canned pineapple by Dole and discusses the factors responsible for the phenomenal development, stressing particularly the contribution of advertising programs.

Until 1912, the fruit was trimmed, sliced and packed by hand. Then Dole mechanized the peeling and coring process by installing the first Ginaca machine, which was improved in 1922 and again in 1925. During 1903 to 1908, only sliced pineapple was packed. Grated pineapple was introduced in 1908; tidbits in 1912; broken slices in 1913; unclarified juice in 1921; crushed (formerly called grated) pineapple in 1922; gems or chunks in 1931; the new clarified juice in 1932; frozen pineapple in 1946; frozen concentrated juice in 1952 and pasteurized concentrated juice about the same time.

The popularity of pineapple juice increased so rapidly that in less than ten years after its introduction the pack in Hawaii and the Philippines had risen to an average of 10,700,000 cases by 1939, being exceeded only by tomato and grapefruit juice and accounting for 20% of the hot pack of all single-strength juices (Table 12). During the war, the Hawaiian pack of pineapple was maintained, but the juice pack dropped a little and govern-

TABLE 13

PINEAPPLE JUICE (HAWAIIAN PACK[1])

Pack—Actual Cases

1935–36	4,086,930	1947–48	8,890,454	1959–60	11,921,815
1936–37	6,811,475	1948–49	10,043,475	1960–61	12,950,725
1937–38	7,161,918	1949–50	10,404,518	1961–62	13,508,064
1938–39	8,870,987	1950–51	11,699,088	1962–63	13,581,854
1939–40	8,555,896	1951–52	10,797,160	1963–64	13,094,372
1940–41	10,808,302	1952–53	15,139,248	1964–65	12,301,964
1941–42	8,563,012	1953–54	14,654,428	1965–66	13,625,755
1942–43	8,829,949	1954–55	14,291,984	1966–67	13,266,885
1943–44	8,297,598	1955–56	14,212,874	1967–68	13,370,495
1944–45	7,957,424	1956–57	14,855,372	1968–69	N.A.
1945–46	8,671,204	1957–58	11,248,651		
1946–47	8,206,789	1958–59	13,464,622		

Pack by Size of Container—Actual Cases

	1964–65	1965–66	1966–67	1967–68	1968–69
Indiv. 6Z	840,246	926,683	885,438	833,795	
8Z	367,198	246,647	247,503	304,959	
No. 211 cyl.	1,215,205	1,385,207	1,326,025	1,496,876	
No. 2	1,248,894	1,247,175	972,374	921,030	N.A.
No. 3 cyl.	8,382,595	9,513,951	9,532,215	9,529,307	
No. 10	247,826	306,092	303,330	284,528	
Total	12,301,964	13,625,755	13,266,885	13,370,495	

From Canned Food Pack Statistics 1968 National Canners Assoc., Washington, D.C.

[1] Reported by Pineapple Growers Association of Hawaii; includes both U.S. and foreign operations of its members. Data for 12 months beginning June 1.

ment purchases for military forces were so large that civilian consumption in the United States was cut about 40%.

During 1947–1951, the pineapple pack of Hawaii and the Philippines averaged 15,400,000 cases on a No. 2 can basis, while pineapple juice had risen to 12,700,000 cases. The juice accepted for one-eighth of the total hot pack of single-strength fruit and vegetable juices and about 9% of the total of all juices, including hot and frozen concentrates and lemonade.

Pasteurized single-strength pineapple juice now ranks third among the different kinds of single strength pasteurized juices canned in the United States, being exceeded only by tomato and grapefruit juice (Tables 11 and 13.

Data indicating the annual pack of pineapple juice are given in Table 13.

During the period 1960–1968, the annual pineapple juice production averaged about 13 million cases (Anon. 1969B).

TOMATO JUICE

Tomato juice, introduced in the middle 1920's and first distributed in significant commercial amounts in 1928, held a striking leadership among individual juices until citrus juices gained ascendency during the Second

World War. No other juice or other processed food had as spectacular a growth as tomato juice until frozen concentrated orange juice was introduced after the war. Even since the war, it has shown a continuous marked upward trend and in 1968 exceeded the combined hot pack of cit-

TABLE 14

TOMATO JUICE

Year	Actual Cases	Basis 24/2's Cases	Year	Actual Cases	Basis 24/2's Cases
1931	4,583,635	4,720,000	1951	31,625,534	36,160,291
1933	4,170,492	4,528,105	1952	31,416,590	35,807,067
1934	5,703,920	6,192,998	1953	32,733,466	37,754,370
1935	9,286,590	11,255,854	1954	23,465,873	27,034,309
1936	13,104,809	16,001,820	1955	23,699,438	26,921,365
1937	13,444,972	16,979,057	1956	39,032,309	43,551,768
1938	8,988,028	11,234,567	1957	29,307,511	32,589,549
1939	11,091,068	13,658,619	1958	33,578,929	37,467,126
1940	12,414,186	15,086,168	1959	28,302,919	31,116,076
1941	19,046,257	23,390,935	1960	29,936,714	33,017,987
1942	20,738,394	25,177,653	1961	28,844,786	31,594,291
1943	19,251,559	22,848,901	1962	36,456,839	40,157,886
1944	26,487,392	30,809,202	1963	31,283,810	34,519,313
1945	24,552,853	28,389,140	1964	32,396,978	35,301,128
1946	30,525,274	34,899,677	1965	30,563,532	32,825,343
1947	16,880,277	19,506,182	1966	29,752,599	31,891,207
1948	23,701,199	27,774,403	1967	33,151,208	35,094,076
1949	20,559,673	23,541,854	1968[1]	31,358,746	N.A.
1950	22,740,658	26,179,619			

Pack by Size of Container—Actual Cases

	Units per Case	1964	1965	1966	1967	1968[1]
Indiv. 5–6Z	48	4,720,159	5,679,006	5,590,060	7,049,313	
8Z	48	57,599	[3]	[3]	[3]	
No. 211 cyl	48	1,474,004	1,269,348	1,346,592	1,421,760	N.A.
No. 300(a)	24	2,178,184	1,566,309	1,881,984	1,684,858	
No. 2	24	1,948,165	1,326,654	1,639,213	1,148,019	
29, 32, & 36Z	12	461,885	930,338	539,626	804,608	
No. 3 cyl	12	18,006,150	16,942,898	15,804,126	17,515,633	
No. 10	6	409,410	264,695	314,726	288,633	
Misc. tin and glass		3,141,422	2,584,284	2,636,272	3,238,384	
Total		32,396,978	30,563,532	29,752,599	33,151,208	31,358,746

From: Canned Food Pack Statistics 1968 National Canners Assoc., Washington, D.C.
[1] 1968 figure does not include tomato vegetable juice combinations which were included in previous years.
[2] Includes 303 and 17½ oz.
[3] Included in 5–6 oz.

rus juices which have declined greatly in the face of the spectacular growth of citrus concentrate since 1945. Single-strength tomato juice has never had to compete with concentrated tomato juice for consumer favor. Unlike citrus concentrate, concentrated tomato juice, neither pasteurized nor frozen, has proved popular, although concentrated tomato juice has been made commercially and used in food processing. Factors responsible for the spectacular rise in the popularity of tomato juice are its distinctive and pleasing flavor, its suitability for use at breakfast and also as an appetizer at any meal, and its relatively high vitamin C content together with its timely introduction when the public was vitamin conscious. Also tomato juice is the lowest priced of any single-strength canned juice. Moreover, the tomato being an annual plant, it was possible, in response to the rapid increase in the demand for the juice, to expand the production ot the crop quickly.

Table 14 on the supply and distribution of canned tomato juice and combination vegetable juices containing 70% or more of tomato juice shows that the total pack of these vegetable juices rose rapidly from a beginning in 1929 to 231,000 cases, equivalent of 24 No. 2 cans, to an average of over 12 million cases a year during 1934–1938, when it accounted for 40% of the national total juice pack and per capita consumption of 2.4 lb. Stimulated by war time demands, by 1942–1946 the pack had risen to 28 million cases (30% of all juices or considerably more than double its pre-war average, with a per capita consumption of over 4.5 lb.

From Table 14, which summarizes the annual production of canned hot pack of tomato juice from 1929–1930 to 1968–1969, it will be seen that the annual pack reached its peak in 1956–1957 when more than 43 million cases were processed. Since then, production has been fairly steady averaging more than 31 million cases annually.

OTHER VEGETABLE JUICES

Nearly all of the national pack of vegetable juices is tomato juice, which term as used in industry statistics includes combinations containing 70% or more tomato juice. Tomato juice constituted almost 94% of the 1958 pack and 98% of the 1954 pack of all vegetable juices. In 1967, 33,151,000 cases of tomato juice were packed (Anon. 1969B) whereas only an estimated 1,400,000 cases of "Other Vegetable Juices" were packed.

No data are available on the composition of the pack of vegetable juices other than tomato juice. However, most of this pack is believed to be tomato-vegetable blends in which tomato juice constitutes the largest part of the blend (but less than 70% or otherwise it would be classified as tomato juice). A few unblended vegetable juices were also introduced in the 1930's, mostly carrot and sauerkraut. No statistics are available on their pack. While small in total volume, they are popular sellers in health food stores and some are also sold in retail groceries.

By H. R. LÜTHI[2] | PART 2. THE EUROPEAN FRUIT JUICE INDUSTRY

Introduction

At the end of the last century Switzerland was the birthsite of the European fruit juice industry. At the time a strong movement against excessive alcohol consumption greatly aided its origin and expansion. It soon was able to take a hold in Germany and Austria as well.

In central Europe the development was characterized by a great number of small enterprises operating with the most primitive of means. In general, it consisted in the expansion of the preparation of hard cider. Doubtlessly, this fact was greatly responsible for the faster expansion of the fruit juice market, especially of apple juice, in central Europe rather than in other regions. In the thirties, there were still well over 3000 production sites. During the last decade a strong concentration has set in, yet more than one-third of the enterprises still exists today. Most of them have only small capacity and in most recent times have been an impediment to further technological development and quality standards, and thus to the extension of the fruit juice market.

The actual industrial development of European fruit juice production set in after World War II, especially in the marginal states of Europe. There the first stages of development were skipped. The number of enterprises has shrunk and their technical equipment equals the capacity of the larger central European ones.

Prior to World War II, practically only apple and pear, grape, and berry juices were produced in Europe. Only afterwards the citrus juice industry started expanding in the Mediterranean countries. Most of these enterprises originated during the last ten years. Their models are in America—and often they are economically connected with them.

During the past 20 years, the European fruit juice industry has been organized within the International Federation of Fruit Juice Producers (Head office: Rue de Liège 10, Paris IXe, France). At regular intervals it publishes reports of its symposia.

Production

It is not surprising that the fruit juice industry has its origins in Switzerland. This country has the greatest per capita production in the world of apples and pears. The problem of a large surplus stimulated the production of fruit juice. The raw material used for the preparation of apple and pear juices stems largely from production of fruit not suitable for fresh consumption but solely for the preparation of fruit juice and fruit wines. A great number of varieties used in suitable combinations gives

[2]Federal Agricultural Research Station, Wädenswil, Switzerland.

TABLE 15

FRUIT JUICE PRODUCTION IN SOME EUROPEAN COUNTRIES

	Apple and Pear Juice		Grape Juice		Berry Juice		Citrus Juices		Other Juices	
	1965	1967	1965	1967	1965	1967	1965	1967	Tomato, 1965	Apricot, 1967
	*In Hectoliters**									
Austria	39,262	90,000	2,102	[1]	22,467	25,000	...[2]	...	...	...
Germany	1,100,000	[1]	12,000	[1]	548,900	[1]	...	...	...	...
France	408,398	603,551	545,216	465,242	11,245	9,358	...	...	131,502	80,662
Switzerland	512,343	777,000	110,800	97,000	[1]	2,000	...	...	...	...
Mediterranean countries	301,928	[1]	240,050	9,645	16,000	[1]	724,085	30,658	212,168	67,951
Total	2,361,931	1,470,551	910,168	571,885	598,612	36,358	724,085	30,658	343,670	148,613

All Juices

	Austria		Germany		France		Switzerland		Mediterranean Countries	
	1965	1967	1965	1967	1965	1967	1965	1967	1965	1967
Total Production	63,831	133,200	1,760,000	[1]	1,101,580	1,161,242	623,143	876,000	1,249,105	108,254

Source: International Federation of Fruit Juice Producers, Paris.
* One hectoliter = 26.42 U.S. gal.
[1] No data available.
[2] ... = no production.

excellent juice qualities. Only recently, the surplus of apples and pears intended for fresh consumption is taking on greater importance in the European fruit juice industry. Thus problems of preparation and juice treatment have arisen which up until now were unknown to industry.

The previously mentioned foundations for production as well as geographical conditions have characterized the European fruit juice enterprises. In the Mediterranean sector, the citrus industry produced mainly concentrates, which are partly marketed in individual containers and partly sold in bulk. These have entered the frozen food market. The other fruit juice products are stored in large tanks. The previously customary storage of single-strength juice is slowly being replaced by storage in concentrated form. Depending upon further use the juice is stored as "half concentrate" at approximately 35–50°Brix, or as "full concentrate" at approximately 70°Brix at temperatures near the freezing point. The "half concentrate" plays the part of an intermediate product which finds any number of further uses. For industrial use the fruit juices are packed in returnable bottles.

Development of Production and Consumption of Fruit Juice in Europe

It is extremely difficult to get accurate data on the fruit juice production in Europe. The indicated figures must, however, be considered minimal values. The reasons lie in the political structure of Europe as well as in the greatly varied legislations or organizations of industry. Apple juice still holds first place among fruit juices. Its main producers are in Germany, Switzerland, and France. In second place, we find grape juice, the most important producers of which are in France, Italy, Switzerland, and Spain. The production of citrus juices ranks third, concentrated mainly in Spain and Italy. Next we have berry juices, with Germany, Austria, and Poland as most important producers. Pulpy juices are produced in great quantities in Italy. Tomato juice and tomato juice concentrate are produced mainly in Italy as well as in other Mediterranean countries, including France, Spain, and Portugal. On the European market, however, tomato juice has not yet become of importance. The same is true of vegetable juices, the production of which is only just beginning in a few countries.

Per Capita Consumption of Fruit Juices in Some European Countries in 1969 (All Juices)

Switzerland	14 liters = 3.69 U.S. gal
Germany	8.5 liters = 2.23 U.S. gal

Austria	2.5 liters = 0.66 U.S. gal
France and Italy less than	2 liters = 0.5 U.S. gal

The International Federation of Fruit Juice Producers has made attempts at collecting statistical data of fruit juice production from all over Europe. The figures in Table 15 are taken from the latest available information.

BIBLIOGRAPHY

ANON. 1964. The story of pineapple. Western Canner and Packer *26,* No. 2, 19–30.

ANON. 1969A. Florida Agricultural Statistics: citrus summary *1969.* Fla. Dept. Agr., Tallahassee, Fla.

ANON. 1969B. Canned and bottled juice, juice drink, and concentrate pack. Canner/Packer *138,* No. 10, (Yearbook No.) 85–86.

ANON. 1969C. Frozen juice and concentrate pack. Canner/Packer *138,* No. 10 (Yearbook No.) 97.

ANON. 1970. Summaries of trade and tariff information. Schedule 1. Animal and vegetable products, *10,* Beverages. TC Publ. 317, Washington D.C.

CALIFORNIA PRUNE ADVISORY BOARD. 1960. Prune juice purchases and availability in retail stores in the U.S. Oct. 1949–Dec. 1959. Mimeo. San Francisco, Calif.

CANCO MARKETING DIVISION. 1960. Summer Servings in Urban American Homes of Fruit Juice Drinks and Fruit and Vegetable Juices. American Can Co., New York.

CHARLEY, V. L. S., *et al.* 1950. Recent advances in fruit juice production. Commonwealth Bur. Hort. Plant Crops Tech. Comm. *21.*

COMMONWEALTH ECONOMIC COMMITTEE. 1960. Fruit: A review of production and trade relating to fresh, canned and dried fruit, fruit juices and wine. Annual Rept. London.

DALRYMPLE, D. G. 1958A. Marketing of fresh apple juice and cider. Conn. Agr. Expt. Sta. and Agr. Exten. Serv. Prog. Rept. *27.*

DALRYMPLE, D. G. 1958B. Marketing of apple juice in Europe. Conn. Agr. Expt. Sta. and Agr. Exten. Serv. Supplement No. 1 to Prog. Rept. *27.*

DALRYMPLE, D. G. 1959A. Flavor ratings and chemical analysis of apple juice and cider. Conn. Agr. Expt. Sta. and Agr. Exten. Serv. Supplement to Prog. Rep. *27.*

DALRYMPLE, D. G. 1959B. Marketing fresh apple juice and cider—some recent developments. Conn. Agr. Expt. Sta. and Agr. Exten. Serv. Supplement to Prog. Rept. *27.*

DALRYMPLE, D. G. 1960. Marketing potentials for apple juice and cider. Mich. State Univ., Dept. Agr. Econ. Agr. Econ. *804.*

GACHOT, H. 1948. Fruit Juices—A Practical and Theoretical Manual for the Preparation and Preservation of Fruit Juices. Editions P. H. Heitz, Zurich, Switzerland.

HAMILTON, H. G. 1959. Major changes in the Florida citrus industry. *In* Economic Leaflets, Bureau of Economic and Business Research, Univ. Florida. *28:* Nos. 9 and 10.

HAVIGHORST, C. R. 1948–1949. Advanced methods of Hawaiian Pineapple Co.-Agriculture-Processing-Distribution. Food Inds. *20,* 1725–1730, 1864–1866, *21,* 3–7, 167–170, 754–757, 868, 870, 872.

HIEMSTRA, S. J. 1970. Food consumption, prices and expenditures. Agr. Economic Service, U.S. Dept. Agr. Supplement to Agricultural Econ. Rept. *138.*

HOOS, S. 1956. Tomato and tomato products. Economic trends and f.o.b. price relationships. Calif. Agr. Expt. Sta. Giannini Foundation of Agricultural Economics. Mimeo. Rept. *185.*

HOOS, S. 1960. The lemon industry. Economic Situation. California Citrograph *45,* No. 9, 284–285.

HOOS, S., and BOLES, J. N. 1952. Oranges and Orange Products. Changing Economic Relationships. 1952. Calif. Agr. Expt. Sta. Bull. *732,* 1–68.

HOOS, S., and MEISSNER, F. 1952. California canning tomatoes. Economic trends and statistics. Calif. Agr. Expt. Sta. Giannini Foundation of Agr. Econ. Mimeo. Unnumbered Rept.

HOOS, S., and SELTZER, R. E. 1952. Lemons and lemon products: changing economic relationships, 1951–1952. Calif. Agr. Expt. Sta. Bull. *729.*

MEHLITZ, A. 1951. Unfermented Juices. Serger and Hempel. Braunschweig, Germany.

NATIONAL CANNERS ASSOCIATION. 1969. Canned food pack statistics for 1968. 72–79.

PUBOLS, B. H. 1960. Trends in consumption of citrus fruits. U.S. Agr. Mkting. Serv. Fruit Situation TFS-*135.* 24–33.

REDIT, W. H., *et al.* 1951. Transportation of frozen citrus concentrate by railroad and motor truck from Florida to northern markets. U.S. Dept. Agr. Information Bull. *62.*

SUNKIST GROWERS. 1960. Statistical information on the citrus industry. Supplement *1960.* Marketing Research Dept., Los Angeles, Calif.

TIMMONS, D. E. 1950. Citrus canning in Florida. Early history and current statistics. Univ. Fla. Agr. Expt. Series, Agr. Econ. Dept., E Series 50–4.

TRESSLER, D. K. 1938. Fruit and vegetable juices. Fruit Products J. *17,* 196–198, 210, 235–237, 249.

U.S. DEPT. AGRICULTURE. 1969A. Handbook of agricultural charts. Agr. Handbook *373.* Washington, D.C.

U.S. DEPT. AGRICULTURE. 1969B. Citrus fruits by states, 1967–1968 and 1968–1969. Production, use, value. Statistical Reporting Service, Fr Nt 3–1 (10–96). U.S. Dept. Agr., Washington, D.C.

U.S. DEPT. AGRICULTURE. 1969C. Agricultural Statistics 1969. U.S. Dept. Agr., Washington, D.C.

U.S. DEPT. AGRICULTURE. 1970. The Fruit Situation, Economic Research Service *TFS 174,* U.S. Dept. Agr., Washington, D.C.

WESTERN CANNER AND PACKER. 1936. Product Survey No. 11. Canned and bottled fruit juices, *28,* No. 6, 9–13.

WESTERN CANNER AND PACKER. 1960. Yearbook Number Western Edition *129,* No. 10, San Francisco, Calif.

WINKLER. 1959. Methods of commercial juice production—present and past. Industrial Obst.-U. Gemüseverwert *44,* 563–565.

CHAPTER 2

Matthew K. Veldhuis

Orange and Tangerine Juices

INTRODUCTION

"Breakfast without orange juice is like a day without sunshine," is a slogan of a state agency promoting citrus products. Indeed, orange juice is a favorite for breakfast and at many other times during the day. It is known for its good flavor as well as its nutritional value. The flavor of orange is favored, not only in natural fruit juices, juice drinks, and ades but in synthetic drinks as well. Natural orange juice products (canned, chilled, frozen or juice drinks) compete very well with synthetic products and it is considered unlikely that natural citrus beverages will be largely replaced. A recent survey shows that natural orange juices and orange juice drinks account for nearly 40% of all fruit juices and fruit-flavored drinks consumed at home.

The production of orange juice products has undergone a remarkable development in the past 25 to 30 years. Previous to the World War II orange juice production was 3 million cases a year or lower and blends of orange and grapefruit about the same, while frozen concentrated juices and tangerine juices were nonexistent. Since that time the volume of citrus juice products has increased until it has reached the equivalent of over 175 million cases (24 cans 18 oz) per year and has become a very important factor in the diet.

During the 1968–69 season there were about 194,000,000 boxes[1] of oranges (including tangerines) produced in the United States. Of the total crop approximately 72% was raised in Florida, 23% in California and the remaining 5% in Arizona and Texas. About 87% of the crop was processed into juices and concentrates. In Florida, only 8% of the orange crop was marketed as fresh fruit, the remainder being processed. Figure 8 illustrates the production of single-strength canned and chilled juices and frozen concentrated orange juice during the past 25 years. The most outstanding fact is the rapid increase in frozen concentrated orange juice. It seems that the market still has not been saturated and each time orange production goes up, the added crop is marketed largely in this form. Reduction in yields in 1962–63 and 1967–68 were due to freezes in the citrus-

MATTHEW K. VELDHUIS, is Chief, U.S. Fruit and Vegetable Products Laboratory, Winter Haven, Fla., a laboratory of the Southern Utilization Research and Development Division, Agricultural Research Service, U.S. Department of Agriculture.

[1] Net content of box varies: in California and Arizona, average is 77 lb; in Florida and other states, 90 lb.

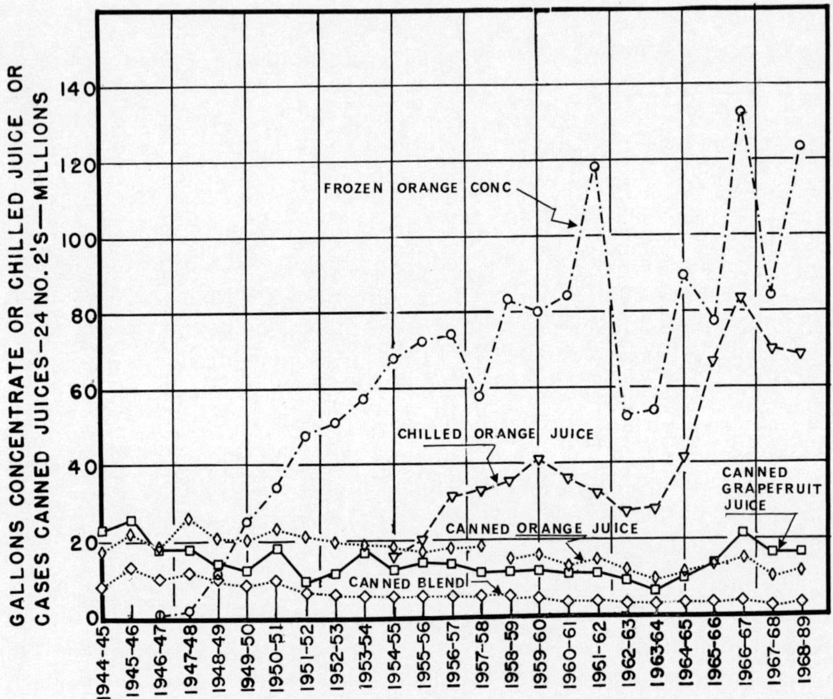

Fig. 8. Production of Canned Orange Juice, Grapefruit Juice, Chilled Orange Juice, and Frozen Concentrated Orange Juice

producing areas of Florida. Fortunately, carry-over from bumper production from the preceding years was available to supply most of the demand. Another remarkable item is the outstanding growth of the convenience food, chilled orange juice (in 1- and 2-qt jars) which is second only to frozen concentrate in using oranges. Canned single-strength juices have experienced some decrease during this period, but they still are important outlets for citrus fruit and bring the nutritive value of the fruit to the consumer in a very satisfactory way. For comparison, a gallon of concentrate equals 4 gal of juice and a case of juice equals $3^3/_8$ gal. Tangerine juices have ranged from 50,000 to 500,000 cases in recent years but more and more is used in frozen concentrated orange juice, or in single-strength juice where up to 10% may be used to improve color and adjust acidity to more desirable levels.

COMMERCIAL VARIETIES OF ORANGES

Commercial varieties of oranges for processing can be classified conveniently according to the time required between blossoming and harvesting. Blossoming in all areas in the United States is normally at about the same time, in March and April. In Florida and Texas, the early season oranges mature in October to December and are characterized by the *Parson Brown* and *Hamlin.* Mid-season oranges in Texas and Florida mature during January, February and March and the usual variety is the *Pineapple orange,* so designated because of the fragrance in the grove on certain occasions. The late season varieties mature in March, April and May and the usual variety is *Valencia.*

In California and Arizona, the predominant varieties are *Washington Navel* which matures from November to May and *Valencia* which matures there from March to October. The cooler temperatures in California result in longer times between bloom and harvest; it is well over a year for Valencia. Unfortunately a bitter substance, limonin, usually forms in the juice from the Navel orange shortly after extraction so the fruit is used in beverage bases and other products where the slight bitterness is not objectionable. Valencia oranges are favored for processing. California fruit tends to be somewhat more acid or tart than that from Texas and Florida. Emphasis is placed on the use of oranges for marketing as fresh fruit in California and Arizona and anything extra is used for processing. In Florida and Texas, the principal use for the fruit is for processing, particularly the mid-season and late-season types.

There are a number of minor varieties which have special merits for fresh market use, but for processing they generally resemble the varieties listed which mature at the same time.

Mandarin Type Oranges

These are "loose-skinned" types that peel easily by hand. They are generally blended with oranges and serve useful purposes in permitting the processing of more uniform, pleasing products.

Dancy tangerines are grown largely in Florida and are the common type found on fresh fruit markets. They are grown primarily for fresh market use and surplus fruit is processed for juice or concentrate .

Temple oranges, a hybrid, are raised mainly in Florida. Usually they are blended with other oranges for juice.

The *Tangelo,* a hybrid of tangerine and grapefruit, is chiefly a Florida fruit, but its unusual flavor limits its use for processing.

ANATOMY OF THE FRUIT

Citrus fruits belong to the *Rutaceae* family and are classified by Swingle (Webber and Batchelor 1943) as follows:

Citrus medica—citron
C. limon—lemon
C. reticulata—mandarin (including tangerine)

C. *indica*—Indian wild orange
C. *grandis*—pummelo
C. *paradise*—grapefruit
C. *aurnatifolia*—lime
C. *sinensis*—sweet orange
C. *aurantium*—sour orange

The orange consists of an outer peel which serves largely as a cover to the inner pulp or juice-bearing bodies of the fruit. Viewing these facts in more detail, the inner flesh of the ripe fruit consists of segments (carpels, locules) distributed about a soft pithy core forming the central axis of the fruit. Each segment is surrounded by a thin wall (carpellary membrane, locular wall) which is a tissue of epidermal origin. The juice-containing bodies of the mature fruit are closely compacted, club-shaped vesicles which completely fill the segments and are attached to the walls with small hair-like papillae. Multicellular in structure, the extremely thin-walled cells contain, besides juice, the color-bearing yellow chromatophores. Oil droplets embedded within the cellular tissue occur in the

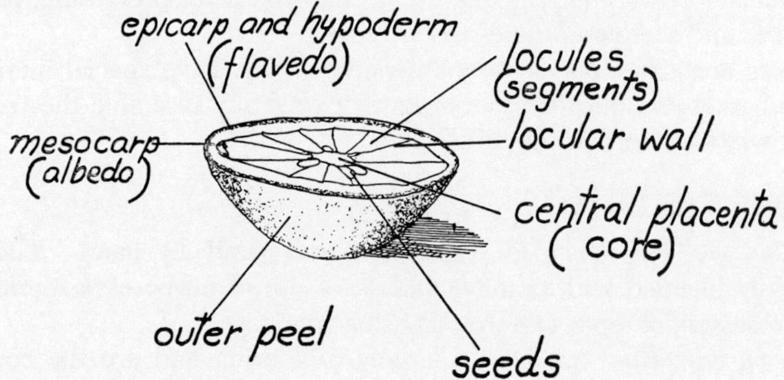

Fig. 9. Macroscopic Structure of Halved Orange

central part of each juice vesicle (Davis 1932). In addition, the segments of most varieties contain seeds attached by means of placentae to the walls (carpellary membrane) where these come in contact with the pithy core of the fruit (Fig. 9). The surrounding rind, or peel, consists of an outer colored portion (flavedo) and an inner white, spongy layer of parenchymatous cells (albedo) closely adherent to the outer walls of the segments. The epidermal layer of cells comprising the flavedo contain numerous oil vesicles and chromtaophores. The oil vesicles are balloon-shaped cells which are more or less easily ruptured; oil from these cells furnishes the familiar orange oil of commerce. The chromatophores are green in young fruits and yellow in mature fruits. The cells of the spongy

TABLE 16

PHYSICAL AND CHEMICAL COMPOSITION OF GRAPEFRUIT AND ORANGES[1]

Physical		Chemical	
Component	Per Cent	Component	Per Cent
Juice	40–45	Water	86–92
Flavedo (outer peel)	8–10	Sugars	5–8
Albedo (inner peel)	15–30	Pectin	1–2
Rag and pulp	20–30	Glycosides	0.1–1.5
Seeds	0–4	Pentosans	0.8–1.2
		Acids (essentially citric)	0.7–1.5
		Fiber	0.6–0.9
		Protein	0.6–0.8
		Fat	0.2–0.5
		Essential oil	0.2–0.5
		Minerals	0.5–0.9

[1] From Hendrickson, R., and Kesterson, J. W. 1951. Citrus by-products of Florida. Fla. Agr. Expt. Sta. Bull. *487*.

tissue underlying the epidermal cells are loosely arranged toward the inner portion. An extensive system of radially branching vascular bundles extends throughout this whole tissue.

Substances responsible for some of the bitterness developing in the juice are located chiefly in the carpellary membranes, the vascular bundles, the spongy pith, and the inner spongy tissues (albedo) of the peel. The seeds also contain limonin, which is intensely bitter: Pectic substances and pectic enzymes are present largely in the inner peel. The oxidizing enzyme, peroxidase, is also largely present in the vascular bundles of the peel.

COMPOSITION OF THE FRUIT

The composition of citrus fruits is affected by such factors as growing conditions, various treatments and practices, maturity, rootstock and variety, and climate. The same variety grown in different citrus areas will also vary in composition. As an example, California Valencia juice is, in general, more deeply colored and more acid than Florida Valencia juice. Table 16 gives an indication of the range of the physical and chemical composition of grapefruit and oranges (Hendrickson and Kesterson 1951), and Table 17 gives the approximate composition of the juice of oranges. In this connection, it has been found that mature oranges (and grapefruit) have a considerably higher concentration of total soluble solids in their stylar than in their stem halves, and concentration of total soluble solids in the segments of a given fruit may differ greatly in mature fruit (Bartholomew and Sinclair 1941). More detailed data on the chemical composition of the orange, including environmental and cultural factors and scions and rootstock are given in a recently published monograph edited by Sinclair (1961).

TABLE 17

APPROXIMATE COMPOSITION OF ORANGE JUICE

Variety	Total Soluble Solids (Brix), %	Total Acid as Citric, %	pH	Ratio Solids/Acid	Vitamin C, mg/ml	Reducing Sugars, %	Sucrose, %	Total Sugars, %
Parson Brown (Florida)[1]	9.5–11.6	0.55–0.87	3.4–4.3	10.9–21.2	0.56–0.58	3.7–4.3	3.1–4.4	6.8– 8.7
Hamlin (Florida)[1]	8.4– 9.6	0.70–0.89	3.4–4.2	9.4–13.7	0.46–0.50	3.0–2.6	2.4–3.7	5.4– 6.3
Homosassa (Florida)[1]	8.1–10.7	0.57–1.5	3.0–4.0	5.4–18.7	0.47–0.53	3.5–3.3	1.9–2.8	5.4– 6.1
Pineapple (Florida)[1]	7.8–12.0	0.75–1.2	3.3–3.9	6.5–16.0	0.42–0.48	3.1–3.7	2.3–3.5	5.4– 7.2
Seedlings (Florida)[1]	8.9–13.1	1.0 –2.1	2.8–3.6	4.2–13.1	0.53–0.54	...	...	...
Valencia (Florida)[1]	10.1–12.5	0.40–1.5	3.1–4.3	6.7–31.2	0.29–0.45	3.5–4.7	2.5–5.1	6.0– 9.8
Valencia (California)[2]	9.1–13.7	0.96–2.2	3.0–3.6	4.7–12.4	0.41–0.75	4.3–5.8[3]	...	7.3–10.5[3]
Navel (California)[2]	7.2–14.4	0.85–1.3	...	9.2–14.4	0.29–0.80	...	...	...

[1] Compiled from Harding, P. L., Winston, J. R., and Fisher, D. F. 1940. Seasonal changes in Florida oranges, U.S. Dept. Agr. Tech. Bull. *753*.
[2] Compiled from data supplied by C. G. Beisel, Real Gold Citrus Products, Anaheim, California.
[3] Compiled from data of Sinclair, W. B., and Bartholomew, E. T. 1944. Effect of rootstock and environment on the composition of oranges and grapefruit, Hilgardia, *16*, No. 3, 125–176.

Inasmuch as in the process of juice extraction, pressure, and tearing forces are exerted upon the various tissues of the orange in varying degrees, the extracted juice contains substances from these tissues. Some of these elements may be responsible for undesirable changes occurring in processed orange juice, and a knowledge of some of the constituents of the fruit would be of value in helping combat these changes.

Peel Oil

In the extraction of orange juice a certain amount of oil from the peel will be extracted at the same time. The amount of oil incorporated can be controlled by the settings of the extractor, or excessive amounts can be removed in a vacuum deoiler before canning. The oil vaporizes during the manufacture of concentrate and cold-pressed peel oil must be added before final packing. Opinions vary but a peel oil content of 0.020 to 0.025% v/v in juice is generally preferred. Peel oil is essential to good flavor of any citrus juice, but like most things it can be overdone. Most people object to 0.050% v/v as being much too strong.

The composition of orange and other peel oils has been the subject of many investigations. It has long been known that *d*-limonene is the principal component, comprising from 90 to 95% of the oil. A number of aldehydes, ketones, terpenes, and sesquiterpenes were also known to be present. The development of gas chromatography, together with infrared, ultraviolet, nuclear magnetic resonance and mass spectroscopy has permitted the examination for components present in much more detail than before.

A list of compounds that have been shown to be present in cold-pressed orange peel oil is given in Table 18. The 87 compounds listed illustrate the complexity of the product. Most of the compounds have some odor and contribute something to the overall effect but the oxygenated constituents such as aldehydes, ketones, esters and alcohols probably are the more important. Which compounds are essential to optimum quality and in what amounts still remains to be determined. Earlier tests stressed total aldehyde content, but some of the aldehydes may be detrimental to optimum flavor, especially if the straight chain aldehydes of 8 to 12 carbons are present in high amounts.

Changes occur in the composition of oil in orange juice as shown by Kirchner and Miller (1957). During storage for three years the main changes were a loss in total volatile oil, conversion of hydrocarbons to alcohols and losses in esters, aldehydes, and terpene aliphatic alcohols. They came to the conclusion that off-flavor of stored canned orange juice appears to come from nonvolatile precursors. They noted some of the compounds reported in Table 18 and in addition reported β-myrcene,

TABLE 18

COMPOSITION OF COLD-PRESSED ORANGE PEEL OIL

α-β-Unsaturated aldehydes[1]
- α-Hexyl-β-heptyl acrolein
- α-Hexyl-β-octyl acrolein
- α-Heptyl-β-heptyl acrolein
- α-Octyl-β-heptyl acrolein
- α-Hexyl-β-nonyl acrolein

Aldehydes[2]
- *n*-Hexanal
- *n*-Heptanal
- *n*-Octanal
- *n*-Nonanal
- *n*-Decanal
- *n*-Undecanal
- *n*-Dodecanal
- Citronellal
- Neral
- Geranial
- Perillaldehyde
- α-Sinensal
- β-Sinensal

Ketones[2]
- 6-Methyl-5-hepten-2-one[3]
- Carvone
- Piperitenone[3]
- Nootkatone

Oxides[2]
- *trans*-Limonene oxide
- *cis*-Limonene oxide

Esters[2]
- Octyl acetate
- Perillyl acetate
- 1,8,*p*-Menthadiene-9-yl acetate

Alcohols[4]
- *n*-Heptanol
- *n*-Octanol
- *n*-Nonanol
- *n*-Decanol
- *n*-Undecanol
- *n*-Dodecanol
- Linalool
- Citronellol
- α-Terpineol
- *trans*-Carveol
- Geraneol
- Nerol
- *cis*-2-8-*p*-Menthadiene-1-ol
- *trans*-2-8-*p*-Menthadiene-1-ol
- *cis*-Carveol
- 1-*p*-Menthene-9-ol
- 1-8-*p*-Menthadien-9-ol
- 8-*p*-Menthene-1,2-diol
- Elemol

Paraffins[5]
- n-$C_{21}H_{44}$
- 2-Methyl-$C_{21}H_{43}$
- n-$C_{22}H_{46}$
- 2-Methyl-$C_{22}H_{45}$
- n-$C_{23}H_{48}$
- 3-Methyl-$C_{23}H_{47}$
- n-$C_{24}H_{50}$
- 2-Methyl-$C_{24}H_{49}$
- n-$C_{25}H_{52}$
- 3-Methyl-$C_{25}H_{51}$
- n-$C_{26}H_{54}$
- 2-Methyl-$C_{26}H_{53}$
- n-$C_{27}H_{56}$
- 3-Methyl-$C_{27}H_{55}$
- n-$C_{28}H_{58}$
- 2-Methyl-$C_{28}H_{57}$
- n-$C_{29}H_{60}$

Terpenes[6]
- α-Pinene
- Camphene
- 2,4-*p*-Menthadiene
- Sabinene
- Myrcene
- Δ-3-Carene
- α-Phellandrene
- α-Terpinene
- *d*-Limonene
- β-Terpinene
- *p*-Cymene
- Terpinolene
- α-Thujene

Sesquiterpenes[6,7]
- α-Cubebene
- Copaene
- Farnesene
- β-Elemene
- β-Cubebene
- β-Copaene
- Caryophylene
- α-Humulene
- β-Humulene
- Valencene
- Δ-Cadinene
- Pentadecane

[1] Moshonas and Lund (1969A).
[2] Moshonas and Lund (1969B).
[3] Moshonas (1967).
[4] Hunter and Moshonas (1965).
[5] Hunter and Brogden (1966).
[6] Hunter and Brogden (1965).
[7] Veldhuis and Hunter (1967).

ethyl isovalerate, methyl alpha-ethyl *n*-caproate, citronellyl acetate, terpinyl acetate, *n*-terpinol and *l*-hexanol.

Tangerine peel oil contains α-pinene, β-pinene, myrcene, *d*-limonene, γ-terpinene, *p*-cymene, terpinolene, Δ-elemene, copaene, pentadecane, α-elemene, caryophylene, β-elemene, α-humulene, β-humulene, and Δ-cadinene (Hunter and Brogden 1965 and Veldhuis and Hunter 1968). It also contains linalool, octanol, *cis*- and *trans*-2,8-*p*-methadiene-1-ol, nonanol, nerol, geraniol, *trans*-carveol, 1-*p*-menthene-9-ol, dodecanol, 1-8-*p*-menthadiene-9-ol, elemol, thymol, 8-*p*-menthene-1,2-diol, and *o*-phenyl phenol (Hunter and Brogden 1966).

Volatile Constituents

The commercial recovery of fragrant volatile essences from orange juice has become an established practice. Perhaps half the plants in Florida have one type or another of essence recovery equipment. Recovered essence may be used along with cold-pressed peel oil to supplant or supplement fresh "cut-back" juice in imparting a fresh flavor to frozen concentrated orange juice. It also permits the manufacture of full-flavored, high-Brix (55°–65°Brix) concentrates which would conserve shipping and storage space and weight. The first essence recovery units operated separately, under high vacuum. Later units were developed which were a part of the evaporator and operate at atmospheric conditions or nearly so. These later units cost much less to build and since they use much less energy, they are less expensive to operate.

The chemical composition of the water soluble constituents in orange essence is of interest. It is desirable to know which constituents are present and which are the more important from a flavor standpoint. Compounds isolated from orange juice essence are given in Table 19. In view of the number of compounds, it is not surprising that a clear picture of the significance of each compound has not been established. A few things can be said, however. The most abundant compound by far is ethanol and essence of 100-fold concentration (1 volume will flavor 100 volumes of juice) may contain as much as 10% ethanol, while everything else may be well below 0.1%. Obviously ethanol contributes little to flavor.

Several methods of control have been suggested for evaluating essence including a modification of the COD method by Dougherty (1968) in which any insoluble oil is eliminated in a trap before the determination is made. The main compound responding to this method is ethanol so the value of the results is limited except in that it does give an overall estimation on how well the volatiles are being collected. Another approach has been the estimation of oxygenated terpenes as $C_{10}H_{18}O$, saturated aliphatic aldehydes as octanal, α,β-unsaturated aldehydes as citral and for esters as ethyl butyrate (Attaway *et al.* 1967). These methods are helpful in judging the effectiveness of a given recovery method, but as yet do

TABLE 19

COMPOSITION OF NATURAL ORANGE JUICE ESSENCE

Aldehydes and Ketones
Acetone
Acetaldehyde
n-Hexanal
2-Hexenal
1-Octanal
1-Nonanal
1-Decanal
Neral
Geranial
Carvone
2-Octenal
Methyl heptenone
Undecanal
Citronellal
Esters
Ethyl butyrate
Ethyl caproate
Ethyl caprylate
Linalyl acetate
Terpinyl formate
Citronellyl butyrate
Alcohols
Methanol
Ethanol
1-Propanol
2-Butanol
1-Butanol
2-Pentanol
1-Pentanol
1-Hexanol
cis-3-Hexen-1-ol
Linalool
3-Hepten-1-ol
1-Octanol
Terpinen-4-ol
1-Nonanol
α-Terpineol
1-Decanol
Citronellol
Nerol
Geraniol
Carveol
Terpene Hydrocarbons
α-Pinene
β-Pinene
D-Limonene
Myrcene
γ-Terpinene
α-Terpinene
Valencene
Acids
Formic
Acetic
Propionic
Butyric
Caproic
Capric
Valeric
Oxides
cis-Linalool oxide
trans-Linalool oxide
cis-Limonene oxide
trans-Limonene oxide

Source: Wolford and Attaway (1967).

not provide an accurate measure of quality. It is thought that ethyl butyrate is important in imparting a fresh floral characteristic to citrus juices. Other esters probably contribute. The aldehydes and volatile acids have distinctive flavors, and probably contribute to the overall fragrance. Probably the lower molecular weight alcohols and terpene hydrocarbons contribute the least. Valencene, a sesquiterpene hydrocarbon is a very predominant peak in the gas chromatogram. While it has little aroma, it can be used to make nootkatone, which has a strong odor of grapefruit.

Many of the same compounds are found in both cold-pressed orange oil and in essence. Theoretically one might expect a distribution of all compounds between the oil and aqueous phases in proportion to the solubility in the two phases. The relative abundance in one or the other phase according to solubility would make a given compound easier to detect in that phase. It is observed that there are more terpenes, sesquiterpines, aldehydes and paraffins in the oil and more alcohols, esters and volatile acids in the essence.

Kirchner *et al.* (1950) found hydrogen sulfide in California Navel and Valencia orange juice. This is also probably present in orange juices from other growing regions.

Sugars

Early work by Scurti and dePlato (1909) indicated that sugars in oranges were glucose, levulose, and sucrose. Of interest in this connection is their statement that glucose and levulose are used up during ripening, and sucrose diminishes. If this were true, total sugars would decrease during ripening, which is not in accordance with the facts as we now know them. Curl and Veldhuis (1948) found that 50.5% of the total sugars in Florida Valencia concentrated orange juice was sucrose, 23.7% glucose, and 25.8% levulose. McCready *et al.* (1950) showed glucose, levulose, and sucrose and quantities of acid-hydrolyzable glycoside containing galactose, glucose, and rhamnose to be present in California orange juice.

Enzyme Technology[2]

Enzyme technology in food processing was recently reviewed in a book (Reed 1966) and in several articles (Joslyn 1963; Underkofler 1960; and Schwimmer 1969). These general reviews do not include the trends and prospects of using enzymes in citrus processing. Development of an enzyme technology in citrus processing follows from fresh approaches to the problems of (1) juice clarification, (2) flavor degradation, (3) grapefruit bitterness, and (4) juice acidity.

Juice Clarification.—When juice is extracted from citrus fruit, the cellular integrity of the juice cell is destroyed. Most of the enzymes that synthesize the sugars, acids and myriad of flavor compounds are not active in the acidic juice. However, the activity of some enzymes are potentiated by extraction. Unless controlled, the activated enzymes destroy the appearance and flavor of the juice.

Pectinesterase (PE) is an enzyme whose activity is released from control when juice is extracted. The activity of PE in the intact fruit has not been studied but much has been written about its activity in juice. Sinclair (1961) reviewed the extensive literature on the relation between PE activity, pectic changes, and clarification and gelation in orange juice and orange juice concentrate. PE demethylates pectin which triggers the formation of calcium pectate and the subsequent colloidal and physical changes resulting in clarification of the juice.

Heat inactivation is relied upon in commercial processing to control PE

[2] The assistance of Joseph H. Bruemmer, U.S. Fruit and Vegetable Products Laboratory, Winter Haven, Fla. in preparing the part on Enzyme Technology is acknowledged.

activity and prevent clarification during storage and distribution. PE is inhibited by plant extracts (Kew and Veldhuis 1960, 1961) but commercial use of inhibitors has not developed. Removing the substrate, pectin, was recently proposed to control PE mediated clarification (Baker and Bruemmer 1970). This proposal was based on evidence that soluble pectin is not required for support of orange juice cloud. Baker and Bruemmer showed that the subcellular particles that form the natural cloud in orange juice also formed a stable cloud in water and in simulated orange juice without pectin. The subcellular particles also formed a stable cloud in orange juice serum (clarified orange juice) in which the pectin has been depolymerized with the commercial pectin-enzyme, Klerzyme 200. Klerzyme 200 contains polymethylgalacturonase (PMG) and polygalacturonase (PG) activities (Baker and Bruemmer 1970). PMG hydrolyzes pectin to mono- and digalacturonic acids; it does not hydrolyze pectic acid, the demethylated pectin containing free carboxylic acid groups. PG, which required free carboxylic acid groups for activity, hydrolyzes only pectic acid and not pectin. In removing soluble pectin by depolymerization, Baker and Bruemmer (1969) interrupted the chain of reactions leading to clarification without destroying PE. These observations suggest that PE-mediated clarification of citrus juices can be prevented without heat by depolymerizing pectin and pectic acid to oligogalaturonic acids, which do not form insoluble calcium salts.

Numerous degrading enzymes are released into citrus juices but the high acidity of the juice, combined with heat pasteurization, destroys or minimizes their activity. PE is the only enzyme in citrus juices that has been identified unequivocally with deterioration of commercial packs.

Flavor Degradation.—An oxidoreductase that catalyzes the reduction of aldehydes to alcohols is released into juice during extraction (Bruemmer and Roe 1970A). Both saturated and unsaturated aldehydes are reduced but α,β-unsaturated aldehydes are reduced faster (Bruemmer and Roe 1970B). The enzyme requires the coenzyme, reduced nicotinamide adenine dinucleotide (NADH) for reduction. The coenzyme is destroyed in the acidic juice but oxidoreductase activity can be detected in concentrated protein fractions of citrus juices when commercial NADH is added. However, the enzyme is probably not active in stored juice because of the absence of NADH.

The formation of α,β-unsaturated aldehydes is a serious problem in citrus processing because these compounds contribute to the "citrus-oxidized flavor" (COF) of off-flavored frozen citrus products. Blair *et al.* (1957) produced COF in grapefruit seed oil by chemical dehydration, and identified formation of COF with α,β-unsaturated aldehydes. The nonoxidative development of COF suggested to them that α,β-unsautrated aldehydes in the juice are not oxidized products of unsaturated fatty acids, but are biochemical dehydration products of "aldol-like" intermediates of fatty acid biosynthesis. Blair *et al.* (1957) also presented the following evidence that the redox level in the juice controls this dehydration reaction: first, decreasing the redox level by vigorously aerating the citrus product before storage increased COF; secondly, "extra" ascorbic acid added during processing decreased COF. Presumably, ascorbic acid increased the redox level and inhibited biochemical dehydration of the aldol intermediates.

The NADH-dependent reduction of α,β-unsaturated aldehydes is an example of the potential for use of native enzymes in citrus to overcome off-flavors. The "extra" ascorbic acid could be inhibiting accumulation of α,β-unsaturated aldehydes by initiating reactions to reduce the aldehyde to the alcohol through the NADH-oxidoreductase. Bruemmer and Roe (1970C) showed that the quinone reductase system in orange juice can use ascorbate to reduce NAD to NADH. The NAD is the "storage form" of the coenzyme in citrus juice and is stable under the acidic conditions (Bruemmer 1969). Reduced glutathione, reduced quinones, and other substrates of NAD-dehydrogenases can enzymically generate NADH from NAD in the presence of their specific enzyme. If these dehydrogenases are active in the processed juice, addition of these biochemical reductants would probably be as effective as ascorbate in decreasing development of the α,β-unsaturated aldehyde-type COF.

Glucose oxidase is the only commercial enzyme that has been formulated into citrus drinks to prevent flavor deterioration (Underkofler 1968). Glucose oxidase requires molecular oxygen to oxidize glucose to gluconic acid. The rate of oxidation at low O_2-tensions is high enough that the oxidase can actively scavenge minute traces of oxygen from a solution containing glucose when catalase is present to remove the hydrogen peroxide that is formed in the reaction. By removing oxygen in the glass packed citrus drinks, the enzyme prevents light dependent oxidative reactions.

Grapefruit Bitterness.—Naringin is the bitter component of grapefruit. Naringinase is a rhamnosidase that hydrolyzes naringin to prunin, the nonbitter 7-glucoside of naringenin, and rhamnose. Ting (1958) detected naringinase activity in a commercial pectic enzyme preparation and proposed its use in debittering grapefruit juice. Selective destruction of the pectic enzymes in an enzyme preparation from *A. niger* has made available a highly active preparation (Omura *et al.* 1963) for process development work on both grapefruit juice and sections (Olsen and Hill 1964; Wenzel 1970).

Juice Acidity.—Citric acid, the major organic acid in citrus fruit, accumulates in young fruit to $2^1/_2\%$ (w/v) of the juice before decreasing to about 1% at commercial maturity. Acidity in grapefruit frequently remains high when the soluble solids approach a plateau at commercial maturity. The need exists for an inexpensive method of decreasing acidity in citrus fruit.

Bruemmer (1969) observed that the redox ratio of the dehydrogenase coenzyme, NADH/NAD, increased as the respiratory rate of oranges and grapefruit declined with maturity. Bruemmer and Roe (1970A) showed that NAD-dependent orange malic dehydrogenase was inhibited completely when the redox ratio was 0.05 or higher. Theorizing that the redox ratio controls the rate of synthesis of citrate through malic dehydrogenase, they speculated that anaerobic metabolism of fruit would increase the NADH/NAD ratio and decrease the citric acid-determined acidity. When oranges and grapefruit were heated to 100°F for 16 hr in 100% N_2 or CO_2 atmospheres, the coenzyme redox ratio increased and acidity of the juice declined about 10% (Bruemmer and Roe 1969B). When the experimental environment contained 20% NH_3, the acidity declined about 50%. These observations could lead to development of a process of lowering grapefruit acidity that might be commercially advantageous.

The rapid response of intact fruit to change in gas environment suggests that post-harvest treatment of fruit with specific biochemical agents may be a useful experimental tool for other problems in citrus processing, such as grapefruit bitterness and poor flavor and color in early season fruit.

Lipids

Matlack (1940) found oleic, linoleic, linolenic, palmitic, and stearic acids, glycerol, a phytosterol (sitosterol) and a phytosterolin in the pulp and locular tissue of California Valencias. The phytosterolin was probably β-sitosteryl-D-glycoside, later isolated by Swift (1952A) from Florida Valencias. A rather extensive investigation of the fatty constituents of the peel (Matlack 1929) showed that the composition of the lipids was similar to that in the pulp with the exception that ceryl alcohol was present in the peel and not in the pulp, and pentacosane was present in the pulp but not in the peel.

Nolte and von Loesecke (1940) were probably the first to suggest that off-flavors in canned orange juice might be related to changes in the fatty constituents. Curl (1946) and Curl and Veldhuis (1947) indicated that off-flavors developing in tangerine and orange juices were associated with the lipids. Subsequent studies by Swift and Veldhuis (1951), Swift (1952A and B), and Huskins *et al.* (1952) have contributed significantly to our knowledge of the composition of the lipids of orange juice and the changes they undergo in stored, canned orange juice. Huskins and Swift (1953) also reported that changes in lipid composition of orange juice due to pasteurization are very slight and are not related to changes in fla-

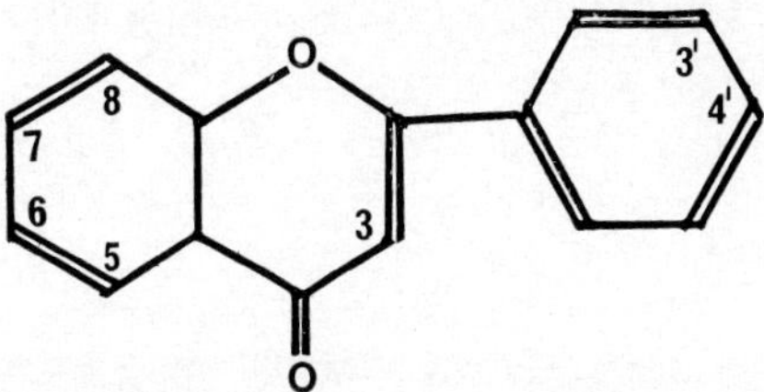

FIG. 10. FLAVONE NOMENCLATURE

vor. Addition of antioxidants to canned orange juice did not stop flavor change (Nolte *et al.* 1942).

Nordby and Nagy (1969) made an extensive study of the C_{12}–C_{26} fatty acids of lipids in tangerine and orange juices. They found that the normal chain fatty acids comprise 97–99% for grapefruit, orange and tangerine, unsaturated acids account for 25–31%, and every even and odd carbon number from C_{12} to C_{26} is present. Small quantities of a number of iso- and anteiso acids in the C_8 to C_{12} and C_{27} to C_{29} ranges were observed. There were present saturated, mono-, di-, and triunsaturated fatty acids. In Valencia orange juice there were found 74 acids plus traces of 17 more, in tangerine juice 70 acids plus traces of 11 more, in Marsh seedless grapefruit juice 73 acids plus traces of 16 more, and in Duncan grapefruit 72 acids plus traces of 5 more. Traces indicated less than 0.001% of the acid present. Total lipids ranged from 0.067 to 0.10% of the juices.

Flavones

Tangeretin (5,6,7,8,4′-pentamethoxyflavone) was isolated from orange juice by Nelson (1934). Sinensetin (5,6,7,3′,4′-pentamethoxyflavone was found by Born (1960) and more fully characterized by Swift (1964). Other flavones in orange juice includes nobiletin (5,6,7,8,3′,4′-hexamethoxyflavone) (Swift 1960) tetra-O-methyl-scutellarein (5,6,7,4′-tetramethoxyflavone) (Swift 1965) and 3,5,6,7,8,3′4′-heptamethoxyflavone (Böhme and Völcker 1959). The nomenclature of flavones is illustrated in Fig. 10. Swift (1967) reported that the most abundant flavone in six samples of orange peel juice was nobiletin followed by sinensetin, tetra-O-methyl-scutellarein, heptamethoxylflavone and tangeretin. The average total flavonoid content was 244 ppm and the juice was quite unpleasant in flavor. Veldhuis, Swift and Scott (1970) reported on the flavone content of commercial frozen orange concentrates packed over a period of 19 years and found the flavone content to average 5.1 ppm, on a reconstituted basis, well below the taste threshold level, and concluded that flavones in citrus juices from orange peel were not significant to flavor. While there were differences between samples, there was no obvious trend with increased yield of juice from oranges.

Nobiletin and tangeretin appear to have some interesting physiological properties both to plants and animals. Nobiletin is the most active, but tangeretin also has some activity. Ben-Aziz (1967) found that these com-

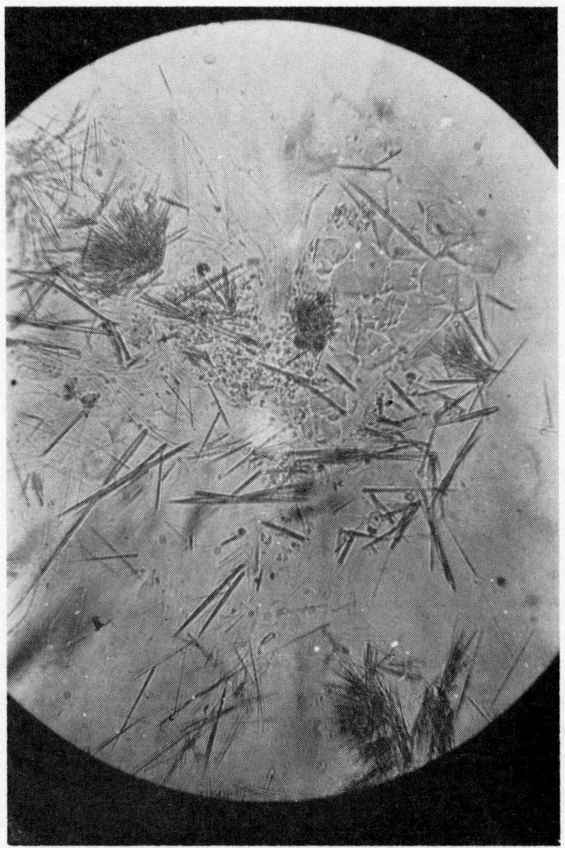

FIG. 11. PHOTOMICROGRAPH OF HESPERIDIN CRYSTALS IN CANNED ORANGE JUICE

This photograph was taken of crystals in a commercial pack three months old.

ponents were effective in controlling the "Mal Secco" disease of citrus trees in the Mediterranean area. Wattenberg *et al.* (1968) found that nobiletin and, to a lesser degree, tangeretin were active inducers of benzypyrene hydroxyla activity in the liver and lung of the rat. Of still greater interest is the possibility that these compounds may reduce blood clotting; at least preliminary experiments so indicate.

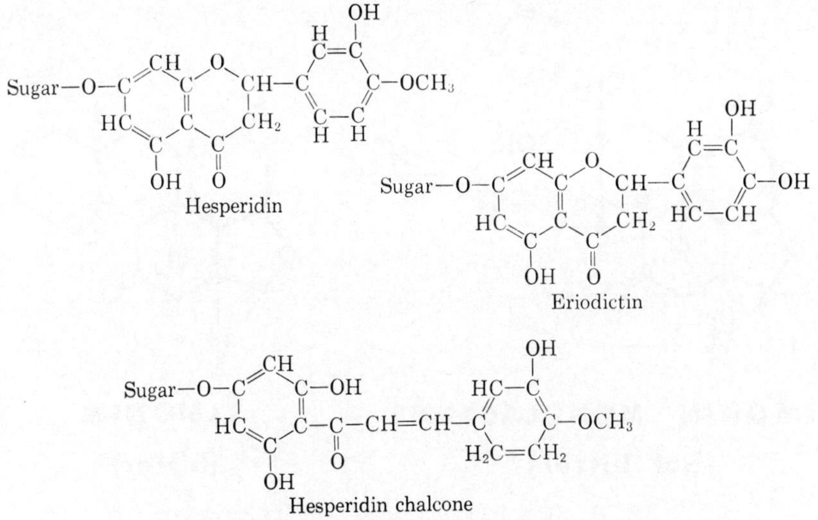

Hesperidin

Eriodictin

Hesperidin chalcone

FIG. 12. STRUCTURAL FORMULAS OF FLAVANONE GLYCOSIDES IN ORANGES

The sugar portion of the molecule consists of 1 mol of glucose and 1 mol of rhamnose.

Flavanone Glycosides

The most important flavanone glycoside is hesperidin. It has been known for over a century (Libreton 1928). It can be readily crystallized from orange juice, particularly from fruit that is immature, or from fruit that have been frozen on the tree. Sometimes crystals of hesperidin will collect on the surface of heat exchangers used in processing orange juice such as on the tubes of falling film evaporators or in pasteurizers where they can affect the heat exchange capacity. Crystals of the glycoside can sometimes be found in the sediment of aged, canned juice (see Fig. 11) or frozen orange concentrate. Hesperidin has little or no effect on the flavor of orange juice, probably because it is so insoluble. Typical flavanone glycoside formulas are given in Fig. 12. Hesperidin and eriodictin have been found in oranges and hesperidin can be converted readily to hesperidin chalcone.

Dunlap and Wender (1960) found naringin and isosakuranetin 7-rhamno-glucoside in orange peel, as well as hesperidin. Evidence of possible presence of several other glycosides was obtained.

Much has been said about the possible physiological effects of flavonoids and there are many articles in the literature. Effects on capillary fragility of the flavonoids and also of chalcones obtained from them are reported. For a time these compounds were designated as "Vitamin P" but it soon developed that this term was not warranted. More recently

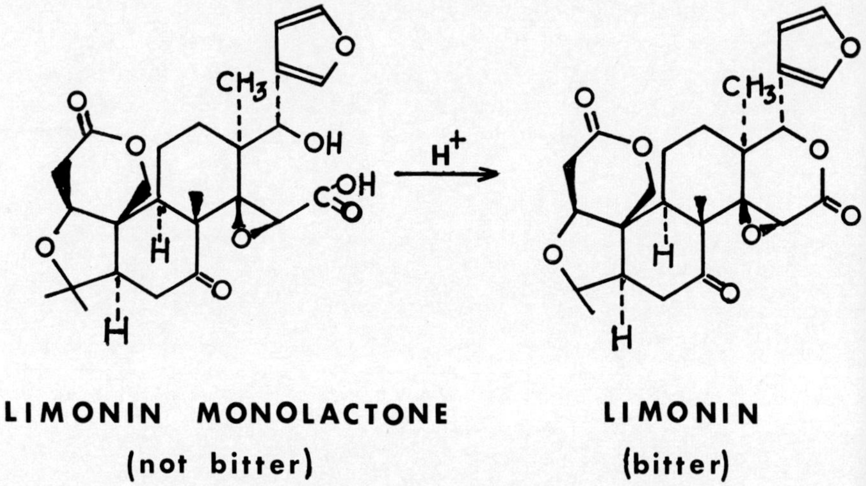

LIMONIN MONOLACTONE (not bitter) → LIMONIN (bitter)

FIG. 13. STRUCTURE OF LIMONIN AND ITS PRECURSOR

Limonin is responsible for delayed bitterness in Navel orange juice.

the term "bioflavonoids" has come into use. The literature is confusing partly because of the difficulties involved in measuring capillary fragility and in attempting to interpret the results. Suggested benefits have ranged from cold remedies to protection from frostbite and radiation injury.

Albach and Redman (1969) examined the flavanone composition of 41 citrus varieties representing 18 recognized species of citrus. An analysis of the data showed a quantitative and qualitative consistency, with minor variations, of individual species and crosses. They developed rules of probable relationships among varieties and species and used them to evaluate probable relationships.

Limonin

The juice of certain oranges such as Washington Navel, and Australian Valencia turns bitter shortly after extraction, even though the fruit or freshly extracted juice is not bitter. Higby (1938) isolated limonin from the tissue of Navel oranges and partially characterized it. Arigoni *et al.* (1960) completed the proof of structure. It remained for Maier and Beverly (1968) to establish the structure of the precursor, limonin monolactone. This delayed bitterness is quite different from the bitterness in grapefruit which is due to naringin in the juice before extraction.

The structures of limonin and its nonbitter precursor, limonin monolactone, are shown in Fig. 13 and it will be noted that limonin is a di-lactone while the precursor has only one such group. As indicated, the conversion from the precursor occurs in acid solution, such as orange juice. It appears that juice extraction and maceration of the tissue brings the precursor into the acid juice and the conversion begins. Limonin monolactone is nonbitter at 50 ppm while limonin is detectably bitter at 2.7 ppm and extremely bitter at 15–20 ppm. Maier *et al.* (1969) found evidence of an enzyme which also promotes the conversion of the precursor to limonin. They proposed the name limonoic acid A-ring lactone for the compound previously called limonin monolactone.

Pigments

These are carried chiefly in the plastids, and the size and shape of these appear to be characteristic of the species from which they are obtained. Anthocyanin occurs in red-fleshed oranges known as blood oranges (Matlack 1931), while pigments of orange and tangerine juices are probably chiefly carotenes and xanthophylls (Matlack 1928, Zechmeister and Tuzson 1933, 1937). As chlorophyll in citrus peel decreases, carotenoids increase (Miller *et al.* 1940). In mature green fruit, xanthophylls predominate; later when the fruit has attained it highest carotenoid content, cryptoxanthin and carotene are in higher concentrations than xanthophylls. Natarajan and Mackinney (1952) identified alpha, beta, and zeta carotenes, and phytofluene in California orange juice and observed pigments with absorption maxima similar to lutein epoxide and flavoxanthin.

Curl (1953) and Curl and Bailey (1954, 1955, 1956, and 1959) have conducted extensive investigations on the carotenoid pigments of fresh, canned, and powdered orange juice, orange peel, and orange pulp. They reported phytoene, phytofluene, alpha-carotene, beta-carotene, zeta-carotene, hydroxy-alpha-carotene, cryptoxanthin, lutein, zeaxanthin, lutein 5,6-epoxide, antheraxanthin, flavoxanthin, mutatoxanthins, violaxanthins, luteoxanthins, auroxanthins, valenciaxanthins, sinensiaxanthis, tollein, valenciachromes, sinensiachrome, and evidence of the presence of several other carotenoids. Curl and Bailey (1957) applied their techniques to tangerines. They attributed the redder color as compared to the orange as being due to higher concentrations of cryptoxanthin, beta-carotene, and a hydroxy-canthaxanthin like substance. As a minor constituent, lycopene was observed.

Recently Yokoyama and associates (1965A,B,C, 1966, 1968A,B) studied the composition of carotenoids in citrus products. Among products isolated and identified were citranaxanthin, reticulaxanthin, sinthaxanthin, semi-β-carotenone, β-carotenone, and 8′hydroxy-citranaxanthin. They also found ergosterol.

Acids

Orange juice like other citrus juices is characterized by a pleasantly acid (tart) taste. Not only does the acidity contribute to flavor, but the acid medium (pH 3.5 to 4.0) is such that organisms grow slowly, especially at refrigerated temperature and heat treatment under atmospheric conditions (ca 185°F) is sufficient to render the product commercially sterile and to inactivate pectinesterase enzymes. It has long been known that citric acid is the principal acid in the edible portion of citrus fruit (Scurti and de Plato 1909). Braverman (1933) reported traces of tartaric, benzoic and succinic acids in orange juice. Clements (1964) found that while citric acid was the principal acid in the juice of oranges and tangerines, oxalic acid was the more abundant in peel. He also reported malonic acid in orange peel and tangerine peel. Wolf (1958) found quinic acid as a minor acidic component in orange tissue (locules) in addition to citric and malic acids. Ting and Deszyck (1959) and Ting and Vines (1966) found quinic acid in the peel and pulp of Pineapple and Hamlin oranges. It will be remembered that Wolford and Attaway (1967) reported formic, acetic, propionic, butyric, caproic and valeric acid in orange essence, which came from orange juice. Ascorbic acid is always present, and galacturonic acid from the degradation of pectin.

Vitamins

The principal vitamin in citrus fruit is vitamin C (ascorbic acid). The amount varies with variety, maturity, and other factors. Early season varieties such as Hamlin and Parson Brown are highest, and late season varieties like Valencia are lowest. As fruit matures the amount gradually decreases. During the harvesting seasons values ranged from 0.3 to 0.6 mg per ml (Harding *et al.* 1940). In tangerines Harding and Sunday (1949) found the ascorbic acid content to range from about 0.25 to 0.40 mg per ml.

Ascorbic acid is relatively stable in citrus products during processing and storage. Sale (1947) in an extensive survey found the retention of ascorbic acid averaged 98.3% during canning of orange juice and during storage at room temperature for 12 months, the retention averaged 75%. Kew (1957) observed no appreciable loss in this vitamin during 5-year storage of frozen concentrated orange juice.

Bissett and Berry (1970) studied the retention of ascorbic acid in frozen concentrated orange juice and chilled juice in commercial packages. There was no measurable loss in ascorbic acid in the frozen concentrate at 0°F over a period of a year whether packed in tin cans, aluminum cans, cans with laminated fiberboard bodies (layers of paper and aluminum with a polyethylene liner) or, as an added check, a simple polyethylene bag. There was no significant loss of ascorbic acid at 40°F in chilled, single-strength juice in glass jars over a period of six months, but when packed in cardboard (milk) cartons or in some plastic containers there was a marked decrease in ascorbic acid within a month. It is understood that plastic containers are available that form a better barrier for oxygen and prevent loss of ascorbic acid.

Dehydroascorbic acid has been reported in oranges (Frankenthal 1939; Krehl and Cowgill 1950). Biotin, folic acid, pyridoxine, inositol (Krehl and Cowgill 1950), and riboflavin, provitamin A, thiamin and niacin (Watt and Merrill 1963) are known to be present in orange juice.

Amino Acids and Proteins

The composition of the amino acids and proteins in citrus juices has been the subject of numerous investigations. It has been known for some time that much of the nitrogen in citrus juices is present in soluble form and as amino acids. Nelson *et al.* (1933) undertook a study of the soluble nitrogen distribution in fresh and deteriorated orange juice. Half the soluble nitrogen present was in the amino form. Stachydrine, arginine, choline, asparagine, and aspartic acid were found, and there was evidence of histidine. No change was detectable, however, in the nature of the bases present in deteriorated juice from those in the fresh juice.

Rockland *et al.* (1950) using paper chromatography technique, report alanine, asparagine, arginine, proline, serine, and tentatively identified lysine and glutamine in California Valencia juice. Ratios of amino acids in orange juice may vary with stage of maturity (Underwood and Rockland 1953). Glutathione has also been reported in oranges (Coulson *et al.* 1950).

Clements and Leland (1962) studied the free amino acids in several citrus varieties and found the same amino acids as Rockland in Valencia oranges and Washington Navel oranges, Eureka and Lisbon lemons, Dancy tangerines and Marsh grapefruit. In addition, aspartic acid, glutamic acid, and γ-aminobutyric acid were formed. Proline was the most abundant except in grapefruit. Nitrogen calculated from the amino acids accounted for 70% of the Kjeldahl nitrogen. Isolated amino acids totaled 4.5% of the soluble solids for Valencia oranges, 3.3% for Navels and 3.4% for the tangerines. Watt and Merrill (1963) reported protein as 1% in orange juice of 12.2% soluble solids. Amino acids are important compounds in citrus juices and contribute significantly to the nutritive value.

Ivan Stewart and coworkers have obtained interesting information on some nitrogen compounds in citrus fruit. Stewart *et al.* (1964) isolated and identified 1-synephrine from citrus leaves and fruit. They found 3.1 mg/gm fresh tangerines and lesser amounts in other fruits. Wheaton and

Stewart (1965) found 125 mg synephrine, 15 mg *n*-methyltyramine, 1 mg tyramine and 1 mg octopamine per liter Dancy tangerine juice; and 21 mg synephrine, 4 mg feruloylputrescine and 1.5 mg *n*-methyltryramine, per liter on the average in Hamlin, Navel, Pineapple, and Valencia orange juices.

Suspended Matter

The suspended matter in citrus juices has long been regarded as essential to good quality. Efforts were first made to pack a clear orange juice but it was of poor quality and not characteristic of the fruit. Cloudy juices were much more satisfactory.

Scott, Kew, and Veldhuis (1965) made a study of the composition of the suspended matter in orange juice cloud. They found that dry weight of the suspended matter to be 0.67% of original juice weight. They reported about 25% lipids (hexane-soluble), 3% cellulose, 4% hemicellulose, 86%, pectin, 7.7% nitrogen, 1.3% P_2O_5 and 2.6% ash in the suspended matter. The cloud appeared to originate mainly from juice cells rather than from mechanical disintegration of structural tissue. They also found immediately after extraction from the fruit, the peel oil could be concentrated in the lightest fraction by centrifuging, but after a few hours it was to be found largely in the centrifuge sediment. For instance, as much oil was to be found after standing in the 2.5% of sediment as in the 97.5% of supernatant fluid. This indicates that the peel oil is free from extraction, but gradually becomes associated with the suspended matter where much of it dissolves in lipids. This probably accounts for the rapid change of flavor of orange juice in the first few hours after extraction. It may also explain why cloud is important to flavor in that the lipids act as a storage point for peel oil components. Cloud from freeze damaged oranges was somewhat higher in total amount and lower in lipids and nitrogen.

Cloud and cloud loss has received a great deal of attention in relation to pectin content, type of pectin, pectinesterase activity and heat treatment. Pectin has long been regarded as a stabilizer of cloud and when changed the cloud may settle rapidly. The general formula for pectin is given in Fig. 14, which shows three galacturonic anhydride units. Pectin may contain several hundred of these units. Pectinesterase facilitates the removal of the methyl groups with the formation of pectic acid (illustrated by the anhydride unit to the left); a reaction which can be followed with a pH meter. This may be followed by the formation of calcium pectate (with calcium already in the juice), cloud loss, and gelation in frozen concentrated orange juice (Rouse 1949) if the storage temperature is allowed to rise.

At first frozne concentrated orange juice was made without heat treatment, only the very best oranges were used and storage was maintained at 0°F or below. As time went on and the size of the pack trebled year after year it was impossible to be as select in choosing fruit, and adverse storage became more frequent, so heat treatment of the juice or concentrate became the rule. A number of studies were made on the temperatures and times required for the heat treatment (Atkins and Rouse 1953 and Bissett *et al.* 1957A,B).

The chemistry of pectin is very complex as would be expected from the lengths of the chains, possibilities of removing methyl groups, breaking the chains into shorter lengths and various combinations. The protopectin in the peel and in the cell walls may be brought into solution by heat, acid, alkali, or enzymes. Further treatment by these chemicals or enzymes can form pectates, pectinates, pectic acid, or *d*-galacturonic acid, and all can be expected to a greater or lesser degree in citrus juice products.

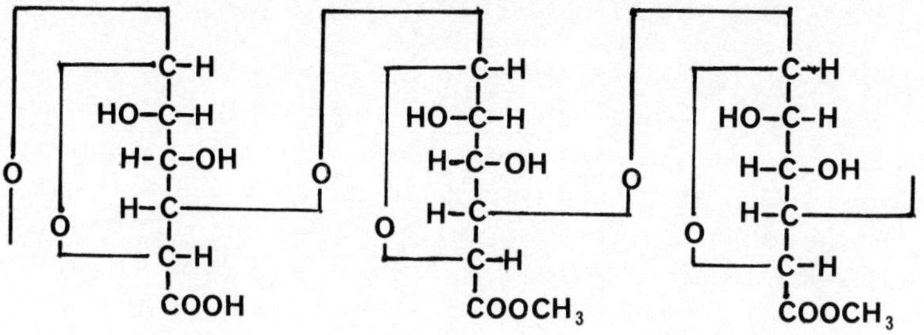

FIG. 14. LINKAGE OF GALACTURONIC ANHYDRIDE UNITS IN PECTIN

Baker and Bruemmer (1970A and B) obtained some of the washed cloud from Scott *et al.* (1965) and examined it further with regard to the 86% pectin value. This "pectin" fraction (alcohol-precipitate) was found to be 47% protein. The protein had precipitated with the pectin when the alcohol was added.

Rouse (1953) studied the distribution of total pectin in citrus fruit and found it to be highest in the albedo (2.7–8.7% wet basis calculated as calcium pectate) and lowest in the juice (0.1–0.11%). He also found the pectinesterase value to be highest in the juice sacs (7.1–25.6 PEμ/gm $\times$ 10^3) and lowest in juice (0.01–0.4 PEμ/gm $\times$ 10^3). Atkins and Rouse (1953) found that different methods of juice extraction caused water soluble pectin to vary from 0.01–0.026%, ammonium oxalate soluble pectin from 0.023–0.036% and total pectin from 0.047–0.083%, all calculated as anhydrogalacturonic acid.

Minerals

Roberts and Gaddum (1937) studied the mineral content of the juice of a number of orange varieties grown in Florida. Primo and Royo-Iranzo (1968) also investigated the mineral composition of the serum from commercial varieties of oranges grown in Spain and the United States and reported 0.24–0.45 gm/100 ml ash, 0.20–1.55 mg/100 ml sodium, 2.4–200 mg/100 ml potassium, 7.40–19.6 mg/100 ml calcium, 4.15–17.63 mg/100 ml magnesium, 7.25–21.75 mg/100 ml phosphorus, and 0.05–0.79 mg/100 ml iron. These values are in agreement with the older values of Roberts and Gaddum, except that they found 0.007–0.009% sodium in orange juice; they also reported values for many minor elements. It is to be expected that the mineral content of the juice will vary to a certain extent with the fertilizer program.

SELECTION AND PREPARATION OF FRUIT FOR PROCESSING

Harvesting

Methods for harvesting fruit for processing have been the same as for shipment as fresh fruit. That is, the fruit was pulled (or clipped) from the tree. To do this a ladder was laid against the tree and the picker climbed the ladder carrying a canvas bag which would hold 50 or 60 lb of fruit. Fruit was picked by hand and placed in the bag and the worker then descended, carrying the load. The bottom of the bag opened so the worker could dump the contents in a box or larger container (Rose *et al.* 1951). He was paid according to the amount of fruit picked. This was hard work and the cost increased until it is by far the largest single item in the cost of producing fruit.

Oranges are rather tough fruit, comparatively speaking and can stand dropping from the tree to the ground and be quite satisfactory for processing, if used promptly (24 to 48 hr). If the ground is soft sand, as is frequently the case in Florida, the tendency toward bruising is lessened. A number of mechanical tree shakers are in various stages of development and a number of abscission chemicals are being tried to loosen the fruit. Normally citrus fruits are attached firmly and it takes quite a "snap" to free them. Some degree of success is being experienced with these mechanical harvesters and it may be that a number of models will emerge as being reasonably satisfactory, especially if combined with an abscission treatment. It will be necessary to clear the ground of dropped fruit before harvesting. Some bruising will be natural, some enzymes will be released, and a possible entry for microorganisms may be provided, so processing plant operators will have to watch carefully to avoid loss in quality. Tangerines and Temple oranges have loose skins and must be picked by hand, as must all fruit for fresh shipment.

The realization that fruit can be dropped has brought another procedure into being and this is picking by hand and dropping to the ground. More fruit can be picked in this fashion, and the picker need not be so strong. Women can pick in this fashion and harvesting may become a family affair.

Mechanical devices have been developed for raking the fruit to the center of the aisle between tree rows and loading the fruit into trucks, so this is no particular labor problem. The same equipment may be used to clear the grove before harvesting.

Variety

In Florida, the principal varieties of oranges used for processing are Pineapple (mid-season) and Valencia (late season). Considerable quantities of Parson Brown and Hamlin (early season varieties) are also used but are considered less desirable because of somewhat lower soluble solids content, color and flavor. Partial concentration has been suggested by Moore *et al.* (1947) as a means of improving quality of canned juice.

In California, the principal variety used for canning is Valencia although the Washington Navel orange is suited for certain types of beverage bases where the tendency for bitterness is not objectionable. In Texas, the practices largely parallel those in Florida.

When citrus processing began, the fruit used consisted largely of packing house eliminations or "rejects" which were not the best suited for fresh market because of size, shape, lack of optimum skin color, etc. Such fruit continues to be used and constitutes the principal supply in California. In Florida, where most of the crop is processed, much of the fruit moves directly from the grove to the cannery.

Fruit Quality and Preparation

All major citrus producing areas have regulations concerning the maturity of the fruit that may be harvested. These are concerned for the most part with Brix/acid ratio and are designed to deter harvesting until good flavor has developed. In order to insure optimum quality, further selection is made and most fruit used is well above the minimum values listed in the regulations. Attention is further given to the blending of different lots to achieve optimum balance in flavor and color.

Upon reaching the processing plant the fruit goes through inspection lines, where bruised or broken fruit are removed, and then is conveyed to storage bins which permit an accumulation of fruit sufficient for continuous operation of the cannery over a reasonable length of time. These bins are constructed so that the fruit is never piled to a depth of more than 3 to 4 ft. Fruit should not be kept in bins longer than required to permit orderly plant operation.

Courtesy of FMC Corp.

Fig. 15. Battery of FMC In-Line Citrus Juice Extractors

As the fruit is conveyed to the bins, automatic devices divert a small portion to a laboratory where the titratable acidity, Brix, and juice yield are determined. These values are used in determining which bins are to be blended. Juice yield is frequently estimated by extracting a sample with a full-scale juice extractor.

From the bins the fruit passes to the washer. The fruit is soaked briefly in water containing a detergent, scrubbed by revolving brushes, and rinsed with clean water. The fruit is inspected again to remove damaged fruit missed before or subsequently bruised or broken. The fruit is then separated into sizes automatically and enters the juice extractors. In the early days of orange juice canning, juice was extracted by hand reaming, one operator being able to extract about 10 gal per hour and production was limited. The automatic juice extractor has been a major factor in the development of the industry.

Extracting and Finishing Juice

FMC In-Line Extractor.—This machine is used extensively in all citrus producing areas and a battery of them is shown in Fig. 15. The principle of the operation of the machine is shown in Fig. 16. In the first position,

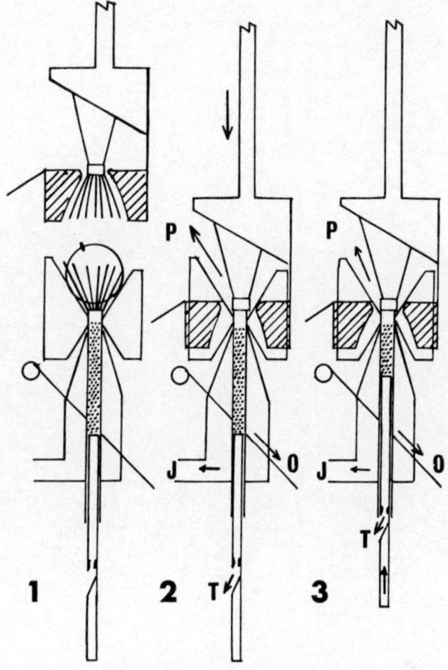

Courtesy of FMC Corp.

FIG. 16. SKETCH SHOWING PRINCIPLE OF FMC IN-LINE JUICE EXTRACTOR

This model is arranged for simultaneous collection of cold pressed peel oil (O), shredded peel (P), and juice (J).

the fruit has been deposited in the bottom cup and the upper half has begun to descend. As it does, the sharp upper end of the tube in the lower half of the machine cuts a hole in the bottom of the fruit and as the many fingers of the two halves mesh, the crushed, juice laden segments pass into the tube as shown in the second position. There is a restrictor in the lower end of the tube to prevent loss of juice which is forced through the perforated tube and emerges at "J." When the upper cup is firmly seated, the central tube containing the restrictor rises to compress the contents of the tube, recover remaining juice and eject the plug at "T," as shown in the third position. The machine illustrated is designed for simultaneous recovery of cold-pressed peel oil. As the fruit is squeezed, the peel oil runs down the outside of the fruit and water sprays wash it down the sloping plane until it drops into a conveyor at "O." To make recovery of oil easier, the pulp is discharged separately. An annular space between the center tube and the "fingers" has been provided in the upper cup to facilitate separate discharge of peel upward at "P." The yield of

Courtesy of Brown International Corp.

FIG. 17. BATTERY OF BROWN MODEL 400 CITRUS JUICE EXTRACTORS

juice and the type of juice obtained can be varied by changing the type of cup, by using perforated tubes with holes of different size, by changing restrictors to reduce clearance in the passage for pulp and seeds and finally by changing the height to which the central tube rises in the last operation. From the extractor the juice passes to a finisher where excess pulp is removed. A five-head machine will handle from 200 to 400 fruit per minute.

Brown Model 400.—This machine (Fig. 17) has been used for many years in the citrus industry and continues to be a favorite. It produces a high quality juice very low in peel oil content. The machines are arranged in batteries adjusted to the size of the fruit being used. Each fruit is sliced in half, the two halves going to opposite sides of the machine. The fruit halves are carried in synthetic rubber cups revolving on a horizontal plane and reamed by revolving reamers mounted on a synchronized carrier revolving on an inclined plane. The juice collects in the machine and is conveyed to the finishers, while the peel is diverted to the waste conveyer. The maximum capacity is 350 fruit per minute.

Brown Model 700.—This excellent machine (Fig. 18) operates on the same principle as the Brown Model 400 in that the fruit is halved and the juice removed with a rotating reamer. It produces a juice with the same high quality, low oil standards as the older model. In the older machine the cups and reamers are mounted on rotating discs but in the new machines the cups are mounted on tracks, which permit programming of the

Courtesy of Brown International Corp.

Fig. 18. Battery of Brown Model 700 Citrus Juice Extractors

approach of the reamer into the fruit. The reamer can be made to penetrate rapidly at first and then more slowly as the point of maximum penetration is reached. This machine handles up to 700 fruit per minute. In common arrangement, the Brown Model 700 is used for those sizes comprising the bulk of the fruit and the Brown Model 400 for the largest sizes comprising only a small portion of the fruit.

Brown Model 1100 Juice Extractor.—Three parallel lines of single file fruit are fed into this extractor (Fig. 19). Each fruit drops to its proper position as it becomes wedged between pairs of revolving, tapered, circular, synthetic rubber discs. The smaller fruit falls nearer the center and the larger sizes are engaged nearer the periphery. The discs carry the fruit through a stainless steel knife which slices it in half. Each half travels a converging path between a perforated stainless steel grid and the disc as the disc rotates. Spent peel is discharged out of the rear of the machine after having traveled approximately 320° around its circular path. Juice flows to the bottom of the collector and can be divided into

Courtesy of Brown International Corp.

FIG. 19. BATTERY OF BROWN MODEL 1100 CITRUS JUICE EXTRACTORS

Three parallel lines of single file fruit are fed into this extractor. Each fruit drops to its proper position as it becomes wedged between pairs of revolving, tapered, circular, synthetic rubber discs. The smaller fruit falls nearer the center and the larger sizes are engaged nearer the periphery. The discs carry the fruit through a stainless steel knife which slices it in half. Each half travels a converging path between a perforated stainless steel grid and the disc as the disc rotates. Spent peel is discharged out of the back of the machine after having traveled approximately 320° around its circular path. Juice flows to the bottom of the collector and can be divided into two fractions, i.e., that which has been expressed lightly, containing low peel oil and pulp, and the juice recovered from the tighter extraction which contains higher levels of peel oil and pulp. The juice flows out two outlets which are located at the bottom of the stainless juice collector. The spacing between disc and grid is adjustable, providing for variation in fruit thickness. The extractor has a capacity of up to 12 tons/hr of fruit. Maximum juice yields can be obtained with the machine.

two fractions, i.e., that which has been expressed lightly, containing low peel oil and pulp, and the juice recovered from the tighter extraction which contains higher levels of peel oil and pulp. The juice flows out two outlets which are located at the bottom of the stainless juice collector. The spacing between disc and grid is adjustable, providing for variation in fruit thickness. The extractor has a capacity of up to 12 tons/hour of fruit. Maximum juice yields can be obtained with the machine.

Photo by M. K. Veldhuis

FIG. 20. SCREW TYPE CITRUS JUICE FINISHER

Finishing

A typical screw-type citrus juice finisher is shown in Fig. 20. While this model is a small one, the larger ones are built in the same manner. The machine is shown disassembled so the construction can be visualized. In the center there is a large screw which turns rapidly and carries the pulp and juice along. In operation, the reinforced screen is placed over the screw and bolted in place. As the material is carried along, the juice passes through the screen and the excess pulp, bits of peel and rag, and seeds pass out an annular orifice at the right. The screw floats and even pressure is maintained by air against a flexible diaphragm pushing against the left end of the shaft. The annular opening opens just enough to let the excess pulp and seeds pass.

An example of a commercial screw-type finisher of somewhat different design is shown in Fig. 21. This is Brown Model 2503, of 100 to 200 gallons per minute capacity. Separation is accomplished by means of a rotating screw within a cylindrical screen. The liquids and a controlled amount of solids pass through the screen. The balance of the solids is discharged through a nonrotating air-loaded valve. Dryness of discharged pulp can be accurately controlled by simply varying the air pressure on the discharge valve. This model gives highly efficient liquid-solids separation with a minimum degradation of solids.

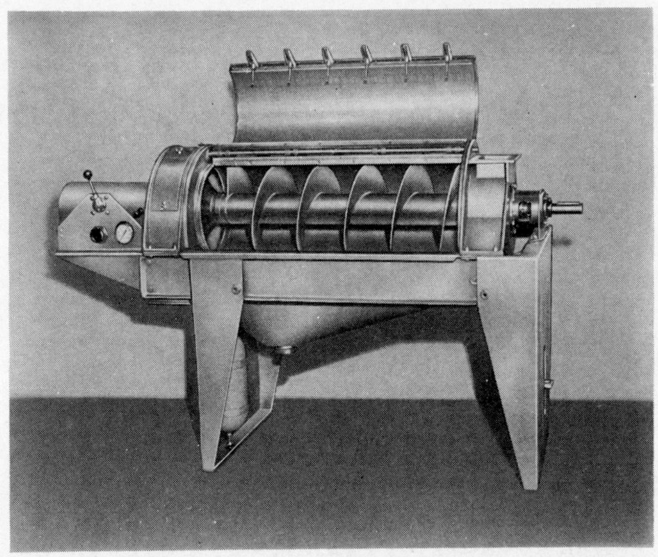

Courtesy of Brown International Corp.

FIG. 21. BROWN MODEL 2503 SCREW FINISHER FOR CITRUS JUICES

The FMC In-Line citrus juice extractor does a preliminary job of pulp removal in the perforated tube, so there is less pulp to be removed in the final finisher. This means that different settings must be made than for juice from Brown juice extractors where everything but the peel must pass through the finisher.

In some cases finishers with paddles rotating within a cylindrical screen (paddle finishers) have been used. Simple rotating octagonal or hexagonal screens have been used for special purposes as finishers.

The juice finisher, along with the juice extractor, are important pieces of equipment and must be properly adjusted to yield the product known to the public as juice or concentrate. In some cases the manufacturer may wish to provide some larger pieces of pulp in the juice to simulate the appearance of fresh juice. This can be done by increasing the size of the openings in the finisher and decreasing pressure on the finisher shaft. Also, the perforated tube in the FMC machine may be replaced by one with larger sized openings. This may be done for only part of the juice.

Yield is important to the grower who wants the highest return for his fruit and to the processor who is also responsible for the quality of the finished product. In Florida, yield is regulated by law. Test extractors are located in each processing plant and are used by State Inspectors to determine a reasonable yield and the processor must comply. If fruit has been damaged by cold weather, permissible yield is reduced as a safeguard of quality.

Canning of Single Strength Juices

Blending and Sweetening.—After finishing, the juice flows to large stainless steel tanks where it is checked for acidity and soluble solids. Sugar is added, if needed.

Deoiling.—Deoilers were developed in order to be able to control the peel oil level in canned citrus juices. Previously, the only methods of controlling oil level was in the adjustment of the extractor or by softening the peel by immersing the fruit for a minute or two in hot water (Scott 1941). The oil in the juice varied from lot to lot and control was difficult. Deoilers are essentially small vacuum evaporators in which the juice is heated to about 125°F and from 3 to 6% of the juice evaporated. The vapors are condensed, the oil separated by centrifuging or by decantation and the water layer returned to the juice. This treatment is sufficient to remove about three-fourths of the volatile peel oil present. Government standards for U.S. Grade A orange juice permit not more than 0.035% by volume. Normally the value is kept between 0.015 and 0.025%. Recently a new method of estimating recoverable oil was developed by Scott and Veldhuis (1966) which is more precise and more rapid than previously available tests. It can be completed in seven minutes and involves distillation of juice with 2-propanol and oxidation of the recovered *d*-limonene with a standard potassium bromide-potassium bromate solution under acid conditions.

Deaeration.—Deoilers simultaneously deaerate juice so deaerators are seldom seen in juice canneries. Oxidation has long been considered as a mechanism of flavor deterioration in citrus juices and the tendency has been to recommend that the oxygen level be kept low. Pulley and von Loesecke (1939) and Henry and Clifcorn (1948) have observed that dissolved oxygen disappears rapidly in canned juice, especially at high temperature. This reaction has been associated with loss in vitamin C. Some workers have questioned the value of deaeration (Kefford *et al.* 1950). A decided benefit is a decrease in frothing in the filler bowl if deaeration is used. The Pulley (1936) deaerator has been the most widely used.

Pasteurization.—Pasteurization of citrus juices accomplishes two things. First, it destroys microorganisms which would otherwise cause fermentation in the can and second, it inactivates enzymes which would otherwise cause cloud loss and other changes in the juice. Generally, higher temperatures are needed for enzyme inactivation than for destruction of microorganisms. Kew *et al.* (1957) observed that heating to about 160°F was sufficient to prevent fermentation in experimental packs, but from 185° to 210°F was required to achieve cloud stability.

The temperatures required depended on time of heating and pH of the juice. Kew and Veldhuis (1950) proposed a rapid method for checking the effectiveness of pasteurization. Earlier references to pasteurization of citrus juices include Mottern and von Loesecke (1933), von Loesecke *et al.* (1934), Heid and Scott (1937), and Loeffler (1941A and B).

In plant, juices are heated in tubular or plate type heat exchangers in which the heating medium is either steam or hot water. Heating is accomplished in 30 to 60 sec and the juice then piped hot directly to the filling machine. From time to time more rapid but higher heating procedures called "Mallorizing" have been used, but they have not been widely adopted.

Filling.—Juice is maintained hot (about 185°F) in the filler bowl and filled directly into cans. Juice is in the filler bowl from 1 to 2 min in most cases. This time should be kept short to minimize flavor damage. Cans are closed in automatic machines, inverted for about 20 sec and rapidly cooled by spraying with cold water while spinning in a conveyer. High speed filling and closing machines have been developed and some will handle up to 500 cans a minute.

It is considered desirable to minimize the amount of oxygen in the final container. Riester *et al.* (1945) have shown that the volume of oxygen entrapped in the headspace may be greater than that in the juice. Live steam injected into the headspace as the can is closed will replace the air with steam (Peterson 1949).

Plain tin cans are used for single strength orange juice as well as other single strength citrus juices because they are satisfactory and least expensive.

Storage of Orange Juice.—Changes in flavor and other factors influencing quality of canned orange juice are only slight during the actual canning procedure. Changes during storage are more profound. The temperature under which the product is held from canning to consumption is a major factor influencing flavor and vitamin content of the juice when consumed. At a storage temperature of 70°F there is slight flavor change and approximately 85 to 90% of the ascorbic acid is retained for one year (Freed *et al.* 1949; Riester *et al.* 1945). At higher temperatures deterioration in flavor and loss of the ascorbic acid progress more rapidly. At lower temperatures (30° to 40°F) quality and ascorbic acid content remain little affected in canned orange juice during storage for 1 or 2 years (Riester *et al.* 1945; Ross 1944).

As cans leave the juice cooler and are cased they are at about 100°F. Some warmth is desirable to insure drying of the cans to prevent rust. Riester *et al.* (1948) observed that 2 to 3 weeks are required for the temperature in palletized stacks to cool to that in the warehouse. Feaster *et al.* (1950) considered changes in flavor and ascorbic acid content during cooling of stacks as minor in comparison to subsequent changes during storage for 7 to 12 months.

CHILLED ORANGE JUICE

Substantial packs of orange juice are made especially for infant feeding. Fruit is selected for high ascorbic acid content and generally processed in the usual manner. Pulp is reduced by finisher adjustment or by use of continuous centrifuges. Peel oil is reduced to 0.001% or less by volume by de-oiling or by centrifuging. Juice is packed in small cans for individual servings.

Canned Orange Juice for Infants

Chilled orange juice has enjoyed a good and continuing growth during the past 15 years (Fig. 8). It started with delivery of fresh juice to restaurants and on milk routes (Lister and Fay 1956). Gallon jugs or paper milk cartons were the usual containers, and these are still used to some extent, but the more popular containers are now 1- and 2-qt jars. These jars are made in the citrus producing areas and in some cases in the chilled juice processing plants. They are relatively inexpensive per ounce of juice, the product can be pasteurized, and the quality of the product remains high for long periods of time if kept at 50°F or below. A substantial portion of the pack is packed aseptically. The jars and caps are sterilized with hot water, with a chlorine solution or with an iodophor solution, and allowed to drain briefly before filling. The juice is heated to about 240°F for a few seconds in a pasteurizer made of small tubes (Mallorizer) and then cooled to about 40°F. Filling is done in aseptic chambers with special equipment. The product is much like canned juice, except that glass containers are used in place of tin, and it is refrigerated to maintain good flavor. Reconstituted concentrate can be used in chilled juice.

The quality of properly prepared and stored, chilled juice should be at least as good and perhaps a little better than reconstituted juice from properly prepared frozen concentrate. Convenience and the appearance of orange juice in clear glass containers are important factors.

Considerable quantities of concentrated orange juice in bulk are sold to manufacturers in distant cities where it is used in part to make chilled juice. Figures on the amounts so used are not available and they are not included in Fig. 8.

CANNED TANGERINE JUICE

Tangerines are quite fragile and must be handled with care. They cannot be hauled at the usual depth in citrus trucks or placed in bins. They are handled in boxes or in shallow layers in trucks. Some orange conveyers and washers would crush tangerines and would need remodeling or replacing in order to efficiently handle the latter fruit. Regular citrus juice extractors can be used, especially those fitted to handle small fruit After finishing, the juice is usually centrifuged to remove excess pulp which would otherwise contribute to off-flavor development in storage. The capacity of a given plant handling tangerines is about half that when handling oranges.

Tangerine juice has a distinctive flavor preferred by some. The crop is limited (about $^1/_{30}$ that of oranges) and so is the pack of tangerine juice. The crop of tangerines varies quite widely from year to year and the pack has ranged from 50,000 to 500,000 cases in the last ten years. The pack comes almost exclusively from Florida and the Dancy tangerine is the predominant variety. Some tangerines are used in the manufacture of frozen concentrate.

During the 1968–69 season approximately 90,000 cases of tangerine juice were packed, but at the same time over ten times as many tangerines were used to make over a million gallons of concentrate. The pack of concentrate has remained more or less constant for the past ten years, while the pack of canned juice has declined. One factor is that canned tangerine juice has a very limited shelf-life while frozen concentrate is quite stable. Another is that many of the volatiles of unusual flavor are removed during vacuum concentration and the product is not as harsh in flavor. Tangerines are grown primarily for fresh market use and only the surplus is available for processing.

INSTANT ORANGE JUICE

The "puff-drying" method of preparing powdered orange juice was developed by Strashun and Talburt (1954). In this process concentrated orange juice was made to "puff" into a porous structure under high vacuum and the product dried in a vacuum shelf drier. The material from the drier has about three per cent moisture. The product is hygroscopic. It was packaged with an "in package" desiccant which further reduced the moisture content to below 1% in which condition it has excellent stability at room temperature (Mylne and Seamans 1954). Most of the volatile flavors were lost during drying, but typical orange flavor was restored by adding cold-pressed orange oil entrapped in sorbitol (Griffin 1951). Later Schultz *et al.* (1956) developed a method of preparing "locked-in" oil in sugars for the same use.

The Chain-Belt vacuum drier was developed to adapt the puff-drying method to a commercial scale. At Plant City, Florida, such a unit has been operating for several years (Bonnell *et al.* 1955).

Recently a new process has been developed called "Foam-mat" drying (Morgan *et al.* 1959). Edible stabilizers such as fatty acid monoglycerides are added to aid in the formation of a stiff foam produced by a wire beater. The foam is spread in a thin layer on a drying tray or belt and dried in a blast of hot air at atmospheric pressure. As in the puff-drying procedure the porous structure aids in rapid drying. Very little, if any flavor damage is done during the drying process.

A further adaptation of the process is called the "crater" technique in which foam is spread on a perforated sheet and the holes opened by passing the sheet over an air blast. Drying is accomplished by passing air through a stack of loaded sheets (Berry *et al.* 1967). The time of drying is 10 to 12 min and a moisture content of 1% is achieved which eliminates the need for an in-package desiccant. One-half per cent of methyl cellulose serves as a tasteless foam stabilizer. The dried foam breaks into an exceedingly fine impalpable powder, but by flaking between rolls at high pressure (80,000 lb on a 3 in. width) and subsequent grinding, coarse granules are obtained, which dissolve in cold water with ease. The product is flavored with locked-in, cold-pressed orange peel oil and concentrated orange essence to produce a very acceptable product. The cost of foam-mat drying is about 11¢ per pound soluble solids. Foam-mat drying, and variations thereof, have excellent potentialities.

FROZEN CONCENTRATED ORANGE JUICE

The development of frozen concentrated orange juice has been most remarkable. While eight years from research laboratory to production is considered normal, this product saw substantial commercial production in less than two years and rapid increases since then until in 1968–69 over 79% of the orange crop in Florida was converted to this single product. Frozen concentrated orange juice was a cooperative development of the Florida Citrus Commission (now State of Florida, Department of Citrus) and the Winter Haven, Florida, Fruit and Vegetable Products Laboratory of the U.S. Department of Agriculture.

On or about April 19, 1944, Dr. L. G. MacDowell, Research Director of the Florida Citrus Commission, sent an outline of a series of experiments he wished conducted by Commission Research Fellows, Dr. E. L. Moore and Mr. C. D. Atkins, then stationed at the U.S. Dept. Agr. laboratory. This outline contained the essential features of concentration at low temperature, the addition of fresh "cutback" juice to the concentrate to restore fresh flavor and aroma, and packing as a frozen product. Up until a month or so previously this laboratory had no concentrate program such as this, but equipment at hand permitted preliminary studies. These studies were favorable and much of the effort of the laboratory was directed on this product.

Dr. MacDowell, Dr. Moore and Mr. Atkins were granted U.S. Patent No. 2,453,109 covering the method. This was assigned to the U.S. Government as represented by the Secretary of Agriculture. In 1956, the U.S. Department of Agriculture favored the Winter Haven Laboratory with its highest honor, the Distinguished Service Award for the development of frozen concentrated orange juice. The group was listed as Dr. L. G. Macdowell, Dr. E. L. Moore, Mr. C. D. Atkins and Miss Eunice Wiederhold for the Florida Citrus Commission, and Dr. M. K. Veldhuis, Dr. R. Patrick and Dr. A. L. Curl for the U.S. Dept. Agr. The research work was well done and timely, ample raw material was at hand and an outlet was needed; industrial know-how was available to develop the necessary processing equipment, and last, but not least, a frozen food distribution system and a market for frozen foods had already been developed.

Juice Extraction and Finishing

Juice extraction and finishing is done in essentially the same manner as for canned juice, with some variations. For the preparation of fresh "cut-back" juice, to be added to restore fresh flavor after the bulk of the juice has been over-concentrated, the strainer tube in the FMC extractor or the screen in the finisher used after the Brown extractor may have larger holes to permit larger pulp pieces to give the appearance of juice freshly extracted in the home. In Florida, State regulations prohibit the addition of sugar to frozen concentrated orange juice, the idea being to delay harvesting until the juice is naturally sweet and to permit marketing a product which is 100% orange juice.

Large automatic "desludging" centrifuges are used at times to reduce the amount of finely divided pulp, if an adequate job is not done at the finisher. These are disc-type units with nozzles at the periphery of the bowl which open periodically to discharge a thick slurry. These centrifuges are helpful in reducing viscosity in juice passing through an evaporator and are used particularly after a freeze when the fruit tissue tend to disintegrate more readily.

Pulp washing was practiced for several years in Florida, but has been prohibited because many thought it yielded an inferior product. The process consisted of washing the finisher pulp in a countercurrent fashion with water in about five stages. A product of about 6% soluble solids was obtained, but it contained a higher percentage of fine pulp and only a limited amount could be added without affecting the viscosity of the concentrate. It is still permitted in certain concentrates for manufacture.

Evaporators

Citrus juice evaporators form the heart of the frozen, concentrated orange juice industry and much engineering skill has gone into the develop-

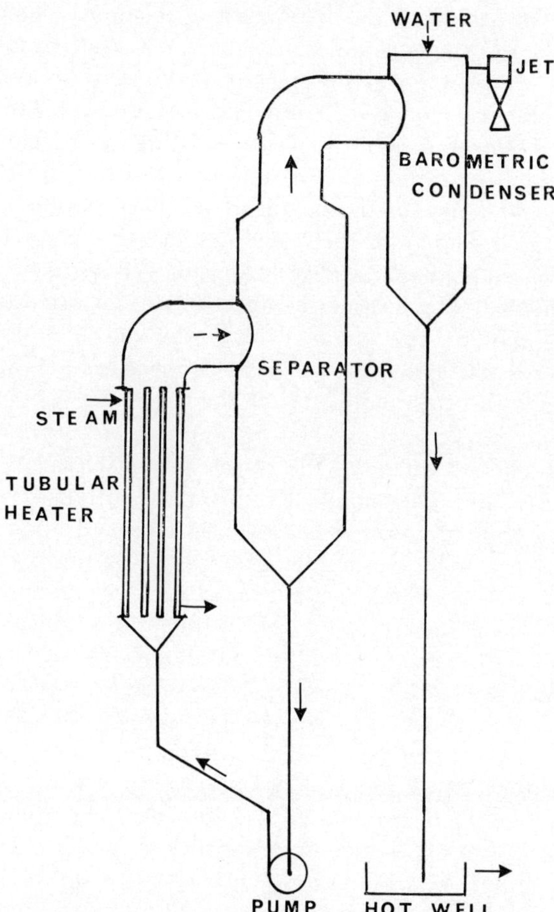

FIG. 22. TYPICAL FORCED-CIRCULATION EVAPORATOR USED FORMERLY IN THE MANUFACTURE OF "HOT-PACK" ORANGE CONCENTRATE

ment. The start came just after World War II which had generated much skill in high vacuum techniques, as in the manufacture of penicillin. It also saw the introduction of the falling-film evaporator into the juice industry. Because of the significance of the development and close relationship of other fruit juice and liquid food products, the history will be sketched briefly.

Before frozen citrus concentrates came into being, a typical evaporator was like that shown in Fig. 22. A centrifugal pump forced the juice through the heat exchanger where some of the water was vaporized on each pass. The vapors and liquid were separated in the large chamber and the vapors passed to the barometric condenser. Noncondensibles were removed and the vacuum maintained by a small steam jet system. This type of evaporator was inexpensive to build and easy to operate. The lowest practical operating temperature was about 120°F and was limited by the temperature of the water available for the barometric condenser. There was a substantial rise in the temperature of the juice in the heat exchanger because of the height of the juice column. About $1^1/_3$ lb of steam were required for each pound of water evaporated. The temperature in the evaporator was ideal for pectinesterase activity, so this enzyme was inactivated by heating the juice before it was fed to the evaporator. The evaporator was operated batchwise and juice was fed to the unit until a sizeable batch of the desired concentration was obtained. The concentrate was then pumped from the unit and a new batch started.

The first commercial low-temperature orange juice evaporator designed especially to take advantage of the research work of the Winter Haven laboratory was built at Plymouth, Fla., by Vacuum Foods (later Minute Maid, Minute Maid Division of Coca Cola Corp., and Foods Division of Coca Cola Corp.). This was a falling-film type and consisted of series of vertical stainless steel cylinders about three feet in diameter and 30 ft tall arranged so that the juice sprayed against the inside surface of the top of the cylinders. The juice flowed down the inside surfaces and was warmed by a water jacket. The vapors were drawn upward into large steam jet boosters which discharged into barometric condensers. The jackets of the large tubes were heated with warm water from the barometric condenser. Water vaporized continuously as the juice flowed down the tube without significant rise in temperature. Since the tube was so large, vapors did not impede the downward flow of juice. There were 13 of these large tubes in a row to form an evaporator and the juice passed down each tube only once. The evaporation temperature was 50°F. The unit was placed in production on April 1, 1946, with about half the output consigned to frozen concentrate and half to the production of orange juice powder. Concentrate of 42°Brix was filled into 6 oz cans at a rate of $5^3/_8$ fl oz per can and packed 96 cans per case under the Snow Crop label. This evaporator furnished the 226,000 gal of concentrate of the 1945–46 season. The following year a second similar evaporator of 14 tall cylinders was used and the evaporation temperature was raised to 65°–70°F (Roy 1970). The evaporators were effective in evaporating at low temperature but were not especially efficient and were soon replaced, but they did help establish the practice of falling-film evaporation. Two of these units produced the frozen concentrate manufactured in 1946.

Some falling-film Skinner evaporators were already in existence at Citrus Concentrates, Inc., Dunedin, Fla., but were designed for use at some-

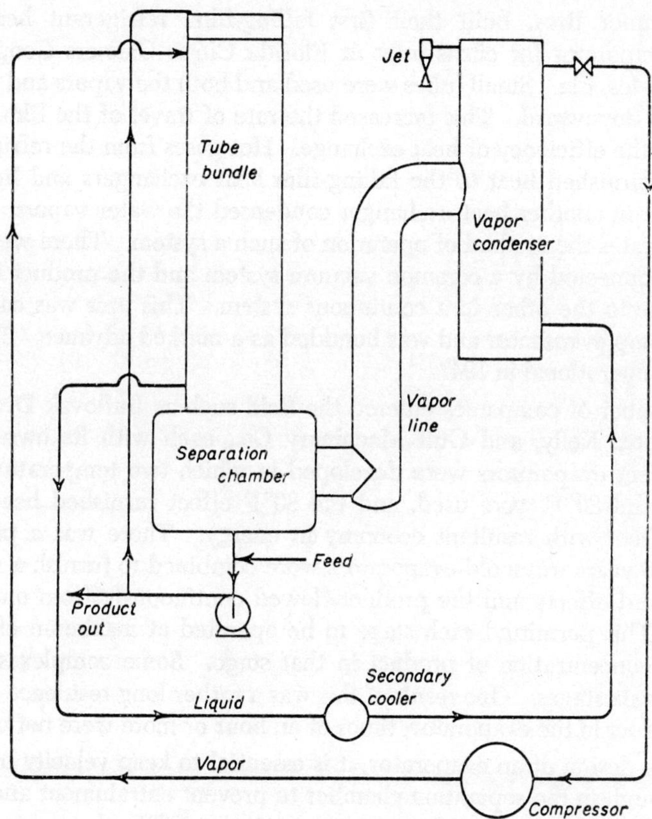

Fig. 23. Heat Pump Cycle Using Primary Refrigerant

what higher temperatures for hot-pack concentrate. When the quality of the product from the Plymouth plant had been demonstrated, the Skinner evaporators were modified to lower the evaporation temperature. To make the falling-film tubes, stainless steel sheets 4 ft wide and 12 ft long were slit lengthwise and each half rolled into an eight inch tube and welded. A considerable number of these tubes were rolled into heads and arranged in a shell. Vapors went up while the juice went down the inside surface. Part of the vapors were raised in temperature and pressure with steam jets and used to heat the evaporator in a form of the heat pump cycle. The remaining vapor was drawn off by another steam booster and passed to a barometric condenser. At least a dozen of these evaporators were built and used for 5 to 10 years. The first of these modified units began full-scale operation on frozen concentrate in 1947. They contributed a major portion of the pack in the earlier years.

Mojonnier Bros. built their first falling-film, refrigerant heat-pump cycle evaporator for citrus juice at Florida Citrus Canners Cooperative, Lake Wales, Fla. Small tubes were used and both the vapors and the film traveled downward. This increased the rate of travel of the film and increased the efficiency of heat exchange. Hot gases from the refrigeration system furnished heat to the falling-film heat exchangers and liquid refrigerant in another heat exchanger condensed the water vapors. Figure 23 illustrates the method of operation of such a system. There were three stages connected by a common vacuum system and the product traveled from one to the other in a continuous system. This unit was called the Low-Temp evaporator and was heralded as a marked advance. This unit became operational in 1947.

A number of companies entered the field such as Buflovak Division of Blaw-Knox, Kelly, and Gulf Machinery Co., each with its own design. Two-effect evaporators were developed in which two temperatures such as 60° and 80°F were used, and the 80°F effect furnished heat to the 60°F effect with resultant economy in energy. There was a period of about 10 years when old evaporators were combined to furnish a series of stages and effects and the product flowed continuously from one to the other. This permitted each stage to be operated at maximum efficiency for the concentration of product in that stage. Some complexes had as many as six stages. One result of this was a rather long residence time for the product in the evaporator; times of an hour or more were not unusual.

In the design of an evaporator, it is essential to keep velocity of vapors low enough in the separation chamber to prevent entrainment and loss of liquid droplets. In an evaporator operating at 75°F, the recommended vertical vapor velocity is 40 ft/sec. As the temperature in the evaporator increases, the recommended velocity decreases. The recommended velocities are 30 ft/sec at 100°F, 17 ft/sec at 150°F, and 9 ft/sec at 200°F. However, increased density of vapors at higher pressures and temperatures overcomes the velocity factor and the higher the temperature, the smaller the separator that can be used for the same vapor capacity. At 200°F the size of a separation chamber need only be about one-fifth that at 75°F. The use of cyclone separators permits higher vapor velocities and many separation chambers are designed to promote circular motion.

When frozen concentrated orange juice was first developed, only the highest quality of unblemished fruit was used and there were no significant freezes for several years. With limited production it was possible to guard the commodity to see that it was kept at 0°F or below. As volume increased it was not possible to select only the very best fruit, and eventually it became necessary to use fruit that had received slight freeze damage. Also, it was realized that in actual distribution channels it was not always possible to ensure 0°F temperature. In order to provide a degree of protection the juice was heated in a tubular heat exchanger to reduce the pectinesterase activity. At the same time the microbial population was reduced. Several studies have been conducted on the times and temperatures needed (Bissett *et al.* 1957 A,B, and Atkins and Rouse 1953 A and B, Rouse and Atkins 1953). Gradually it became standard practice to pasteurize juice for frozen concentrate. A temperature of approximately 180°F for 30 sec to a minute was used. Some pasteurizers were tubular and some were of the plate type. In most cases the juice was pasteurized before being fed to the evaporator and this has the advantage of decreasing bacterial count in the entire evaporator as well as inactivating enzymes. In a few plants, pasteurization was after partial concentration (Carroll *et al.* 1957). This decreased the energy needed as the weight of material to be heated was much less. In a few cases heating of the concentrate between stages was by direct steam injection, a method which involved very little equipment and permitted very rapid heating.

As pasteurization came into general use, it was realized that a good product could be prepared in this manner, and the possibilities of using higher evaporator temperatures but for shorter times became obvious. Such a unit was designed by Cook (1963 and 1964) of Dunedin, Fla., and designated as the TASTE evaporator for Temperature Accelerated Short Time Evaporator. In a typical design there are seven stages and four effects plus a flash cooler. The juice passes through each stage only once so the time the juice is in the evaporator can be measured in minutes instead of an hour or two in a usual low-temperature unit. One or more stages operate at 200° to 212°F and one result is the pasteurization of the product. Other stages and effects range down to about 105°F. Table 20 shows approximate operating conditions in an evaporator of 65,000 lb/hr water evaporating capacity. These evaporators are of the falling-film type using fairly small tubes in bundles.

TABLE 20

TASTE EVAPORATOR[1]

Stage	Product, lb	Temperature, °F	Concentration, °Brix
Feed	80,000	70	12
First	75,000	105	13
Second	60,000	205	16
Third	40,000	190	33
Fourth	25,000	170	40
Fifth	20,000	145	48
Sixth	18,000	115	56
Seventh	15,200	105	63
Flash	15,000	60	65

[1] Approximate operating conditions 65,000 lb/hr.

Photo by M. K. Veldhuis

FIG. 24. THREE EVAPORATORS AT CITRUS WORLD, INC., LAKE WALES, FLA.

At left a 28,000 lb/hr (water vaporizing capacity) Mojonnier Lo-Temp Evaporator. At center a 32,000 lb/hr Kelly Low Temperature Evaporator. At right a 60,000 lb/hr TASTE (Temperature Accelerated Short Time Evaporator) Evaporator.

Installed evaporation capacity in Florida of TASTE evaporators is estimated at 1.5 million pounds water vapor per hour (equals production capacity of 1.5 million gallons four-fold concentrate per 24 hr), more than all other types combined. These evaporators are remarkably efficient in that three pounds of water are vaporized per pound of steam. Units range in capacity from 20,000 to 80,000 lb per hr evaporating capacity. Smaller units usually have fewer stages. Most new construction has been of this type and some old, less efficient units have been replaced by TASTE evaporators.

TASTE evaporators have advantages in a minimum of product residence time, comparatively low initial cost, high efficiency and relative ease in cleaning "in place." They also have some disadvantages. They are relatively inflexible because the product goes through each stage only

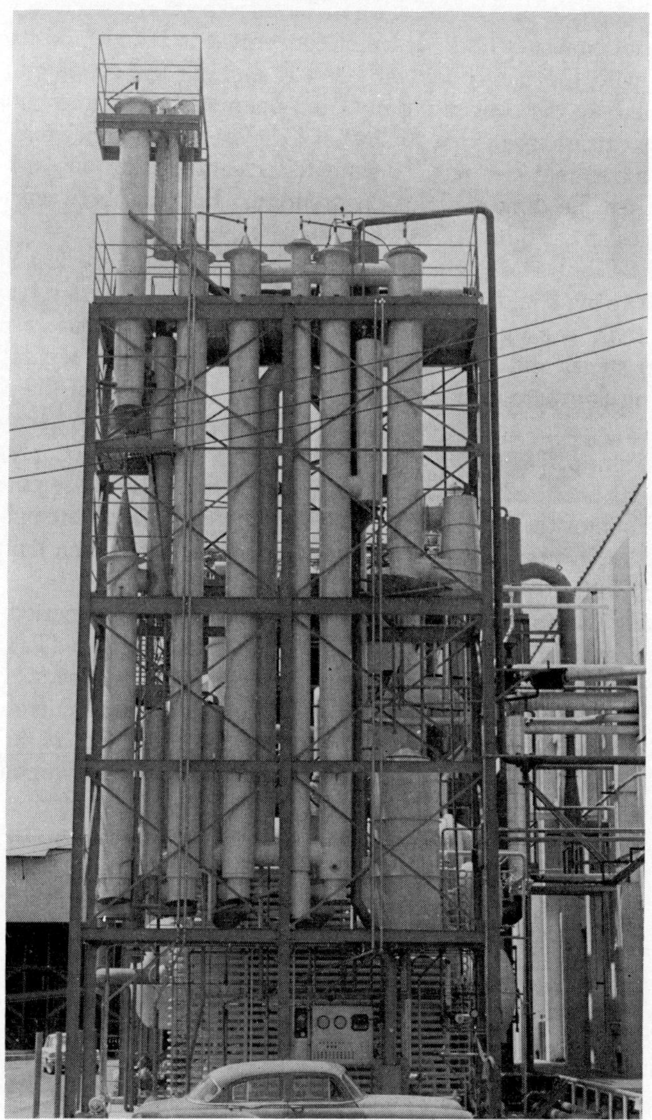

Photo by M. K. Veldhuis

Fig. 25. Taste (Temperature Accelerated Short Time Evaporator) Evaporator Showing Arrangement of Tube Bundles and Separating Chambers

This is another view of the unit shown at right in Fig. 24.

once and changes in concentration of feed are soon reflected in a change in pumpout concentration. It is not convenient to blend "add-back" concentrate with the feed juice and send it through the evaporator as this would increase the concentration of the pumpout. Also, the higher temperatures cause more rapid fouling of heat exchanger tubes and necessitate more frequent cleaning. Fortunately cleaning takes only a few minutes and can be done without disassembly. Intervals between cleaning may be as short as 6 hr.

Figure 24 shows three citrus evaporators. The center one is a Kelly low temperature unit and the left one is a Mojonnier Lo-Temp evaporator. Both of these use mechanical refrigeration, have heat pump cycles and have four stages and two effects. The large vapor-liquid separators and connecting ducts are characteristic of the type. The unit of the right is a TASTE evaporator and its capacity is equal to that of the other two combined. Figure 25 is another view of the same TASTE evaporator. The tall, slender heat exchangers and "coffee pot" vapor liquid separators are characteristic of the type. These three units form a flexible combination. Either of the low temperature evaporators may be used when limited production is desired and all three for maximum production.

Cleaning Evaporators.—Citrus juice evaporators require periodic cleaning because of microbial buildup on the interior surfaces (Patrick and Hill 1959) or because of scaling on the heat exchanger surfaces. The low temperature evaporators usually encounter difficulties in microbial contaminations and the required cleaning interval will depend on the design. Some of the old Skinner evaporators could be run a week without cleaning, while other types could be run only 2 or 3 days. Spattering of juice onto upper surfaces due to high vapor velocity is one cause. In TASTE evaporators, a scale of hesperidin forms on the surface of the heat exchanger in 6 to 10 hr and must be removed. In either case primary cleaning is by circulating hot caustic solution in the evaporator. In low temperature evaporators some surfaces may require cleaning by hand and visual inspection. Of course the caustic must be thoroughly rinsed from the evaporator.

Microbial growth can be detected in an evaporator by analysis for diacetyl in the evaporator product (Hill *et al.* 1954). Another method is to use plate counts on orange serum agar. Such tests should be used extensively when a new evaporator is being started and periodically thereafter. During warm weather fruit will naturally contain more microorganisms and more precautions are necessary.

Scaling of heat exchangers can be detected by checking for small flakes in the concentrate or by decrease in evaporating capacity.

Essence Recovery.—Essence recovery has been introduced into many plants in the citrus industry. A method of recovery under vacuum was developed by Wolford *et al.* (1968). This is particularly applicable to the low-temperature evaporators and the essence is recovered before the juice is fed to the evaporators. About 15% of the juice is evaporated and the volatiles concentrated in a series of condensers until the volume is approximately one-hundredth that of the original juice. The product is very fragrant and used to impart fresh flavor to frozen concentrated orange juice. Other methods include the recovery of essence from the vapors from the first stage of a low-temperature evaporator (Byer and Lang 1964) and the use of a pump with a liquid seal to recover vapors (Bomben *et al.* 1966 and Brent *et al.* 1966). The most popular method is to recover the essence from the first effect of a TASTE evaporator. Essence recovery does not pose any particular technical difficulties. The first item is to strip off the essence and this can be done by evaporating from 15 to 25% of the juice either under vacuum or at atmospheric conditions. Once volatilized it is comparatively easy to separate the water in a packed column and let the fragrant vapor pass to the last condenser where it is condensed in a refrigerated condenser.

Separate essence recovery units suffer from an energy standpoint because they are single effect and represent substantial increases in energy requirements, if 15% or more of the juice is to be vaporized. It is better to incorporate the essence unit as a part of a multi-effect evaporator. The units incorporated with the TASTE evaporators have the added advantage of operating at atmospheric pressure or nearly so. Thus, the volumes of vapor are much smaller, the size of the fractionating columns can be much smaller, and the condensers can be smaller and require less refrigerant.

The quality of essence varies and it is desirable to blend extensively to improve uniformity. Essence should be kept under refrigeration in filled containers. Essence seems to improve high quality concentrate more than that of lesser quality. Also the benefit to flavor gradually diminishes with time even in frozen storage.

Concentration by Freezing

Concentration by freezing ice crystals and separation of these crystals from the concentrate by centrifuging has been tried a number of times on an experimental scale and on full commercial scale. There are a number of patents on supposedly superior modifications. All commercial efforts have been abandoned, but the possibilities continue to challenge the imagination. A chief advantage is that it tends to concentrate certain soluble fragrant components in the liquid product. It takes less energy to separate water by freezing than by evaporation, but multi-effect evaporators tend to nullify this advantage. Freezing water out is a relatively slow

Photo by M. K. Veldhuis

FIG. 26. VOTATOR FOR CHILLING CONCENTRATED ORANGE JUICE PRIOR TO FILLING INTO CANS

process in comparison to evaporation and less susceptible to speeding up. Another difficulty is that suspended matter and some soluble solids tend to be separated with the ice and such losses are large enough to require recovery. For a time, one plant used such a process to recover partially concentrated juice for blending in the final product to improve fresh flavor. The development of essence recovery equipment has made freeze-concentration less attractive.

Addition of Fresh Cut-Back Juice.—Concentrate from the evaporators is collected in cold-wall tanks. Cut-back is added at this point and the concentrate adjusted to 45° Brix. In order to assure optimum flavor, cold-pressed peel oil may be added to bring the recoverable oil value to about 0.025% v/v on a reconstituted basis.

While in the mixing tank, the temperature of the concentrate is reduced to 30° to 40°F. Further cooling may be achieved by pumping through Votators (Fig. 26) before filling into the final containers. In some plants automatic blending units replace the blending tanks.

Containers.—The familiar 6-oz can which reconstitutes to 24 oz when 3 volumes of water are added is still the most popular size. Some 12-oz cans are also marketed and offer savings in container cost per unit of product. Consideration has been given to containers which would reconstitute to a quart or other convenient size. The trade is reluctant to use anything other than the size that has been so popular.

Enamel-lined tin cans were the regular container for the first dozen years. Then a series of changes began to occur, including the replacement of the soldered side seam with a heat sealed side seam, aluminum bodies, aluminum ends, and finally composition bodies. Zip tops were introduced and then modified so that concentrate was not flipped about on opening. Composition bodies are in general use and a favorite combination is a fiberboard body with polyethylene liner, aluminum ends and a zip-strip in the body where it joins an end. Rectangular cardboard boxes with plastic liners are being made and they offer advantages in a savings in space.

The introduction of a wide variety of containers prompted a renewed study on the retention of ascorbic acid and flavor over a period of a year. No differences were noted at 0°F (Bissett and Berry 1970).

Add-Back.—During the manufacture of frozen concentrated orange juice advantage is taken of "add-back" to maintain uniform color and flavor. "Add-back" concentrate is high density concentrate which has been packed in polyethylene lined 55-gal barrels and stored at 0°F until needed. For example, Valencia concentrate of high color and low acidity might be stored for blending with juice of low color and high acidity at the beginning of the following season. Usually the add-back concentrate is defrosted and added to the feed juice to the evaporator. Then if any off-aroma has developed in storage, it will be removed during subsequent concentration.

In Florida, no sugar is added to frozen concentrated orange juice in accord with State regulations and the minimum sugar/acid ratio must be maintained by the selection of fruit. In California, sugar may be added.

Storage Temperatures.—Storage of frozen concentrated orange juice should be at 0°F, or below to maintain quality (Moore *et al.* 1950; Dubois and Kew 1951; Kew 1955, 1957; McColloch and Rice 1955). Storage at temperatures 5° and 10°F for extended periods or at higher temperatures for brief periods of time will result in flavor damage, loss of cloud, and possibly the formation of a gel.

FROZEN TANGERINE AND BLENDED CONCENTRATES

Frozen tangerine concentrate and frozen blended concentrated orange and grapefruit juice have been manufactured by similar methods. Production and popularity of these products has been limited, however.

HIGH-BRIX FROZEN CONCENTRATES

It has been pointed out by Rice *et al.* (1954), Dubois and Murdock (1955), and Bissett *et al.* (1957A), that there are advantages to concentrates of higher than 45° Brix. Concentrations most frequently mentioned are $53^1/_3$°, 58.5°, and 65° Brix. At these concentrations the tendency to clarify and form gels is less and flavor stability is somewhat better than at 42° Brix. There would also be some savings in containers, freight, and storage costs.

No serious attempt has been made to market frozen high-Brix orange concentrates to date, mainly because it is felt that the trade is accustomed to the present product and producers are reluctant to risk a change. High-Brix concentrate is commonly marketed in larger containers for institutional use. The development of essence recovery makes possible the packing of a full-flavored, high-Brix product.

PASTEURIZED CONCENTRATES

Pasteurized "hot pack" concentrates are made by essentially the same methods as frozen concentrates. A few differences should be noted, however. In some cases evaporators are operated at higher temperatures (100° to 120°F) to decrease costs and in these cases, the juice fed to the evaporators should first be thoroughly pasteurized to prevent excessive enzyme activity during concentration. Usually concentration is continued until 65° Brix is obtained. No cut-back juice is used, but some cold-pressed peel oil may be added for flavor. The finished concentrate is heated to 160° to 180°F and filled hot into cans to prevent subsequent fermentation (Bissett *et al.* 1953). Gallon cans are the usual container. Most of the product is used in manufacturing other products such as beverage bases, bakery products, etc.

PRESERVATION WITH SULFUR DIOXIDE

Preservation of orange juice with sulfur dioxide is practiced more in citrus producing areas other than in the United States. Sulfur dioxide may be introduced either as a salt of sulfurous acid, or as gaseous sulfur dioxide. Juice preserved with sulfur dioxide cannot be packed in tin containers since the gas will darken the tin plate and the tin may reduce sulfur dioxide to hydrogen sulfide. In most cases, sulfured juice is packed in paraffin-lined oak or fir barrels.

When sulfur dioxide is added to citrus juices, there is a combination of the sulfurous acid with certain organic constituents of the juice (Downer 1943; Ingram and Vas 1950A and B; Ingram 1949). Combined sulfurous acid has little or no preservative effect. Besides such combination, there is probably an oxidation of sulfite to sulfate, and a volatilization of free sulfur dioxide. The lower the temperature of storage, the lower these losses.

Sulfured orange juice should contain from 800 to 1000 ppm total sulfur dioxide and 500 ppm free sulfur dioxide (Downer 1943). Some states do not permit sale of foods containing sulfur dioxide even though the Federal Food, Drug, and Cosmetic Act permits its use in certain fruits and fruit juices with proper labelling.

SANITATION—QUALITY CONTROL

Sanitation and quality control involve numerous State and Federal regulations in addition to specifications for specific brands and companies. In general, Federal regulations are in broad terms and designed to accommodate the fruit from all areas while State regulations have been prepared with only the fruit of that area in mind.

The Food and Drug Administration, U.S. Department of Health, Education, and Welfare, has recently established Standards of Identity for orange juice and concentrate and similar Standards are being developed for a number of other citrus products including orange juice drinks, orange drinks, and ades. The Food and Drug Administration has also issued the so-called standards for "Good Manufacturing Practice" (Ley 1969) which describe in considerable detail what will be acceptable as good sanitation in the manufacture of processed foods. Citrus products are included, of course.

The Consumer and Marketing Service, U.S. Dept. Agr. has Grade Standards for fresh citrus fruit and for 13 different citrus juice products. Grade classifications for processed citrus products are Fancy, Choice, Standard and Substandard, but either the Choice or Standard grade is omitted from some series. The grades refer to the quality of the product, not the food value.

State regulations generally cover the same areas but are designed to take advantage of particular properties of the fruit from the region. For example, oranges from California produce more deeply colored products and oranges from Texas and Florida produce products which are sweeter to taste. The respective State regulations are designed to see that manufactured products take advantage of these characteristics. In Florida where over 90% of the orange crop is processed there are elaborate regulations designed to promote the production of quality products from the fruit available. For instance, sugar may not be added to frozen concentrated orange juice produced in the State. These regulations are developed by the State of Florida, Department of Citrus (formerly Florida Citrus Commission). Maturity regulations also vary among the different areas of production.

In judging maturity the most important factors are Brix, acid, Brix/acid ratio, and juice yield. The fruit may be tested in the grove, in the packing house or as unloaded at the processing plant.

In the grading of processed citrus juices, score points are given within specified ranges for three factors: color, defects and flavor. Color is judged by comparison with standard plastic tubes. The factor of defects concerns the degree of freedom from small seeds, dissolved specks, excessive amounts of juice sacs or fruit parts, and excessive recoverable oil. All of these are evaluated by visual inspection, except for recoverable oil which must be measured by the "Bromate Titration Method." The flavor factor is scored by measurement of Brix and acid, and by tasting. The product should have a characteristic flavor and be free of off-flavors.

Other tests commonly used in quality control include suspended solids (pulp) which may be estimated by centrifuging and observing the volume of sediment. An estimation of pectinesterase activity may be made to check effectiveness of pasteurization in frozen concentrate or chilled juice. "Cloud" may be measured by centrifuging and measuring light transmission in a colorimeter with a red filter. Tendency for gel formation in frozen concentrate may be observed by incubating a few cans at 80°F for 24 hr, cutting the cans and checking the contents. The contents should not show more than a few small gel formations.

International standards, "Codex Alimentarius," are being developed for citrus juices and concentrates. It is anticipated that these will be used in foreign trade and that local standards will be modified to conform, when possible.

BIBLIOGRAPHY

Albach, R. F., and Redman, G. H. 1969. Composition and inheritance of flavanones in citrus fruit. Phytochem. 8, 127–143.

Arigoni, D. *et al.* 1960. The constitution of limonin. Experientia *16,* 41–49.

Atkins, C. D., and Rouse, A. H. 1953A. Time-temperature relationships for heat inactivation of pectinesterase in citrus juices. Food Technol. *7,* 489–491.

Atkins, C. D., and Rouse, A. H. 1953B. The effect of different methods of juice extraction on the pectic content of Valencia orange juice. Proc. Fla. State Hort. Soc. *66,* 289–292.

Atkins, C. D., Rouse, A. H., and Moore, E. L. 1956. Effect of thermal treatment and concentration on pectinesterase, cloud and pectin in citrus juices. Proc. Fla. State Hort. Soc. *69,* 181–184.

ATTAWAY, J. A., WOLFORD, R. W., DOUGHERTY, M. H., and EDWARDS, G. J. 1967. Methods for the determination of oxygenated terpene, aldehyde, and ester concentrations in aqueous citrus essence. J. Agr. Food Chem. *15*, 688–692.

AXELROD, B. 1947A. Citrus juice phosphatase. J. Biol. Chem. *167*, 57–72.

AXELROD, B. 1947B. Phosphatase activity as an index of pasteurization in citrus juices. Fruit Products J. *26*, 132–133.

BAKER, R. A., and BRUEMMER, J. H. 1969. Cloud stability in the absence of various orange juice soluble components. Proc. Fla. State Hort. Soc. *82*, 215–220.

BAKER, R. A., and BRUEMMER, J. H. 1970. Unpublished observations. Winter Haven, Fla.

BARTHOLOMEW, E. T., and SINCLAIR, W. B. 1941. Unequal distribution of soluble solids in the pulp of citrus fruits. Plant Physiol. *16*, 293–312.

BEN-AZIZ, A. 1967. Nobiletin is main fungistat in tangerines resistant to Mal Secco. Science *155*, 1026–1027.

BERRY, R. E., BISSETT, O. W., WAGNER, C. J., JR., and VELDHUIS, M. K. 1967. Conditions for producing foam-mat-dried grapefruit crystals. Food Technol. *21*, 293–296.

BISSETT, O. W., and BERRY, R. E. 1970. Ascorbic acid retention in orange juice as related to container type. J. Food Sci. Submitted for publication.

BISSETT, O. W., VELDHUIS, M. K., GUYER, R. B., and MILLER, W. M. 1957A. Stability of frozen concentrated orange juice. III. The effect of heat treatment in the production of high-Brix frozen concentrate. Food Technol. *11*, 96–99.

BISSETT, O. W., VELDHUIS, M. K., GUYER, R. B., and MILLER, W. M. 1957B. Stability of frozen concentrated orange juice. IV. Effect of heat treatment on Hamlin, Pineapple, and Valencia juices at different stages of maturity. Food Technol. *11*, 512–515.

BISSETT, O. W., VELDHUIS, M. K., and RUSHING, N. B. 1953. Effect of heat treatment on the storage life of Valencia orange concentrates. Food Technol. *7*, 258–260.

BLAIR, J. S., GODAR, E. M., REINKE, H. G., and MARSHALL, J. R. 1957. The "COF Effect" in frozen citrus products. Food Technol. *11*, 61–68.

BÖHME, H., and VÖLCKER, P. E. 1959. The nonvolatile principles of orange peel oil. Arch. Pharm. *292*, 529–536.

BOMBEN, J. L., KITSON, J. A., and MORGAN, A. J. JR. 1966. Vacuum stripping of aromas. Food Technol. *20*, 1219–1222.

BONNELL, J. M., STRASHUN, S. I., and DORSEY, W. R. 1955. Commercial production of orange and grapefruit crystals. Proc. Fla. State Hort. Soc. *68*, 114–116.

BORN, R. 1960. 3′,4′,5,6,7 penta-O-methyl-flavone in orange peel. Chem. and Ind. *1960*, 264.

BRAVERMAN, J. B. S. 1933. The chemical composition of the orange. Hadar *6*, 62–65.

BRENT, J. A., DUBOIS, C. W., and HUFFMAN, C. F. 1968. Essence Recovery. U.S. Pat. No. 3,248,233.

BRUEMMER, J. H. 1969. Redox state of nicotinamide-adenine dinucleotides in citrus fruit. J. Agr. Food Chem. *17*, 1312–1315.

BRUEMMER, J. H., and ROE, B. 1969. Post-harvest treatment of citrus fruit to increase Brix/Acid ratio. Proc. Fla. Hort. Soc. *82*, 212–215.

Bruemmer, J. H., and Roe, B. 1970A. Regulation of NAD and NADP oxidoreductases in Oranges. Phytochem., in press.

Bruemmer, J. H., and Roe, B. 1970B. Unpublished observations.

Bruemmer, J. H., and Roe, B. 1970C. Enzymic oxidation of simple diphenols and flavonoids by orange juice extracts. J. Food Sci. *35*, 116–119.

Byer, E. M., and Lang, A. A. 1964. Production of flavor-enhanced citrus concentrates. U.S. Pat. No. 3,118,776.

Carroll, E. A., Guyer, R. B., Bissett, O. W., and Veldhuis, M. K. 1957. Stability of frozen concentrated orange juice. V. The effect of heat treatment at intermediate stages of concentration on juices prepared from Valencia oranges. Food Technol. *11*, 516–519.

Clements, R. L. 1964. Organic acids in citrus fruits. I. Varietal differences. J. Food Sci. *29*, 276–286.

Clements, R. L., and Leland, H. V. 1962. An ion-exchange study of the free amino acids in the juices of six varieties of citrus. J. Food Sci. *27*, 20–25.

Cook, R. W. 1963. High temperature short time evaporator. Proc. Citrus Eng. Conf., Fla. Sect. Am. Soc. Mech. Eng. *9*, 1–7.

Cook, R. W. 1964. Vacuum evaporator. U.S. Patent No. 3,141,807. July 21.

Coulson, D. M., Crowell, W. R., and Friess, S. L. 1950. Polarography of reduced glutathione and glutathione-ascorbic acid mixtures. Anal. Chem. *22*, 525–529.

Curl, A. L. 1946. Off-flavor development in processed tangerine juice. Fruit Products J. *25*, 356–357.

Curl, A. L. 1953. Application of countercurrent distribution to Valencia orange juice carotenoids. J. Agr. Food Chem. *1*, 456–460.

Curl, A. L., and Bailey, G. F. 1954. Polyoxygen carotenoids of Valencia orange juice. J. Agr. Food Chem. *2*, 685–690.

Curl, A. L., and Bailey, G. F. 1955. The state of combination of the carotenoids of Valencia orange juice. Food Research *20*, 371–376.

Curl, A. L., and Bailey, G. F. 1956. Orange carotenoids. Part I—Comparison of carotenoids of Valencia peel and pulp. Part II—Carotenoids of aged canned Valencia orange juice. J. Agr. Food Chem. *4*, 156–162.

Curl, A. L., and Bailey, G. F. 1957. The carotenoids of tangerines. J. Agr. Food Chem. *5*, 605–608.

Curl, A. L., and Bailey, G. F. 1959. Changes in the carotenoid pigments in preparation and storage of Valencia orange powder. Food Technol. *13*, 394–398.

Curl, A. L., and Veldhuis, M. K. 1947. The origin of the off-flavor which develops in processed orange juice. Fruit Products J. *26*, 329–330, 342.

Curl, A. L. and Veldhuis, M. K. 1948. The composition of the sugars in Florida Valencia orange juice. Fruit Products J. *27*, 342–343, 361.

Davis, W. B. 1932. Deposits of oil in the juice sacs of citrus fruits. Am. J. Botany, *19*, 101–105.

Davis, W. B. 1942. The distribution of citrus peroxidase. Am. J. Botany *29*, 252–254.

Dougherty, M. H. 1968. A method for measuring the water-soluble volatile constituents of citrus juices and products. Food Technol. *22*, 1455–1456.

Downer, A. W. E. 1943. The preservation of citrus juices with sulfurous acid. J. Soc. Chem. Ind. *62*, 124–127.

DuBois, C. W., and Kew, T. J. 1951. Storage temperature effects on frozen citrus concentrates. Refrig. Eng. 59, 772–775, 812.

DuBois, C. W., and Murdock, D. I. 1955. The effect of concentration on quality of frozen orange juice with particular reference to 58.5° and 42° Brix products. I. Chemical and physiological effects. Food Technol. 9, 60–63.

Dunlap, W. J., and Wender, S. H. 1960. Purification and identification of flavanone glycosides in the peel of the sweet orange. Arch. Biochem. and Biophys. 87, 228–231.

Feaster, J. F., Braun, O. G., Riester, D. W., and Alexander, P. E. 1950. Influence of storage conditions on ascorbic acid content and quality of canned orange juice. Food Technol. 4, 190–193.

Frankenthal, L. 1939. The methylene blue-reducing system of Palestine orange peels investigated by the Thunberg method. Enzymologia 6, 287–306.

Freed, M., Brenner, S., and Wodicka, V. O. 1949. Prediction of thiamin and ascorbic acid stability in stored canned foods. Food Technol. 3, 148–151.

Griffin, W. C. 1951. Solid essential oil concentrate and process for preparing same. U.S. Pat. 2,566,410. Sept. 4.

Harding, P. L., and Sunday, M. B. 1949. Seasonal changes in Florida tangerines. U.S. Dept. Agr. Tech. Bull. 988.

Harding, P. L., Winston, J. R., and Fisher, D. F. 1940. Seasonal changes in Florida oranges. U.S. Dept. Agr. Tech. Bull. 753, 1–88.

Heid, J. L., and Scott, W. C. 1937. The processing of citrus juices. Observations on heating and cooling operations. Fruit Products J. 17, 100–104, 121.

Hendrickson, R., and Kesterson, J. W. 1951. Citrus by-products of Florida. Fla. Agr. Expt. Sta. Bull. 487.

Henry, R. E., and Clifcorn, L. E. 1948. The problem of deterioration in flavor of canned orange juice. Canning Trade 70, No. 31, 7–8, 22.

Higby, R. H. 1938. The bitter constituents of Navel and Valencia oranges. J. Am. Chem. Soc. 60, 3013–3018.

Hill, E. C., Wenzel, F. W., and Barreto, A. 1954. Colorimetric method for detection of microbial spoilage in citrus juices. Food Technol. 8, 168–171.

Hunter, G. L. K., and Brogden, W. B. Jr. 1965. Terpenes and sesquiterpenes in cold-pressed orange oil. J. Food Sci. 30, 1–4.

Hunter, G. L. K., and Brogden, W. B. Jr. 1966. Analysis of cold-pressed orange oil paraffin waxes. Phytochem. 5, 807–809.

Hunter, G. L. K., and Moshonas, M. G. 1965. Isolation and identification of alcohols in cold-pressed Valencia orange oil by liquid-liquid extraction and gas chromatography. Anal. Chem. 37, 378–380.

Hunter, G. L. K., and Moshonas, M. G. 1966. Analysis of alcohols in essential oils of grapefruit, lemon, lime and tangerine. Food. Sci. 31, 167–171.

Huskins, C. W., and Swift, L. J. 1953. Changes in the lipid fraction of Valencia orange juice during pasteurization. Food Research 18, 305–307.

Huskins, C. W., Swift, L. J., and Veldhuis, M. K. 1952. Constituents of the lipids from stored Florida Valencia orange juice. Food Research 17, 109–116.

Hussein, A. A. 1944. Respiration in the orange—a study of systems responsible for oxygen uptake. J. Biol. Chem. 155, 201–211.

Ingram, M. 1949. Behavior of sulfur dioxide in concentrated orange juice. Food Research 14, 54–71.

INGRAM, M., and VAS, K. 1950A. Equilibrium state. J. Sci. Food Agr. *1*, No. 1, 21–27.

INGRAM, M., and VAS, K. 1950B. Combination of sulfur dioxide with concentrated orange juice. II. The rate of reaction. J. Sci. Food Agr. *1*, No. 2, 63–66.

JANSEN, E. F., JANG, R., and BONNER, J. 1960. Orange pectinesterase–binding and activity. Food Research *25*, 64–72.

JANSEN, E. F., JANG, R., and MACDONNELL, L. R. 1947. Citrus acetylesterase. Arch. Biochem. *15*, 415–431.

JANSEN, E. F., JANG, R., and MACDONNELL, L. R. 1949. Isolation of acetylesterase from citrus waste. U.S. Pat. 2,458,171. Jan. 4.

JOSLYN, M. A. 1963. Enzymes in food processing, *in* Food Processing Operations, Vol. 2, J. L. Heid, and M. A. Joslyn (Editors). Avi Publishing Co., Westport, Conn.

KEFFORD, J. F., MCKENZIE, H. A., and THOMPSON, P. C. O. 1950. The effect of oxygen on flavor deterioration and loss of ascorbic acid in canned orange juice. Food Preservation Quart. Sept. 44–47.

KEW, T. J. 1955. Changes in commercial frozen orange concentrate stored at several temperatures. Proc. Fla. State Hort. Soc. *68*, 167–170.

KEW, T. J. 1957. Five-year storage of frozen concentrated orange juice at −4°, 5°, and 10°F. Proc. Fla. State Hort. Soc. *70*, 182–184.

KEW, T. J., and VELDHUIS, M. K. 1950. An index of pasteurization of citrus juices by rapid method of testing for residual enzyme activity. Proc. Fla. State Hort. Soc. *63*, 162–165.

KEW, T. J., and VELDHUIS, M. K. 1961. Cloud stabilization in citrus juice. U.S. Patent No. 2,995,448. Aug. 8.

KEW, T. J., and VELDHUIS, M. K. 1960. Citrus pectinesterase inhibitor in grape leaf extract. Proc. Fla. State Hort. Soc. *73*, 293–297.

KEW, T. J., VELDHUIS, M. K., BISSETT, O. W., and PATRICK, R. 1957. The effect of time and temperature of pasteurization on the quality of canned citrus juices. U.S. Dept. Agr. ARS-72-6.

KIRCHNER, J. G., and MILLER, J. M. 1957. Volatile water soluble and oil constituents of Valencia orange juice. J. Agr. Food Chem. *5*, 283–291.

KIRCHNER, J. G., RICE, R. G., MILLER, J. M., and KELLER, G. J. 1950. The presence of hydrogen sulfide in citrus juices. Arch. Biochem. *25*, 231–232.

KREHL, W. A., and COWGILL, G. R. 1950. Vitamin content of citrus products. Food Research *15*, 179–191.

LEBRETON, 1928. On the crystalline material of small oranges and the analyses of immature fruit of the hesperides family. J. Pharm. Chim. *14* (series 2), 377–392.

LEY, L. L. JR. 1969. Part 128–Human Foods; current manufacturing practice (sanitation) in manufacture, processing, packing, or holding. Federal Register *34*, 6977–6980.

LISTER, L. J., and FAY, A. C. 1956. The quality control of chilled orange juice from the tree to the consumer. Proc. Fla. State Hort. Soc. 69, 136–138.

LOEFFLER, H. J. 1941A. Processing of orange juice—effect of storage temperature on quality factors of bottle juice. Ind. Eng. Chem. *33*, 1308–1314.

LOEFFLER, H. J. 1941B. Maintenance of cloud in citrus juice. Proc. Inst Food Technol. 29–36.

MACDONNELL, L. R., JANSEN, E. F., and LINEWEAVER, H. 1945. The properties of orange pectinesterase. Arch. Biochem. *6*, 389–401.

MAIER, V. P., and BEVERLY, G. D. 1968. Limonin monolactone, the nonbitter precursor responsible for delayed bitterness in certain citrus juices. J. Food Sci. *33*, 488–492.

MAIER, V. P., HASEGAWA, S., and HERA, E. 1969. Limonin D-ring lactone hydrolase. New enzyme from citrus seeds. Phytochem. *8*, 405–407.

MACDOWELL, L. G., MOORE, E. L., and ATKINS, C. D. 1948. Method of preparing full-flavored fruit juice concentrates. U.S. Pat. 2,453,109. Nov. 9.

MATLACK, M. B. 1928. Some preliminary observations on the coloring matter of citrus juices. Am. J. Pharm. *100*, 243–246.

MATLACK, M. B. 1929. A chemical study of the rind of California orange. J. Am. Pharm. Soc. *18*, 24–31.

MATLACK, M. B. 1931. Observation on the red color of the blood orange. Plant Physiol. *6*, 729–730.

MATLACK, M. B. 1940. The fatty constituents of California Valencia pulp. J. Org. Chem. *5*, 504–507.

MCCOLLOCH, R. J., and RICE, R. G. 1955. Properties of stored frozen orange concentrate observed by differential cloud determination. Food Technol. *9*, 70–73.

MCCREADY, R. M., Walter, E. D., and MACLAY, W. D. 1950. Sugars in citrus juices. Food Technol. *4*, 19–20.

MILLER, E. V., WINSTON, J. R., and SCHOMER, H. A., 1940. Physiological studies of plastic pigments in rinds of maturing oranges. J. Agr. Research *60*, 259–267.

MOORE, E. L., HUGGART, R. L., and HILL, E. C. 1950. Storage changes in frozen concentrated citrus juices. Proc. Fla. State Hort. Soc. *63*, 165–174.

MOORE, E. L., MACDOWELL, L. G., ATKINS, C. D., and HUGGART, R. L. 1947. An experiment on partial concentration as a means of standardizing low solids orange juice. Fruit Products J. *27*, 72–74.

MORGAN, A. I., JR., GINNETTE, L. F., RANDALL, J. M., and GRAHAM, R. P. 1959. Technique for improving instants. Food Eng. *31*, No. 9, 86–87.

MOSHONAS, M. G. 1967. Isolation of piperitenone and 6-methyl-5-hepten-2-one from orange oil. J. Food Sci. *32*, 206–207

MOSHONAS, M. G., and LUND, E. D. 1969A. Isolation and identification of a series of α,β-unsaturated aldehydes from Valencia orange peel oil. J. Agr. Food Chem. *17*, 802–804.

MOSHONAS, M. G., and LUND, E. D. 1969B. Aldehydes, ketones and esters in Valencia orange peel oil. J. Food Sci. *34*, 502–503.

MOTTERN, H. H., and VON LOESECKE, H. W. 1933. Deaeration and flash pasteurization of orange and grapefruit juices. Fruit Products J. *12*, 325–326.

MYLNE, A. M., and SEAMANS, V. S. 1954. Stabilized orange juice powder II. Changes during storage. Food Technol. *8*, 45–50.

NATARAJAN, C. P., and MACKINNEY, G. 1952. Carotenoid pigments of orange juice. J. Sci. Ind. Research (India) *11B*, 416–418.

NELSON, E. K. 1934. The occurrence of a pentamethyl flavonol in tangerine peel. J. Am. Chem. Soc. *56*, 1392–1393.

NELSON, E. K., and MOTTERN, H. H. 1934. Occurrence of citral in Florida Valencia orange oil. J. Am. Chem. Soc. *56*, 1238–1239.

NELSON, E. K., MOTTERN, H. H., and EDDY, C. W. 1933. Nitrogenous constituents of Florida Valencia orange juice. Fruit Products J. *12*, 231–235, 250.

NOLTE, A. J., PULLEY, G. N., and VON LOESECKE, H. W. 1942. Experiments with antioxidants for preventing flavor deterioration in canned orange juice. Food Research *7*, 236–243.

NOLTE, A. J., and VON LOESECKE, H. W. 1940. Chemical and physical characteristics of the petroleum ether soluble material of fresh and canned Florida Valencia orange juice. Food Research *5*, 457–467.

NORDBY, H. E., and NAGY, S. 1969. Fatty acid profiles of citrus juice and seed lipids. Phytochem. *8*, 2027–2038.

OLSEN, R. W., and HILL, E. C. 1964. Debittering of concentrated grapefruit juice with naringinase. Proc. Florida Hort. Soc., *77*, 321–325.

OMURA, H., CHIKANO, T., ISHIZAKI, G., and YAMAFUJI, K. 1963. Removal of pectinase activity in naringinase preparations. Kyushu Daigaku Nogakubu Gakugei Zasski *20*, 321–327.

ONSLOW, M. W. 1921. XIII. Oxidizing enzymes. V. Further observations on the oxidizing enzymes of fruits. Biochem. J. *15*, 113–117.

PATRICK, R., and HILL, E. C. 1959. Microbiology of citrus fruit processing Fla. Agr. Expt. Sta. Bull. *618*.

PETERSON, G. T. 1949. Methods of producing vacuum in cans. Continental Can Company Bull. *18*.

PRIMO, Y. E., and ROYO-IRANZO, J. 1968. Detection of adulterations in citrus juices. IX. Mineral composition of the whey of single-strength orange juices manufactured in Spain and the United States. Revista de Agroquimsica y Tecnologia de Alimentos. *1*, No. 3, 364.

PULLEY, G. N. 1936. Apparatus for deaerating liquids. U.S. Pat. 2,060,242. Nov. 10.

PULLEY, G. N., and VON LOESECKE, H. W. 1939. Gases in the commercial handling of citrus juices. Ind. Eng. Chem. *31*, 1275–1278.

REED, G. 1966. Enzymes in Food Processing, Academic Press, New York.

RICE, R. G., KELLER, G. J., MCCOLLOCH, R. J., and BEAVENS, E. A. 1954. Fruit concentrates, flavor-fortified high-density frozen citrus concentrates. J. Agr. Food Chem. *2*, 196–198.

RIESTER, D. W., BRAUN, O. G., and PEARCE, W. E. 1945. Why canned citrus juices deteriorate in storage. Food Inds. *17*, 742–744, 850, 852, 854, 856, 858.

RIESTER, D. W., WILES, G. D., and COATES, J. L. 1948. Temperature variations in warehousing citrus fruits. Food Inds. *20*, 372–375, 494, 496.

ROBERTS, J. A., and GADDUM, L. W. 1937. Composition of citrus fruit juices. Ind. Eng. Chem. *29*, 574–575.

ROCKLAND, L. B., UNDERWOOD, J. C., and BEAVENS, E. A. 1950. Nitrogenous constituents of citrus fruit juices. Calif. Citrograph *35*, 490–492.

ROSE, D. H., COOK, H. T., and REDIT, W. H. 1951. Harvesting, handling and transportation of citrus fruits. U.S. Dept. Agr. Bull. *13*.

ROSS, E. 1944. Effect of time and temperature of storage on vitamin C retention in canned citrus juices. Food Research *9*, 27–33.

ROUSE, A. H. 1949. Gel formation in frozen citrus concentrates thawed and stored at 40°F. Proc. Fla. State Hort. Soc. *62*, 170–173.

ROUSE, A. H. 1953. Distribution of pectinesterase and total pectin in component parts of citrus fruit. Food Technol. *7*, 360–362.

ROUSE, A. H., and ATKINS, C. D. 1953. Further results from a study of heat inactivation of pectinesterase in citrus juices. Food Technol. *7*, 221–223.

Roy, W. R. 1970. Personal communication. Orlando, Fla.

Sale, J. W. *et al.* 1947. Ascorbic acid in grapefruit juice, orange juice, and their blends: 1943. J. Assoc. Offic. Agr. Chemists *30,* 673–680.

Schultz, T. H., Dimick, K. P., and Makower, B. 1956. Incorporation of natural flavors into fruit juice powders. I. Locking of citrus oils in sucrose and dextrose. Food Technol. *10,* 57–60.

Schwimmer, S. 1969. Trends and perspectives in the enzymology of foods. Lebensm. Wiss. u. Technol. *2,* 97–104.

Scott, W. C. 1941. Pretreatment of grapefruit for juice canning. Canner *98,* 11.

Scott, W. C., Kew, T. J., and Veldhuis, M. K. 1965. Composition of orange juice cloud. J. Food Sci. *30,* 833–837.

Scott, W. C., and Veldhuis, M. K. 1966. Rapid estimation of recoverable oil in citrus juices by bromate titration. J. Assoc. Offic. Anal. Chem. *49,* 628–633.

Scurti, F., and DePlato, G. 1909. (1) The chemical process of ripening; (2) the ripening of oranges; (3) the presence of asparagine and glutamine in lemons. Staz. sper. Agrar. Ital. *41,* 456–470.

Sinclair, W. B. (ed.). 1961. The Orange, Its Biochemistry and Physiology. Univ. of Calif. Press, Berkeley, Calif.

Sinclair, W. B., and Bartholomew, E. T. 1944. Effect of rootstock and environment on the composition of oranges and grapefruit. Hilgardia. *16,* No. 3, 125–176.

Sinclair, W. B., Bartholomew, E. T., and Ramsey, R. C. 1945. Analysis of the organic acids of orange juice. Plant Physiol. *20,* 3–18.

Sinclair, W. B., and Eny, D. M. 1947A. Ether soluble organic acids and buffer properties of citrus peels. Botan. Gaz. *108,* 398–407.

Sinclair, W. B., and Eny, D. M. 1947B. Ether soluble acids of mature Valencia oranges. Plant Physiol. *22,* 257–269.

Smith, A. H. 1925. A protein in the edible portion of orange. Preliminary paper. J. Biol. Chem. *63,* 71–73.

Stanley, W. L., Ikeda, R. M., Vannier, S. H., and Rolle, L. A. 1961. Determination of the relative concentrations of the major aldehydes in lemon, orange and grapefruit oils by gas chromatography. J. Food Science *26,* 43–48.

Stewart, I., Newhall, W. F., and Edwards, G. J. 1964. The isolation and identification of l-synephrine in the leaves and fruit of citrus. J. Biol. Chem. *239,* 930–932.

Strashun, S. I., and Talburt, W. F. 1954. Stabilized orange juice powder. I. Preparation and packaging. Food Technol. *8,* 40–45.

Swift, L. J. 1952A. Isolation of betasitosteryl-D-glucoside from the juice of Florida Valencia oranges. J. Am. Chem. Soc. *74,* 1099–2000.

Swift, L. J. 1952B. Fatty acids of the lipids from freshly canned Florida Valencia orange juice. Food Research *17,* 8–14.

Swift, L. J. 1960. Nobiletin from the peel of the Valencia orange. (Citrus sinensis L.) J. Org. Chem. *25,* 2067–2068.

Swift, L. J. 1964. Isolation of 5,6,7,3′,4′ pentamethoxyflavone from orange-peel juice. J. Food Sci. *29,* 766–767.

Swift, L. J. 1965. Tetra-O-methylscutellarein in orange peel. J. Org. Chem. *30,* 2079–2080.

Swift, L. J. 1967. TLC-Spectrophotometric analysis for neutral fraction flavones in orange peel juice. J. Agr. Food Chem. *15,* 99–101.

SWIFT, L. J., and VELDHUIS, M. K. 1951. Constitution of the juice lipids of the Florida Valencia orange. *Citrus sinensis* L. Food Research *16*, 142–146.

TING, S. V. 1958. Enzymatic hydrolysis of naringin in grapefruit. J. Agr. Food Chem. *6*, 546–549.

TING, S. V., and DESCYCK, E. J. 1959 Isolation of 1-quinic acid in citrus fruit. Nature *183*, 1404–1405.

TING, S. V., and VINES, H. M. 1966. Organic acids in the juice vesicles of Florida "Hamlin" orange and "Mash Seedless" grapefruit. Proc. Am. Soc. Hort Sci. *88*, 291–297.

UNDERKOFLER, L. A. 1968. Enzymes *in* Handbook of food additives. T. E. Furia (Editor). Chem. Rubber Co., Cleveland, O.

UNDERWOOD, J. C., and ROCKLAND, L. B. 1953. Nitrogenous constituents in citrus fruits. I. Some free amino acids in citrus juices determined by small-scale filter-paper and chromatography. Food research *18*, 17–29.

VELDHUIS, M. K., and HUNTER, G. L. K. 1968. Nomenclature of ylangene, copaene and cubebene. J. Food Sci. *32*, 697.

VELDHUIS, M. K., SWIFT, L. J., and SCOTT, W. C. 1970. Fully methoxylated flavones in Florida orange juice. J. Agr. Food Chem. *18*, 590–592.

VON LOESECKE, H. W., MOTTERN, H. H., and PULLEY, G. N. 1934. Preservation of orange juice by deaeration and flash pasteurization. Ind. Eng. Chem. *26*, 771–773.

WATT, B. K., and MERRILL, A. L. 1963. Composition of foods—raw, processed, prepared. U.S. Dept. Agr. Handbook No. *8*, Rev.

WATTENBERG, L. W., PAGE, M. A., and LEONG, J. L. 1968. Introduction of increased benzpyrene hydroxylase activity by flavones and related compounds. Cancer Research *28*, 934–937.

WEBBER, H. J., and BATCHELOR, L. D. 1943. The Citrus Industry. 1. History. Botany and Breeding, pp. 133–474. Univ. Caif. Press. Berkeley, Calif.

WENZEL, F. W. Personal communication. Lake Alfred, Fla.

WENZEL, F. W., MOORE, E. L. ATKINS, C. D., and PATRICK, R. 1955. Chilled citrus products. Proc. Fla. State Hort. Soc. *68*, 161–166.

WHEATON, T. A., and STEWART, I. 1965. Quantitative analysis of phenolic amines using ion-exchange chromatography. Anal. Chem. *12*, 585–592.

WILLIMOTT, S. G., and WOKES, F. 1926. Oxidizing enzymes in the peel of citrus fruits. Biochem. J. *20*, 1008–1012.

WOLF, J. 1958. Organic acids in citrus fruit. Fruchtsaft-Ind. *3*, 93–97.

WOLFORD, R. W., ATKINS, C. D., DOUGHERTY, M. H., and MACDOWELL, L. G. 1968. Recovered volatiles from citrus juices. Trans. 1968 Citrus Engr. Conf. Fla. Sect. Am. Soc. Mech. Engr. *14*, 64–81.

WOLFORT R. W., and ATTAWAY, J. A. 1967. Analysis of recovered natural orange flavor enhancement materials using gas chromatography. J. Agr. Food Chem., *15*, 369–377.

YOKOYAMA, H., and WHITE, M. J. 1965A. Citrus carotenoids. II. The structure of citranaxanthin, a new carotenoid ketone. J. Org. Chem. 30, 2481–2482.

YOKOYAMA, H., and WHITE, M. J. 1965B. Citrus carotenoids. IV. The isolation and structure of sinthaxanthin. J. Org. Chem. *30*, 3994–3996.

YOKOYAMA, H., and WHITE, M. J. 1966. Citrus carotenoids. V. The isolation of 8′-hydroxy-citranaxanthin. J. Org. Chem., *31*, 3452–3454.

YOKOYAMA, H., and WHITE, M. J. 1968A. The occurrence of ergosterol in citrus. Phytochem. 7, 493–494.

YOKOYAMA, H., and WHITE, M. J. 1968B. Citrus carotenoids. VIII. The isolation of semi-β-carotenone and β-carotenone from citrus relatives. Phytochem. 7, 1031–1034.

YOKOYAMA, H., WHITE, M. J., and VANDERCOOK, E. C. 1965. Citrus carotenoids. III. The structure cf reticulataxanthin. J. Org. Chem. *30*, 2482–2483.

ZECHMEISTER, L., and TUZSON, P. 1933. Mandarin pigments. Zeit. Physiol. Chem. *221*, 278–280.

ZECHMEISTER, L., and TUZSON, P. 1937. Polyene pigments of the orange. Ber. *70B*, 1966–1969.

CHAPTER 3

Matthew K. Veldhuis

Grapefruit Juice

INTRODUCTION

The grapefruit, *Citrus paradisi:* Macf. is closely related to the pumulo or shaddock, *Citrus grandis* Osbeck. The origin of the grapefruit is unknown but it is presumed by many to be mutation or sport from the shaddock. The shaddock is known to have been cultivated in the West Indies about 1696 and the grapefruit was first reported as growing in the Barbados island in 1750 (Webber and Batchelor 1943).

The name grapefruit comes from a tendency of the fruit of some varieties to grow in clusters. It is the largest of the commercial citrus fruit and is easily recognized when mature by its bright yellow color, large size, and characteristic pleasing bitter acidic taste. An average grapefruit tree is 20 to 25 ft high, produces 15 to 30 eighty-pound boxes of fruit per year and has leaves of a shiny dark green color, somewhat larger in size than those of the orange tree.

The blossoms are large, white, and may be borne singly or in clusters in the axils of the leaves. They are quite similar to orange blossoms in both odor and appearance. Grapefruit are generally more susceptible to damage by low temperatures than oranges, but considerably more resistant than limes and lemons; the trees being damaged by temperatures lower than 26°F and the fruit by temperatures lower than about 28°F. The freezing points of the rind of Florida grapefruit were found to range between 26.9° and 29.7°F, and the flesh between 28.9° and 30.0°F by Whiteman (1958). The symptoms of freeze damage in grapefruit have been described by Burdick (1951). As a result, grapefruit are grown only in the warmer regions of Florida, Texas, Arizona, and California. Grapefruit are grown commercially in other regions of the world with a similar warm climate.

COMMERCIAL VARIETIES

Horticulturists and citrus growers have greatly improved the originally thick skinned, seedy, and intensely bitter grapefruit. Nineteen cultivated varieties of grapefruit having pallid or white pulp and four pink or red fleshed varieties have been described by Webber and Batchelor (1943). More recently Maurer *et al.* (1950) reported studies on several additional

MATTHEW K. VELDHUIS is Chief, U.S. Fruit and Vegetable Products Laboratory, Winter Haven, Fla., a laboratory of the Southern Utilization Research and Development Division, Agricultural Research Service, U.S. Department of Agriculture.

FIG. 27. TYPICAL VARIETIES OF GRAPEFRUIT

Left to right: Duncan, Foster, Marsh White, Marsh Pink, Ruby Red.

red fleshed varieties developed in Texas. The Duncan (seedy) and the Marsh (seedless) are the most important white fleshed grapefruit; the Foster Pink (seedy) and the Marsh Pink (seedless) are the most important pink fleshed grapefruit; and the Ruby Red (seedless) along with the Redblush (seedless) are the most important red fleshed grapefruit. The development of these pink and red fleshed grapefruit is one of the most significant developments in grapefruit since that of the Marsh seedless and its full economic effect has not yet been felt by either the fresh fruit or the processed grapefruit industries. The Duncan and the Marsh are the principal varieties in Florida with the Duncan being the one most commonly processed. The Marsh seedless greatly exceeds in volume that of Duncan processed in Texas. Formerly, the red fleshed grapefruit were almost entirely limited to Texas; however, the volume in Florida has rapidly increased lately.

Pink grapefruit are produced in both Florida and Texas, but only Texas packs any appreciable volume of juice made wholly from pink fleshed grapefruit. In Florida, the juice from pink fruit is blended with substantial quantities of juice from white fruit. At times the pulp (and pink color) may be removed from the pink juice by desludging centrifuges before blending. Unfortunately the pink color changes during storage of juice to a rather muddy, rusty color which is unattractive. In Texas, this is compensated to a degree by adding an extra amount of high-colored pulp. The color change takes place much less rapidly in frozen concentrate and the improvement in color by pulp fortification is more successful (Lime et al. 1954; Griffith and Lime 1959). The preference of pink grapefruit is an example of judging quality by color rather than by flavor. Pink grapefruit is favored in comparison to white grapefruit when the flesh can be seen. The same thing is observed in orange juice where an improved flavor score is given after a little tasteless red food color is added. The flavor of juice from seeded fruit is generally preferred to that from seedless fruit. Usually seedless fruit is preferred when fruit is used to prepare fresh juice or sections as the seeds are considered bothersome in the home.

ANATOMY OF THE GRAPEFRUIT

The juice is present in small, multicellular spindle- or club-shaped juice sacs, which completely fill the segments or sections of the fruit. These segments, or carpels, are distributed radially about the soft pithy core. The core is often associated with a large air space (see Fig. 27). Each segment is completely surrounded by a carpellary membrane and closely adherent to the outercarpellary membrane are the vascular elements. The seeds and pips (immature or abortive seeds which are present even in seedless fruit), are located in the segments along the side nearest the core.

Segments and vascular elements are surrounded by a whitish sponge-like layer called the albedo. The outer layer, or flavedo, contains the yellow coloring matter and the oil cells or sacs. Naringin, the bitter tasting glucoside, is found in all parts of the fruit, but it is most highly concentrated in the albedo, seeds, and segment membranes. The red coloring (lycopene) of the red fleshed grapefruit is concentrated in the segment membranes (rag) and occurs also in the flavedo of the blushing varieties, which gives them their name. The albedo is quite thick and contains large amounts of pectin, pectic enzymes, and oxidizing enzymes that should be avoided during juicing. The albedo layer also contains a considerable amount of soluble solids. The oil glands are balloon shaped cells located in the inner portion of the flavedo.

History and Commercial Production of Fruit and Products

Grapefruit were introduced in Florida about 1810 but they were little more than backyard curiosities for the next 50 years and were considered by some to be inedible. Gradually people came to know and to relish the fruit. The first shipments were made to Philadelphia and New York be-

TABLE 21

PRODUCTION OF GRAPEFRUIT AND GRAPEFRUIT JUICE PRODUCTS IN THE UNITED STATES

	Grapefruit Production[1]				Grapefruit Juice Production[2]			Blended Juice Production[2]			Frozen Grapefruit Concentrate (Fla.)[3]
	Fla.	Tex.	Ariz.	Calif.	Fla.	Tex.	Calif.-Ariz.	Fla.	Tex.	Calif.-Ariz.	
1899 only	12		1	18							
1909 only	1,000		1	120							
1919 only	5,900	3	29	360							
1920–1924	7,600	650	66	380							
1925–1929	7,210	680	200	790	190 (2)	18 (1)					
1930–1934	12,900	1,800	680	1,600	850	120					
1935–1939	16,700	10,700	2,300	1,800	3,800	3,800	340	600	24 (2)		
1940–1944	24,900	17,400	3,300	3,000	12,500	7,100	1,100	4,500	80	38 (3)	
1945–1949	27,700	17,700	3,300	2,000	9,700	6,900	1,000	10,200	310	350	630 (3)
1950–1954	35,600	2,400	1,700	2,500	11,600	1,000	700	6,500	260	260	1,000
1955–1959	34,400	3,600	2,300	2,500	10,620	1,000	400	4,800	30	90	3,100
1960–1964	30,800	2,400	2,500	3,000	12,750	400	800	3,000	30	60	3,200
1965–1969	38,000 (4)	5,300	2,820	4,820							4,300 (4)

Source: Agricultural Statistics. U.S. Dept. Agr.
[1] 1,000 boxes. Size of box varies—Florida = 80 lb; Texas = 80 lb; Ariz. = 68 lb; Calif. = 65–68 lb.
[2] 1,000 cases. Cases: 24 No. 2 cans equivalent.
[3] 1,000 gal.
Figures in parentheses indicate length of period if it is less than 5 years.

tween 1880 and 1885. Initial developments in California came at about the same time (Webber and Batchelor 1943).

Production of grapefruit in the United States is summarized in Table 21. As can be seen, production was limited until the turn of the century, and in Florida the trend has been generally upward. A peak was reached in the 1950–1954 period, but this has been exceeded in the 1965–1969 period. While Florida had the largest crops, Texas production has also been an important factor. Severe freezes on three occasions in the citrus growing areas of Texas destroyed trees, and greatly limited the crop for a number of years. Severe freezes have also occurred in Florida, Arizona and California which reduced the crop, but the effects have not been so drastic.

Some efforts were made by several individuals to process grapefruit beginning in about 1915. None of these early efforts were successful due in part to lack of technical information, partly to lack of adequate financing and partly because of a lack of knowledge of business methods. Some of the early efforts included cutting the grapefruit flesh into chunks (bitter flavor from locular walls resulted) and canning clarified juice as with grape juice (good flavor was lacking) or use of glass instead of tin cans. During the mid-1920's more and more people began to process grapefruit juice in a very limited way but it was not until late in the twenties that anything resembling commercial production was realized (May 1937).

Table 21 also contains statistics on the production of grapefruit juice, blended juice and frozen concentrates calculated where possible as five-year averages. Production grew to a point in 1928 when grapefruit juice was first considered worth recording at 205,000 cases for the season. Production of grapefruit products was the greatest in Florida while that in Texas was a good second and lesser quantities were processed in California and Arizona. Production of grapefruit juice increased and reached a maximum in 1943 when a total of over 26 million cases were packed in the United States. The requirements of World War II greatly increased the demand for grapefruit juice. At this time and previously more grapefruit were processed than oranges, but this was changed shortly with the development of frozen concentrated orange juice and improvement in the technology of processing and storage of juice products. The pack of grapefruit in 1943 in Florida is one remembered as demand was high but quality was only fair because of a heavy "June bloom" which resulted in fruit on the tree of two distinctly different maturities which could not be readily distinguished from external appearance. Labor was scarce and all the fruit was harvested in one picking. It was several years before confidence was restored in the quality of grapefruit juice products.

In recent years, another unusual factor has influenced the marketing of fresh grapefruit and grapefruit juices. These products began to be used

Table 22

COMPOSITION OF GRAPEFRUIT JUICE

	Florida,[1] %	California,[1] %	Arizona,[1] %	Texas, %
Water				
Average	90.1	89.3	89.9	88.9
Maximum	92.4	92.5	91.6	90.6
Minimum	87.1	86.1	88.5	86.5
Protein				
Average		0.4		0.6
Fat				
Average		0.1		0.1
Ash				
Average	0.4	0.4		0.25
Sugar (as invert)				
Average	6.65	7.03	6.69	7.9
Maximum	9.66	9.51	8.02	10.2
Minimum	4.54	3.38	5.27	5.4
Citric acid				
Average	1.42	1.77	1.61	1.25
Maximum	2.43	2.64	1.92	1.8
Minimum	0.70	0.85	1.24	0.4

[1] Chatfield and McLaughlin (1931).

in so-called "grapefruit diets" in which fresh grapefruit or grapefruit juice (unsweetened) are used in abundance. The idea seems to be that the use of grapefruit in abundance will decrease the use of other foods. The idea has many adherents and the market for grapefruit products has improved greatly.

Blended grapefruit and orange juices (approximately half and half) were first produced in quantities large enough to be recorded in 1935 and the product improved in popularity until 1945 when over 12 million cases were packed in Florida and about 13.5 million cases in the United States. The popularity of the product then decreased slowly, probably because of the increasing popularity of frozen concentrated orange juice.

Frozen concentrated grapefruit juice began to be packed shortly after the orange product began to become popular. The pack has increased slowly but steadily until now over 4 million gallons per year are packed. About a tenth of the grapefruit crop is marketed in this fashion.

GENERAL COMPOSITION OF GRAPEFRUIT

Acidity

Citric acid derives its name from the fact it is found in citrus fruit; grapefruit contains large amounts of this acid. The compositions of grapefruit and grapefruit juice are quite variable. Only the major constituents are given in Tables 22 and 23. The ratio of the Brix reading to the total titratable acidity expressed as per cent citric acid is widely used as a criterion of maturity (Capel 1960) in spite of its limitations. The average Brix

TABLE 23

CHEMICAL ANALYSIS OF GRAPEFRUIT JUICES

	Florida Marsh Seedless[1]	Florida (Duncan) Seedy[1]	Texas Marsh Seedless[2]
Citric acid, %	0.89	1.35	1.25
Sp. gr., 68°/68°F	1.028	1.039	1.043
Degree Brix	6.95	9.74	11.2
pH	3.0	3.0	3.2
Water, %	93.05	90.26	88.8
Organic matter, %	6.73	9.33	10.95
Nitrogen:			
Organic, %	0.043	0.052	....
Protein, %	.....	.....	0.10
Non-protein, %	.....	.....	0.09
Protein (N × 6.25)	0.27	0.33	0.625
Reducing sugar, %	3.44	3.96	5.0
Sucrose, %	1.34	2.24	3.0
Total sugar, %	4.78	6.20	8.0
Pectic acid, %	0.004	0.004	....
Ash, %	0.218	0.414	0.25
Ash constituents in juice			
K	0.089	0.171	0.17
P	0.010	0.030	0.011
Ca	0.008	0.012	0.005
S	0.002	0.004	0.002
Mg	0.005	0.009	0.005
Na	0.004	0.007	0.002
Fe	0.00009	0.00008	0.0019
Al	0.0003	0.0007	....
C	0.019	0.037	....
Cl	0.001	0.002	0.0012
Cu	.....	.....	0.00002
I	.....	.....	>0.0001
Mn	.....	.....	0.00002

[1] From Roberts and Gaddium (1934).
[2] Commercially canned Texas grapefruit juice.

of mature California grapefruit is about 12 and the acidity about 2.0, so that the ratio is about 6.0. Thus, Poore (1934) reported that the juice of California Marsh seedless grapefruit picked early in February tested 12.1° Brix and contained 1.87% citric acid, giving a ratio of 6.47 to 1. The Brix of Texas grapefruit is intermediate to that of California and Florida, its average being slightly over 11 degrees. The acidity of Texas fruit is considerably lower than that of the other states. Thus, Texas grapefruit juice generally has a higher ratio and a correspondingly sweeter taste. The naringin content of Texas grapefruit likewise is generally lower than that of fruit grown elsewhere.

Acidity is most simply determined by titration against a standard sodium hydroxide and is generally reported as grams of anhydrous citric acid per 100 ml of juice. The degrees Brix is the grams of soluble solids per 100 gm of juce and is most simply determined by means of a Brix hydrometer and temperature corrected. The degrees Brix is roughly proportional to the sugar content with which it is often confused. The Brix of citrus juices can also be determined by means of a refractometer according to Stevens and Baier (1939) and Scott and Veldhuis (1961). The sugar content of grapefruit juice is approximately 55 to 75% of the Brix value. The principal sugars present in freshly extracted juices are sucrose, glucose, and fructose. The reducing and nonreducing sugars are present in about equal proportions in the fruit, but the sucrose undergoes inversion, due to the acidity, so that canned juice contains only traces of sucrose. This point is of interest since invert sugar is somewhat sweeter than sucrose.

Grade standards have been established by the U.S. Department of Agriculture stipulating acid content, Brix, ratio of Brix to acid peel oil, flavor and color. Copies of these standards can be obtained by writing to the U.S. Dept. Agr., Washington, D. C.

The processor can blend juice of high acid content with that of low acid content; he can blend with orange juice; or he can sweeten, that is, add sugar to produce the most satisfactory product from the type fruit available.

Color

Freshly extracted grapefruit juice has a bright whitish oyster shell color. It contains only traces of carotene and xanthophyll, which are largely responsible for the color of citrus juices. Juices from pink and red fleshed fruit contain only a fraction of the color of the intact fruit, since most of the pigment is located in the segment membranes and pulp. The red coloration of these is due to the hydrocarbon lycopene and the deeper orange color of these varieties is due to beta carotene, according to Matlack (1935). According to Khan and MacKinney (1953), the following carotenoids are present in the flesh of Texas Pink, Arizona Red Blush, Coachella Pink (Marsh Pink), Coachella White (Marsh White) grapefruit: lycopene, beta carotene, zeta carotene, and phytofluene. The lycopene contents in micrograms per 100 gm were: 237, 176, 20, and 0 in the order given. The beta carotene contents were: 207, 142, 129, trace; the zeta carotene contents were 18, 10, 14, and 6; and the phytofluene contents were: 5, 20, 3, and 9. The carotinoids of the Ruby Red grapefruit have likewise been studied by Curl and Bailey (1957) who found lycopene and beta carotene to be the principal pigments of the pulp. They also identified various xanthophylls such as hydroxy-alpha-carotene, cryptoxanthin in the peel, and lutein, antherxanthin in pulp only, luteoxanthins, mutatoxanthins, valenciachromes and auroxanthins. Red fleshed grapefruit thus present preculiar processing problems: first, the color is not pronounced in extracted juice; secondly, the canned juice develops an unappetizing brownish appearance upon aging. On the other hand, the delicate pink color is very appealing and the mild taste (due to low naringin) is especially pleasing. The color of pink juices varies with the season. It is most highly colored about mid-season, and considerably lighter toward the beginning and end of the season (Lime *et al.* 1954). New technics have recently been developed by Griffiths and Lime (1959) which should eliminate these problems. Pulp that is highly colored is processed during the most favorable periods. This highly colored pulp contains excessive amounts of the bitter tasting naringin, which is debittered by means of the enzyme naringinase. The highly colored debittered pulp is stored so it can be added as needed throughout the season to produce a uniformly colored product.

Properly selected and processed grapefruit juice should have the same color and appearance as freshly extracted juice immediately after canning and it should maintain this color for at least six months under normal storage conditions. Sometime between 7 and 9 months storage it begins to darken slightly and a brownish coloration increases gradually throughout the storage life. A great deal of work has been done on the discoloration of citrus juices and it is variously attributed to a reaction between the sugars and the amino acids, oxidation and decomposition of ascorbic acid to furfural-amino acid polymers. With the development of off-colors there is a simultaneous reduction in the ascorbic acid as well as a loss of flavor. Storage at low temperatures, 32°F or lower, will prevent these adverse effects. Proper deaeration and pasteurization offer the most practical means of controlling satisfactory color.

COMPOSITION OF GRAPEFRUIT PEEL OIL

The composition of grapefruit peel oil has been studied extensively in recent years because of the availability of efficient gas chromatographs together with infrared, ultraviolet, mass and NMR spectrographs. Techniques have become possible to identify compounds without having enough to detect by flavor or aroma.

Hydrocarbons

The principal terpene hydrocarbon is *d*-limonene which comprises from 90 to 95% of the oil. Other hydrocarbons include the terpenes, α-pinene, sabinene, myrcene, and α-terpinene, and the sesquiterpenes, α-cubebene, copaene, β-cubebene, β-elemene, caryophylene, α- and β-humulene, *p*-cadinene, Δ-cadinene and $C_{14}H_{24}$ (Hunter and Brogden 1964, 1965A; Veldhuis and Hunter 1968). Attaway *et al.* (1967) obtained information on the percentage composition of grapefruit peel oil at monthly intervals from April to January. They observed α-pinene, sabenene, myrcene, α-terpinene, *d*-limonene and ocimene. The most abundant was *d*-limonene, followed by myrcene, sabinene and α-pinene. As time passed the percentage of some compounds increased (*d*-limonene, myrcene, α-pinene) while some decreased (ocimene and sabinene).

Carbonyl Compounds

The most significant carbonyl compound in grapefruit peel oil is nootkatone. The compound was discovered in a variety of cedar by Erdtman and Hirose (1962) and the compound was first observed in grapefruit oil by MacLeod and Buigues (1964). They also found the aroma to be characteristic of grapefruit. MacLeod (1965) proved the structure of the compound. Nootkatone is a solid at room temperature when highly purified but most preparations have the appearance of a thick clear syrup. If a drop or two is left in an open vial for months, the characteristic grapefruit aroma remains undiminished and there is no obvious loss of material. Only an extremely small quantity is needed to impart an aroma. Studies by Berry *et al* (1967) indicate that 1–2 parts per million is enough to impart a significant aroma. Strangely enough, this beneficial compound can be deleterious if too much is added. The compound is bitter in taste and if over about 7 ppm is added an objectionable bitter flavor develops. The aroma of the compound is like that one notices upon leaning over a bin of fresh grapefruit. Nootkatone is used extensively to impart a fresh grapefruit flavor to carbonated beverages. Sufficient nootkatone is not available from grapefruit peel oil to meet all demands. Fortunately somewhat larger quantities of valencene are present in distilled orange oil and it is a comparatively easy matter to convert valence to nootkatone by careful oxidation with tertiary-butyl chromate (Hunter and Brogden 1965B) as shown in Fig. 28.

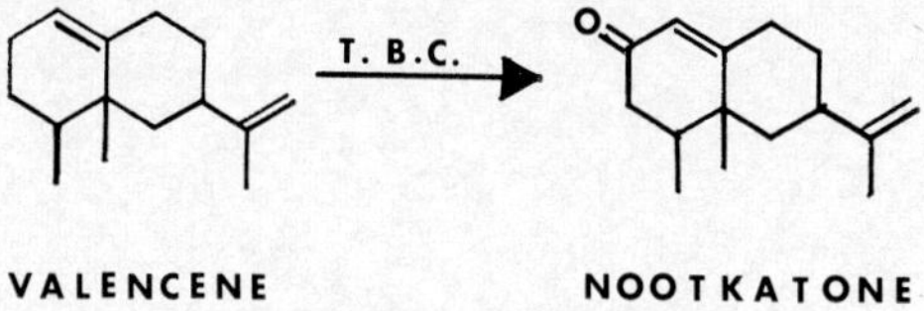

T. B. C.

VALENCENE NOOTKATONE

FIG. 28. CONVERSION OF VALENCENE TO NOOTKATONE WITH TERTIARYBUTYL CHROMATE

Stanley *et al.* (1961) reported on the relative concentrations of aldehydes in grapefruit peel oil. He noted the normal C_7, C_8, C_9, C_{10}, C_{11} and C_{12} aldehydes. The C_8 and C_{10} aldehydes were the most abundant. Attaway *et al.* (1967) observed octanal and geranial in grapefruit peel oil.

Alcohols

An analysis of grapefruit peel oil (Hunter and Moshonas 1966) showed *cis*-and *trans*-linalool oxide, linalool, octanol, *cis*- and *trans*-2,8-*p*-menthadiene-1-ol, nonanol, decanol, citronellol, nerol, geraneol, *cis*- and *trans*-carveol, dodecanol, 1,8-*p*-mentadiene-9-ol, nerolidol, elemol, 8-*p*-menthene-1,2-diol and ortho-phenyl phenol. Of these octanol, decanol, citronellol, geraneol, and elemol were the most abundant. Attaway *et al.* (1967) observed octonal and geranial, both of which decreased in percentage as the season progressed.

Naringin

Naringin, the bitter tasting substance so characteristic of grapefruit, is a white to yellowish-white crystalline glucoside.

Acid hydrolysis yields glucose, rhamnose, and naringenin (5,7,4′-trihydroxyflavanone); and the latter yields phloroglucinol and *p*-coumaric acid on alkaline hydrolysis as shown below:

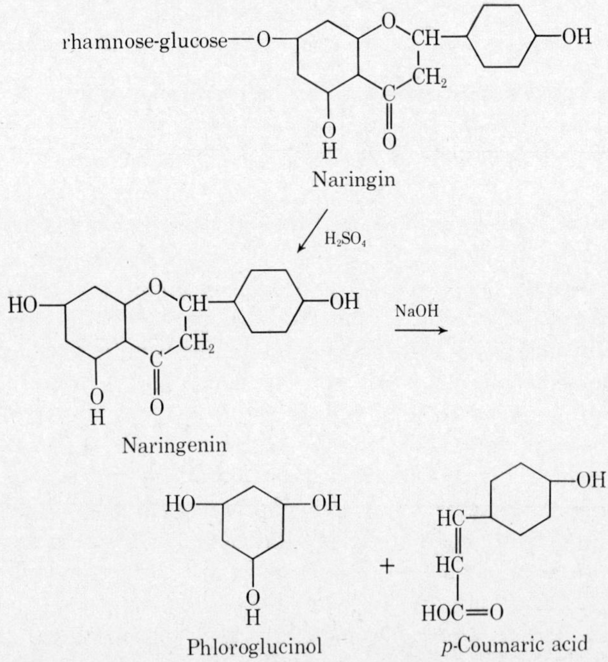

rhamnose-glucose—O— ... —OH

Naringin

↓ H_2SO_4

Naringenin

→ NaOH

Phloroglucinol + *p*-Coumaric acid

In spite of the many claims made, its pharmacological and physiological properties are quite obscure. For example, its vitamin P-like activity is both claimed and denied. The phosphatase inhibiting activity of naringin has been studied quite extensively by Rebate (1935), and Rebate and

TABLE 24

DISTRIBUTION OF NARINGIN IN TEXAS GRAPEFRUIT[1]

Date Picked	Flavedo, %	Albedo, %	Sec. Mem., %	Core, %	Juice, %
Duncan (seedy)					
10/13	1.73	4.00	2.92	3.51	0.095
11/17	0.56	2.52	0.89	1.13	0.049
12/23	0.57	2.00	0.79	1.20	0.035
1/27	0.45	1.49	0.69	1.28	0.015
Marsh (seedless)					
10/13	2.38	5.35	2.91	2.42	0.130
11/17	0.61	2.04	0.74	0.97	0.043
12/23	0.67	2.69	1.35	1.07	0.054
1/27	0.67	2.37	1.38	1.67	0.019
Ruby Red (Henninger)					
10/13	1.25	4.02	3.07	5.42	0.074
11/17	0.41	2.46	1.15	1.48	0.019
12/23	0.51	4.10	1.16	2.24	0.019
1/27	0.59	2.75	1.27	1.58	0.039
Redblush (Webb)					
10/13	2.43	4.95	1.70	2.92	0.086
11/17	0.55	2.53	1.26	2.06	0.023
12/23	0.71	3.75	1.56	1.56	0.019
1/27	0.54	1.88	0.99	1.19	0.016

[1] Data from Maurer *et al.* (1950).

Courtois (1940, 1941A and B). It was formerly thought that naringin occurred only in the grapefruit and the very closely related shaddock; however, it is now known to exist in several other plants such as the Japanese bitter orange, *Citrus aurantium* (Shizuo-Hattori *et al.* 1952). Pulley (1936) thoroughly investigated the effect of temperature upon its solubility in water. He found it relatively insoluble in cold water but quite soluble in warm or hot water. Its bitter taste persists and can be detected at dilutions in excess of 1 part in 10,000.

Naringin is found in all parts of the fruit and in greatest abundance in the albedo layer. Its distribution in the various parts of grapefruit has been reported by Maurer *et al.* (1950), the results are summarized in Tables 24 and 25. It is quite well known that as maturity is approached the naringin concentration and bitterness decrease in extracted juice. Various investigators have suggested the possibility of using naringin as a measure of maturity (Wood and Reed 1938; Maurer *et al.* 1950). The latter found naringin content offered certain advantages as a measure of maturity over the usual acid and Brix standards. Harvey and Rygg (1963) found California grapefruit peel to average 7.3% naringin, the flavedo layer to average 6.38% (4.17 lowest to 7.87% highest) and the albedo layer to average 8.26% (5.96 to 10.35%) for the Marsh variety grown in the Corona-Fontana area. Their data for the flavedo layer averaged 4.80% (3.01 to 8.24%) and for the albedo layer 8.15% (6.85 to

10.17%) for the same variety grown in the Oasis area. The Florida fruit was found to contain 0.40% naringin in the peel and 0.10% in the rag. Maurer *et al.* (1950) found Texas Marsh averaged 1.08% naringin (0.61 to 1.73%) in the flavedo layer, and 3.11% (2.04 to 5.35%) in the albedo layer. They found the Duncan variety grown in Texas averaged 0.83% (0.45 to 1.73%) naringin in the flavedo layer, while the albedo layer averaged 2.50% (1.49 to 4.00%).

Davis (1947) has reported a value of 0.102% naringin for a sample of California canned juice. Commercially canned Florida grapefruit juices have been found to contain somewhat more naringin than those of Texas, which average between 0.015 and 0.03% naringin. The pink and red fleshed varieties contain less naringin than the white varieties. In general, grapefruit processing residue consisting principally of peel, membrane,

TABLE 25

EFFECT OF STORAGE ON NARINGIN CONTENT OF FLORIDA GRAPEFRUIT[1]

Variety of Fruit	Age of Fruit	Weight of Fruit, gm	Weight of Naringin from Peel, gm
Indian River	Fresh market	770	0.62
	Old market	715	0.35
Walters	Fresh market	682	0.50
	4 mos. at 59°F.	695	0.24
Marsh Seedless	Fresh market	539	0.36
	Old market	570	0.08

[1] Data from Zoller (1918).

and seeds contains about 0.75% naringin, the amount depending largely upon the maturity of the fruit. Methods for recovering this valuable material from grapefruit by-products have been described by Baier (1947), Higby (1947), and Burdick and Mauer (1953). Naringin is more abundant in immature fruit, so that fruit processed early in the season is more likely to have not only a poor flavor, but also a milky turbid appearance. The same applies to frost damaged fruit.

Kesterson and Hendrickson (1952, 1953) found that in the 5 most common varieties of grapefruit, the total naringin per fruit reached a maximum by the time they were 2 in. in diameter and then remained virtually constant. The naringin content of the whole fruit ranged from 3.2% for fruit of 2.3 in. diameter to 0.4% in mature fruit. About 62% of the naringin was in the peel, 36% in the pulp and rag and 2.4% in the juice. This illustrates how improper juice extraction and finishing could easily extract additional naringin from the pulp, rag or even peel and increase bitterness. They used the Davis (1947) test which includes small amounts of other flavanone glycosides.

Hagen *et al.* (1966) reported a rapid and nearly proportionate decrease in the content of naringin, neohesperidin, poncirin, naringenin-7-β-rutinoside, hesperidin, and isosakuranetin-7-β-rutinoside in juice sacs of Texas Ruby Red grapefruit harvested from July through November and a slower decrease thereafter. These results are in agreement with previous results using nonspecific methods. Hagen *et al.* also reported that the naringenin-7-β-rutinoside was the principal flavanone other than naringin and the amount of this compound was nearly half that of naringin. They used chromatographic-fluorometric methods in estimating these flavanone glucosides. Albach *et al.* (1969) studied the production of rhamnoglucosides in grapefruit and concluded that they are produced and accumulated during the entire growth of the fruit, but the rate of production of these compounds is several times greater during the first month of fruit growth. Fisher *et al.* (1966) developed a method for estimating naringin and naringenin-7-β-rutinoside (the tasteless isomer) using thin-layer chromatography and an ordinary laboratory colorimeter. This method places the determination of naringin by a specific method within the capability of the average laboratory. A survey of the occurrence of naringin in grapefruit and grapefruit juice products using this method is now underway at the U.S. Dept. Agr. Fruit and Vegetable Products Laboratory, Winter Haven, Fla.

The composition and inheritance of flavanones in citrus fruit was studied by Albach and Redman (1969). In grapefruit they observed the 7-rutinosides of naringenin, isosakuranetin, hesperetin, and naringenin-4′-glucoside; and the 7-neohesperidosides of naringenin (naringin), isosakuranetin, hesperetin (neohesperidin), and naringenin-4′-glucoside. They suggest that these data may be of value in evaluating relationships of citrus varieties and species.

Ting (1958) found that commercial pectic enzyme preparations such as Pectinol contained an enzyme which would hydrolyse naringin to glucose, rhamnose and naringinin and thereby reduce the bitterness in grapefruit. Limited quantities of a commercial purified product "naringenase" were produced by Rohm & Haas Company in which nearly all the pectic enzymes had been removed. The possibilities of using this enzyme were studied by Griffiths and Lime (1959) who indicated that the breakdown products were naringenin and prunin. They stated that optimum conditions were 122°F, pH 3.1, enzyme concentration of 0.05 to 0.10% and an incubation period of 1 to 4 hr. The pectinesterase in the juice must be inactivated before treatment with naringinase or there will be loss of cloud. Olsen and Hill (1964) worked with concentrated grapefruit juice (55° Brix). Optimum conditions were 32 hr at 80°F with 0.08% naringinase when 89% reduction of naringin was obtained.

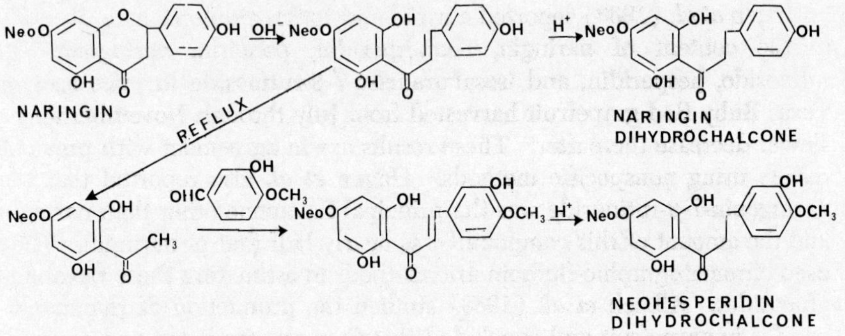

NARINGIN

REFLUX

NARINGIN DIHYDROCHALCONE

NEOHESPERIDIN DIHYDROCHALCONE

Fig. 29. Structure of Naringin and Synthesis of Dihydrochalcone Sweeteners

Horowitz and Gentili (1969) have been engaged in extensive investigations on the relation of structure to bitterness and sweetness. While naringin is extremely bitter, naringin dihydrochalcone is very sweet. It is much sweeter than sugar but sodium saccharin is about 2.5 times sweeter. Of more interest is neohesperidin dihydrochalcone which is about 19 times as sweet as naringin dihydrochalcone. Neohesperidin is not present in citrus fruit in sufficient quantities to be of interest but naringin is relatively abundant and easy to recover from grapefruit peel. Horowitz and Gentili (1968) developed a method of converting naringin to neohesperidin chalcone in reasonably good yield. Not only is the product much sweeter, but because so much less is required, the chances of toxicity are less. The structure of the various compounds and methods of synthesis are sketched in Fig. 29. Neohesperidin is about 1500 times as sweet as sugar and the sweetness is comparatively slow in onset. It is characterized as being of a licorice-like quality, a property shared by some other nonsugar sweeteners. Probably neohesperidin dihydrochalcone would need be blended with other materials to achieve the best flavor balance. The subject of bitterness and sweetness of phenolic glycosides in relation to structure has been reviewed by Horowitz and Gentili (1969). They have found the linkage in the sugar portion of these compounds to be important. If the sugar group has a rutinosyl structure, the compound will likely be bitter as naringin or poncirin; but if it has a neohesperidosyl structure, it will likely be tasteless as neohesperidin or neoeriocitrin. Since poncrin dihydrochalcone is not sweet (slightly bitter it is concluded that there must be at least one hydroxyl group in the β-ring for sweetness.

Phenolic Compounds

Williams *et al.* (1967) found in grapefruit peel the sterols β-sistosterol, stigmasterol, campesterol, cycloeucalenol, 24-methylene lophenol,

TABLE 26

VITAMIN CONTENT OF CANNED GRAPEFRUIT JUICE[1]

	Mg per 100 Ml	Method
Vitamin A	Trace	Chemical
Carotene	Trace	Chemical
Thiamin HCl (vitamin B_1)	0.036	Thiochrome
Riboflavin (vitamin B_2)	0.028	Microbiol.
Pyridoxine (vitamin B_6)	0.030	Microbiol.
Calcium *d*-pantothenate	0.57	Microbiol.
Inositol	66.8	Microbiol.
p-Aminobenzoic acid	0.0037	Microbiol.
Ascorbic acid (vitamin C)	39.6	Chemical
Biotin (vitamin H)	0.0013	Microbiol.
Vitamin D	Trace	Rat assay
Choline chloride	Trace	Chemical

[1] Analyses of Texas commercially canned grapefruit juice.

24-ethylidene lophenol (citrostadienol), cycloartenol and 24-methylene cycloartanol.

Maier and Metzler (1967 A,B) found dihydrokaempferol, kaempferol, umbelliferone, esculetin, scopoletin, bergaptol, *p*-coumaric acid, caffeic acid, ferulic acid, naringenin, isosakuranetin, eriodictol, hesperetin, apigen-in quercetin, and isorhamnetin in grapefruit peel and endocarp after enzymatic hydrolysis of glycosides and esters. They suggest a pathway leading from *p*-coumaric acid to coumarin, furocumarin, flavanone, flavone, and flavenol.

Coumarins and psoralines can be isolated from grapefruit oil. Umbelliferone was observed by Markley *et al.* (1937) and 7-geranoxy coumarins by Kariyone and Matsuno (1953). Stanley (1963) also found 7-dihydroxygeranoxy coumarin, 7-methoxy-8-isopentyl coumarin, bergaptol and 5-methoxy-8-dihydroxy-isopentanoxy psoralin. He observed that the solids recovered from cold-pressed grapefruit oil and containing the coumarins totaled 1.37%.

Vitamin and Amino Acid Content

Grapefruit juice is an excellent source of ascorbic acid (vitamin C). In spite of this, approximately 83% of the vitamin C content of the white fruit is located in the peel and thus not generally consumed (Atkins *et al.* 1945). Almost all (97%) of the original vitamin C content of grapefruit juice is retained during commercial processing (Moore *et al.* 1944).

Nelson and Keenan (1933) reported they were able to isolate only about 3 mg of inositol from 100 ml of juice, which is considerably less than the 66.8 mg listed as being present in Table 26. Grapefruit appears to be an excellent source of this vitamin. Table 27 shows a typical analysis of commercially canned grapefruit juice. All of the essential amino acids are

TABLE 27

AMINO ACID CONTENT OF CANNED GRAPEFRUIT JUICE[1]

	Mg per 100 Ml	Method
Arginine	76.3	Microbiol.
Aspartic acid	470.0	Microbiol.
Cystine	0.18	Chemical
Glutamic acid	280.0	Microbiol.
Histidine	13.8	Chemical
Isoleucine	10.9	Microbiol.
Leucine	12.6	Microbiol.
Lysine	16.4	Microbiol.
Methionine	0.35	Chemical
Phenylalanine	11.9	Chemical
Serine	310.0	Microbiol.
Threonine	10.0	Microbiol.
Tryptophane	4.2	Chemical
Tyrosine	6.4	Chemical
Valine	24.0	Microbiol.

[1] Analyses of Texas commercially canned grapefruit juice.

present, as well as the more common nonessential ones. Approximately one-half of the amino acid content is present in the uncombined form; that is, they are not combined in the form of protein molecules.

A study of the amino acids of Marsh grapefruit juice by Underwood and Rockland (1953) indicated the presence of aspartic, asparagine, serene, alanine, proline, γ-aminobutyric acid, glutamine and arginene in the order of decreasing abundance. Their study included California, Arizona, Texas and Florida fruit and they used paper chromatography. Clements and Leland (1962) used ion-exchange to study the free amino acids in California Marsh grapefruit juice. They observed alanine, γ-aminobutyric acid, arginine, asparagine, aspartic acid, glutamic acid, glycine, lysine, phenylalanine, tyrosine, proline, serine and valine as well as ammonia. They accounted for two-thirds of the Kjeldahl nitrogen by these compounds.

COMMERCIAL PROCESSING

Formerly the grapefruit canning industry depended on packing house rejects, (fruit that had external blemishes, were misshapen, off size or of uneven color) and these are still used, but the majority of the fruit moves directly from the grove to the processing plant. When received at the plant, a sample is taken by an automatic device and the fruit checked by a State or Federal Inspector to see if it meets maturity requirements and is otherwise suited for food use. A sample is extracted on a machine much like those in the commercial line and checked for yield, Brix and acid.

In Florida and Texas, the Duncan is preferred because it is slightly better in flavor. The Marsh seedless variety is increasing in volume be-

TABLE 28

CITRIC ACID CONTENTS OF GRAPEFRUIT JUICES

	Minimum %	Maximum %	Average %
Texas	0.40	1.8	1.25
Florida	0.7	2.2	1.32
California[1]	0.8	2.6	1.8
Arizona[1]	1.2	1.9	1.6
Israel[1]	1.8	2.4	2.1
South Africa[2]	...	...	1.9
Jamaica[2]	...	...	1.6
British Honduras[2]	1.2	1.4	1.3
Algeria[2]	1.6	2.9	2.2

[1] From Braverman (1949).
[2] From Burke (1950).

TABLE 29

SUGAR CONTENT OF GRAPEFRUIT JUICE

	Minimum %	Maximum %	Average %
Arizona[1]	5.27	8.02	6.69
California[1]	3.38	9.51	7.03
Florida[1]	4.54	9.66	6.65
Texas	5.10	10.55	8.20

[1] From Chatfield and McLaughlin (1931).

TABLE 30

SEASONAL CHANGES IN BRIX, ACID AND RATIOS OF GRAPEFRUIT JUICE

	Texas[1]			Florida[2]		
	Acid, %	Brix	Ratio	Acid, %	Brix	Ratio
November	1.35	10.80	8.00	1.47	10.05	6.84
December	1.45	11.10	7.65	1.44	10.25	7.12
January	1.41	11.35	8.05	1.38	10.25	7.43
February	1.31	11.30	8.62	1.34	10.30	7.69
March	1.18	11.20	9.48	1.29	10.30	7.95
April	1.07	11.00	10.28	1.22	10.15	8.32
May	0.95	10.75	11.32	1.11	9.80	8.84
Average	1.245	11.07	9.05	3.32	10.15	7.79

[1] Data covers five normal seasons in Texas.
[2] Data obtained from Harding and Fisher (1945).

cause it is preferred for fresh use and naturally surplus quantities become available for processing. Tables 28 and 29 show the effect of locality on some of the more significant constituents of grapefruit juice. Table 30 shows how the acid, Brix and ratio change during the canning season in Texas and Florida. Texas fruit is more mild, being lower in acidity and the fruit from California is more tart since it is higher in acidity. The Florida fruit is in between. Naringin contents have not been well estab-

Courtesy of FMC Corp.

FIG. 30. WASHER AND ELEVATOR TO SIZING AND GRADE ROOM

lished, but experience indicates that this value depends on maturity. It is under the control of the operator to a certain extent. Severe freezes tend to give juice of higher naringin content and close control is necessary.

When received, the contents of a single truck load (about 32,000 lb) are usually placed in a separate bin and tagged with the Brix, acid, ratio and any other value of interest at the time. This information is used in blending fruit to achieve as much uniformity as possible. Seldom is the fruit from a single bin processed by itself. As the fruit goes to the bin, it passes over grading tables where split or decayed fruit is removed and returned to the shipper. This fruit is deducted from the weight of the load. If the fruit requires excessive culling, the whole load may be rejected. As the season progresses, the fruit becomes less firm and culling must be watched more closely (Hill *et al.* 1960). The fruit is again inspected as it is conveyed from bins to the extractors. At the same time the fruit is given a thorough washing to remove dirt that might otherwise get into the juice. These washers generally consist of a soak tank and a washer with revolving transverse brushes where the extraneous material is removed and washed away by the water. Formerly hot water was used in the soak tank at times to soften the outer flavedo and decrease the oil in the juice. This practice has been abandoned in favor of vacuum deoilers which strip off excess peel oil. The latter method is more easily controlled and eliminates softening the fruit which made it more susceptible to mechanical damage. Detergents may be added to the soak tank if needed when the extraneous material is not easily removed. The final rinse water in the washer may be chlorinated to reduce the microbial count on the fruit and

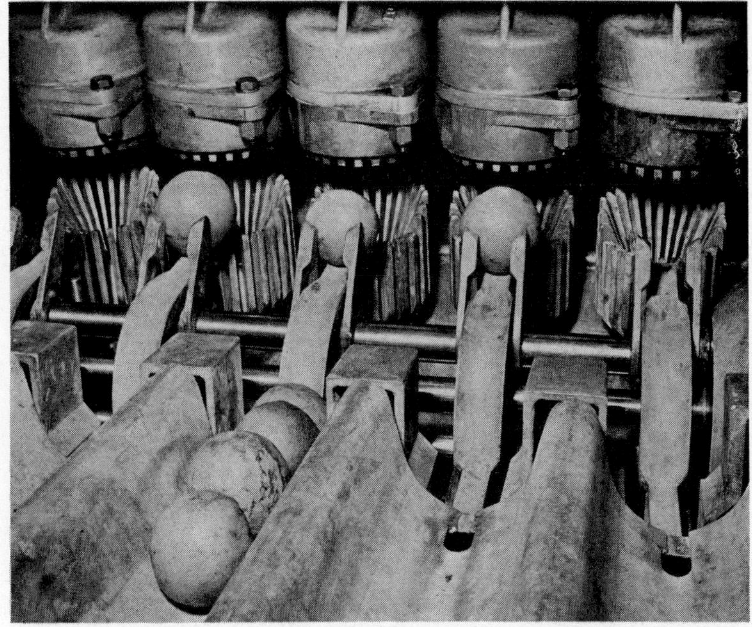

Courtesy of FMC Corp.

FIG. 31. FMC IN-LINE JUICE EXTRACTOR

Feeder assembly complete rear view—fruit entering cup.

help keep the conveyors in a sanitary condition. A typical washer-conveyor system of a small plant is shown in Fig. 30.

Extraction and Yield

Modern juice extractors have made large scale processing of grapefruit juice possible. The same machines may be used but the heads and cups must be changed to accommodate the larger fruit, else yield would be low and quality poor. At present the two types of extractors which dominate the market are the FMC In-Line and the Brown. The In-Line extractors are illustrated in Fig. 31 and Fig. 32 and the Brown in Fig. 33. The flowsheet of a typical large Florida grapefruit processing plant is shown in Fig. 34. Yield of juice may vary from a low of about 80 gal per ton of fruit at the beginning of the season to a high of about 130 gallons at midseason, and then drops considerably toward the end of the season. Average yield is about 115 gal or 36 cases (24 No. 2 cans) per ton. This would be in Texas where statistics are kept in tons while in Florida the statistics ranged from 1.06 to 1.37 cases of 24 No. 2 cans (473 oz) per

Courtesy of FMC Corp.

FIG. 32. FMC IN-LINE JUICE EXTRACTORS

Tandem extractors, one with, one without front cover.

80-lb box over the past 25 years. Once the juice is extracted it must be handled in stainless steel or aluminum (only if the juice is cold), since ascorbic acid (vitamin C) is catalytically oxidized in the presence of copper (Chace *et al.* 1940). Most equipment is of stainless steel as it is inert, is easily cleaned, and gives an excellent appearance. Inert plastics are quite satisfactory where the equipment or parts need not be so rugged.

A detailed flowsheet of a grapefruit juice cannery is given in Fig. 35 and the sequence of the various steps can be readily understood by reference to it.

Finishing

Mechanically extracted juice contains seeds, pips and segment membranes (rag) that must be removed. This is usually accomplished by means of a screw type press or finisher where the size of the perforations and the pressure applied has a marked effect on yield, and taste of the juice. Naringin is abundant in the peel and fruit tissues and if the extraction and finishing procedures are too rigorous, a bitter juice will result. It

Courtesy of Brown International Corp.

FIG. 33. BROWN MODEL 400 GRAPEFRUIT JUICE EXTRACTORS

is imperative that raw grapefruit juice be finished promptly or the juice will leach naringin from the pulp and again bitterness will develop.

Deaeration and De-Oiling

Deaeration and de-oiling constitute one of the most important operations in the canning of grapefruit juice. Freshly extracted juice contains between 2 and 4% by volume of gases according to Pulley and von Loesecke (1939), and at least the oxygen must be removed because of its adverse effect on color, vitamin C, and the citrus oils. Complete removal of oxygen does not entirely eliminate these but it does reduce them to a minimum and insures longer storage life. The gases are easily removed by subjecting the juice in thin films to a high vacuum. Mechanical extractors generally incorporate too much peel oil in the juice, which must be removed or reduced to a low level. For optimum flavor and storage life, the juice should contain between 0.003 and 0.005% recoverable oil. The main constituent of grapefruit oil is *d*-limonene, a terpene, that is easily oxidized and polymerized to produce a terebinthic taste. Blair *et al.* (1952) have shown the acid catalyzed hydration-dehydration of *d*-limo-

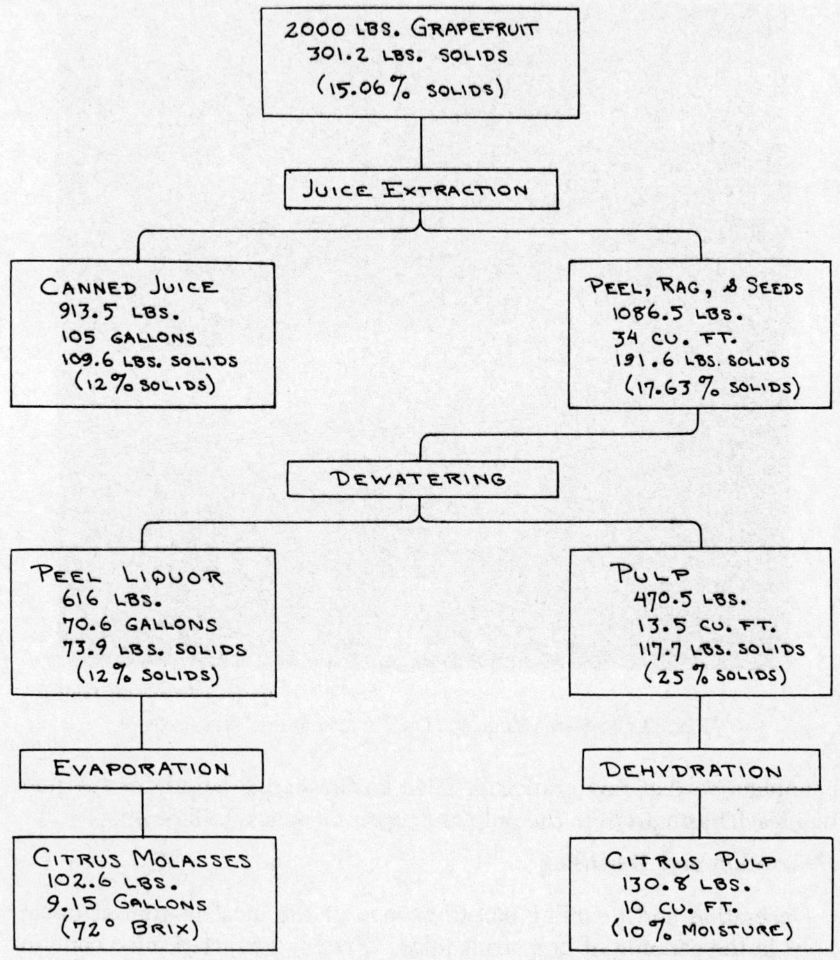

FIG. 34. GRAPEFRUIT JUICE FLOWSHEET AND MATERIAL BALANCE

nene produces a terebinthic taste even in the absence of molecular oxygen. Excessive amounts of peel oil are readily removed by means of vacuum steam distillation by the usual commercial procedure. The technical and engineering phases of deaeration and de-oiling have been discussed by Shearon and Burdick (1948). Approximately 80% of the peel oil can be removed by evaporation of only four per cent of the volume of the juice. Less evaporation removes less oil; more evaporation removes more oil; yet it requires abnormally large evaporation to reduce the oil content below 0.003%. Deaeration and the de-oiling evaporation are generally done continuously in a vacuum of 26 in. or higher. The vaporized oils

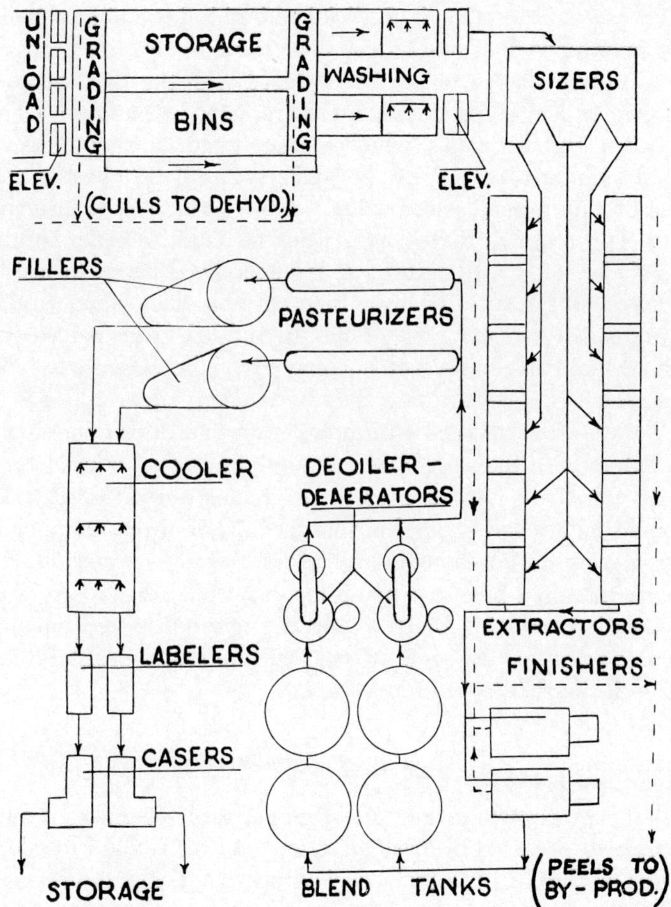

Fig. 35. Flowsheet of Grapefruit Juice Cannery

and water are condensed, the oil separated and the water recombined with the original juice. The oil content has long been used as a measure of quality, since it is closely related to flavor and storage life. The peel oil content can readily be determined by the bromate method of Scott and Veldhuis (1966). This method is precise and permits the determination to be completed in about seven minutes.

Sweetening and Blending

Much of the grapefruit juice of commerce is sweetened since the natural juice of most grapefruit is too acid to suit most people. Burke (1950) studied grapefruit juice packed in six foreign countries and found all good quality juices were sweetened. Judicial and ethical use of sweetening and blending operations does much to standardize and improve product quality. The sugar contents, not to be confused with the Brix, of grapefruit juices grown in various producing areas are listed in Table 22. The juice is collected in suitable tanks, which are equipped with agitators and the calculated amount of dry sugar or sugar syrup of 65° Brix is added to bring the Brix up to the desired value. When syrup is used instead of dry sugar, the law requires that it be at least 65° Brix in order to minimize dilution of the juice with water. It is generally cheaper to use glucose than sucrose, but the latter seems to be preferable since when it is inverted it is considerably sweeter. Sugar is often added to grapefruit juices to make them more palatable, yet not enough to be classified as "sweet." In such cases it is necessary that they be labeled "sugar added." Grapefruit juices are often blended with orange juice and this operation is generally conducted in the same tanks or equipment that is used for sweetening. If grapefruit juice is present in greater proportion, the blended juice should be labeled "grapefruit-orange"; while if orange juice is present in greater proportion it should be labeled "orange-grapefruit."

Recently there has been a demand for unsweetened grapefruit juice for use in so-called reducing diets. Only the naturally sweet juice can be used in this purpose. In some cases it will be found profitable to delay harvest until the Brix/acid ratio improves.

Pasteurization

The high acid content or low pH of grapefruit juice makes it one of the most simple to preserve by pasteurization. In turn, this caused difficulties in loss of cloud in the early packed juices. Temperatures as low as 165°F will destroy the microorganisms, but it is necessary to destroy the pectic enzymes likewise. Pectin is responsible for the cloud or milky appearance of the juice, which is essential. Thus it is necessary to inactivate the pectin degrading enzymes to prevent its conversion into pectinic acids, which would later separate, leaving a clear supernatant liquid. The effect of heating citrus juices is discussed by Joslyn and Sedky (1940), and Loeffler (1941) states that the cloud is increased by flash pasteurization, now almost universally used. Flash pasteurization is used to designate short times and high temperatures. Phaff and Joslyn (1947) explain the loss of cloud in improperly pasteurized juice by the action of pectin esterase on pectin to destroy its protective colloidal action. Kew *et al.* (1957) conducted extensive tests on the effect of time and temperature of pasteurization on the cloud stability of canned grapefruit juice. They obtained cloud stability at 210°F in a high speed (1.75 sec) pasteurizer,

Courtesy of Will Shearon, Jr.

FIG. 36. FILLING AND CLOSING GRAPEFRUIT JUICE CANS

at 195°F in a 12.75 sec pasteurizer and at 185° to 190°F in a 42.6 sec pasteurizer. The temperature at which cloud stability was achieved increased about 0.9°F with each increase of 0.1 pH unit on the average. All microbial life was destroyed at 160°F. No consistent difference was observed between orange and grapefruit juices except that the heat imparted more cloud stability to grapefruit juices in the lower temperature ranges and more cloud stability to orange juices in the upper part of the temperature ranges.

Filling, Closing, and Cooling

Immediately after pasteurization, the juice should be filled into clean and preferably steam-treated cans (Fig. 36). The temperature nust be at least 165°F if a good vacuum is to be obtained; 180° to 185°F s desirable; higher temperatures produce excessively high vacua that often cause panelling or can collapse. These high filling temperatures prompted the can manufacturers to use beads on the No. 3 special (46-oz) can which is the most commonly used for grapefruit juice. The filled cans are lidded or closed and the cans inverted by means of twists to allow pasteurization of the inside of the lids. The inverted cans should be sprayed with a small quantity of chlorinated water to wash off any juice that might have been spilled during the filling and closing operations. Fifteen to thirty seconds in the inverted position is adequate to insure a good seal and pasteurization of the lid. During this brief period the lid seal "breathes"; the use of chlorinated water is imperative to prevent later spoilage, which generally shows up as "swells" the second or third day. Final cooling is effected by the use of large volumes of chlorinated water sprayed over the cans, which are rolled or spun to assist in the heat transfer. Temperatures between 90° and 110°F should be reached as soon as possible (2 min or less). Too much cooling may not permit proper can drying; while insufficient cooling is detrimental to flavor (produces "stack burning") and often causes labelling difficulties. Often too low filling temperatures are responsible for subsequent "swells" and must be avoided. It is obvious the proper quantity of juice must be added not only for legal reasons but to provide the proper headspace.

Plain tin cans are used for grapefruit juice as suitable enamels have not as yet been developed and the slight reducing action of the tin has a beneficial effect on color and storage life. Filling in an inert atmosphere such as nitrogen is employed by some processors, but its use in grapefruit juice processing is not essential to good quality.

Storage

Canned or bottled grapefruit juice will retain its normal flavor almost indefinitely when stored at 32° to 40°F. However, even under the best practical conditions it is not completely stable and will deteriorate. The rate of deterioration increases rapidly with increases of temperature. Cold storage is desirable; cooled storage is preferable to uncooled; while extended storage at high temperatures is undesirable. Chilled or frozen single-strength juices can be stored for years without serious deterioration. Improperly cooled juice is subject to "stack burn" during the early storage period. Canned juice should be warehoused or stored in such manner that adequate ventilation or air circulation is achieved. Under normal storage temperatures and conditions, properly processed juice should retain its normal flavor and appearance about nine months; it should still possess a good flavor for about 15 months, after which definite off-flavors and off-colors develop. High temperature storage in fast aging tests can be used in predicting quite accurately the storage life of citrus juices. Ross (1944) has shown storage temperatures to be very important in vitamin C retention.

Kirchner *et al.* (1953) and Kirchner and Miller (1953) reported investigations of the chemical nature of the volatile constituents of fresh grapefruit juice and the effect of canning and storage on these constituents. The volatile water-soluble constituents of fresh juice contained acetaldehyde, ethyl alcohol, methanol, and a trace of hydrogen sulfide. The freshly canned juice had a small amount of acetic acid and other volatile acids and a trace of furfural, which was not present in the fresh juice. The stored canned juice contained less acetaldehyde, less of the volatile acids but much more acetic acid, and in addition contained acetone, furfural slightly more ethyl alcohol and considerably more methanol. The oil constituents of the volatile flavoring material from freshly canned and stored canned grapefruit juice were separated into 21 compounds and three complex fractions. Some were found in all three juices, others only in the fresh and freshly canned juice. The most significant changes in stored canned juices were a decrease in limonene and an increase in linalool monoxide, α-terpineol, and furfural.

CHILLED GRAPEFRUIT JUICE

Chilled citrus juices, although by no means new, have gained commercial importance. The volume of chilled orange juice has far outdistanced that of chilled grapefruit juice but its volume is significant and is expected to increase. It has previously been pointed out elsewhere in this chapter that properly processed grapefruit juice when stored at low temperatures will retain its normal flavor and color almost indefinitely. The chilled juice industry makes full use of this fact. Chilled juices are manufactured by proceses very similar to single strength juices up to the point of filling. Immediately after pasteurization the juices are chilled by refrigeration and generally filled into waxed paper containers similar to those used by the milk industry. Large volumes of chilled juices are transported by means of refrigerated tank trucks. The shelf-life of chilled juice in cardboard cartons is limited as measured by flavor and retention of ascorbic acid. Sealed one- and two-quart jars provide long shelf-life and are generally favored.

FROZEN CONCENTRATED GRAPEFRUIT JUICE

The volume of frozen concentrated grapefruit juice has lagged far behind its Cinderella sister, frozen concentrated orange juice. Probably the chief reason for this is the flavor of the frozen product is only slightly, if at all, superior to the cheaper single-strength canned juice. The production of frozen concentrated grapefruit juice involves the same general principles in processing single-strength juice up to the point of filling. The frozen concentrated juices, which have not been pasteurized or heat treated to inactivate the pectic enzymes, are subject to "gelation," that is, solidification in the can to a jelly-like mass which is difficult or impossible to reconstitute. Grapefruit juice is more susceptible to gelation than is orange juice since it contains more pectin and pectic enzymes. For this reason it must be heat treated, prior to concentration, to inactivate these enzymes. This heat treatment varies from mild pasteurization for a fraction of a second to about one minute at temperatures ranging from 160° to 265°F. Rouse and Atkins (1952) have reported the pectinesterase in grapefruit juice to be completely inactivated by heating 0.8 sec to temperatures of

195°, 200°, and 205°F when the pH of the juices is 3.0, 3.5, 3.8, respectively, and immediately cooled by flash evaporation. The juice is then concentrated under high vacuum at temperatures below 80°F to about five-fold, diluted or "cut-back" with fresh unconcentrated, deaerated, heat treated juice having a higher pulp and oil content to about four-fold. Often cold-pressed grapefruit oil is added to replace that lost during the concentration. It is filled into lithographed cans, sealed, and frozen. Often the concentrated juice is frozen to a slush before filling to lower the freezing load of the final freezing system. Freezing is effected by immersion in very cold solutions such as alcohol or by a refrigerated air blast. Most frozen concentrated grapefruit juice produced to date has been sweetened by the addition of sugar. Excellent tasting and unique appearing products have been made on an experimental scale from the red fleshed grapefruit, the color of which is stable when frozen.

Concentration is accomplished in the same evaporators used for frozen concentrated orange juice and the multistage, multieffect TASTE (Temperature-Accelerated-Short-Time-Evaporator) has largely replaced the older low-temperature evaporator. Concentration and pasteurization are achieved in the same equipment.

NONFROZEN CONDENSED GRAPEFRUIT JUICES

The introduction of nonfrozen condensed citrus juices a few years back caused no little concern to both single-strength juice processors and frozen concentrators. Their most important feature is the economy offered, which was reported to be as high as 22% at the consumer level. The economy is due to a savings of approximately one-half of the costs of cans, cartons, labels, handling, and the freight in the case of a two-fold concentrate. Cans, cartons, and labels normally account for about 80% of processing costs, exclusive of the fruit cost. With a three-fold product approximately two-thirds can be saved, while with a four-fold product approximately three-fourths. It is necessary to heat treat or pasteurize to inactivate the enzymes prior to concentration and preferably following deaeration. Evaporation should be as rapid as possible and at temperatures below 80°F to the desired concentration and cut back with deaerated pasteurized juice. The products should be filled aseptically or again pasteurized before filling and sealing. Cooling should be as rapid as possible, preferably with chilled water. The products are packed in lithographed cans. Although lacquered cans are sometimes used for orange products they are not necessary in grapefruit juices. Grapefruit juice is sometimes "hot-packed" as is orange juice, that is, it is concentrated to about 65° Brix at temperatures between 100° to 105°F. These products are generally packed in 1- and 5-gal tin cans. Cold storage is necessary (temperatures from 34° to 45°F) to insure retention of quality.

BARRELLED JUICE

Small quantities of grapefruit juice are preserved in barrels for export purposes, where it is converted into "ades," "squashes," etc. The juice is packed in good grade fir barrels, which should be silicated and double paraffined. It is preserved either by the addition of potassium or sodium metabisulfite or sulfurous acid, about 1000 ppm as sulfur dioxide, alone or by the addition of 350 ppm of sulfur dioxide gas and 0.05% sodium benzoate. The latter procedure is recommended. Flash pasteurization improves the appearance by inhibiting the cloud clearing and clotting brought about by pectic enzymes.

BIBLIOGRAPHY

ALBACH, R. F., JUAREZ, A. T., and LIME, B. J. 1969. Time of naringin production in grapefruit. Am. Soc. Hort. Sci. *94,* 605–609.

ALBACH, R. F., and REDMAN, G. H. 1969. Composition and inheritance of flavanones in citrus fruit. Phytochem. *8,* 127–143.

ATKINS, C. D., WIEDERHOLD, E., and MOORE, E. L. 1945. Vitamin C content of processing residue from Florida citrus fruits. Fruit Products J. *24,* 260–262, 281.

ATTAWAY, J. A., PIERINGER, A. P., and BARABAS, L. J. 1967. The origin of citrus flavor compounds—III. A study of the percentage variations in peel and leaf oil terpenes during one season. Phytochem. *6,* 25–32.

BAIER, W. E. 1947. Methods for recovery of naringin. U.S. Pat. 2,421,063.

BERRY, R. E., WAGNER, C. J., JR., and MOSHONAS, M. G. 1967. Flavor studies of nootkatone in grapefruit juice. J. Food Sci. *32,* 75–78.

BLAIR, J. S., GODAR, E. M., MASTERS, J. E., and RIESTER, D. W. 1952. Flavor deterioration of stored canned orange juice. Food Research *17,* 235–260.

BRAVERMAN, J. B. S. 1949. Citrus Products—Chemical Composition and Chemical Technology. Interscience Publishers, New York.

BURDICK, E. M. 1951. Symptoms of freeze damage in citrus fruit. Proc. 5th. Rio Grande Val. Hort. Inst. 117–120.

BURDICK, E. M., and MAURER, R. H. 1950. Removal of naringin from solutions containing the same. U.S. Pat. 2.510,797. June 6.

BURDICK, E. M., and MAURER, R. H. 1953. Process for the isolation of flavanone glucosides. U.S. Pat. 2,630,432. Mar. 3.

BURKE, J. H. 1950. Foreign market notes—citrus fruits. An analysis of certain foreign processed citrus juices. Foreign Agricultural Circ., FCF-4-50.

CAPEL, G. L. 1960. The quality of Florida grapefruit. Citrus Industry *41,* 16, 18–19.

CHACE, E. M., VON LOESCKE, H. W., and HEID, J. L. 1940. Citrus fruit products. U.S. Dept. Agr. Circ. *577.*

CHATFIELD, C., and MCLAUGHLIN, L. I. 1931. Proximate composition of fresh fruits. U.S. Dept. Agr. Circ. *50,* Rev.

CLEMENTS, R. L., and LELAND, H. L. 1962. An ion-exchange study of free amino acids in the juice of six varieties of citrus. J. Food Sci. *27,* 20–25.

CURL, A. L., and BAILEY, G. F. 1957. The carotenoids of Ruby Red grapefruit. Food Research *22,* 63–68.

DAVIS, W. B. 1947. Determination of flavanones in citrus fruits. Anal. Chem. *19*, 476–478.

ERITMAN, H., and HIROSE, Y. 1962. The chemistry of the natural order cupressales 46. The structure of noookatone. Acta. Chem. Scand. *16*, 1311–1314.

FISHER, J. F., NORDBY, H. E., and KEW, T. J. 1966. A thin-layer chromatographic-colorimetric method for determining naringin in grapefruit. J. Food Sci. *31*, 947–950.

GRIFFITH, F. P., and LIME, B. J. 1959. Debittering of grapefruit products with naringinase. Food Technol. *13*, 430–433.

HAGEN, R. E., DUNLAP, W. J., and WENDER, S. H. 1966. Seasonal variation of naringin and certain other flavone glycosides in juice sacs of Texas Ruby Red grapefruit. J. Food Sci. *31*, 542–547.

HARDING, P. L., and FISHER, D. F. 1945. Seasonal changes in Florida grapefruit. U.S. Dept. Agr. Tech. Bull. *886*.

HARVEY, E. M., and RYGG, G. L. 1936. Field and storage studies on changes in the composition in the rind of a Marsh grapefruit in California. J. Agr. Research *52*, 747–787.

HIGBY, R. H. 1947. Methods for recovery of naringin. U.S. Pat. 2,421,062. May 27.

HILL, E. C., WENZEL, F. W., and HUGGART, R. L. 1960. Microbiology of citrus juice. Food Technol. *14*, 268–270.

HOROWITZ, R. M., and GENTILI, B. 1968. Conversion of naringin to neohesperidin and neohesperidin chalcone. U.S. Pat. No. 3,375,242 March 26.

HOROWITZ, R. M., and GENTILI, B. 1969. Taste and structure in phenolic glycosides. J. Agr. Food Chem. *14*, 696–700.

HUNTER, G. L. K., and BROGDEN, W. B., JR. 1964. A rapid method for isolation and identification of sesquiterpene hydrocarbons in cold-pressed grapefruit oil. Anal. Chem. *36*, 1122–1123.

HUNTER, G. L. K., and BROGDEN, W. B., JR. 1965A. Analysis of terpene and sesquiterpene hydrocarbons in some citrus oils. J. Food Sci. *30*, 383–387.

HUNTER, G. L. K., and BROGDEN, W. B., JR. 1965B. Conversion of valencene to nootkatone. J. Food Sci. *30*, 876–878.

HUNTER, G. L. K., and MOSHONAS, M. G. 1966. Analysis of alcohols in essential oils of grapefruit, lemon, lime and tangerine. J. Food Sci. *31*, 167–171.

JOSLYN, M. A., and SEDKY, A. 1940. The relative rates of destruction of pectin in macerates of various citrus fruits. Plant Physiol. *15*, 675.

KARIYONE, T., and MATSUNO, T. 1953. Constituents of orange oil. I. Structure of auraptene. Pharm. Bull. Japan *1*, 119–122 (Chem. Abstr. *48*, 6080 1954).

KESTERSON, J. W., and HENDRICKSON, R. 1952. The glucosides of citrus. Proc. Fla. State Hort. *Soc. 65*, 223–226.

KESTERSON, J. W., and HENDRICKSON, R. 1953. Naringin, a bitter principle of grapefruit. Univ. Florida Agr. Expt. Sta. Bull. *511*.

KEW, T. J., VELDHUIS, M. K., BISSETT, O. W., and PATRICK, R. 1957. The effect of time and temperature of pasteurization on the quality of canned citrus juices. U.S. Dept. Agr. Research Ser., Processed Pub. *ARS-72-6*, Winter Haven, Fla.

KHAN, M., and MACKINNEY, G. 1953. Carotenoids in grapefruit. *Citrus paradisi*. Plant Physiol. *28*, 550–552.

KIRCHNER, J. G., and MILLER, J. M. 1953. Citrus flavoring. Volatile oil constituents of grapefruit juice. J. Agr. Food Chem. *1*, 512–518.

KIRCHNER, J. G., MILLER, J. M., RICE, R. G., KELLER, G. J., and FOX, M. M. 1953. Citrus flavoring. Volatile water-soluble constituents of grapefruit juice. J. Agr. Food Chem. *1*, 510–512.

LIME, B. J., STEPHENS T. S., and GRIFFITHS, F. P. 1954. Processing characteristics of colored Texas grapefruit. 1. Color and maturity of Ruby Red grapefruit. Food Technol. *8, 566.*

LOEFFLER, H. J. 1941. Maintenance of cloud in citrus juices. Proc. Instit. Food Technologists, 29–36.

MACLEOD, W. D., JR. 1965. The constitution of nootkatone, nootkatene and valencene. Tetr. Letters *52,* 4779–4783.

MACLEOD, W. D., JR., and BUIGUES, N. M. 1964. Sesquiterpenes I. Nootkatone, a new grapefruit flavor constituent. J. Food Sci. *29,* 565–568.

MAIER, V. P., and METZLER D. M. 1967A. Grapefruit Phenolics–I. Identification of dihydrokaempferol and its co-occurrence with naringenin and kaempferol. Phytochem. *6,* 763–765.

MAIER, V. P., and METZLER, D. M. 1967B. Grapefruit Phenolics–II. Principal aglycones of endocarp and peel and their possible biosynthetic relationship. Phytochem. *6,* 1127–1135.

MARKLEY, K. S., NELSON, E. K., and SHERMAN, M. S. 1937. Some waxlike constituents from expressed oil from the peel of Florida grapefruit, *Citrus grandis.* J. Biol. Chem. *118,* 433–441.

MATLACK, M. B. 1935. Pigments of pink grapefruit. J. Biol. Chem. *110,* 249–253.

MAURER, R. H., BURDICK, E. M., and WAIBEL, C. W. 1950. Distribution of naringin in Texas grapefruit. Proc. 4th Rio Grande Val. Hort. Inst. 147–151.

MAY, E. C. 1937. The Canning Clan. The Macmillan Co., New York.

MOORE, E. L., WIEDERHOLD, E., ATKINS, C. D., and MACDOWELL, L. G. 1944. Ascorbic acid retention in Florida grapefruit juices during commercial canning. Canner *98,* No. 9, 24–26.

NELSON, E. K., and KEENAN, G. L. 1933. i-Inositol in citrus fruit. Science *77,* 561.

OLSEN, R. W., and HILL, E. C. 1964. Debittering of concentrated grapefruit juice with naringenase. Proc. Fla. State Hort. Soc. *77,* 321–325.

PHAFF, H. J., and JOSYLN, M. A. 1947. The newer knowledge of pectic enzymes. Wallerstein Labs. Commun. *10,* 133–148.

POORE, H. D. 1934. Recovery of naringin and pectin from grapefruit residue. Ind. Eng. Chem. *26,* 637–639.

PULLEY, G. N. 1936. Solubility of naringin in water. Ind. Eng. Chem., Anal. Ed. *8,* 360.

PULLEY, G. N., and VON LOESECKE, H. W. 1939. Gases in the commercial handling of citrus juices. Ind. Eng. Chem. *31,* 1275–1278.

REBATE, J. 1935. Biochemistry of the salicaceae V. Relation of salipurposide to naringinoside and isohesperidoside. Bull. Soc. Chem. Biol. *17,* 314–318.

REBATE, J., and COURTOIS, H. 1940. Action of phlorosides and some related heterosides on various phosphates. Compt. Rend. Soc. Biol. *134,* 468–469.

REBATE, J., and COURTOIS, H. 1941A. The action of phlorizoside and some related heterosides on renal phosphatase. Bull. Soc. Chim. Biol. *23,* 184–189.

REBATE, J., and COURTOIS, H. 1941B. Is it possible to utilize phlorosides and related heterosides for differentiating between phosphatases? Bull. Soc. Chim. Biol. *23,* 190–195.

ROBERTS, J. A., and GADDIUM, L. W. 1934. Composition of citrus fruit juices. Ind. Eng. Chem. *29,* 574–575.

ROSS, E. 1944. Effect of time and temperature of storage on vitamin C retention in canned citrus juices. Food Research *9,* 27–33.

ROUSE, A. H., and ATKINS, C. D. 1952. Heat inactivation of pectinesterase in citrus juices. Food Technol. *6,* 291–294.

SCOTT, W. C., and VELDHUIS, M. K. 1961. The determination of soluble solids in citrus juices. III. Empirical factors for converting refractometer and density values to soluble solids. Food Technol. *15,* 388–391.

SCOTT, W. C., and VELDHUIS, M. K. 1966. Rapid estimation of recoverable oil in citrus juices by bromate titration. J. Offic. Anal. Chem. *49,* 628–633.

SHEARON, W. H., JR., and BURDICK, E. M. 1948. Citrus fruit processing. Ind. Eng. Chem. *40,* 370–378.

SHIZUO-HATTORI, SHIMOKORIYAMA, M., and KANAO, M. 1952. Studies on flavanone glycosides IV. The glycosides of ripe fruit peel and flower petals of *citrus aurantium* L. J. Am. Chem. Soc. *74,* 3614–3615.

STANLEY, W. L. 1963. Recent developments in coumarin chemistry in Aspects of Plant Phenolic Chemistry. Proc 3rd. Ann. Symp. P.P.G.N.A, Toronto, Ont.

STANLEY, W. L., IKEDA, R. M., VANUIR, S. H., and ROLLE, L. A. 1961. Determination of the relative concentrations of the major aldehydes in lemon, orange and grapefruit oils by gas chromatography. J. Food Sci. *26,* 43–48.

STEVENS, J. W., and BAIER, W. E. 1939. Refractometric determination of soluble solids in citrus juices. Ind. Eng. Chem. Anal. Ed. *11,* 447–449.

TING, S. V. 1958. Enzymic hydrolysis of naringin in grapefruit. J. Agr. Food Chem. *6,* 546–549.

UNDERWOOD, J. C., and ROCKLAND, L. B. 1953. Nitrogenous constituents in citrus fruits. I. Some free amino acids in citrus juices determined by small-scale filter-paper chromatography. Food Research *18,* 17–29.

VELDHUIS, M. K., and HUNTER, G. L. K. 1968. Nomenclature of ylangene, copaene and cubebene. J. Food Sci. *32,* 697.

WEBBER, H. J., and BATCHELOR, L. D. 1943. The citrus industry. Vol. I. History, Botany, and Breeding. Univ. of Calif. Press, Berkeley, Calif.

WHITEMAN, T. M. 1958. Freezing points of fruits. The Citrus Industry *39,* No. 3, 12–14.

WILLIAMS, B. L., GOAD, L. J. and GOODWIN, T. W. 1967. The sterols of grapefruit peel. Phytochem. *6,* 1137–1145.

WOOD, J. F., and REED, H. M. 1938. Maturity studies of Marsh seedless grapefruit in the Lower Rio Grande Valley. Texas Agr. Expt. Station Bull. *562.*

ZOLLER, H. F. 1918. Some constituents of the American grapefruit. Ind. Eng. Chem. 10, 364–373.

CHAPTER 4

H. E. Swisher
and L. H. Swisher

Lemon and Lime Juices

LEMON JUICE

Lemon juice occupies a unique position among the several citrus juices produced in the home and factory in the United States. The fruit is grown commercially only in California, Arizona and Florida, while production areas for oranges and grapefruit are well distributed in Arizona, California, Florida, Louisiana and Texas. In Florida, lemon growers have best results with the Bearss and Lisbon varieties, while the groves in California are mostly the Eureka and some Lisbon. The composition of lemon juice is distinctly different, in quantitative degree at least, from other citrus, excepting limes, which makes its processing problems and uses far more varied, and in some cases more complex technically.

Because of the high acidity of lemon juice, smaller quantities are used at any one time and for many more purposes than may be true of other fruit juices. This accounts for the general desire of consumers to keep some lemon fruit or juice on hand at all times for various applications as a flavorful and healthful household acidulant. Except for sugar and salt, lemon juice has probably been used more extensively to enhance and develop inherent food flavor than any other food item.

Relation of Fresh Fruit Practices to the Products Industry

Fresh fruit marketing practices as dictated by consumer demand and the unique nature of California lemons have led to fruit handling practices which have had a marked effect on the lemon products industry.

Eurekas and Lisbons, the two principal commercial varieties, bloom year-round and the fruit takes about seven months to develop fully. It was found early that fruit allowed to ripen on the tree is not as satisfactory for packing and shipment as fruit picked to size when still green or silver in color and then "cured" through use of controlled storage conditions.

Under optimum storage conditions of 58°F and 85% relative humidity, with ample fresh air, the green color of the rind disappears, giving way to a translucent, whitish yellow. An extra thick layer of waxy cutin is formed, lessening fruit shrinkage caused by evaporation of moisture and thus extending the useful life of the fruit. During this storage period, the albedo and membranes become thinner and the juice sacs increase in size,

---

H. E. Swisher is Director of Research and Development Division, and (Mrs.) L. H. Swisher is formerly Research Librarian, Sunkist Growers, Inc., Ontario, Calif.

TABLE 31

WORLD PRODUCTION OF LEMONS, BY COUNTRIES[1]

Crop Year	United States 1	Greece 2	Italy 3	Spain 4	Syria and Lebanon 5	Israel 6	Turkey 7	Argentina 8	Chile 9	Australia 10	Republic of So. Africa 11	All Other 12	Total World 13
	Million Cartons												
1959–60	36.4	3.6	20.8	5.6	1.0	0.8	2.4	5.2	2.4	1.0	0.6	3.2	83.0
1960–61	28.6	4.6	19.6	5.0	1.4	1.2	3.2	5.0	2.4	0.8	0.6	4.2	76.6
1961–62	33.4	5.0	28.6	5.4	1.6	1.4	3.0	4.8	2.6	0.8	0.6	3.0	90.2
1962–63	26.0	5.2	20.8	3.2	2.0	1.8	3.2	4.6	2.6	1.0	1.0	4.2	75.6
1963–64	38.0	4.8	28.2	3.4	2.2	1.8	3.4	4.6	2.6	1.0	1.0	3.6	94.6
1964–65	28.4	5.2	32.4	6.4	2.2	1.8	2.2	4.6	2.6	1.0	1.4	3.8	92.0
1965–66	31.5	5.7	32.5	5.4	2.7	2.0	4.6	4.1	2.6	1.0	1.1	2.9	96.1
1966–67	35.8	6.2	35.0	5.5	2.8	2.4	4.9	5.2	2.7	1.2	1.1	3.3	106.1
1967–68	33.7	5.4	38.9	6.5	2.9	2.4	5.2	4.3	1.8	1.1	1.1	3.4	106.7
1968–69	33.2	3.5	45.4	4.6	2.9	2.1	6.4	10.4	4.0	1.3	0.7	1.2	115.7

[1] Source: Statistical Information on the Citrus Fruit Industry, Table 17, 1969 Supplement. Compiled by Sunkist Growers from data in the Foreign Agricultural Circular of the Foreign Agricultural Service, U.S. Dept. Agr.

TABLE 32

U. S. EXPORTS AND IMPORTS OF LEMON JUICES

	Lemon Juice	
Year, Nov.–Oct.	Exports Pasteurized and Frozen Concentrate, Million Gal[1]	Imports Pasteurized Concentrate, Million Gal[1]
1959–60	2.25	0.17
1960–61	1.94	0.16
1961–62	1.88	0.84
1962–63	1.03	2.39
1963–64	0.88	0.96
1964–65	[2]	[3]
1965–66	[2]	[3]
1966–67	[2]	[2]
1967–68	[2]	[2]

Source: Statistical Information on the Citrus Fruit Industry, Table 35, 1969 Supplement. Compiled by Sunkist Growers.
[1] Gallons of single strength equivalent.
[2] Data not available.
[3] 1964–65 — 9,000 gal — 1965–66— 1,000 gal.

making the juice more readily available. It was shown by early experimental evaluation of the Sunkist research department, which was completed in 1934, that light green lemons, properly cured, develop more juice of higher quality than the same fruit allowed to develop to a yellow color on the tree.

Lemons are usually picked according to size rather than color and although they may be green, they nevertheless are required to meet a maturity standard before being packed for consumption within the United States. According to State regulations in California, lemons are considered mature when they have a juice content of 30% or more by volume.

Oranges, on the other hand, are picked commercially when they are ripe as defined by maturity standards and thus pose an entirely different storage problem. In contrast to lemons, oranges are best shipped immediately after washing, packing and precooling.

The details of current methods used in the various operations involved in the picking and handling of lemons in the grove and packing house have been described by Harding, MacRill and Nixon (1959).

The fresh lemon market is year-round, peaking during the hot summer months when cold lemonade and iced tea are in strong demand. Peak storage of lemons occurs in late spring or early summer, nearly coinciding with this period of high demand. Thus, the practice of lemon storage benefits the consumer in two ways. Adequate supplies when demand is high prevent excessive price increases and a source of better quantity and quality of juice is provided.

The lemons picked for storage are carefully segregated at the packing house according to size, color and condition. Fruit which has become highly colored, is badly misshapen, scarred, or not within the desired size range is moved directly to the products plants. The remaining lemons, after washing, treating, rinsing and color sorting, go into storage in a wet condition. On coming out of storage, the fruit is graded and sized before packing. Stored fruit graded out because of defects or blemishes or not packed because of changing market conditions also goes to products plants.

In recent years, a vastly increased demand for lemon products (see Table 31) and the economics of an increased average crop (see Table 32) made it both necessary and desirable at times to process large quantities of lemons which have not had the benefits of a storage period. Such fruit may be field-run in addition to that resulting from the washer elimination at the packing house. Depending upon the season, this source of fruit may represent approximately 80% of the lemons received by processors at a given time. In other cases, the fruit received may be almost entirely derived from grading operations before and after the curing process. When field-run or washer culls are processed in the products plants, the total juice yield and the citric acid content of the juice run lower than those obtained from stored fruit.

Selection and Grading of Fruit for Juice Production

In the early days of the lemon products industry, when it was purely a salvage operation, there was little concern over the matter of different types of fruit coming into the products plant. Since one of the chief products of manufacture was crystalline citric acid, variations in the acidity and nature of the fruit were not considered to be of great importance. Because of unfavorable economics, the production of citric acid from lemon juice was largely discontinued in 1958. Most juice now goes into concentrated juices and compounded juice products where flavor and standardization are primary considerations.

Concentrated juice can, of course, be manufactured to any desired acid content by adjustment of the volume concentration ratio. In concentrates intended for nonfrozen storage, where full-flavor is usually neither expected nor necessary to the ultimate use, considerable variation in the raw material can be tolerated. Today, however, frozen concentrate-for-lemonade and other frozen juice products, which are manufactured from single strength and concentrated juices, are a major outlet for lemon juice. It is especially important to give due consideration to the fruit used in order to control flavor and other properties of such products effectively. Very immature fruit that has not gone through the curing process may at

Courtesy of Lemon Products Div., Sunkist Growers

FIG. 37. GRADING LEMONS IN PREPARATION FOR JUICE EXTRACTION

times impart a so called green-fruit taste, whereas fruit stored too long may impart an overmature or stale taste. When either of these or other undesirable conditions prevail, such offending fruit must be diverted to other uses. In addition, blending of fruit may be necessary at times, to obtain satisfactory, uniform flavor and acidity.

Lemons used for juice production in commercial operation are graded and washed before going to the juice extractors, as has been described by Kieser and Havighorst (1952). Beisel (1951) has described in detail methods for controlling microorganisms in citrus processing plants.

Fruit that is delivered to the lemon products plant is placed in bins which contain fruit-protecting baffles, for temporary storage. From the bins the lemons are conveyed on belts to an area where they are sprayed with a solution containing chlorine of strength 25 to 35 ppm. Following this sanitizing treatment they are run over roller conveyors where unsound fruits are removed manually. The fruit is next brush-and-spray-washed with mild detergent solution and rinsed. After a second grading, the lemons are conveyed to sizers so that the fruit which is delivered to each of the various types of extractors falls within the proper size range for efficient handling. Finally, the lemons are again sprayed with a chlorine solution so that the fruit and belt are kept wet with the sanitizing solution up to the time the fruit enters the extractors.

A problem, which at one time was very serious, occurred in the grading of lemons for the purpose of removing those infected internally with Alternaria and certain other species of fungi. Because such infections may affect flavor but give no indication by external damage, it is highly desirable but difficult to eliminate this fruit. Improved packing house practices in addition to careful inspection and sampling of the fruit at the processing plants have nearly eliminated this problem.

The trend in the use of lemons for products purposes is definitely toward better grading (Fig. 37), and gentler, more prompt handling of better quality fruit. To reduce time in transit, lemons are transported by both truck and rail car with bin storage time being reduced to a minimum thereby averting deterioration from handling. Ordinarily lemons are hauled less than 100 miles but occasionally the distances may be as much as 400 miles. In recent years improvements have been made which involve padding and the spacing of baffles so that the free fall of an individual fruit does not exceed 18 in. Thus the energy of falling, which can be injurious is absorbed as the fruit changes direction by deflection.

This trend is a reflection of the greater need for upgrading the quality of manufactured products and the development of higher revenue consumer items from juice. From $^1/_3$ to $^1/_2$ of the entire crop may find its way into products bearing nationally advertised brand names. To the extent that lemon products displace the sale of fresh fruit, they are a liability to the citrus grower. It is fresh fruit sales that pay the major production costs, not the salvage operation of products.

In Florida, grower interest in the production of lemons increased with the introduction in 1949 of frozen concentrate for lemonade in California as described by Cole (1955). Although the production of lemons in Florida at that time was limited, Wenzel *et al.* (1958) discussed the several factors of importance in the use of Florida lemons for the production of frozen concentrate for lemonade. Since Florida now has about 7,000 acres of commercial lemon plantings, lemon juice products are now of increased importance. In December 1953, the United States Standards for Grades were first issued covering the product designation, Frozen Concentrate for Lemonade. Presently US standards of identity and a label statement of optional ingredients for this product have been stayed pending further hearings.

The soluble solids-acid ratio, which is the best single objective criterion of quality for orange and grapefruit juice, is quite unimportant in the case of lemon juice. Citric acid is the most important single constituent of the lemon and consequently concentrated juices are standardized on the basis of acidity, rather than on the basis of total soluble solids, or degrees Brix, as in the case of orange juice. The acidity is standardized at the desired number of grams citric acid per liter of concentrate. The total soluble solids is measured as degrees Brix and this value may be determined with a Brix spindle or a refractometer. Usually soluble solids values are measured by the refractometer sugar scale, with a correction for acid being applied as suggested by Stevens and Baier (1939). In the manufacture of concentrate for lemonade, where large quantities of sugar are dissolved in the juice, the ratio of soluble solids to acid in the finished beverage becomes very important.

TABLE 33

COMPOSITION OF LEMON JUICE

Constituent	Source of Juice[1]	Number of Samples	Content per 100 Grams			
			Range		Average	
Protein (total N × 6.25)	C, X	26	0.26–0.77	gm	0.42	gm
Amino nitrogen	C	31	0.019–0.046	gm	0.035	gm
Fat (ether extract)	C, X	...	None—0.6	gm	0.2	gm
Soluble solids, total (°Brix)	C	2746	7.1–11.9	gm	9.3	gm
Acid, total, as anhyd. citric	C	3123	4.20–8.33	gm	5.97	gm
Malic acid	C	15	0.15–0.41	gm	0.26	gm
Sugar, total, as invert	C, X	368	0.77–4.08	gm	2.16	gm
Reducing sugar	C	95	0.78–2.63	gm	1.67	gm
Sucrose	C	47	0.03–0.63	gm	0.18	gm
Minerals, total ash	C, X	50	0.15–0.35	gm	0.25	gm
Calcium	C, X	26	5.6–27.9	mg	9.88	mg
Phosphorus	C, X	27	5.3–16.6	mg	9.35	mg
Iron	C, X	20	0.14–0.69	mg	0.23	mg
Magnesium	C, X	19	5.8–11.3	mg	6.7	mg
Potassium	C	24	99–128	mg	103	mg
Sodium	C, X	19	1.0–5.0	mg	1.3	mg
Sulfur	C, X	20	2.0–8.0	mg	3.36	mg
Chlorine	C, X	4	2.3–4.0	mg	3	mg
Vitamin A (as carotene)	C, X	...	None or trace		None	
Thiamine (B_1)	C, X	34[2]	0.004–0.125	mg	0.043	mg
Riboflavin (B_2)	C, X	30[3]	0.005–0.073	mg	0.0183	mg
Niacin	C, X	26	0.056–0.196	mg	0.089	mg
Inositol	C	17	56–76	mg	66.5	mg
Folic acid	C	17	0.00082–0.00094	mg	0.00091	mg
Flavanones	C	2	46–54	mg	50	mg
Ascorbic acid (vitamin C)	C	357	31–61	mg	45	mg
pH	C	93	2.11–2.48		2.30[4]	

[1] C denotes juice from California-Arizona fruit; X, juice from fruit of other or unknown sources.
[2] Includes 8 samples of edible portion (excluding peel and seeds).
[3] Includes 6 samples of edible portion.
[4] Representative value.
Note: Original references used, weighted with data from the Wisconsin Alumni Research Foundation, W.A.R.F.

Other constituents of lemon juice also are important for their effect on flavor, their health value and for purpose of identification of the kind and amount of juice in a product. A compilation of data on the composition of lemon juice, prepared by Sunkist research laboratory personnel, is shown in Table 33.

In addition to the constituents listed in Table 33, considerable interest has been directed in recent years towards minor constituents which have important nutritional significance.

The analytical work reported by Joseph *et al.* (1961) has shown that the elements aluminum, copper, lithium, titanium, manganese, cobalt, zinc, strontium, boron, tin, nickel, chromium, vanadium, zirconium, molybdenum, and barium all are present in lemon juice. All of these except aluminum occur in quantities amounting to less than 0.01% of the ash.

Investigating nitrogenous constituents of lemon juice, Miller and Rockland (1952) found cysteine and glutathione to be present at levels of 0.32 and 2.8 mg per cent, respectively. Clements and Leland (1962) determined free amino acids in the juices of mature Eureka and Lisbon lemons. The principal amino acids found in the Eureka lemon juice, and reported in mg/100 ml juice, are proline 41, aspartic acid 36, glutamic acid 19, serine 17, asparagine 16, alanine 9, γ-aminobutyric acid 7, and arginine 3.

Flavonoids known to be in lemons include hesperidin, eriocitrin, diosmin and naringenin rutinoside. The flavonoid content of lemon juice is largely dependent upon the extraction method used, since the peel and pulp contain much greater amounts of these compounds. For fresh centrifuged lemon juice, McCready *et al.* (1950) have reported 0.046% calculated "as hesperidin." Bryant (1959) found 0.10–0.12% on fresh natural-strength pulp-containing lemon juice.

On the basis of recent work by Maier and Grant (1970), it has now been established by analytical method that lemon juice, as well as Navel orange and grapefruit juices, contains limonin, the intensely bitter triterpenoid dilactone formed during the delayed bittering of citrus juices. Limonin levels from 4.2 to 14.2 ppm were found in reconstituted commercial lemon juice concentrates. Lemon juice often has a slightly bitter taste, thus emphasizing the importance of gentle extraction procedures and short contact time between juice and pulp to minimize limonin content.

Juice Extraction and Oil Recovery

Extraction of lemon juice is accomplished with several different types of equipment. Formerly, corrugated rolls and screw presses were quite widely used in processes by which the whole fruit was crushed to accomplish a separation of peel and pulp from a mixture or emulsion of peel oil and juice. To accomplish separation of most of the oil from juice so obtained, it was necessary to pass the juice through centrifugal machines. Juice of this type is limited to uses in which a high oil level is acceptable.

Most of the juice produced at the present time is extracted with automatic machines made by The Brown International Corporation and The

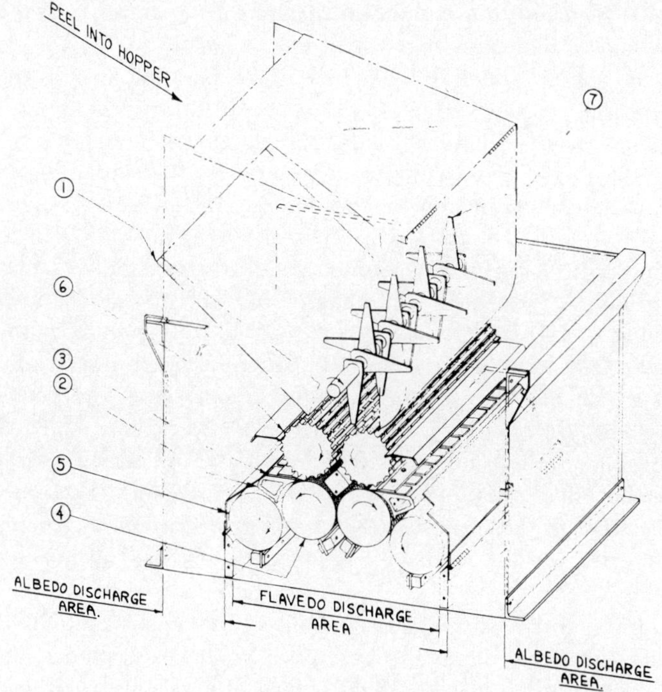

Courtesy of Brown International Corp.

FIG. 38. CITRUS PEEL SHAVER

(1) Peel chute; (2) knife holder manifold; (3) knife shaving; (4) roll-knurled; (5) roll-pressing; (6) roll-cleated; (7) agitator.

Food Machinery and Chemical Corp. (FMC). For purposes of obtaining peel oil, however, other types of machines may be preferred, although the FMC In-line machine is adapted to simultaneous recovery of both juice and oil.

The amounts of peel oil, pulp and pectic enzyme introduced into the juice during the extraction process are determinants in selecting the type of extractor for specific products. Usually one can expect to obtain a juice yield of from 90 to 100 gal per ton of lemons.

Of the several Brown machines available, the Model 1100 (see Fig. 19, p. 60) is most commonly used for extracting lemon juice, although the Model 700 also has application. For purposes of obtaining peel oil, the Brown Extractor Systems includes the Model 2300 peel shaver which is shown in Fig. 38. The shaver automatically orients and shaves the oil bearing flavedo to liberate the peel oil. The water, oil and pressed flavedo slurry is then fed to a paddle finisher which separates the oil bearing liquor, which is then centrifuged.

With the Brown Model 1100 machine, three paralled lines of single file lemons are fed into this extractor. Each fruit drops to its proper position as it becomes wedged between pairs of revolving, tapered, circular, synthetic rubber discs. The smaller fruit falls nearer the center and the larger sizes are engaged nearer the periphery. The discs carry the fruit through a stainless steel knife which slices it in half. Each half travels a converging path between a perforated stainless steel grid and the disc as the disc rotates. Spent peel is discharged out of the back of the machine after having traveled approximately 320° around its circular path. Juice flows to the bottom of the collector and can be divided into two fractions, i.e., that which has been expressed lightly, containing low peel oil and pulp, and the juice recovered from the tighter extraction which contains higher levels of peel oil and pulp. The juice flows out of two outlets which are located at the bottom of the stainless juice collector. The spacing between disc and grid is adjustable, providing for variation in fruit thickness. The extractor has a capacity of up to 12 tons of fruit per hour with good yields.

The FMC In-line machine is now one of the most widely used of the citrus juice extracting units. Because of its general acceptance, its operation will be described in more detail. Basically, it consists of upper and lower cups, the sides of which are slotted so as to intermesh. Individual fruits held in the lower cup are compressed by the descending upper cup. Simultaneously, circular plugs are cut in the top and bottom of the fruit and the contents of the fruit forced through the hole left by the bottom plug into a strainer tube. The rag, seeds and cell sacs in the strainer tube are then squeezed between the bottom plug and the top plug to remove substantially all of the juice. Finally, the compressed disc of peel is ejected. Oil recovery by this machine comes about through collection of the liquor squeezed from the exterior of the fruit as it is compressed.

Screening of the extracted juice is important in controlling its pectic enzyme content and the tendency for flocculation of suspended solids and gelation. Flocculation of insoluble solids and the resultant clearing are caused by the action of pectinesterase on soluble pectin in the juice, which causes the demethoxylated pectinic acids formed to precipitate in the presence of cations such as calcium. The pectic enzyme and much of the calcium which accelerates the enzyme action are associated with the insoluble solids. The amount of these solids left in the juice after screening thus may have an important effect on the flocculation characteristics of the juice. Pectic enzymes are much less active at the pH of lemon juice than is the case with orange juice, but nevertheless the length of time

Courtesy of Lemon Products Div., Sunkist Growers

FIG. 39. MOJONNIER DE-OILER USED IN CONTROL OF THE OIL CONTENT OF LEMON JUICE

the juice is allowed to stand between the juicing and screening operations also is important with respect to flocculation tendency in that long standing tends to increase the soluble pectin content of the juice. Some of the insoluble solids also contain leachable substances which may tend to impair the flavor and color stability of the juice.

In the interest of better juice yields, screening in paddle finishers or screw presses became the general practice for removal of coarse pulp. As was previously noted, however, to minimize juice bitterness from extracted limonin, gentle separation procedures and short contact time between juice and pulp are desirable.

Courtesy of Lemon Products Div., Sunkist Growers

FIG. 40. COLD WALL, STAINLESS STEEL TANKS USED FOR HOLDING LEMON JUICE AT 40°F OR LOWER

For certain specific products, the major one of which is bottled lemon juice, the sediment layer that normally separates from the juice upon long standing is considered undesirable. It is possible to reduce greatly the amount of sediment by removing from the juice most of the fine pulp remaining after normal screening. This can be accomplished by several methods: passing the juice through large continuous centrifuges; hot filtration with an appropriate filter aid; cold filtration of the stabilized reconstituted juice.

It frequently is necessary to use a deoiling process to control the oil content of juice for certain uses. Deoiling is usually accomplished by injecting preheated juice into a vacuum chamber, as is done in the Mojonnier deoiler (Fig. 39). Lemon juice is being used in increasing amounts as an acidulant in varietal juice beverages distributed chilled or as frozen concentrates. The juice character, mild full-bodied tartness, and nutritional values are highly desirable, with an optimum of lemon oil flavor or a regulated degree of such flavor being preferred.

The length of time of standing and the temperature of the juice in the interval between extraction and processing are very important in maintaining the original fresh flavor in frozen products. Lemon juice, like most other citrus juices, changes in flavor rather rapidly when held at ordinary temperatures and exposed to atmospheric oxidation. These changes are greatly reduced by rapidly chilling the juice to 50°F or lower and by holding in cold-wall storage tanks under vacuum sufficiently long to remove entrapped air. Deaeration is important because oxygen dissolved in the juice greatly increases loss of ascorbic acid during subsequent heat processing. This method of handling has an additional advantage in that the low temperature prevents appreciable growth of microorganisms (Fig. 40).

All modern equipment used in processing plants utilizes corrosion resistant materials in parts that come in contact with juice. Such equipment is customarily constructed of stainless steel No. 316 or No. 320. Metallurgy has played a most important part in the development of lemon juice products, these being very sensitive to contamination with copper, iron and other metals. Much of the excessive darkening and off-flavor development which took place in the concentrated lemon juices produced during the early days of the industry can be attributed to the use of copper-bearing alloys, which were the only materials then available.

Lemon Oil in Juice Products

The lemon oil content of juice is very important from the standpoints of flavor and stability. Some oil usually is desirable from the flavor standpoint but the amount must be adjusted in accordance with the type of product, the processing conditions employed, and the storage conditions to which the product will be subjected.

Frozen juice products can desirably carry substantial amounts of the natural peel oil, as much as may be found in the juice after extraction, or as much as may be necessary to give the optimum flavor. Products that are to be stored at room temperature must be kept relatively low in natural oil content. If more oil is required for flavor, it should be added as concentrated oil or as terpeneless oil. These latter types of oil are more stable against oxidation than the natural oil.

Several changes take place in lemon oil in contact with the juice, especially during long standing at elevated temperatures. Lemon peel oil is known to be sensitive to oxidation and to acid-catalyzed rearrangements, yielding products which impart undesirable flavors and odors. There is evidence that several of the terpene hydrocarbons, on oxidation, give rise to rather unpleasant turpentine-like products which are described as having terebinthinate character.

In an investigation of the deterioration of lemon oil, Ikeda *et al.* (1960) found that *p*-cymene was formed from γ-terpinene when lemon oil samples were stored in inadequately stoppered bottles. More recently, Rockland and DeBenedict (1969) reported marked alterations among the monoterpene hydrocarbons that occur during light-induced deterioration of lemon oil during storage in flint glass bottles. In either amber or Pyrex glass bottles, these changes were not noted.

With the finding of two new oxygenated compounds in the oil exposed to light, these authors believe that such compounds represent reduced products formed from other oxygenated compounds (i.e., aldehydes) by abstraction of hydrogen during the formation of *p*-cymene and concurrent losses of α- and γ-terpinene and α-phellandrene.

Although the role of citral in the development of the "cymey" off-flavor found in stored lemon juice is still obscure, nevertheless, the new methods of gas-phase chromatography should make it possible to clarify this point. It is known that many variables including pH, oxygen, certain metallic ions and light influence the pathway of chemical alteration.

The onset of the oxidative changes in lemon oil is retarded by the addition of a suitable antioxidant. The protective value of oil-soluble hindered phenolic antioxidants in lemon oil has been reported by several investigators, including Rusoff and Common (1953) and Swisher (1954).

These oxidation reactions are known to be accelerated by hydrogen-ions and since lemon juice has a high content of acid, the development of off-flavors is favored. As a practical means of reducing the hydrogen-ion concentration and thereby effecting some improvement, Stevens (1934) suggested buffering the juice with sodium citrate or other salt.

In addition to the chemical changes that take place in lemon oil, lipid oxidation has been implicated as a causative factor in flavor deterioration of processed and stored citrus juices. To determine the nature of fatty compounds which might be involved in off-flavor development, Nordby and Nagy (1968) analyzed several citrus juices, including lemon and lime. The fatty acid composition of lemon and lime juices is extremely complex. The range of the fatty acids chain lengths is from 16 to 26 carbon atoms with trace amounts of odd-carbon and branched-chain acids detected.

Since it is often desirable to prepare clear lemon or lemon-lime flavored beverages of good stability, concentrated or terpeneless oils are often used. Lemon oils low in terpenes can be prepared by fractional distillation or by "washing" in low-proof alcohol.

Pasteurization

The use of flash pasteurization to stabilize the cloud in citrus juices in a controlled and reproducible manner was first described by Stevens (1940). This process was later reviewed by Stevens, Pritchett, and Baier (1950), as applicable for citrus juices either to be stored at normal temperatures or to be stored at freezing temperatures. It is desirable to destroy substantially all of the pectic enzyme (pectinesterase) in juice products, such as natural strength lemon juice, concentrate for lemonade and bottlers bases that are to be stored at ordinary room temperature. Enzyme action is much less pronounced in cold storage and consequently partial stabilization whereby only 75 to 95% of the enzyme is inactivated is all that may be necessary for frozen products. Among the latter are frozen natural strength juice, frozen concentrate for lemonade, which is a mixture of lemon juice and sugar, and frozen low-temperature concentrated juice.

Lemon juice appears to contain a simple system involving only one enzyme with pectinesterase activity which can be inactivated within a relatively narrow temperature range of about 156° to 165°F, the specific temperature required being a function of holding time and enzyme concentration. Because of this, the temperature range for partial stabilization is not far different from that required for complete stabilization. A higher temperature of 170°F, with 30 sec holding time, is used in commercial operation, where precision control is not obtainable, to provide an adequate margin of safety. Immediate cooling after pasteurization, accomplished by passing the juice through a heat exchanger or by flashing it into a vacuum chamber, is essential to prevent rapid quality loss.

For maximum cloud stability it is preferred to inactivate pectinesterase by pasteurizing juice before concentration, and then, if sterility is required, pasteurizing the concentrate at 150°F. This avoids the damaging effect of high acidity combined with high temperature. In commercial operation, however, it sometimes is desirable or necessary to pasteurize concentrated juice prepared from raw juice, a concentrate inadequately stabilized in manufacture, or one inadvertently mixed with raw juice during manufacture. In cases where the raw juice is concentrated before pasteurization, somewhat better preservation of vitamin C is obtained because of the fact that the juice is largely deaerated before pasteurization temperatures are employed. It should be possible to use lower tempera-

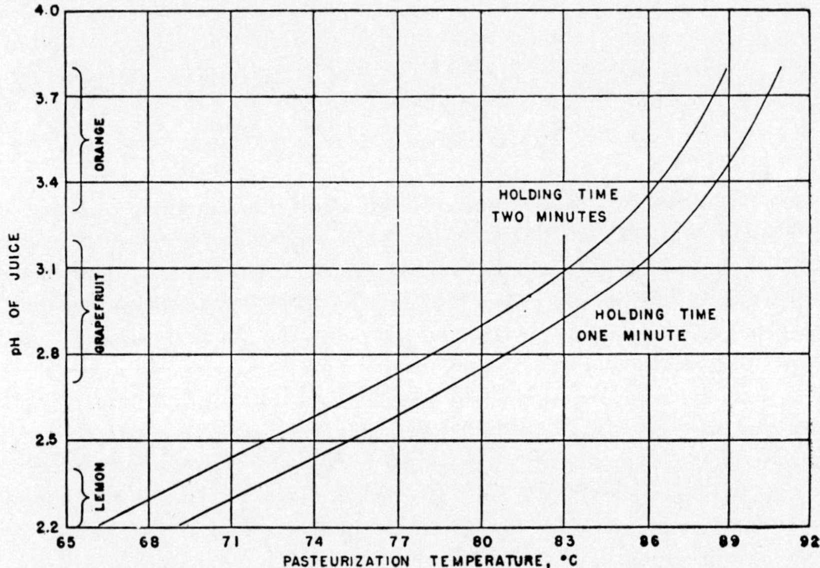

Courtesy of Research Div., Sunkist Growers

FIG. 41. TREND CURVES REPRESENTING MINIMUM TEMPERATURE REQUIRED TO PROVIDE SATISFACTORY INACTIVATION OF PECTIC ENZYMES IN NATURAL STRENGTH CITRUS JUICES

tures in this operation, because of the higher acidity and lower pH, but in actual practice the increased viscosity of the concentrates tends to promote uneven heating, especially in older type pasteurizers, which may largely offset the favorable effect of the increased acidity. For this reason the same pasteurization temperature and holding time are usually recommended with concentrates as with natural strength juice.

Pasteurization of lemon juice that has been stored for an appreciable length of time at other than optimum frozen conditions after the original processing frequently is much more deleterious in its effects than is the case with freshly extracted or freshly processed juice. Such processing brings about undesirable changes in flavor, color, and cloud stability.

The curves in Fig. 41 and 42 show some of the essential findings respecting the stabilization of cloud in citrus juices.

A reliable method of testing for pectinesterase (P.E.) is essential in commercial processing of lemon juice. The method described by Lineweaver and Ballou (1945), based on the titration of liberated carboxyl groups first used by Kertesz (1937), is valuable in the estimation and control of the enzyme in frozen products. The flocculation test devised by Stevens (1941) is more reliable in testing for small amounts of residual enzyme,

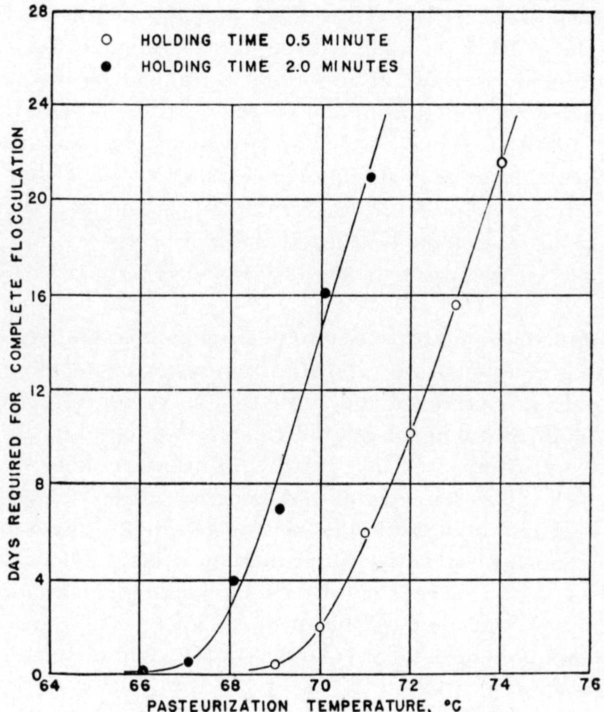

Courtesy of Research Div., Sunkist Growers

FIG. 42. THE EFFECT OF PASTEURIZATION TEMPERATURE ON THE INACTIVATION OF PECTIC ENZYMES IN BURRED LEMON JUICE

Flocculation time was determined by an accelerated test in which four days' stability indicates commercially satisfactory juice.

such as may be of importance only in products stored at ordinary temperatures. Determination of residual methoxyl group content of pectinic acids or direct determination of methanol produced by sensitive colorimetric methods based on chromotropic acid, as suggested by Doesburg (1966), is used also for determination of P.E.

Spoilage organisms are of importance in lemon juice, but because of its higher acidity, are less of a factor than in most other citrus juices. Sanitary significance of microorganisms in frozen citrus juices has been discussed by Vaughn and Murdock (1956). Several species of yeast and one or more species of bacteria are capable of profuse growth in natural strength lemon juice. Molds will grow in it whenever air is present. At least two species of yeast have been encountered that can cause spoilage in concentrated juice containing 27 to 28% anhydrous citric acid (pH 1.80 to 1.90). The yeast and molds are the most resistant to pasteurization.

Laboratory studies, using an accurately controlled pasteurization process, have indicated that the minimum temperature required to obtain commercial sterility is about 144°F with 30 sec holding time. In practical operation where commercial sterility is essential, experience has indicated that the minimum safe pasteurization conditions are about 150°F, with 30 sec holding time. Complete heat inactivation of pectinesterase, as heretofore described, assures practical sterility provided recontamination is not permitted.

The bacteriological methods used to determine the sanitary condition of juice handling equipment, to estimate the number of microorganisms in unpasteurized juice products and to detect the presence of spoilage organisms in products are in general the same as those used in the manufacture of other citrus juices: Hays (1951); Murdock, Folinazzo, and Troy (1952); Rowell (1954); Stevens and Manchester (1944); Stevens (1954).

Sodium benzoate and sulfur dioxide are frequently used to preserve lemon juice. Such preservatives are generally added after heat stabilization, merely as a precaution against recontamination. Sulfur dioxide also serves to preserve the color and flavor of the juice. The range from 0.05 to 0.2% of sodium benzoate, or from 200 to 500 ppm of sulfur dioxide is quite often used.

For several years, diethylpyrocarbonate (DEPC), has been used in Europe as a cold sterilant for such products as carbonated drinks and fruit based beverages. The US Food and Drug Administration has approved the use of DEPC up to 300 ppm in several beverages since it decomposes within hours to ethyl alcohol and carbon dioxide. Its use is limited to beverages having a low initial bacterial count.

Concentration

Concentrated juice products for general use in shelf items, bottlers bases, and the like are usually prepared from lemon juice in which the pectic enzyme system has been completely inactivated by pasteurization. The concentration of the heat stabilized juice is carried out in vacuum evaporators.

The final concentrate is standardized on the basis of grams of anhydrous citric acid per liter, usually about 325 gm per liter, of finished product. This corresponds to about 2.7 lb of acid per gallon and gives an average volume-concentration ratio of about 5.7:1. See Table 34 for volume concentration ratio data.

Concentrated juices prepared for use in frozen products are ordinarily made from unpasteurized juice, or from juice that has been partially heat

TABLE 34

COMPOSITION OF NATURAL STRENGTH AND CONCENTRATED CITRUS JUICES

LEMON JUICES					
Grams/Liter C.A.	57	250	325	380	400
°Brix	8.90	35.06	43.82	49.92	52.03
Lb/Gal at 20°C	8.617	9.601	9.975	10.249	10.347
Grams/Liter at 20°C	1032.6	1150.5	1195.3	1228.1	1239.8
Lb/Gal Sol. Solids	0.767	3.367	4.371	5.116	5.383
Grams/Liter Sol. Solids	91.9	403.5	523.8	613.0	645.1
% C.A. Anhydrous	5.52	21.73	27.19	30.94	32.26
Lb/Gal C.A.	0.476	2.086	2.712	3.171	3.338
Vol. Conc. Ratio (Fold)	1:1	4.39:1	5.70:1	6.67:1	7.02:1

Source: Beverage formula data from Sunkist Research Division (1965).

stabilized by pasteurization, and are concentrated at intermediate temperatures in an APV pan. This type of concentrate is also standardized on the basis of acidity, usually with a volume concentration ratio averaging either about 5.7:1, or about 7.0:1. Considerably more of the original fresh flavor is maintained in the finished product if a low concentration ratio such as 4:1 is used in preparing the concentrate. These products are stored at 0°F, or lower. Contrary to the increased storage stability obtained in concentrated orange juice through ascorbic acid addition, ascorbic acid added to concentrated lemon juice promotes browning. This is apparently due to the low pH of lemon juice since the adverse effect can be prevented by increasing the pH of 5.7-fold concentrate to about 3.2 from the normal 2.0 or lower.

The ultimate in concentration, the complete removal of water, results in a completely dehydrated product. For many years mixtures of lemon juice, dextrose, gums and other materials have been spray dried. Such products, while serving a definite need, have never, when reconstituted, sufficiently resembled fresh lemon juice to be competitive with frozen products.

A more recent technique developed by Morgan *et al.* (1959, 1960), of the U.S. Dept Agr., involves making a foam from concentrated juice, then drying a mat of the foam by passing hot, dry air through it. While more applicable to drying other juices than lemon, the foam-mat process holds promise.

Any one of several drying procedures makes products which when combined with good quality "locked-in" flavoring lemon oils such as those described by Swisher (1957) and Schultz (1958) approach frozen concentrates in quality.

Packaging

Packaging of lemon juice in its various forms has involved, at one time

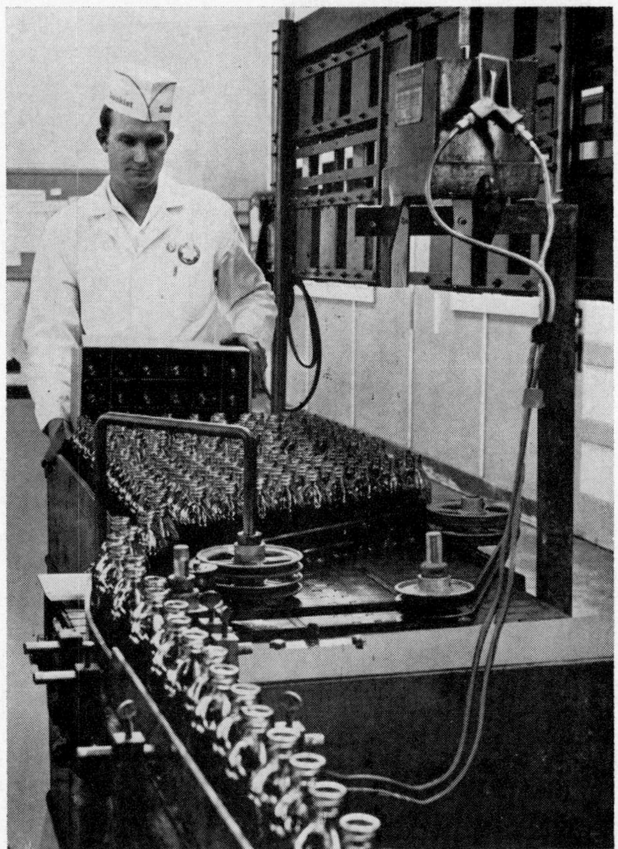

Courtesy of Lemon Products Div., Sunkist Growers

FIG. 43. EQUIPMENT USED FOR FILLING LEMON JUICE INTO BOTTLES

or another, nearly all the accepted food containers and some that are not commonly used.

Paraffin-lined fir or oak barrels and kegs were for a long time the predominant container for movement of concentrated lemon juice under refrigeration to reprocessors and food manufacturers. A weakness of the keg or barrel is that even though paraffin-lined, they are not airtight and this allows the headspace air to be replenished with oxygen as oxidation of the juice proceeds. For this reason, best results are obtained with these containers when the juice is sulfited to prevent discoloration of the topmost layer.

In most cases wooden barrels and kegs have now been replaced as shipping containers by steel drums with heavy-walled polyethylene liner insert. The drum is filled and emptied through a bung, so that the concentrated juice is well protected for atmospheric oxidation. Also used, primarily for inplant storage, are plain steel, removable-head drums lined with polyethylene bags.

Several small size glass bottles including 5-, 8-, 16-, and 32-ounce (see Fig. 43) have come into widespread use for packing and distribution of natural strength juice made and preserved directly or prepared by reconstituting concentrated juice. Also used widely for the latter purpose are injection-molded, polyethylene containers made to simulate the shape and color of lemons. The small consumer packages of preserved natural strength lemon juice have the advantages of good storage life and easy reseal with vinylite-lined screw caps. These features make for versatility, including condiment uses, and such products are widely accepted.

Some friction top and slip cover cans have been used for juices but the sanitary can is much more standard for all types of natural strength and concentrated lemon juice. Cans lined with a special enamel, commonly referred to as citrus enamel, are preferred for various shelf items. In recent years foil-lined fiber cans have come into general usage for the frozen product in sizes up to 32 oz. Above this size tinned cans are preferred. Several types of containers constructed of flexible materials are now used for individual servings of concentrate for lemonade. One is a packet made from a laminate of aluminum foil and polyethylene.

For dehydrated juices and juice products both plastic lined, aluminum foil pouches and hermetically sealed cans are used.

The process of filling juice into containers has been described by Kieser and Havighorst (1952) and varies according to the type of pack.

Frozen, single-strength juice is first chilled to 30°F in a Votator, canned, quick frozen and then stored at −10°F. Frozen, concentrated juice may be drawn directly into drums from the vacuum pan and frozen during storage at −10°F, or it may be chilled, canned and frozen. Frozen concentrate for lemonade is prepared in cold-wall tanks, where sugar is added to a standardized juice blend, then chilled, canned and frozen.

Single-strength, hot pack juice is piped while still hot from the deoiler to the canning line. After closing, the cans are cooled by water to about 75°F in rotary coolers and placed in 40°F storage. Hot pack concentrated juice, made from completely stabilized juice, is either filled directly into drums or, if canned, is heated to 160°F in a heat exchanger, filled hot, and cooled. All hot pack products are stored at 40°F.

Exclusion of head-space oxygen during canning of lemon juice, natural strength or concentrated, is accomplished by either of two methods. When hot fill is used, displacement of the head-space air with pure nitrogen by the gas flow process is quite effective. In the canning of a semisolid frozen natural strength juice or frozen concentrate the steam flow method should be used to insure sufficient vacuum to compensate for the further expansion of the juice during freezing to a solid condition.

Vacuum pack is satisfactory but is is rarely used. The steam exhaust method which has been used in the canning industry for other fruits is generally considered to be the method of choice for handling lemon juice products.

Storage and Distribution

All types of lemon juice products should be kept at as low a temperature as is practical. Lower storage temperatures for all canned products is the trend today and canned citrus products stand to benefit most by it. Probably it was the advent of canned citrus juices as much as any other factor that motivated this trend.

A low storage temperature is more essential for lemon juice, particularly concentrated juice, than for most citrus juices to maintain good flavor and color and a high retention of vitamin C. Storage at unfavorable temperatures tends to destabilize the cloud in concentrated juice, presumably by acid hydrolysis of the natural pectin which makes it susceptible to precipitation by calcium and other cations. The retention of vitamin C is generally higher in citrus juices than in most other products and the consumers rely upon the canned product as a source of vitamin C which is only slightly inferior to the corresponding fresh fruit juice.

Deteriorative changes and the rate of loss of vitamin C are logarithmic functions of temperature. As a result, there is a gradually increasing rate of change from the freezing point up to about room temperature and much more rapid changes at higher temperatures. So far as possible, therefore, storage temperatures should be kept below 60°F.

Frozen juices are preferably handled at −10°F; 0°F is satisfactory, and +10°F should be considered the maximum allowable for frozen storage. There is no sharp line of demarcation below which microbial and enzyme activity cease completely. Neither is there an upper temperature reached by a product still in the frozen state when it suddenly loses its fresh quality. Certain of the deteriorative processes in the frozen juice are accumulative so that all mishandling has its adverse effect on the final quality whether such effect is always perceptible or not.

Uses

Since the consumer must rely upon proper label declaration when purchasing lemon juice products, deceptive substitution of undeclared citric acid for lemon juice is obviously an economic fraud.

With the development by Vandercook *et al.* (1963) of means to characterize lemon juice in terms of constituents other than citric acid, the detection of adulteration is now possible. These analytical methods, which were adopted by the AOAC (Association of Official Agricultural Chemists), depend upon measurement of citric acid, amino acids by formol titration, *l*-malic acid by optical rotation and phenolics by UV absorbance.

There are many uses of lemon juice that are quite distinct from those of other citrus varieties. Several such uses are covered in pamphlets by Sunkist Growers (1952 and 1959). These specialty applications are best classified as condiment uses in which the lemon juice contributes acidity, flavor, and antioxidant action. Typical of these is its use in mayonnaise as a complete or partial replacement for vinegar. Lemon juice has been used for many years in the homemade product and was first advocated in commercial mayonnaise by Joseph (1929). Use in canned tomato juice cocktail, fruits for salad, breakfast prunes and other products was described by Baier and Stevens (1932). Lemon juice has application in such items as lemon butter, avocado pastes and in pickle solutions for curing hams, also for preventing darkening in fresh fruits and in processing dietetic olives. For the purpose of providing extra natural juice acidity to many low acid vegetable and fruit products, lemon juice has usefulness in shortening the safe processing time required. It is well-known that pH is a critical factor that determines the efficacy of the heat processing so far as acid-tolerant organisms are concerned.

Historically, seafoods and lemon juice have been associated so long that they are now generally considered as being complementary. For solving many of the special treating, storage and packaging problems of seafoods, the use of lemon juice is indicated. The natural balance of chemical and physical properties in lemon juice gives it the unique ability to maintain quality in many kinds of seafood.

Lemon juice has particular utility for blending with such flavors as pineapple, apple, grape, berry, etc., as an acidulant to enhance the natural fruit flavor of beverages (see also Chap. 10). Several of these products are sold as fruit juice punches in the food service and dispenser fields.

Juice beverages, of course, account for the largest outlet for natural strength and concentrated lemon juice. Among the favorite mixed drinks containing lemon juice are "Tom Collins," planters punch, whiskey sour, and "Bloody Mary."

A delicious sauce, which can be served with a wide variety of hot vegetables, is prepared by combining equal parts of softened butter, mayonnaise and lemon or lime juice.

LIME JUICE

Limes are grown to some extent in most of the areas that are favorable for the production of citrus fruits. The only two acid fruits of the lime

TABLE 35

COMPOSITION OF LIME JUICE

Constituent	Number of Samples	Content per 100 Grams Range		Average	
Protein (total N × 6.25)	11	0.3–0.7	gm	0.4	gm
Fat	...	0.0–0.11	gm	Trace	
Soluble solids, total (°Brix)	93	8.3–14.1	gm	10.0	gm
Acid, total, as anhyd. citric	129	4.94–8.32	gm	5.97	gm
Sugar, total, as invert	13	0.0–1.74	gm	0.72	gm
Non-reducing sugar	7	0.02–0.26	gm	0.14	gm
Ash, total	5	0.25–0.4	gm	0.35	gm
Calcium	2	4.5–10.4	mg	7	mg
Phosphorus	2	9.3–11.2	mg	10	mg
Iron	2	0.19–0.92	mg	0.6	mg
Carotene	2	0.003–0.005	mg	0.004	mg
Thiamine (B_1)	2	0.011–0.028	mg	0.020	mg
Riboflavin (B_2)	2	0.011–0.018	mg	0.015	mg
Niacin	5	0.090–0.275	mg	0.19	mg
Ascorbic acid (vitamin C)	13	23.6–32.7	mg	29	mg
pH	20	1.7–3.2		...	
Food energy (calories)	...	24–33		...	

group that have attained commercial importance are the Key (Mexican or West Indian) lime and the large-fruited Persian (Tahitian) seedless lime. In California, small plantings are principally located in the San Diego County area. However, most of the limes used on the Pacific Coast are imported from Mexico. There are two chief production areas in Florida, where most of the limes of this country are grown. The Key lime is produced almost entirely on the coastal islands or "Keys" south of the mainland. In recent years the industry has extended to the mainland where the main plantings, which are of the Persian variety, are located around Goulds and Homestead in the Redlands fruit growing area of Dade County. In Mexico, the principal lime growing areas are in Michoacan, Colima and Veracruz.

The lime resembles the lemon in structure and composition, but it usually is smaller in size. The Key or common lime is nearly round or oval in shape and averages slightly over one inch in diameter. The Persian lime is considerably larger in size, varying from about $1^3/_4$ to $2^1/_2$ in. in diameter and is shaped much like the lemon.

The composition of lime juice varies considerably with the variety of fruit and with the location where the fruit is grown. The citric acid content seems to average about the same as that of California lemon juice as shown by the compilation of data in Table 35 which is based on analyses of juice from different varieties and from different production areas, as reported in the literature. The citric acid content of 89 samples of juice prepared from Persian limes grown in Florida and analyzed by Lynch (1942) varied from 4.94 to 7.66%, with a mean value of 5.73%. The degrees Brix of 72 of these samples varied from 8.3 to 14.1, with an average of 10.1.

Because of the difference in size of the two principal types of limes, the methods of handling for processing vary. With the larger Persian variety, standard juicing equipment is used. However, since the Key or Mexican lime is smaller, the use of conventional extractors becomes impractical; therefore, juice is generally obtained by crushing the whole fruit in a screw press.

According to Lewis (1951), in a typical canning procedure for the manufacture of frozen juice in Florida, the fruit is carefully graded, washed and sometimes sterilized before passing to the high speed juice presses. The expressed juice is screened, analyzed, blended, deaerated and deoiled before the final canning operation. The juice is precooled before filling in cans for freezing.

The methods used in Florida for lime processing have been largely those developed for handling citrus in general. In one processing plant of California, lime juice is handled and pasteurized in the same way as lemon juice.

With the Persian variety, the juice is passed through a finisher, after extraction with standard juicing equipment. In these steps it is important to keep the pressure comparatively light to avoid extraction of bitter constituents from the peel. Pruthi and Lal (1951) have observed that deaeration combined with flash pasteurization of 195° to 205°F gave the best retention of vitamin C and overall juice quality.

In the case of the lime juice obtained by crushing the whole fruit in a screw press, it may be desirable to reduce the peel oil content by vacuum deoiling. The lime juice also may be clarified by mixing with a filtering aid and passing through a plate-and-frame press. Clarified juice is useful in compounding formulas for bottled drinks and fountain use.

As compared to other citrus juices, the marketing of canned lime juice has been limited, mainly because the products deteriorated rapidly at room temperature.

Single strength, pasteurized, canned limeade was known to develop off-flavors which were described in part at least, as "terpeney," a difficulty believed to be caused by the peel oil present in the juice. Macfie (1953) found a close correlation between peel oil content and the development of terpeney flavors. With respect to the general off-flavors, however, he found that pulp was a major factor.

Because of the similarity in chemical composition between lime and lemon oil, it is not surprising that lime oil in contact with juice under unfavorable conditions develops off-flavors. As was shown by Ikeda and co-workers (1960) for lemon oil, gamma-terpinene under oxidative conditions is readily converted to the off-flavored product, *p*-cymene. Whereas Stanley *et al.* (1960) found *p*-cymene to represent 0.7% of the hydrocarbon fraction of cold pressed lime oil, it represented 6.5% in distilled lime oil. Further, lime oil is high in the relatively unstable pinenes which may in part contribute to the development of off-flavors.

Bissett, Veldhuis and Rushing (1954) have shown that during production of canned lime juice, sufficient heat to inactivate pectinesterase and destroy bacteria is desirable, and that refrigerated storage of the canned juice favors retention of highest quality. Sweetened and unsweetened lime juices were heated to temperatures ranging from 120° to 200°F, and tested for stability in storage at 35°F. Effects of the treatments were judged on the basis of bacterial counts, flavor, destruction of pectinesterase and cloud stability. Pasteurization at a minimum temperature of 170°F is required to inactivate pectinesterase enzyme and insure cloud stability of the juice in 35°F storage. In commercial practice pasteurization temperature is usually about 195°F. Such products stored at 35°F for 15 months retain flavor practically unchanged, but in unheated samples some changes occurred. At 80°F storage life is limited to about $4^1/_2$ months.

Procedures for processing lime juice into space-saving superconcentrates, from which limeade of true flavor can be prepared, were developed and pilot-plant-tested by Bissett, Veldhuis and Scott (1954). The products are an 8-fold, sweetened concentrate, requiring only water for reconstitution, and 35-fold unsweetened concentrate needing addition of sugar and water. In preference rating tests, these authors established that a limeade should have a soluble solids content of about 11°Brix and a soluble solids-acid ratio in the range of 14 : 1 to 16 : 1. The best flavor was obtained by adding lime purée to concentrated lime juice to give a peel oil content of 0.003% to 0.004% in the prepared limeade.

Frozen concentrate for limeade was introduced to the trade in 1951. In its preparation, sucrose is added to lime juice until the Brix is raised to about 48°. It is usually considered desirable to apply a mild heat treatment during preparation, followed by freezing and storing the product at 0°F or lower.

The commercial production of lime juice products in this country has been fairly stable the past several years. These products include both sweetened and unsweetened lime juice concentrates, frozen concentrate for limeade, frozen single-strength lime juice and single-strength pasteurized canned limeade.

As an acidulant, lime juice is used for some of the same purposes as lemon juice. A major outlet for lime juice is in syrups and concentrates for beverage uses. Lime beverages are quite distinct in character from the corresponding lemon product and appeal to different consuming groups. In general, lime beverages seem to be more popular with adults than with children.

For beverage uses, lime juice is very popular as a thirst quencher in the preparation of coolers and cocktails as well as in citrus flavored punches. Favorite mixed drinks which contain lime juice include gin rickey, gin and tonic, gimlet, rum and soursop, and "Scarlett O'Hara." Many other drinks, such as the "Margarita" and daiquiri may contain either lime or lemon juice.

Although not as popular as their lemon counterparts, preserved lime juice is sold domestically in both bottles and plastic containers molded to the shape and color of a lime. "Rose's Lime Juice," a British product having a characteristic musty lime flavor, is found in many bars throughout the world. Of interest is the fact that similar products with natural fresh lime oil flavor are not acceptable on the British market.

In mixed juice beverages, lime blends well with other citrus juices, with apple and with apricot purée to give an unusual mellow taste. Among the several applications in food products, lime juice is used in lime cream chiffon pie and the popular Key lime pie, soufflés and parfaits.

In South Florida and the Keys, many old timers use "Old Sour" which is fermented lime juice seasoned with salt. This preparation is used on all fish and shellfish dishes, on meats and in salad dressing.

BIBLIOGRAPHY

ANON. 1962. Chemistry and Technology of Citrus, Citrus Products and By-Products. Agriculture Handbook 98, Agr. Res. Serv., U.S. Dept. Agr.

BAIER, W. E. 1949. Vitamin-acid complex of lemon juice plays unique nutrition and food preservation role. Nutr. Res. 7, No. 1, 1–3. Sunkist Growers, Los Angeles, Calif.

BAIER, W. E., and STEVENS, J. W. 1932. Lemon juice in packaged foods. Canner 75, No. 10, 9–11.

BARTHOLOMEW, E. T., and SINCLAIR, W. B. 1951. The lemon fruit. Univ. Calif. Press, Berkeley and Los Angeles, Calif.

BEISEL, C. G. 1951. Working out the fruit bugs. Food Eng. 23, No. 11, 82–84, 202, 204, 205, 207.

BISSETT, O. W., VELDHUIS, M. K., and RUSHING, N. B. 1954. Pasteurization and storage of sweetened and unsweetened lime juice. Food Technol. 8, No. 1, 136–138.

BISSETT, O. W., VELDHUIS, M. K., and SCOTT, W. C. 1954. Lime juice superconcentrates. Food Eng. 26, No. 6, 56–58, 190–195.

BRAVERMAN, J. B. S. 1949. Citrus Products. Chemical Composition and Chemical Technology. Interscience Publishers, New York.

BRYANT, E. F. 1959. Unpublished Report. Sunkist Growers, Ontario, Calif.

CHACE, E. M., WILSON, C. P., and CHURCH, C. G. 1921. The composition of California lemons. U.S. Dept. Agr. Bull. 993.

CHANDLER, L. C. 1957. Trends in the production of limes for processing. Proc. Fla. State Horticultural Soc. *70,* 228–331.

CHATFIELD, C., and MCLAUGHLIN, L. I. 1931. Proximate composition of fresh fruits. U.S. Dept. Agr. Circ. *50,* Rev. 1–19.

CLEMENTS, L. C., and LELAND, H. V. 1962. An ion-exchange study of the free amino acids in the juices of six varieties of citrus. J. Food Sci. *27,* 20–26.

COLE, G. M. 1955. Concentrates for lemonade. Food Technol. *9,* No. 1, 38–45.

DAVIS, W. B. 1947. Determination of flavanones in citrus fruits. Ind. Eng. Chem. Anal. Ed. *7,* 476–478.

DOESBURG, J. J. 1966. Pectic substances in fresh and preserved fruits and vegetables. Inst. Res. Storage Processing Horticultural Produce Communication, 152 pp. Wageningen, The Netherlands.

EXCHANGE LEMON PRODUCTS COMPANY. Laboratory Reports. Corona, Calif.

GOLDMAN, M. E. 1949. The pH of fruit juices. Food Research *14,* 275–277.

HARDING, P. L., MACRILL, J. R., and NIXON, H. W. 1959. Citrus Fruits. Am. Soc. Refrig. Eng. Data Book *1,* No. 1, Chapter 25, 1–32.

HAYS, G. L. 1951. The isolation, cultivation and identification of organisms which have caused spoilage in frozen concentrated orange juice. Proc. Fla. State Horticultural Soc. *64,* 135–137.

HODGSON, R. W., and EGGERS, E. R. 1938. Rootstock influence on the composition of citrus fruits. Calif. Citrograph *23,* No. 12, 499, 531.

HULME, A. C. 1970. The Biochemistry of Fruit. In press. Academic Press, New York.

IKEDA, R. M., STANLEY, W. L., and COOK, S. A. 1960. Investigations of the hydrocarbons in lemon oil. Presented Ann. Meeting Inst. Food Technologists, San Francisco, May.

JOSEPH, G. H. 1929. Mayonnaise and other salad dressings. Spice Mill *52,* 1887–1889.

JOSEPH, G. H., *et al.* 1961. Nutrients in California lemons and oranges. J. Am. Dietet. Assoc. *38,* 552–559.

KASSAB, M. A. 1951. Experiments on clarification and preservation of lime juice. Canner *112,* No. 16, 10–11.

KERTESZ, Z. I. 1937. The determination of pectin-methoxylase activity. J. Biol. Chem. *121,* 589–598.

KIESER, A. H., and HAVIGHORST, C. R. 1952. They use every part of fruit in full product line. Food Eng. *24,* No. 9, 114–116, 156–159.

KULKARNI, V. H. 1930. The manufacture of lime juice and its economic value. Poona Agr. Coll. Mag. *22,* 89–92.

LEWIS, J. A. 1951. Lime juice—A promising new comer. Quick Frozen Foods *13,* No. 12, 86–87.

LINEWEAVER, H., and BALLOU, G. A. 1945. The effect of cations on the activity of alfalfa pectinesterase (pectase). Arch. Biochem. *6,* No. 3, 373–387.

LYNCH, S. J. 1942. Some analytical studies of the Persian lime. Fla. Agr. Expt. Sta. Bull. *368.*

MACFIE, G. G., JR. 1953. Lime oil is a factor in the deterioration of flavor of lime juice. Proc. of the Fla. State Horticultural Soc. *66,* 258–264.

MCCREADY, R. M., WALTER, E. D., and MACLAY, W. D. 1950. Sugars of citrus fruits. Food Technol. *4,* 19–20.

Maier, V. P., and Grant, E. R. 1970. Specific thin-layer chromatography assay of limonin, a citrus bitter principle. J. Agr. Food Chem. *18,* No. 2, 250–252.

Miller, J. M., and Rockland, L. B. 1952. Cysteine and glutathione in citrus juices determined by small scale filter paper chromatography. Arch. Biochem. and Biophys. *40,* 416–423.

Morgan, A. I., Ginnette, L. F., Randall, J. M., Graham, R. P., and Mariani, P. Jr., 1960. Foam mat drying. Food Processing *21,* No. 6, 34–35.

Morgan, A. I., Jr., Ginnette, L. F., Randall, J. M., and Graham, R. P. 1959. Technique for improving instants. Food Eng. *31,* No. 9, 86–87.

Munsell, H. E., Williams, L. O., Guild, L. P., Troescher, C. B., Nightingale, G., and Harris, R. S. 1950. Composition of food plants of Central America. III. Guatemala. Food Research *15,* No. 1, 34–52.

Murdock, D. S., Folinazzo, J. F., and Troy, V. S. 1952. Evaluation of plating media for citrus concentrates. Food Technol. *6,* 181–185.

Mustard, M. J. 1946. The ascorbic acid content of fresh and commercially canned Tahiti (Persian) lime juice. Fla. State Hort. Soc. Proc. 125–126.

Nordby, H. E., and Nagy, S. 1968. Differential fatty acid studies of seeds and juice from several citrus species. Proceedings of the 1968 conference on citrus chemistry and utilization. Agr. Res. Service 72–73, May.

Peterson, W. H., and Elvehjem, C. A. 1928. The iron content of plant and animal foods. J. Biol. Chem., *78,* 215–223.

Pilnik, W., and Charley, V. 1970. Citrus products. In press.

Poore, H. D. 1932. Analysis and composition of California lemon and orange oils. U.S. Dept. Agr. Tech. Bull. *241.*

Pope, W. T. 1923. The acid lime fruit in Hawaii. Hawaii Agr. Expt. Sta. Bull. *49.*

Pruthi, J. S., and Lal, G. 1951. Preservation of citrus fruit juices. J. Sci. Ind. Tes. *10B,* 36–41.

Rockland, L. B. 1961. Nitrogenous constituents, Chapter 8, 247, Table 91, "The Orange." W. B. Sinclair, University of Calif. Press.

Rockland, L. B., and DeBenedict, C. 1969. Studies on the stability of lemon oil. I. The hydrocarbon fractions of raw, cold-pressed California lemon oil. Abstracts of papers, citrus research conference, U.S. Dept. Agr. Pasadena, California, December 2, 1969.

Rowell, K. M. 1954. The slide plate method of estimating the number of viable microorganisms in orange juice. Food Technol. *8,* 459–461.

Rusoff, I. I., and Common, J. L. 1953. Stabilized citrus oil and method of producing the same. U.S. Pat. 2,657,997. Nov. 3.

Russell, W. C., Taylor, M. W., and Beuk, J. F. 1943. The nicotinic acid content of common fruits and vegetables prepared for human consumption. J. Nutr. *25,* 275–284.

Schultz, T. H. 1958. Preparation of solid flavoring compositions. U.S. Pat. 2,856,291. Oct. 14.

Sinclair, W. V., and Eny, D. M. 1945. The organic acids of lemon fruits. Botan. Gaz. *107,* 231–242.

Stahl, A. L. 1935. Composition of miscellaneous tropical and subtropical Florida fruits. Fla. Agr. Expt. Sta. Bull. 283, 1–20.

Stanley, W. L. 1960. Unpublished work.

STANLEY, W. L., IKEDA, R. M., VANNIER, S. H., and ROLLE, L. A. 1960. Gas chromatographic analysis of the major aldehydes in lemon, orange, and grapefruit oils. Presented Ann. Meeting Inst. Food Technologists, San Francisco.

STEVENS, J. W. 1934. Beverages and beverage materials and the preparation thereof. U.S. Pat. 1,955,864. Apr. 24.

STEVENS, J. W. 1940. Method of conserving fruit juices. U.S. Pat. 2,217,261. Oct 8.

STEVENS, J. W. 1941. Method of testing fruit juices. U.S. Pat. 2,267,050. Dec. 23.

STEVENS, J. W. 1954. Preparation of dehydrated agar media containing orange juice serum. Food Technol. *8*, 88–92.

STEVENS, J. W., and BAIER, W. E. 1939. Refractometric determination of soluble solids in citrus juices. Ind. Eng. Chem., Anal. Ed. *11*, 447–448.

STEVENS, J. W., and MANCHESTER, T. C. 1944. Methods for direct count of microorganisms in citrus products. J. Assoc. Offic. Agr. Chemists *17*, 302–307.

STEVENS, J. W., PRITCHETT, D. E., and BAIER, W. E. 1950. Control of enzymatic flocculation of cloud in citrus juices. Food Technol. *4*, 469–473.

SUNKIST GROWERS. 1952. Basic information for the food server on California citrus fruit and other fruit and vegetables. Sunkist Growers, Los Angeles, Calif.

SUNKIST GROWERS. 1959. Fresh citrus quantity serving handbook. Los An-Angeles, Calif.

SUNKIST GROWERS, Research Department, Ontario, Calif. Rept. Files.

SWISHER, H. E. 1954. Improving citrus oils with antioxidants. California Citrograph *39*, 354–355.

SWISHER, H. E., 1957. Solid flavoring composition and method of preparing the same. U.S. Pat. 2,809,895. Oct. 15.

TEPLEY, L. J., STRONG, F. M., and ELVEHJEM, C. A. 1942. The distribution of nicotinic acid in foods. J. Nutr. *23*, 417–423.

VANDERCOOK, C. E. 1967. Chemical characterization of lemon juice products. Proc. of 1967 conference on citrus chemistry and utilization. Agr. Res. Service, U.S. Dept. Agr. Oct. 13.

VANDERCOOK, C. E. *et al.* 1963. Lemon juice composition. J. Assoc. Offic. Agr. Chemists *46*, No. 3, 353–365.

VAUGHN, R. H., and MURDOCK, D. I. 1956. Sanitary significance of microorganisms in frozen citrus juices. Am. J. Public Health *46*, 886–894.

WATT, B. K., and MERRILL, A. L. 1963. Composition of foods—Raw, processed, prepared. U.S. Dept. Agr., Agriculture Handbook *8*.

WEBBER, H. J. 1932. The lime in California. Calif. Citrograph *17*, 456–457, 478–479.

WELLS, A. H., AGCAOILI, F., and OROSA, M. Y. 1925. Philippine citrus fruits. Philippine J. Sci. *28*, No. 4, 453–527.

WENZEL, F.W., OLSEN, R. W., BARRON, R. W., HUGGART, R. L., and HILL, E. C. 1958. II. Use of Florida lemons in frozen concentrate for lemonade. Proc. Fla. State Hort. Soc. *71*, 129–132.

CHAPTER 5

F. P. Mehrlich,
revised by G. E. Felton

Pineapple Juice

IMPORTANCE

Pineapple juice is the most important noncitrus fruit juice used in the American diet. Some 10 million to 15 million cases of single-strength canned pineapple juice have been consumed annually during each of the last 20 years in the United States. The retail value of an annual pack is approximately $50,000,000.

Recently the use of pineapple juice has expanded in several areas. The most important is as an ingredient in blended fruit drink and juice products in either the canned or frozen forms. Its use as a packing media for unsweetened pineapple slices, chunks, and crushed has increased significantly. Pineapple wine is also being produced from frozen concentrated pineapple juice.

VARIETIES AND PRODUCTION CENTERS

Four horticultural varieties account for virtually all pineapple grown for canning. These are: Cayenne, the major canning variety, and Singapore, Queen, and Red Spanish. Cayenne is grown exclusively in Hawaii, Taiwan, and the Philippines, and is on the increase in many other centers of production throughout the world. Singapore (also known as Singapor Canner) is grown in the Malaysian Peninsula. Commercial production of Queen is principally in Australia and South Africa, while Red Spanish is confined to the Caribbean Region.

The chief sources of the world's canned pineapple and pineapple juice are Hawaii, the Philippines, Taiwan, Malaysia, South Africa, Australia, the Ryukyus (Okinawa) and the Ivory Coast. Other production centers of lesser importance are in Mexico, Puerto Rico, Kenya, Swaziland and Thailand. There is not a fixed relationship between the amount of solid pineapple items and juice items packed in various regions of the world. Technology and marketing patterns are different for the various production centers. For example, while Hawaii produces only 35–40% of the world's solid packed pineapple products, around 80% of world's production of pineapple juice comes from Hawaii.

FERDINAND P. MEHRLICH is the Director, Food Laboratory, Department of the Army, U. S. Army Natick Laboratories, Natick, Massachusetts.

DR. GEORGE E. FELTON is the Vice-President, Technical Division, Dole Company, Honolulu, Hawaii.

Courtesy of Dole Company

Fig. 44. Hawaiian Pineapple Fields

GROWING AND HARVESTING OF PINEAPPLE

The commercial production of pineapple juice is an integral part of the processing of sliced pineapple and other solid items of pack. In the total production of pineapple and pineapple products in Hawaii, very close coordination is maintained between processing in the canneries and production on the plantations. For the great majority of Hawaiian pineapple production, a system of vertical integration of operations exists with agricultural production, processing and manufacturing sharing the same management and ownership within the individual pineapple companies. Typical Hawaiian pineapple fields ars shown in Fig. 44.

The pineapple is an herbaceous monocot, more closely resembling in its gross morphology such plants as corn, sisal, and bananas than it does the tree or bush fruits such as apples, pears, or raspberries. In its first fruiting year, some 18–22 months following planting, the plant bears a single compound fruit on a central stalk or peduncle. Subsequently one or more axillary suckers give rise to ratoon fruit. The first fruit or "plant crop" is illustrated in Fig. 45. Figure 46 shows a whole plant split along its cen-

Fig. 45. A Mature Cayenne Plant Crop Pineapple Fruit

tral axis illustrating, at the bottom of the picture, the stem or stump of the "mother plant." On close examination, the dried peduncle can be seen at the apex of this stump. This was the attachment for the "plant crop" fruit. Arising from the stump of the mother plant are two axillary suckers; the one on the right bearing a "first ratoon" fruit. At the base of the ratoon is a slip, in cross section, and at the top of the fruit, the crown is shown. Crowns and slips, from either the "plant crop" or ratoons are commonly used as sources of planting material. Nonfruiting suckers may also be used for planting.

The quality of pineapple fruit is dependent upon a number of important factors, including: (1) variety; (2) nutrition; (3) exposure to light; (4) weather—(a) light intensities, (b) day and night temperatures, (c)

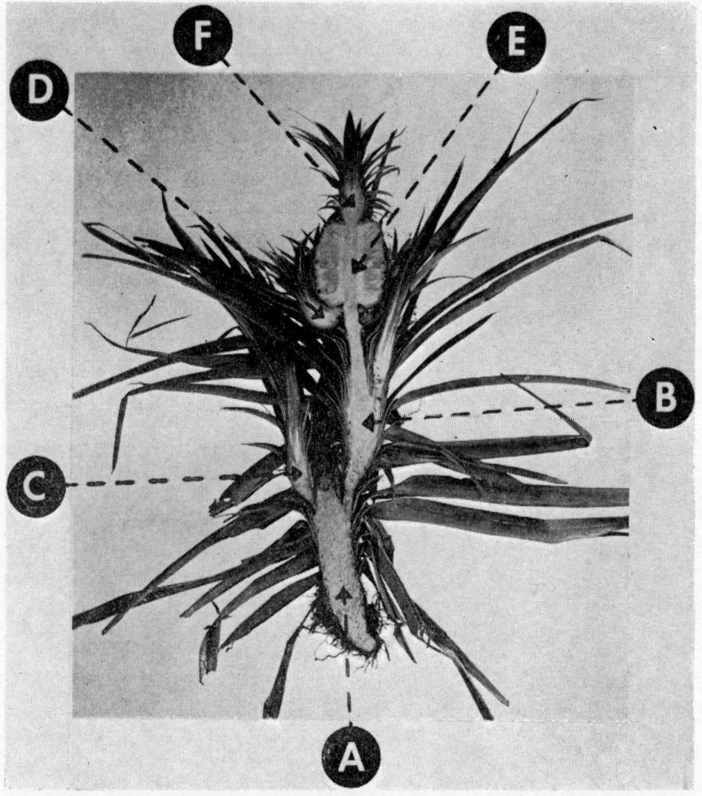

FIG. 46. PINEAPPLE PLANT SPLIT ALONG CENTRAL AXIS

(A) Stump of plant crop; (B) fruiting; first ratoon sucker; (C) nonfruiting sucker; (D) slip; (E) fruit; (F) crown.

rainfall (or irrigation), (d) season; (5) ripeness; and (6) freedom from blemishes, insects, or diseases.

The flavor and composition of pineapple juice reflects in considerable degree, the flavor and composition of the fresh fruit from which it is processed.

It is possible through a manipulation of the kind of planting material used, the time of planting, the number of plants per acre, fertilization, judicious application of irrigation, and other agricultural techniques to alter the quality of pineapple fruits. Thus it is possible in some degree to affect the color, flavor, and appearance of pineapple juice and influence acceptability by the consuming public. Varietal differences, effects of weather, climate and season, and the relative ripeness of fruit are the more important elements affecting pineapple juice quality.

Plant Nutrition

The nutrition of the pineapple plant is controllable to a considerable degree depending upon limits imposed by soil, water, and climatological factors. To a limited extent fruit composition reflects the level of nitrogen nutrition, for example. It is no doubt affected also by the relative levels of other essential elements, both major and minor, as well as the carbohydrate status of the plants from which the fruit are harvested. Levels of adequacy for nitrogen, phosphorus, potassium, iron, zinc, and magnesium as well as for carbohydrates have been established for maximizing fruit size.

Fruit Exposure

Fruit exposure plays an important role in determining fruit quality as well as rate of ripening. The mechanism, no doubt, is one of permitting fruit temperature to rise during daylight hours. The most direct measure of higher temperatures through increased exposure is an increase in the Brix-acid ratio of the juice in the fruit. Shading through excessive leaf growth, high plant densities, or low sunlight occurring in winter or at higher elevations, have the effect of reducing Brix-acid levels. Levels of esters and other flavor constituents are lower in fruit receiving low exposure to sunlight.

Weather

One of the many factors that contribute to the excellence of Hawaii's climate for the growing of pineapple is the intensity of sunlight and its favorable effect on photosynthesis. Much of the year and particularly the warm summer months, is characterized by clear, cloudless skies. Only at the very highest elevations at which pineapples are grown, does cloud cover constitute a possible limiting factor in photosynthesis.

Day and night temperatures also play a role in determining fruit size and composition. There is ordinarily a marked decrease in temperature from day to night. This affects respiration rate which in turn affects many metabolic processes of the plant during its vegetative phase, flowering and fruit maturation. Warm days and cool nights are considered ideal for maximum fruit quality.

Adequate soil moisture is essential to proper development of the pineapple plant and of the fruit. It occurs as a result of rainfall or may be supplied by means of irrigation. Soil moisture, of itself, is of little consequence unless the plant has a healthy, functional root system. Water plays an essential role in the growth of the plant as well as in the transport of nutrients and other dissolved substances among the tissues of the plant. Moisture supply is important in determining fruit size and weight. The

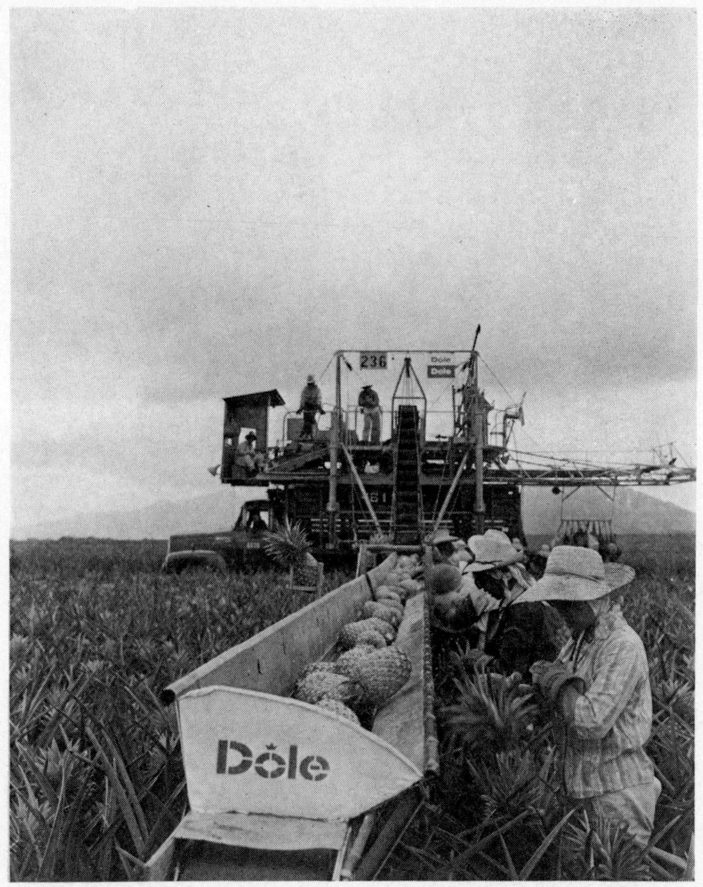

Courtesy of Dole Company

FIG. 47. HARVESTING CAYENNE PLANT CROP PINEAPPLES IN HAWAII

pineapple plant is admirably adopted to withstand relatively long periods of low rainfall, but both yield and quality are adversely affected by prolonged drought.

Fruit quality in Cayenne pineapple grown in Hawaii reaches a peak during the early summer months of June and July. Every effort, therefore, is made through management practices by providing an adequate labor supply and cannery capacity to maximize production during the high quality period of the year. During winter, fruit tends to be paler, lower in Brix, higher in acid, and somewhat lacking in volatile flavor constituents.

Courtesy of Dole Company

FIG. 48. BULK FRUIT UNLOADING PRIOR TO SIZE GRADING

Fruit Ripeness

Since the relative ripeness of the fruit can be of primary importance in determining the ultimate quality of all products derived from pineapple, harvest control is a vital factor in the total production process. In general, pineapples do not improve following harvesting. If fruit are harvested prior to prime ripeness they remain inferior with respect to quality. Also, over-ripe fruit must be rejected or down-graded because of the deterioration of physical and chemical properties and accordingly of taste and appearance.

Blemishes, Diseases and Insects

Every effort is made to control the diseases and insects which adversely affect the growth, productivity and quality of pineapple. Among the important diseases are those which affect root health and thus interfere with normal plant development. Others invade the fruit and render it unfit for processing or of limited value. Insect control is important to avoid direct plant damage and to avoid secondary effects such as diseases transmitted by mealybugs and thrips.

Courtesy of Dole Company

Fig. 49. Graded Pineapple Being Washed and Elevated into Cannery

Fruit blemishes which can impair recovery and quality may be caused by bacteria and other parasitic microorganisms or may be physiological in nature. Great effort is expended to minimize losses from these as well.

This historical development and present status of pineapple production is discussed in a monograph by Collins (1960), one of a series dealing with world crops. More detailed information in the botany, culture, production and marketing of pineapple fruit and pineapple products is presented in the monograph.

Fig. 50. Modern High Speed Ginaca Machines Which Remove Shells, Ends, Cores and Eradicator Meat in Preparation of Pineapple Products

THE PROCESSING OF PINEAPPLES

The fruit when harvested in the manner shown in Fig. 47 is transported to the cannery where the identity of its origin is maintained up to the point of introducing it into the processing line.

Figure 48 shows fruit being unloaded from bulk bins to pass over graders for introduction into the conveyors (Fig. 49) which will carry it to the Ginaca machines.

The Ginaca machines, as shown in Fig. 50, perform several important functions. The machines are of several sizes to accommodate the different grades of fruit which are segregated on the basis of their diameters. The Ginaca machine removes the inedible portions of the fruit from the edible parts. The outer skin, known as the "shell," is first taken off. Figure 51 shows a plant crop pineapple of the Smooth Cayenne variety cut longitudinally. A number of superimposed black lines are drawn on the surface of the fruit section to illustrate the utilization of the various parts of the fruit. The scale shown on Fig. 51 is in inches.

The tissues lying outside lines A-A adhere to the shell when it is re-

FIG. 51. PLANT CROP PINEAPPLE CUT LONGITUDINALLY

Lines AA represent diameter of circular knife which cuts the central cylinder of fruit for production of $2^1/_2$ size of slices. Lines BB delimit the diameter of 2-T size of slices. Central line C is axis of fruit. The two lines DD define diameter of core removed by 2-T Ginaca. Lines EE delimit diameter of core $2^1/_2$ size Ginaca.

moved and pass through other parts of the machine known as the "eradicator."

The bottom of each fruit is removed in another operation of the Ginaca machine and the top is also removed. Approximately one-half inch is cut from the bottom of the fruit and approximately three-fourths inch is

FIG. 52. A GENERAL VIEW OF THE TRIMMING, SLICING AND PACKING DEPARTMENT OF A LARGE HAWAIIAN PINEAPPLE CANNERY

removed from the top. These cuts also contain edible tissues which may be used for beverage juice production. The final operation of the Ginaca machine removes the core from the center of the fruit. The Ginaca machine peels some 90 fruits per minute, removes the ends from them, cuts the edible flesh from the shells and the ends and removes the core from each fruit.

The cores, it will be seen from Fig. 51, contain a considerable amount of longitudinal conducting tissues. Hence, the percentage of juice extracted from cores is somewhat lower than that extractable from the more fleshy portions of the fruit. The cores, however, yield juice of very attractive quality, generally somewhat lower in sugars, lower in acids and in volatile flavoring constituents than from some of the other tissues. The cores contribute "body" as well as flavor to the beverage juice.

Trimming, Slicing, Grading and Packing Operations

Figure 52 is a general view of the trimming and packing department of one of the large Hawaiian pineapple canneries. On the left of the picture are seen trimming tables and on the right are shown the packing tables; separating the two are the slicing machines. One of these is shown in the left foreground of Fig. 51.

The pineapple cylinders are cut from the individual fruits by the Ginaca machines as already noted. These pass onto trimming tables, the detail of which is shown in Fig. 53. Each of the cylinders is hand-trimmed to remove the last traces of shells and blemishes of various sorts. The edible portion of these trimmings may be used as a constituent in juice pro-

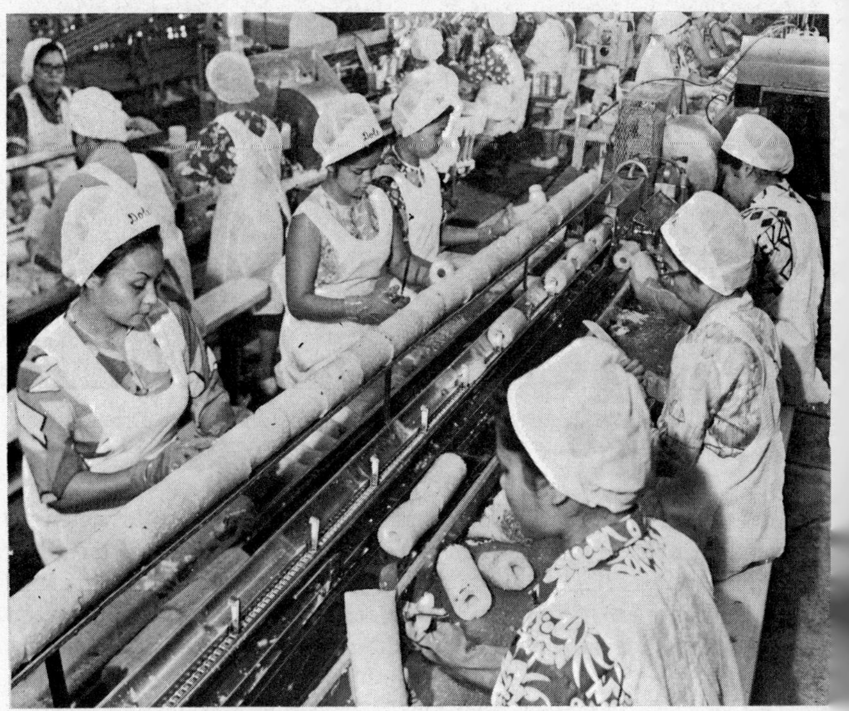

Fig. 53. A Pineapple Trimming Table

duction. The inedible portions are trimmed off and placed on separate belts to be conveyed to by-products manufacture. The trimmed cylinders pass through slicing machines and are carried by conveyors to the packing tables (Fig. 54). At the packing tables, the cylinders which have been sliced are graded visually and are manually packed into the several grades. Slices which have been cut either too thick or too thin, and broken pieces too small to be used in the solid pack, pass over the end of the packing table. From this point they are conveyed either to the crushed department or in part to the beverage juice department.

Fig. 54. A Pineapple Packing Table

HISTORY OF PINEAPPLE JUICE DEVELOPMENT AND OF MACHINERY USED TO PROCESS IT

Pineapple production in the Hawaiian Islands is said to have originated about 1882. However, there are no accurate statistics available prior to 1903. As early as 1903 there existed the desire to develop pineapple beverages, and in that summer a few cans were packed containing juice which separated from "grated pineapple" in the course of its production. Since this product lacked the characteristic pineapple flavor, there was little interest in it.

About 1909, Elton R. Shaw of San Jose, a canner of highgrade specialties, was employed by the Hawaiian Pineapple Company to develop a pineapple juice. This resulted in the introduction of a filtered juice in clear glass bottles under the name of "Dole's Pure Hawaiian Pineapple Juice." During 1910 this product was marketed.

It was withdrawn from the market in 1913 owing to lack of demand. Subsequently, small quantities of pineapple juice consisting of the liquids drained from the crushed pineapple were packed and sold.

During 1909 and 1910, efforts were made to extract beverage juice from pineapple pulp using hydraulic presses under high pressure. This effort was without success, inasmuch as the extraction percentage was exceedingly low. The product was without characteristic pineapple flavor and lacked "body."

In 1932, a renewed effort was made to develop a potable juice derived from the Cayenne pineapple in an effort to stimulate lagging sales of pineapple products. In the spring of 1932, the first successful extraction of a desirable beverage resulted from the work of Simes T. Hoyt and Richard Botley. This process involved the addition to pineapple pulp of substantial quantities of inert, coarse, sharp quartz. The mixture of pulp and quartz when subjected to moderate pneumatic pressures, yielded a pineapple beverage juice of excellent quality. The extraction level was of the magnitude of 90% of the weight of ingoing pulp. Juice flowed freely from the combined pulp and quartz. A part of the process involved the recovery and washing of the quartz for re-use. This pioneering process is no longer used commercially.

In recent years, a number of the producers of pineapple juice have utilized equipment reasonably similar to that designed for tomato juice production. Such equipment, available from canning equipment manufacturers such as FMC Corporation of San Jose, California, is referred to in more detail in succeeding paragraphs.

Sources of Beverage Juice

In general, there are six types of fruit portions or derivatives used in the preparation of commercial pineapple beverage juice. These constituents are derived from various stages in the processing of the solid packs of pineapple. The six common constituents are: (1) cores; (2) juice trimmings; (3) eradicator meat; (4) small fruit; (5) juice drained from crushed pineapple; and (6) juice drained from eradicator meat.

(1) **Cores.**—The cores are removed from the central axis of the individual fruits by the Ginaca machine.

(2) **Juice Trimmings.**—The cylinders of fruit prepared by the Ginaca machine for subsequent trimming and slicing yield portions suitable for juice.

(3) **Eradicator Meat.**—The eradicator meat produced at the Ginaca machine as has been described is employed either totally or in part as a primary constituent of beverage juice.

(4) **Small Fruit.**—Fruit primarily from older ratoons which, owing to small size, is unsuited to the production of slices is generally used as a juice constituent in its entirety.

(5) **Juice Drained from Crushed Pineapple.**—During the cutting or dicing of pineapple tissues in the preparation of crushed pineapple, a surplus of liquids is frequently developed. This excess, if left in the crushed

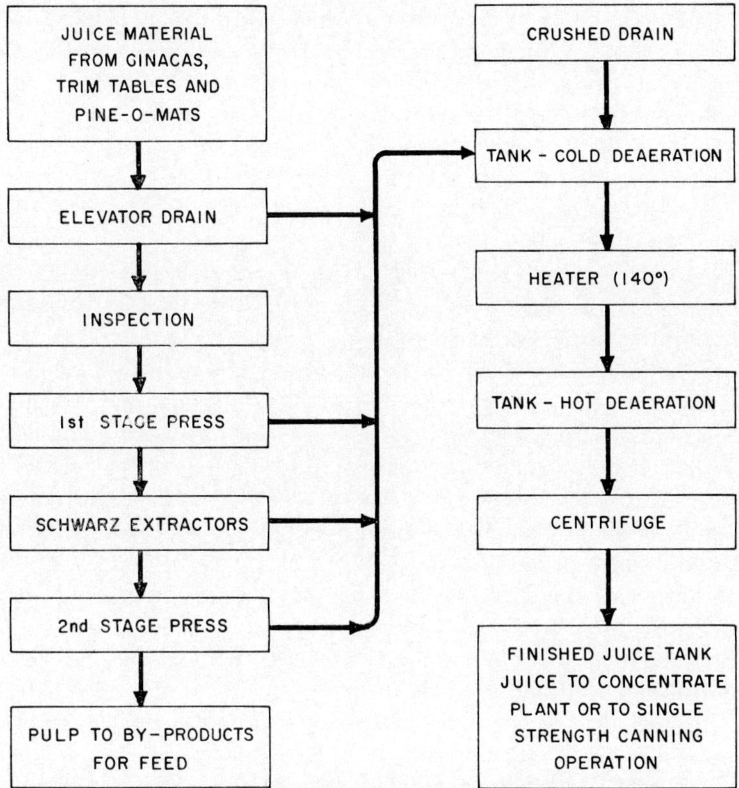

Fig. 55. Flow Chart of a Typical Pineapple Beverage Juice Plant

product, would dilute the solids disproportionately. Therefore, part of this juice is drained to become a component of the beverage juice.

(6) **Juice Drained from Eradicator Meat.**—In the removal of the flesh adhering to the shells, a surplus of juice is developed which can be pumped to the Juice Department to become a constituent of the beverage juice product.

Pineapple Beverage Juice Steps

Figure 55 is a flow chart of a typical pineapple beverage juice plant. It shows the six sources of juice materials noted above.

Liquid Constituents.—The liquid constituents are carried to a holding tank in which they are blended with the juices extracted from the solid portions of the fruits.

Solid Constituents.—In many of the canneries, all of the solid constituents are combined prior to comminution and extraction. An exception is the small fruit of sub-1T size ($3^3/_4$ in. diam and smaller) which are processed in special equipment designed for this purpose by the Citrus Equipment Corporation of Whittier, California.

In this machine, the "Pine-O-Mat," small, ratoon fruits are single-filed and lead into the extractor. Women workers remove defective fruit and those with crowns attached. In the extractor, the fruit is cut in two, then guided between the feed drum and an extraction drum. The extraction drum acts on the skin (shell) to draw the half fruit into a contracting chamber between the extractor drum and perforated grid. In this position the meat is sheared and pressed from the shell, without substantially disrupting the tissues of the inedible portions of the fruit. Thus a clean juice is obtained, low in bacterial count, and high in quality.

A yield of 50–55% of total ingoing fruit weight is possible, and this is as good as obtained on somewhat larger fruits using other extraction devices.

Production from a single machine is up to 150 tons of fruit daily, from which approximately 20,000 gal of juice are derived. Pineapples of several sizes (diameters less than $3^3/_4$ in.) can be commingled and need not be classified prior to processing.

The output of the Pine-O-Mat is a juice-slurry combination which is finished through a No. 300 Finisher (Citrus Equipment Corp.). The resultant juice is low in pulp and may be blended with other juices having a higher content of insoluble solids.

The processing of the solid portions of fruit for beverage purposes is generally accomplished in several successive operations.

Operation 1—Inspection.—Quality inspection of the combined juice constituents is accomplished at a central location.

Operation 2—First Stage Pressing.—A first stage screw press may be used to remove a part of the extractable juice before the fruit tissue is disintegrated. This operation reduces the amount of fine solids that must be removed later in the process in order to produce a palatable juice.

Operation 3—Extraction.—Some canneries use disintegrators for this operation, whereas others use a Schwarz extractor that produces a liquid portion which goes directly to the juice tank and a coarse pulp that is the feed for the second stage presses.

Operation 4—Second Stage Pressing.—Specially designed pressure screw extractors of the general type frequently used in tomato juice production are employed in many canneries to separate the liquids from comminuted solids of pineapple. Other canneries use the slow speed Jones press for their final stage of extraction.

Operation 5—Blending.—The juices from the liquid sources and those expressed from the solid portion of the fruit are blended in large tanks. These tanks serve as cold de-aerators. Since pineapple juice is prone to

Courtesy of Dole Company

FIG. 56. A WESTPHALIA CENTRIFUGE INSTALLATION

foam badly, antifoaming agents are often added at this point in order to facilitate the separation of the entrained air. Some pineapple juice components will oxidize and one canner blankets the extraction equipment and the de-aerating tanks with nitrogen in order to preserve the natural pineapple flavor.

Operation 6—Heating.—The juices derived from whatever source are heated to approximately 140° to 145°F in suitable heat exchangers.

Operation 7—Finishing.—The hot juices are passed into centrifuges to remove the excess of fiber and other material which may have been carried through prior processing steps. Control of the quantity and character of the suspended solids is one of the important operations affecting quality. It is possible by controlling the centrifuge cycle to control both the amount and size distribution of cellular fragments remaining in the beverage juice. These suspended solids are very important in giving body to the juice and have a discernible effect upon flavor perception by the consumer. The centrifuges generally used are the Sharples, Merco, or Westphalia continuous types. A typical installation is shown in Fig. 56.

After centrifuging the juice is generally passed into a blending tank of considerable capacity. The blending tank obviously allows for a mixing

Courtesy of Dole Company

FIG. 57. REFRIGERATED STORAGE TANKS FOR SINGLE STRENGTH JUICE SUPPLY TO CONCENTRATE EVAPORATORS

of the constituents of several lots of fruit having their origin presumably in different ecological situations—these lots, hence, may be of different compositions.

Operation 8—Pasteurizing.—From the blending tank the juice may be handled according to either of two alternative processes. In the first alternative, the juice passes directly into the filling machines and thus is filled at a temperature of approximately 140°F. The filling machines commonly employed are manufactured by the FMC Corp. of San Jose, California.

Following the filling of the juice at a temperature approximating 140° F, the filled cans pass through the usual double seamers and then the juice receives its final pasteurizing in the can. This is generally accomplished by passing the cans through a standard reel cooker and cooler combination. The processing time of the several can sizes is regulated to bring the temperature of the contents to no less than 190°F.

The second alternative procedure for handling the juice during its final

Courtesy of Dole Company

Fig. 58. Pineapple Juice Concentrate Evaporator

pasteurizing is to pump it directly from the centrifuge discharge tank into a flash pasteurizer which heats the product to approximately 195°F. The cans are filled with the juice at this temperature, and the filled cans are conveyed to allow a brief lag of 1 to 3 min prior to cooling them in various types of high-speed coolers.

Users of the cool-fill process favor this process since there is some reason for believing that a greater portion of the volatile flavoring constituents of the juice are preserved by closing the can before elevating the temperature of the juice to the final pasteurizing point.

Pineapple Concentrate

About one third of the pineapple juice produced in Hawaii is converted into concentrate. As is shown in the flow-chart (Fig. 55), the juice used for concentrate production is exactly the same as that used for single strength juice, up to the point following the centrifuge operation. The pineapple concentrate is produced from single strength juice in equipment similar to that used for the production of orange and other fruit juice concentrates. In order to maintain production through a full 24 hr day while the cannery is operating only a few hours, large refrigerated storage tanks (Fig. 57) are used to store the single strength juice supply. The first step in the concentrating operation is to strip out the volatile flavoring materials. These are separated as about a 100 fold product and added back to the final concentrate. The concentrate evaporators (Fig. 58) may either be low temperature or high temperature short retention time types (Smyser 1952; Jefferson and Lloyd 1952).

Pineapple concentrate is produced as a 3 to 1 product which has a Brix of about 46.5°, as a $4^1/_2$ to 1 product with a Brix of 61°, or a 6 to 1 product with a Brix of 72°. The concentrates are produced in both sterile and frozen forms. However, even the sterile product is usually stored and sold under refrigeration in order to preserve quality. Some unsterilized concentrate is held under storage using preservatives to limit microbial action and may be handled in bulk containers. The primary use for concentrate is as an ingredient in blended fruit drinks and fruit juice products. The most important of these blended products is the combination with grapefruit juice.

The canned fruit drink market in 1969 had a volume approximately half the size of that for all canned and bottled fruit juices. The expansion in the drink market has been spurred in those years when freezes in the orange producing area have restricted supplies and increased prices of straight juice products. Another factor that may have influenced growth in the fruit drink area, is the increase in fortification with vitamin C to give the consumer a fruit drink that is comparable to the fruit juices in supplying this essential vitamin. It is also possible with these manufactured products to adjust to individual tastes by providing a sweeter product that may be more appealing to the young consumers.

JUICE COMPOSITION AND DIETETIC PROPERTIES

Pineapple juice is consumed because it is a food product of attractive appearance,of pleasing aroma, and of good flavor, which contains several vitamins and other known and unknown nutritional factors.

Extensive research has been conducted respecting many of the important aroma, flavor, and nutritional constituents. The accumulated information is so voluminous, however, that only a few of the analyses can be referred to herein. Reference will be made to some of the more important nonvolatile and volatile flavoring constituents; to some of the vitamin assays, ash components, and to certain other compounds of general interest.

Table 36

CHEMICAL COMPOSITION OF CANNED PINEAPPLE JUICE

	Minimum	Maximum	Average	Standard Deviation
Soluble solids, %	12.3	16.8	15.2	1.32
Ash, %	0.243	0.452	0.364	0.054
K, mg/100 gm	100	214	164	30.2
P, mg/100 gm	4.0	11.7	6.9	1.7

Source: Osborn (1964).

Table 37

PROXIMATE, MINERAL AND VITAMIN COMPOSITION OF FROZEN PINEAPPLE JUICE

Proximate Composition, %	Maximum	Minimum	Average
Solids	15.1	13.4	13.8
Ash	0.39	0.31	0.35
Ether extract	0.04	0.03	0.03
Protein	0.50	0.36	0.41
Crude fiber	0.19	0.08	0.11
Total carbohydrate	14.3	12.6	13.0
Calories per 100 gm	53	47	49
Minerals, mg/100 gm			
Calcium	12.8	9.0	10.8
Total iron	0.52	0.24	0.32
Phosphorus	9.6	7.6	8.3
Magnesium	10.7	4.6	8.9
Potassium	170	135	143
Sodium	1.0	0.6	0.8
Vitamins, mg/100 gm			
Ascorbic acid	16.6	11.0	13.0
β-Carotene	0.011	0.006	0.009
Folic acid	0.002	0.001	0.001
Niacin	0.29	0.20	0.25
Pantothenic acid	0.157	0.094	0.125
Riboflavin	0.019	0.012	0.016
Thiamine	0.069	0.058	0.066
Vitamin B_6	0.098	0.053	0.074

Source: Burger *et al.* (1956).

The composition of pineapple fruits and, hence, of the juice derived therefrom is known to vary widely as a function of variety, ripeness, season, crop, locale, plant status, weather, fruit portions used, and of blemishes. Additionally, the manner in which the product is processed and stored exerts a profound influence on juice quality as does also the type of container in which the juice is held. Pineapple juice is a semiperishable product and its quality deteriorates on prolonged storage, even at room temperatures.

Chemical Composition

The chemical composition of canned pineapple juice as reported on 27 authentic samples in 1964, is shown in Table 36.

TABLE 38

SUGAR AND ACID CONTENT OF HAWAIIAN PINEAPPLE JUICE

Year	Samples No.	Brix Avg	Brix Std. Dev.	Acid Avg	Acid Std. Dev.
1963	222	14.00	0.49	0.78	0.09
1964	208	14.31	0.71	0.84	0.13
1965	194	13.89	0.63	0.83	0.10
1966	196	14.44	0.73	0.86	0.11
1967	425	14.17	0.76	0.81	0.12
1968	342	14.16	0.50	0.81	0.10
1969	335	14.65	0.69	0.83	0.09

TABLE 39

SUGAR AND ACID CONTENT OF PHILIPPINE PINEAPPLE JUICE

Year	Samples No.	Brix Avg	Brix Std. Dev.	Acid Avg	Acid Std. Dev.
1967	16	12.82	0.38	0.73	0.10
1968	43	12.95	0.28	0.77	0.04
1969	150	12.99	0.34	0.69	0.09

TABLE 40

THE COMPARATIVE PROXIMATE OXALATE CONTENT OF CERTAIN FOOD PRODUCTS

Product	Oxalates % Fresh Weight
Spinach	0.892
Oranges	0.240
Canned Hawaiian pineapple	0.0063
Prunes	0.0058
Peaches	0.0050
Pears	0.0030

Source: Kohman (1939).

A more complete measure of the proximate, mineral and vitamin composition of frozen pineapple juice is shown in Table 37. Pineapple juice is a fair source of ascorbic acid, thiamine, riboflavin and vitamin B_6. It is also a fair source of potassium and is quite low in sodium even though grown in areas close to the ocean. Sodium is usually found at levels less than 100 ppm in processed pineapple juice.

Nonvolatile Acids

Citric acid is the most prevalent of the nonvolatile organic acids occurring in pineapple juice. Malic acid is also present at a level of about 0.2% throughout the last three months of fruit development. Citric acid occurs at a low concentration until the last 60 days, and then increases rapidly to a level several times as high as malic acid (Singleton and Gortner 1965).

Free acid as determined by titration of juice does not measure the total acid present; a variable percentage of it occurs in combined forms. Fruits highest in total acid generally are characterized by the highest concentrations of free acid. Those samples generally also display higher ash contents, but are lower in pH.

The free acid content of Hawaiian pineapple juice averages slightly over 0.80% (Table 38). Studies have shown that consumers tend to discriminate against juice with acidities less than 0.4 or more than 1.0%. It is common practice to use juice with high acidity for the production of concentrate. This product is then utilized in fruit drinks or other diluted products where the high acid level is an economic advantage and sugar can be added to give a desirable flavor balance. Juice from pineapple producing areas that are warmer than Hawaii tend to have lower acid and sugar levels (Table 39).

Ascorbic acid is another important nonvolatile acid constituent of pineapple juice. This acid tends to fluctuate markedly during fruit development and its level does not seem to be directly related to the physiological stage of development. Sunlight and fruit temperatures are implicated in the changes. Winter juice is higher than summer juice in total acid and in ascorbic acid. There are varieties of pineapple that have much higher levels of ascorbic acid than Smooth Cayenne. However, none of these varieties is currently being grown commercially although they do present the opportunity to produce new hybrid types that have levels of ascorbic acid comparable to oranges.

As a result of studies by Clark (1939) it was determined that oxalic acid is usually present in Cayenne pineapple at levels less than 0.01% and probably less than 0.005%. Kohman (1934) came to the conclusion that the concentrations of oxalate in pineapple are so low that it has no physiological importance. Selected data from this study are shown in Table 40.

pH

Pineapple juice is well buffered. The pH of various lots ranges from 3.3 to 3.7. Acid and pH variations in the Cayenne pineapple are discussed by Spiegelberg (1936) in relation to the spoilage of canned pineapple products and by Singleton and Gortner (1965) in a report on chemical changes during fruit development.

Sugars

Singleton and Gortner have studied the changes in sugar composition during the development of pineapple fruit. In the early stages the sucrose level is low and more than 80% of the sugar is present as invert. From this level the reducing sugars decrease during the last 60 days of

TABLE 41

VARIATION IN SUGAR CONTENT OF PINEAPPLE SLICES WITH FRUIT SIZE AND QUALITY

Fruit Type	Samples No.	Brix Average	Standard Deviation
1T Fancy	346	17.9	1.03
2T Fancy	1044	17.5	1.04
2-1/2 Fancy	793	17.1	0.96
1T Choice	346	16.9	0.97
2T Choice	1040	16.2	1.12
2-1/2 Choice	794	16.1	0.96

TABLE 42

A COMPARISON OF RIPENING DATE AND FINAL COMPOSITION OF TWO LOTS OF PINEAPPLE FRUIT

Harvest Date	Translucence (Avg % of Fully Translucent)		Shell-yellowness (Avg % of Full Yellow)		Volatile Esters in Juice (ppm EtOAc)		Pigment in Flesh (ppm Carotene)	
	Older	Younger	Older	Younger	Older	Younger	Older	Younger
July 14	50	28	0	0	5	2	0.88	0.80
July 21	52	48	22	0	5	1	1.12	0.88
July 28	70	48	76	20	51	2	1.91	1.37
Aug. 4	78	72	92	72	161	45	1.95	1.82

Source: Singleton (1965).
Underlined values indicate the comparable stages considered commercially ripe.

fruit development to about 30% with a slight upturn in the final week of ripening. Fully mature Cayenne pineapple therefore contains about two-thirds sucrose and one-third reducing sugars. The reducing sugars are composed of approximately equal amounts of glucose and fructose. During processing of pineapple juice there is some inversion of the sucrose and during storage this inversion continues until the sugar is practically all in the reducing form. Measurements of the sugar composition can be utilized as a means of checking on the age of canned pineapple juice up to the time that it is completely inverted.

A rapid method for measuring the sugar content of pineapple juice is to subtract from the Brix reading a value of three times the per cent acidity. Since the reducing sugar is essentially invert sugar, the optical rotation of clarified juice together with corrected Brix readings can be used to calculate both sucrose and invert sugar. Singleton and Gortner reported that sugars determined by this method compared to the conventional methods gave a correlation coefficient of 0.993.

The sugar content varies markedly in different parts of the same fruit. From top to bottom there will be an increase of about 1° Brix per inch of fruit length. The sugar concentration is also appreciably higher in the areas of the fruit used for the production of slices as contrasted to the

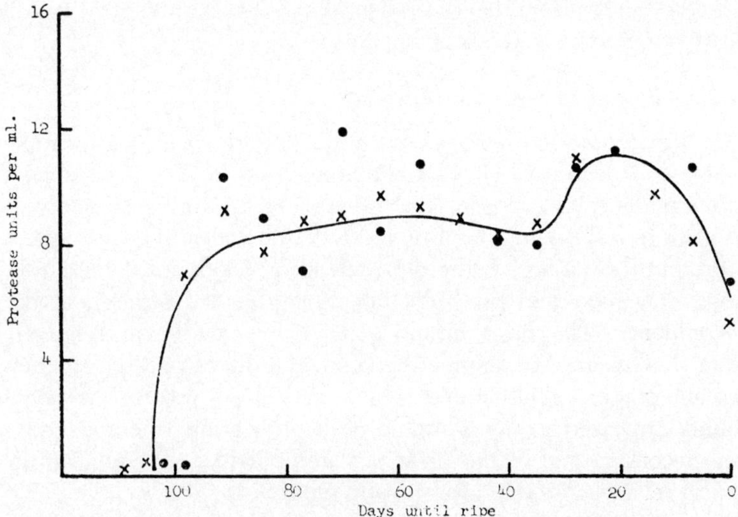

FIG. 59. PROTEASE ACTIVITY (MILK-CLOTTING UNITS PER MILLILITER OF JUICE) DURING FRUIT DEVELOPMENT

areas closer to the shell that are utilized for juice. Sugar concentration on the average is also appreciably higher in small fruit as compared to large. Table 41 shows the extent of this variation in samples gathered throughout a commercial canning season. During the same season the average juice Brix was 14.16.

Pigments

The amount of yellow pigment in pineapple flesh is an excellent measure of quality. The increase in pigment level along with the increases in sugar and volatile flavoring as fruit ripens are quite rapid (Table 42).

Fruit picked too early will be unacceptable in flavor. Some of the ripening changes will continue even after the fruit is removed from the plant; however, the desirable changes take place to a much smaller degree and the sugar level will not improve at all in the separated fruit. The pigments in pineapple have been extensively studied by Gortner (1965) and by Singleton *et al.* (1961). These studies showed that the chlorophyll in the shell of the pineapple decreased very rapidly in the last few days of maturation and at the same time the carotenoid pigments in the flesh of the fruit increased just as rapidly. The carotenoid pigments were shown to contain a high proportion of epoxide groups which are readily isomerized to furanoid forms in contact with acid. It is, therefore, not possible to compare directly pigments in fresh fruit with those in processed fruit. Advantage can be taken of this isomerization to measure quantitatively the amount of bruising that has taken place in the commercial handling of pineapple (Gortner and Singleton 1961).

Nitrogenous and Enzyme Constituents

The nitrogenous and enzyme constituents in developing pineapple fruit have been measured by Gortner and Singleton (1965). A relatively small portion of the total nitrogen is accounted for the form of protein. At 90 days prior to full ripeness slightly more than 0.2 mg/ml of nitrogen was in the protein form whereas the total nitrogen was about 0.9 mg/ml. The changes in amino acid concentration were followed throughout the fruit development. The basic amino acids were present in relatively low amounts. Glycine and alanine increased rapidly during the ripening and senescent stages. Methionine which had been present in only trace amounts appeared in considerable amounts during ripening and senescence becoming one of the principal amino acids. The pineapple flesh was also relatively rich in aspartic and glutamic acids.

About one-half of the protein in pineapple flesh is accounted for by the protease bromelin. The enzyme is not present at all during the early stages of fruit development and then increases very rapidly and stays at a high level until decreasing slightly as the fruit ripens (Fig. 59). Pineapple is unique among fruits in having a high concentration of protease in the ripe fruit. Papayas which are the source of commercial papain, have high levels of enzyme while in the green stage, but become completely inactive when the fruit is fully ripe. Although bromelain is inactivated by heat and, therefore, is not present in canned juice, it is an important pineapple constituent and is being produced from pineapple stems and is finding many uses in the pharmaceutical and food areas. A small amount of bromelain is usually present in concentrated juice. This product is not heated to as great an extent as the canned single strength product. For some concentrate uses a small amount of additional heating is required in order to inactivate completely the protein digesting enzyme.

The other enzyme in pineapple which was studied by Gortner and Singleton was peroxidase. This is present during the early stages of fruit development and gradually decreases in amount as the fruit matures but is still present in moderate quantities in the ripe fruit.

Volatile Flavoring Constituents

No combination of sugars and acids can yield the flavor of pineapple juice. The flavor of pineapple products is owing to a variable mixture of "nonvolatile" and volatile constituents. These differ from season to season and are profoundly affected by relative ripeness, processing, and storage conditions.

TABLE 43

REPORTED VOLATILE PINEAPPLE COMPONENTS
(1945–68)

Ethyl formate[1]	Δ-Octalactone[3]
Methyl acetate[1,2]	Ethyl hexanoate[2,4,5]
γ-Butyrolactone[3]	Methyl 3-hydroxyhexanoate[3]
1-Propyl formate[1]	Ethyl 3-methylthiopropionate[5,8]
Ethyl acetate[1,2,4,5]	Methyl *cis*-4(?)-octenoate[3]
Ethyl acrylate[4]	Methyl octanoate[2,4,5]
1-Butyl formate[1]	Ethyl 3-hydroxyhexanoate[3]
2-Methyl-1-propyl formate[1]	Ethyl octanoate[2]
1-Propyl acetate[1]	Pentyl hexanoate[5]
Ethyl propionate[1]	Methyl 3-acetoxyhexanoate[3]
Methyl butyrate[2]	Ethyl 3-acetoxyhexanoate[3]
Methyl 2-methylpropionate[1]	Formaldehyde[9]
γ-Caprolactone[6]	Acetaldehyde[1,4,9]
Acetoxyacetone[3]	Acetone[1,9]
2-Methyl-1-propyl acetate[1]	2,3-Butanedione[5]
Ethyl butyrate[2,5]	2-Pentanone[4]
Ethyl 2-methylpropionate[1]	Furfural[9]
Methyl pentanoate[4]	5-Hydroxymethylfurfural[9]
Methyl 3-methylbutyrate[4,5]	2,5-Dimethyl-4-hydroxy-2,3-dihydro-3-furanone
Ethyl lactate[5]	
Methyl 3-hydroxybutyrate[3]	Methanol[5]
2-Propyl 2-methylpropionate[1]	Ethanol[1,4,5]
Ethyl 3-methylbutyrate[4]	1-Propanol[5]
Methyl 4-methylpentanoate[4]	2-Methyl-1-propanol[5]
Methyl hexanoate[1,2,5]	1-Pentanol[5]
Dimethyl malonate[3]	*para*-Allyphenol[6]
Methyl 3-methylthiopropionate[5,7,8]	*trans*-Tetrahydro-α,α,5-trimethyl-5-vinylfurfuryl alcohol[3]
γ-Octalactone[3]	

[1] Howard and Hoffman (1967).
[2] Mori 1963 (see Connell 1964).
[3] Creveling *et al.* (1968).
[4] Haagen-Smit *et al.* (1945*b*).
[5] Connell (1964).
[6] Silverstein *et al.* (1965).
[7] Haagen-Smit *et al.* (1945*a*).
[8] Rodin *et al.* (1966).
[9] Gawler (1962).
[10] Rodin *et al.* (1965).

The first significant information on the volatile flavoring constituents in pineapple was gathered by Haagen-Smit (1946) and Haagen-Smit *et al.* (1945A and B). These investigators identified a number of the more prominent components in pineapple flavor. These components were largely esters. A unique sulfur containing ester was identified as methyl 3-methylthiopropionate. This identification has been confirmed by other investigators including Rodin *et al.* (1966) who found also the corresponding ethyl ester. Although these sulfur containing volatile compounds are unique, it is not felt that they are very significant contributors to the typical pineapple aroma. Haagen-Smit and coworkers came to the conclusion that the esters in summer fruit were primarily ethyl whereas winter fruit was primarily methyl. Recent work has shown that this conclusion is not valid. Both methyl and ethyl esters of the same acids are found in all pineapple. As a general rule the ethyl esters are

TABLE 44

ESTER COMPONENTS OF PINEAPPLE ESSENCE

1. Methyl acetate	18. Methyl pentanoate
2. Ethyl acetate	19. Ethyl pentanoate
3. 2-Propyl acetate	20. Methyl hexanoate
4. 1-Propyl acetate	21. Methyl 3-hydroxyhexanoate
5. 2-Methyl-1-propyl acetate	22. Methyl 3-hexanoate
6. 3-Methyl-1-butyl acetate	23. Ethyl hexanoate
7. 2-Methyl-1-butyl acetate	24. Ethyl 3-hydroxhexanoate
8. Methyl propionate	25. Methyl 3-acetoxyhexanoate
9. Methyl 2-methyl propionate	26. Ethyl 3-acetoxyhexanoate
10. Ethyl propionate	27. Methyl heptanoate
11. Methyl 3-methylthiopropionate	28. Ethyl heptanoate
12. Ethyl 3-methylthiopropionate	29. Methyl octanoate
13. Methyl butyrate	30. Ethyl octanoate
14. Methyl 2-methylbutyrate	31. Diethyl carbonate
15. Ethyl butyrate	32. Dimethyl malonate
16. Ethyl 2-methyl butyrate	33. Ethyl benzoate
17. Ethyl 3-methyl butyrate	

Source: Flath and Forrey (1970).

present in higher concentrations but the flavor intensity of the related methyl esters is greater so that both types are appreciable contributions to pineapple aroma.

The most comprehensive study of the volatile components of Smooth Cayenne pineapple has been reported by Flath and Forrey (1970). Their summary of compounds reported between 1945 and 1968 on constituents of pineapple essence are listed in Table 43. They were able to identify 45 components including 21 which had not been reported previously. This work was carried out on an isopentane extract of pineapple essence and the resulting extract was examined by combination gas chromatography, mass spectrometry.

Thirty-three of the identified compounds were esters and they are listed in Table 44 grouped according to their acid components. It will be noted that this list tends to disprove the early hypothesis advanced by Haagen-Smit that the pineapple esters were products of amino acid metabolism. It also casts some doubts on the hypothesis that the acids are formed by a β-oxidation of a C_{10} or larger fatty acid. However, the C_2, C_4, C_6 and C_8 acids are present in larger quantities than the acids with an odd number of carbon atoms. Ethyl acetate appears to be the end product in the metabolic chain involved in pineapple ester synthesis and its level becomes extremely high in overripe fruit. The relative relationship between major ester components in two commercial essence samples is shown in Table 45. The methyl and ethyl decanoate shown in this table may have been erroneously identified, since more refined studies have failed to confirm their presence in pineapple essence.

The alcohol and miscellaneous components identified by Flath and Forrey are listed in Table 46. Probably the most interesting feature of this

TABLE 45

APPROXIMATE RELATIVE AMOUNTS OF MAJOR PINEAPPLE ESSENCE COMPONENTS

Component	Commercial Essence A	Commercial Essence B
Ethyl acetate	61.1	27.9
Methyl butyrate	3.4	4.0
Ethyl butyrate	3.6	5.3
Methyl hexanoate	1.2	0.7
Ethyl hexanoate	1.2	0.7
Methyl octanoate	12.9	26.6
Ethyl octanoate	10.0	23.9
Methyl decanoate	1.2	4.5
Ethyl decanoate	5.4	6.4
Total	100	100

TABLE 46

ALCOHOL AND MISCELLANEOUS COMPONENTS OF PINEAPPLE ESSENCE

1. Isopentane (solvent)	7. 2-Methylbutan-1-ol
2. Benzene	8. 2-Methyl-3-buten-2-ol
3. 3-Pentanone	9. 2-Methyl-1-propanol
4. 1,1-Diethoxyethane	10. Linaloöl
5. Ethanol	11. Terpinen-4-ol
6. 3-Methylbutan-1-ol	12. α-Terpineol

Source: Flath and Forrey (1970).

work was the identification of three terpene alcohols, linalool, α-terpineol and terpinen-4-ol. They also separated a number of compounds that they have not been able to identify including some with molecular weights in the sesquiterpene region. The sensitive methods utilized by Flath and Forrey can be employed to identify components in the essence from a single fruit and hence this technique may be of considerable value in studying new varieties that have unique flavor components.

Four compounds which had been previously reported in pineapple, were tested by Flath and Forrey and found to be unstable in the equipment that they used. These compounds were ethyl lactate, 2,5-dimethyl-4-hydroxy-2,3-dihydro-3-furanone, 5-hydroxymethyl-furfural and *para*-allylphenol. The high-boiling, unstable compound 2,5-dimethyl-4-hydroxy-2,3-dihydro-3-furanone was first identified by Rodin *et al.* (1965) and was found to have a very intense odor described as "burnt pineapple." This compound has since been reported as being a flavor constituent of beef broth by Tonsbeek *et al.* (1968). The instability of important flavor components undoubtedly accounts for some of the difference in taste between fresh and processed pineapple products. In addition the esters tend to slowly hydrolyze during storage.

A substantial percentage of the volatile flavoring elements of pineapple juice is frequently lost in the commercial disintegration, extraction, heating and centrifuging of it. A factory survey indicated that some 20 to 30% of the "essence" is lost if appropriate precautions are not taken to prevent the losses. In general, processing should be done in closed systems at as low temperatures as are practical.

Pineapple does not have a single component that accounts for most of the characteristic flavor. Even the total volatile flavor fraction is not easily recognized as being distinctly pineapple although it does have a fruity character. On the other hand the pineapple residue from which the volatiles have been stripped is always identifed as being pineapple. However, the addition of the distilled essence to the stripped base gives a superior product. The volatile flavor components in processed pineapple products cover up the cooked flavor and are important contributions to high quality pineapple juice. This observation stresses the importance of storing and handling pineapple juice under conditions that will retain a maximum of its desirable flavor constituents.

BIBLIOGRAPHY

BURGER, M., HEIN, L. W., TEPLEY, L., DERSE, P. H., and KRIEGER, C. H. 1956. Vitamin, mineral and proximate composition of frozen fruits, juices, and vegetables. J. Agr. Food Chem. *4*, 418–425.

CITRUS EQUIPMENT CORPORATION. 1960. Unpublished personal communications. Winter Haven, Fla.

CLARK, H. E. 1939. Oxalates in pineapples. Food Research *4*, 75–79.

COLLINS, J. L. 1958. Medical and dietetic properties of the pineapple. Bromeliad Soc. Bull. *8*, 84–86.

COLLINS, J. L. 1960. The Pineapple. Interscience Publishers, New York.

CONNELL, D. W. 1964. Volatile flavoring constituents of the pineapple. (I. Some esters, alcohols, and carbonyl compounds). Australian J. Chem. *17*, 130–140.

CREVELING, R. K., SILVERSTEIN, R. M., and JENNINGS, W. G. 1968. Volatile components of pineapple. J. Food Sci. *33*, 284–287.

FLATH, R. A., and FORREY, R. R. 1970. Volatile components of Smooth Cayenne pineapple. J. Agr. Food Chem. *18*, 306–309.

GAWLER, J. H. 1962. Constituents of canned Malayan pineapple juice (I. Amino-acids, non-volatile acids, sugars, volatile carbonyl compounds and volatile acids). J. Sci. Food Agr. *13*, 57–61.

GORTNER, W. A. 1965. Chemical and physical development of the pineapple fruit. IV. Plant pigment constituents. J. Food Sci. *30*, 30–32.

GORTNER, W. A. and SINGLETON, V. L. 1961. Carotenoid pigments of pineapple fruit. II. Influence of fruit ripeness, handling and processing of pigment isomerization. J. Food Sci. *26*, 53–55.

GORTNER, W. A., and SINGLETON, V. L. 1965. Chemical and physical development of the pineapple fruit. III. Nitrogenous and enzyme constituents. J. Food Sci. *30*, 24–29.

HAAGEN-SMIT, A. J. 1946. Flavor studies on pineapple. Am. Perfumer Essent. Oil Rev. *1946*, 62–69.

HAAGEN-SMIT, A. J., KIRCHNER, J. G., DEASY, C. L., and PRATER, A. N. 1945A. Chemical studies of pineapple (*Ananas sativas* Lind.). II. Isolation and identification of a sulfur containing ester in pineapple. J. Am. Chem. Soc. *67*, 1651–1652.

HAAGEN-SMIT, A. J., KIRCHNER, J. G., PRATER, A. N., and DEASY, C. L. 1945B. Chemical studies of pineapple (*Ananas sativas* Lind.). I. The volatile flavor and odor constituents of pineapple. J. Am. Chem. Soc. *67*, 1646–1650.

HAAGEN-SMIT, A. J., STRICKLAND, A. G. R., JEFFREYS, G. E. P., and KIRCHNER, J. G. 1946. Studies on the vitamin content of canned pineapple. Food Research *11*, 142–147.

HOWARD, G. E., and HOFFMAN, A. 1967. A study of the volatile flavoring constituents of canned Malayan pineapple. J. Sci. Food Agr. *18*, 106–110.

JEFFERSON, H. D., and LLOYD, R. H. 1952. The world's largest plant for freezing pineapple juice. Refrig. Eng. *60*, 1167–1171.

KOHMAN, E. F. 1934. Organic acids and acid-base relationship. Oxalic acid in foods. J. Am. Dietet. Assoc. *10*, 100–106.

KOHMAN, E. F. 1939. Oxalic acid in foods and its behavior and fate in the diet. J. Nutr. *18*, 233–246.

OSBORN, R. A. 1964. Chemical composition of fruit and fruit juices. J. Assoc. Offic. Agr. Chemists *47*, 1068–1086.

RODIN, J. O., COULSON, D. M., SILVERSTEIN, R. M., and LEEPER, R. W. 1966. Volatile flavor and aroma components of pineapple. III. The sulfur-containing components. J. Food Sci. *31*, 721–725.

RODIN, J. O., HIMEL, C. M., SILVERSTEIN, R. M., LEEPER, R. W., and GORTNER, W. A., 1965. Volatile flavor and aroma components of pineapple. I. Isolation and tentative identification of 2,5-dimethyl-4-hydroxy-3(2H)-furanone. J. Food Sci. *30*, 280–285.

SILVERSTEIN, R. M., RODIN, J. O., HIMEL, C. M., and LEEPER, R. W. 1965. Volatile flavor and aroma components of pineapple. II. Isolation and identification of chavicol and α-caprolactone. J. Food Sci. *30*, 668–672.

SINGLETON, V. L. 1965. Chemical and physical development of the pineapple fruit. I. Weight per fruitlet and other physical attributes. J. Food Sci. *30*, 98–104.

SINGLETON, V. L., and GORTNER, W. A., 1965. Chemical and physical development of the pineapple fruit. II. Carbohydrate and acid constituents. J. Food Sci. *30*, 19–23.

SINGLETON, V. L., GORTNER, W. A., and YOUNG, H. Y 1961. Carotenoid pigments of pineapple fruit. I. Acid-catalyzed isomerization of the pigments. J. Food Sci., *26*, 49–52.

SMYSER, A. A. 1952. Dole launches frozen concentrated pineapple juice. Food Eng. *24*, No. 8, 72–73, 169, 170, 172.

SPIEGELBERG, C. H. 1936. Acid and pH variations in *Ananas comosus* Merr. in relation to swells caused by *Clostridium Sp. J. Bacteriol. 31*, 85.

TONSBEEK, C. H. T., PLANCKEN, A. J., and v. D. WEERHOF, T. 1968. Components contributing to beef flavor. Isolation of 4-hydroxy-5-methyl-3 (2H)-furanone and its 2,5-dimethyl homolog from beef broth. J. Agr. Food Chem. *16*, 1016–1021.

CHAPTER 6

J. C. Moyer
and H. C. Aitken

Apple Juice

INTRODUCTION—JUICE APPLES

Commercial production of canned and bottled apple juice started in North America about 1937 but had developed earlier in Europe. In North America, it did not enjoy the rapid growth of some other juices but has gradually increased in importance until it now constitutes a substantial portion of the fruit juice pack (see Chapter 1). Apple juice is generally understood to be sweet cider that has been treated by some method to prevent spoilage as long as the can, bottle or other type of container is kept hermetically sealed. Sweet cider is generally thought of as the product sold fresh without any permanent preservative treatment.

Owing to the relatively low price obtained for apple juice and to the fact that it is a by-product, the manufacturer is limited to those varieties that are surplus and to such quantities of available varieties that are classed as second grade or culls. In the early days of apple juice production, little attention was paid to the maturity or quality of the fruit used in the production of juice; actually in some cases it was thought that some rotten apples were necessary to give the finished product a "cider flavor." This has changed. All successful manufacturers now stress proper maturity and specify a definite quality of apples. In the United States the quality of apples used for juice is subject to regulations under the Federal Food, Drug and Cosmetic Act, while in Canada the apples are subject to inspection by the Dominion Department of Agriculture.

Soundness

A satisfactory apple juice cannot be made from wholly or partially decayed fruit. A very small proportion of such apples will influence the flavor of a large quantity of juice. Some rots have a very strong "moldy" flavor. To make a top-ranking product great care must be taken to make certain that no decayed or partially decayed apples are ground for pressing.

The common blemishes and defects, other than rots, seem to have little effect on the quality of juice. External worm stings, small scab spots and

---

Dr. James C. Moyer is Professor, Food Science and Technology, N.Y.S. Agricultural Experiment Station, Cornell University, Geneva, New York.

Mr. Herbert C. Aitken is Manager, Ashner Food Products, Ltd., Mississauga, Ontario, Canada.

aphid injury do not noticeably change the quality of the final juice. Sometimes slightly blemished and deformed apples give a juice that has slightly higher specific gravity than that from normal apples. This can be partially attributed to the fact that such abnormal apples are usually somewhat more mature than normal apples at the same date.

Maturity

The maturity of the apples is important not only for its influence on the quality of the finished juice but also because of its effect on the economy of plant operations.

Immature apples produce an unsatisfactory juice, lacking in apple flavor and have a "starchy" or "green-apple" taste. The juice tends to be acid and astringent in character and lacking in sweetness and body. These characteristics are due to the high percentage of starch in the immature apples. As the fruit matures this starch changes into sugars with a resulting improvement in the quality of the apple juice.

Overmature apples give a low yield of poor quality juice, lacking in flavor. They are also very difficult to press as the full press cloths tend to slip under pressure in the press. Another difficulty with overmature fruit is that the pressed pomace tends to adhere to the press cloths making cleaning very difficult. This slows down the whole pressing operation. Juice from overmature apples is also more difficult to clarify and filter. The low yield, difficulty of pressing and difficulty of clarifying or filtering all combine to make overmature apples uneconomical for juice purposes.

Varietal Suitability.—Generally, with the exception of the very early or "summer" apples, most of the varieties of apples grown in North America can be used for making a saleable apple juice. Most varieties do not make a satisfactory juice when used singly but are excellent when blended with other varieties. In most cases, processors distribute their products over an area where consumer tastes for apple juice correspond closely to that of the taste of the varieties of apples available.

In any given area a good general blending rule is to make apple juice from a combination of not less than three varieties that are at approximate "eating" maturity. If and when large quantities of a single variety are received they should be stored separately for future mixing with other varieties at grinding time, or they can be dumped into bins with other varieties to make an approximate blend at once. It is much easier to blend the apples than it is to keep the juices separate from each variety and combine them later for a blend.

Each apple producing area has its own favorite juice apples. Varieties vary greatly in their juice characteristics which vary from one region to another. An outstanding example of this variation is the McIntosh variety which is considered a juice apple of mediocre quality in most of the eastern part of North America but seems to make satisfactory juice in Quebec and the western part of the continent.

Apple juice that is acceptable in one area may be considered poor in another. Apple juice made in Virginia tastes flat and rather insipid to a consumer in Pennsylvania or New York where more acid juices are favored. Pennsylvania juice tastes sweet and flat to a consumer in Nova Scotia where a still more acid juice is common. A Nova Scotia juice would taste almost like vinegar to a consumer of Virginia apple juice. Generally, a Western apple juice tastes somewhat flat and sweet to eastern consumers while Eastern juice tastes sharp and acid to western consumers. The same general relationship holds for Southern and Northern juices.

Fabian and Marshall (1935) classified varieties into five classes as shown in Table 47.

TABLE 47

VARIETIES GROWN IN MICHIGAN, CLASSIFIED FOR BLENDING PURPOSES

Group I Acid to Sub-acid	Group II Sub-acid to Mild	Group III Aromatic	Group IV Astringent	Group V Neutral
Duchess	Jonathan	Delicious	All Crab Apples	Stark
Yellow Transparent	Baldwin	McIntosh		Ben Davis
Wolf River	Wagener	Snow		Gano
Gideon	Wealthy			
Maiden Blush	Northern Spy			
Northwestern Greening	Rhode Island Greening			
Red Astrachan	Grimes			
Alexander	Hubbardson			
	King			
	Winter Banana			
	Canada Red			
	Chenango			
	Golden Russet			
	Winesap			
	Opalescent			
	Seek-no-further			
	Fall Pippin			
	King David			
	Fallawater			

Source: Fabian and Marshall (1935).

Referring to the table they suggest that any of the varieties listed in Groups II and III make a very good apple juice without the addition of any other varieties but, such juice will be improved by the addition of about five per cent of any of the varieties in Group IV. Group III apples supply a spicy agreeable flavor and Group IV apples will add astringency. Varieties in Group I do not make very good juice, being generally too acid.

Juice from these varieties should be blended with 10 to 20% of juice from Group II or III or both, to dilute the acidity and then add some of Group IV. Varieties in Group V, being neutral, can be used for reducing acidity and should be mixed with Group I. Juice from apples in Group IV and V alone is not a good product and should be blended with other juices.

Charley and Harrison (1939) emphasize that the flavor of an apple juice is based on two factors: (a) sugar-acid balance and (b) aroma or bouquet. The juices from different varieties will vary with respect to these two characteristics. They maintain that the major differences will be in relative sharpness or sweetness of the different juices and that the actual apple character of the juice will be more constant. By carefully blending to give a relatively constant acid-sugar balance variations in actual apple flavor will not be very noticeable.

Clague and Fellers (1936) emphasize the fact that there is no rule for blending that will prove infallible. Factors to be considered in blending according to these workers are the degrees Brix, the tannin content, the total acidity and a factor not stressed by other investigators, namely the pH.

A general observation that covers the position of most apple juice manufacturers is that they take what apples are available from the growers. In some cases it is possible to maintain a limited control over the varieties delivered but more generally the deliveries are mixed varieties. This is a good thing because it avoids the problem of single variety juice. The ideal situation for any juice packer would be to have complete control of all the necessary apples and schedule the deliveries of the varieties so that a proper and uniform blend could be maintained at all times. Where necessary certain varieties could be held in cold storage and withdrawn as required to complete the blend. Generally it is not economical to store "juice" apples because the narrow margin of profit in the final product will not allow for the additional expense. Where a processor packs canned apples or apple sauce it is possible to keep a juice plant operating for a lengthy season by using the "juice" apples sorted from the processing apples that have been cold stored.

JUICE PREPARATION

Washing

The use of a leaf-eliminator section in a conveyor previous to the storage bins, or at least previous to washing and sorting, prevents the accumulation of leaves and grass in the plant. Where large quantities of drops or windfall apples are used the leaf-eliminator is a necessity to prevent leaves and grass being ground up with the apples. A high proportion of leaves or grass ground up with the apples causes an off-flavor in the juice. In one plant the leaf-eliminator was placed on a platform outside the plant and all apples as received had to pass over it. While this meant that all leaves and grass were removed outside the plant it also meant that all the apples could be observed for condition by plant personnel as well as by the trucker. Poor apples could be removed immediately, returned to the truck and weighed back to the grower.

Before apples are used for juice they should be thoroughly washed to remove all adhering dirt. This washing may be done by dumping the apples into troughs of moving water in which they are conveyed into the plant, after which they are separated from the water and given a final spray-wash on a roller type conveyor. They may be washed by strong water sprays as they move along a roller type conveyor. Or as is done on the Swiss type washer, receive a soak plus a thorough rinse as they move through a vertical worm conveyor on the way to the grinder.

In areas where spray residues are heavy, extra precautions must be taken to assure the removal of the chemicals. Special washers that operate with hydrochloric acid solutions are available or can be built for the removal of lead and arsenate residues. Generally, little difficulty can be expected from spray residues because a large proportion of the material remains on the pomace and is not carried in the juice.

Sorting

Sorting the apples to remove all partially or wholly decayed fruit is possibly the most important operation in the production of a first quality apple juice. It should be noted that even a few partially decayed apples can impart a characteristic "rotten" apple flavor to a large volume of juice. The days when any apple, complete with adhering dirt and showing numerous rot spots, could be used for making apple juice have long since passed. Quality juice can only be made from carefully selected quality fruit.

One manufacturer of high quality apple juice in Pennsylvania used three men to sort the apples as they were transferred from the grower's truck to the holding bins and then four women sorters to inspect the apples again as they travelled to the apple grinder. While this may seem extreme, yet it was probably the most important single factor in the production of an outstanding apple juice.

Grinding

The washed and sorted apples are elevated to the equipment that reduces them to a pulp suitable for juice extraction. Two types of equipment are most commonly used for this process, one type grates the apples to a pulp, the other type is a hammer mill. The former type of equipment is most common in Europe but is now being introduced into North America. The hammer mill or similar equipment has been most common in North America. Regardless of the type of equipment used, care must be taken to see that the apples are reduced to the proper consistency for economical juice extraction. If the pulp contains too many large pieces of apple, the yield of juice will be low but the juice will be relatively low in suspended solids. If the pulp is too fine and "soupy," pressing will be difficult and the juice will contain a high percentage of finely divided solids. As there are several methods for extracting the juice from apples, some of them very new, it is necessary for the operator to determine the exact method of grinding the apples to give the most economical operation with his particular type of extraction equipment. The hammer-mill type of equipment is easily adjusted by changing speed and/or the size of the openings in the screen. Some of the grater types of equipment are not easily adjusted and therefore may be only suitable for certain types of extraction equipment.

Juice Extraction

This step in the manufacture of apple juice has always been the most laborious and most unattractive of all the steps in the complete process. Because of this, there has always been great interest in developing more satisfactory methods of extracting the juice from apples. The most commonly used methods are: (1) hydraulic cider press; (2) pneumatic fruit juice press; (3) continuous screw-type press; (4) a continuous plate press; (5) a horizontal basket press; (6) a screening centrifuge.

(1) **Hydraulic Press.**—This is the old-fashioned method of pressing out apple juice. With this method two sets of accessories are necessary, namely, cider press cloths and cider press racks.

Cider press cloths are large coarsely woven cloths varying in size with the press for which they are required. They vary in size from about 36 inches to as large as 90 inches square. The cloths are made of cotton, wool or nylon. The latter material is the most satisfactory as it is very light, very strong, easy to clean, nonabsorbent and resistant to stains and mildew. The nylon or related material used for cider press cloths should be "heat-set" so that it will not harden when washed in hot water during cleaning.

Press racks are square lattices of wooden slats varying in total dimension according to the press for which they are required. The wooden slats are approximately three-quarters of an inch wide by one quarter of

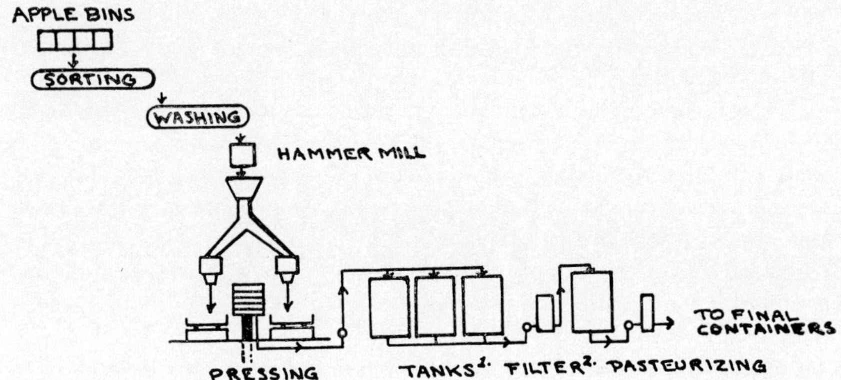

FIG. 60. FLOW SHEET FOR MAKING APPLE JUICE USING HYDRAULIC PRESSES

(1) Used for holding or treating juice; (2) centrifuge may be substituted for filter.

an inch thick and are spaced about one quarter of an inch apart. The outer slat on each side is usually about three inches wide for added strength. The top surface of each slat should be rounded for easy cleaning and rapid draining. The usual wood used for racks is either elm or poplar, although oak has proved very strong and durable. In all cases a coat of chemical resistant varnish on the racks will make them nonabsorbent and more easily cleaned. Nails used for the racks should be brass or, preferably stainless steel.

In loading a press, a rack is placed in the press truck; a form or bottomless box (slightly smaller than the rack) is placed on the rack; a press cloth is placed on the rack so that the corners hang over the sides of the form and then sufficient apple pulp is allowed to run on to the cloth so that the evenly spread depth of apple pulp fills the volume of the form. The apple pulp is then wrapped up in the cloth by foldng the corners across the top. Another rack is then placed on the filled cloth and the whole process repeated until a sufficient number of "cheeses" have been made for the capacity of the press. The truckload of "cheeses" is then pushed under the press and pressure is applied (Fig. 60).

The quantity of apple pulp loaded into each cloth varies with the plant and the condition and type of apples. The quantity to use is established by experience. Ripe apples require the use of thinner layers than hard apples. Thinner layers give higher juice yields but a lower production rate than thick layers. Whatever the amount used it should be uniform throughout the whole truckload of "cheeses" to insure efficient pressing and to avoid slipping under pressure. While some plants leave the quantity of pulp to the judgment of the operators, others have developed measuring devices that eliminate the chance of uneven loading. Some of these devices operate on a volumetric principle while others operate on a weight principle.

The usual cider press is operated by hydraulic pressure using very compact electric oil pumps in two stages. In the first stage the pressure is applied rapidly to about 500 to 700 psi on the ram and the free-run juice is pressed out rapidly. During the second stage the pressure is increased very slowly until it reaches 2500 to 3000 psi on the ram. When the pressure reaches the desired maximum an automatic valve maintains it at that point until released by the operator, or some automatic timing device. The average pressing cycle for single press is 20 to 30 min. The actual time under pressure has to be determined by the operating conditions in the plant and is affected by production and yield desired. When the juice has been pressed from the pulp, the pressure is released and the truck pushed from under the press. Another truck is immediately placed in position for pressing.

European presses have been designed somewhat differently to those in North America. It is claimed that this difference in design gives a higher yield of juice and higher labor efficiency. The large presses of this design have two separate presses for the two stages of pressure. These presses operate on the turntable principle with the platforms carrying the trucks moving around a center post. A press load is built up of racks and filled cloths and is placed in the first or low pressure press. As this load is moved to the first press another platform or truck comes into position for loading. When this load is completed it is placed under the first press and the partially pressed load is moved on to the second or high pressure press. When another load is completed it moves to stage one and the others also move bringing the finished load into position for unloading and reloading. The loading station is supported on a hydraulic jack which allows the working level to be adjusted to suit the press-men.

In all cases the pressed apple pomace is removed from the cloths by shaking and the cloths set aside until needed for refilling. The pomace is then discarded, or dried for pectin manufacture or cattle feed. Some good results have been obtained by using the wet pomace as cattle feed, either fresh or as silage if free of pesticides.

When overmature apples are pressed it is often difficult to shake the pomace from the cloths. This difficulty can be reduced by the use of diatomaceous earth or filter aid. The filter aid is scattered over the press cloth before it is loaded with apple pulp or the filter aid may be incorporated continuously at the hammer mill by some automatic feeding device. The filter aid forms a layer between the pomace and the cloth

Courtesy of Hubert Stollenwerk

FIG. 61. WILLMES PRESSER

and prevents the pomace from sticking. Another advantage is that a slightly higher in yield of clearer juice is obtained when filter aid is used. Still another advantage is that there is less tendency for the "cheese" to slip when filter aid is used. The correct quantity of filter aid to use can only be determined by actual test under operating conditions.

(2) **Pneumatic Press.**—The Willmes Presser (Fig. 61) is essentially a horizontal, cylindrical screen, lined with press cloth material, within which there is a large rubber tube which can be inflated by compressed air. The inflated inner tube exerts pressure on the material to be pressed when it is present in a layer between screen and tube. After the fruit pulp is filled into the press, the whole assembly is revolved as the air is admitted. This spreads an even layer of pulp between the rubber tube and the screen. Pressure on the tube reaches a maximum of 6 atmospheres or approximately 90 psi.

For pressing apple pulp some adjunct is needed to give free draining and to prevent the pressed apple pulp or pomace from adhering to the inner cloth. The most satisfactory material for this purpose is cleaned rice hulls. However, a good grade of well disintegrated wood pulp will work well but is more absorbent.

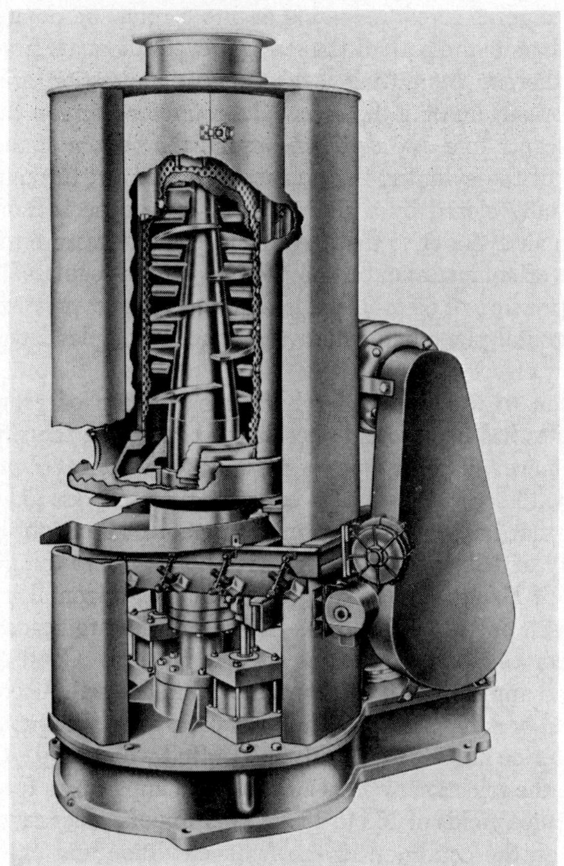

Courtesy of Jones Div., Beloit Corp.

FIG. 62. A CONTINUOUS SCREW PRESS COMMONLY USED FOR PRESSING APPLES

(3) **Continuous Screw Press.**—As long ago as 1928 Warcollier reported that a continuous screw press had been used in Normandy to reduce the labor associated with the hydraulic pressing of apples. However until recently the use of a continuous screw press with apples has not been successful because of low juice yields and large amounts of suspended solids in the juice, although its use has been widespread in the manufacture of grape and other juices. These difficulties have been overcome through changes in press design, use of press aids, and newer methods of solids separation from the juice.

A continuous screw press commonly used for pressing apples in the United States is shown in Fig. 62. A mixture of finely ground apples and press aid is fed into the top of the press and is gradually propelled downwards by a tapered screw revolving at 3 to 5 rpm. Stationary paddles or interrupter bars in the path of the screw prevent the mass from slipping on the screw thereby permitting a continued compression of the pomace. The cylinder surrounding the screw is a reinforced screen through which the juice escapes to a drainage pan around the bottom of the screen. At the bottom of the cylinder, the pomace is forced out through an annulus that is partially closed by a sliding cone. The cone is mounted on the piston of an air cylinder so that by varying the air pressure to the cylinder the amount of compression on the pomace can be regulated. Usually an air supply pressure of 80 to 90 psi is required. Screw presses that operate in the horizontal plane and utilize the above principles have been found to be equally effective.

In addition to the interrupter bars, the addition of press aid to the ground apples has been found necessary to overcome the slippery nature of apple pomace. Various types of press aids or mixtures of press aids have been used with screw presses. A common type of press aid is a purified wood pulp that has been fluffed in a hammer or attrition mill to give a bulk density of 1 lb/cu ft. This press aid is added to the ground apples at the rate of $1^1/_2$ to 4% as the pulp enters a horizontal mixing trough equipped with open-loop paddles. These paddles are spaced around the shaft to form a helix that revolves at 50 to 60 rpm. Good mixing of the press aid and apple pulp is usually achieved in 45 sec. Rice hulls and extracted wood bark have also been used as press aids. Frequently a mixture of 0.5 to 1% rice hulls is used with 2% fluffed wood pulp. Care must be exercised in the selection of press aids to avoid imparting a foreign flavor to the juice. Juice yields of 165 to 185 gal per ton of apples may be obtained depending on the condition of the fruit, condition and amount of press aid used. The suspended solids content of the juice range from 2 to 6%.

(4) **Continuous Plate Press.**—The Willmes Co. has recently introduced a press in which a layer of apple pulp is squeezed between moving vertical plates. A mixture of apple pulp and press aid is spread on a horizontal nylon belt having a weave similar to that used for press cloths on hydraulic presses. As the belt moves forward the outer edges are brought together by converging chains to form a continuous U-shaped pocket before it passes between vertical panels attached to heavy roller type chains. The sprockets supporting the chain are adjusted to that increasingly greater pressure is exerted on the pulp. The juice flows out between the plates and is collected in a pan beneath the press. At the other end of the press the cloth belt diverges until it passes over horizontal rollers for pomace discharge and cleaning before return to the point of feed. The rate of pulp feed to the press should be carefully controlled to insure the optimum thickness of cake between the plates. In one installation of a

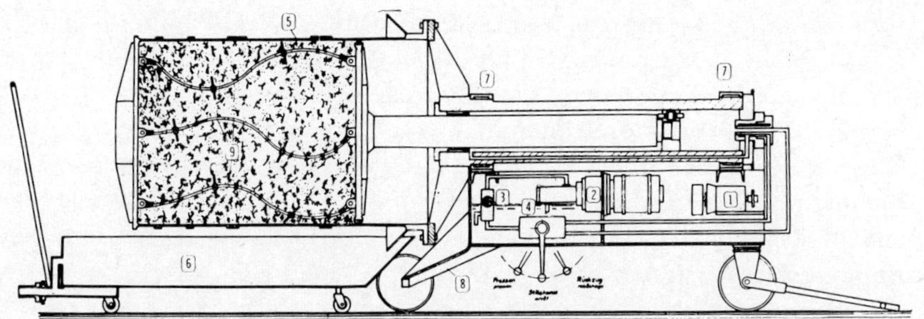

Courtesy of Bucher-Guyer Co.

FIG. 63. SCHEMATIC DIAGRAM OF A HORIZONTAL BASKET PRESS

This drawing shows working method of press and mechanism for loosening pomace. (1) Rotary motor; (2) pump with motor; (3) regulating valve; (4) control valve; (5) filling lid; (6) collecting basin; (7) bearing; (8) truck; and (9) loosening device.

continuous plate press about one per cent of shredded extracted wood bark was blown into the hammer mill as the apples were being ground. A juice yield of 175 gal per ton of apples was obtained and the juice had a suspended solids content of two per cent.

(5) Horizontal Basket Press.—The Bucher-Guyer Co. of Switzerland has introduced the basket press as a means of automating the hydraulic pressing of apples (Fig. 63). A horizontal perforated cylinder with a hinged cover is filled with apple pulp and pressure is exerted on the mass by a circular platen mounted on the piston of a hydraulic cylinder at one end of the basket. As the piston moves into the basket the juice is forced out through the perforated cylinder and also through perforated nylon hoses strung between the stationary head and the platen. These hoses also serve to break up the pomace cake when the platen is retracted. Usually the pomace is alternately compressed and broken during a single press cycle. At the end of the cycle, the basket is revolved so that the spent pomace is discharged through the opened cover. Usually a press cycle is one hour duration and the capacity of the basket is approximately five tons of ground apples.

(6) Screening Centrifuge Plus Some Type of Press.—In recent years the screening type centrifuge has been used to extract a large part of the juice from apple pulp with the final extraction being done by pressing the ejected pulp in some type of cider press. The screening type centrifuge is essentially a revolving, cone-shaped, self-cleaning screen through which the juice is squeezed by centrifugal force.

A typical equipment arrangement and process would be for the ground up apple pulp to be pumped into a supply tank above the centrifuge from which a steady flow of pulp feeds into the centrifuge. The extracted juice runs into a holding tank for clarification treatment. The pulp discharged from the bottom of the centrifuge is conveyed to a press where the remaining juice is pressed out. For this pressing operation both the standard hydraulic cider press and the Willmes pneumatic press have been used. The juice from the pressing is combined with the centrifuged juice in the holding tank. If the centrifuge is not being fed to capacity it is sometimes advantageous to feed pressed juice back into the pulp supply tank and through the centrifuge for screening.

Centrifugal juice of this type contains more solids than juice from a regular cider press. The volume of suspended solids will vary with the type of screen used, the condition of the apples and the character of the pulped fruit. With the usual screen recommended for apple juice the suspended solids will vary between 2 and 5% by volume of the juice. If adequate pre-treatment is used these additional solids do not seem to cause any great difficulty in filtering. Factories that have a cider vinegar operation find that the heavy sludge remaining in the settling tanks after filtering can be fermented out for cider vinegar stock.

Aitken (1960) has found that the yield of juice by this process is reduced below that usually obtained by the traditional methods of juice extraction. The reduction being between 10 and 15 gal per ton of apples.

Yield of Juice

The yield of apple juice to be expected is from 7.0 to 8.5 US gal or 6.0 to 7.0 Imperial gallons per 100 lb of apples. The yield will vary with such factors as variety, season, location, condition of the fruit, type of grinder, and method of extraction or pressing. Freshly picked fruit will yield more juice than similar apples that have been stored. A general observation is that after a dry season the juice will be higher in soluble solids but less in quantity than after a wet season.

Screening

Apple juice, as it comes from the press, contains more or less finely divided pomace and if the Willmes press is used, some rice hulls. To remove these particles the juice is usually screened. This is most commonly done by means of a "cider" screen. This screen is a cylinder of monel or stainless steel screen of approximately 100- to 150-mesh which revolves on a system of rollers. The juice flows in from a pipe at one end and passes through the screen into a tank below while the particles are retained by the screen. The revolving action keeps the screen clean and unplugged by causing the pomace to gather into small balls and finally into a continuous roll which falls off the end of the screen. To facilitate this self-cleaning action the screen is set at a slight slope toward the outlet end. The screened juice is pumped to the holding tanks for further treatment.

Vibratory screens having an 80-mesh (US Standard) are also used to remove the larger particles from apple juice. These screens will reduce the suspended solids content to around 2% and reduce the load on the filter.

Filtration

In the United States, a large proportion of processed apple juice is sold in the filtered or brilliantly clear condition. This product is produced by passing the juice through some type of filter that removes all particles, giving a final product that is brilliantly clear (Neubert 1943).

Filtering freshly pressed apple juice is very difficult unless the juice is treated to reduce the pectinaceous nature of the product. Much of the suspended solid material is colloidal and can only be retained on a very retentive filter. Such filters are easily clogged and therefore have a low production rate. Various treatments have been developed to overcome this difficulty by making the juice more easily filtered.

Filtered juice is produced in the following general types: untreated, tannin and gelatin treated, enzyme treated, heat treated, and bentonite treated.

Untreated Juice.—A filtered juice that will have a superior flavor with excellent body can be produced without any pretreatment if the freshly pressed and screened juice is filtered and processed rapidly. Modern filters with large filter areas and resultant large capacity which are easily and quickly cleaned have been used successfully for this method. One-half to two per cent of a filter aid is usually added to juice before filtration. The juice carries a slight haze but has the full flavor of the original fruit. The finished product develops no objectionable sediment during storage although a slight increase in cloudiness may occur. A rotary vacuum precoat filter may be used but the filtration rate will be about one-third that with juice that has been enzyme treated.

Enzyme Treatment.—There are a number of enzyme preparations recommended for the clarification of apple juice. Some of the new products are much more concentrated than those available several years ago and are therefore more economical. The action of all these enzymes depends on their ability to hydrolyze pectin, and thereby reduce the viscosity of the juice making it more easily filtered. Also as the pectin is a high molecular weight colloid that acts as a protective colloid in suspending the particles in apple juice, when it is hydrolyzed these particles are released and settle out of the juice leaving the supernatant juice clear.

The most concentrated enzyme preparations are in liquid form while the more dilute types are in dry powder form. The dry forms are usually composed of the enzyme material diluted with dextrose, filter-aid or gelatin. The gelatin also acts as a clarifying agent. All these enzyme preparations are subject to the usual conditions that can influence enzymatic action, such as pH, temperature, enzyme concentration, and length of reaction time.

In general, because of the variables involved in enzymatic clarification, it is recommended that the individual operator make tests to establish the proper concentrations and conditions for his own operations.

In some cases, trouble due to after-precipitation in bottled or canned apple juice has occurred with enzyme treated juice. Marshall (1946) reported on previous work on this problem and from new data suggested a method for preventing the formation of the unsightly sediment. He states that if such juice is to go into consumption within 30 days no added precautions are necessary to prevent precipitation. Also, he doubted whether it is necessary to prevent sedimentation because the sediment tends to adhere to the bottom of the cans and is not noticeable in dark bottles. However, to prevent sediment in enzyme clarified apple juice, during storage, he recommended that 5 to 10 oz of nonacidulated, starch-free, liquid, apple pectin of 50 grade be added to each 100 gal. of juice. The liquid pectin should be added to the juice and thoroughly stirred before pasteurizing and filling.

Tannin and Gelatin Treatment.—Apple juice contains tannins to which much of its astringency is due. If a solution of gelatin is added to apple juice a heavy flocculant precipitate is formed. As this precipitate settles it carries down the suspended particles in the juice and leaves a nearly clear supernatant liquid. The reason for this precipitating action is that the colloidal material in apple juice is negatively charged and when the positively charged gelatin is added the oppositely charged particles coalesce and precipitate. In actual practice, before the gelatin is added some additional tannic acid is added to the juice. This is done to prevent a reduction in flavor and color that would result from the removal of the natural tannins from the juice by the gelatin. After the juice has settled it is filtered to produce a brilliantly clear light amber colored juice.

Walsh (1934) has described the procedure for determining the proper proportions of tannin and gelatin to be used:[1]

Solution 1. Dissolve $^1/_3$ oz (9.45 gm) of tannin (tannin acid) in 5.95 fluid ounces (176.0 cc) of 95% ethyl alcohol. Then add 23.8 fl oz (704.1 cc) of water and mix thoroughly.

Solution 2. Dissolve $^3/_4$ ounce (21.2 gm) of gelatin in 23.8 fl oz (704.1 cc) of water and add 5.95 fl oz (176.0 cc) of 95% ethyl alcohol

Heat a portion of the water and add the gelatin slowly, stirring continuously. Then add the rest of the water and dissolve the gelatin by heating in a pan of hot water or double boiler and stirring. Add the alcohol and mix well.

These solutions should be kept in stoppered bottles and may be used as needed, the alcohol acting as a preservative in both cases. In some cases the gelatin will gel when cold, but can be liquefied when needed by putting the container in hot water.

Four white glass quart bottles should then be filled up to the neck with apple juice and numbered 1, 2, 3, and 4. Then add to each bottle the following amounts of Solution 1 (tannin) and Solution 2 (gelatin).

	Bottle No. 1	Bottle No. 2	Bottle No. 3	Bottle No. 4
Sol. 1, cubic centimeters	10	10	10	10
Sol. 2, cubic centimeters	5	10	15	20

Measure and add the amounts of solution shown to each bottle, adding the tannin first in all cases and shaking well after the addition of each solution. Let the bottles stand for ten minutes and the bottle showing the most clear juice is the one to which the proper proportions of tannin and gelatin were added.

The quantities of tannin and gelatin to use for 100-gal. (US gallon) batches of apple juice are then found by referring to the table below. For smaller amounts of cider, proportionate amounts of tannin and gelatin are used. For example, if bottle 3 showed the greatest amount of clear juice at the end of the 10 min period, 1.25 oz of tannin and 4.5 of gelatin should be added to each 100 gal. of cider; for 50 gal., one-half these amounts, or 0.63 oz of tannin and 2.1 oz of gelatin, should be added to the cider.

AMOUNTS OF GELATIN AND TANNIN TO BE USED FOR 100 GALLONS US (83.3 IMPERIAL GALLONS) OF CIDER

	Bottle No. 1	Bottle No. 2	Bottle No. 3	Bottle No. 4
Tannin, ounces	1.25	1.25	1.25	1.25
Gelatin, ounces	1.50	3.00	4.50	6.00

The actual clarification of apple juice according to this procedure is carried out by first stirring into the apple juice a solution containing the proper amount of tannin. A few minutes later the correct quantity of gelatin, dissolved in hot water, is added, stirring constantly. It is most essential that the juice be very thoroughly stirred after the addition of the treating chemicals. After standing overnight, the clear supernatant liquid is drawn off and filtered. In some plants the liquid is not separated from the sludge as the sludge is held by the filter. This speeds up the operation and eliminates the waste due to discarding juice with the sludge.

The tannin-gelatin method of clarification is not fool-proof. Its successful use depends to a considerable extent on experience. If incorrect amounts of gelatin are used and a surplus remains in the juice, not only will filtering be more difficult but the finished juice may develop a cloud or precipitate during storage.

Heat Treatment.—This method of clarification is based on the principle that the components which make apple juice difficult to filter are coagulated by flash heating to between 180° and 185°F. The heated juice is rapidly cooled and filtered or centrifuged to remove the coagulated particles. The efficiency of this method of clarification seems to vary with the variety of apples used. Therefore, the method should only be used when tests have shown that it will be satisfactory with the apples available. One disadvantage to the heat treatment method is that the juice is subjected to two heatings. After the first heating, cooling and filtering it is necessary to pasteurize the juice before filling the containers. This drastic heat exposure can have a detrimental effect on the flavor of the finished product.

The final pasteurization should be done at a temperature slightly below that used for the initial heating, otherwise still further material will be precipitated.

Bentonite Treatment.—This method of clarification was developed by Sipple, McDonnell and Lueck (1940). It is a modification and improvement on the flash heating treatment.

The freshly pressed, screened apple juice is flash heated to 180° to 190°F and immediately cooled to 80°F. This is done most efficiently if a regenerative heat exchanger is used, wherein the first section of the unit is the heating section and the last section is the cooling section. The incoming juice is used as the cooling medium in the second section and at the same time it is heated before passing into the first section. This results in considerable saving of fuel.

The juice passes from the heat exchanger to tanks where a suspension of equal parts of bentonite and filter aid is added with vigorous stirring. The quantity of materials used is usually 7 to 8 oz each, of fine mesh bentonite and medium grade filter aid for each 100 gal of juice. The treating materials are suspended in a small quantity of juice and the suspension added to the large volume. After treatment the juice is allowed to stand for at least an hour and then is filtered.

Marshall (1947) discounts reports that off-flavors may develop due to inferior bentonite but does state that great difficulties have developed in filtering some lots of apple juice after bentonite treatment. Experience seems to be an important factor in the successful use of the bentonite treatment.

Filtering.—Regardless of the treatment used in preparing the apple juice the filtering procedure is basically the same. A large assortment of different types of filters are available in capacities to suit any scale of production. Generally those using filter aid are the best for filtering apple juice. The types of filters that use disposable pads or sheets, while being very easy to clean, are too easily plugged in filtering apple juice and are therefore not recommended.

The filter should be of a type and capacity to be capable of supplying sufficient filtered juice to maintain the production of the plant. As apple juice is a rather difficult liquid to filter, this point should be stressed in obtaining equipment, to be certain that equipment with adequate capacity is supplied. There should be no iron parts to come in contact with the juice. The best material of construction, as with all apple juice equipment, is stainless steel.

A filter is essentially a support for a filtering medium with some method of forcing or drawing the liquid through the medium. The particles are retained by the medium and the clear filtrate is removed after passing through the medium. The interior of many filters contains a set of plates which may be the support for the medium or upon which cloth may be placed to support the medium. Some filters have plates covered permanently with fine stainless steel wire mesh. On the support a pre-coat of filter medium is deposited and the unfiltered juice, containing a small percentage of filter medium, is passed through the filter. The medium builds up a porous non-plugging cake which is still retentive enough to sieve out the suspended particles. Eventually the medium and trapped particles build up sufficiently to reduce flow of filtrate to the point where further operation of the filter is uneconomic. When this point is reached the filter is shut down, dismantled. cleaned and reassembled for another cycle. In some plants a sheet of relatively porous filter paper is placed over the support medium before the precoat layer is applied. These paper sheets are discarded with the cake. The use of filter paper prevents blinding of the support medium during prolonged operation.

The usual filter medium used for apple juice is diatomaceous earth. This material consists of microscopic shells of single-celled plants known as diatoms. This material is especially processed to remove any "earthy" flavor that might affect the flavor of the apple juice. Diatomaceous earth or filter aid can be obtained in many grades, each with definite characteristics. Experience will determine which grade is best to use under individual plant conditions.

The operation of the filter in any plant is a procedure that requires a skilled and experienced operator. A general description of the filtering process is as follows: The filter is properly assembled. Sufficient juice, equal to slightly more than the volume of the filter, is placed in a small tank equipped with an agitator. Filter aid is added to this juice at the rate of approximately one pound for each square foot of filter area. This filter aid is thoroughly mixed with the juice and then circulated through the filter. This is referred to as "precoating" and builds up a layer of filter-aid in direct contact with the filter plates. The precoating juice is circulated until it becomes clear, showing that a proper precoat has been formed.

As soon as the precoating is finished the flow of juice is changed from the precoat tank to one of the tanks containing juice to be filtered. This juice has filter aid added to it at the rate of 0.1 to 0.2% by weight and is kept thoroughly mixed to keep the filter aid in suspension. The change from precoat tank to juice tank must be carried out carefully and slowly to make certain that no sudden change in the pressure in the filter occurs to cause the filter cake to break loose from its support. If this should happen the filtrate will become cloudy and very likely it will be necessary to disassemble the filter, wash it out, reassemble and precoat again to get proper filtering.

Most filters are equipped with centrifugal type pumps which give a high flow under low pressure but a low flow under high pressure. Because of this, flow from the filter will be high at first but as the filter cake builds up and increases the pressure, the flow will decrease. When the pressure has reached the maximum permitted for the filter the flow through will be so low that further operation of the filter becomes uneconomical. At this point the filter is cleaned out and a new cycle started.

Some filter installations have special pumps for adding a concentrated slurry of filter aid to the juice before it enters the filter. The concentrated slurry of filter aid and juice is made in a separate small tank from which it is pumped into the feed line to the filter pump. It is best to add the filter aid ahead of the pump so that it will be well mixed before it enters the filter. This arrangement permits very uniform addition of filter aid.

It is also possible to add filter aid in a similar manner without the use of a special pump. The slurry is made in a small tank and allowed to run by gravity through a regulating valve into the suction side of the filter pump. The valve is used to adjust the flow of filter aid slurry.

Rotary vacuum precoat filters are gradually replacing plate and frame or pressure leaf filters for clarification of apple juice. A vacuum is applied to the inside of a revolving drum covered with a reinforced wire mesh. Over this wire a cloth is placed and when the drum dips into a tank of filter aid suspension a cake three inches deep is built on the drum. The filter aid suspension is then replaced with apple juice and a knife is moved towards the cake so that a layer of filter aid and apple solids 0.001 in. thick is removed with each revolution of the drum. In this manner a fresh filter surface is exposed continually to the juice. A single precoat layer may last for 12 hr continuous filtration and require less filter aid than would be consumed in a plate and frame or pressure leaf filter. An average filtration rate for depectinized juice would be 10 gal/hr/sq ft and the filtrate would contain 0.1% or less suspended solids. A relatively small polishing filter is required to produce a sparkling juice.

In the grape juice industry, rotary vacuum belt filters have been used with press aid to reduce the suspended solids in the juice to 0.75%. In this application the precoat layer is replaced by an endless belt made of synthetic fiber. Juice from a continuous press is mixed with 0.5% fluffed wood fiber and added to the filter tank. The vacuum draws a layer of press aid and juice solids onto the belt and this layer is discharged when the belt departs from the drum to pass over a small roller. The belt is then washed under sprays of water before it reenters the tank. The filter cake is then added to incoming pulp to serve as a press aid in the pressing operation. Attempts to apply a rotary vacuum belt filter to apple juice have not been very successful. The filtrate contains 1 to 2% suspended solids and the cake must be broken up finely in a hammer mill in order to disperse it in the relatively thick apple pulp coming from the grinder if the wood fiber is to be reused as press aid.

Centrifuged Apple Juice

A type of apple juice that is slightly clearer than the unclarified juice, but is considerably more opaque than the filtered juice can be made by passing the pressed, screened juice through a centrifuge. The use of a centrifuge to clarify the juice makes it possible to process juice by an almost continuous method and plants of this type were designed with this in mind. No large storage or holding tanks are required so the juice can usually be turned out in its final container within 30 min. of being pressed from the apples.

The original process for this type of juice used a centrifuge having a tubular bowl through which the juice was forced by gravity flow or by pumping. As the juice passes through the rapidly spinning bowl (speeds of 15,000 rpm are used) it is subjected to centrifugal force many times that of gravity with the result that the suspended particles are forced out of the juice and adhere to the side of the bowl. The centrifuge is stopped periodically and the sediment removed. To eliminate long delays in the process two interchangeable bowls are used for one machine or three bowls used for two machines.

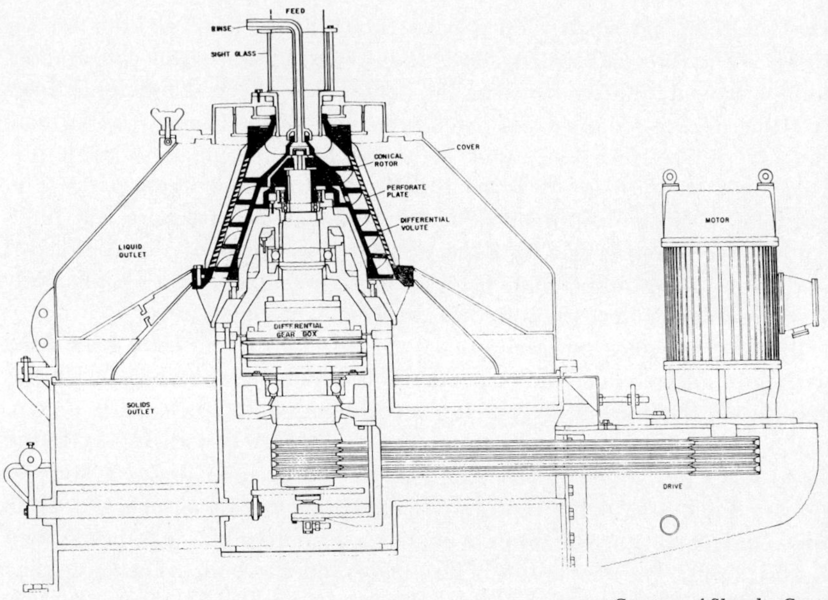

Courtesy of Sharples Corp.

FIG. 64. DRAWING SHOWING CONSTRUCTION OF THE SHARPLES SUPER CENTRIFUGE

More recently continuous centrifuges have become available and can be used to give a continuous operation. These are self-cleaning so that no interruption of the process is necessary as with the tubular type machine.

Centrifuged apple juice is more viscous and has more body than any of the juices prepared with pretreatments followed by filtration. This type of juice is cloudy, but free from visible suspended particles. It is relatively stable, especially if a small residual quantity of ascorbic acid remains after pasteurization. Sediment that may settle out during storage is light, fluffy and easily shaken back into suspension.

One serious disadvantage to centrifuging apple juice has been the excessive aeration that can occur during the process. This has largely been overcome by the development of special centrifuges. Another possible method of prevention is to use inert gas such as nitrogen as an atmosphere within the machine, as described by Chambers (1949, 1950).

Between 1945 and 1952 large qualities of centrifugally clarified apple juice were marketed in the Eastern United States. However, since that time the centrifuging process has been coupled with or superseded by direct filtration, to produce a somewhat clearer apple juice with no sediment.

Since most of the particles that will form a sediment in the bottled juice are less than 10 microns in size and have a density that varies by only 0.02

units of specific gravity from the juice, any method employing centrifugal force for separation must use a substantially long retention time with high centrifugal energy.

Unclarified Juice

Apple juice in the unclarified state is generally sold in the fresh state or preserved by chemical preservatives for prompt consumption. Juice of this type has the coarse particles removed by screening or settling but is not otherwise treated. The essential step in the production of this type of juice is the treatment of the apples during grinding with ascorbic acid (vitamin C). The ascorbic acid acts as an antioxidant and prevents darkening of the juice. The prevention of oxidation seems to influence the amount of sediment developing in the juice during further processing and storage.

Pederson (1947) carried out tests on the production of apple juice whereby solutions of ascorbic acid were sprayed on the apples as they were ground up or on the pomace immediately after grinding. The resulting juice was light in color, being the color of apple flesh with no evidence of oxidation. The flavor was that of fresh apples, being unlike the usual "cider" flavor. A small quantity of sediment formed in the finished pasteurized juice but it was light and fluffy and therefore easily dispersed by gentle shaking of the container. An outline of the suggested process is as follows:

> "Good quality mature apples are essential to good apple juice. Flavor will depend on the flavor of the apples. They must be washed free of dirt and spray residue. It is most desirable to chill the apples, even as low as 30°F. They should be ground rapidly in a mill that has no exposed corrosive iron or copper. A Fitzpatrick stainless steel mill was used experimentally. The apple juice solution of ascorbic acid, 12 gm per pint, should be sprayed on the pomace during or immediately after milling and the operation from here on should be as rapid as possible. (The quantity of ascorbic acid solution used was sufficient to add 12 gm of ascorbic acid per bushel of apples.) Press racks and cloths should be clean. A stainless steel base with slanting troughs and a stainless steel slanting box below the racks for building the cheese are essential to cleanliness, rapid handling of the juice, and reducing the exposure to air. The deaerator and water-heated flash pasteurizer should be near the press to speed handling. High temperature and prolonged heating changes the character of the juice. If the juice is to be clarified, this should be done after flash pasteurization and cooling. Deaeration simplifies filling of the containers. Containers should be filled hot and full at 165° to 175°F, closed, and cooled immediately in water. Containers of juice should be stored in the cold since apple and all other fruit juices are not as stable as more solid processed foods."

Holgate, Moyer and Pederson (1948) continued the investigations started by the preceding author. Factors investigated were the influence of the method of adding ascorbic acid, strength of solution, varieties of apples, and speed of operation. Varieties used were Caville Blanc, Northwestern Greening, Jonathan, McIntosh, Baldwin, Rome and Ben Davis. A summary of their results is as follows:

"For all varieties tested ascorbic acid added at the rate of 6 gm per bushel of apples (40 to 45 lbs) was sufficient to produce high-colored, true-flavored apple juice. This quantity leaves about 20 to 25 mg of ascorbic acid per 100 gm of pasteurized juice, and will protect the juice for at least 2 hr. between deaeration and pressing, provided the pomace is held in the racks and covered with the press cloths. Rapid handling of the crushed apples and juice in all stages of the operation is highly desirable for quality production and pasteurization must be sufficient to inactivate the enzymes, or darkening will eventually occur in storage."

"Several methods of adding ascorbic acid were devised but adding directly to the mill, so that it is applied and mixed with the tissue as soon as the tissue is exposed to the air, was found to be the best of those tried."

Atkinson and Strachan (1949B) report development of a commercial method for producing unclarified or "natural" juice that was a compromise between filtered juice and crushed juice. Their work was similar to that of the previous authors but carried further to obtain additional information applicable to the apples of British Columbia. In this process the apples are sprayed with ascorbic acid solution as they enter the hammer mill. The juice is pressed out, strained, pasteurized, and filled into containers with subsequent cooling and storage. These workers state that the amount of ascorbic acid must be determined for the apples being used. A standard solution of ascorbic acid can be made and the quantity added to the fruit can then be varied by changing the volume sprayed on the fruit at the mill. Maturity of the apples and variety have an influence on the effectiveness of the ascorbic acid. Apples of "eating" maturity lend themselves best to this type of process. Overripe apples cannot be used. These workers emphasize the fact that varieties such as Newtown, Rome Beauty, and Delicious have not been successfully handled by this method because these varieties contain a large quantity of oxidative enzymes. Success of the process depends on adjusting the whole operation so that a residual of not less than one mg of reduced ascorbic acid remains in the final extracted juice. Further fortification with ascorbic acid was an added protection.

A process for making "opalescent" apple juice has been patented in Canada and the United States by Walrod (1957A and B) and this process uses the antioxidant effect of ascorbic acid to prevent oxidation of apple juice by adding the ascorbic acid solution to the juice immediately after it has been extracted and before oxidative changes have become irreversible. This process has been used extensively by one processor in British Columbia. This type of juice appeals to the consumer who does not like the more

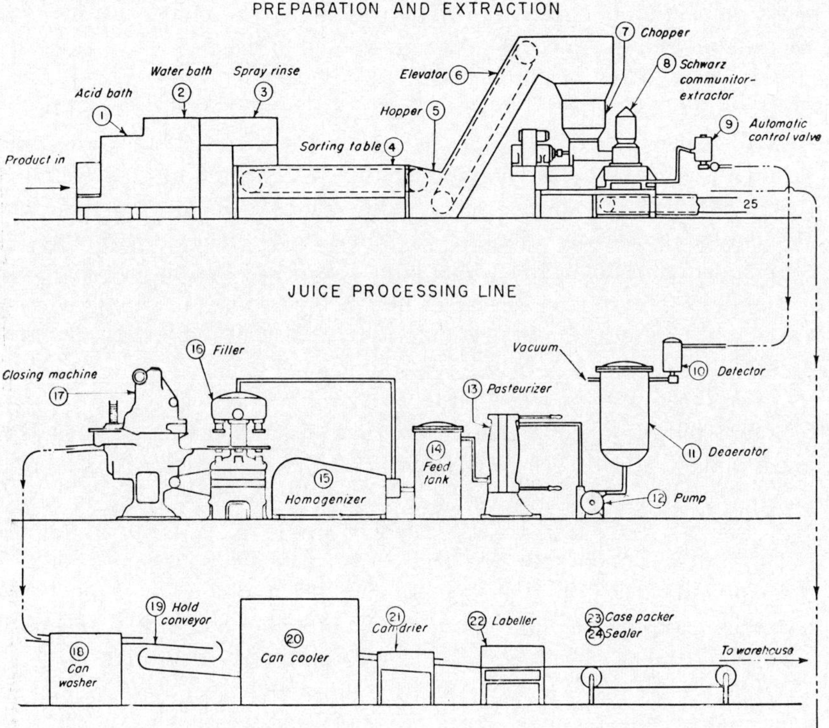

Courtesy of Food Engineering

FIG. 65. STEPS IN THE MAKING OF CRUSHED APPLE JUICE

common brilliantly clear filtered apple juice, or the heavier "crushed" apple juice.

"Crushed" Apple Juice

"Crushed" apple juice is an extreme type of unclarified apple juice containing a large quantity of fine cellular material. In this process no cider press is used; instead the sorted and washed apples are passed through a rough slicer and then into a Schwartz comminutor extractor. This is a vertical mill which grinds the fruit and forces the juice and fine particles through a special rubber screen. The perforations in the screen vary from 1600 to 3600 psi. The Schwartz machine may be varied to give any desired amount of pulp in the extracted juice. The amount of solids is usually between 3 and 10%. The pulpy juice is drawn by vacuum into a deaerator and then through a homogenizer to the pasteurizer. The juice is pasteurized at 190°F and filled into the containers, cooled and cased. As this type of juice should be very light or pale in color it is essential that every precaution be taken to prevent oxidation. The process is, therefore, continuous with the juice never being exposed to the air.

Bertuzzi (1960), of Milan, Italy, has developed a novel process for pulpy fruit juices which is schematically represented in Fig. 65 and briefly described here. After having been washed and sorted the fruit passes through a grinder to the Thermobreak where enzymes are inactivated by steam. After that the pulp is separated in a juice extractor from the coarse elements of the core as well as of seeds and stems. The hot pulpy juice is centrifuged, thus eliminating other large particles. Then it is deaerated in a cylinder. The sudden release of the vacuum causes most pulp cells to explode, thus producing a very fine pulp. The cells which do not break up are disintegrated afterward by an ultrasonic homogenizer. After this treatment the product is flash pasteurized and bottled.

Before and after centrifuging, citric acid, sugar solutions or other fruit juices may be added. Usually, ascorbic acid also is added.

DEAERATION

This process removes the dissolved air from the juice. The efficiency of removal varies with the type of equipment. Essentially deaeration is effected by exposing the juice in a thin film or spray to a partial vacuum in a special chamber. This causes the entrapped air to "boil" off.

While it is accepted practice to deaerate some juices, the advantage of such a procedure for apple juice is controversial. Marshall (1947) reports little advantage in deaerating apple juice. In fact, there was some evidence that flavor was lost during the process as shown by the presence of a pronounced apple odor in the deaerator exhaust. Conclusions from his work indicated that even though deaerated apple juice was slightly superior in appearance and taste to the nondeaerated apple juice nevertheless it could not be recommended because of the extra expense of equipment and operation plus the possible loss of flavoring materials.

PREVENTION OF OXIDATIVE CHANGES

The oxidative changes in apple juices due to enzymatic and nonenzymatic browning are well known. A good description of these reactions was given by Lavollay (1950). The "tannins" of juices form the substrates that are mainly involved in enzymatic reactions, chlorogenic acid and leucoanthocyanins being of major importance. Amino acids, sugars and organic acids participate in non-enzymatic browning reactions.

The intensive browning reactions occurring immediately after grinding and pressing are almost exclusively enzymatic ones. Associated with the formation of the brown color there is a decrease in flavor. The typical fruit flavor disappears, and the juice takes on the flavor of old-fashioned cider.

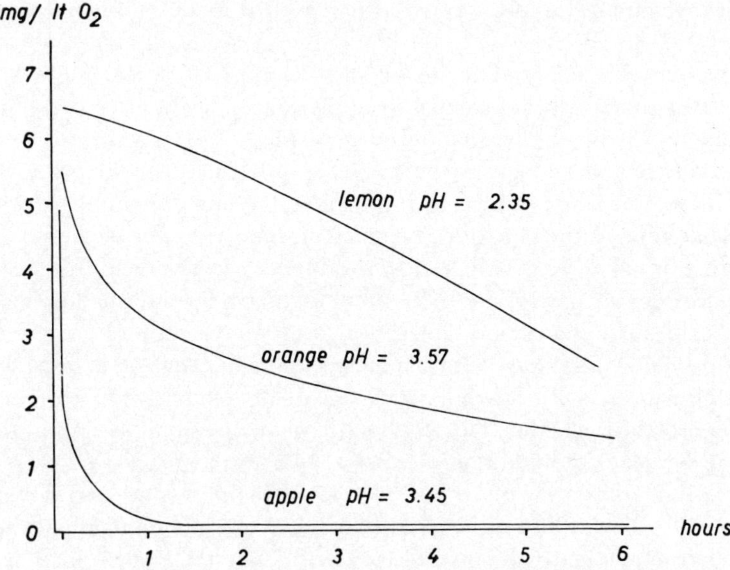

Fig. 66. Oxygen Up-Take of Different Fresh Fruit Juices

Juices are saturated with oxygen. Their concentration is continuously determined in closed system by polarography. These curves show distinctly that oxygen transmission to substrates takes place most rapidly in apple juices. Therefore, apple juices should be immediately flash-heated after pressing, if effective protection against a too-intensive oxidation is wanted.

Measurements of oxygen uptake in apple juices (Lüthi 1953, 1954, 1960; Biedermann 1956) showed that oxidation occurs more rapidly than in orange or lemon juices (see Fig. 66). Since these oxidation processes continue at unreduced speed in the absence of air, it is absolutely necessary to inactivate the oxidases as quickly as possible. Unfortunately, the pressing operation creates almost ideal conditions for an intense aeration of the juices. Normally, heating the juice at 185°F for 30 sec is sufficient to inactivate the oxidating enzymes (Dimick *et al.* 1950). After this heat treatment the oxygen uptake in apple juices will be considerably lower (Biedermann 1956).

The successful use of ascorbic acid in reducing oxidative changes in apple juice has been discussed in the preparation of unclarified juice. However, as Atkinson and Strachan (1949B) point out, amount of ascorbic acid required may be almost prohibitive if the apples have very active oxidative enzyme systems.

The destruction of added ascorbic acid appears to be caused by peroxides which are rapidly formed after the fruit tissue is broken in grinding.

Polarographic analyses made by Merck and Co. (1949) showed that there was practically no oxygen in apple juice shortly after pressing but that there was a definite quantity of peroxides. These peroxides were an important factor in the destruction of ascorbic acid in the apple juice. When ascorbic acid is added to apple juice a certain amount disappears at the same time as the peroxides. The color and the flavor of the juice will remain normal as long as there is a residual of ascorbic acid to react with the peroxides as they form or with those that have been formed previously.

Peroxides being an important factor in the destruction of ascorbic acid in apple juice, attempts were made to eliminate them or at least lessen their effect. As sulfur dioxide is an active antioxidant, tests were carried out to ascertain whether the addition of small amounts, as sodium bisulfite, previous to the addition or mixed with, the ascorbic acid would be effective in conserving the ascorbic acid. This procedure did not prove successful. It was also discovered that relatively small amounts of sulfur dioxide can eliminate all apple flavor even before the characteristic flavor of sulfur dioxide is detectable. Another serious drawback to this method was that small quantities of sulfur dioxide cause serious off-flavors in canned apple juice.

A preparation of pure catalase was tried with small lots of apple juice. This enzyme has an affinity for peroxides but seemed to have no effect in reducing the ascorbic acid losses in fortified apple juice.

Citric acid in combination with ascorbic acid has a sequestering effect on traces of iron and copper in some products so it was thought it might be useful in reducing ascorbic acid losses. In actual practice this did not prove to be the case.

It is well known that iron and copper in trace amounts catalyse the oxidation of ascorbic acid. This suggested the possibility of using ethylenediamine tetra-acetic acid as a sequestering agent. There was some indication that this was at least partially effective, but the cost of the sequestering agent was about equal to the saving in ascorbic acid. More recently with the introduction of several salts of ethylenediamine tetra-acetic acid, these tests were repeated with filtered juice in cans. The chemicals had no effect as far as the losses in the can after packing were concerned. No tests were done to determine the effect of the sequestering agent in the raw juice with ascorbic acid added.

PRESERVATION

The commonest methods used to preserve apple juice are based on pasteurization, chemical treatment, refrigeration, and sterile filtration.

Heat Preservation

The most important commercial method of apple juice preservation is pasteurization. This method is based on time and temperature relationships. The juice is heated to a temperature, such that when held for an adequate length of time, will cause the destruction of microorganisms in the apple juice. Pasteurization does not kill all organisms but does eliminate those that can develop if the juice is put hot into containers which are completely filled and then hermetically closed. When containers are closed at relatively high temperatures a partial vacuum develops in the headspace on cooling. The low oxygen content of the headspace prevents the growth of all but especially adapted organisms. Occasionally trouble will occur when such facultative organisms are present in the juice as was the case with part of a commercial pack reported by Aitken (1951B). In this case the organism was *Spicaria divaricata* (Thom) which developed on the surface of apple juice in bottles with vacua as high as 14 in.

Flash pasteurization or HTST pasteurization involves rapid heating of the juice to temperatures just below the boiling point. The usual temperatures are between 170° and 190°F with times of between 25 and 30 sec. Under usual operating conditions the juice is exposed to high temperatures for not over three minutes including heating, holding and filling. Numerous types of HTST heat exchangers are available in capacities to suit various needs and the basic procedure in all of them is to heat the juice very rapidly by passing it in a thin film between plates or through small diameter tubes that are heated by steam or hot water. The high speed flow causes turbulence in the juice which prevents scorching the product. The hot juice is filled into containers which are immediately sealed and cooled. The HTST method causes little reduction in the flavor of apple juice because the short exposure to heat causes no scorched flavor. This method is the one most commonly used because of its adaptability to continuous operations.

Canning

Cans for apple juice are generally lined with special enamel or lacquer which is resistant to the corrosive action of the juice. Special techniques have now been developed which make it possible to cover all breaks in the enamel of the side-seam by side-seam striping. In this process a thin coat of enamel is sprayed on the side-seam of the can after it has been formed; this has greatly reduced the possibility of metal contamination in apple juice.

As the cans travel along the line to the filler they should pass through a can washer where all dust particles or other debris are removed. The cans are filled on special filling machines and immediately sealed with covers in a can-closing machine. The closed cans should be inverted or rolled on their sides for approximately three minutes to bring the hot juice into contact with the cover to sterilize it. The cans are then cooled in a cooler to between 100° and 90°F. If the cans are not cooled sufficiently there will be a definite reduction in quality due to the effect of the heat remaining in the product. If the cans are cooled too much there will be difficulty in labeling them because they will not dry sufficiently. Also if they are too cool going into the final cartons they may rust because there will not be sufficient heat remaining in the container to dry off the outside. From the cooler the cans are labeled and cased. All operations from the filling machine to the final casing are carried on continuously with the cans passing uninterruptedly from one operation to another.

Bottling

Bottling apple juice requires specialized equipment and more supervision than canning because of the fragile nature of the containers and because of their susceptibility to thermal shock. Conveyor lines for glass containers must be designed and operated so that the bottles are not "bruised" or broken by impact. Glass containers may be "bruised" so that while no visible damage is evident, nevertheless, breakage will occur later with any impact or sudden temperature change. Because glass containers are subject to thermal shock, good practice dictates that temperature changes of more than 20°F should be avoided to prevent excessive breakage.

Previous to filling glass bottles with hot apple juice they should be cleaned by passing them through a special cleaning unit to remove all dust particles. If new bottles are used it is rarely necessary to wash them as Aitken (1951B) found that the number of viable organisms in new bottles was very low. This is especially so with bottles that are placed neck-down in cartons immediately after they leave the annealing furnace at the factory. The bottles should be preheated to within 20°F of the filling temperature before filling. This can be done in a special section of conveyor in which steam jets impinge on the containers. Fillers of several types are available but the most satisfactory type is that which draws the juice into the container by evacuating the container. This type of filler reduces oxidation of the product.

Closures for bottles and jugs can be screw caps, crown caps or vacuum caps. The latter are the most satisfactory because there is less chance of breakage during application and the headspace vacuum is slightly higher than with other types. Also if fermentation does happen to occur in any containers, the vacuum type cap will blow off before the bottle explodes due to internal gas pressure.

Hot, filled glass containers must be cooled gradually in a special cooler, usually of the spray type. Where bottles enter the cooler the sprayed water is hot and as the bottles move through the cooler the sprayed water is gradually reduced in temperature. The water spray should be very fine so that cooling can be done by evaporation as well as by conduction. Bottles emerging from the cooler should still be warm enough to dry completely but not above 100°F to avoid deleterious heat effects during storage.

Refrigerated Bulk Storage

Apple juice has been stored in bulk in Europe by heating; then pumping while hot into storage tanks. These tanks, having capacities up to 2000 gal, are vented with an air filter and allowed to cool. However due to the slow cooling rate, the quality of the juice is not high. This method of bulk storage has been replaced largely by presterilizing the tanks with hot water, steam or sulfite solution. The air in the tank is replaced by CO_2 at 1.5 psi to prevent fungal growth and then pasteurized and cooled juice is pumped into the tank. The success of this storage depends on the maintenance of aseptic conditions following pasteurization and during transfer of the cooled juice into the tank. The lack of personnel trained in aseptic handling has limited its application to apple juice. The temperature of a European tank room is usually 60°F or less. In recent years increasing quantities of single-strength pasteurized citrus juice have been shipped long distances in refrigerated trucks for repackaging and sale in refrigerated dairy counters and a similar procedure might be used in the retailing of apple juice. Bulk storage of pasteurized apple juice at 30°F would extend the supply and permit blending to achieve a desirable flavor.

To overcome the difficulties encountered in maintaining sterility in bulk storage, the Boehi process was developed in Switzerland for the "return" bottle trade. Clean tanks are completely filled with water which is then forced out with 45 psi CO_2. When empty, juice at 40°F impregnated with 0.6 to 0.8% CO_2 is pumped in until the tank is 95% full. The head space of the tank is further purged with CO_2 to eliminate oxygen before it is sealed through a safety valve. If the storage temperature is maintained below 40°F yeast and lactic acid bacterial growth will be inhibited.

Preservation with Chemicals

The principal preservatives[1] in commercial use are salts of benzoic acid, some benzoate derivatives, sulfurous acid or its salts, and recently also sor-

---

[1]Any person planning to use chemical preservations in apple or other fruit juice should check with the U.S. Food and Drug Administration and also local health authorities to determine the amounts allowed.

bic acid. Sodium benzoate is used chiefly to increase the shelf life of unpasteurized apple juice and frequently used in the United States for juice packed in one-and two-gallon jugs and often labelled apple "cider." Benzoate prevents spoilage when present in concentrations of 0.1 to 0.3%, the quantity necessary varying with the acidity of the juice (see below). The salt is dissolved in water and added to the juice at the time of preparation. Sulfurous acid is used mainly for preserving juice in bulk for export or for manufacturing purposes. Concentrations necessary to prevent spoilage vary from 0.02 to 0.1% calculated as sulfur dioxide, depending on the juice preserved. It is added in the form of sulfites or sulfur dioxide, as gas from a cylinder, or as a solution in water.

In many countries benzoic acid and SO_2 or their salts are the only preservatives permitted by law. When added they have to be declared on the label. Indiscriminate use of chemical preservatives in the past to mask the impaired quality has resulted in a marked prejudice against them. They are, however, still used widely in the beverage industry all over the world.

Sodium Benzoate.—Pure sodium benzoate, when added in concentrations of 0.05 to 0.1%, generally does not impart any objectionable flavor to fruit juices or to a fruit juice beverage base, particularly when they are to be diluted before use. Some individuals may, however, have a higher or lower taste threshold. The concentration perceptible to taste depends also on the ratio of benzoate ion to benzoic acid. In concentrations of 0.1% or above, sulfurous acid, whether added as such or as potassium metabisulfite, does have an objectionable flavor. Sulfur dioxide has the undesirable property of bleaching the juice. In addition it strongly retards oxidation and the resulting discoloration and loss of flavor. The amount of preservative required depends on the extent and type of infection and the character of the juice, particularly its acidity. Thus Cruess *et al.* (1929, 1931) found that in acid juices, 0.1% of sodium benzoate was sufficient, but in less acid juices, such as those from very ripe apples or grapes, at least 0.3% was necessary. The concentration of metabisulfite or sulfite required to prevent growth in an acid juice is about 0.1% calculated as SO_2. When only used to inhibit oxidation, about 0.02% of SO_2 is sufficient under ordinary conditions, when the juice is stored in sealed containers. The preservative should be completely dissolved and thoroughly mixed with all the juice to be treated.

When used in high concentration for preservation in bulk, color may fade to a very high degree. However, color is largely restored when the sulfurous acid is removed later on. At the same time SO_2 has the favorable effect of retarding oxidation of ascorbic acid and many other substances.

Recent studies prove that benzoic acid accelerates discoloration. This explains why these two preservatives may be used to advantage in combination with each other; sulfurous acid to retard oxidative changes and benzoic acid chiefly to check spoilage organisms (Anand *et al.* 1958). Nevertheless, they both increase sedimentation, influencing the colloidal balance of the juice.

Sulfites and Sulfurous Acid.—SO_2 is frequently used in fruit juices. However, in the United States it is seldom used in apple juice. In some states its use is not permitted. Even in cases where it is not intentionally added, minor amounts may become included in the final products. This SO_2 originates in the SO_2 being used for disinfecting utensils and equipment, particularly in smaller juice factories.

Sulfurous acid, sometimes used as preservative for fruit juices, is more effective against mold spores and bacteria than yeast. Monier-Williams (1937), in a report of the British Ministry of Health, gave a detailed review of various papers published up to this time and dealing with the nature of the combination between sulfurous acid and certain constituents of food such as aldehydes, ketones, sugars etc. Downer (1943), investigating the preservative capacity of free and bound sulfur dioxide in citrus fruit juices, found that 55 per cent of the sulfur dioxide combines with the carbonyl group of the sugar in the juice. This leaves only part of the SO_2 free to act as a preservative. The germicidal effect of free sulfur dioxide as contrasted to the lack of such an influence on the part of combined sulfur dioxide was discussed by Ingram (1948).

Sulfur dioxide is much more effective in dilute than in concentrated juices, in which products only a fraction of the added sulfur dioxide remains in the free state (Ingram 1949A and B). Only this fraction is effective in preventing the growth of microorganisms (Downer 1943). Concentrates with addition of sulfurous acid consequently are more likely to ferment than corresponding dilute juices (Pruthi and Lai 1951).

Sorbic Acid.—Sorbic acid is a 2,4-hexadienic acid and is metabolized to carbon dioxide and water, the only known preservative with this important characteristic (Saller 1957).

Sorbic acid or sodium sorbate is effective for the inhibition of yeast fermentation in unpasteurized apple juice (Salunkhe 1955; Ferguson and Powrie 1957; Weaver *et al.* 1957). It is also effective against many common molds, but generally not against bacterial fermentation. The specific mechanism whereby sorbic acid exerts its suppression of microbial growth seems to be by the blocking of the normal functioning of certain sulfhydryl-enzymes (Whitaker 1959). Emard and Vaughn (1952) made the important discovery that sorbic acid is selective, suppressing catalase-positive microorganisms such as most bacteria, actinomycetes, molds and yeasts, but not interferring with catalase-negative species, such as lactic acid bacteria and clostridia. The resistance of *Clostridium parabotulinum* to sorbic acid is particularly noteworthy (York and Vaughn 1955). On this basis Lück (1958, 1960) has developed a most useful appraisal of most organic acids used as preservatives. The degree of efficiency with which they disturb the catalase enzymes determines their usefulness.

Sorbic acid has the advantage of not impairing the taste of fruit juices, to the same extent as benzoic acid (Dryden and Hills 1959). The sodium salt of sorbic acid is, however, not quite as effective as that of benzoic acid (Weaver *et al.* 1957). Sodium sorbate was, nevertheless, able to maintain the freshness of apple juice for seven days at 70° to 75°F and for 10.5 days at 50°F. At higher temperatures molds and yeasts remained under control while bacteria developed. They utilize sorbic acid in their metabolism and thus reduce its amount in the juice and diminishes its preserving influence (Melnick and Luckmann 1954). Sodium hydrosulfite blocks this mechanism but cannot for obvious reasons be used as a food additive. Consequently the effectiveness of sorbic acid is enhanced by reducing the initial load of yeasts.

A recent study confirmed three important aspects of the use of sorbic acid. It is active against the entire group of blastomycetes, including yeasts. The minimum amount is 1 gm per liter which can be reduced when the initial load is lowered below certain values. Finally a growth stimulating effect is evident through minor quantities, e.g. 25–30 mg per liter (Tarantola 1958).

A mild heat treatment improves the effectiveness of added sorbic acid or its salts. Thus by combining sodium sorbate (0.06 to 0.12%) with heat treatment the storage life of fresh apple juice is greatly increased (Robinson and Hills 1959).

Added to apple juice for an effective suppression of yeast the limit value for sorbic acid is 0.6 gm per liter when a normal pH of approximately 3.2 prevails (Burmeister 1958).

Preservation by Freezing

In 1910, Gore of the U.S. Department of Agriculture suggested the freezing preservation of apple juice. The idea was too new, and about the only refrigeration facilities available for holding frozen products were those of commercial cold storages; consequently, little fruit juice was frozen until 1930 when the freezing of orange juice in small containers for sale at retail was tried on a large scale by the then two largest dairy products companies in the United States. The products were of good quality, but the distribution and sale of the juice were found to be too difficult, and therefore, these operations were not continued.

Freezing is the ideal method of preserving apple juice, since after thawing it cannot be distinguished from the fresh product. Nevertheless, very little single strength juice is frozen commercially. The probable reason for this is the length of time required to thaw as small a quantity as one quart.

Unlike canning, freezing does not sterilize fruit juices, it merely reduces the temperature to the point where microorganisms do not multiply and chemical and enzymatic changes take place very slowly. Actually, microorganisms not only do not multiply in frozen fruit juices, but decrease in number until only 5 to 10% of those originally present in the fresh juice remain. The probable reason for this destruction of microorganisms is the concentration of the fruit acids because of the freezing of a large proportion of the water as nearly pure ice crystals.

The more rapidly a juice is frozen, the smaller the ice crystals formed, and the less the amount of colloidal matter coagulated. When rapidly frozen juice is held under fluctuating storage temperatures, the fine ice crystals gradually grow in size. The reason for this is that with each rise in temperature, some of the very small crystals melt. During the subsequent drop in temperature, this water freezes onto other crystals causing them to increase in size. The wider the range of fluctuation and the higher the temperature, the more rapidly the crystals grow (Tressler, Van Arsdel, and Copley 1968).

As the temperature of a juice is slowly lowered during freezing without agitation, the sugars and other dissolved substances move to the center of the container as nearly pure ice freezes around the exterior (Pederson and Beattie 1947). When the juice reaches 0°F, practically all of the juice will be solid except for a little thick syrup in the center of the container.

Storage of the Frozen Juice.—In general, it can be said that the lower the storage temperature, the longer any particular frozen juice may be held without noticeable change in flavor, appearance, or vitamin content. However, unless frozen juices are to be held for more than a year, a storage maintained uniformly at 0°F is entirely satisfactory. Temperatures of 10°F or above permit slow changes in flavor and a gradual loss of vitamin C.

Other factors influencing storage changes are (1) uniformity of storage temperature, (2) oxygen content of the container, and (3) the permeability of the container to air. Maintenance of uniformly low storage temperatures permits less crystal growth and less change in the colloidal state of the juice components (less coagulation) than will occur if the storage temperature is permitted to fluctuate. Frozen juice packed under nitrogen or some other inert gas, or under a high vacuum, deteriorates less rapidly than the same frozen juice packed under air. Juice evacuated prior to freezing will not deteriorate during freezing and subsequent storage as rapidly as that which contains dissolved air. Citrus juices, especially orange juice, are especially subject to oxidative changes caused by the oxygen of the air (Charles and Van Duyne 1952). Oxidation may cause (1) the development of undesirable off-flavor, (2) loss of flavor, (3) destruction of vitamin C, (4) change in color, and (5) coagulation of suspended and colloidal material which will settle when the juice is thawed (Braverman 1949).

In the early work on frozen orange juice, Joslyn and Marsh (1934) reported rapid deterioration of flavor in presence of oxygen and best retention of flavor in juices that were deaerated or those deaerated and treated with nitrogen. Oxidized flavors associated with aeration before freezing have been encountered in certain frozen citrus concentrates (Blair *et al.* 1957). Although complete removal of oxygen was found to improve retention of ascorbic acid and flavor during processing it was found to have little effect on the retention of these quality factors during storage by Kefford *et al.* (1959). They found, however, that in frozen orange juice oxygen does not disappear as rapidly as in heat processed canned juice and efficient deaeration is justified in terms of improved retention of flavor and ascorbic acid.

Thawing Frozen Juices.—If the original quality of the juice is to be retained unimpaired, it is important not only to thaw the juice quickly, but also to keep all of the juice cold, e.g., 50°F or lower, during and after thawing. Small water-tight cartons, jars, or cans of juice can best be thawed by placing them in running cold water, and shaking from time to time. About 15 min is required to thaw a small container by this method. Another rapid method of thawing is to place the containers in front of an electric fan, shaking occasionally to mix the contents. The fan should be stopped just as soon as the juice is completely thawed.

If ample time is available, the simplest method of thawing small cartons and cans of juice is to place the containers in a household refrigerator. From 8 to 24 hr will be required to thaw the juice in a refrigerator, the time needed will vary with the size of container, the temperature of the juice, the temperature and amount of air circulation in the refrigerator, etc. Thawing of small containers of juice by allowing them to stand at room temperature without the benefit of forced air circulation should not be undertaken unless the containers are shaken frequently and the product is either consumed almost immediately after thawing or is removed to a refrigerator.

The thawing of large containers of juice is much more difficult. About the best way is to thaw the juice in warm water or before a fan just sufficiently to permit the cake of ice to be slipped out. After removal, the

TABLE 48

ACID CONTENT OF APPLES

Variety	Malic Acid, %	Citric Acid, %
Crab	1.02	0.03
Delicious	0.27	nil
Grimes Golden	0.72	"
Jonathan	0.75	"
McIntosh	0.72	"
Rome Beauty	0.78	"
Yellow Transparent	0.97	0.02

Source: Joslyn (1950).

cake should be crushed, and the crushed ice rapidly melted in a steam or hot-water-jacketed aluminum or stainless steel kettle, agitating the slush throughout the thawing operation, then shutting off the heat just before all of the ice has been melted, since the flavor of the juice is likely to change if the juice is permitted to become warm. However, if the juice is to be used in the making of jelly, there is no danger in heating it, since it will be necessary to boil it during the jelly making operation.

COMPOSITION OF APPLE JUICE

Apple juice contains a considerable portion of the soluble constituents of the original apple, as for example, sugars, acids, other carbohydrates and minerals. The water content of the fruit affects the quality and composition of the juice, because of its affect on the percentage of soluble solids or specific gravity. Some varieties give a low yield of high soluble solids juice while others give a high yield of low soluble solids juice. The pectin and "pectin-like" compounds have a marked effect on the "body" or viscosity of the juice. The presence of these latter substances influence the ease or difficulty encountered when the juice is filtered and also affect the stability of the juices packed without being brilliantly filtered.

The predominant sugar in apple juice is levulose with small amounts of sucrose and glucose. Hulme (1958) gives the sugars in mature apples as fructose (4.37 to 8.24%), glucose (1.34 to 1.95%) and sucrose (1.72 to 4.18%). The quantity of sugar varies with variety as does the proportion of each sugar. On the basis of geographical location too, there is a variation in the sugar content. A variety grown in one area will have a different sugar content from the same variety grown in another area. Joslyn (1950) gives the maximum reducing sugars in apples as 15.9% and the minimum as 6.6%, with an average of 11.1%.

Malic acid has been the only generally recognized acid present in apple juice. When the acidity of an apple juice is referred to, it is usually stated in terms of malic acid. However, Joslyn (1950) indicates that in some varieties small amounts of citric acid are present as shown in Table 48.

Hulme (1958) lists the following acids as being present in the apple fruit or juice: quinic, glycolic, succinic, lactic, galacturonic and citramalic. Kenworthy and Harris (1960) have shown that apples in Michigan and Washington states in the United States contain malic, oxalacetic, glyoxylic, m-tartaric, uronic and indole-3-acetic acids as determined by chromatographic analysis.

The quantity of acid varies, as do the sugars, with variety, condition of fruit, growing conditions and location. In the eastern regions of North America there seems to be a definite increase in the acidity of apples from south to north. In Virginia the acidity tends to be low with a range of 0.25 to 0.45%, in Pennsylvania the acidity is usually medium with a range of 0.30 to 0.55%, while in Nova Scotia the acidity tends to be high with a range of 0.40 to 85%; all calculated as malic acid. The acidity of apples decreases during storage and ripening. Soft-ripe apples will usually contain only $^{1}/_{2}$ to $^{2}/_{3}$ the acidity of green apples. Apples grown in warm, sunny seasons are as a rule higher in sugar and acid than those grown in a cool, cloudy season, according to Caldwell (1922).

The odorous constituents of the apple have received increased attention with the interest in the production of "full-flavored" apple juice concentrate and apple essence or natural apple flavor. Kirchner (1949) published a comprehensive review of the data on fruit and vegetable flavors, including apple flavor. The publication by White (1950) gives methods of investigation and reports that the constituents of apple flavor are as follows: alcohols (92%): methyl alcohol, ethyl alcohol, propyl alcohol, 2-propanol, butyl alcohol, isobutyl alcohol, *d*-2-methyl-l-butanol, and hexyl alcohol; carbonyl compounds (6%): acetaldehyde, acetone, caproaldehyde, and 2-hexenal; esters (2%): ethyl butyrate and ethyl caproate. Methanol, ethanol, 2-propanol, butanol and formic, acetic, propionic, butyric and caproic acids were identified as components of other esters. These compounds are present in the original fruit at a total concentration of approximately 50 ppm. As these compounds are volatile they are lost to some extent during the processing of apple juice, especially where heating takes place. The extent to which these compounds are "flashed-off" during processing markedly influences the flavor of the finished juice. Every possible precaution should be taken to reduce exposure to heat under conditions where these volatile flavoring components may be lost if a full-flavored apple juice is to be produced.

Tannin is also present in small amounts in apple juice. This group of compounds has a marked effect on the flavor of juice because of their astringency. Tannins are also partially responsible for the rapid darkening of macerated apple tissue and apple juice when they are exposed to the air. Joslyn and Ponting (1951) have published a very comprehensive review on the enzymatic-oxidative browning in fruit products. According to these authors, two enzyme systems are responsible for the oxidative browning of ground up apple tissue and apple juice. These are polyphenol oxidase and peroxidase. Polyphenol oxidase is responsible for the greater part of the discoloration as it oxidizes the catechol and pyrogallol of the tannins in apple juice. Peroxidase is responsible for only a small part of the darkening and it is not required to produce discoloration. There still remains the possibility that other enzyme systems may be present to catalyze the darkening of apple tissue. Hulme (1958) states that plant phenolics or tannins known to be present in apples include; leucoanthocyans, epicatechin, *dl*-catechin, chlorogenic acid, isochlorogenic acid, quinic acid, shikimic acid, *p*-coumaryl quinic acid, quercitrin, isoquercitrin, avicularin, rutin and quercetin-xyloside. According to this author catechin and chlorgenic acid are involved in phenolase catalyzed oxidations.

Atkinson and Strachan (1949A), Charley and Harrison (1939) and Clague and Fellers (1936) have all published analyses of apples that are typical for their particular geographic region. These data are given in Tables 49, 50, and 51.

In freshly pressed apple juice, in addition to the soluble constituents, there are suspended solids ranging from pieces of apple, through pulp and broken cellular material to colloidal particles. Data on the composition of this material as separated by centrifuging are shown in Table 52 from Smock and Neubert (1950).

FORTIFICATION WITH ASCORBIC ACID (VITAMIN C)

The fortification of apple juice with ascorbic acid has been of considerable interest to both the manufacturer and the consumer. This is especially of interest to the consumer because apple juice is naturally low in this vitamin and it is used interchangeably with high vitamin C juices in the diet. In Canada, during World War II, regulations were introduced that made it compulsory to fortify all commercially processed apple juice. In 1946 the regulations were rescinded and for several years fortified apple juice disappeared from the Canadian market. However, commencing in 1954, there has been a steady increase in the volume of fortified apple juice. During this same period there was also an increased interest in the fortified product in the United States.

Fortified apple juice in Canada shall contain not less than 35 mg of biologically active vitamin C per 100 cc of juice as determined by the indophenol titration at any time within 12 months from the date of packing. All containers must be coded to indicate the date of packing.

In the United States, several manufacturers fortified their apple juice but about 1949 this practice was discontinued because they did not feel

TABLE 49

COMPOSITION OF APPLE GROWN IN BRITISH COLUMBIA (1934–45) AND ANALYZED AT OPTIMUM RIPENESS FOR JUICE MANUFACTURE

Variety	Soluble[1] Solids, %	pH	Malic Acid, %	Invert Sugar, %	Tannin,[2] %
Delicious (14)[3]	13.16	3.91	0.27	11.79	0.0261
Golden Delicious (4)	14.26	3.60	0.41	12.39	0.0275
Jonathan (7)	13.56	3.33	0.64	11.45	0.0233
Jubilee (3)	14.94	3.53	0.40	12.60	0.0341
McIntosh (10)	12.72	3.35	0.54	10.89	0.0375
Newtown (5)	13.76	3.31	0.61	11.67	0.0169
Stayman (3)	13.81	3.37	0.59	11.69	0.0236
Winesap (1)	14.83	3.47	0.58	12.82	0.0271
Wealthy (1)	11.90	3.10	0.84	9.85	0.0230

Source: Atkinson and Strachan (1949).
[1] Soluble solids by refractometer.
[2] Tannin by method of Hartman, B. G., *J. Assoc. Off. Agr. Chem. 26*, 452–462.
[3] ( ) Number of samples averaged for result.

TABLE 50

AVERAGE CHEMICAL COMPOSITION OF JUICES OF SOME VARIETIES OF ENGLISH GROWN APPLES

Variety	Type of Fruit	Specific Gravity	Malic Acid, %	Tannin, %
Bramley's Seedling	Culinary	1.046	0.90–1.30	0.12–0.1
Lane's Prince Albert	"	1.045	0.87	0.08
Newton Wonder	"	1.043	0.55	0.08
Stirling Castle	"	1.040	0.64	0.03
Wellington	"	1.043	0.90	0.09
Annie Elizabeth	"	1.052	0.81	0.13
Edward VII	"	1.046	0.77	0.09
Cox's Orange Pippin	Dessert	1.057	0.62	0.06
Laxtonls Superb	"	1.051	0.53	0.05
Allington Pippin	"	1.048	0.70	0.05
Blenhein Orange	"	1.051	0.53	0.05
Wealthy	"	1.040	0.70	0.06
Worcester Permain	"	1.043	0.27	0.10
Vintage				
Kingston Black	Cider	1.060	0.68	0.24
Foxwhelp	"	1.048	0.70	0.24
Sharp				
Frederick	"	1.048	1.00	0.09
Cap of Liberty	"	1.050	0.85	0.22
Dymock Red	"	1.052	0.55	0.22
Sweet				
Sweet Alford	"	1.053	0.26	0.14
Woodbine	"	1.057	0.30	0.16
Bittersweet				
Knotted Kernel	"	1.060	0.38	0.35
Dabinett	"	1.053	0.20	0.25
Yarlington Mill	"	1.050	0.25	0.24
Medaille d'Or	"	1.053	0.25	0.45

Source: Charley and Harrison (1939).

Table 51

COMPOSITION OF SOME NEW ENGLAND VARIETIES USED FOR APPLE JUICE

Variety	Specific Gravity	Degrees Brix	pH	Malic Acid, %	Tannin, %
Baldwin	1.0499	11.8	3.5	0.48	0.06
Ben Davis	1.0450	11.5	3.7	0.43	0.06
King	1.0500	12.9	3.6	0.53	0.07
McIntosh	1.0400	11.5	3.5	0.48	0.08
Northern Spy	1.0452	12.0	3.4	0.49	0.08
Rhode Island Greening	1.0450	12.0	3.5	0.47	0.07
Rosbury Russet	1.0652	16.0	3.3	0.67	0.06
Wealthy	1.0470	12.4	3.3	0.61	0.05

Source: Clague and Fellers (1936).

Table 52

COMPOSITION OF CENTRIFUGED MATERIAL FROM APPLE JUICE

Component	Northern Spy, %	Rome Beauty, %	Russet, %
Dry material, grams[1]	22.0	37.40	43.30
Ash	2.80	4.85	5.50
Fiber	4.24	2.66	2.80
Protein (Nx 6.25)	19.05	30.70	24.75
Protopectin[2]	1.58	3.64	2.72
Pectic material[3]	33.02	24.00	22.80
Tannin	1.58	1.46	0.96
Ether extract	8.19	6.57	5.06
Total sugars	11.60	3.84	2.91
Total	82.06	77.72	67.50

Source: Smock and Neubert (1950).
[1] Centrifuged material in all cases was obtained from 5 gal. of raw juice and dried to a constant weight at 215°F.
[2] Protopectin (pectose) extracted by M/75 HCl and reported as calcium pectate.
[3] Pectic material extracted by M/75 NaOH and reported as calcium pectate.

the added expense of ascorbic acid was justified when their surveys showed that the consumer would not pay a premium for the nutritionally superior fortified products. As mentioned in a previous paragraph there is some indication that the trend is now toward an increased pack of fortified apple juice.

Some packers use small amounts of ascorbic acid in their apple juice for its antioxidant effect. No nutritional claims are made in such cases. This procedure produces a light colored juice and in the cloudy type juices it tends to reduce the amount of sedimentation. Also the flavor of the product is better when a small residual of ascorbic acid is maintained in the finished product. It has also been shown by Aitken (1951B) that with added ascorbic acid in the juice there is less material "baked" on the interior of the pasteurizer.

Strachan (1942), Johnson (1943), Andreae (1943), and Esselen, Powers and Fellers (1946) have reported on the experimental fortification of apple juice on the laboratory scale while Aitken (1942, 1956, 1957), Merck & Co. (1949), Hoffman-LaRoche (1946) and Pfizer (1946) have published on commercial procedures for fortification with ascorbic acid.

Regardless of the method used for fortification, every precaution should be taken to prevent aeration of the apple juice, as oxygen, through the production of peroxides, is the most potent agent in the destruction of ascorbic acid. This detrimental effect of oxygen is catalyzed by traces of iron and copper.

Usually if 50 mg of ascorbic acid per 100 ml of juice are added the finished product will contain approximately 40 mg or 80% of the original amount.

CONCENTRATED APPLE JUICE

Much apple juice is concentrated in vacuum evaporators similar to those used for concentrating orange juice (see Chap. 2). The industry is concentrated in Nova Scotia and Switzerland. The product is a heavy syrup resembling molasses in consistency and appearance and keeps well provided it is filled hot into containers which can be sealed hermetically.

BIBLIOGRAPHY

AITKEN, H. C. 1942. Fortified apple juice. Can. Food Packer *13,* No. 7, 20.

AITKEN, H. C. 1951A. Apple juice. Chemical tests and some notes on their application. Can. Food Inds. *22,* No. 9, 31–36.

AITKEN, H. C. 1951B. Report of laboratory for quality control and research 1947 to 1951. Unpublished report to Berks-Lehigh Cooperative Fruit Growers, Inc. Fleetwood, Pa.

AITKEN H. C. 1956. Vitaminized apple juice. Can. Food Inds. *27,* 34–36.

AITKEN, H. C. 1957. "C"–Enriching tips for cost-watchers. Food Eng. *29,* No. 3, 127.

AITKEN, H. C. 1960. Unpublished data. Canada Vinegars Limited.

ANAND, J. C., SOUMITHRI, T. C., and JOHAR, D. S. 1958. Effectiveness of some chemical food preservatives in controlling fungal spoilage in mango squash. Food Science (Mysore) 7, No. 11, 319–322.

ANDERSON, W. 1949. Inversion of sucrose in candy making. Confectionery Production *15,* 660.

ANDREAE, W. A. 1943. Recent developments on fortification of apple juice with vitamin C. Can. Food Packer *14,* No. 2, 13–14.

ANON. 1953. Series of analyses of fruit varieties for sweet must. Flüssiges Obst. *20,* No. 3, 10–14.

ARENGO-JONES, R. W. 1939A. Carbonation of cider with dry ice. Fruit Products J. *18,* 297.

ARENGO-JONES, R. W. 1939B. The preparation and preservation of apple juice. Fruit Products J. *19,* 327, 330, 356–358, 375, 377; *20,* 7–9, 23, 47–51.

ATKINSON, F. E., and STRACHAN, C. C. 1939. Preparation of fruit juices. Can. Food Packer *10,* No. 8, 9–12.

ATKINSON, F. E., and STRACHAN, C. C. 1940. Chemical constituents of some fruits grown in British Columbia. Sci. Agri. *20*, No. 6, 321–328.

ATKINSON, F. E., and STRACHAN, C. C. 1949A. Production of juices. Dominion of Canada, Dept. Agr. Tech. Bull. *63*.

ATKINSON, F. E., and STRACHAN, C. C. 1949B. The manufacture of natural apple juice. Fruit Products J. *28*, 132–133, 157.

ATKINSON, F. E., and STRACHAN, C. C. 1950. Preservation of color in the milling of apples for natural apple juice. Food Technol. *4*, 133–135.

BAUMANN, J. 1959. Handbook of the sweet must manufacturer. Verlag Ulmer. Stuttgart.

BERTUZZI, A. 1960. "Bertuzzi system" for making dietetic fruit sauces for ice cream. Notizario *18*, No. 140.

BIEDERMANN, W. 1956. Oxidation in fruits and fruit juices. Mitt. Lebensmittelunters. Hyg. *47*, 86–112.

BLAIR, J. S., GODAR, E. M., REINKE, H. G., and MARSHALL, J. R. 1957. The "COF effect" in frozen citrus products. Food Technol. *11*, 61–68.

BOEHI, A. 1912. A new process of making alcohol-free fruit and grape wines (carbonic acid process). Verlag Huber and Co. Frauenfend, Switzerland.

BORGSTRÖM, G. 1954. Preservation of fruit juices by sterilization filtration, chemical preservatives, etc. *In* The Chemistry and Technology of Fruit and Vegetable Juice Production, D. K. Tressler, and M. A. Joslyn (Editors). Avi Publishing Co., Westport, Conn.

BRAVERMAN, J. B. S. 1949. Citrus Products. Chemical Composition and Chemical Technology. Interscience Publishers, New York.

BROWN, H. D., and BEACH, F. 1936. Sweet cider. Ohio State Agr. College Mimeo.

BROWN, H. D., FITZGERALD, C., and NEUMAN, F. 1939. Preserving cider by carbonation. Am. Soc. Hort. Sci. *36*, 371–373.

BRUNNER, H. 1957. A space-saving method of storage for sweet must. Schweiz. Ztschr. Obst- und Weinbau *66*, 274–275.

BRUNNER, H., and SENN, G. 1958. Contribution to the qualitative analytical determination of aromatic substances. Schweiz. Ztschr. Obst- und Weinbau, *67*, 8–11.

BÜCHI, W. 1958. Origin, chemical properties and test for aromatic substances. 16. Jahresber. Schweiz. Obst- und Weinfachschule, Wädenswil (German).

BÜCHI, W., ULLMANN, F., and PFENNINGER, H. 1959. Determination of glucose and fructose in stone-fruit juices. Flüssiges Obst *4*, 46–52.

BUCHLOH, G. 1956. The influence of "air-wash" on the storage of apples. Angew. Bot. *30*, 169.

BURMEISTER, H. 1958. Preservation of raw pressjuice of fruit. Flüssiges Obst. 25, No. *12*, 13–17 (German).

CALDWELL, J. S. 1922. Farm manufacture of unfermented apple juice. U.S. Dept. Agr. Farmers Bull. *1264*.

CARPENTER, D. C. 1933. Carbonated apple juice. Fruit Products J. *13*, 37, 59.

CARPENTER, D. C., PEDERSON, C. S., and WALSH, W. F. 1932. Sterilization of fruit juices by filtration. Ind. Eng. Chem. *24*, 1218–1223.

CARTWRIGHT, R. A., ROBERTS, E. A. H., FLOOD, A. E., and WILLIAMS, A. H. 1955. The suspected presence of p-coumarylic-quinic acid in the apple and pear. Chem. and Ind. 1062.

Celmer, R., and Cruess, W. V. 1937. Carbonated fruit juices in cans. Fruit Products J. *16,* 229, 251.

Chambers, G. F. 1949. Nitrogen processing of apple juice. Linde Air Products Co. Tech. Memo. *8–28.*

Chambers, G. F. 1950. Juice color is bettered by gas blanket. Food Inds. *22,* No. 1, 88–90.

Charles, V. R., and Van Duyne, F. O. 1952. Comparison of fresh, frozen, concentrated and canned orange juice. J. Am. Dietet. Assoc. 534–538.

Charley, V. L. S., and Harrison, T. H. J. 1939. Fruit juices and related products. Imp. Bur. Hort. and Plant Crops, Tech. Commun. *11.*

Cheldelin, V. H., and Williams, R. J. 1942. The B-vitamin content of foods. Univ. Texas Publ. *4237.*

Clague, J. A., and Fellers, C. R. 1936. Apple cider and cider products. Mass. Agr. Expt. Sta. Bull. *336.*

Cruess, W. V., and Richert, P. H. 1929. The effect of H-ion concentration on the toxicity of sodium benzoate to micro-organisms. J. Bacteriol. *17,* 363–371.

Cruess, W. V., Richert, P. H., and Irish, J. H. 1931. The effect of hydrogen-ion concentration on the toxicity of several preservatives to micro-organisms. Hilgardia *6,* 295–314.

Dimick, K. P., Ponting, J. D., and Makower, B. 1951. Heat inactivation of polyphenolase in fruit purées. Food Technol. *5,* 237–241

Downer, A. W. E. 1943. The preservation of citrus juices with sulphurous acid. J. Soc. Chem. Ind. *62,* 124–127.

Dryden, E. C., and Hills, C. H. 1959. Taste thresholds for sodium benzoate and sodium sorbate in apple cider. Food Technol. *13,* 84–86.

Duman, K. 1957. The most valuable fruit varieties. Verlag G. Fromme, Wien.

Eggenberger, W. 1949. Biochemical examination of apples during development and storage. Diss. ETH Zürich, Ber. Schweiz. Bot. Ges. *59,* 91–154.

Emard, L. O., and Vaughn, R. H. 1952. Selectivity of sorbic acid media for the catalase negative lactic acid bacteria and clostridia. J. Bacteriol. *63,* 487–494.

Esselen, W. B., Jr. 1945. A study of methods of clarification and blends of Massachusetts apples for apple juice. Fruit Products J. *24,* 165–168, 189.

Esselen, W. B., Jr., Powers, J. J., and Fellers, G. R. 1946. The fortification of fruit juices with ascorbic acid. Fruit Products J. *26,* 11–13 29.

Fabian, F. W., and Marshall, R. E. 1935. How to make, clarify and preserve cider. Mich. Agr. Expt. Sta. Circ. Bull. 98 Rev.

Ferguson, W. E., and Powrie, W. D. 1957. The preservation of fresh apple juice with sorbic acid. Appl. Microbiol. *5,* 51–43.

Gennerich, M. 1938. Contribution to the production of sweet must bv carbonic acid pressure process. (Boehi-Seitz). Diss. Techn. Hochschule München.

Hadorn, H., und Högl, O. 1945. Statistics of the stone-fruit juices of 1944. Mitt. Lebensmittelunters. u. Hyg. *36,* 216–231.

Heller, M. E., Nold, T., and Willaman, J. J. 1947. Survey of apple juice packed in 1946. U.S. Dept. Agr. Bur. Agr. and Ind. Chem. Mimeo AIC 161. Also Fruit Products J. *27,* 77–79, 87–89.

Heller, M. E., Nold, T., and Willaman, J. J. 1949. Survey of apple juice packed in 1947. Fruit Products J. *28,* 164–166.

HEUPKE, W. 1949. Fruit and fruit juice diets for the healthy and the sick. Umschau-Verlag Frankfurt a.M.

HOFFMAN-LAROCHE. 1946. Vitamin C (ascorbic acid) enriched apple juice. Vitamin Div., Hoffman-LaRoche, Inc., Nutley, N.J.

HOLGATE, K. C., MOYER, J. C., and PEDERSON, C. S. 1948. The use of ascorbic acid in preventing oxidative changes in apple juice. Fruit Products J. *28*, 100–102, 112.

HULME, A. C. 1958. Some aspects of the biochemistry of apple and pear fruits. Advan. Food Research *8*, 297–413.

INGRAM, M. 1948. The germicidal effect of free and combined sulfur dioxide. J. Soc. Chem. Ind. (London) *67*, 18–21.

INGRAM, M. 1949A. Fermentation in concentrated orange juice. Food Manuf. *24*, 121–124.

INGRAM, M. 1949B. Behavior of sulfur dioxide in concentrated orange juice. Food Research *14*, 54–71.

IRISH, J. H. 1933. Juice ratios for carbonated beverages. Fruit Products J. *12*, 196–197, 220.

JACKSON, S. F., CHICHESTER, C. O., and JOSLYN, M. A. 1960. The browning of ascorbic acid. Food Research *25*, 484–490.

JACQUIN, P. 1955. The pear. Bull. Soc. Sci. Hyg. Aliment. *43*, 1.

JACQUIN, P., and TAVERNIER, J. 1954. Contribution to a study of the principal constitutents of perry pears during growth and maturation. Ann. technol. agr. (Paris) *3*, 209.

JENNY, J. 1952. The scientific basis for the preservation of grape and stone fruit juices under carbon dioxide pressure. Ind. Agric. Alim. *69*, 1–14.

JOHNSON, F. P. 1943. Vitamin C fortification of apple juice. Fruit Products J. *22*, 195–197.

JOSLYN, M. A. 1950. Methods in Food Analysis applied to Plant Products. Academic Press, New York.

JOSLYN, M. A., and MARSH, G. L. 1934. The keeping quality of frozen orange juice. Ind. Eng. Chem. *26*, 295–299.

JOSLYN, M. A., MIST, S., and LAMBERT, E. 1952. The clarification of apple juice by fungal pectic enzyme preparations. Food Technol. *6*, 133–139.

JOSLYN, M. A., and PONTING, J. D. 1951. Enzyme-catalyzed oxidative browning of fruit products. Advances in Food Research *3*, 1–44.

KEFFORD, J. F., MCKENZIE, H. A., and THOMPSON, P. C. O. 1959. Effects of oxygen on quality and ascorbic acid retention in canned and frozen orange juice. J. Sci. Food Agr. *10*, 51–63.

KENWORTHY, A. L., and HARRIS, N. 1960. Organic acids in the apple as related to variety and source. Food Technol. *14*, 372–375.

KESSLER, H. 1945. Swiss Apple Varieties. Verbandsdruckerei A.G. Bern, Switzerland.

KESSLER, H. 1948. Swiss Pear Varieties. Verbandsdruckerei A.G. Bern, Switzerland.

KIESER, M. E., POLLARD, A., and WILLIAMS, A. H. 1953. The occurrence of leuco-anthocyanins in perry pears. Chem. and Ind. *1953*, 12, 60.

KIRCHNER, J. G. 1949. The chemistry of fruit and vegetable flavors. Advances in Food Research *2*, 259–296.

KRÜMMEL, GROH, FRIEDRICH. 1956. German Fruit Varieties. Deutsch. Bauernverlag, Berlin.

LAVOLLAY, J. 1950. Oxidation during the production and preservation of fruit juices. Rapp. IIme congrès Fd. Int. Producteurs de Jus Fruits, Zürich, 53–81.

LAWLER, F. K. 1961. New juice process cuts costs. Food Eng. *33*, No. 2, 71–72.

LÜCK, H. 1958. The effect of preservatives on hemin enzymes. I. General effects. Z. Lebensm. Forsch. *108*, No. 1, 1–9.

LÜCK, H. 1960. The effect of preservatives on hemin enzymes. II. Investigation of the correlation between the preservative effect of organic acids and their catalase inhibition. Z. Lebensm. Unters. Forsch. *3*, No. 3, 190–198.

LÜTHI, H. 1953. Recent analyses of the significance and preservation of oxidative reactions in apple juice. Int. Fruchtsaft-Union, Zug. 1953.

LÜTHI, H. 1954. The significance of the oxidation of our fruit juices by enzymes. Schweiz. Ztschr. Obst- und Weinbau *63*, 455, 469, 494.

LÜTHI, H. 1958A. Concerning some causes of incomplete fermentation of fruit juice concentrates which have become brown. Bet. Int. Fruchtsaft-Union, Symposium Bristol, 391–399.

LÜTHI, H. 1958B. The significance of the continual pressing of fruit and grape juices. Flüssiges Obst. *25*, No. 4, 16–19.

LÜTHI, H. 1959A. Progress in the making of fruit juices. Flüssiges Obst. *26*, No. 7, 8.

LÜTHI, H. 1959B. The elimination of the metallic taste in sweet must stored under carbonic acid pressure. Landw. Jahrb. Schweiz. *73*, 108–111.

LÜTHI, H. 1960. The determination of some qualitative factors in alcohol-free fruit juices. Schweiz. Ztschr. Obst-u-Weinbau, *69*, 407–412, 490–495.

LÜTHI, H., and HOCHSTRASSER, R. 1952. Concerning two new infections recently becoming common in the farm production of sweet must. Schweiz. Ztschr. Obst- und Weinbau *61*, 301–307, 359–361.

LÜTHI, H., and HOTZ, E. 1960. Concerning the utilization of ascorbic acid in the home and farm sweet must industries. Schweiz. Ztschr. Obst- und Weinbau *69*, 506–508.

LÜTHI, H., and STEINER, K. 1957. The storage of fruit juice half-concentrates. Schweiz, Ztschr. Obst- und Weinbaur *66*, 269–274.

LÜTHI, H., and VETSCH, U. 1955. Concerning the occurrence of temperature resistant fungi in the sweet must industry. Schweiz. Ztschr. Obst- und Beinbau *64*, 404–409.

LÜTHI, H., and VETSCH, U. 1960. A simplified method for the determination of germ numbers and for biological manufacturing control. Mitt. Lebensmittelunters. u. Hygiene *51*, 394–399.

MACFARLANE, W. D., and DAVIS, M. B. 1941. Fruit and vegetable juices and processes of producing the same. Can. Pat. 395,770.

MARSHALL, R. E. 1943. Prevention of precipitation in processed apple juice. Fruit Products J. *23*, 40–42.

MARSHALL, R. E. 1946. Prevention of sedimentation in apple juice clarified by the enzyme method. Proc. Am. Soc. Hort. Sci. *47*, 75–78.

MARSHALL, R. E. 1947. Apple juice. Preparation and preservation. Mich. Sta. College. Agr. Expt. Sta. Circ. Bull. *206*.

MEHLITZ, A. 1951. Sweet must. Serger und Hempel, Braunschweig.

MEHLITZ, A. 1959. Composition of fruit juices. V. Int. Fruchtsaftkongress, Wein.

MEHLITZ, A., und MATZIK, B. 1956. The recognition of volatile acids occurring in fruit juices. Fruchtsaft-Industrie, *1*, 130–146.

Mehlitz, A., and Matzik, B. 1958. Aromatic substances in apple juice. Flüssiges Obst. *10*, 18–23.

Melnick, D., and Luckmann, F. N. 1954. Sorbic acid as a fungistatic agent for foods. II. Spectrophotometric determination of sorbic acid in cheese and in cheese wrappers. Food Research *19*, 20–27.

Merck and Company, Inc. 1949. Ascorbic acid as an antioxidant in fruit and fruit products. Merck and Company, Rahway, N.J.

Meyer, A., and De Vos, L. 1959. Determination of total titrable acid (TTA) content of fruit juices. Proceedings Int. Fruit Juice Union *2*, 64–68.

Miller-Thurgau, H. 1896. The production of unfermented and alcohol-free fruit and grape juices. Verlag Huber & Cie., Frauenfeld (Schweiz).

Milleville, H. P. 1960. Continuous apple pressing. Food Processing *21*, No. 9, 38–39.

Monier-Williams, G. W. 1937. The determination of sulfur dioxide. Min. Health Rept. *43*. His Majesty Stationery Office, London, England.

Mottern, H. H., Nold, T., and Willamen, J. J. 1941. Survey of apple juice packed in 1940. Fruit Products J. *21*, 68–71.

Neubert, A. M. 1943. Effect of filtration on appearance, viscosity, and alcohol-insoluble fraction of apple juice. Food Research *8*, 477–488.

Neubert, A. M., Carter, G. H., and Ingalsbe, D. W. 1956. A study of commercial juice apples of the Pacific Northwest. Food Technol. *10*, 396–399.

Pederson, C. S. 1947. Apple juice with original character retained. Fruit Product J. *26*, 294, 313.

Pederson, C. S., and Beattie, H. G. 1947. Concentration of fruit juices by freezing. N.Y. State Agr. Expt. Sta. Bull. 727.

Pfizer, C. and Co., Inc.. 1946. The use of ascorbic acid in the food industry in frozen fruits and fruit juices. Tech. Service Chas. Pfizer and Company, New York.

Phillips, J. D., Pollard, A., Whiting, G. C. 1956. Organic acid metabolism in cider and perry fermentations. J. Sci. Food Agr. *7*, 31–40.

Pollard, A. 1959. Organic acid and amino-acid in fruit juices. 5. Int. Fruit Juice Congrès, Vienna.

Power, F. B., and Chestnut, V. K. 1920. The odorous constituents of apples. J. Am. Chem. Soc. *42*, 1509–1526.

Pruthi, J. S., and Lal, G. 1951. Preservation of citrus fruit juice. J. Sci. Ind. Research (New Delhi) *10*, No. 2, 36–41.

Rentschler, H., and Tanner, H. 1956. Concerning tannins of some fruit juices. Fruchtsaft-Industrie *1*, 30–35.

Rentschler, H., and Tanner, H. 1960. Concerning a hitherto unexplained copper tarnishing of alcohol-free stone-fruit juices. Schweiz. Ztschr. Obst- und Weinbau, *69*, 368–371.

Robinson, J. F., and Hills, C. H. 1959. Preservation of fruit products by sodium sorbate and mild heat. Food Technol. *13*, 251–253.

Saller, W. 1957. Sorbic acid–a new preservative for fruit juices. Fruchtsaft-Industrie 2, 14–19.

Salunkhe, D. K. 1955. Sorbic acid as a preservative for apple juice. Food Technol. 9, 590.

Schaller, A. 1959. The location of the equilibrium point in potentiometric determinations of acidity of fruit juices by titration. Fruchtsaft-Industrie *4*, 160–163.

SCHMITTHENNER, F. 1949. The action of carbonic acid on yeasts and bacteria. Der Weinbau. Wiss. Beihefte *3,* 147–187.

SCHUBERT, E. 1951. The evaluation of filtration-enzymes. Schweizer Brauerei-Rundschau *62,* Nos. 3–4.

SCHUBERT, E. 1952. The action of pectinase on apple juice and pectin solutions. Schweizer Brauerei-Rundschau *63,* 95–101.

SCHWILCH, W. 1959. The making of sweet must. Wetzikon/Kempton, Schwiez.

SIPPLE, H. L., MCDONNELL, G. H., and LUECK, R. H. 1940. The canning of apple juice. Fruit Product J. *19,* 167–171, 180–183, 187.

SMOCK, R. M., and NEUBERT, A. M. 1950. Apples and Apple Products. Interscience Publ., New York.

SOCIÉTÉ POMOLGIQUE DE FRANCE. 1947/48. The French Orchard. B. Arnoud, Paris.

STRACHAN, C. C. 1942. Factors influencing ascorbic acid retention in apple juice. Can. Dept. Agr. Tech. Bull. *40.*

STRACKENBROCK, K. H. 1961. Investigations concerning the aroma of apples. Diss. Friedr. Wilhelm, Universität, Bonn.

TANNER, H., and RENTSCHLER, H. 1954. The synthesis of fruit acids from Swiss fruit juices. 2. The fruit acids of Swiss apple ciders. Mitt. Lebensmittelunters. u. Hyg. *45,* 305–311.

TANNER, H., and RENTSCHLER, H. 1956. Concerning the phenol of stonefruit and grape juices. Fruchtsaft-Industrie *1,* 231–245.

TARANTOLA, C. 1958. Action of sorbic acid on yeasts. Acad. ital. vite e vino, Siena, Atti *10,* 147–167.

TÄUFEL, K., and MÜELLER, K. 1957. The oxidiometric determination of sorbitol in wine using the paper-chromatography approach. Z. Lebensmitteluntersuch. Forschung *106,* 123–128.

TAVERNIER, J., and JACQUIN, P. 1955. Quality of apples and pears varieties. Ann. Nutrition et Alimentaire *9,* 5–6.

TAYLOR, H. V. 1946. The Apples of England. Crosby Lockwood, London.

TRENKLE, R. 1950. Work in fruit varieties. The fruit varieties of Bavaria most worthwhile to develop. Bayr. Landesverb. Obst- und Gartenbau, München.

TRESSLER, D. K., VAN ARSDEL, W. B., and COPLEY, M. J. 1958. The Freezing Preservation of Foods. 4 Volumes. Avi Publishing Co., Westport, Conn.

WALSH, W. F. 1934. Cider making on the farm. N.Y. State Agr. Expt. Sta. Circ. 149.

WALROD, R. P. 1957A. Process for the production of fruit juice in the natural state thereof. Can. Pat. 549,526, Dec. 3.

WALROD, R. P. 1957B. Process for the production of fruit juice in the natural state thereof. U.S. Pat. 2,817,589, Dec. 24.

WARCOLLIER, G. 1928. The Cider Factory. J. B. Bailliere and Sons, Paris.

WEAVER, E. A., ROBINSON, J. F., and HILLS, C. H. 1957. Preservation of apple cider with sodium sorbate. Food Technol. *11,* 667–669.

WHITAKER, J. R. 1959. Inhibition of sulfhydryl enzymes with sorbic acid. Food Research *24,* 37–43.

WHITE, J. W., JR. 1950. Composition of a volatile fraction of apples. Food Research *15,* 68–78.

WHITING, G. C., and COGGINS, R. A. 1960. Organic acid metabolism in cider and perry fermentations. 2. Non-volatile organic acids of cider-apple juices and sulphited ciders. J. Sci. Food Agr. *11*, 337–344.

YORK, G. K., and VAUGHN, R. H. 1955. Resistance of *Clostridium parabotulinum* to sorbic acid. Food Research *20*, 60–65.

CHAPTER 7

C. S. Pederson

Grape Juice

INTRODUCTION

The processed fruit juice industry originated in 1869 when a dentist, Dr. Thomas B. Welch, and his 17 year old son, Charles, gathered grapes from their trellis in Vineland, New Jersey, prepared juice, filtered it, filled it into bottles and pasteurized it in hot water long enough to kill the yeasts. Dr. Welch was using the principles expressed in Louis Pasteur's theory of pasteurization. He thus established a new and great industry.

The juice so prepared was placed on the communion table in the local Methodist church for sacramental use in the fall of 1869. The orders for juice, primarily for communion purpose, increased to such an extent that much of the time of Dr. Welch and his son, Dr. Charles E. Welch, was occupied with preparing juices. In 1896, Dr. Charles Welch transferred operations to Watkins Glen, N.Y., and the following year to Westfield, N.Y. Some 300 tons of grapes were pressed that year. Five years later production had increased to 3,000 tons. A gradual increase in production has occurred since then (see Chap. 1).

In 1967, 95,485 tons of a total crop of 141,134 tons were converted to grape juice in New York State (Table 53; see also Chap. 1). Yearly production of grapes has increased steadily since 1949 (Fig. 67) in the Lake Erie and Finger Lakes grape belts and even more rapidly in Washington. The development of concentrated juice, grape drinks, jellies, and other products have been valuable outlets. The streamlining of processing, improved pressing, continuous pasteurizing, cooling and transfer to cool storage tanks has speeded processing and improved quality. Mechanical harvesting has reduced picking costs and transfer of grapes to the factory.

No grape has rivalled the Concord variety for grape juice quality. Relatively few grapes produce juices with such a balance of sugars, acids, flavoring substances and astringent characteristics, resulting in such a palatable and wholly satisfactory juice. Although it is sweet, the acid, astringent characteristic yields a juice which is not only refreshing but also thirst quenching. The strong, tangy and somewhat astringent flavor does not appeal to all individuals. Few, however, have realized that the juice is more highly flavored than most other fruit juices and that if it is subjected to dilution and sweetening, it will still impart a rich flavor. Many in-

Carl S. Pederson is Emeritus Professor, Food Science and Technology Department, New York State Agricultural Experiment Station, Cornell University, Geneva, N. Y.

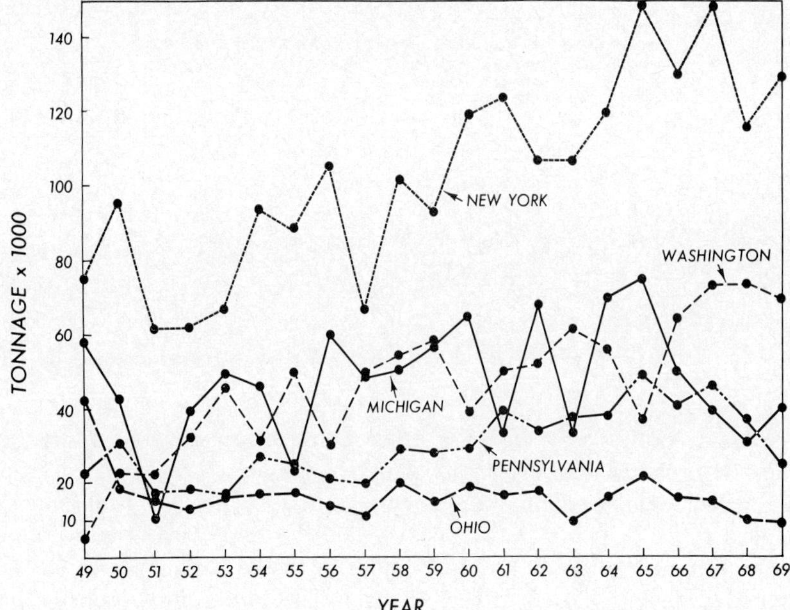

Fig. 67. Grape Production in New York, Michigan, Washington, Pennsylvania 1949–1969

dividuals who do not care for the rich, tangy, astringent flavor of the undiluted juice prefer the sweeter grape juice drinks or drinks made from frozen concentrates.

Varieties

There are three distinct broad classes of grapes grown in the three principal grape growing areas of the United States, the northeastern or native euvitis or bunch grape *Vitis lubrusca*, the western grape common to the California area, *Vitis vinifera*, and the southeastern Muscadine grape, *Vitis rotundifolia*.

One species, *Vitis vinifera*, supplied all the grapes that were used by civilized man prior to the discovery of America. It is the grape of the Bible, of myths and poets; the grape from which wines, raisins and table grapes are produced. Its varieties are still important varieties throughout the world. When North America was colonized, it was soon found that the varieties of this species could not stand the severe winters and the attacks of insects and diseases. The Colonists found many native grapes which thrived despite the insects and which could develop in the relatively cold climate. Selection of hybrids of *Vitis labrusca* crossed with the American species gave us new types of grapes.

Table 53

UTILIZATION OF GRAPES IN NEW YORK STATE IN TONS

Variety	Sweet Juice		Wine		Other Products	
	1967	1968	1967	1968	1967	1968
Concord	91,922	54,118	16,386	15,576	4,454	3,898
Fredonia	1,036	ND[1]	87	...		
Clinton	4	ND	33	15		
Niagara	1,734	ND	7,917	5,158	12	
Catawba	107	237	6,221	3,866		
Delaware	565	ND	3,654	ND		
Elvira	29	ND	1,798	ND		
Ives, Riesling, Dutchess, Isabella and others	88	372	5,086	1,293	1	

Source: U. S. Dept. Agr., Agricultural Marketing Service, New York State Crop Reporting Service, Jan. 1969.
[1] ND = Data not available.

Ephraim Bull, a horticulturist, tried for years to develop a superior grape by crossing many varieties of native grapes. The Concord grape was an accidental seedling of unknown parentage which Mr. Bull found in his garden.

The unfermented grape products industry in the United States has developed from one variety, the Concord. The grape juice industry has been built around this variety to the extent that no other grape is welcome to the manufacturers. Its varieties are still the important juice varieties throughout the world and are now being used both straight and in blends. It is grown throughout the cooler areas of the United States and Canada. Washington has now become one of the leading states in production. When hot pressed, Concord grapes yield a highly colored and flavored juice which is deep red by transmitted light and reddish purple by reflected light. When bottled juice is shaken, the purple red color of the foam in the neck of the bottle is distinctive. Its aroma and flavor, due to a considerable extent to methyl anthranilate, is characteristic. Relatively few grapes produce juices having the balance of sugar, acid, flavor, and astringent constituents so that they are wholly satisfactory for making juice. Concord grapes are easily grown throughout the cooler climates and yield well year after year. Although they vary slightly from year to year and in different sections of the country, the almost exclusive use of this variety has standardized the product. The use of earlier or even later varieties would make it possible to spread the processing season and to harvest more grapes at their optimum maturity.

Among the many natural crosses or hybrids of the native species, the Fredonia and Van Buren yield equally as well as the Concord, and since the latter ripens as much as three weeks earlier, their use would extend the season. The use of the Sheridan, as well as many others would also extend the season. However, in spite of their similarity to the Concord,

Courtesy of Welch Grape Juice Co.

FIG 68. MECHANICAL HARVESTING OF CONCORD GRAPES

their lack of typical flavor and methyl anthranilate decreases their acceptability for juice (Robinson, Shaulis and Pederson 1949). Thus approximately 96% of the juice made in New York State is prepared from Concord grapes (Agricultural Marketing Service, New York Crop Reporting Service, Jan. 1969). The Ives and Clinton yield juices of unusual flavor and good color. Catawba and Delaware juices are light red when hot-pressed and nearly colorless when cold-pressed. Catawba and Isabella have fragrance peculiar to the variety. During prohibition some unfermented juices were prepared from Catawba and other varieties. Because of the demand for these grapes for wine making, little is used for unfermented juices.

Recently excellently flavored opalescent juice has been prepared by cold pressing Niagara, Ontario, Seneca, and other white or green grapes, using ascorbic acid to inhibit or delay undesirable oxidative changes (Pederson, Robinson, and Shaulis 1953). These grapes, however, are finding still greater acceptance in the wine industry.

The grapes of Northern United States are either selections from natural crosses or hybrids produced by crossing native species with the European *Vinifera* species. The climate of the West is suitable for growing varieties of the species *Vitis vinifera.* Although California produces more grapes than all of the other states, relatively little unfermented juice is preserved in this region. At least one large winery in California produces grape juice commercially. In general, the *Vinifera* grapes of the West are much higher in sugar and lower in acidity than the types grown in the East, and with the exception of the Muscat varieties, possess no characteristic flavor. It is probable that this lack of tartness and flavor is the reason why California grape juices have not met with popular favor as have the stronger flavored Concord juices. Mixtures prepared recently by blending juice from Concord grapes with juices from some of the other varieties have met with more favor (Anon. 1951). The Pierce Isabella, a tart highly colored "foxy" grape, and a new variety, Scarlet, come closer to giving a juice resembling that of the Northern grapes than any other variety growing in California.

The *Vitis vinifera* varieties of grapes commonly grown in California, must be blended in order to obtain a desirable juice. Juice produced from the Muscat has a strong flavor but is colorless and insufficiently tart. It lends itself to blending with suitable red wine grapes, e.g., Barbera, Valdepenas, St. Macaire, and Crabbe's Black Burgundy. Other blends may be prepared with some of the more common varieties, Petite Sirah, Zinfandel, Alicante Bouschet, and Carignane.

Tokay grapes have been used in producing a white grape juice in California. This juice may be blended with Muscat. The Muscat yields a rich musky flavored juice. Zinfandel juice is sprightly and Mission juice is sweet.

In the Southeastern States, varieties of *Vitis rotundifolia* are grown. These are Muscadines and not true grapes. The berries are borne singly or in very small clusters, mature irregularly, and drop when ripe. Nevertheless, they are important since they are hardy under hot and humid conditions. Muscadine grape juice, properly prepared, has a bouquet said to be equalled by few other fruit juices. Blends have a beautiful deep red color and a refreshing taste. Varieties vary in color from almost white to pink, red, blue, and purple. Scuppernong and Hunt varieties are most popular. Murphy *et al.* (1938) also recommend the Brownie, Creek, Dulcet, Hunt, and Yuga.

Varieties of *Vitis vinifera* are used in Europe for making grape juice. A highly sulfited grape juice is prepared in France. It is assumed that juices produced in other areas of the world were obtained from some of these varieties.

In discussion of varieties of grapes for grape juice, one must compare

TABLE 54

VOLATILE CONSTITUENTS OF CONCORD GRAPE JUICE ESSENCE

Compound	Concentration, mg per ml
Ethanol	35.0
Methanol	1.5
Ethyl acetate	3.5
Methyl acetate	0.15
Acetone	0.30
Acetaldehyde	0.03
Methyl anthranilate	0.33

Source: Holley, Stoyla, and Holley (1955).

their characteristics with Concord. Concord juice has a rich purple red color that presents a good appearance without necessitating clarification and resultant loss of viscous character. Of all fruit juices, it is one of the juices most stable to heat processing and storage.

In processing, the naturally occurring flavoring constituents of grape juice, sugars, volatile constituents, tannins, pigments should be disturbed as little as possible, except for precipitation of excess tartrates. Juices from most varieties of grapes are not so stable as that of the Concord and many are brown, gray or muddy-colored, tending to throw down a muddy unsightly precipitate even after the second processing. Some juices lose their fresh flavor and acquire an unpleasant cooked taste when subjected to pasteurization (Winkler 1949). Clarification and filtration, therefore, are almost a necessity; of the major juices of commerce marketed today, only apple and grape juice are clarified.

COMPOSITION OF GRAPE JUICE

Grape juice is the liquid expressed from suitably ripened fruit of the grape. Grape juice differs little in composition from the grapes except for the content of crude fiber and the oils which are primarily present in the seed. The principal flavor constituents include the sugars, acids, anthranilate, volatile esters, acids, alcohols, and aldehydes. An analysis presented by the Welch Grape Juice Company has shown that grapes also contain in addition to the mineral elements, sodium, potassium, calcium, phosphorus, iron, copper, and manganese, the organic substances; biotin, niacin, inositol, pantothenic acid, pyridoxine hydrochloride, thiamine, folic acid, ascorbic acid, choline and even trace amounts of riboflavin and vitamin B_{12}. Berg (1940) listed among other compounds, vitamins C and B_2, and the enzymes, invertase, oxidase, protopectinase, and pectase. Sastry and Tischer (1952A) have shown that in addition to the anthocyanin pigments, Concord grapes contain chlorophyll, carotenes, and water soluble yellow pigments.

TABLE 55

CHEMICAL COMPOSITION OF HOT- AND COLD-PRESSED CONCORD GRAPE JUICE

Juice Pressed Before or After Heating	Solids	Sugar (as Invert Before Inversion)	Non-sugar Solids	Total Acid as Tartaric	Total Tartaric Acid Free and Combined	Free Tartaric Acid	Cream of Tartar	Ash	Tannin and Coloring matter	Alkalinity of: Soluble Ash	Alkalinity of: Insoluble Ash
	Gm per 100 ml									N/10 Acid per 100 ml	
Maximum											
Before	17.20	14.36	2.84	0.84	0.65	0.24	0.62	0.27	0.08	33.2	3.6
After	18.50	15.12	3.63	1.16	1.04	0.35	1.05	0.46	0.24	55.8	4.8
Minimum											
Before	15.66	13.38	2.25	0.74	0.55	0.09	0.42	0.20	0.06	22.4	2.6
After	16.44	13.29	3.15	1.01	0.94	0.12	0.71	0.33	0.19	38.0	3.8
Average											
Before	16.36	13.93	2.43	0.78	0.61	0.16	0.50	0.23	0.07	26.9	3.1
After	17.43	14.03	3.40	1.09	0.99	0.22	0.88	0.39	0.21	46.7	4.2
Average Increase	1.07	0.10	0.97	0.31	0.38	0.06	0.38	0.16	0.14	19.8	1.1

Source: Hartmann and Tolman (1918).

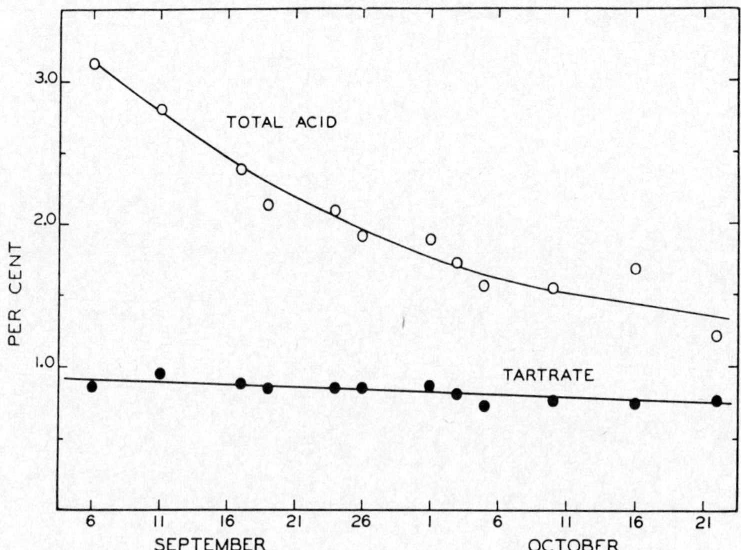

FIG. 69. CHANGES IN ACID CONTENT OF CONCORD GRAPES DURING RIPENING

The sugars are the principal constituents of the soluble solids. While grape sugar and glucose are synonymous, grapes actually contain invert sugar and, in some instances, a considerable amount of sucrose. As much as one-third of the total sugar has been found to be sucrose in certain samples of grapes (Table 55). However, other samples contain little or no sucrose (Caldwell 1925). The smaller quantity of acids, flavor substances such as methyl anthranilate and volatiles, tannins and color substances have a greater effect upon the quality of the juice (Table 54). The changes that occur in grapes during growth markedly affect the quality of the juice.

The natural acidity, color, and aroma of the fresh grapes provide the characteristic fruitiness in single-strength Concord juice. If the juice is above 0.85% acidity the juice tends to be too tart; if sugar must be added to make the juice pleasantly sweet, the processed juice must be labelled *sugar added.* Sufficient pigment must be present to give the foam a deep color. Sufficient quantities of specific esters must be present to give a pronounced Concord aroma. Flavor and aroma reach a peak during the ripening process. The Brix measurement is the most satisfactory method for grading grapes according to Robinson and Shaulis (1968).

The principal acids of grape juice are tartaric and malic, although small amounts of citric, succinic, lactic, and other acids have been reported. The tartaric acid may be present as free tartaric acid or as salts such as potassium bitartrate. Robinson, Shaulis, Smith, and Tallman (1959) ob-

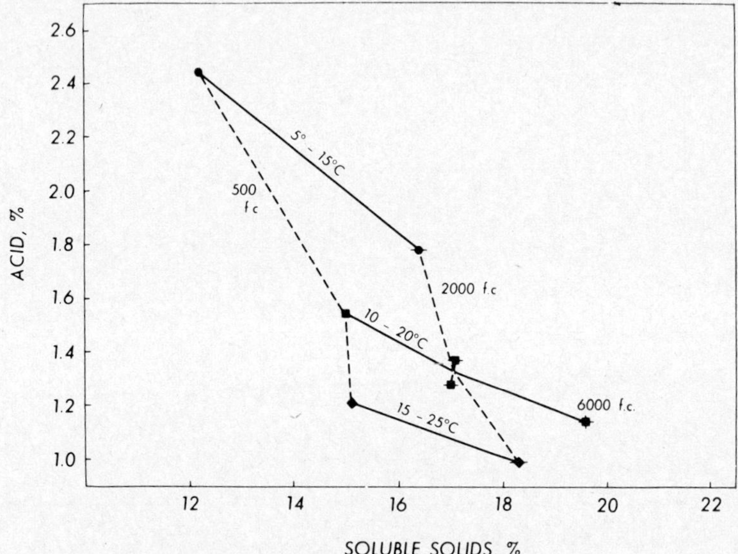

FIG. 70. EFFECT OF TEMPERATURE AND LIGHT ON SUGAR AND ACID IN CONCORD GRAPES

served that the decrease in total acid during ripening was primarily due to decrease in malic acid (Fig. 69) but a decrease in tartrate also occurs. There are several possible explanations for these changes. Amerine, Berg, and Cruess (1967), state that the most rational explanation is that malates are respired during the latter stages of ripening and that even tartrates may be respired. Amerine *et al.* (1967) further add that there are relative changes in proportions of acids and acid salts during ripening. There is evidence indicating that the amount of potassium bitartrate may be related to the amount and availability of the potassium in the soil.

The aroma of grapes consists of a variety of volatile organic compounds including esters, alcohols, acids, aldehydes, lactones and others (Table 54). The aroma of Concord grapes closely resembles that of methyl anthranilate. Several varieties of American grapes contain anthranilic esters but Concord contains an exceptional quantity. Robinson, Shaulis and Pederson (1949) observed a marked increase of methyl anthranilate during ripening (Fig. 71) that was correlated with development of flavor. Closely allied varieties contain considerably less anthranilate. The presence of this ester is important. Recently Mattick, Robinson, Weirs, and Barry (1963) devised a quick and accurate method for determination of this ester.

The color of Concord juice is largely due to the anthocyanin pigments located in and adjacent to the skin. Mattick, Weirs, and Robinson (1967)

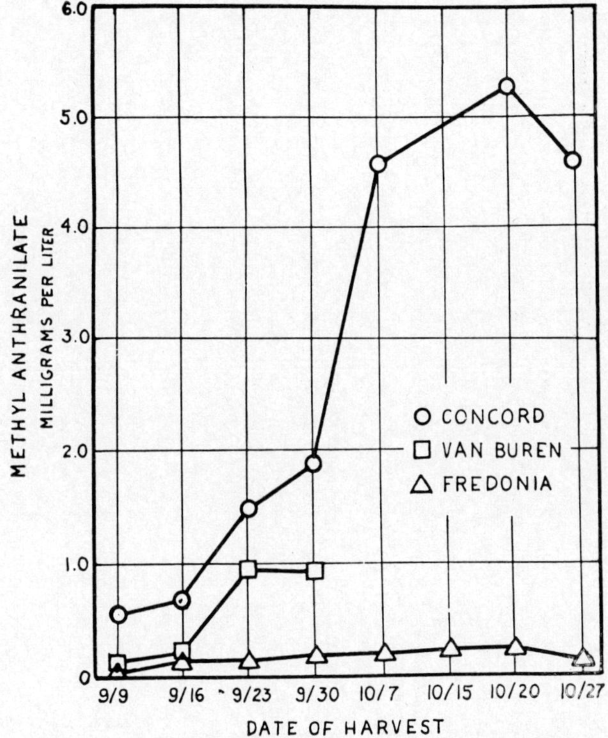

From Robinson, Shaulis and Pederson (1949)

Fig. 71. Changes in Methyl Anthranilate During the Ripening of Concord, Fredonia, and Van Buren Varieties of Grapes

identified seven color components in Concord juice as mono- or diglucosides. Delphinidin monoglucoside is the major component and based upon this fact a method was proposed for detection of adulteration of Concord juice. Sastry and Tischer (1952B) previously identified malvidin 3-monoglucoside in Concord grapes. The anthocyanin pigment of *Vitis rotundifolia* grapes was reported by Brown (1940) to be 3,5-diglucosidyl-3′-0-methyldelphinidin. The composition of pigments of *Vitis vinifera* grapes are varied and reference is made to Amerine, Berg, and Cruess (1967).

The analysis of grapes means very little unless based upon statistical analysis of a number of analyses. Only then can an accurate approximate composition of a given variety of grapes be obtained. The results presented by Kertesz (1944), Robinson, Avens, and Kertesz (1949), Robinson, Shaulis, Smith and Tallman (1959), and Robinson, Einset, and Shaulis

TABLE 56

CHEMICAL COMPOSITION OF NEW YORK STATE GRAPES 1947

Location	Ash Per Cent			P_2O_5 mg per 100 gm			K_2O mg per 100 gm			Soluble Solids Brix			pH Acidity			Acidity Tartaric Acid Per Cent		
	Avg	Min	Max	Avg	Min	Max	Avg	Min	Max	Avg	Min	Max	Avg	Min	Max	Avg	Min	Max
Hudson Valley	0.435	0.36	0.50	32.7	22.0	52.8	237	139	308	15.1	12.9	17.8	2.81	2.52	3.11	1.24	0.97	2.02
Finger Lakes	0.496	0.36	0.62	31.4	22.8	45.2	237	123	335	16.4	13.1	19.5	2.95	2.62	3.17	1.36	0.94	1.75
Chautauqua	0.420	0.25	0.64	26.7	14.0	44.0	215	105	311	16.7	11.7	20.0	2.95	2.51	3.32	1.26	1.04	1.65

Source: Robinson, Avens and Kertesz (1949).

TABLE 57

CHEMICAL COMPOSITION OF GRAPE JUICES OF NEW YORK STATE 1939

	Comparative Color			Relative Viscosity Ostwald	Refractometer Reading	Specific Gravity at 59°F	Hydrogen Ion Concentration	Total Acid, gm per 100 ml	Total Sugar as Invert, gm per 100 ml	Protein gm per 100 ml
	Dilution	Red	Yellow							
Fredonia F	1–9	7.3	0.3	2.71	15.3	1.063	2.92	1.04	13.9	0.13
Hungarian	1–9	9.7	0.5	3.14	18.4	1.077	2.93	1.36	17.1	0.35
Van Buren	1–9	8.4	0.4	4.85	17.8	1.072	3.36	0.73	16.4	0.23
#7002	1–9	4.4	0.3	3.74	19.5	1.080	3.37	0.73	18.7	0.20
Fredonia G	1–9	6.5	0.3	2.08	13.6	1.056	2.97	1.22	12.1	0.33
Ontario	1	1.4	3.5	2.30	19.2	1.080	3.93	0.41	19.2	0.30
Delaware	1	6.4	6.5	2.85	20.8	1.088	3.33	0.72	21.0	0.32
Westfield	1–9	15.0	0.5	2.36	18.8	1.079	3.01	1.11	18.3	0.23
Clinton	1–9	7.0	0.4	2.11	19.3	1.080	3.15	1.61	17.3	0.92
Ives	1–9	3.6	0.2	3.00	11.6	1.048	3.31	0.87	9.6	0.43
Concord	1–9	7.6	0.3	3.14	19.4	1.079	3.30	0.81	18.0	0.34
Catawba	1	18.0	4.0	2.77	20.0	1.083	3.10	1.08	18.1	0.34
Concord	1–9	7.5	0.1	3.00	18.6	1.076	3.20	0.76	17.6	0.32

Source: Unpublished data of Tressler, D. K., and Pederson, C. S. New York State Agr. Expt. Station.

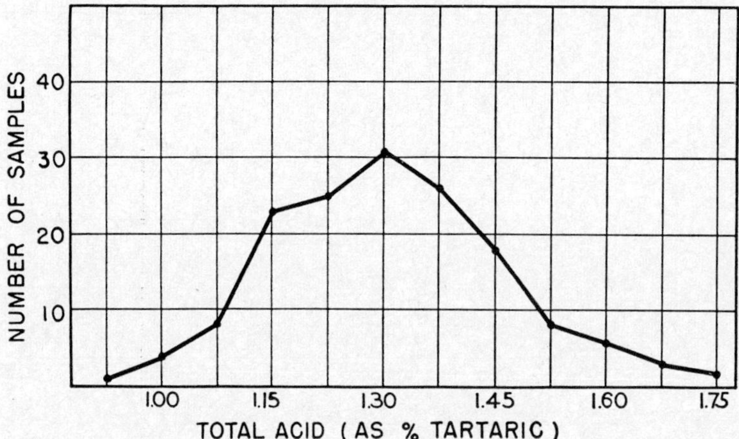

Fig. 72. Distribution of the Total Acid Values of 155 Samples of Concord-Type Grapes

(1970) show that grape juices prepared from Concords not only vary from year to year, but that the composition changes considerably during ripening. These facts must be considered in analyzing the data presented in (Tables 54 and 57).

Two of the seven figures presented by Robinson *et al.* (1949) are presented (Figs. 69 and 70) to illustrate the great variation in composition that might be expected. In general, as the fruit matures, the sugar and color increase and the titrable acidity decreases. In a warm sunny season, grapes are generally higher in sugar and lower in acid and astringency than in a cool cloudy season. Likewise, the composition of a given variety will vary from area to area depending upon the soil, location, and climatic conditions. The recent report of Robinson *et al.* (1970) (Fig. 70) shows the effect of sunlight and temperature and emphasizes the importance of site and season. Vines growing in shallow soils on the eroded hillsides are relatively small and fruit and foliage are well exposed to sunlight. Early and unusually high content of soluble solids result. In contrast, vines grown in deep soil in bottom land are vigorous and highly productive but the grapes are lower in sugars, color and tannins.

Among the numerous analyses of grapes and grape juices reported, both those of Kertesz (1944) and Robinson, Avens, and Kertesz (1949) are of particular interest (Table 56). Their results show that grape juices of the Concord type not only vary from year to year as reported by numerous workers, but that the composition changes considerably during ripening. In general, the pH increases, the titratable acid decreases, and sugar increases as the fruit matures. Otherwise, their results, although

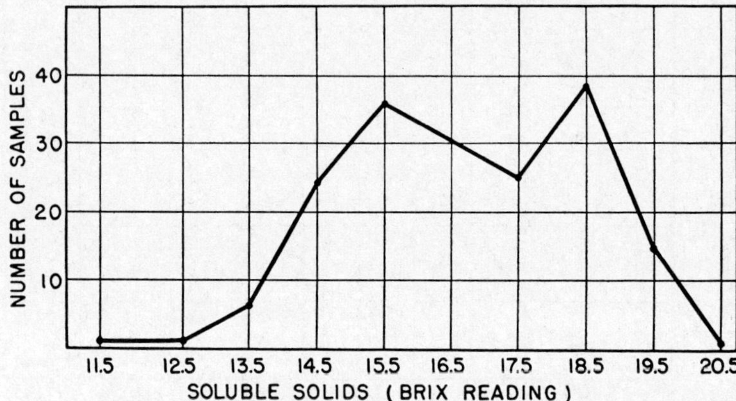

Fig. 73. Distribution of Soluble Solids Values for 156 Samples of Concord-Type Grapes

showing a somewhat higher acidity and lower sugar content, do not differ considerably from the analyses presented in Tables 54, 55, 56 and 57. In a warm, sunny season, grapes are higher in sugar and lower in acid and astringency than in a cool cloudy year. Likewise, the composition of a given variety will vary from place to place, depending upon the soil, the location and the climatic conditions. Robinson *et al.* (1949) have shown that this variation not only applies to sugars, total solids, and acids but also to mineral constituents.

The analysis of grapes means very little unless based upon statistical analysis of a number of analyses. Only then can an accurate approximate composition of a given variety of grapes be obtained.

Maturity

The acidity, color, and aroma of fresh grapes provide the characteristic fruitiness to the juice. These characters are influenced by the maturity of the grapes. The development of color and flavor, particularly that due to methyl anthranilate has been discussed. Quality characteristics of marketed juice must be uniform and therefore juice from underripe grapes must be blended with juice from well-ripened fruit. Needless to say the latter juice has the greater appeal. The quality factor that has been used most frequently is the Brix reading. Color can be measured by optical density on hot-extracted juice. The amount of pigment is directly related to the light absorbed. Acidity can be determined readily. If the juice is above 0.85% acidity it tends to be too tart. Sugar must be added to balance the flavor. Astringency is related to the amount of tannins present in the grapes. The tannins can be measured by chemical analysis. Fla-

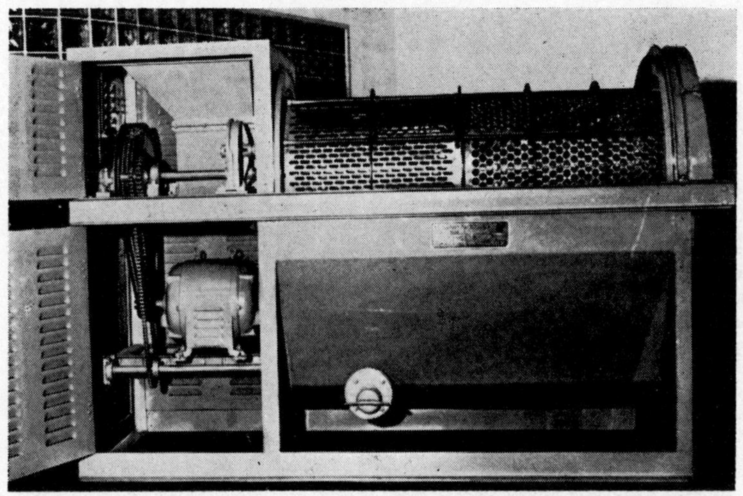

Courtesy of Healdsburg Mfg. Co.

FIG. 74. ROTARY GRAPE CRUSHER

The hood has been removed and inspection door closed.

vor is a complex quality, embracing sweetness, tartness, aroma and astringency. Flavor can be determined by organoleptic methods only. Fortunately these factors are all interrelated. Therefore, the Brix measurement is a satisfactory method in that it is simple, accurate and adaptable.

THE PREPARATION OF GRAPE JUICE

Nearly all grape juice prepared in the United States is made from Concord grapes. Of the major juices of commerce marketed today, only grape and apple juice are clarified. Grape and apple differ materially in their characteristics and by experience apple juice is expressed cold while grape juice is expressed hot. Hot pressing of Concord grapes is essential in order to bring into solution the color and other ingredients of the fruit. The chemical composition of the juice will depend upon the method of extraction and the average composition of hot-pressed Concord juice will be quite different from cold-pressed juice (Table 55). Hot-pressed juice is much higher in total solids, nonsugar solids, tannin, coloring matter and other substances. Since the astringency of the juice will depend upon the amount of tannins, the temperature and time of extraction are important factors in determining the quality of the juice. In commercial production, the primary aim is to produce a juice with the most desirable characteristics of flavor, aroma, color, and nutritive qualities.

Grape juice is essentially a solution of all soluble ingredients of the fruit. In order to solubilize as much of the juice as possible and to

Courtesy of Chisholm Ryder Co.

Fig. 75. Steam-Jacketed, Vacuum Preheater for Grapes Equipped with Thermostatic and Vacuum Controls

Steam circulates around the tubes, heating the grapes to approximately 145°F.

stream-line the processing, considerable changes have been made during the past 15 to 20 years in methods of extraction. Pressing by means of a hydraulic press is a tedious, time consuming, unsanitary operation requiring considerable labor. The method has been replaced throughout the industry by continuous pressing.

Hot Pressing

The fully ripened grapes, usually harvested on orders from the factory fieldman, are unloaded at the receiving platform. They may be allowed to stand for a time in order to permit them to mellow. The grapes are emptied into the hopper of a bucket elevator which carries them to an upper floor of the plant. As they travel up the conveyor, they are washed with powerful sprays of water.

The conveyor empties the grapes into the hopper of a machine similar to Fig. 74 where they are forcibly moved into the receiving end of the drum by a rotating worm. When the grape enters the drum it will fall into the path of the rotating beater blades, which not only beat the fruit but also throw it outwardly against beating bars and the apertured surface of the drum. In view of the spacing provided, however, the seeds and stems will not be crushed. This forcible beating and propulsion of

TABLE 58

CHEMICAL COMPOSITION OF CONCORD GRAPE JUICES OBTAINED AT VARIOUS PRESSURES[1]

Pressure	Experiment	Time	Solids	(As Invert) Before Inversion	Non-Sugar Solids	Ash	Total Acid as Tartaric	Total Tartaric Acid Free and Combined	Tannin and Coloring Matter
		Min	Gm per 100 Ml						
Free run	1	15	16.62	13.48	3.14	0.410	1.11	0.99	0.27
	2		16.78	13.36	3.42	...	1.04	0.99	0.26
0 to 25 tons	1	15	17.30	13.82	3.48	...	1.20	1.01	0.28
	2		16.91	13.34	3.57	...	1.17	1.06	0.28
25 to 75 tons	1	15	17.48	13.86	3.62	...	1.25	1.04	0.31
	2		...	...	...	...	...	...	...
75 to 100 tons	1	5	17.41	13.88	3.53	...	1.25	1.07	0.33
	2		16.78	13.07	3.71	...	1.28	1.15	0.29
Drainings as 100 tons	1	25	17.48	13.66	3.82	0.484	1.27	1.12	0.36
	2		16.73	12.93	3.80	...	1.31	1.17	0.32

[1] From Hartmann, B. G. and Tolman, L. M. (1918).

the fruit will result in breaking up the berries, separating the juice therefrom. Furthermore, the centrifugal action set up and the air current produced by the rotating beating blades will cause the juice and pulp to escape outwardly through slots and the opening in the drum, leaving the stems substantially dry, until they are discharged from the outlet end by the propelling action of the spiral blades. The juice and pulp gravitate to the large receiver beneath the cylindrical drum. The pulp and juice are pumped to stainless steel single-tube vacuum preheaters (Fig. 75) and thence to steam-jacketed aluminum or stainless steel kettles equipped with rotating paddles designed to mix the grape mass. Some plants are not equipped with the preheaters and thus do all heating in the kettles. The grape mass is heated to extract color and other solubles and to convert the product to a fluid mass. The temperature and times of heating used in preheater and kettles will depend somewhat on the maturity of the grapes. Ordinarily, the temperatures range from 140° to 145°F. Heating the grape solubilizes much of the pectin and the coloring matter and some of the tannins from skins and seeds. Consequently within limitations the higher the temperature and the longer the grapes are heated, the darker the juice and the heavier its body will be. Hard pressing also tends to increase the acidity and color of the juice (Table 58). Most juice factories attempt to produce juices of uniform color. During the early part of the season, therefore, before maximum color has been developed in the grape or when light colored grapes are being pressed, grapes are heated to higher temperatures or for longer times than when the more fully matured grapes, or more highly colored grapes are being pressed. In some plants, temperature and time of heating are automatically controlled and recorded by suitable instruments.

Excessive heating must be avoided or else excessive amounts of tannin will be extracted from seeds and skins. The anthocyanin pigments are extracted more readily than are the tannins. Experience in commercial operations as well as experimental studies shows that in commercial practice 150°F should not be exceeded in heating, considering the time juice is ordinarily held.

Pressing.—Considerable change has been effected during the recent years in the methods of pressing the heated grape mass.

The old, well-standardized method of pressing with a hydraulic press is still used in many operations. The method lends itself to small scale operation such as in experimental work and in making grape juice in the home. The heated grape mass is run onto press cloths for pressing. The exact procedure varies in different plants. A wooden rack of special construction is placed in position beneath the pipe outlet for the grapes. A press blanket, usually made of heavy cotton cloth, or a lighter nylon cloth is placed in a frame over the rack. A valve is opened releasing enough of the grape mass or pulp to fill the cloth. In some plants, a filter aid such as infusorial earth may be placed upon the cloths or mixed with the pulp to aid pressing and later removal of the pomace from the cloths. Four deft folds of the cloth over the mass of pulp and juice enclose it, and the first layer of the "cheese" has been made. The frame is removed, a second rack and cloth is placed upon the first and filled. This is repeated layer upon layer until the complete "cheese" is built, enough for pressing with the hydraulic press.

As much as one-half or more of the juice drains out from the heated pulp during the making of the "cheese." This is due not only to the fact that the juice runs easily from the pulp at this stage, but also to the pressing action of the racks and cloths on the pulp as the cheese is built. This juice, usually called free-run juice is somewhat lighter in color, and contains less acid (see Table 58) and more sugar than that which is pressed out subsequently. A short settling period may be allowed. In many plants heavy weights are placed upon the "cheese" before it is transferred to the hydraulic press. The transfer of the "cheese" to the hydraulic press is expedited by use of special rails upon which to roll the "cheese" to the press. Hydraulic pressure is applied gradually until it reaches 3200 lb on the ram or a pressure of 250 to 300 psi. The yield of juice is about 75%, or from 175 to 185 gal per ton of grapes. The expressed and free-run juices flow down into holding tanks for blending.

The residue in the cloths, called pomace, consisting of skins and seeds, is dry and tough. It contains about 60% moisture. The pomace is readily removed and the cloths are placed in large washing machines for washing. In some factories, the cloths are washed each time they are used while in others, cloths are washed at less frequent intervals.

Extraction of juice by means of hydraulic presses is not only tedious

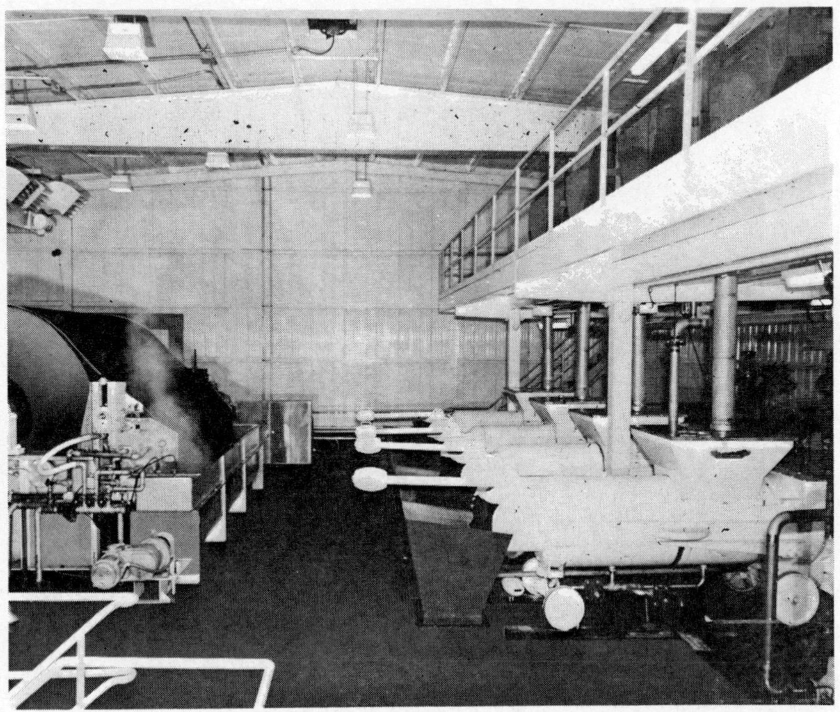

Courtesy of Welch Grape Juice Co.

Fig. 76. A Battery of Garola Presses

and time consuming but requires considerable labor and is far from sanitary. Pederson (1936A) found that the juice coming from the fruit juice press contains large numbers of yeasts. Fermentation sometimes was observed in fruit in the presses and occasionally alcohol contents of freshly pressed juice exceeded allowable tolerances. When cool storage, 24°–28°F was first used and before the practice of pasteurizing and cooling before transferring to the storage tanks was practiced, yeast growth continued at times, but more often the numbers of yeasts decreased. Molds frequently developed on the surfaces of these tanks. With the introduction of the general practice of pasteurizing before cooling, the yeasts and molds were killed. The yeasts that developed in these juices were psychrophilic species and increased in numbers during storage. This will be discussed further in the section on low temperature storage.

Continuous Fruit Juice Pressing

The need for a method for expressing juice by a continuous process to obviate some of the objections to hydraulic pressing was obvious in the in-

Fig. 77. A Grape Pressing Room

The "cheeses" are first pressed with weights, then by hydraulic pressure.

dustry. Many types of continuous methods were tried. Amerine and Joslyn (1951) in reviewing the status of continuous methods in wineries observed that much of the juice coming from the presses was filled with organic matter; however the first juice was usually clear while the later juice was murky. They found that higher yields of juice could be obtained. Continuous pressing presented few difficulties after the juices were fermented. This suggested that some type of clarification was essential. Clarification by use of enzymes had been suggested, but until Kertesz (1930) and Willaman and Kertesz (1931) perfected methods of preparation of clarifying enzymes, little use had been made of this method of clarification. This enzyme preparation was obtained by growth of a mold which had previously been isolated from clarified carboyed grape juice.

In the early 1950's, the grape juice processors united in an effort to develop a continuous processing method engaging R. F. Celmer to carry on the experimental work. These studies resulted in the use of enzyme preparations and fibres to aid in holding back the pulps and ultimately the method patented by Wolcott (1958).

As a result more recently, hydraulic presses have been replaced by continuous screw presses which require destruction of the naturally occurring pectin in the grapes and the addition of wood fiber for their successful operation. At present the Garolla press, or a variation of this press, (Fig. 77) has found greatest acceptance. The Zenith, Willmes, Vincent and other types have been used experimentally. The hot pulp is pumped into large holding tanks equipped with slowly moving agitators which facilitate the mixing of 0.2 lb of pectic enzyme preparation and 10 to 20 lb of purified wood fiber per ton of grapes. A 30-min holding period allows the enzymes to break down the pectin, thereby reducing the slipperiness of the pulp and also dispersing the wood fiber which acts as a bulking agent and permits the screw to exert a pressing action.

The digested pulp is partially drained (approx. 30%) of the free-run juice in either revolving screens having a 40-mesh or finer screen, or on sloping vibrating decks equipped with trapezoidal shaped rods. This free-run juice may have 40 to 10% suspended solids as determined by centrifuge tests. The remainder of the pulp is then pumped to a continuous screw press. The expressed juice from the screw press may have 4 to 6% suspended solids and the cake a moisture content of 45 to 50%.

The free-run and expressed juice are combined and the suspended solids removed by pressure leaf filtration, rotary vacuum filtration or by centrifugation. In pressure filtration ample space (4 to 7 in.) between the leaves is provided for cake formation since 1 to 2% diatomaceous filter-aid is used and pressures of 70–80 psi are applied by the filter pumps. Continuous desludging centrifuges may also be used to remove the suspended solids followed by plate and frame filters using diatomaceous filter-aids. Under normal operating conditions, 190 to 195 gal of juice are obtained from a ton of grapes. In some instances, the cake from the screw press may be extracted with water in a countercurrent system so that the final extract contains approximately 14% soluble solids which may represent a 5% increase in juice yield.

The extracted juice may be run directly through pasteurizers and coolers but it is usually centrifuged or filtered to remove some of the suspended solids before pasteurization and cooling.

Unlike the paddle and the screw principle used in some of the continuous presses, the Willmes Press consists of a perforated rotating cylinder with an inner rubber sleeve into which compressed air is applied to inflate it and press the juice cake. Clarification with a pectinase previous to pressing, as well as use of filter aid is recommended.

The newer methods in general require fewer operators, the juice is extracted more quickly and therefore is subjected to high temperatures for a shorter time and the equipment is more easily cleaned than are press cloths and racks.

A method has been described by Tischer (1951) for preparation of

Table 59

CHANGES IN CHEMICAL COMPOSITION OF CONCORD GRAPE JUICE RESULTING FROM 4 MONTHS' STORAGE

	Solids	Sugar (as Invert) Before Inversion	Sugar (as Invert) After Inversion	Non-Sugar Solids	Total Acid as Tartaric	Total Tartaric Acid Free and Combined	Free Tartaric Acid	Cream of Tartar	Tannin and Coloring Matter	Ash	Alkalinity of Soluble Ash	Alkalinity of Insoluble Ash
	gm per ml										N/10 Acid per 100 ml	
Before												
Maximum	19.76	16.39	16.55	3.76	1.27	1.03	0.31	0.86	0.28	0.44	45.0	8.0
Minimum	16.99	13.25	13.38	3.06	0.98	0.85	0.13	0.64	0.15	0.34	33.8	6.4
Average	17.92	14.54	14.62	3.38	1.14	0.94	0.21	0.77	0.22	0.39	41.1	7.5
After												
Maximum	19.18	16.15	16.30	3.07	1.10	0.84	0.28	0.63	0.22	0.32	33.6	4.6
Minimum	16.41	13.34	13.45	2.60	0.83	0.58	0.13	0.47	0.13	0.22	24.8	3.0
Average	17.39	14.52	14.52	2.87	1.01	0.70	0.22	0.53	0.18	0.27	28.3	4.0
Average loss	0.53	0.02	0.10	0.51	0.13	0.24	−0.01	0.24	0.04	0.12	13.0	3.5

Source: Hartmann, B. G. and Tolman, L. M. (1918).

grape juice. The grapes are heated at temperatures from 190° to 205°F in the absence of air in a special type annular cylindrical vessel. The juice is removed as it is formed, while that remaining with the pulp is extracted with a centrifuge. A yield of 85% of juice, equivalent to regular Concord juice in chemical analysis and palatability is reported.

Pasteurization and Storage of Juice

Two methods are commonly employed for storage of juice for settling of argols. The older method, carboy storage, is now almost entirely replaced by cool storage at 22° to 28°F. A small amount of juice is stored in the frozen state similar to the method used for storage of grape pulp for jam manufacture. When grape juice prepared from the *Labrusca*-type grapes is pasteurized and stored immediately after pressing, potassium bitartrate, tannins, and some colored substances will deposit during storage. The deposit is referred to as crude argols and although undesirable in bottled juices, it is the source of much of the tartrates for baking powders. The juices are ordinarily stored for from 1 to 6 months or more to allow complete deposition of the argols (Table 59). The juice bottled after storage will not deposit sediment.

Low Temperature Storage.—The grape juice industry has changed almost entirely from the old method of storing juice in 5-gal carboys to cool storage in tanks at 22° to 28°F. By this method of storage, heating effects are minimized. A general improvement in quality has been effected and at this temperature argols are formed and are precipitated more rapidly than at the higher temperatures used for carboy storage. Although relatively few microorganisms can grow at these temperatures, at times, problems of yeast and mold contamination are serious.

After the juice is extracted, it is flash-heated at 175° to 185°F in a plate-type or tubular heat exchanger and then cooled to about 32°F by one of several methods, before pumping it into storage tanks. When the method was first used, the juice was not pasteurized.

Development of mold colonies on the surfaces of the juices in the vats usually occurred resulting in a more rapid clarification and in a more rapid deposition of argols. The numbers of yeasts, however, actually decreased at first and later the psychrophilic yeast flora developed and some serious losses occurred, Pederson (1936B), Pederson, Albury, Wilson and Lawrence (1958). The method of storage favors the retention of natural aroma and flavor.

In the first coolers used, the juice is pumped through the first stage of the cooling apparatus where water serves as the cooling medium. The juice passes immediately through the second stage of cooling in which liquid ammonia is used as the cooling medium. In the third stage, the juice

FIG. 78. A PLATE-TYPE HEAT EXCHANGER FOR PASTEURIZING AND COOLING

This is a continuous flow heat exchanger in which the juice may be partially cooled for storage, or it may be used for heating for final bottling in which case the juice is not cooled.

is cooled quickly and uniformly to near the freezing point, 27° to 28°F, by means of surface-type coolers (Fig. 79). These coolers are housed in a separate refrigerated room where uniform and sanitary conditions can be maintained. Usually ultraviolet lamps are installed in this room. It is most essential to attain rapid uniform cooling at this stage since it would require long periods of time to attain the proper temperature in the storage tanks. Recording thermometers, with their bulbs in the line flow, are installed to keep an accurate record of cooling of all juice.

In many installations now in use, the entire pasteurizing and cooling of juice is accomplished in single unit heat exchangers (Fig. 78).

From the cooler, the juice flows or is pumped into glass-lined metal, concrete, or wood storage tanks in refrigerated rooms, where it is held at uniform, automatically controlled temperatures. The concrete and wood tanks are lined with one of several types of wax-like or plastic coatings to

FIG. 79. INTERIOR OF A BAUDELOT ROOM IN WHICH THE THIRD STAGE OF COOLING TAKES PLACE

prevent penetration of the juice or action of the acid upon concrete. Practices vary in regard to covering the tanks. In some factories, open tanks are used; ultraviolet lamps are employed to inhibit mold growth on the surface of the juice. In other plants, the tanks are covered and sealed. The juice is held in these tanks for a month or more to allow crystallization of argols.

On occasion, yeasts or molds will develop in the juices stored in this manner. The mere presence of the yeasts or molds is unimportant in itself. If the yeasts or molds grow and multiply sufficiently to alter the product, they will cause an economic loss to the producer. Lawrence *et al.* (1959) have shown that contamination in the handling and storage of grape juice arises from yeasts harbored in the pores of wood or coating of tanks, the air in the room, foam on the surface of containers, intermediate holding tanks, valves, improper gaskets and similar places where microorganisms may accumulate and grow. Four types of yeast capable of growing at the low storage temperature were described by Lawrence, Wilson and Pederson (1959), one of which is a true psychrophile. In further study Pederson, Albury and Christensen (1961) have shown that several organic acids are effective fungistats in controlling this yeast growth at the low temperature even when used in very low concentrations.

Carboy Storage.—In the older method of storage the juice is pasteurized, placed in carboys or jugs and allowed to stand three months or longer in a cool cellar. It is necessary to sterilize the juice and fill it into carboys while hot to prevent fermentation during this period. The following procedure is used:

When the juice flows from the presses it is strained through several thicknesses of cloth, or through special roller shaker screens, to remove any particles of skin or seeds which may have passed through the press cloths. The shaker screens consist of stainless steel cloth screens in a frame which is vibrated by a balanced eccentric pulley. The juice is then run into large steam-jacketed aluminum or stainless steel kettles equipped with agitators. The juice may be heated in these kettles, or it may pass through special tubular or plate-type heat exchangers to bring about pasteurization (Fig. 78). Juice is heated to 170° to 185°F, the temperature employed depending on practice in the particular plant. The foam and solid particles which rise to the surface during heating are removed from the juice, since it is impossible to heat this scum sufficiently to sterilize it. The heated juice is run by tubes leading to the bottoms into hot carboys or jugs which have been gradually brought up to this temperature of filling by heating in steam boxes. In filling the containers, sufficient juice is added to cause the foam formed during filling to flow over the top and out of the container. The cork used in closing the carboy is dipped in melted paraffin about half way up, immediately before use, and then pushed in all the way. Melted paraffin is poured over it to obtain a tight seal. In some plants, vacuum seals are now used instead of corks. In some factories, the carboys of hot juice are placed on a conveyor which slowly carries them through mist sprays of cool and then cold water. This cooling may reduce the temperature of the juice to as low as 120°F.

The carboys or jugs are then transferred and placed on large racks in cool cellars. The cellars are kept cool during the winter after the grape season has passed, but during the season when warm carboys of juice are being constantly placed in them, the temperature rises well above 80°F. Although it is protected from the deteriorating effect of oxygen of the air, the high temperature storage causes some deterioration of the juice.

In some plants, the hot, pasteurized juice is run into sterile barrels at a temperature of 175° to 185°F. These barrels may be stored in a cool place where they may be turned a little each day to prevent drying out of the upper staves. Such drying out will cause shrinking and consequently permit air to enter the barrel. Juice stored in this manner cools very slowly and consequently is subjected for a longer time to the deteriorating effects of heating.

Pederson, Beattie, and Stotz (1947) have shown that grape juice is one of the most stable of all fruit juices but will deteriorate over a period of time if exposed to high temperature storage.

Sastry and Tischer (1952A) have indicated a protective action of the tannins of grape juice on the anthocyanin pigments.

CONCENTRATION OF JUICE FOR STORAGE

Concentration of grape juice has many advantages regardless of how the juice will be used. The practice has assumed an important role in the industry. Concentration reduces the bulk and permits economies in storage and transportation. This is important when one considers the tank volume required to store the juices processed within a relatively short harvest season. Concentration results in a more complete deposition of tartrates. During low temperature storage, 22° to 28°F there is less possibility of yeast growth. The concentrate can be converted readily to the frozen grape juice beverage that is now second in sales only to frozen orange juice concentrate. The grape juice beverage appeals to many people who prefer the sweeter more dilute beverage to the highly flavored foxy bottled grape juice.

Concentration of juices can be accomplished by heating in an open kettle, in a vacuum pan, with or without volatile flavor recovery or by freezing concentration (Tressler and Joslyn 1961). The possibility of growth of psychrophilic yeasts in grape juices stored at 22° to 28°F has hastened the practice of concentrating juices for storage. The cool storage tanks merely serve in a temporary capacity as a surge tank before the juice is pumped to the concentrator. Concentration is carried out in two steps, first, the volatile flavors are stripped from the juice and then the stripped juice is concentrated by heating under vacuum to the desired density. The concentrate is cooled to about 70°F and the concentrated volatile flavors and about 10% of single strength juice is added to give a final concentration of 45° to 47° Brix. Sugar, ascorbic acid, fruit acids, and even concentrate prepared from other varieties of grapes may be added to prepare the final frozen grape juice beverage concentrate.

Volatile Flavor Separation

The volatile components are removed by heating the single strength juice to 220°–230°F for a fraction of a minute in a heat exchanger, flashing a percentage of the liquid into vapor in a jacketed tube bundle and then discharging the liquid and vapor through an orifice tangentially into a separator. The separator should be of sufficient size that the vapor velocity is reduced to 10 ft per sec or less for minimal entrainment. From 20 to 30% by weight of the original juice flashes off as a vapor that is led into the base of a fractionating column filled with ceramic saddles or rings. A reflux condenser on the vapor line from the column and a reboiler section at the base of the column are used to provide the necessary reflux ratio. The vent gases from the reflux condenser are then chilled in a heat exchanger and the condensate containing the essence is collected at a rate equivalent to 1/150 of the volume of entering flavoring material.

Concentration of Juice

The unflashed juice from the separator may be concentrated in a forced circulation, falling film or a single pass evaporator having a relatively short retention time. Forced circulation evaporation may be carried out in one or several stages using temperatures ranging from 135° to 160°F and with a retention time in the evaporator of possibly an hour's duration. This retention time and heat exposure have been reduced by use of falling film evaporators to approximately 15 to 20 min to 100° to 150°F while under vacua of 27 to 29 in. More recently in a single-pass evaporator of special design, the exposure time has been further reduced to approximately 2 to 3 min for complete concentration to 48° Brix in a multiple stage unit using temperatures of 150° to 160°F in the first effect, and 115°F in the second effect. The same type of evaporator may be used to achieve concentrations of 72° Brix if the juice has been depectinized.

Methyl Anthranilate

The essence recovery process has been applied successfully to the production of fruit juice concentrates. Fruit aroma consists of a variety of volatile organic compounds such as esters, alcohols, acids, aldehydes, lactones, and others. In a conventional flavor recovery process, the aqueous distillate is assumed to contain most of the volatile components.

An important flavor component of Concord grape juice is methyl anthranilate that has a boiling point of 512°F and is only slightly soluble in water. This high boiling point and low solubility in water has resulted in losses of methyl anthranilate when the efficiency of the stripping column is low. It has been suggested that these losses may be reduced by increasing the vaporizing temperature.

Moyer and Saravacos (1968) demonstrated that the volatility of each compound depends upon its physicochemical properties and the interaction with other components. Methyl anthranilate is not easily recovered. Moyer and Saravacos (1968), and Saravacos, Moyer and Wooster (1969) found that methyl anthranilate required high boil-up rates and several distillation plates which must be designed for this compound and that high sugar content reduces the efficiency of high boiling compounds. They credit Roger and Turkot (1965) for applying the principles of distillation to the design of an essence rectification column for Concord grape juice.

Concentration by freezing has theoretical advantages over concentration by evaporation. The energy required for freezing per unit of water is only about one-seventh of that required for evaporation. The loss of volatile flavor constituents and alterations of flavor and color due to chemical reactions induced by heating are minimized. The grape juice processors are equipped with the expensive refrigeration equipment required to remove the latent heat of fusion.

Monti in Italy patented a process in 1903 for concentration of grape juice by freezing. Jackson patented a similar process in the United States in 1911, and Gore suggested freezing concentration of apple juice in 1910 (Tressler and Joslyn 1961). The relative simplicity of freezing grape juice in the cold rooms seems to suggest this concentration method.

In general, the methods used may be classified as slow or quick freezing. Quick freezing reduces the temperature rapidly to a point at which microorganisms will not grow. The more slowly a juice is frozen, the larger will be the ice crystals. This is actually the condition that occurs in many instances in grape juice held at 22° to 28°F. As the temperature is decreased, the juice solids concentrate toward the center of the container and the major share of the fruit solids form a thick syrup in the center of the container. There is a gradual increase in solids from the relatively pure ice at the periphery to the heavy syrup at the center. Rapid freezing does not afford an opportunity for migration of juice solids and conversely the more slowly a juice is frozen the greater the opportunity is afforded for such migration. Pederson and Beattie (1947) used this principle and obtained grape juice concentrate as high as 63° and 64° Brix. The objection to the process is the necessity of several successive freezings and separation of ice from concentrate to obtain satisfactory recovery of a high degree concentrate. By centrifuging or hydraulic pressing, 90 to 95% of the total solids was obtained, and by a draining procedure 60 to 70% was obtained. The principle has been used experimentally in preparing juice for jelly. In commercial operation, a combination of concentration by freezing and evaporation of the remaining ice fractions may have possibilities.

Other Methods of Removing Argols.—Many rapid methods of removing the crude tartrates from juice have been proposed. The simplest of these involves the freezing and thawing of the juice, followed by the siphoning of the cold juice from the crystalline sludge formed during freezing. The general procedure consists of filling the cooled juice into carboys or barrels, filling about nine-tenths full to allow for expansion. The containers are then placed in a sharp freezer at about 0°F. At the end of the freezing period, from 4 to 7 days, the juice is removed to a warm room and thawed as rapidly as possible in the air (Table 60). Circulation of air with electric fans will hasten thawing. When thawed and settled, the clearer juice at the top should be siphoned off taking care not to disturb the sludge. The sludge must be filtered with a filter press using a filter aid.

Another method involves the addition of calcium acid malate, lactate or acid phosphate to the juice. A rapid precipitation is said to occur.

The addition of dipotassium tartrate to grape juice will cause a reaction between this salt and tartaric acid to produce two parts of the less soluble potassium acid tartrate. The insoluble crystals will settle out rapidly.

Another procedure which speeds up the formation of argols involves the treatment of the juice with a pectic enzyme preparation such as Pectinol, followed by a short storage period in a cool place before filtration. The removal of the protective colloids accomplished by this treatment facilitates crystallization of the crude tartrates. Obviously, this method can be used only when a clear grape juice is desired. When grape juice is clarified and treated for removal of argols by the enzyme method, 20 oz of an enzyme preparation such as Pectinol W are added to each 100 gal of cool juice. The juice is then held at about 45°F for 3 days. The clear juice is then carefully siphoned from the sediment, heated to 170°F, cooled and filtered. The clarified grape juice is then pasteurized and bottled without further treatment. However, Concord juice may require a longer period of refrigeration, or cooling to a lower temperature, to permit crystallization of argols.

Table 60

COMPOSITION OF FRESHLY PRESSED JUICE BEFORE AND AFTER STORAGE AT 25°F FOR SIX DAYS

	Fresh Juice	Frozen Juice
Soluble solids, %	15.6	14.50
Sugars (as invert)	12.10	12.19
Ash	0.427	0.185
Alkaline number ash	11.7	10.8
Phosphorus pentoxide ash	5.92	13.3
Magnesium phosphorus pentoxide	24.30	24.31
Cubic centimeters N/10 acid	162.7	110.7
Acidity (as tartaric), %	1.22	0.83
Alcohol precipitate	0.442	0.412
Pectic acid	0.273	0.260
Sulfur in ash	1.94	4.62
Potassium oxide in ash	19.75	22.68
Reduction in acidity, %	...	32.0
Reduction in ash, %	...	56.7
Reduction in potassium oxide, %	...	51.4

Source: Lathrop and Walde (1928).

Another procedure suggested for rapidly eliminating argols is based on the principles described above, i.e., the potassium bitartrate crystallizes more rapidly from clarified juice than from cloudy juice. The method involves the use of casein for clarification and the addition of citric acid to prevent further separation of cream of tartar.

Cold Pressing

Light colored grapes may be pressed without previous heating, thus obtaining a nearly colorless juice. The grapes may or may not be stemmed since tannins will not be extracted during a heating operation. After washing, they pass to the crusher from which they fall directly to a press and are then handled in the same way as hot pressed juice. Screw expeller presses have been used for cold pressing. They have the advantage of continuous operation and thus require less labor than the rack and frame hydraulic press. Screw expeller presses have been improved in design to avoid some of their previous disadvantages, such as crushing of seed and the low yields obtained unless pulp is forced through the screen.

Cold pressing of grapes has an advantage over hot pressing in that a fresh grape flavor is more readily obtained from many varieties of grapes than is obtained by hot pressing. Some color will be extracted from many varieties of grapes. Even Concord will yield a pink colored juice. However, yields of juice from Concord type grapes may be as much as 20% lower than yields obtained by hot pressing. These proportional yields will depend on the character of the grape. Moreover, and possibly of even greater importance, is the appearance of the juice. Cold-pressed, light-colored juices are invariably muddy and may have an unsightly sediment. This necessitates clarification to produce an appealing product. Clarified grape juice does not have the desirable flavor and body characteristic of the natural juice.

To overcome the objectionable changes that occur in cold-pressed grape juices, the principle used by Pederson (1947) for preparing opalescent apple juice was adapted for preparing opalescent grape juice from several of the green and light colored varieties of grapes (Pederson, Robinson and Shaulis 1953). Ascorbic acid was added to the washed and stemmed grapes immediately before crushing. The processed juices were excellent in flavor, aroma, color and body, so much so that the variety of grape used in preparing the juice could be identified readily. Retention of ascorbic acid was good. Yields from some varieties were as high as 76% and usually averaged 66 to 70%. This is only slightly lower than that obtained by hot pressing. The juice pasteurized and bottled at 175° F did not deposit tartrates. The slight sediment that formed had the same color as the juice and blended with it. Thus clarification was not considered necessary.

MUSCADINE GRAPE JUICE

Muscadine grape juice is prepared by blending hot-pressed and cold-pressed juices (White 1950; Woodroof 1952[1]). White (1950) observed that the addition of ascorbic acid to Muscadine grapes before pressing helped prevent oxidation of color and flavor. The juice of several varieties is usually blended to give the most desirable color and flavor. After the well-ripened grapes are washed and crushed between wood rollers, one-third of the grapes are heated by simmering in a stainless steel or aluminimum steam-jacketed kettle, without addition of water. Constant stirring is necessary for uniform heating. The one-third heated portion of grape is pressed and the juice is blended with the juice obtained by cold pressing the other two-thirds of the grapes. The former has more color and is more acid and the latter has the flavor of fresh grapes. The blend is said to be a product more pleasing in color, flavor, and aroma that can be obtained from either hot-pressed or cold-pressed juices alone. This is especially true if ascorbic acid is added to the crushed grapes immediately before pressing.

Yield from Muscadine grapes is somewhat lower than obtained with Concord. About 60 to 62% yields may be obtained by hot pressing and 50 to 55% by cold pressing. Tartrates settle rapidly. Juice cooled to 40°F will have the tartrate crystallized and settled within a few days.

The Final Processing of Grape Juice

The juice may be reprocessed at any time after all of the argols have formed and settled out so that a large portion of the juice may be siphoned off. Siphons in carboys extend low enough to siphon off most of the clear juice without disturbing the sediment below. After removal of the clear juice, the thick juice and argols are partially filtered through a screen or through several thicknesses of heavy cotton cloths on a frame. The juice flowing through is still muddy and thick and must either be resterilized and stored again to permit a second precipitation of argols, or filtered in a filter press using infusorial earth or other substances as a filter aid. Juice stored in large containers by the low temperature storage method is more easily handled. Draw-off pipes in the sealed storage tanks extend sufficiently above the bottom to prevent disturbance of the argol sediment. After the contents of the tank have been drawn off, the juice and argols remaining in the bottom of the tank are drained and treated as described for carboy juice, or are separated by means of a continuous bowl centrifuge. A continuous stream of centrifuged juice is ob-

[1] This information concerning the preparation of Muscadine grape juice was furnished by Dr. J. G. Woodroof, Georgia Experiment Station.

From Tressler and Pederson (1936)

FIG. 80. BOTTLES OF GRAPE JUICE WHICH SHOW DETERIORATING EFFECTS OF OXYGEN AND HEAT AFTER PROLONGED STORAGE

Note the deposit of colored sediment in the bottle on its side and the deposit in the neck of the upright bottle.

tained from one part simultaneously with discharge of partially dry argols.

Juices extracted by continuous or semi-continuous methods are often treated with clarifying enzymes previous to pressing. Although such juices may contain greater quantities of insoluble solids, since the viscosity

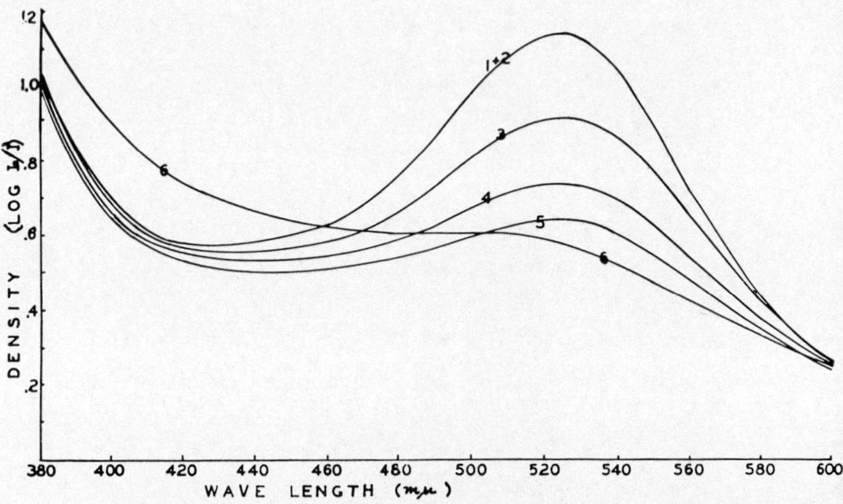

From Pederson et al. (1947)

FIG. 81. THE DETERIORATION OF GRAPE JUICE DUE TO HEAT OF STORAGE AT 113°F AS SHOWN BY SPECTROPHOTOMETRIC COLOR ANALYSIS MADE ON JUICE

(1) Original juice; (2) stored 2 days; (3) 1 week; (4) 2 weeks; (5) 3 weeks; and (6) 9 weeks. Decrease in density at 520 mμ is due to development of a yellow color.

has been reduced by action of the clarifying agent, the separation of argols is effected more readily.

During storage for elimination of argols, there is a decrease in solids, about one-half of which is accounted for by precipitation of potassium and sodium tartrates. Tannins, coloring matters (Table 59) gums, and pectins are included in the other half.

Marked improvements have been made also in some factories in methods of pasteurizing and bottling grape juice. These are designed to overcome some of the deteriorative effects caused by the presence of oxygen of the air, and those caused by prolonged heating (Fig. 80 and 81). Juice from which argols have been removed is conveyed to holding tanks above or adjacent to the bottling room. From there it flows by gravity or is pumped through the tubular or plate heat exchanger and into the filler. Hot water is used as a heating medium and the temperature employed is high enough to obtain a temperature in the bottled juice of 170°F or above. Suitable recording and control instruments are used with the equipment. The hot juice from the heat exchanger is filled by means of an automatic filler into preheated bottles which have passed through an air cleaner and preheating hood. The air cleaner using filtered air removes particles of lint or foreign matter from the inverted bottles. In the preheating hood, the bottles are subjected to steam heating.

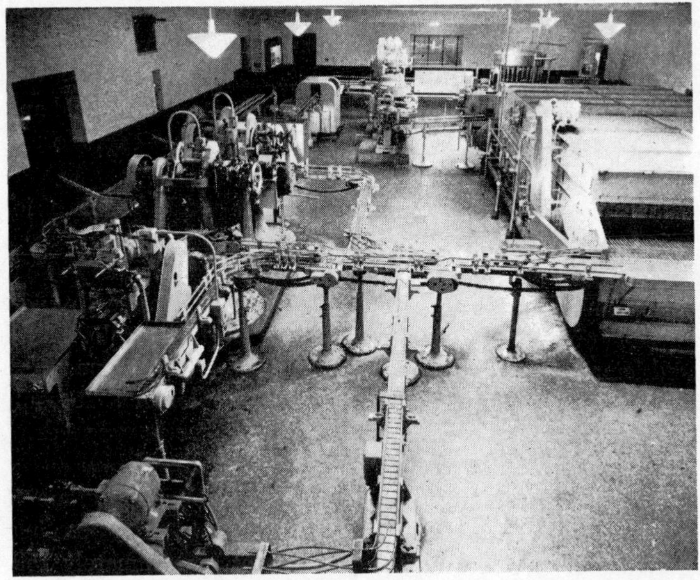

Courtesy of Welch Grape Juice Co.

FIG. 82. VIEW OF GRAPE JUICE PASTEURIZATION ROOM

Equipment shown includes juice heat exchanger for pasteurizing before filling, bottle preheater, air cleaner for cans or bottles, bottle filler, can filler, bottle crowner, can closer, pasteurizer and cooler, and conveyors, labelers, and other essential equipment necessary to handle bottles or cans from time of filling until cased for shipment.

After filling, the bottles are capped under atmospheres of steam or carbon dioxide and are then discharged to a converter which carries the bottles to the pasteurizer. Since the bottles are filled hot, the pasteurizer serves to hold the bottles at pasteurizing temperature. In the latter part of this line the bottles are subjected to mist sprays of cool and then cold water so that they are discharged from the pasteurizer at the desirable temperature for drying and labeling.

Considerable quantities of grape juice are still preheated or even pasteurized in kettles. Preheated juices are then given final pasteurizing in conveyors which carry the bottles of juice first through hot water and then through cooling water (Fig. 82).

METHODS OF PRESERVATION OTHER THAN BY HEAT

Although pasteurization is by all means the most common method employed for the commercial preservation of grape juice, some juice is preserved in other ways. Grape juice is now being preserved in large quantities by concentration and freezing. The volume of frozen concentrated grape juice has expanded considerably during the past several years. Standardization of concentrate should be effected in this part of the industry. There is little doubt that the high concentration of acid and sugar is effective in the preservation of the concentrate but little information as to their effectiveness is available.

The utilization of grape juice in grape drinks and in blends of juice has also expanded considerably; some are fortified with vitamins, even using the fat soluble vitamins in emulsion form. Blends of apple and Concord grape juices have found a great outlet. Blends of apple with juices from other grape varieties have been found to be most desirable. A blend of grape and lemon juices has been marketed. Blends of grape with grapefruit and other juices have been found to be very pleasing. It would seem desirable to standardize the content of grape juice in grape drinks and blends with juices from other fruit(see Chapters 10 and 11).

In Germany, Switzerland, and South Africa clarified grape juice is often preserved by filtering it through a sterilizing "germ-proofing" filter and holding under carbon dioxide pressure of approximately 150 psi.

In 1865, Prandtl observed that fermentation of grape juice sealed in a vial ceased as the pressure of carbon dioxide increased and long before sufficient alcohol was formed to stop fermentation. This was believed to be a specific pressure effect of carbon dioxide. In 1884, Certes and Cochin reduced the fermentative powers through pressures of 300 to 400 atm. The use of carbon dioxide under pressure to suppress fermentation of grape juice was conceived and patented by Gräger in 1896. The first report on the carbonic acid or Boehi impregnation process was published by Boehi in 1912. In this it was stated that under 6 to 7 atm of carbon dioxide all microbial activity ceased and the juice retained its natural aroma and flavor. Unfortunately, this carbon dioxide pressure does not inactivate enzymes, nor does it kill yeasts and bacteria, and lactic acid bacteria can grow. Lüthi (1959) demonstrated production of lactic, acetic and carbonic acids in unpasteurized juices stored under carbon dioxide pressure. This may be due to a malo-lactic fermentation. The so-called tank flavor may be similar to the flavor developed in unpasteurized Concord juices sterilized by filtration, filled, and sealed in glass. Tressler and Pederson (1936) observed that detrimental changes in aroma and flavor as well as haze formation and color change occurred in unpasteurized juices that have been sterilized by filtration. Although noncitrus juices have been stored in sealed tanks under 77 atm of carbon dioxide held at 59 F, the risks of obtaining flavor changes are greater if the Boehi process is used without previous sterilization of the juices. Pasteurization and low temperature storage is essential in maintaining flavor and avoiding undesirable fermentation even when carbon dioxide is used. The low pressure tanks are costly and the necessity of storage at 32° to 39°F under 45 psi pressure to inhibit fermentation approach the nonpressure methods commonly employed for Concord juice.

In the same areas, large quantities of grape juice are filtered through a "germ-proofing" filter and bottled under aseptic conditions into sterile bottles. Carpenter, Pederson and Walsh (1932) have shown that clarified Concord juice is more easily sterilized by filtration through a Seitz filter than are juices from other fruits. However, Pederson and Tressler (1936) have shown that Concord grape juice must be heated sufficiently to inactivate the enzymes if it is to be preserved in this way; otherwise undesirable changes in flavor occur.

Freezing storage is used to a limited extent to hold juice for manufacture of jelly and jam. Frozen juice holds its flavor well, but deposits a greater amount of argols than juice held in other ways. This causes a loss of acidity which may result in a juice which is lacking in tartness. Frozen juice soon becomes substantially sterile and also does not deteriorate materially due to oxidation. The excessive deposition of tartrate crystals is not necessarily objectionable if the juice is to be used in jelly making or for beverage purposes. Juice to be held in freezing storage should be precooled before freezing by the same methods employed for cool storage. This will result in more rapid freezing, resulting in greater uniformity due to less separation of ice from juice. It will also prevent any possibility of fermentation during freezing.

Some grape juice is preserved by addition of chemicals. Sulfur dioxide and the various sulfites are commonly used in combination since sulfur dioxide alone may be slowly dissipated. Many strains of yeasts used for wine making are tolerant to sulfur dioxide and will effect fermentation in presence of high concentrations of the chemical. Grape juice is occasionally preserved with sodium benzoate which is inhibitive even to chemically tolerant wine yeasts.

BIBLIOGRAPHY

AMERINE, M. A., BERG, H. W., and CRUESS, W. V. 1967. The Technology of Wine Making, 2nd Edition. Avi Publishing Co., Westport, Conn.

AMERINE, M. A., and JOSLYN, M. A. 1951. Table Wines—The Technology of Their Production in California. Univ. Calif. Press, Berkeley, Calif.

ANON. 1951. California becomes important grape juice producer. Western Canner Packer *43*, No. 9, 39–40, 42.

BERG, V. A. 1940. Composition of grapes. Kultur Rastanii 7, 105–119.

BROWN, W. L. 1940. The anthocyanin pigment of the Hunt Muscadine grape. J. Am. Chem. Soc. *62*, 2808–2810.

CALDWELL, J. S. 1925. Some effects of seasonal condition upon the chemical composition of American grape juice. J. Agr. Res. *30,* No. 12, 1133–1176.

CARPENTER, D. C., PEDERSON, C. S., and WALSH, W. F. 1932. Sterilization of fruit juices by filtration. Ind. Eng. Chem. *24,* 1218–1223.

HARTMANN, B. G., and TOLMAN, L. M. 1918. Concord grape juice; Manufacture and chemical composition. U.S. Dept. Agr. Bull. *656.*

HOLLEY, R. W., STOYLA, B., and HOLLEY, A. D. 1955. The identification of some volatile constituents of Concord grape juice. Food Research *20,* 326–331.

KERTESZ, Z. I. 1930. A new method for enzymatic clarification of unfermented apple juice. N. Y. State Agr. Expt. Sta. Bull. *589.*

KERTESZ, Z. I. 1944. The chemical composition of maturing New York State grapes. N. Y. State Agr. Expt. Sta. Tech. Bull. *274.*

LATHROP, C. P., and WALDE, W. L. 1928. Change in Concord grape juice composition by freezing storage. Fruit Products J. *7,* No. 5, 26–27.

LAWRENCE, N. L., WILSON, D. C., and PEDERSON, C. S. 1959. The growth of yeasts in grape juice stored at low temperatures. II. The types of yeast and their growth in pure culture. Appl. Microbiol. *7,* 7–11.

LÜTHI, H. 1959. The progress realized in the production of fruit juices. Fruit *14,* 447–457.

MATTICK, L. R., ROBINSON, W. B., WEIRS, L. D., and BARRY, D. L. 1963. Determination of methyl anthranilate in grape juice by electron affinity-gas chromatography. J. Agr. Food Chem. *11,* No. 4, 334–336.

MATTICK, L. R., WEIRS, L. D., and ROBINSON, W. B. 1967. Detection of adulterated Concord grape juice with other anthocyanin-containing products. J. Assoc. Offic. Agr. Chemists *50,* 299–303.

MOYER, J. C., and SARAVACOS, G. D. 1968. Scientific and Technical Aspects of Fruit Juice Recovery. N. Y. State Agr. Expt. Sta. Journal Paper *1647.*

MURPHY, M. M., JR., PICKETT, T. A., and COWART, F. F. 1938. Muscadine grapes: culture, varieties and some properties of juices. Georgia Expt. Sta. Bull. *199,* 1–32.

PEDERSON, C. S. 1936A. The preservation of grape juice. I. Pasteurization of Concord grape juice. Food Research *1,* 9–27.

PEDERSON, C. S. 1936B. The preservation of grape juice. III. Studies on the cool storage of grape juice. Food Research *1,* 301–305.

PEDERSON, C. S. 1947. Apple juice with original character retained. Fruit Products J. *26,* 294, 313.

PEDERSON, C. S., ALBURY, M. N., and CHRISTENSEN, M. D. 1961. The growth of yeasts in grape juice stored at low temperature. IV. Fungistatic effects of organic acids. Appl. Microbiol. *9,* 162–7.

PEDERSON, C. S., ALBURY, M. N., WILSON, D. C., and LAWRENCE, N. L. 1958. The growth of yeasts in grape juice stored at low temperatures. I. Control of yeast growth in commercial operation. Appl. Microbiol. *7,* No. 1, 1–6.

PEDERSON, C. S., and BEATTIE, H. G. 1947. Concentration of fruit juice by freezing. N.Y. State Agr. Expt. Sta. Bull. *727.*

PEDERSON, C. S., BEATTIE, H. G., and STOTZ, E. H. 1947. Deterioration of processed fruit juices. N.Y. State Agr. Expt. Sta. Bull. *728.*

PEDERSON, C. S., ROBINSON, W. B., and SHAULIS, N. J. 1953. Opalescent juice from white grapes. N.Y. State Agr. Expt. Sta. Farm Research *19,* No. 1, 2.

PEDERSON, C. S., and TRESSLER, D. K. 1936. Improvements in the manufacture and preservation of grape juice. N.Y. State Agr. Expt. Sta. Bull. *676.*

ROBINSON, W. B., AVENS, A. W., and KERTESZ, Z. I. 1949. The chemical composition of ripe Concord-type grapes grown in New York in 1947. N.Y. State Agr. Expt. Sta. Tech. Bull. *285*.

ROBINSON, W. B., EINSET, J., and SHAULIS, N. J. 1970. The relation of variety and grape composition to wine quality. Proc. New York State Hort. Soc. *111*, 283–287.

ROBINSON, W. B., and SHAULIS, N. J. 1968. Measure of quality in grapes. Proc. New York State Hort. Soc. *113*, 280–285.

ROBINSON, W. B., SHAULIS, N. J., and PEDERSON, C. S. 1949. Ripening studies of grapes grown in 1948 for juice manufacture. Fruit Products J. *29*, 36–37, 54, 62.

ROBINSON, W. B., SHAULIS, N. J., SMITH, G. C., and TALLMAN, G. F. 1959. Changes in the malic and tartaric acid contents of Concord grapes. Food Research *24*, 176–180.

ROGER, N. F. and TURKOT, V. A. 1965. Designing distillation equipment for volatile fruit aromas. Food Technol. *19*, 62–72.

SARAVACOS, G. D., MOYER, J. C., and WOOSTER, G. D. 1969. Stripping of high-boiling aroma compounds from aqueous solutions. N.Y. State Agr. Expt. Sta. Res. Circ. *21*.

SASTRY, L. V. L., and TISCHER, R. G. 1952A. Stability of the anthocyanin pigments in Concord grape juice. Food Technol. *6*, 264–268.

SASTRY, L. V. L., and TISCHER, R. G. 1952B. Behavior of the anthocyanin pigments in Concord grapes during heat processing and storage. Food Technol. *6*, 82–86.

SHEPARDSON, E. S., SHAULIS, N. J., MOYER, J. C., BOURNE, M. C., SPLITTSTOESSER, D. F., FRIEDMAN, I. E., JORDAN, T. D., TASCHENBERG, E. F., and DOMINICK, B. A., JR. 1969. Mechanical harvesting of grapes varieties grown in New York State. Fruit and vegetable mechanization. Rural Manpower Center, Michigan State Univ., East Lansing, Mich.

TISCHER, R. G. 1951. A high temperature process for the extraction of Concord grape juice. Food Technol. *5*, 160–163.

TRESSLER, D. K., and JOSLYN, M. A. 1961. Fruit and Vegetable Juice Process Technology. Avi Publishing Co., Westport, Conn.

TRESSLER, D. K., and PEDERSON, C. S. 1936. Preservation of grape juice. II. Factors controlling the rate of deterioration of Concord juice. Food Research *1*, 87–97.

WHITE, E. D. 1950. Reveal new uses for Muscadine grapes. Food Inds. *22*, 1719–1721.

WINKLER, A. J. 1949. Grapes and wines. Econ. Botany *3*, 46–70.

WILLAMAN, J. J., and KERTESZ, Z. I. 1931. The enzymatic clarification of grape juice. New York State Agr. Expt. Sta. Tech. Bull. 178.

WOLCOTT, S. K., JR. 1958. Process for conditioning grape and analogous berry and fruit materials prior to extraction of juice therefrom. U.S. Patent 2,837,431.

WOODROOF, J. G. 1952. Private communication. Experiment, Ga.

CHAPTER 8

D. K. Tressler,
V. L. S. Charley,
and B. S. Luh

Cherry, Berry and Other Miscellaneous Fruit Juices

CHERRY JUICE

Cherry juice has an attractive color and a pleasing flavor; nevertheless its manufacture and use is very limited when compared to the more popular juices. Perhaps the reason for this is because it is so strong that it requires dilution to be pleasing to most persons.

It is produced chiefly in Wisconsin although small amounts are made in New York, Colorado, and Pennsylvania. Statistical data on the production of cherry and berry juices are not available by kind but are included with data on miscellaneous fruit and berry juice packs.

Varieties Suitable

Ordinarily, no single common variety of cherry yields a juice which is of the proper acidity and sugar content for an ideal beverage. As a rule, the unsweetened juice of some varieties, Montmorency, Early Richmond, and English Morello is too high in acidity and too low in sugar content to be entirely pleasing to the average palate. If Montmorency cherries, however, are allowed to reach full maturity, their sugar content increases and the acidity becomes proportionally less. Such well matured fruit produces a very desirable juice without blending. It may be necessary, however to spray the fruit on the trees with a hormone solution to prevent dropping.

Sweet cherries, on the other hand, may be too low in acid to yield juice of pleasing flavor (Isham and Mottern 1938).

The flavor of juice made from the Montmorency and English Morello varieties is excellent, although the Morello juice is preferred by many persons. Early Richmond juice is inferior in flavor (Tressler 1941A; Tressler *et al.* 1941).

Quality of Fruit

If juice of excellent flavor and color is desired, the best quality of cherries must be used. Juice prepared from cull fruit is not lacking in flavor and color, but generally possesses an off-flavor usually resembling benzaldehyde, derived from spoiled or spotted fruit. The benzaldehyde-

VERNON L. S. CHARLEY is Director, Product Development, Beecham Foods Limited, Brentford, England.

B. S. LUH is Lecturer, Food Science and Technology Department, University of California, Davis, Calif.

TABLE 61

COMPOSITION OF THE JUICES OF SEVERAL VARIETIES OF CHERRIES

	Montmorency	Early Richmond	English Morello	Bing
Specific gravity (68°F)	1.0637	1.0456	1.0786	1.0475
Total solids, %	15.23	13.37	18.00	14.84
Volatile acidity[1]	6.1	4.2	2.7	3.0
Total acidity as malic acid, %	1.32	1.51	1.86	0.47
Reducing sugars, %	9.70	7.88	10.17	10.56
Nonsugar solids, %	5.53	5.49	7.83	4.28

Source: Swisher and Poe (1935).
[1] Cubic centimeters of tenth normal sodium hydroxide per 100 gm of juice.

like flavor is probably derived from the enzymatic hydrolysis of cyanogenic glucosides similar to amygdalin. Juice made from under-ripe fruit is sour and of poor color. It is of low density, and deficient in sugar and other soluble components which contribute to flavor.

Mushy fruit yields juice which contains so much suspended material that filtration is difficult. Moreover, such juice usually becomes cloudy during storage.

Composition of Cherry Juice.—The proximate analysis of the three common varieties of sour cherries and one sweet variety is presented in Table 61. It will be noted that although there is little difference between the sugar content of the several varieties, the total acidity varies widely. The sweet varieties yield juice which is low in acid, whereas the common sour varieties contains 3 to 4 times as much. Malic is the principal acid present. However, Bridges (1941) reports that cherries also contain small amounts of citric, succinic and lactic acids. Chatfield and Adams (1940) found 0.10% of volatile acids in the juice of Black Tartarian cherries. The principal sugars of cherry juice are dextrose and levulose with but only small amounts of sucrose.

The Preparation of the Juice

Sorting and Washing.—Cherries for juice production may be harvested with stems or picked without stems. The freshly harvested cherries should be sorted to eliminate spoiled, wormy and damaged fruit. The cherries should then be washed in very cold water (50°F) preferably with some time allowed for soaking. However, the soaking period should not be longer than 12 hr as otherwise there will be a notable loss in soluble solids and some change in flavor. Zubeckis (1955–1956A) proposed that cherries be stemmed before washing, but the washing of stemmed fruit should be carefully controlled to minimize loss of soluble solids. He recommended pitting before juice expression. The pitting loss in a mechanical pitter amounts to about 7%.

Three methods may be used for obtaining juice from cherries: hot pressing or cold pressing of fresh cherries and the cold pressing of the previously frozen fruit.

Hot Pressing.—In many ways the simplest method of making cherry juice is by heating the washed cherries to approximately 150°F in a steam-jacketed stainless steel or aluminum kettle and then pressing the fruit before it cools. The heating extracts a large proportion of the pigments of the cherries, and in the case of Montmorency and Early Richmond varieties produce a deep red juice. The English Morello yields a very dark red juice (Tressler, Pederson and Beavens 1941).

Zubeckis (1955–1956A) recommends that the pitted cherries be heated to 140°F in a jacketed stainless steel kettle fitted with a double motion agitator.

A hydraulic press of the type often used for pressing grapes is suitable for the pressing of cherries. However, the press cloths should not be of coarse weave, as otherwise much pulp passes into the juice. Zubeckis suggests the use of Nylon cloths.

The hot juice coming from the press should be strained through a fine wire screen made of corrosion resistant metal, or a muslin bag. The strained juice should be chilled to 50°F or lower and allowed to settle overnight. The clear juice should be siphoned from the sludge, and then mixed with a small amount of filter aid, e.g., Hyflo Super Cel[1] or Dicalite[2] and filtered through canvas in a plate and frame filter press or some other filter (Tressler *et al.* 1943). The yield obtained by hot pressing Montmorency cherries varies from 62 to approximately 68%.

Cold Pressing.—Hot pressing yields a beautiful juice which is easily filtered. However, its flavor is not that of fresh cherries but rather that of canned cherries. Cold-pressed juice is not so brilliantly colored as the hot-pressed product, but its flavor closely resembles that of fresh cherries and so is preferred by many persons.

The washed fruit is drained and then cut to a coarse pulp. This may be done in an ordinary apple grinder, such as is used for the making of cider, provided the knives are set so that the pits are not crushed during the operation of maceration. This comminution of the fruit results in a better extraction of color, for if whole Montmorency cherries are pressed without heating, their juice will be but pale red. The cold, macerated cherries are pressed in a rack and cloth hydraulic press, such as is often used for grapes. The yield obtained by cold pressing varies from 61 to approximately 68%. According to the process commonly used in Wisconsin

[1] Hyflo Super Cel is made by Johns-Manville Corp., New York 16, N. Y.

[2] Dicalite is made by Dicalite Division, Great Lakes Carbon Corp., New York 16, N. Y.

(Martin 1936), the freshly pressed juice is rapidly heated to 190° to 200°F, and then cooled. This operation inactivates enzymes and kills most of the microorganisms of the juice. It also helps to coagulate the colloidal matter.

Even when using this heat treatment, it is usually necessary to give the juice a special clarification treatment before filtration or else the filter is soon clogged by fine particles of pulp. A simple method of preparing the juice for filtration is to treat it with the pectic enzyme preparation, Pectinol, according to the following procedure: The juice is cooled to 100°F, then 0.1% by weight of Pectinol M is added and permitted to act on the juice held at this temperature for 3 hr. After this period, the juice is heated to 180°F, then cooled and filtered through a plate and frame filter press.

Cold Pressing Thawed Fruit.—Deep red juice having a color nearly as dark as that obtained by hot pressing and yet possessing the fresh flavor of cold-pressed juice may be obtained by pressing frozen cherries. The cherries may be prepared for freezing either by packing pitted cherries, with or without added sugar, into enamel-lined tin cans or barrels, or by crushing the unpitted fruit just sufficiently to release enough juice to cover the cherries when packed in enamel-lined tin cans or barrels. The cherries are frozen and stored at 0°F or lower. When needed for juice they are thawed at room temperature, preferably before a fan, until the fruit reaches a temperature of 40° to 50°F, then the thawed fruit is pressed in a hydraulic press. Juice obtained from thawed cherries should be treated with Pectinol and filtered as described above for cold-pressed juice. Thawed Montmorency cherries yield 70 to 76% and Early Richmond from 60 to 75% of juice, the higher yields being obtained at 145°F.

Sweetening and Processing.—It has already been indicated that cherry juice from the sour varieties, Montmorency, Early Richmond and English Morello, is usually too sour to please the average palate. Therefore, unless the juice has been produced from especially sweet cherries, it is necessary to sweeten it by adding dry sugar or sugar syrup. Sufficient sugar should be added to bring the density of the juice to about 17°Brix (Zubeckis 1955–1956A; Tressler *et al.* 1941). This procedure takes the edge off the sourness but does not reduce the acidity sufficiently. A more palatable beverage may be obtained by diluting the juice with half its volume of water and adding sufficient sugar to bring the percentage of total solids back to the original point. This procedure reduces the total acidity to 1% or less and yet maintains the solids content at approximately 10%.

If sugar, sugar syrup, or water is added to cherry juice, the addition should be clearly indicated on the label or else the product may be considered by the Food and Drug authorities to be adulterated. Further, it should be noted that a diluted product cannot be labeled "juice" (Tressler *et al.* 1941).

On the other hand, the juice of the sweet cherries, such as the Bing, is somewhat lacking in acidity. Further, most sweet cherries yield a juice which is not deeply colored. Sweet cherries are ordinarily more valuable than sour cherries and so are seldom used for juice. If the juice of sweet cherries is available, it may be greatly improved by blending with an equal volume of the juice of a sour variety such as the Montmorency.

Since hot-pressed cherry juice is of better color and cold-pressed juice of superior flavor, a blend of the two is more attractive than either one alone. Equal parts of each or two parts of cold-pressed juice blended with one part of hot-pressed juice gives a product more desirable than either alone.

Cherry juice may be packed in either cans or bottles. Because of its beautiful red color, bottled juice has a greater aesthetic appeal than canned juice. However, cans are cheaper and lighter. If cans are used, they should be lined with a fruit or berry enamel.

Cherry juice and cherry beverages, containing half water and half cherry juice may be preserved by either holding or flash pasteurization methods (see Chapter 10). The procedures described for the pasteurization of apple juice (pp. 213 and 214) are applicable to cherry juice and cherry beverages. Flash pasteurization temperatures as low as 165°F may be used if care is taken to eliminate air in the headspace of the bottled product.

Pasteurized cherry juice should be held under refrigeration if it is to be stored long, otherwise its flavor deteriorates markedly.

Factors Affecting Stability and Color of Cherry Juices

Louvric (1965) studied the storage stability and color of blackberry and cherry juices. Blanching cherries for one minute at 185°F before expressing the juices yielded a more intensely red color than from unblanched fruit. The subsequent degradations of the color during storage was less in the blanched fruit juices. With diatomite filtration, anthocyanin pigments were absorbed, decreasing the color of the juices. No significant color loss was observed following a treatment with a pectinolytic enzyme to clarify the juices. The color of concentrated juice was more stable than that of diluted juice. The concentrated juice was more stable at temperatures approaching 32°F. Exclusion of oxygen also had a beneficial effect on the color stability of the fruit juices at all storage temperatures, but more markedly at the lower temperatures.

Louvric (1962) reported on factors influencing hydroxymethylfurfural in sour cherry and blackberry juices. The effects of concentration, addition of sucrose, repeated pasteurization and storage at various temperatures on the amount of hydroxymethylfurfural (HMF) were studied to elucidate the degradation in commercial sour cherry and blackberry juices. The amount of HMF depends on its simultaneous formation from the carbohydrate and its decomposition or combination with other reactive juice components. Anthocyanin is most probably one of the factors which cause the decrease in HMF during storage at 32° and 65°F. Another factor may be oxygen remaining in the cans after filling and sealing.

Detection of Adulteration

The official paper-chromatographic method for detecting adulteration in Concord grape juice was applied to cherry juice and other dark colored fruit juices by Fitelson (1968). In contrast to the complicated anthocyanin patterns on the paper chromatograms of grape juices, these juices show simple patterns of 1 or 2 major red bands. Since most adulterants have more complicated anthocyanin patterns, they can be readily detected by this method, even at low concentrations. If adulteration cannot be detected by the anthocyanin patterns, it can usually be shown by the anthocyanidin patterns. In this paper-chromatographic test, three separate anthocyanidin spots are formed. The dark-colored juices tested here showed most of the anthocyanidin color in the central spot, whereas the possible adulterants showed other patterns. Therefore, mixtures will have abnormal anthocyanidin patterns in this test.

Carbonated Cherry Juice

Cherry juice carbonated with about three volumes of carbon dioxide is a very pleasing beverage. Cold-pressed juice does not yield a satisfactory carbonated beverage, since the carbonation causes the deposition of a great deal of sediment. On the other hand, carbonated hot-pressed juice remains clear during carbonation, pasteurization and subsequent storage.

The methods described for the carbonation of apple and other fruit juices may be used in preparing the product. Pasteurization may be effected by holding the bottled carbonated juice at 140° to 145°F for 30 min.

Cherry Syrup

Cherry syrup of good quality may be made (Tressler 1941A) by first concentrating cherry juice prepared from frozen Montmorency cherries, by either low temperature vacuum evaporation or freezing concentration to a 2 to 1 or greater concentration, and then sweetening the concentrate either with sugar or a mixture of sugar and enzyme converted corn syrup.

An excellent cherry syrup may be made from such a 2 to 1 concentrate, which contains approximately 30% total solids, by sweetening it with an

TABLE 62

AVERAGE COMPOSITION OF SOME BERRY JUICES IN PER CENT

	Blackberry[1]	Blueberry[1]	Cranberry[2]	Loganberry[1]	Raspberry Black[1]	Raspberry Red[1]	Strawberry[1]
Sugars (as invert)	5.4	12.4	3.31[3]	6.5	7.6	7.3	3.6
Acid (as citric)	0.92	0.19	3.60	1.89	1.04	1.40	1.01
Ash	0.39	0.19	0.16	0.40	0.80	0.46	0.45
Protein	0.3	0.1	...	0.6	0.2	0.4	0.2
Water	92.3	85.9	93.3	88.9	88.4	90.8	94.2

[1] From Chatfield and McLaughlin (1931).
[2] From Rice, Fellers, and Clague (1939).
[3] By difference.

equal weight of enzyme converted corn syrup and one-sixth of its weight of granulated sugar. The product contains about 64% solids and will not ferment, but may spoil because of mold growth, especially after the container has been opened and exposed to air. Therefore if it is to be used in soda fountains, it is advisable to add 0.1% of sodium benzoate to aid in its preservation and to fill while hot, taking care to fill each container completely.

A somewhat sweeter cherry syrup may be made by dissolving sufficient granulated sugar in a 2 to 1 concentrate to bring the total solids content to approximately 64%.

Cherry syrups of excellent color and fair flavor may be prepared by dissolving granulated sugar in warm hot-pressed cherry juice, preferably made from the Montmorency variety of cherries, until the total solids concentration reaches approximately 64%. Filtration of the juice, prior to the addition of the sugar, is desirable as the syrup obtained should be sparkling clear.

BERRY JUICES

There has been a considerable increase in interest in the manufacture of berry juices because several important soft drink manufacturers market carbonated beverages flavored with pure fruit juices. As yet, however, the total annual production of these juices is not great. Blackberry, loganberry, and raspberry juices are packed on the Pacific Coast. Youngberry juice is prepared and preserved in certain Southern States. Cranberry juice is bottled in Massachusetts. Strawberry juice is packed on a small scale in Tennessee and Oregon.

Many berry juices possess an excellent flavor and are attractive in color. They have been used for many years for the preparation of fruit jellies, fruit punches, ice cream sodas, milk shakes, fruit wines, and other fruit beverages and products (Tressler 1938, 1942; Charley 1932; Charley and

TABLE 63

SOME TYPICAL CHEMICAL ANALYSES OF CHERRY, CURRANT AND BERRY JUICES

Juice	Active Acidity, pH	Malic Acid, gm per 100 ml	Specific Gravity	°Brix
Strawberry (Culver)	3.48	1.18	1.041	10.1
Cherry (Montmorency)	3.52	1.56	1.080	19.3
Red raspberry (Marcy)	3.12	2.00	1.081	19.5
Purple raspberry (Sodus)	3.13	1.93	1.044	11.1
Black raspberry (Bristol)	...	0.55	1.049	11.8
Currant, red	3.19	1.92	...	...

Source: Pederson *et al.* (1947).

Harrison 1939; Charley 1950). Considerable quantities of many berry juices are prepared for commercial use in making these products, but with the exception of blackberry, loganberry, and cranberry juices, none is commonly used as a table beverage.

Composition

The common berries, with the exception of blueberry and raspberry, are low in sugar, running from about 4 to 8% (see Tables 62 and 63). The acidity of most of the berries is approximately 1%, calculated as citric acid (Beattie *et al.* 1943; Tressler *et al.* 1943; Pederson and Beattie 1943A and B; Pederson *et al.* 1947). An exception is blueberry juice which not only is relatively high in sugar but also is very low in acid. Cranberry and loganberry juices are other exceptions being much higher in acid, running 1.9% or above.

Because of their relatively high acid and low sugar content, the palatability of most berry juices is improved by dilution with a half volume of light sugar syrup (see Chapter 10). Most people like a juice containing 10 to 12% of sugar and 0.6 to 0.7% of acid. If the juice is diluted, labeling regulations must be met.

Method of Preparation

Cold Pressing Fresh Strawberries.—The method suggested by Walker *et al.* (1954) for preparing juice from fresh strawberries is to put the cold berries through a hammer mill fitted with a one-quarter-inch screen. Then filter aid is added to the crushed berries in amounts varying from 3 to 10%, after which the slurry is immediately pressed in a bag-type press. The amount of filter aid used depends on the firmness of the berries, and this is added in sufficient quantity to produce a firm, dry cake in the press. The yield of juice varies from 70 to 80% depending upon the variety, maturity etc. of the berries. The cloudy juice from the press is treated immediately with a pectic enzyme preparation in order to remove the pectin component in the jelling reaction. Treatment for 3 hr at 75°F with 0.5% Pectinol was found by Walker *et al.* (1954) to degrade the pectic substances sufficiently to produce a clear stable juice. After this treatment it should be filtered under pressure using filter aid precoated plates and an addition of 0.25% of filter aid to the juice.

Zubeckis (1955–1956B) suggests the preparation of cold-pressed juice by first crushing fresh red raspberries then depectinizing the purée by treatment with 0.05% Pectinol 100 D, after which the slurry is pressed in a hydraulic press. The juice obtained is flash pasteurized at about 207°F for 15 sec.

Cold Pressing Thawed Berries.—Frozen berries, usually those prepared without sugar, are sometimes used for juice. Their use has five definite advantages (Pederson and Beattie 1943A). Freezing effects a coagulation of the mucilaginous components which otherwise make pressing difficult, thus making heating of the berries unnecessary. On the average a higher yield of juice (65 to 79% of the weight of the fruit) is obtained from frozen berries than is the case when heated fresh berries are pressed in a hydraulic press. A third advantage is that when frozen berries are used as raw material, the juice plant may be operated throughout the year instead of only during the season when fresh berries are available. Juice obtained by cold pressing thawed berries has a much deeper color than that produced by cold pressing fruit that has not been frozen, and is nearly equivalent in this regard to hot-pressed juice. Further, it has a fresh fruit flavor and lacks the astringency often characteristic of hot-pressed juice.

Hot Pressing Fresh Berries.—When fresh fruit is used, the process generally employed for blackberries, boysenberries, loganberries, raspberries, strawberries and youngberries is the following: Fully ripe, washed and sorted berries are placed in a steam jacketed kettle where they are heated to 140° to 180°F. During heating the fruit is agitated either mechanically or by hand paddles. The agitation and heating partially crushes the berries, thus aiding in the extraction and fixation of the color. The heating also reduces the mucilaginous character of the partially crushed berries and so facilitates the pressing. As soon as the berries reach the desired temperature, they are pressed preferably in an hydraulic rack and cloth press. Long continued heating should be avoided as otherwise tannin and other disagreeably flavored substances may be extracted from the seeds. The following yields were reported by Pederson and Beattie (1943A): Red raspberry 68% at 180°F; blackberry 65% at 142°F; strawberry 69% at 170°F.

Continuous screw expeller presses are sometimes used, but because of the excessive maceration of the pulp the resulting juice is very pulpy and is usually difficult to clarify. Pederson and Beattie (1943A) extracted juice from heated berries in a tapered screw juice extractor, obtaining the following yields of pulpy juice: Red raspberries 70%; black raspberries 55%; dewberries 82%; strawberries 58%.

Clarification.—Since most berry juices are ordinarily marketed as clear juices, filtration is necessary. During the heating required to effect pasteurization, clouding, and possibly coagulation and deposition of colloidal matter, may occur if the juice has not been preheated at a temperature slightly above that used in pasteurization. For this reason, berry juices should be heated to a temperature of approximately 190°F and then cooled, and filtered through an aluminum or wooden filter press using Hyflo Super Cel, Dicalite or some similar substance as a filter aid.

If neither the crushed berries nor the freshly extracted juice has been treated with pectic enzymes, treatment with commercial enzyme preparations, such as Pectinol and Clarase, aids materially in effecting clarification. Digestion with pectic enzymes aids clarification in two ways: (1) It causes coagulation and sedimentation of the suspended material and much of the colloidal content of the juice, and (2) the digestion of the pectin reduces the viscosity of the juice and consequently, permits filtration at a more rapid rate (Simpson 1957–1958).

The same general procedures described for the enzymatic clarification of apple juice (p. 212) may be used for treating berry juices.

Loganberry and boysenberry juices are usually not filtered prior to canning but are merely carefully strained.

Deaeration.—Deaeration of berry juices prior to pasteurization is recommended in order to prevent undesirable changes caused by oxidation during storage of the pasteurized juice. These changes include loss of color and flavor, and the clouding of the clear juice. Deaeration may be accomplished either by the batch process in which the juice is run into a tank and then subjected to a high vacuum (28 inches or higher) for 30 min, or by a continuous process. By the latter process the juice is sprayed into an evacuated chamber, thus deaerating the juice almost instantaneously.

Pasteurization.—Formerly a large proportion of the berry juice was put in bottles which were then crowned and pasteurized at 170° to 180°F for 20 to 30 min, the time and temperature of pasteurization depending on the type of juice, the size of bottle, and the practice of the particular factory in which the juice is packed.

In recent years, it has been generally recognized that flash pasteurization of berry juices yields products which will not spoil because of the growth of microorganisms, and are less subject to oxidative changes if care is taken to fill the containers completely, than are the juices preserved by holding pasteurization. The flash pasteurization procedure is entirely satisfactory for berry juices. Temperatures of 175°F or above applied for 30 sec or longer are usually recommended. The hot juice may be filled either into hot bottles or into cans lined with fruit or berry enamel, taking care to fill each container completely and close immediately. Regardless of the method of pasteurization, prompt cooling is an important factor in obtaining a good quality of preserved juice.

Pasteurized berry juices should be held under refrigeration if they are to be stored for longer than a month or two (Lee *et al.* 1950) otherwise serious flavor deterioration may occur. The loss in quality of pasteurized strawberry juice is especially rapid.

Berry Syrups

Syrups for pancakes, waffles, etc. are prepared from frozen raspberries, blackberries, and other berries (Lamb 1950). The berries are thawed, then pressed. Sugar and dextrose are dissolved in the hot juice and the syrup diluted with water to reduce the acidity to the desired point. The hot juice is filled into warm bottles.

BLUEBERRY JUICE

Blueberry juice is a pleasing product of high color and body, but as far as is known has not been packed for beverage purposes. The blueberry contains much more mucilaginous material than any of the berries considered thus far. For this reason the preparation of the juice is rather difficult. Clear blueberry juice, like clarified tomato juice, possesses relatively little flavor. Therefore, the unclarified product is the type considered best.

According to the process worked out at the New York State Agricultural Experiment Station, the washed blueberries are heated in a steam-jacketed aluminum or stainless steel kettle, agitating the berries slowly during the heating process. When the berries reach 180°F, they are put through a screw impeller type of tomato juice extractor. The temperature of the extracted juice is raised to 180°F by passage through a heat interchanger. The hot juice is then run into carboys which are completely filled and then closed with a paraffined cork according to the process formerly used for grape juice. After standing in a cool cellar for at least two months, the juice is siphoned from the heavy sludge on the bottom of the carboys. It is then flash pasteurized at 180°F according to the usual procedure, filled into bottles or cans which are promptly cooled.

Chandler and Highlands (1950) have suggested an improvement in the method of preparing blueberry juice. Instead of heating the berries to release the juice, Chandler and Highlands macerate the fresh blueberries, then mix the macerated product with 0.1% Pectinol M. After standing for 2 hr at 65° to 70°F the product is pressed in a hydraulic press, using a pressure approximately 6000 psi. A yield of nearly 88% of juice was obtained, which is slightly more than when the berries were heated prior to pressing. Thus, 1 bu of blueberries yielded approximately 4 gal. of juice. Juice prepared by this method is red in color and translucent in layers approximately 2 in. in thickness. By contrast, the juice from cooked blueberries is almost opaque in layers of this thickness. Chandler and Highlands recommend flash heating the juice and closing the containers at a temperature of at least 180°F.

CRANBERRY JUICE BEVERAGES

Although small amounts of cranberry beverages and syrups have been offered since 1895, the business was very limited until 1929 when the manufacture of cranberry cocktail began. This product is a diluted cranberry juice with added sugar.

Methods Employed in Extraction of Juice

When the very simple and rapid heat extraction method (Rice *et al.* 1939) is used, cranberries are heated with water for 8 to 10 min. Approximately 6.5 gal of water are used for each 100 lb of berries. The heat softens the berries so that the juice can be pressed out in a rack and cloth hydraulic press. About 8 gal of a viscous, brilliant red juice containing much pectin are obtained from each 100 lb of cranberries. It is either strained or filtered and diluted with from $1^1/_2$ to 2 parts of water and then sufficient sugar added to make it test 15° to 20° Brix.

Another method sometimes employed for separating the juice from the heated pulp is to run it into a basket-type centrifuge lined with paper pulp. When this method of extracting the juice is employed, approximately 35 gal of water are used for each 100 lb of cranberries; 32 to 34 gal of "juice" are obtained.

According to Rice, Fellers, and Clague (1939), the best method of extracting the raw cranberry juice by the cold press method is to grind the berries and then allow them to stand several hours before pressing in a rack and cloth hydraulic press. In this way approximately 7 gal of juice are obtained from 100 lb of berries. The product is of almost syrupy consistency, and, without dilution, is very difficult to filter. This juice it too tart for use as a beverage and should be blended with a sugar syrup. The procedure followed in converting it into a palatable beverage is described in Chapter 10.

Table 64

ANALYSES OF BERRY JUICES OBTAINED FROM VARIOUS ENGLISH FRUITS

Fruit	Variety	Specific Gravity	Acidity (as Malic Acid)	Tannin
			%	%
Green gooseberry	Keepsake	1.034	1.96	0.32
Red gooseberry	Ironmonger	1.036	0.80	0.10
Strawberry	Royal Sovereign	1.054	0.95	0.19
Raspberry	Baumforth A	1.041	2.23	0.13
Raspberry	Baumforth A	1.032	1.88	0.17
Raspberry	Baumforth A	1.030	1.57	0.10
Blackberry	Mixed Seedling	1.033	1.42	0.21
Loganberry	...	1.035	2.70	0.26

Source: Charley (1932).

Table 65

PROXIMATE COMPOSITION OF CERTAIN FRUIT JUICES

Component	Currant Black[1]	Currant Red[1]	Passion Fruit	Pome-granate[2]	Quince[1]
Sugars (as invert)	10.9	6.2	11.5	13.9	9.1
Acid (as citric)	2.89	2.00	2.14	1.47	1.20[3]
Ash	0.68	0.54	0.52	0.42	0.36
Protein	0.50	0.30	1.42	0.23	0.30
Water	85.05	89.1	81.0	82.9	89.04

[1] From Chatfield and McLaughlin (1931).
[2] From Nelson (1927).
[3] Calculated as malic acid.

RED CURRANT JUICE

Although currant juice is extensively used for making jelly and is used in a limited way for punches and other mixed fruit beverages, its use for beverage purposes is not of great importance in this country.

The methods used for making Concord grape juice (Chapter 7) may be employed in making currant juice. However, since the juice does not contain potassium bitartrate, it is not necessary to hold currant juice to eliminate argols. The hot-pressed juice may be bottled immediately after filtration (Charley 1950).

Red currant juice often varies in acidity (see Tables 63 and 65) from 1.9 to about 2.9%. Juice of such high acidity is not suitable for use as a beverage without dilution with a sugar solution.

BLACK CURRANT JUICE PRODUCTS[3]

During the last 30 years black currants have become of importance in Europe largely as a result of their high ascorbic acid content. The various

[3] This section prepared by Vernon L. S. Charley, Director, Product Development, Beecham Foods Limited, Brentford, England.

processes which are now associated with the production of a variety of black currant juice products were developed primarily at the Geisenheim National Institute in Germany, the Research Foundation for Fruit Growing and Fruit Juice Production at Ober-Erlenbach in Germany and the Long Ashton Research Station in England. In Germany, the development of a sweetened diluted juice beverage was emphasized and in England a black currant syrup with a high vitamin C content was developed.

Development Work in England

The publications on black currant juice processing in England have all emanated from the Long Ashton Research Station of the University of Bristol. A very brief description of the work which led up to commercial production in 1936 is provided here in the form of references to the original papers.

Charley (1932) first studied methods for the extraction of juice from fresh black currants without the application of heat. The same worker (Charley 1935A) studied the conditions for producing syrups from juices extracted from the fruit either by alcoholic fermentation or pectinase enzymes. White cane sugar was invariably used to make a syrup, and the finished products, where the sugar content by itself was insufficient to inhibit completely yeast action, were stabilized by pasteurization at 165°F for half an hour. Syrups with 65% total soluble solids retained their fresh black currant flavor for over four years. Provided that a juice filtered to a brilliant condition was used for making the syrup, such high sugar contents provided syrups which possessed safe keeping qualities without pasteurization or preservation.

At this stage the black currant syrup was considered for use in flavoring milk. The optimum sugar content for this purpose was found to be 55% by weight. At a dilution of one part of syrup with four parts of milk the pH of the fruit milk mixture was about 5.0, and this was quite satisfactory if held at a temperature of 45°F to avoid curdling (Charley 1935A).

The next stage in the development of black currant products was suggested by the popularity in England of citrus fruit squashes, i.e., syrups containing a suitable proportion of fruit tissues (Charley 1935B).

As a result of all these studies at Long Ashton a large-scale commercial enterprise was initiated to produce a range of pure fruit syrups from strawberries, raspberries, loganberries, blackberries and black currants. The syrups were primarily intended for use in milk. Charley (1936A) published a detailed description of the operation of the processes which had been taken from a purely laboratory-scale straight through to full-scale commercial production with no intervening pilot-scale operations. The black currants were picked on the strig and brought to the factory in wooden boxes or, later, aluminum trays, the depth of the fruit being 10 in. and 4 in., respectively. After a close inspection to demonstrate the absence of spontaneous fermentation or mold growth, the fruit was milled through a grater mill as used in the cider-making industry, metallized with a layer of 1/1000-in. of stainless steel. Initially an alcohol content of 0.8–1.2% was allowed to develop and the juice could then be pressed out with ease. Later, either because of protracted fermentation periods or excessively quick and uncontrollable fermentations, the removal of pectin was achieved by adding Pectinol or Filtragol to the fruit as it entered the mill. The progress of enzyme action was followed by checking the viscosity of the expressed juice at regular intervals. The pulp could be rendered suitable for pressing in a matter of 24 to 36 hr using 0.3% of single-strength pectinase of commerce. With the black currant fruit, very little separation of juice from tissue occurred, and the entire quantity of pulp was pressed out in the normal type of cider press using cotton (later nylon or terylene) cloths and ash wood racks. Using pulp which had been properly treated with enzyme, yields of 150 to 160 gal of juice could be obtained from one ton of fruit. This juice was centrifuged and converted into a 55° Brix syrup by the addition of solid cane sugar. The necessary quantity of edible color and preservative (0.035% by weight of sulfur dioxide) was added and the syrup clarified through a diatomaceous earth filter. The syrup produced in this way had a safe shelf-life of 18 months. Its acidity of approximately 1.3 to 1.6% citric acid by weight proved to be an important feature in its stabilization. Strawberry syrups, however, repeatedly developed fermentation at lower acidities, natural to the fruit of 0.5 to 0.8%, and the lowest safe acidity for a total soluble solids content of 55% was shown to be 1.1% by weight.

Black currant syrup of this type can be used for milk shakes at the rate of three-quarters of a fluid ounce of syrup added to 7 oz of milk with constant agitation at 40°F. It is important to add the syrup to the milk and not vice versa.

The syrup made as described above could be acidified where necessary to 1.5% of citric acid by weight and diluted with carbonated water in the proportion 1 + 5 for bottling and distribution as a sparkling fruit juice.

Sills (1939) examined the effect of varying preservatives on the retention of ascorbic acid in black currant juices and syrups over a period of 15 months. For juice the best retention of 77.7% was achieved by the use of the fully permitted quantity of SO_2, but 0.06% by weight of benzoic acid showed a retention of only 62.3%. (The untreated juice retained 57.8% of the vitamin after 15 months.)

TABLE 66

MAIN CONSTITUENTS OF BLACK CURRANT JUICES FROM FIVE VARIETIES

Variety	Acidity, % by Weight	"Tannin," % by Weight	Ash, % by Weight	Ascorbic Acid, mg/100 ml
Baldwin	3.40	0.24	0.574	161
Boskoop	3.20	0.23	0.516	132
French	2.86	0.33	0.416	128
Edina	3.34	0.46	0.533	99
Westwick Choice	2.91	0.25	0.683	147

Source: Charley (1936B).

Fifty degrees Brix black currant syrups prepared without pasteurization retained 84% of the initial vitamin C content and benzoic acid-preserved products 60.8% after the full storage period. Commercial experience, however, has shown that with much closer attention to the prevention of contact of the juice throughout its processing history with metals such as copper, the stability of the vitamin can be very greatly improved.

A further development in the black currant work at Long Ashton related to the production of sweetened juices rather than heavy syrups (Charley and Sills 1940). The specific gravity of the products was about 1.100 with acidities varying between 3% (as citric acid) and 1.65% for a sweetened juice in which approximately half of the original acidity had been neutralized with some alkaline calcium salt. The full reduction of acidity by neutralization gave a definite saline taste, and a heavy granular white deposit was formed after only short-term storage in bottle. The juices of minimum acidity retained remarkably full and fresh fruit characters after 20 months storage. During this period the ascorbic acid of a typical sweetened juice fell from its initial figure of 149 mg/100 ml to 106.6 mg. The method of production of these products ensures a very high juice content in the product, thus distinguishing it from the German sweetened and diluted Süssmost types of drink, but the overall flavor is such that it is not likely to appeal to a wide section of the public.

Charley *et al.* (1942) studied the optimum conditions for the extraction of residual juice from the pomace. They showed the effect of temperature and time of extraction on the efficiency of recovery of juice and ascorbic acid from the residues. Where water had to be added for this purpose it was possible later to remove the extractant by vacuum evaporation and recover a pure juice.

Throughout these investigations analyses were made on some of the chemical constituents which were of importance. Charley (1936B) reported a number of these and they are presented below in Table 66. Associated with these analyses was the observation that the flavors of

TABLE 67

ORGANIC ACIDS IN BLACK CURRANTS

	Milli-equivalents/100 Gm of Fruit			
Variety	Total Organic Acids	Malic Acid	Citric Acid	Oxalic Acid
Cotswold Cross	38.6	3.9	32.3	0.5
	42.4	3.9	35.6	0.6
Mendip Cross	39.9	8.9	28.6	0.3
	42.8	8.9	31.0	...

Source: Bryan (1946).

French and Edina varieties of black currants had richer fruit characters than those of the other varieties.

Bryan (1946) examined the organic acids in black currants, and her data are given in Table 67.

Pollard (1943) carried out at Long Ashton a comprehensive examination of some physiologically active constituents in black currants which had an effect on the capillary resistance of cell walls. A physiologically active fraction similar to the so-called vitamin P complex was obtained from black currants. Various substances were prepared from the crude black currant material, and whereas some had no activity, one of the materials had an activity of 10,600 G.L. units per gm compared with 100 units for hesperidin.

Recent Advances in Production Methods

For the production of a black currant juice intermediate product destined to be converted into a syrup with a high vitamin C content, the fundamental production methods remain generally very similar to those which were originally developed as described above from the Long Ashton original experimental studies. Such improvements in technique as have occurred in recent years have been largely concerned with the necessity to streamline the processing and make the fullest possible use of modern factory techniques which were not available when the original processes were being developed. Generally speaking, the methods of juice extraction, clarification, pasteurization and storage are similar to those used in other branches of the fruit juice industry, and no techniques other than those described earlier in this book are needed.

However, it is appropriate to refer to four points in processing techniques which have a special technical interest:

(a) The enzyme action is usually carried out discontinuously on large batches of milled pulp held in stainless steel tanks with tapering sides leading to outlets to the hydraulic presses. Figure 83 shows a battery of such tanks.

Courtesy of Beecham Foods Ltd., London

FIG. 83. TANKS FOR TREATING BLACK CURRANT PULP WITH ENZYME

(b) It is usual in modern practice to flash pasteurize all centrifuged, filtered fruit juices for syrup production at temperatures up to 200°F for 15 sec. Machines fitted with specially-constructed plates now carry out this duty with an extremely high efficiency, and can subsequently in the same operation reduce the temperature in one or two stages to 34°F. The lower temperature is necessary when juices are to be impregnated with CO_2 and filled under pressure into tanks which will be maintained at 32° to 34°F throughout the storage period (the Boehi method). Figure 84 illustrates a recently developed machine of this type of plate pasteurizer, and Fig. 85 shows the interior view of a large, modern cool store maintained at 32° ± 2°F containing 44 mild steel Prodorglas-lined tanks of 5,000 gal. capacity each, the juice being impregnated with CO_2 at 45 psi pressure.

(c) Black currant residues from the first pressing operation are now re-pressed in a continuous fashion in expeller presses fabricated in stainless steel. Such presses are recent developments of older types of machines used in the French cider industry to reduce the moisture content of apple pomace before it was dried. Figure 86 shows a Colin continuous press of this type.

(d) The final treatment of black currant residues is to dry the second-pressed pomace in a continuous machine in which the pomace is tossed over a circularly arranged battery of steam heated pipes. These pipes are fitted with angled "shoes" which pick up the pomace and direct it slowly forward through the machine. The moisture content is reduced to

Courtesy of APV Co., Crawley, England

FIG. 84. FLASH PASTEURIZER FOR BLACK CURRANT AND OTHER JUICES

below 12%. The final product has some value as a minor constituent in animal feeding stuffs.

Modern Techniques for Enzyme Treatment

The earlier work at Long Ashton on which various commercial processes were based involved the use of pectinase enzymes at ambient temperatures. The main difficulty with such a process arose from the perishable nature of the milled fruit and the likelihood of the onset of spontaneous fermentation during the period of enzyme action. The developments in Germany, where enzyme action is carried out at relatively elevated temperatures, led to similar conditions being adopted in England in what was originally known as the Long Ashton cold process, and temperatures up to about 110°F were employed. The time required for enzyme treatment at such a temperature could be reduced to as short a period as one or two hours by increasing the quantity of enzyme used. One considerable advantage accrued from the use of this higher temperature, for fermentation was considerably inhibited, and in cases where enzymes were available which had an optimum activity at 110°F or even 130°F, fermentation was entirely obviated.

Courtesy of Beecham Foods Ltd., London

FIG. 85. COOL STORAGE (32°F) FOR PRESSURE TANKS OF JUICE

It is known that pectinase enzymes in general are closely associated with certain fruit tissues. In order to obtain the maximum possible interaction between the innate and the added enzymes it is essential to insure the maximum contact between the enzymes, added either in solid or liquid form, and every part of the milled pulp.

Commercial Processing

There are a number of variations in the processing of black currants by methods generally similar to those referred to in connection with the work of Baumann (1951) and Koch (1955, 1956). The best process will be the one which provides finished juices with the specific flavor required. The steaming operation can be increased or decreased to give stronger or weaker flavors as desired, although it is essential to avoid the extraction of bitter compounds from the strigs. For juices of the Muttersäfte type which are eventually destined to be broken down into consumable drinks with 25% of juice, it is obviously necessary to extract the maximum

Courtesy of Pressoirs Colin, Paris

Fig. 86. Colin Continuous Juice Press

amount of clean, fruity flavoring substances from the fruit. A satisfactory process could be considered along the following lines: the fruit is steamed at 176°F in a machine similar to the one illustrated in Fig. 87. In Germany this apparatus is often made in aluminum, the rotating central screw being hollow and perforated along its length. The screw rotates at approximately three rpm. At this temperature undesirable astringent materials are not extracted, but enzyme systems in general are inactivated. The pulp from the steamer can be pressed immediately by the addition of 2 to 3% of kieselguhr. Even if an enzyme action is not used it is nevertheless possible to operate a pressing system in which the yield of juice plus the 20% of steam condensate gives a final yield of diluted juice of approximately 110%.

The pomace from the press cloths is disintegrated and re-pressed with water. The first and second pressings can be mixed together or stored separately. It is also known that in certain installations the second pressings are obtained from the first-pressed pomace by a further enzyme action to facilitate removal of the residual juice. In either case, the diluted juice is centrifuged, flash pasteurized and stored in sterile tanks without the application of pressure or low temperatures. This system avoids the use of pressure vessels and cold or cool stores which add appreciably to the costs of the process.

The use of such an extensive steaming treatment suggests that the use of low temperature storage for the final juice product may not provide such a distinct advantage from an organoleptic point of view as would be the case with the English process where the temperatures used are much

Courtesy of Sëissmost-Geräte-Zentrale, Bad Homburg

FIG. 87. GERMAN BERRY STEAMER FOR BLACK CURRANT JUICE PRODUCTION

lower. The operation of this method of storage at ambient temperature and atmospheric pressure calls for extreme care in the sterilizing of the tanks, the efficiency of flash pasteurization of the juice and in effecting a sterile transference of the juice from the flash pasteurizer to the inlet of the storage tank. In Germany, storage tanks of this type are mostly prepared of mild steel with one or other of a variety of plastic linings. The use of aluminum alloys of specialized composition is very prevalent on the Continent. Quite large horizontal or vertical tanks are widely utilized for black currant juice intermediates storage. Since 1955, there have been a

Courtesy of Weinkellerei H. Müller, Rastatt, Germany

FIG. 88. CENTRIFUGAL FRUIT JUICE PRESS

number of types of tanks constructed by new methods which are rapidly gaining in favor. Resin-reinforced fiberglass tanks are prominent amongst the newcomers, but stringent testing of the tank material is necessary to ascertain whether there is full compatibility between the surface material of the tank and the product to be stored. It is not usual to filter the juice before filling into these tanks and consequently a considerable amount of solid deposition occurs during storage.

Although the berry steamer in one or other of its forms still represents the chief means of producing materials for the very large production of black currant Süssmost-type drinks in Germany, development work is constantly proceeding to obtain quicker methods of processing combined with other advantages. For example, Wucherpfennig (1956) has described a process for the continuous removal of juice from black currants by using a centrifugal separator. This machine, however, does not permit a completely continuous removal of juice to be effected, for the thick pulp which is, indeed, continuously ejected from one part of the machine has then to be pressed in a discontinuous fashion in a traditional form of hydraulic press. The black currants are milled in a grater mill similar to that used for cidermaking. Even the skins are finely disintegrated, but the seeds are not destroyed. The centrifugal separator consists of a non-perforated drum revolving at high speed into which the enzyme-treated pulp is fed. The action of centrifugal force separates the solid tissues from the juice inside the drum. The thick mass of tissue is removed from the inside of the drum by a feed screw which extends over the whole of the inside of the drum. This feed screw works continuously to expel the more solid parts of the black currant pulp from the drum. It is claimed that the yield of juice from the centrifugal separator alone is about 75% and if a continuously operating screw press is used on the discharged residue the total yield of pure juice can rise to 80 to 82%. If, however, a hydraulic press with racks and cloths is used with the residue from the centrifugal separator, a total juice yield of 90%, with a maximum of 94% by weight, has been obtained. Machines of this type can operate at rates of up to six tons per hour.

BEVERAGE (SÜSSMOST) MANUFACTURE

The pure juice from the large tanks or the balloons is suitably diluted to contain approximately 25 to 30% of juice and then sweetened. (This is a general statement, for some high quality products of this type are known to contain up to 40% of juice.) The beverage is filtered and heated to 158° to 165°F and transferred in a continuous fashion to the reservoir of the bottle filler. Carefully washed bottles are finally rinsed in water at 120°F and the hot beverage is filled into the warm, clean bottles. The bottles are usually filled almost to the top, and the caps applied at once. The additional precaution of previously sterilizing the caps with formaldehyde vapor is often taken, but this is not necessary with the hot-filled method if the bottles are inverted after filling.

COMPOSITION OF BLACK CURRANT INTERMEDIATES

References have been made to the German procedures whereby fruit is steamed in a continuous apparatus and a juice diluted with condensed steam is stored prior to formulation of desirable beverages containing 25 to 30% of juice and added sugar in amounts sufficient to balance the acidity of about one per cent by weight. A very thorough examination of the composition and formulation of such Süssmost-type products has been made by Koch and Zeyen (1957). Reference here will be restricted to the results for one variety of black currants which is well known throughout Europe. Boskoop Giant fruit was processed by the hot, quick enzyme process. The method used yielded 100 liters of blended juice and condensate from 100 kg of berries, this yield being considered a satisfactory one in commercial practice. The berries for this experimental work were passed through the Fryma mill and the pulp heated to 130°F in a tubular heater. The pulp was treated with 0.3% liquid Pectinol for 1 hr and the pure juice expressed therefrom. The pomace was passed through the Fryma mill with the addition of water. The weight of water used was equal to that of the first pressings originally associated with the pomace, plus an addition of ten per cent. After standing for a short time the mash is pressed to provide an extract of the pomace. The pure juice and pom-

TABLE 68

CHEMICAL COMPOSITION AND OTHER DATA FOR PURE AND DILUTED BLACK CURRANT SEMIPROCESSED RAW MATERIALS[1]

	Boskoop Giant		
	Pure Juice	Pomace Extract	Blend
Specific gravity at 68°F	1.0577	1.0286	1.0458
Total extract gm/100 ml	14.99	7.41	13.83
Sugar (after inversion) gm/100 ml	8.06	4.06	7.33
Total acid gm/100 ml	3.59	1.35	3.21
Ash gm/100 ml	0.62	0.36	0.57
Alkalinity of ash: ml n-NaOH/100 ml	6.08	4.30	5.63
Ascorbic acid mg/100 ml[2]	151.2	69.0	137.5
Copper mg/100 ml[3]	0.11	0.03	0.09
Iron mg/100 ml[4]	0.86	0.41	0.78
Pure pectin gm/100 ml	0.41	0.07	0.35
Esterification of pectin	57.7	57.2	54.3
Viscosity at 68°F cP	2.99	1.37	2.77
Yield of juice % by weight	85.0	16.5	99.5

[1] Koch and Zeyen (1957).
[2] Koch and Bretthauer (1957).
[3] Koch and Breker (1955).
[4] Bretthauer (1956).

ace extract were blended together and stored as raw material for the finally diluted, sweetened juice. Table 68 taken from Koch and Zeyen (1957) gives the details of the chemical composition and other data for black currant products from the Boskoop Giant variety.

CHEMICAL COMPOSITION OF DILUTED BLACK CURRANT BEVERAGES

The intermediate products referred to in Table 68 above were formulated into the sweetened, diluted black currant drinks after three months' storage. Table 69 gives the chemical composition of the beverage made from the Boskoop black currant, which thus compares directly with the figures given in Table 68. As a comparison for these data, minimum, maximum and mean values are also set out in the table for commercially produced black currant beverages of the Süssmost type.

The figures for black currant beverages taken from the market are under constant review by the appropriate organizations in Germany which control the overall quality of black currant Süssmost-type drinks. Strong recommendations have been made to the industry by Koch and Zeyen (1957) to store the pure juice together with any diluted material. It is not practicable in all circumstances to produce a beverage of the quality understood by the phrase "Schwarz Johannisbeere Süssmost" from oncepressed pomace alone. Apart from the fact that the aroma, fruit flavor and body of the beverage will be noticeably deficient, chemical analyses

Table 69

CHEMICAL COMPOSITION OF SWEETENED, DILUTED BLACK CURRANT BEVERAGES (SÜSSMONT TYPE)

	From Boskoop Giant Fruit	Commercial Black Currant Beverages		
		Minimum	Maximum	Mean
Specific gravity at 68°F	1.0590	1.048	1.0641	1.0573
Total acid %	1.03	0.97	1.27	1.04
Extract %	15.75	12.51	16.96	15.04
Sugar %	13.65	10.32	14.31	12.88
Sugar-free extract %	2.10	1.33	4.45	2.22
Ash %	0.234	0.176	0.482	0.204
Alkalinity of ash: ml n-NaOH/100 ml	3.36	1.76	4.30	2.41
Alcohol %	0	0	0.48	0.12
Volatile acids %	0.01	0.008	0.035	0.016
Lactic acid %	0.005	0.002	0.017	0.004
Ascorbic acid mg/100 ml	37.1	15.0	54.2	25.0

Source: Koch and Zeyen (1957).

will also indicate the fact of a deficiency in composition. The possibility of sophistication, too, must be considered, and the building-up of a wide range of analytical figures for these sweetened and diluted products is essential so that the necessary organisations can check on the quality of the products on the market. Koch and Zeyen (1957) have suggested that the minimum ascorbic acid content for quality drinks made from the black currant should be 25 mg/100 ml. To prevent the substitution of a diluted product with added synthetic ascorbic acid, it is suggested at the same time that the sugar-free extract should have a minimum value of 1.8 gm/100 ml.

The acidity figure is also of considerable importance, and in general a minimum acidity of 1.0% as tartaric acid should be maintained.

CHEMICAL COMPOSITION OF BLACK CURRANT JUICES AND SYRUPS

The chemical composition of black currants varies very rapidly as the fruit approaches ripeness. The sugar content increases, but the ascorbic acid figure, calculated on a weight basis, decreases throughout the ripening period. It is important, therefore, to choose fruits of similar maturity if comparable figures are to be obtained for the juices expressed from them. It is generally recognized that to produce a quality beverage fruit should be at least 80% black before it is harvested or for the purpose of providing analytical data. Whilst the adoption of this suggestion is imperative if reasonably comparable figures are to be attained for ascorbic acid, it is also of value for the other constituents of the fruit and of its juice. In the author's laboratories over a long period of years analyses of

Table 70

ANALYSIS OF BLACK CURRANT JUICES (OR FRUITS)

	Minimum	Maximum
Specific gravity at 68°F	1.054	1.079
Total sugars (as invert)	4.5% wt/vol	11.5% wt/vol
Acidity (as citric acid monohydrate)	3.1% wt/vol	4.5% wt/vol
"Tannin" (permanganate-reducing figure)	0.24% wt/vol	0.58% wt/vol
pH	2.48	3.60
Nitrogen	0.021% wt/vol	0.098% wt/vol
Total ash	0.55% wt/vol	1.48% wt/vol
P_2O_5	0.026% wt/vol	0.148% wt/vol
Ascorbic acid	90 mg/100 ml	260 mg/100 ml
Pectin (as Ca pectate)		
English juice	...	0.85% wt/vol
English fruit	0.68% wt/vol	1.45% wt/wt
English fruit[1]	0.90% wt/wt	1.25% wt/wt
Russian fruit[2]	0.69% wt/wt	3.15% wt/wt
Potassium	3.1 mg/100 ml (avg)	
Sodium	245 mg/100 ml (avg)	
Calcium	29 mg/100 ml (avg)	
Magnesium	11 mg/100 ml (avg)	
Flavonol in juice: Germany	4.75 mg/100 ml (avg)	
Anthocyanin: Germany	76.0 mg/100 ml (avg)	

[1] Kieser, Pollard, and Sissons (1957).
[2] Bogdanski, Zalewski, and Bogdanska (1956).

pure black currant juices have been carried out from fruits which have satisfied this condition. The minimum and maximum values for pure, mature English black currant juices and some fruits are given in Table 70, together with a few further data from other laboratories.

BIBLIOGRAPHY

Cherry, Berry and Pomegranate Juices

Beattie, H. G., Wheeler, K. A., and Pederson, C. S. 1943. Changes occurring in fruit juices during storage. Food Research *8*, 395–404.

Bridges, M. A. 1941. Dietetics for the Clinician, 4th Edition. Lea and Febiger, Philadelphia.

Chandler, F. B., and Highlands, M. E. 1950. Blueberry juice. Food Technol. *4*, 285–286.

Charley, V. L. S. 1932. Investigations on fruit products. 1. Preparation of juices, syrups, concentrates and wines from some English fruits. Ann. Rept. Agr. Hort. Research Sta. Long Ashton, Bristol, 1932, 175–201.

Charley, V. L. S. 1950. Recent advances in fruit juice production. Commonwealth Bureau of Horticulture and Plantation Crops. Tech. Commun. No. *21*.

Charley, V. L. S. 1961. The use of enzymes in the processing and storage of juices and other products from fruit. Symposium on Enzymes in the Manufacture, Storage and Distribution of Food. Soc. Chem. Ind.

Charley, V. L. S., and Harrison, T. H. J. 1939. Fruit juices and related products. Imperial Bureau of Horticulture and Plantation Crops. Tech. Commun. No. *11*.

CHATFIELD, C., and ADAMS, G. 1940. Proximate composition of American food materials. U.S. Dept. Agr. Circ. *549*.

CHATFIELD, C., and MCLAUGHLIN, L. I. 1931. Proximate composition of foods. U. S. Dept. Agr. Circ. *50*, Rev.

FITELSON, J. 1968. Detection of adulteration in dark-colored fruit juices. J. Assoc. Offic. Anal. Chem. *51*, 937–939.

ISHAM, P. D., and MOTTERN, H. H. 1938. Products from sweet cherries. Fruit Products J. *17*, 264–265.

LAMB, A. F. 1950. Raspberry syrup in new glassed foods pack. Western Canner and Packer *42*, No. 4, 29, 31.

LEE, F. A., ROBINSON, W. B., HENING, J. C., and PEDERSON, C. S. 1950. Low temperature preservation of fruit juices and fruit juice concentrates. N. Y. State Agr. Expt. Sta. Bull. *743*.

LOUVRIC, T. 1962. Influence of some technological factors on the content of hydroxylfurfural in sour cherry and blackberry juices. Kem. Ind. (Zagreb) *11*, 527–530.

LOUVRIC, T. 1965. Factors determining the stability of the color of blackberry and sour cherry juices. Ind. Conserve (Parma) *40*, 208–221 (Italian).

MARTIN, W. M. 1936. Problems involved in packing cherry juice. Fruit Products J. *15*, 166–168, 183, 185, 187.

MENZIES, D. J., and KEFFORD, J. F. 1949. Apple juice blends. Food Preservation Quart. *9*, 31–32.

NELSON, E. K. 1927. The non-volatile acids of the pear, quince, apple, loganberry, blueberry, cranberry, lemon and pomegranate. J. Am. Chem. Soc. *49*, 487–488.

PEDERSON, C. S., and BEATTIE, H. G. 1943A. Preparation and preservation of juices from certain small fruits. Fruit Products J. *22*, 260–264, 281, 287.

PEDERSON, C. S., and BEATTIE, H. G. 1943B. Buffering effect of fruit juices. Food Research *8*, 405–408.

PEDERSON, C. S., BEATTIE, H. G., and STOTZ, E. H. 1947. Deterioration of processed fruit juices. N. Y. State Agr. Expt. Sta. Bull. *728*.

PETERSON, G. T. 1938. Changes in sour cherries resulting from soaking. Canner *86*, No. 12, Part 2, 72, 75.

RICE, C. C., FELLERS, C. R., and CLAGUE, J. A. 1939. Cranberry juice—manufacture and properties. Fruit Products J. *18*, 197–200, 219.

SIMPSON, M. 1957–1958. Viscosity as related to pectin content in strawberry juices. A reprint from the 1957–1958 Rept. Hort. Expt. Sta. and Products Lab., Vineland, Ontario, 126–129.

SWISHER, C. A., and POE, C. F. 1935. Chemical changes accompanying the fermentation of cherry juice. Fruit Products J. *14*, 367–369, 379.

TRESSLER, D. K. 1938. Fruit and vegetable juices. Fruit Products J. *17*, 196–198, 210, 235–237, 249.

TRESSLER, D. K. 1941A. Try making these cherry products. Western Canner Packer *33*, No. 8, 35–43.

TRESSLER, D. K. 1941B. Need for sanitary and other standards for the manufacture and sales of fruit and vegetable juices. Am. J. Public Health *31*, No. 3, (Yearbook Supplement) 101–105.

TRESSLER, D. K. 1942. Using fruit purées to get new flavors in ribbon ice cream. Food Inds. *14*, 49–51, 99.

TRESSLER, D. K., and PEDERSON, C. S. 1940. Result of a demonstration sale of cherry cocktail. Fruit Products J. *19*, 195–197.

TRESSLER, D. K., PEDERSON, C. S., and BEATTIE, H. F. 1943. Fruit and vegetable juice preparation and preservation. Ind. Eng. Chem. 35, 96–100.

TRESSLER, D. K., PEDERSON, C. S., and BEAVENS, E. A. 1941. Cherry juice and cherry beverages. N. Y. State Agr. Expt. Sta. Circ. *180* Rev.

WALKER, L. H., NOTTER, G. H., MCCREADY, R. M., and PATTERSON, D. C. 1954. Concentration of strawberry juice. Food Technol. *8*, 350–352.

ZUBECKIS, E. 1955–1956A. Montmorency cherry beverages. A reprint from the 1955–1956 Rept. Hort. Expt. Sta. and Products Lab., Vineland, Ontario, 111–113.

ZUBECKIS, E. 1955–1956B. Color changes in raspberry juice concentrate. A reprint from the 1955–1956 Rept. Hort. Expt. Sta. and Products Lab., Vineland, Ontario, 114–117.

Black Currant Juice

ANET, E. F. L. J., and REYNOLDS, T. M. 1954. Isolation of mucic acid from fruits. Nature *174*, 930.

BAUMANN, J. 1951. Handbook for Fruit Juice Producers, 7th Edition. Eugen Ulmer, Stuttgart.

BAUMANN, J. 1953. The preservation of vitamin C during the processing of black currants. Flüssiges Obst. *20*, No. 11, 2–3.

BAUMANN, J. 1959. Experiments in black currant growing 1959. Flüssiges Obst., *26*, No. 9, 10–15.

BOGDANSKI, K., ZALEWSKI, W., and BOGDANSKA, H. 1956. Studies on the 1-ascorbic acid content, color and certain other components and properties of black currant varieties. Roczniki Nauk Rolniczych (A) 73, 123–143.

BRETTHAUER, G. 1956. The iron content of fruit juices. Fruchtsaft-Ind. *1*, 184–190.

BRYAN, J. D. 1946. The organic acids of some common fruits. Ann. Rept. Long Ashton Res. Sta. *138*.

BRYAN, J. D., and POLLARD, A. 1947. The effect of manurial treatment on the composition of black currants. Prog. Rept. Ann. Rept. Long Ashton Research Sta. *216*.

CHARLEY, V. L. S. 1932. Investigations on fruit products. 1—Fruit juices and syrups from some English fruits. Ann. Rept. Long Ashton Research Sta. *175*.

CHARLEY, V. L. S. 1935A. Investigations on fruit products. 6—Fruit syrups. Ann. Rept. Long Ashton Research Sta. *162*.

CHARLEY, V. L. S. 1935B. Investigations on fruit products. 7—Production of fruit squashes. Ann. Rept. Long Ashton Research Sta. *184*.

CHARLEY, V. L. S. 1936A. Investigations on fruit products. 10—The commercial production of fruit syrups. Ann. Rept. Long Ashton Research Sta. *213*.

CHARLEY, V. L. S. 1936B. Chemical constituents of fresh juices from single varieties of soft fruits, and the suitability of juices for syrup manufacture. Ann. Rept Long Ashton Research Sta. *207*.

CHARLEY, V. L. S. 1956. The nutritive value of fruit juices. (Lecture to International Federation of Fruit Juice Producers, Stuttgart).

CHARLEY, V. L. S., KIESER, M. E., and STEEDMAN, J. 1942. Production of black currant syrup. Ann. Rept. Long Ashton Research Sta. *110*.

CHARLEY, V. L. S., and SILLS, V. E. 1940. A note on the production of black currant juice and its suitability as a source of vitamin C. Ann. Rept. Long Ashton Research Sta. *125*.

FORE, H. 1957. The ascorbic acid content of black currants. Flüssiges Obst. *24*, No. 11, 14–16.

GANTNER, A. 1955. A continuous process for the steam-heating of berries. Flüssiges Obst *22*, No. 4, 12–13.

HOOPER, F. C., and AYRES, A. D. 1950. The enzymatic degradation of ascorbic substances occurring in black currants. J. Sci. Food Agr. *1*, 5–8.

KIESER, M. E., POLLARD, A., and SISSONS, D. J. 1957. The activity of pectin methylesterase in black currants. Progress Rept. Ann. Rept. Long Ashton Research Sta. 134–137.

KIESER, M. E., POLLARD, A., and STONE, A. M. 1949. The effect of manurial treatment on the composition of black currants and their products. Ann. Rept. Long Ashton Research Sta. 159–162.

KIESER, M. E., POLLARD, A., and TIMBERLAKE, C. F. 1950. The effect of manurial treatment on the composition of black currants. Ann. Rept. Long Ashton Research Sta. 194–196.

KIESER, M. E., POLLARD, A., TIMBERLAKE, C. F., and MOSELEY, M. R. 1953. Factors affecting the quality and stability of concentrated fruit juices. 1.—Black currant . . . concentrates. Ann. Rept. Long Ashton Research Sta. 189–198.

KOCH, J. 1955. Technical improvements in soft fruit juice production: 1954 experimental program. Flüssiges Obst. *22*, No. 1, 9–16.

KOCH, J. 1956. Investigations into the simplification of processing and improvement in quality of soft fruit juices and beverages. Fruchtsaft-Ind. *1*, 66–74.

KOCH, J., and BREKER, E. 1955. The estimation of heavy metals in grape juice. Industrielle Obst.-und Gemüseverwertung *40*, 242–256.

KOCH, J., and BRETTHAUER, G. 1957. Determinations of l-ascorbic acid in various black currant juice intermediates. Fruchtsaft-Ind. *2*, 60–62.

KOCH, J., and ZEYEN, E. 1957. Standardization of black currant juice products by means of chemical analysis. Fruchtsaft-Ind. *2*, 121–127.

POLLARD, A. 1943. The vitamin P activity of black currants. Ann. Rept. Long Ashton Research Sta. 141–147.

SILLS, V. E. 1939. Preservation of vitamin C in English fruit juices and syrups. Ann. Rept. Long Ashton Research Sta. 127–138.

TIMBERLAKE, C. F. 1960A. Metallic components of fruit juices. III.—Oxidation and stability of ascorbic acid in model systems resembling black currant juice. J. Sci. Food Agr. *11*, 258–268.

TIMBERLAKE, C. F. 1960B. Metallic components of fruit juices. IV.—Oxidation and stability of ascorbic acid in black currant juice. J. Sci. Food Agr. *11*, 268–273.

WUCHERPFENNIG, K. 1956. Continuous processing of soft fruits into juice. Flüssiges Obst. *23*, No. 1, 10–13.

CHAPTER 9

B. S. Luh

Tropical Fruit Beverages

INTRODUCTION

The demand for fruit beverages is largely based on their nutritive value, flavor, aroma and color. These quality factors are dependent directly on the structure and chemical composition of the fresh fruit. Fruit juice is a source of vitamins, minerals, carbohydrates, amino acids, flavonoid compounds, and probably other still unidentified constituents. The chemical composition of fruit juice depends largely on the combined influences of genetic regulatory mechanisms and the physical, chemical, and biological environments to which the fresh fruits are subjected during growth and after harvest.

At first glance it would seem that the tropical fruit beverage, by its name, means a drink of pure tropical fruit juice. However, due to their difference in composition and the method of preparation, other names for the fruit beverages are used, such as fruit juice beverages, nectars, fruit punches, squashes, and cordials. Val *et al.* (1959A) stated that fruit juice squash consists essentially juice containing moderate quantity of fruit pulp to which cane sugar is added for sweetening, e.g., orange squash. Fruit juice cordial is a sparkling clear, sweetened fruit juice from which all the pulp and other suspended materials have been completely eliminated e.g., lime juice cordial.

In 1968, the total US packs of single-strength canned juices were 110,-368,000 standard cases (Anon. 1969A,B). These include 15,430,000 cases of grapefruit juice, 13,953,000 cases pineapple juice, 11,372,000 cases orange juice, 9,365,000 cases apple juice, 2,032,000 cases orange-grapefruit juice, and 33,680,000 cases tomato juice. In the same year, 86,885,000 cases of canned single-strength juice drinks were packed (see also Chapter 1).

Tropical fruits have certain characteristics that are different from the temperate zone fruit. They tend to be softer and juicier at processing maturity than many of the temperate fruits. Most temperate zone fruits can be picked at a greener stage, cold stored at 32°–34°F for 2 to 3 weeks or even longer, and brought under control temperature and humidity to ideal maturity for processing. Tropical fruits in general do not store particularly well in cold storage and are not responsive to controlled ripening conditions as would be the case with peaches and pears. The majority of

B. S. Luh is Food Technologist, Department of Food Science and Technology, University of California, Davis, Calif.

tropical fruits must be picked close to their optimum maturity and processed promptly (Seale 1967).

The chemistry and technology of citrus, citrus products, and by-products have been published by the U. S. Dept. Agr. (1962). Canned juices prepared from orange, tangerine, grapefruit, lemon, pineapple, grape, berries, tomatoes, and vegetables are covered in other parts of this book. This chapter covers processing and properties of tropical fruit beverages made from passion fruit, guava, mango, papaya, banana, lemon, and lime. (The latter are discussed on pp. 125 to 154.)

PASSION-FRUIT JUICE

The passion fruit belongs to the genus *Passiflora* (Akamine *et al.* 1956). The purple passion fruit, *Passiflora edulis,* has become a cultivated plant of commercial importance (Kefford 1961; Kefford and Vickery 1961). The yellow passion fruit, *Passiflora edulis,* var. *flavicarpa* was introduced into Hawaii from Australia and became the favored commercial variety in the Hawaiian Islands. The yellow variety appears to grow more vigorously and yield more prolifically (average yield 10 tons per acre) than the purple variety (average yield 1–2 tons per acre).

The passion fruit is an oval or sometimes round fruit weighing approximately one ounce and having, in the case of the purple variety, a dark purple, leathery skin or, in the case of the yellow variety, a bright yellow, waxy skin. Within the fruit are numerous embryo sacs containing black or dark brown seeds enclosed in orange-yellow gelatinous pulp. The pulp has an acid but highly attractive and distinctive flavor. There is a real but subtle difference in flavor between the purple and yellow varieties, and the pulp of the yellow varieties tends to be more acid.

Extraction of Pulp and Purée

A simple procedure of cutting the passion fruit in halves and scooping with spoons is still used for extraction of passion-fruit pulp. The pulp can also be extracted in a manner similar to citrus juice extraction by reaming the halved fruit on a small burr or wire loop. Commercial processors have found that mechanical methods of extraction are essential. A centrifugal extractor has been developed in Hawaii and applied successfully in commercial practice (Kinch and Shaw 1954; Boyle *et al.* 1955; Kinch 1960). The fruit is sliced by means of a gang of rotating knives, and the slices ($^5/_8$ in.) drop directly into a perforated centrifuge bowl. The bowl has sloping sides and four baffles at right angles to the sides. When it is rotated at a speed representing a centrifugal force of 175 g, the pulp and seeds from the slices are thrown out through the holes in the basket while the residual skins climb the walls of the basket and are thrown out over

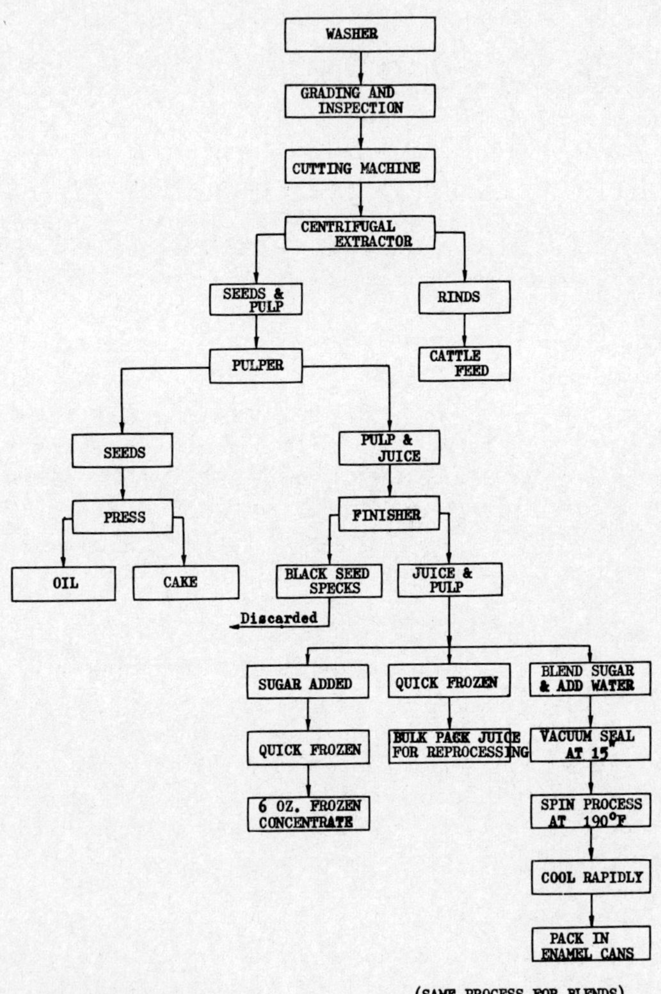

Fig. 89. Flow Sheet for the Processing of Passion Fruit

the edge. The pulp and skins are then collected from separate chutes. The extractor has a capacity of 4000 lb of passion fruit per hour, and an efficiency of extraction of 94% is claimed.

The mechanical extractor used in Australia consists of feeding the fruit into the space between two revolving shallow-pitched cones (Seale 1967). The cones are fitted to the ends of inclined shafts so that fruit, fed into the gap between the spinning cones, rotates and is squeezed to burst the skin and disgorge the contents. The skins and seeds are immediately separated from the resulting pulp.

The extraction method serves only to remove the pulp from the rind; separation of the juice is accomplished in a two-stage process which employs either a brush finisher, or a paddle finisher with the paddles faced with "Neoprene." In the first stage, the pulp passes through a stainless steel screen with 0.033-in. holes, and this is followed by a finishing operation with a screen of 60–80 mesh stainless steel to remove broken seed fragments (Boyle *et al.* 1955). The yield is stated to be similar to that obtained by extraction with spoons (Kefford and Vickery 1961; Seale 1967). In Australia, passion-fruit pulp and the beverage made from it are commonly consumed with the seeds still present. The average yield of juice from the fruit is 30–33%. Yields up to 40% are obtainable from selected strains (Akamine *et al.* 1956). A typical yield of screened juice is 70 gal per ton. Obviously, the method of extraction affects the yield of juice from the passion fruit. A flow sheet for the processing of passion-fruit products is shown in Fig. 89. The details of the procedures appeared in the Hawaii Agricultural Experiment Station Circular No. 58 (Seale and Sherman 1960).

Juice Preservation

Earlier study on the preservation of passion-fruit juice was made by Poore (1935). Poore held frozen juice for two years at 0° to 10°F without noteworthy changes in color, flavor or aroma, but pasteurized bottled juices deteriorated rapidly in flavor during storage. Later workers have found that the distinctive aroma and flavor of passion fruit are elusive and very sensitive to change during heat treatment. It is preferable therefore to avoid heat treatment by preserving the juice by freezing. The preparation of frozen passion-fruit juice in consumer-size cans has been described by Boyle *et al.* (1955).

After mechanical extraction and removal of the seeds, the juice is deaerated to remove air, filled into lacquered cans, sealed under vacuum or steam flow and then frozen at a low temperature. The frozen juice retains satisfactory quality for at least one year at 0°F.

Another alternative to heat treatment for the preservation of passion-fruit pulp or juice is the use of chemical preservatives. African manufacturers have exported large quantities of passion-fruit juice preserved with 1000 to 1500 ppm of sulfur dioxide or benzoic acid, or preferably with a mixture of the two preservatives. The preserved products, however, show marked deterioration of aroma and flavor.

When pasteurization of passion-fruit juice by heat is necessary, best results are achieved by agitated pasteurization in the can (Pruthi 1959A; Seale and Sherman 1960). The screened juice is filled cold into lacquered cans, sealed under mechanical vacuum or steam flow, and processed in atmospheric steam, the cans being rotated axially at 100 to 150 rpm on an inclined belt.

Wang and Ross (1965) reported a spin method of thermal processing whereby cylindrical containers are longitudinally rotated at relatively rapid rates along the axis of the cylinder. Rotation is continuous at constant rate throughout heating and cooling phase. There is no abrupt change in position of the container during processing. The method provides extremely rapid heat transfer for homogeneous liquid. The coaxial rotation gives a tumbling effect to the content of the can. For passion-fruit juice, process times of 1.5 min for No. 1 Tall (301 × 411) cans and 4 min for No. 10 (603 × 700) cans give center temperatures of 170° to 180°F which are adequate for preservation. A commercial pack of sweetened passion fruit pulp in 4-oz cans (211 × 111) is processed 1.25 min to a center temperature of 175°F. After pasteurization the cans are cooled immediately under water sprays at the same rate of rotation. Immediately after processing the "spincooked" juice is very close to fresh juice in flavor. During storage of the canned product some flavor deterioration occurs at a rate dependent upon the storage temperature. Addition of sugar increases flavor stability, and pasteurized juice sweetened to 50° Brix shows satisfactory flavor retention for at least one year at room temperature. Pruthi (1959B,C) has reported on retention of color, flavor, and ascorbic acid in passion-fruit juices preserved by various methods.

Concentrates and Powders

A few workers have investigated the concentration of passion-fruit juice. Morris (1935) prepared a four-fold concentrate by freezing and centrifuging, and Pruthi and Lal (1959B) used a batch-type vacuum evaporator. To restore volatile flavoring substances to their product they concentrated and added back the first 10 to 15% of the distillate. The concentrate was then hot-filled into cans and frozen. Some concentrate prepared in this way was mixed with sugar and dehydrated in a vacuum shelf drier to prepare a passion-fruit powder which was packaged with an in-package desiccant. Both concentrate and powder were claimed to be acceptable products although the flavor was inferior to fresh juice. Seagrave-Smith (1952) prepared a 1 : 1 blend of passion-fruit and pineapple juice with sugar added to bring the solids content to 38.4%. This blend was evaporated under vacuum, diluted with fresh blend or with fresh blend together with the first 10% of distillate, and then the final concentrate was frozen. It was claimed to have satisfactory aroma and flavor although not as good as the initial blend.

The starch in passion-fruit juice introduces difficulties in pasteurization and concentration since gelling of the starch during heating increases the

TABLE 71
COMPOSITION OF PASSION-FRUIT JUICE

Composition of Juice	Purple Variety: India (Pruthi and Lal 1959A) Max	Min.	Mean	Australia	Queensland, Australia	Yellow Variety: Hawaii (Boyle *et al.* 1955) Max	Min.	Mean
Moisture (gm/100 gm)	82.5	76.9	80.4	76.0	71.1	84.2	79.6	82.0
Ether ext. (gm/100 gm)	0.08	0.01	0.05	2.2	...	1.2	0.0	0.6
Soluble solids (gm/100)	21.9	14.4	17.3	...	16.3	18.0	13.0	15.0
Acidity (gm/100 gm)	4.8	2.4	3.4	...	2.1	5.0	3.0	4.0
Brix/Acid ratio	7.7	3.4	5.3	...	...	...	...	...
pH	3.2	2.6	2.8	...	3.3	3.3	2.8	3.0
Reducing sugars (gm/100 gm)	8.3	3.6	6.2	...	5.1	7.8	6.2	7.0
Nonreducing sugars (gm/100 gm)	7.9	2.3	4.6	...	4.2	...	...	...
Total sugars (as invert) (gm/100 gm)	13.3	7.4	10.0	18.4	...	11.6	9.3	10.0
Crude fiber (gm/100 gm)	...	...	...	...	14.2	...	...	0.2
Starch (gm/100 gm)	3.7	1.0	2.4	...	...	...	...	...
Protein (gm/100 gm)	1.2	0.6	0.8	2.4	2.4	1.2	0.6	0.8
Mineral Matter (gm/100 gm)	0.52	0.36	0.46	...	0.70	...	...	...
Ca (mg/100 gm)	18.4	9.7	12.1	11.0	...	...	...	5.0
P (mg/100 gm)	60.4	21.4	30.1	...	...	...	...	18.0
Fe (mg/100 gm)	4.0	2.3	3.1	1.2	...	...	...	0.3
Ascorbic acid (mg/100 gm)	69.9	21.9	34.6	17.0	...	20.0	7.0	12.0
Thiamine (mg/100 gm)	0.04	0.02	0.03	0	...	...	...	...
Riboflavin (mg/100 gm)	0.19	0.12	0.17	0.10	...	...	...	...
Nicotinic acid (mg/100 gm)	1.9	1.5	1.7	1.4	...	...	...	...
Vitamin A (I.U./100 gm)	1547.0	1073.0	1345.0	10.0	...	...	...	570.0

Source: Tressler and Joslyn (1961).

viscosity substantially. Knock (1951) reports that enzymatic degradation of the amylopectin permits the preparation of relatively free-flowing fourfold concentrates, but suggests that centrifugal starch separation may be better for commercial operations.

Composition of Passion-Fruit Juice

The composition of passion-fruit juice has been compiled by Pruthi and Lal (1959A) who examined purple passion fruits grown in India. Their observations are presented in Table 71 together with those of some other workers relating to both purple and yellow varieties (Kefford 1961; Kefford and Vickery 1961).

Among the soluble carbohydrates of passion-fruit juice, sucrose makes up 25% of the total sugars, and glucose and fructose are also present. The principal acid in passion-fruit juice is citric acid, which contributes 93–96% of the total acidity, while malic acid contributes 4–7% (Pruthi 1958). Mucic acid is also present (Anet and Reynolds 1954). Passion-fruit juice contains little pectin but significant amounts of starch, which may settle out as a white or grey precipitate during storage of the juice or beverages made from it (Knock 1951). Cillie and Joubert (1950) found the starch to be almost pure amylopectin with a molecular weight about 7,000,000 and an average chain length of 17 glucose residues.

Benk (1967) studied composition of passion-fruit juices from Kenya. His results are generally comparable to those reported by Pruthi and Lal (1959B). Mollenhauer (1962) studied the chemical and physical properties of passion-fruit pulp. The fruit pulp consisted of juicy arillus tissue and black seeds, had 10–15% sugar, 2.3–3.5% acid as citric acid, and a pH value of 3.4. The viscosity was similar to that of a sugar solution of the same concentration, but deviated from it at higher temperatures. The dry mass of the juice was 12–20%. Data on the technological and microscopic properties, especially the starch characteristic of species, were presented. The amount of pulp and juice corresponding to 1000 kg-fruit were 580 and 426 kg, respectively.

Passion-fruit juice is a useful source of ascorbic acid, and the purple variety appears to show higher ascorbic acid contents than the yellow variety. Ross and Chang (1958) found that the stability of ascorbic acid in passion-fruit juice was comparable to its stability in citrus juices.

The free amino acids in passion-fruit juice have been reported by Pruthi and Srivas (1964). Purple passion-fruit juice contained leucine, valine, tyrosine, proline, threonine, glycine, aspartic acid, arginine, and lysine. However, they found no methionine, phenylalanine, and tryptophan in the product.

The orange-yellow color of passion-fruit juice is due to a complex mixture of carotenoid pigments in which beta carotene predominates (Pruthi and Lal 1958A).

The volatile flavoring substances responsible for the unique aroma and flavor of passion fruit have been studied by Hiu (1959). He found 18 separate components and identified four of these as *n*-hexyl caproate, *n*-hexyl butyrate, ethyl caproate, and ethyl butyrate.

The characteristic flavor of passion fruit was found in the water-insoluble oil, which constituted about 36 ppm of passion-fruit juice (Hiu and Scheuer 1961). Four components, *n*-hexyl caproate, *n*-hexyl butyrate, ethyl caproate, and ethyl butyrate, made up *ca.* 95% of the oil. Among these four, *n*-hexyl caproate was found to be the principal component, accounting for *ca.* 70% of the volatile passion-fruit essence.

The unidentified portion of the oil (*ca.* 5%) very likely contains compounds of greater structural complexity than those identified. Evidence for this assumption comes from the appreciable specific rotation of crude oil. The olefinic unsaturation encountered in the crude oil seems to have its origin in the unidentified portion of the oil.

UTILIZATION OF PASSION-FRUIT JUICE

Because of its unique intense flavor and high acidity, passion-fruit juice has been described as a natural concentrate. When sweetened and diluted it provides a highly palatable beverage and the flavor blends well with other fruits and fruit juices in the preparation of fruit salads and punches.

Consumer preferences in Hawaii and California for frozen sweetened passion-fruit juice intended for dilution before consumption were investigated by Scott (1956). He concluded that for most general acceptance the sugar:juice ratio should not be more than 55:100 nor less than 45:100 and the rate of dilution should be 1 plus 3. In Australian experience, passion-fruit juice sweetened to 50° Brix (sugar:juice ratio approximately 70:100) gives a very pleasing beverage when diluted 1 plus 4. Passion-fruit juice is also highly suitable for flavoring ice cream, cake fillings, frostings, gelatin desserts, sherbets and chiffon pies (Boyle *et al.* 1955; Shaw *et al.* 1955; Seale and Sherman 1960).

Blends

Menzies and Kefford (1949) found that blends of 5 or 10% of passion-fruit juice with apple juice were very attractive in flavor and were most favored among six blends of apple juice tested. In South Africa, blends of passion-fruit juice with pear, apple, peach, and orange juices have been prepared (Anon. 1949). A blended punch which is canned in Hawaii contains orange, pineapple, guava, papaya, and passion-fruit juice (Anon. 1955).

Cordials and Syrups

Passion fruit-cordials and squashes are popular beverage bases in Australia and South Africa. They consist of passion-fruit juice with sugar syrup and acid added so that they normally contain 50 to 55% soluble solids and 1 to 2% acid. Cordials are diluted 1 plus 4 or 1 plus 5 with water for consumption. They are usually artificially colored and preserved with benzoic acid (600 to 770 ppm) or sulfur dioxide (220 to 350 ppm) since they are expected to be stable against spoilage after the bottle is opened. Standard of composition in South Africa require not less than 30% passion fruit by volume (South African Bureau of Standards 1949). In Australia, the minimum juice content varies from 12.5 to 25% by weight in different States. Coetzee *et al.* (1951) described the preparation of blended syrups incorporating passion-fruit juice. Blends of passion-fruit juice with grapefruit, grape, and plum juices were preferred to similar syrups made from passion fruit alone. Pruthi and Lal (1955) present a flow sheet and an analysis of costs in the preparation of passion-fruit squash. The same workers (Pruthi and Lal 1958B) investigated the fortification of passion-fruit squash with ascorbic acid and found that there was 2.5% loss during pasteurization.

Carbonated Beverages

Carbonated beverages based on passion-fruit juice has a very distinctive and attractive flavor. They are made from bottler's syrups similar in composition to the cordials described above. Regulations in New South Wales, Australia, prescribe a minimum fruit juice content of three per cent, and maximum preservative content 114 ppm sulfur dioxide or 385 ppm of benzoic acid or equivalent mixtures of the two preservatives.

Passion-Fruit By-Products

Rinds.—Since passion-fruit rinds made up 50% of the weight of the raw material considerable interest has been shown in possibilities for profitable utilization of the rinds. Martin and Reuter (1949) isolated from the rinds of purple passion fruit a pectic substance which by enzymatic hydrolysis yielded D-galacturonic acid, arabinose, and L-sorbose, but no galactose. Sherman *et al.* (1953) found the pectin content of yellow passion-fruit skins to be 3% on a wet basis or 20% on a dry basis. The pectin showed good jellying properties, comparable to citrus pectins. It contained 76–78% galacturonic acid and 8.9–9.2% methoxyl groups. Pectin-esterase was present in the passion-fruit skin and required to be inactivated by steam blanching for maximum yields of pectin to be obtained.

Otagaki and Matsumoto (1958) have examined the suitability of passion-fruit by-products for utilization as stock feed. The skin of yellow passion fruit is high in carbohydrates, low in ether-extractable material, and contains a moderate amount of crude protein. It is readily dehydrated without lime pretreatment and the dried material is palatable to dairy cattle at 22% of the ration. Laboratory-scale studies by the same workers indicated that it should be possible to produce good-quality silage from passion-fruit rinds.

Seeds.—The seeds of passion fruit contain about 10% protein and about 20% of an edible oil which compares favorably with cottonseed oil in feeding value and digestibility (Otagaki and Matsumoto 1958). The presscake from the seeds is not suitable for feed purposes since it contains about 60% crude fiber and 30–35% lignin.

In Australia, there is a rather extraordinary trade in passion-fruit seeds to pastrycooks who add the seeds to artificially flavored "passion-fruit" icing for cakes (Kefford and Vickery 1961).

GUAVA PURÉE AND NECTAR

Guava

The guava is one of the more important pomiferous fruits of the Myrtle family. The species, *Psidium guajava* L., is grown commercially and has been introduced into the West Indies, Florida, India, West and South Africa, and several of the Pacific island groups (Boyle *et al.* 1957). It grows wild in the wet valleys and on the mountain slopes throughout the State of Hawaii. The ripe fruit can be eaten fresh and has been popular for making nectars, juice drinks, and jams.

The fruit of the common guava tree has a rough-textured yellow skin and varies in shape from round to pear-shaped. In the wild, individual fruits from 1 to 3 in. in diameter are found, but under cultivation the size can be increased to 5 in. and the weight to $1^1/_2$ lb. The color of the inner flesh varies from white to deep pink to salmon-red. Desirable fruits for processing are those with a thick outer flesh and a small seed cavity since they yield more purée per unit weight than the thin-fleshed types. The distinctive musky flavor is more intense in some selections than in others and the acidity varies, too, from those with a pH of 3.0 to a few which have a pH of 4.0. The majority of the common guavas in Hawaii fall into the sour or sub-acid category with pH values ranging from 3.0–3.5.

Guava is a rich source of vitamin C (Goldberg and Levy 1941; Miller and Bazore 1945; Mustard 1945; Asenjo *et al.* 1968) and a fair source of vitamin A, calcium, and phosphorus. Verma and Srivastava (1966) studied pectin in two varieties of guava during growth and maturation. The total pectin content increases as the fruits reach the edible stage, followed by an abrupt decrease with advances in maturity. Ferro and Castelblanxo (1969) studied pectin in two varieties of guava (common and milky species) and found that guava contained less pectin than citrus fruit. Guava pectins showed a high methoxyl index and produced good gels at 65% soluble solids. The gel is stable at pH 2.1–2.4. Milky partially ripe guava showed the highest gel formation capabilities.

From the standpoint of the processor, selected guava varieties grown in orchards would assure him of uniform quality fruit. Since guava trees grow well on land which is considered marginal for other crops, there are many areas in Hawaii where it would be feasible and profitable to grow this fruit as a cultivated orchard crop. Growers could propagate vegetatively one or more of the desirable types of fruits by any of the methods described by Hamilton and Seagrave-Smith (1954). High yields of excellent quality fruit could be expected where good orchard management is practiced, such as fertilizing, irrigating, pruning and control of weeds, insects, and diseases. Harvesting guavas from orchards would be more economical and might be mechanized to some extent. Larger fruits with thick outer flesh and small seed cavities would yield more purée than smaller ones. Guavas with few seeds and small quantities of stone cells are desirable, provided they have the other essential qualities. The more acid fruits, pH 3.3 to 3.5, are better for processing than the sweeter fruits. Good color and flavor and high vitamin C content are more important factors in selecting fruit types for processing. Table 72 shows the quality measurements of fruits from selected Hawaiian guava seedlings (Boyle *et al.* 1957). Processors will not have much control over most of these quality factors; uniform high quality will be attainable only when the best selections are cultivated commercially.

Harvesting.—The bulk of guavas brought to plants will be those collected by the pickers of both cultivated and wild fruit. Firm, yellow, and mature fruit with no signs of insect or fungus damage should be sought. Half-ripe fruit can be stored at 36°–40°F and allowed to ripen. Green fruit should not be processed since it does not have full flavor nor will it yield as much purée as the fully mature fruit. Cost of harvesting will be reduced when sufficient quantities of cultivated guavas become available. Partial mechanization of harvesting as well as greater yield and size of fruits will help to reduce this cost.

Transportation to Processing Plant.—Speed and careful handling are necessary for this phase of the operation. Guavas picked at peak maturity will not keep well, so there should be no delay in getting them to the plant where they can be processed immediately or held in refrigerated storage. Small wooden boxes are preferable to orange crates for carrying the fruit because of the ease with which the ripe fruits are crushed or bruised.

TABLE 72

QUALITY MEASUREMENTS OF FRUIT FROM SELECTED HAWAIIAN GUAVA SEEDLINGS

Seedling No.	No. Fruits Tested	Average Diameter of Fruit, In.	Average Weight of Fruit, Oz	% Seeds	Color of Purée	Flavor	Soluble Solids, %	pH	Vitamin C mg/100 gm Fresh Weight	Comments
B-30	11	2 1/2–3	8.3	1.6	Strong pink	Normal, mildly sour	8.0	3.52	143.8	Good flavor and color, soluble solids low, vitamin C satisfactory
D-31	13	2 1/2–3	6.0	3.7	Light pink	Normal, sour	11.5	3.26	158.2	Good flavor, color weak, soluble solids and vitamin C satisfactory
P-1	3	2–2 1/2	3.5	4.1	Strong pink	Normal, slightly sweet	10.6	4.0	207.9	Small in size, color fine, too sweet
Lupi-1	6	2 3/4	6.3	4.4	Mild pink	Mild, slightly sour	9.8	3.7	492.0	Flavor and color weak, vitamin C outstanding

Source: Boyle *et al.* (1957).

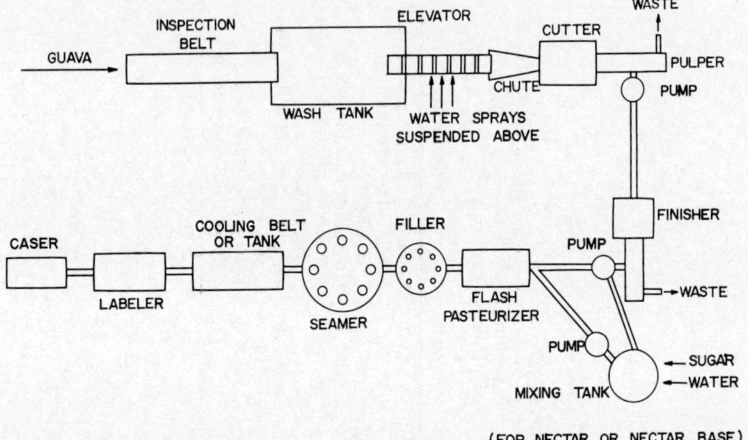

From Boyle et al. (1957)

FIG. 90. FLOW SHEET FOR GUAVA PROCESSING LINE (FOR FROZEN PRODUCTS BYPASS PASTEURIZER AND COOLING BELT)

Damaged fruit deteriorates very rapidly and must be discarded at the plant.

Large quantities of guavas are shipped from one island to another in Hawaii, which poses special problems in transportation. The fruit should be packed in small boxes to prevent damage, and if shipped ripe, should be refrigerated. Transporting by barge at night is preferable to daytime shipping, but if transported during the day some protection from the sun should be provided. The best practice would be to ship only those fruits which are firm and slightly underripe, and to finish off the ripening under controlled conditions at the processing plant.

Storage of Fresh Fruit.—Fully ripe guavas should be processed without delay, but if necessary they can be held for about a week at 36°–45°F. Vitamin C retention may be used as a measure for quality in stored fruits. Data in Table 73 indicate that there appears to be only a small loss in vitamin C after seven days at the two storage temperatures used (Boyle *et al.* 1957).

Green guava fruits can be held at room temperature in boxes or bins until they have ripened. They should be protected from the weather and from insects and rodents. Good ventilation will help to prevent losses due to spoilage.

Guava Purée Processing

Inspecting, Sorting and Washing.—When guavas are ready for processing they should be dumped out on an inspection belt. Here the badly

TABLE 73

RETENTION OF VITAMIN C IN WHOLE GUAVAS STORED AT 36° AND 45°F AND 90% RELATIVE HUMIDITY

No. of Days in Storage	Ascorbic Acid, mg/100 gm Fruit											
	Tree 1 (Pink Flesh)		Tree 2 (Pink Flesh)		Tree 3 (Pink Flesh)		Tree 4 (Pink Flesh)		Tree 5 (White Flesh)		Tree 6 (Pink-Orange Flesh)	
	36°F	45°F	36°F	45°F	36°F	45°F	36°F	45°F	36°F	45°F	36°F	45°F
0	96	96	102	102	95	95	114	114	187	187	90	90
1	99	101	91	98	102	101	119	102	145	177	94	76
2	98	101	97	101	97	98	116	108	170	166	64	81
3	93	99	93	102	90	114	112	98	172	178	80	85
4	...	...	74	105	96	86	110	106	160	188	...	...
6	100	92	...	...	...	...	...	...	96	182	...	...
7	88	106	...	108	...	...	...	...	92	157	...	...

Source: Boyle *et al.* (1957).

spoiled fruit are removed and the green fruit set aside for ripening. Those fruits which have only small defects may be trimmed to make them acceptable for processing. A flow sheet for guava processing is shown in Fig. 90 (Boyle *et al.* 1957).

From the inspection belt the sound fruits drop into a washing tank or onto a washing belt. Mechanical or manual agitation and the addition of a detergent (surface active agent) help to remove dirt, debris, and dried-on flower parts. Tergitol EH (sodium 2-ethyl hexene sulfonate), Duponol (sodium lauryl sulfate) and other anionic surface active agents may be used (Parker and Litchfield 1962). An elevator belt onto which clear water is sprayed removes the fruits from the washing bath and rinses off the detergent from the skins.

Pulping and Finishing.—Guava is one of the easiest fruits to process. The whole fruit can be fed into a paddle pulper for maceration into a purée. If the fruits are rather firm, it may be necessary to attach a chopper or slicer to the hopper which feeds into the machine. Several food machinery companies manufacture pulpers and chopping attachments in enough sizes to fit the needs of different-sized plant operations. To remove seeds and fibrous pieces of skin tissue, the pulper should be fitted with 0.003- or 0.045-in. perforated screens. Chopping of all fruit before feeding into the pulper may be desirable since it allows for a more uniform rate of feed. This is important because the rate of feed, as well as the speed and adjustment of the paddles, controls the amount of waste being discharged from the machine. Nonuniform movement of the material through the pulper may cause discoloration of the purée.

Removal of Stone Cells.—The outer flesh of nearly all guava types found in Hawaii has a considerable number of hard stone or grit cells. Removing the majority of the stone cells not only improves the texture of the final product but also enhances the color. Being yellowish or tan in color, the stone cells "dilute" the bright pink that is sought for finished guava purée. The flesh of guavas grown in Taiwan does not have a bright pinkish color. The nectar made from such fruit resembles milk in appearance, although it is slightly more translucent.

One good method for getting rid of these unwanted cells is to pass the purée through a paddle finisher equipped with 0.020-in. screens. This machine is exactly like the pulper except that the steel paddles are replaced by neoprene rubber strips held in place by stainless steel or hardwood cleats. The rubber paddles can be adjusted so that they almost touch the screen and the angle should be decreased from that at which the paddles are set for the pulping operation. For this operation, the speed of the machine is reduced to 600–800 rpm and the purée is fed into the hopper at a uniform rate. Adjustment of paddles, pitch, speed, and waste gate should be continued until the waste is slightly moist.

Courtesy of APV Co.

FIG. 91. PLATE HEAT EXCHANGER

Another method of finishing is to run the purée through a mustard mill so that the stone cells are pulverized. This does reduce the grittiness but does not improve the color. Both methods are used by guava processors.

Deaeration.—After pulping and finishing to remove the seeds and stone cells, it would be advisable to pump the purée through a deaerator to remove entrapped air. The advantages of deaerating are apparent. First, the removal of oxygen lessens the deterioration caused by this gas during prolonged storage. Oxidation is one of the chief causes for loss in color, breakdown of vitamins, loss of flavor, and production of off-flavors. Second, the removal of air makes for a more uniform and smoother-looking product with improved color. Third, the prevention of foaming, as caused by mixture with air, allows correct and uniform fill of containers. This last advantage of deaeration is important, especially if a mechanical filler is used in the processing line.

Flash Pasteurization.—There are two methods adaptable for heat preservation of canned guava purée. One, the so-called batch process, involves heating the purée in a steam-jacketed kettle until it reaches 185°F. The second method, using a flash pasteurizer or heat exchanger (Fig. 91) to heat the product to a high temperature for a much shorter period of time. For guava purée the recommended time-temperature relationship would be 60 sec. at 195°F. Other time-temperatures can be used. The flash pasteurization does less damage to the flavor of guava purée than the low temperature pasteurization method.

After heating, the purée should be filled immediately into enameled cans. According to Boyle *et al.* (1957), the type "N" enameled container, with two coats of enamel (citrus enamel and vinyl), and type "H", with two coats enamel (fruit enamel and vinyl) are superior to the type "T" (citrus) enamel for guava purée. The cans are sealed, inverted, held for three minutes and then cooled by water sprays or some other method to lower the temperature of the cans rapidly to 100°–120°F. The cans are then air-cooled until they reach room temperature. Prolonged water cooling may result in external rusting of the cans. Casing and stacking in the warehouse while the cans are still hot may result in spoilage by thermophilic bacteria and also lower the quality of the purée due to stack burn.

Canned guava purée is the starting material for a number of other guava products. Sugar and water may be added to make a nectar or juice drink. The purée can be used directly with commercial mixes for making ice cream, sherbet, etc.. As a flavoring for pastries, the straight guava purée or a sweetened purée may be used. Several fruit punch bases are already on the market which use guava purée as an ingredient. This outlet certainly will expand as more of the product becomes available and methods for shipping the purée in bulk are devised.

Guava Nectar

Canned guava nectar has been marketed for a number of years. The purée mentioned above is the basic ingredient. Depending on the soluble solids of the purée, proportioned amounts of sugar and water are added to make the drink. In general, winter fruit contains from 6 to 8% soluble solids and summer fruit from 8 to 10%. The soluble solids of each batch of fruit should be measured with a refractometer in order to control the final soluble solids of the nectar.

The following formula, having 20% purée by weight, is calculated so that the soluble solids of the finished product will be approximately 11%, and the pH (depending on that of the original fruit pulp) will be between 3.3 and 3.5.

Guava purée (average soluble solids 7%)	100 lb
Cane sugar	48 lb
Water	352 lb
Yield of guava nectar	500 lb

In a stainless steel mixing kettle or tank the water and sugar are mixed. The purée is added at a steady rate while mixing thoroughly again. The mixture is pumped through a heat exchanger at 180°–190°F and held there for 60 sec. The product is filled into enameled cans. The cans were sealed, inverted, held for three minutes, and cooled with water to 100°F. After labeling and casing, the cans are ready for shipping or warehousing.

Some processors believe that the addition of a small amount of acid, such as citric acid, enhances the natural flavor of guava.

Sodium benzoate may be added as a preservative up to the limit prescribed by law, provided that such an addition is stated on the label. The use of this or any other preservative, however, does not assure the processor that his product will not spoil. Careful checks for cleanliness in each step of processing and strict adherence to processing times and temperatures give much better assurance.

Yeh (1970) described a procedure for canning guava nectar of 12–14° Brix. The acidity was 0.17–0.20% as citric acid. The nectar contained 15–25% guava juice. The general procedures were similar to that described by Boyle *et al.* (1957), with the exception that guava nectar has to pass through a centrifuge separator to remove coarse particles (Fig. 92). In addition, the nectar was passed through a homogenizer under a pressure of 100 kg/sq cm to make a homogeneous product prior to the flash-pasteurization process.

Rahman *et al.* (1964B) studied the stability of vitamin C in canned tropical fruit juices and nectars. Guava nectar was fortified with vitamin C at seven levels of concentration ranging from the original content to 300 mg/100 ml. The canned products were stored at room temperature and 100°F for six months. The loss of vitamin C was higher in the samples stored at 100°F than at room temperature, regardless of concentration

Courtesy of Westfalia AG.

FIG. 92. CENTRIFUGE SEPARATOR

level. At the end of six months, the loss of vitamin C was less than 30% in samples stored at room temperatures.

Clarified Guava Juice

There are undoubtedly some uses for guava where it is desirable to remove the color and insoluble solids. One possibility is the blending of guava juice with other fruit juices or extracts in which the processor wishes to retain the guava flavor but wants the color removed because the resulting mixture is lacking in color appeal. Other uses for the clarified product would be in the making of clarified guava juice drink.

Two methods for making clarified guava juice have been developed. In the first method, whole guavas are frozen to help break down their internal structure and are kept in frozen storage until needed. In the second method, the starting material is frozen guava purée. From here on both processes are essentially the same, except that when whole guava are used the yield of juice is less due to interference of the seeds in the pressing out of juice. After thawing, the fruits or purée are placed in a press cloth and the clear juice squeezed out by applying mechanical pressure. When purée is used, it is advisable to warm it to about 100°F, and to add a filtering aid before pressing. Celite, a diatomaceous earth, at the rate of one per cent by weight, thoroughly mixed with the purée, is a good filtering aid.

The clarified juice may be blended with other juices, made into jelly or clarified nectar, or heated and stored for future use. Since the flavor and odor of this juice are weaker than that of the guava purée, more of it must be used in juice products.

Waldt and Mahoney (1967) used fungal pectinase to remove the pectin in guava juice. The clarification of guava juice with the aid of fungal depectinizing enzymes was investigated at various temperatures in order to study the properties of fungal pectinases in fruit juice application. Enzyme activity was measured by a simple procedure employing isopropanol as a precipitant of remaining pectin in juice after a period of incubation. The time concentration relationship of enzyme activity was demonstrated. The correlation between depectinization and the phenomenon of flocculation was used to explain the effect of colloidal environment on the clarification of guava juice.

An enzymatic process was used by Sreekantiah *et al.* (1968) to remove pectin in guava juice. An 85% yield of natural flavored juice could be obtained by enzyme treatment of ripe guava pulp. A laboratory-prepared enzyme concentrate produced from *Aspergillus niger* gave results similar to those obtained with commercial pectinolytic enzymes. The best conditions for processing guavas were an enzyme concentration of 0.5%, based on the pulp, and incubation at 104°F for 18 hr. This treatment, which did not completely degrade the pectin, was followed by filter pressing, allowing the expressed juice to stand at 35–37°F for 48–72 hr, and filtering the supernatant liquid. The enzyme-treated juice contained 30–55 mg tannin/100 ml of juice. If the tannin content of the juice was high enough to interface with clarification of the juice, precipitation of the tannins with gelatin was recommended; this might happen with unripe fruits which generally have a high tannin content.

Clarified Guava Nectar

Starting with the clarified guava juice mentioned in the previous section, a palatable but mild-flavored guava juice drink can be manufactured. For a good finished product of 11% soluble solids, one must use 30% by weight of clarified juice as compared to 20% by weight of guava purée for making ordinary guava juice drink. The ingredients are:

	lb
Clarified juice (average soluble solids 7%)	100
Cane sugar	29.5
Water	203.5
Yield of clarified nectar	333.0

The ingredients are mixed thoroughly and pumped through a flash pasteurizer at 190°F at a rate which holds the product at this temperature for 60 sec. Filling, seaming, subsequent cooling, labeling, and casing are carried out exactly as those described in a previous section (see p. 318).

Chilled and Frozen Guava Products

In order to retain the maximum of fresh fruit flavor, aroma, and color, many products are preserved by freezing. With scrupulous care for cleanliness and sanitation, a number of frozen guava preparations may be manufactured without the application of heat.

Frozen Guava Purée.—The steps for making frozen guava purée are essentially the same as that for manufacture of canned purée, omitting, of course, the operations calling for heating and subsequent cooling. After the operation of stone cell removal, a slush freezer may be installed in the processing line to chill the product before it is filled into containers. The advantage of the pre-chilling is that the purée will freeze more rapidly, maintaining higher quality and allowing labeling and casing to take place sooner. Because of the higher acidity of this product, the containers should be enameled or protected with a plastic lining (Feinberg 1968).

Frozen Nectar Base.—Frozen guava nectar base is a combination of purée and sugar in such proportions that it may be diluted with water by the consumer in the same manner that many other fruit juice concentrates are prepared. Because of its natural color and flavor as well as high nutritive value, frozen guava nectar base should become more and more popular as a breakfast drink. The optimum dilution is $2^1/_2$–3 parts of water to 1 part of the base (Boyle *et al.* 1957).

The following formula is recommended for making guava nectar base:

Guava purée (7% soluble solids)	100 lb
Cane sugar	48 lb

If the soluble solids of the purée vary from 7%, the amount of sugar should be adjusted in the formulation. It is advisable to measure the pH of each lot of purée so that the pH range of the finished product will be between 3.3 and 3.5. Most wild guava is in the sour or acid category, but occasionally sweet guavas may be brought to the processor. By blending the purée from sweet guavas with that from the sour types or by adding citric acid, the pH of the final mixture may be kept in the desired range.

After blending the correct amounts of purée and sugar in a mixing kettle, the mixture should be pumped through a slush freezer before going to the filling machine. After filling and closing the containers (preferably enameled), they should be placed immediately in the freezer and kept at 0°F or below. Labeling and casing should take place after freezing without allowing the cans to thaw.

Refrigerated Guava Nectar.—Freshly prepared unheated nectar, when stored at 36°F, will retain its flavor, odor, and color for about two weeks. At 45° its storage life is only one week (Boyle *et al.* 1957). Flash pasteurization at 160°F for 14–18 sec helps considerably in prolonging the storage life of the refrigerated product under the conditions found in retail food stores. A processor or supplier must use a well-organized system of distribution and replacement of refrigerated nectar in retail outlets. A rapid turnover of product with none being retained in the store for more than a few days would be ideal for refrigerated guava nectar.

The product like the canned guava juice drink may be made either from freshly processed fruits or from frozen purée. Artificial food color may be added if desired. The equipment and distribution facilities of a dairy plant seem to be most useful in making and marketing this product. To avoid the formation of clots or clumps, it is suggested that first the sugar be stirred into the purée in small portions. Next, after the mixing is complete, the water can be added. This procedure results in a smooth and homogeneous product.

Quality Control

The food processing plant should have an organized procedure for checking all aspects of its operation, from raw fruit and ingredients to the finished products.

Raw Materials.—As was stated earlier in the discussion of wild versus cultivated guavas, the processor will have little control over quality factors of the fresh fruit until selected seedlings and varieties are cultivated commercially. However, there are a number of checks which a buyer may make on wild fruit for processing. Maturity, of course is important both from the standpoint of juice yield and of quality. Other qualities which should be checked on each lot of fruit are soluble solids, pH, vitamin C content, flavor, and color.

Soluble solids can be measured with a refractometer. This is important in the calculation of formulations and in the blending of different lots of fruits to arrive at a standardized finished product.

The acidity of different lots of guavas should be determined. This factor plays an important part in the flavor acceptance of the fruit and its manufactured products.

The vitamin C content of guava will become more and more important as the public learns the high value of guava products in supplying this essential food factor. Different lots of fruit need to be adjusted for standardization of the vitamin C content of processed guava products.

Color, texture, aroma, and flavor of the fresh fruit can be evaluated by visual observation and actual testing. Instruments or standard color are available for checking color objectively. The use of guavas of poor color and flavor for processing will do more harm to consumer acceptance than any other factor over which a processor has control. It is desirable to check the raw products for these two quality factors on all lots of fruit.

Inspections and tests for molds and bacteria in the equipments and facilities can prevent the spoilage and loss of finished products. Visual examination of the fresh fruits is an important step to eliminate the damaged fruit. It is important that the processor eliminate all sources of contamination in his plant.

Processing.—Plant sanitation is an important matter to be considered in guava product processing. Every piece of equipment that comes in contact with the fruit should be clean. A schedule for regular and thorough cleaning of all equipments should be set up. Water containing 2 to 5 ppm available chlorine should be used to keep down contamination on belts, elevators, and wash tanks. Precautions should be taken to keep down dust and to keep insects and vermin out of the plant.

Each unit operation during the preparation and processing should be studied to learn its effect on quality. At the same time, valuable information on yield and production rate may be gathered. Careful adjustment and checking of such machines as cutters, pulpers, finishers, pasteurizers, fillers, and closing machines will pay off in better quality as well as in more efficient and economical operation. Strict adherence to processing times and temperatures helps to assure a uniform, high quality end product. In case anything goes wrong, the use of a code mark which is changed frequently during a day's operations permits the processor to sort out only those containers which fall below standard in any respect. This device can result in substantial savings to the processor.

Finished Products.—A sampling procedure which allows adequate checks on quality of all lots or batches of each product should be set up. Immediate examination then permits corrections to be made and also allows the processor to isolate any lots which should not be put on the market.

The same sort of tests which were conducted on the raw products may be run on the finished material, such as color, flavor, texture, pH, vitamin content and soluble solids. Measurement of headspace, fill weight, and vacuum should also be made on the canned product.

Any product stored for considerable lengths of time in a warehouse or in frozen storage should be examined periodically. Records of storage times and temperatures should be kept, since all the care during processing can be rendered useless by improper storage.

MANGO PURÉE AND NECTARS

The mango is considered one of the more delicious tropical fruits. According to Kay (1966), certain processed mango products such as pickles, chutney, and canned slices have been available for several years from Jamaica, India, Mexico, and South Africa. Puerto Rico and the Philippines also produce mangoes (Ross 1960). The varieties of mango grown in Hawaii are Haden, Pirie (Yee 1963), Pope (Hamilton 1960), Joe Welch, Zill, and several others (Orr and Miller 1955). Commercial production of mangoes in Hawaii is centered on the island of Maui, although a considerable tonnage is produced from plantings throughout the Hawaiian islands.

Mangoes are marketed chiefly as fresh fruit. Processing has not developed on a large scale, but occasionally small packs of frozen slices or of chutney have been marketed (Brekke *et al.* 1968)

Frozen Mango Purée

A procedure for canning mango purée was described by Brekke *et al.* (1968) as follows:

> "Haden mangoes were sorted, washed in a rotary spray washer, and the seeds removed with knives by hand. A mechanical scraping device (Stafford *et al.* 1966) was used to remove the peel for some of the experimental lots. The fruit was put through a cutting mill and a paddle pulper fitted with a screen with 0.033-in. perforations to remove coarse fibers and particles. The purée was then pumped through a plate heat exchanger for rapid heating and cooling to inactivate the enzyme catalase. In the heat exchanger the purée was heated to 195°–200°F, held at that temperature for one minute, and then cooled to 90°–100°F. It was then filled into 30-pound tins with polyethylene liners and frozen at −10°F."

De Leon and de Lima (1966) studied the acceptability of mango juices canned at various stages of ripening from Katchamita, Piko, Sipsipin and

Carabao varieties. Consumer testing panels indicated a preference for the varieties in the order: Piko, Carabao, Katchamita, and Sipsipin. A slight preference for the yellow and firm stage was indicated over the firm and greenish yellow stage and soft and yellow stage. The color, relative viscosity, acidity, solids and ascorbic acid content of the canned juices after processing and storage were reported. They stated that the soluble solids, pH, and acidity content of fresh mangoes are preferable to penetrometer readings for determining the adequacy of the fruit for processing into juice.

Mango Nectars

Mango nectars can be made either from fresh mangoes or frozen purée. Brekke *et al.* (1968) described a procedure for canning mango purée as follows:

"Frozen purée was thawed overnight at room temperature and transferred to a large stainless steel container in which the ingredients could be mixed with a power stirrer. The basic formula used for the nectar was as follows:

	lb
Mango purée	100
Sugar	30
Water	170
Citric acid	10

After thorough mixing, the nectar was filled into No. 2 cans and vacuum sealed. The cans were processed 3 min at 212°F in a spin cooker (Wang and Ross 1965) in which the cans were rotated at 125 rpm on their long axis. The product was spin cooled with water at 72°F, which was sufficient to reduce the temperature to about 100°F in 4 min."

Frozen mango purées were kept at 0°F for one week and then canned as nectars. The purée which received heat treatment at 195°–200°F for 1 min yielded a nectar of higher aroma and flavor quality than the unheated lot (Brekke *et al.* 1968). The authors concluded that heating the purée to 195°–200°F for 1 min is necessary for quality retention during freezing storage at 0°F. The purpose of the operation is to inactivate the enzyme systems which may cause off-flavor in the product. For industrial production, mango nectar can be made either directly from the fresh fruit at optimum maturity or from frozen mango purée.

A bulletin describing the processing and canning of mango nectars was published by Sanchez-Nieva *et al.* (1959). Particular attention must be paid to maturity of mango for processing. There is a considerable shift in the pH of the fruit during maturation. As pH is also a variable factor between varieties, it is necessary to handle varieties independently and control maturity, so that the pH of canned nectar can be adequately controlled.

The major problem in mango canning is the high labor cost for peeling and that for removing the slabs of flesh from sides of the seed. Mechanical peeling methods have been developed for handling the firm green fruit used in chutney manufacture, but these methods are unsuitable for the mature canning fruit.

The residual flesh adhering to the seed after the initial slabbing cut can be removed and puréed for nectars and for use in frozen ice cream products. The total yield for the larger varieties is in the vicinity of 50%.

The Brix readings of mango nectars are usually at 12–15° Brix, and the acidity at 0.20–0.25% as citric acid. The per cent fruit juice in the beverage may vary from 20–30%.

Storage Stability.—Rahman *et al.* (1964A) studied the factors affecting stability of ascorbic acid in mango nectars and other tropical fruit juices which were fortified with ascorbic acid. A higher rate of destruction occurred when ascorbic acid concentrations was below 200 mg per 100 ml of sample. The rate of destruction was faster in samples of lower ascorbic acid concentration.

The changes in the sugars, vitamins and organic acids in canned mango beverages during preparation and storage was reported by Hamed (1966). The levels of nonreducing sugar decreased and of reducing sugar increased in all the preservation treatments employed, such as pasteurization at 185°F and addition of 0.1% sodium benzoate, 0.1% sorbic acid, 0.1% Na benzoate +0.05% sorbic acid, and 0.02% SO_2. The decrease in ascorbic acid with treatment was not drastic. A significant decrease in sorbic acid occurred during the preparation of the beverage from whole fruit. In contrast to the ascorbic acid levels, the carotene contents did not decrease during preparation and remained nearly constant throughout the eight-month test period. The change was least in the sample receiving SO_2 treatment. Storage at low temperatures following pasteurization also inhibits the chemical changes. The inversion of sugar was suggested as depending upon the enzyme activity rather than the acids since the addition of citric acid to the beverage, followed by pasteurization had little effect on the reducing sugar level. In all cases, the taste did not vary during the first four months of storage.

PAPAYA PURÉE AND NECTARS

Papaya (pawpaw) is a tropical fruit with a definite development potential. The Solo variety is grown in Hawaii for the fresh fruit market. In Australia, it is one of the major components in canned tropical fruit salads

Courtesy of Clarke-Built Ltd.

FIG. 93. SCRAPE-SURFACE HEAT EXCHANGER

for export. Small quantities are used in making nectars and mixed fruit drinks.

Frozen Papaya Purée

The Hawaii Agricultural Experiment Station has developed a procedure for making papaya purée which can be preserved either by canning or freezing (Stafford *et al.* 1966). The procedures are essentially as follows:

"The fresh papayas were inspected and sorted to remove damaged and undesirable ones. The fruits were immersed in water at 120°F for 20 min. The warm water treatment was used to prevent undue spoilage losses during ripening as prescribed by Akamine (1960). The fruits were ripened at room temperature for 5 to 6 days. It is advisable to cool the product to 35°F prior to processing to lessen the possibility of gel formation. The chilled fruits were washed, trimmed with a stainless steel knife or a hydraulic cutter to remove the ends, and then cut into four pieces in a slicer. The skins were separated in a skin separator. The mixture containing the seeds passed a paddle pulper with a 0.033-in. screen. In this operation the seeds are removed. The purée was pumped through a scraped-surface heat exchanger (Fig. 93) at 210°F or higher, and held there for 1 min. It is necessary to heat inactivate the pectin esterase enzyme in the purée immediately after seed removal. The product was cooled to 85°F in a second scraped-surface heat exchanger, and then passed through a paddle finisher with a 0.020-in. screen to remove specks and fibers. The purée is then filled into polyethylene-lined 30-lb cans, sealed, and deep frozen to −10°F or below."

It appears necessary to eliminate the bitter flavor that can occur in papaya purée produced by chopping up whole fruits in a cutting or hammer mill as a first step in purée production. A pilot model machine for separating papaya skins from the seeds and flesh was used by Stafford *et al.* (1966) to determine if this would lessen or eliminate the bitter flavor. Papaya purée made with this machine showed no sign of bitter off-flavor.

The machine consists essentially of two reels rotating at different speeds with the papaya slices fed between them. The upper reel is made of wood covered with a thin sheet of corrugated rubber. The larger lower reel which separates the flesh from the skin is constructed of stainless steel rods which are approximately $^{5}/_{16}$ in. apart. The machine is referred to as a skin separator.

Since the frozen purée will be stored for some time before reprocessing, it was necessary to heat inactivate various enzyme systems which may cause development of off-flavor during storage. Seagrave-Smith and Sherman (1954) reported that gelation in frozen papaya purée can be prevented by heating the product to 200°–210°F for a min and cooling rapidly. Stafford *et al* (1966) reported that heating the papaya purée to 210°F for 1 min immediately after seed removal consistently prevented gel formation. The treatment also inactivated catalase, peroxidase, and papain with minimum effect on flavor and color. Yamamoto and Inouye (1963) and Chang *et al.* (1965) described the use of sucrose to inhibit pectin esterase which can cause gelation in frozen papaya purée when reconstituted.

Aung and Ross (1965) studied heat sensitivity of pectin esterase (PE) in papaya purée. The average PE activity of full ripe papaya was 0.013 meq/min/gm. When the purée was heated to boiling, the PE activity was completely lost. A plot of decimal reduction value (D) in minutes against temperature gave a value of Z (slope of the thermal inactivation curve) of 11°F and $D_{180} = 10$ min for 90% inactivation. They emphasized the possibility of presence of residual PE activity in canned acidified papaya products spin-processed in No. 2 cans for a relatively short time. Demethylation of pectin in papaya caused by PE activity during processing may result in gelation in the final product.

Pilot plant runs were made by Stafford *et al.* (1966) to compare the yield of purée from a processing line utilizing the papaya skin separator with a line utilizing a cutting mill. The yield obtained from the line utilizing the skin separator was 1–2% lower, depending on the spacing between the reels. When the spacing is too close the quality of the purée will be lowered. The use of a hydraulic trimming device lowered the yield by 5 to 10%; however, various types of knives and adjustments can be used on this device to minimize the loss. The balance between the yield and quality must be resolved by the processor.

Papaya Nectars

Papaya nectar was made with approximately 10 parts of purée, 16.4 parts of water, 2.1 parts of sugar, and citric acid sufficient to adjust to pH to 4.0 (Stafford *et al.* 1966). The procedures were similar to those described earlier for making mango nectars (Brekke *et al.* 1968). The product was filled into No. 2 enameled cans, sealed under vacuum, spin-cooked at 212°F for three minutes and cooled in a spin cooler to 100°F in four minutes. The canned nectars were evaluated by a trained taste panel using a 7-point quality scale. Papaya nectars made from heat treated purées (210°F) were superior in flavor to nectars made from purées which had not been heated to inactivate enzymes. Milling the whole fruit resulted in a nectar inferior in flavor and mouthfeel quality to the nectar prepared from skin-separated purée. Removal of seeds by hand prior to mechanical pulping was shown to be unnecessary. Warm water treatment of the fruit before ripening caused no adverse effects on the final nectar quality.

BANANA PURÉE

Bananas belong to the family *Musaceae*, genus *Musa*, comprising 32 or more distinct species and at least 100 subspecies. The majority of edible bananas are from a subsection of *Musa* called *Eumusa* and originate specifically from two wild species, *M. acuminata* and *M. balbisiana*. Most commercial bananas are from the triploid group of *M. acuminata*. In this group are the Cavendish and Gros Michel which are by far the principal bananas in world commerce (Seelig 1969).

World production of bananas is rising. In 1966, it reached 23,708,000 metric tons. The largest part of production is in Latin America, especially in Brazil, Ecuador, Venezuela, Honduras, Panama, and Costa Rica. In 1966, Latin America produced 62% of world's banana crop.

Approximately half of the bananas of the world are eaten as fresh fruit and as salads. The more important banana products are jams, purée, flakes, powder, baby foods, and others. Banana purée canned in 55-gal drums by the aseptic canning process is a new product for the baking and ice-cream industry.

Bananas are harvested when they are still green (0.1–2.0% total sugar and 19.5–21.5% starch). In a period of 10 to 20 days, bananas must be harvested, shipped several thousand miles, ripened and sent to retail stores. The banana ship is air conditioned at 56°–58°F and a relative humidity of 90–95%. The fruit should be ripened at 58°–64°F in 4–8 days to color index No. 5 (green tip) or No. 6 (all yellow) just before reaching the consumer. The best eating quality is at stage 6 (all yellow, 16.5–19.5% total sugar content, 1.0–4.0% starch), and stage 7 (yellow-flecked, 17.5–19.7 total sugar and 1.0–2.5% starch). The controlling factors in banana ripening are generally recognized to be temperature, humidity, and ventilation. During ripening bananas give off small amount of ethylene, volatile esters and carbon dioxide. It is important that these gases be confined to the ripening room particularly during the early stages of the ripening process. The amount of these gases present has a direct bearing on the rate of ripening at a given temperature. To best control the speed of ripening, it is highly desirable to administer ethylene gas artificially. As the fruit colors during ripening, the humidity may be reduced to a point between 75 and 85% (Seelig 1969).

Banana Purée for Bakery Use

A procedure for making refrigerated banana purée suitable for use in bakery products was described by Tonaki *et al.* (1967) as follows:

"The bananas are peeled and immersed for three minutes in a 2.0% solution of sodium bisulfite, which introduces about 200 ppm of SO_2 to the fruit. They are drained several minutes, then milled through $^1/_8$-in. screen to give a coarse purée. For apple bananas, about 0.2% by weight of Pectinol 10-M is added and the purée is allowed to stand for 30 min. The step is not required for Bluefield and Chinese bananas. The purée is pumped to a plate heat exchanger where it is heated very rapidly to 190°F and after about one minute is cooled rapidly to 85°F. It then goes to a finisher with a 0.033 screen which removes seeds and some fibrous material. Citric acid is stirred in to bring the purée to pH 4.2; about 100 gm of citric acid is required for 100 lb of purée. A preservative agent such as potassium sorbate (250 ppm) may be added to increase resistance to spoilage. The purée is filled into 30-lb tins with plastic film bag liners, sealed and placed in cool storage (35° to 40°F)."

"The product retains the natural color and flavor of banana and resists spoilage for several weeks. It is not frozen nor is it heat sterilized. Samples of purée made from Bluefield bananas have remaind unspoiled for 10 weeks; Chinese and Applebanana purées are somewhat less stable but retain good quality for 7 to 8 weeks. A processor or baker can prepare a large quantity of the purée only 4 or 5 times a year and hold it in cool storage until it is used."

Banana Purée Canning

A procedure for canning acidified banana purée was described by Guyer and Erickson (1954) as follows:

"Good mature raw bananas at color index number 6 and 7 were selected and peeled carefully with attention to removal of peel rag and rot. The bananas were blanched whole in steam or boiling water (or a combination of both) until a center temperature of 190°F was reached. A medium size peeled banana requires about 6 to 8 min to attain this center temperature.

The blanched bananas were checked for sugar content and pH value. They were puréed or macerated to the desired viscosity in a comminution machine. Either during the comminuting process or after it the computed amounts of sugar and citric acid were metered and blended into the banana purée to obtain the desired sugar level and the necessary pH of 4.1 to 4.3. The purée was heated to approximately 200°F and filled into enameled No. 1 cans. The cans were closed immediately, inverted and held for 5 min followed by water cooling to 100°F. The entire operation from peeling to filling into cans was carried out as rapidly as possible to insure a high quality product."

Several types of product discoloration have been encountered in the production of banana purée (Guyer and Erickson 1954). A brown discoloration, attributed to a very active oxidative enzyme system, can be eliminated by inactivating the enzyme either with a hot water or steam blanching before pulping. Similar enzyme systems occur in Bartlett pears that may cause brown discoloration in the product if they were not effectively controlled (Luh *at al.* 1963).

Canned acidified banana purée may also undergo pink discoloration which can be intensified by the presence of peel rag and either tin or zinc in the purée (Guyer and Erickson 1954). They reported that the discoloration could be held to a minimum if the temperature of the banana was rapidly raised to 185°F during blanching. Pink discoloration some times occurs in canned Bartlett pears (Luh *et al.* 1960). Pears from certain growing areas had low pH, high acidity and high tannin content. These pears were found to develop pink color after canning especially when excessive heating and delayed cooling processes were used. Canned banana purée may also show pink discoloration especially when the product was acidified. This phenomenon may be related to the level of leucoanthocyanin in the fresh banana. The processor should know the quality of the fresh banana for processing, especially its potential of developing pink color after heat processing. A test for leucoanthocyanins in pears (Luh *et al.* 1960) and peach (Luh and Villarreal 1964) has been reported. It is highly probable that leucoanthocyanins in bananas are related to problem of discoloration in the canned product.

An aseptic canning method for preserving banana purée has been applied commercially in central America where banana is abundant. The product is processed by the high temperature-short time procedure in a scraped-surface heat exchanger, cooled, and canned under aseptic condition in 55-gal drums. The principle of such a process has been described by Luh and Sioud (1966) in aseptic canning of pear purée.

Biochemical Changes in Ripening Bananas

Banana ripening consists of progressive physical and chemical changes starting from the green state in which the fruit is hard, starchy and unpalatable (Seelig 1969). As ripening proceeds, the fruit becomes gradually softer in texture, turns from green to yellow in color and becomes sweeter and pleasant to the taste. The starch originally present is nearly all converted into sugar. During the process, the characteristic pleasing aroma of the ripe fruit develops and numerous other more subtle changes take place. Especially important in controlling ripening is the change in the rate of heat generation as the ripening cycle progresses.

Ripening Temperature.—The ripening process is accomplished at temperatures ranging from 58° to 68°F pulp temperature with relative humidity of 90 to 95%. Ripening temperatures between 58° to 64°F are best when ethylene is used. Within certain limits, the period required for ripening green fruit can be extended or shortened to meet trade requirements by adjusting the temperature.

Ripening temperatures for bananas are varied frequently in contrast to other produce coolers. Ripening characteristics of different lots of bananas vary with country of origin, variety, days in transit, season of the year, maturity when harvested, and other factors. The desired high humidity required for proper ripening can be attained best through the use of automatic humidifiers with humidistats. After coloring is well under way, relative humidity should be lower, about 85%.

Air-circulating fans should be operated continuously when ripening boxed bananas to have a uniform pulp temperature throughout the room. Stacking to allow adequate air circulation is essential for uniform ripening of boxed bananas. Ideally, boxes should be stacked in rows with a four-inch air channel between adjacent rows.

Within certain limits the period required for ripening green bananas can be extended or shortened to meet trade requirements. Under average conditions ripening cannot be accomplished in less than 3 or 4 days nor extended much beyond 8 to 10 days without resorting to drastic treatments harmful to the quality of the fruit. As ripening advances, bananas become progressively softer, and gentle handling is required to prevent bruising. Bruising in the turning or ripe stage may result in discolored pulp without any visible peel injury.

Banana fruits show a typical climacteric rise in respiration after harvest (Murata *et al.* 1965). Sugar, alcohol, and aldehyde contents increased and ascorbic acid decreased during postharvest ripening.

Biochemical Transformations.—The biochemical transformations during ripening of *Musa cavendishi* bananas have been reported by Sgarbieri and Figueiredo (1967). The fruit were harvested at the green stage and then ripened by keeping them in closed chambers at 71°–77°F chambers where sawdust was burned 86°–95°F and then at room temperature; and in 0.1% C_2H_2 at 68°–71°F and over 85% relative humidity.

The last method gave the best results. During ripening, the organic acids increased to a maximum and then decreased, while ascorbic acid and total solids decreased. The soluble solids increased due to transformation of starch into soluble carbohydrates. Fatty acids constitute 0.1–0.25% of the pulp, 50% being palmitic acid, followed by arachidic, linoleic, and oleic acids.

The changes in carbohydrates of banana pulp during ripening was reported by Bazarova (1964). Alcohol extracts of green and ripe bananas were analyzed for sugars by the paper chromatographic method. It was established that bananas contain glucose, fructose, and sucrose. During ripening of bananas, hydrolytic processes take place connected with the accumulation of sugars owing to a decrease of the starch content. The predominant sugar in the fruits is sucrose. During ripening of bananas, the amount of reducing sugars increased. Ghosh and Sarkar (1967) found an increase in reducing sugar and decrease in pectin during ripening of green bananas at 98.6°F for 4–48 hr.

Three pectin methyl esterase fractions were found in ripening bananas (Hultin and Levine 1965). The activities of all three fractions increased with change of skin color from green to yellow. The polymerization of tannins during ripening of banana fruits was shown by de Swardt *et al.* (1967). The leucoanthocyanin-containing fraction extracted from the bananas was shown to be the only pectin methylesterase inhibitory compound present. The authors suggested that low-molecular-weight tannins may be the main enzyme activity controlling compounds in the ripening of bananas.

The nonvolatile organic acids in the ripening bananas were investigated by Wyman and Palmer (1964). Unripe fruit contained about 4.5 meq of total organic acidity per 100 gm fresh weight. In the ripe fruit the total acidity was doubled, with malic about 65%, citric 20%, and oxalic about 10%. The remaining acidity at all stages consisted of traces of glutamic, aspartic, glutaric, quinic, glyceric, glycolic and succinic acids.

Polyphenoloxidase in Bananas.—The enzyme polyphenoloxidase is involved in enzymatic browning of bananas during processing. It is found in both pulp and peel of ripe banana and is readily extracted with phosphate buffer containing ethylenediaminetetraacetate (Palmer 1963). The enzyme was purified by acetone precipitation and chromatography on cellulose. The optimum activity was at pH 7.0 with 3,4-dihydroxyphenylethylamine as substrate.

Volatile Compounds of Bananas.—Volatile compounds in fruits usually increase during ripening (Luh *et al.* 1955; Luh 1961). The volatile components of bananas have been reported by Issenberg and Wick (1963). Gas chromatography of vapors from the homogenate and the

TABLE 74

VOLATILE BANANA CONSTITUENTS (GROS MICHEL)[1]
(20% Ucon 50HB 2000 Column at 185°F)

Fraction		Identification
1	B	Ethyl acetate[2]
...	C	Ethanol[2]
2	...	2-Butanone[3]
3	D	2-Pentanone[2]
...	...	1-Propanol[2]
4	F	Isobutyl acetate[2]
5	H	2-Butanol[2]
6	I	*n*-Butyl acetate
7	J	2-Pentanol acetate[4]
...	...	2-Pentanol[4]
8	...	1-Butanol[2]
9	K	Isoamyl acetate[2]
10	L	Isoamyl alcohol[2]
11	M	*n*-Amyl acetate
12	N	*trans*-2-Hexenal[2]
13	O	An octenone[3]
14	P	2-Pentanol butyrate
15	Q	*n*-Hexyl acetate
16	R	Isoamyl butyrate[2]
17	...	2-Hexanol[3]
18	...	1-Hexanol and an acetate
19–20	...	Unknown

[1] From Wick *et al.* (1966).
[2] From Issenberg and Wick (1963).
[3] Tentative identification.
[4] From Issenberg, Nursten and Wick (1964).

ethyl ether extracts of the distillate showed the presence of the following compounds in bananas: 2-pentanone, iso-BUOAc, iso-BuOH, isoamyl acetate, isoamyl alcohol, trans-2-hexenal, and isoamyl butyrate. Probable identification was obtained for EtOH, EtOAc, and 2-pentanol, and tentative identification based on retention data, for PrOH, amyl acetate, hexyl acetate, and MeOAc.

Wick *et al.* (1966) reviewed the nature of volatile banana constituents, their production during ripening, and their contribution to sensory quality. Table 74 summarizes the volatile components of bananas. Characterization and identification of the components were done by gas chromatography, infrared spectrophotometry, and mass spectrometry. The increase in volatile constituents observed as ripening progresses and flavor develops suggests a fundamental interrelation between these substances and biochemical processes occurring in the fruit.

The volatile alcohols of ripe bananas were separated from other classes of constituents by liquid chromatography on silica gel (Murray *et al.* 1968). The fraction separated thereby contained relatively few components, which were readily identified by combined gas chromatography and mass spectrometry. EtOH, iso-BuOH, BuOH, 2-pentanol, 3-methyl-

1-butanol, 1-heptanol, 2-heptanol, cis- and trans-4-hexen-1-ol, and cis-2-penten-1-ol (tentative) were present.

The gas chromatographic patterns of banana volatiles were related to the flavor profiles of the fruit by McCarthy *et al.* (1963). They determined the contribution of certain compounds to the characteristic banana flavor. Banana-like flavor was found to be due to AmOAc, $EtCO_2Am$, and $PrCO_2Am$, while the fruity and ester-like notes were due to BuOAc, $PrCO_2Bu$, hexyl acetate, and $PrCO_2Am$. Correlations between flavor and odor profiles and chromatographic patterns were consistently observed. Changes in chromatographic pattern and characteristic flavor notes were followed during ripening of Gros Michel and Valery varieties.

LEMONADE AND LIMEADE

Lemonade

Lemonade is a beverage prepared from lemon juice or concentrated lemon juice, with water, sweetener, and optional ingredients (Anon. 1968). The optional ingredients are: lemon oil, cold-pressed lemon oil, concentrated lemon oil, and lemon essence recovered during concentration of lemon juice; sodium benzoate and sorbic acid as preservatives; and buffering salts, emulsifying agents, and weighting oils. The proportion of lemon juice ingredients used is sufficient to yield not less than 0.70 gm anhydrous citric acid/100 ml. It may be heat treated and preserved by refrigeration, freezing, canning, or with preservatives. Colored lemonade is lemonade colored with a color additive. Limeade is similar to lemonade except that fruit and flavoring ingredients are derived from mature limes of an acid variety.

Frozen Concentrate for Lemonade

Frozen concentrate for lemonade contains proper amount of added sugar. It is reconstituted into lemonade when needed. The concentrate is principally a single-strength lemon juice with sugar added. Since most people prefer a tartness in lemonade, the acid content of the product is adjusted by the addition of approximately 10% of concentrated lemon juice to give the proper balance of sugar and citric acid.

According to U. S. Dept. Agr. (1962), a typical frozen concentrate for lemonade can be prepared as follows:

"Add sufficient concentrated lemon juice to 280 gal of single-strength lemon juice and 2,800 lb of granulated sugar so that each 100 gm of the final product will contain from 3 to 3.5 gm of citric acid. This will make approximately

500 gals of 55°-Brix concentrate. The frozen concentrate is reconstituted to lemonade by adding 4 volumes of water to each volume of concentrate."

"It is desirable that some juice cells be added to this concentrate to improve the appearance of the reconstituted lemonade. This is done by screening juice cells from juice after extraction and mixing them into the concentrate."

Lemon Concentrate

Commercial production of lemon products in the United States is confined almost exclusively to California. The Eureka lemon is the principal variety and comprises approximately 88% of the total production. The lemon fruit is picked for size only and held under controlled storage conditions for ripening from green to yellow color. About 40% of the lemon crop is processed into juice and frozen lemonade concentrate (U. S. Dept. Agr. 1967B). The operations in processing involve inspection, washing, sizing and extraction of juice. The extracted juice is pasteurized to inactivate the pectic enzyme system, and then screened to remove rag and seeds. It is held in brine-jacketed tanks to chill. The juice should be deaerated in these tanks by applying a vacuum of 25 in. for 30 min. For canned frozen single-strength juice, the chilled juice is drawn from the cold holding tanks and further cooled to 30°F by passing through a heat exchanger, filled into enamel lined cans, sealed, frozen, cased, and stored at 0° to –10°F.

Frozen lemon juice concentrate is made by concentrating single-strength lemon juice under vacuum in a low temperature vacuum evaporator. Evaporators of various types can be used. They all have several features in common and accomplish approximately the same results (Schwarz 1951). All make use of falling-film heat exchangers, in which the juice runs in a thin film down the inside of a tube while the tube is gently heated from the outside. Since the film of juice is thin, local overheating is prevented. Another advantage is that the heat-exchange rate is high and the temperature of the heating medium can be kept low, so that the chance of overheating is further decreased. The temperature of the juice during evaporation depends on the design of the unit, but is kept in the range of 60°–80°F.

Stainless steel is the standard material of construction for all parts in contact with the juice or concentrate. The lemon juice is concentrated to 43° Brix, chilled to around 30°F by passing through a heat exchanger, filling into drums lined with polyethylene bags, and freezing at —10°F. Sometimes the chilled concentrate is filled into cans, sealed, and frozen at —10°F for institutional use.

Frozen Concentrate for Limeade

Frozen concentrate for limeade is prepared by adding enough sucrose to single-strength lime juice to raise the Brix to about 48°. Some processors apply a mild heat treatment during preparation, and subsequently freeze and store the product at 0°F or lower. On reconstitution with 4 to $4^1/_2$ parts of water, an excellent limeade is obtained. As limes vary somewhat in solids and acid characteristics, some processors concentrate batches of juice for blending to maintain a uniform acid content in the finished product. Then by the addition of sugar to a 48°-Brix level, a uniform composition is attained.

When lime juice is concentrated much of its characteristic aroma and flavor are lost. Efforts to regain the original flavor through the addition of fresh juice, as is the practice in the production of frozen concentrated orange juice, or through the use of emulsified lime oil were unsatisfactory. The use of lime purée in amounts sufficient to give an oil content of 0.003% in the reconstituted limeade proved most satisfactory. The products prepared by this method include an 8-fold sweetened concentrate, which requires only the addition of 7 parts of water to prepare the beverage, and a more concentrated product, which is diluted to 35 times its volume by the addition of sugar and water. The products can be prepared according to the U. S. Dept. Agr. method (1962) as follows:

"To make 100 gal of an 8-fold sweetened superconcentrate, use 6 gallons of lime purée, 42 gal of a 2.06-fold concentrated lime juice, and 691 lb of beet or cane sugar. For the finished beverage add 7 volumes of water to 1 volume of the sweetened superconcentrate."

"To make 100 gal of an unsweetened superconcentrate, use 26.3 gal of lime purée and 73.7 gal of a 5.12-fold concentrated lime juice. For the finished product add $30^1/_4$ lb of sugar to 1 gal of the superconcentrate and dilute to 35 gallons."

VOLATILE ESSENCE RECOVERY

The volatile components are important to the characteristic flavor of fruits. They are easily lost during preheating, evaporation and processing. Various techniques have been used to recover these volatile components, and to add the essence back to the concentrated fruit juice. Volatile essence recovery is now a common procedure in the manufacture of Concord grape concentrate and of pineapple juice concentrate (Walker 1961). Essences of strawberry, Concord grape, apple and others are now available commercially.

The recovery process consists of a method by which these volatile components distilled from a liquid food, concentrated by fractionation in a column and recovered in concentrated form (Walker 1961). The product is usually prepared as a stated concentrate by volume of the ingoing feed; 100-, 150-, or 200-fold being the usual degrees of concentration. Thus one volume of essence (aroma solution) recovered from 100 volumes of juice

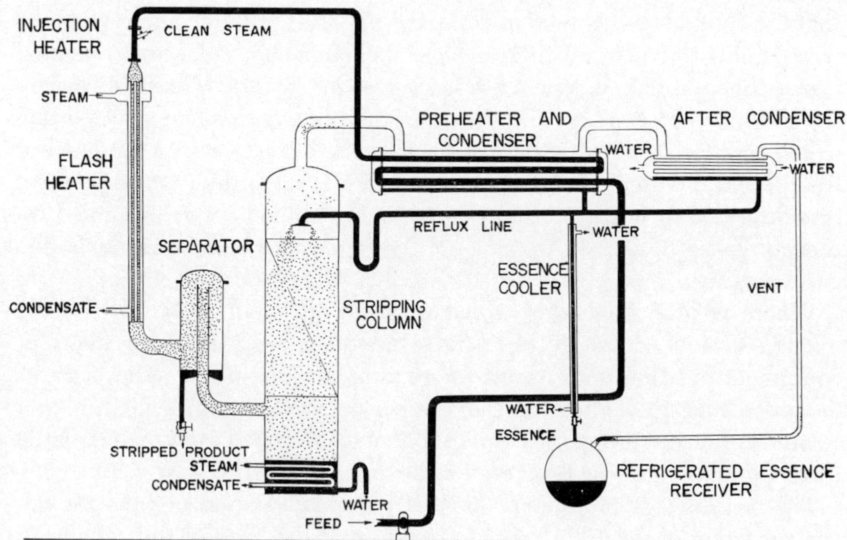

Courtesy of Oscar Krenz, Inc.

Fig. 94. Diagram of Essence Recovery Plant

Juice is preheated by column condensing vapors in the dual preheating-condensing heat exchanger and superheated considerably (250°–275°F) by the steam injection unit. Superheated juice is flashed through an orifice into the flash evaporator where the desired degree of evaporation takes place. Separated juice is ordinarily instantaneously flashed into a vacuum evaporative system. Separated vapors enter the column maintained under partial reflux, where water collects at the bottom and volatile flavors concentrate at the top and in the condensing system. Concentrated volatile flavors (essence) are continually drawn off as a fraction of the condensate flowing back to the head of the column and at a rate directly proportional to the juice feed, i.e., 1:150.

Essence is cooled and held in the receiver at temperatures just above freezing.

will be labeled a 100-fold essence. This does not mean that all of the volatile flavor components in the original 100 volumes of juice are recovered in one volume of the essence. It depends largely on the efficiency of the column and the conditions under which the volatile flavor components are recovered.

An example of a Krenz essence recovery unit is shown in Fig. 94. The feed is heated very rapidly to boiling temperature, the desired percentage of water evaporated in a flash evaporative section and vapor separated from liquid in a vapor liquid separator. The partially concentrated liquid (stripped juice) is very rapidly cooled by some means to eliminate heat damage to it. The vapor from the separator which contains both volatile flavors and water vapor is led to a fractionating column provided with reboiler and a condenser. Operation of the column depends upon the fact that the volatile flavors tend to collect at the head of the column while the water tends to collect in the reboiler. When such a column is operated under partial reflux, it is possible to recover the volatile flavors in concentrated form (essence) by drawing from the refluxing system a set portion of the condensate flowing back from the reflux condenser to the head of the column. Water collecting in the reboiler is discarded. In some cases it is desirable to scrub vent gases with either chilled water or chilled essence in order to recover the volatile flavors which these noncondensable gases contain.

Where volatile flavors are collected from all vapors given off during manufacture of a concentrate, the evaporator replaces these items of equipment together with means for cooling stripped juice. The heart of the process lies in feeding the water-vapor and volatile flavor mixture to a column and in operating the column so that an enriched solution of volatile flavors in water may be recovered in the form of essence.

The process is a continuous one. It requires a period of time for the concentration of volatile flavors to build up at the head of the column so that a fair quantity of feed should be run through a unit before draw-off of essence is commenced. At the end of a run, considerable essence is present at the head of the column when the feed is shut off.

The greater part of the volatile components may be recovered from the fruit juices by evaporating only a small fraction of the water present, for example, 8 to 10% of apple juice, 20% of strawberry juice, 30% of blackberry juice, and 40% of Montmorency cherry juice (Eskew *et al.* 1959). The method has been applied to aseptic canning of pear purée (Luh and Sioud 1966).

A new method for recovering and concentrating heat-sensitive aromas from fruit products was developed by Bomben *et al.* (1966). The feed is boiled under vacuum at 100°F. The vapors are fed to a vacuum sievetray column, where a noncondensable gas is used to strip the volatile aromas from the condensate, which is boiling at 100°F. A liquid-sealed vacuum pump compresses the noncondensable gas and absorbs the aroma in the sealant liquid. The process has successfully produced aroma solutions from orange juice, apple juice, peach purée and apricot purée. It should be applicable to produce aroma solutions from passion fruit, guava, mango, papaya, and other tropical fruit juices.

Fruit volatile flavors consist of minute amounts of a host of different substances, varying widely in amount and types with different type of fruits and with different varieties of the same fruit.

Fruit essence is a very dilute water solution of the many volatile flavors. The individual components of the volatile flavor of a fruit consist largely of alcohols, aldehydes, ketones, ethers, acid, esters, lactones, and others.

Analysis for individual constituents can be done by gas chromatographic methods, infrared spectroscopy and mass spectroscopy.

In Concord grape juice, the methyl anthranilate content runs about 1 to 1.5 ppm. while total esters approximate 50 ppm. However, most authorities agree that the anthranilate is responsible for a major fraction of the flavor sensation. The methyl anthranilate content has been generally accepted as an easily measured component representing the concentration of volatile flavor components. The minimum methyl anthranilate content of a one plus three (4-fold) frozen sweetened grape juice concentrate should be 1.2 mg./l (U. S. Dept. Agr. 1957A). Analysis of several commercial 150-fold Concord grape essences used to restore aroma to the concentrate showed that only about 50% of the original methyl anthranilate in the feed juice was recovered by the essence recovery equipment then available (Roger 1961). In the case of concentrated pineapple juice, ethyl acetate is used as the flavor component to measure the level of volatile flavors, even though its odor is not pineapple-like. Sufficient essence is added to the concentrate so that when diluted back to single-strength level the juice will contain 20 ppm ethyl acetate.

The properties of the various ingredients determine both the process and the modifications needed in the basic process for adequate recovery of volatile flavors. Certain fruits contain, among their flavoring constituents, azeotropic substances which tend to complicate the recovery process. These azeotropes, methyl anthranilate serving as the classic example, tend to remain distributed throughout the recovery system due to the constant boiling mixtures they form with water; some in the stripped juice, some in the column bottoms and some in the essence product. Therefore, the problem of the equipment designer is to set up an essence recovery unit in such a way that a major portion of the azeotrope is stripped from the juice and that as little as possible is lost in the column bottoms. Further, there is no fast rule governing the recovery of volatile flavors which contain azeotropic substances as the proportion of a particular azeotrope remaining in a boiling solution varies widely with different fruits so that a recovery unit suitable for handling the azeotropes in one fruit may or may not be suitable to handle these types of chemicals in a second fruit.

BIBLIOGRAPHY

Akamine, E. K. 1960. Temperature effects in fresh papayas processed for shipment. Hawaii Agr. Expt. Sta. Bull. *122*.

Akamine, E. K., *et al.* 1956. Passion-fruit culture in Hawaii. Univ. Hawaii, Coll. Agr. Ext. Circ. No. *345* Rev.

Anet, E. F. J., and Reynolds, T. M. 1954. Isolation of mucic acid from fruits. Nature *174*, 930.

Anon. 1949. Fruit juices. S. Africa Food Trade J. *2*, No. 1, 38.

ANON. 1955. Hawaiian punch. Food Packer *36,* No. 2, 38–39, 87.

ANON. 1968. Diluted fruit juice beverages: order establishing identity standards for lemonade, colored lemonade, and limeade. Fed. Regist. *33,* 6864–6865.

ANON. 1969A. Canned and bottled juice pack. Canner Packer *138,* No. 10, 85.

ANON. 1969B. The Almanac of the Canning, Freezing Preserving Industries, 54th Annual Compilation. Edward E. Judge and Sons, Westmister, Md.

ASENJO, C. F., HERNANDEZ, E. R., RODRIGUEZ, L. D., and DE ANDINO, N. G. 1968. Vitamins in canned Puerto Rican fruit juices and nectars. University of Puerto Rico., J. Agr. *52,* No. 1, 64–70.

AUNG, T., and ROSS, E. 1965. Heat sensitivity of pectinesterase activity in papaya purée and of catalase-like activity in passion-fruit juice. J. Food Sci *30,* No. 1, 144–147.

BAZAROVA, V. I. 1964. Change of some sugars in the process of ripening of bananas. Sb. Tr. Leningr. Sov. Torgovli No. *23,* 71–80 (Russian); cf. CA *64* No. 1, 1966, No. 1269b.

BENK, E. 1967. Composition of passion fruit juices, particularly juices from Kenya. Ind. Obst-Gemueseverwert. *52,* No. 1, 1–3 (German); cf. CA *66,* No. 9, 1967, No. 75099k.

BOMBEN, J. L., KITSON, J. A., and MORGAN, A. I. 1966. Vacuum stripping of aromas. Food Technol. *20,* 1219–1224.

BOYLE, F. P., SEAGRAVE-SMITH, H., SAKATA, S., and SHERMAN, G. D. 1957. Commercial guava processing in Hawaii. University of Hawaii, Hawaii Agr. Expt. Sta. Bull. *111,* 5–30.

BOYLE, F. P., SHAW, T. N., and HERMAN, G. D. 1955. Wide uses for passion-fruit juice. Food Eng. *27,* No. 9, 94.

BREKKE, J., CAVALETTO, C., and STAFFORD, A. E. 1968. Mango purée processing. Hawaii Agr. Expt. Sta., Univ. of Hawaii, Tech. Progress Rept. *167.*

CHANG, L. W. S., MORITA, L. L., and YAMAMOTO, H. Y. 1965. Papaya pectinesterase inhibition by sucrose. J. Food Sci. *30,* 218–222.

CILLIE, G. G., and JOUBERT, F. J. 1950. Occurrence of an amylopectin in the fruit of the granadilla (*Passiflora edulis*). J. Sci. Food Agr. *1,* 355–357.

COETZEE, N. H. R., HUGO, J. F. DU T., and PRATT, F. F. 1951. Different blends of granadilla syrup. Food Ind. S. Africa *3,* No. 9, 30.

DE LEON, S. Y., and DE LIMA, L. 1966. Acceptability of canned mango juice from four varieties and three color stages of maturity. Philippine J. Sci. *95,* No. 4, 401–409.

DESWARDT, G. H., MAXIE, E. C., and SINGLETON, V. L. 1967. Some relations between enzyme activities and phenolic components in banana fruit tissues. S. Afr. J. Agr. Sci. *10,* 641–650.

ESKEW, R. K., CLAFFEY, J. B., ACETO, N. C., and EISENHARDT, N. H. 1959 Concentrates, strips flavor in 1 pass without vacuum. Food Eng. *31,* No. 1 70–72.

FEINBERG, B. 1968. The manufacture, concentration, and freezing of fruit juices, pulpy fruit juices, and purées. *In* The Freezing Preservation of Foods. Vol. 3—Commercial Food Freezing Operations—Fresh Foods, 139–140, D. K. Tressler, W. B. Van Arsdel, and M. J. Copley (Editors). Avi Publishing Co., Westport, Conn.

FERRO, R. M. L., and CASTELBLANXO, R. H. 1969. Extraction and characterization of pectin from two varieties of guava (*Psidium guajava*). Technologia *11*, No. 57, 30–42 (Spanish); cf: CA *71*, No. 6, 1969, No. 48482b.

GHOSH, B. P., and SARKAR, N. 1967. The content of reducing sugar and pectin in ripe banana (*Musa sapientum*) on storage. J. Nutr. Diet. (Coimbatore, India) *4*, No. 3, 207–210.

GOLDBERG, L., and LEVY, L. 1941. Vitamin C content of fresh, canned, and dried guavas. Nature *148*, 286.

GUYER, R. B. and ERICKSON, F. B. 1954. Canning of acidified banana purée. Food Technol. *8*, 165–167.

HAMED, M. G. E. 1966. Determination and preservation of thick fruit juices from some tropical fruits. Z. Lebensm. -Unters. Forsch. 131, No. 3, 137–144 (German); cf: CA *66*, No. 3, 1967, No. 18135v.

HAMILTON, R. A. 1960. Pope mango. Hawaii Agr. Expt. Sta. Circ. *60*.

HAMILTON, R. A., and SEAGRAVE-SMITH, H. 1954. Growing guava for processing. Hawaii Agr. Ext. Bull. *63*.

HIU, D. 1959. Volatile constituents of passion-fruit juice. Ph. D. Thesis, University of Hawaii.

HIU, D. N., and SCHEUER, P. J. 1961. Volatile constituents of passion-fruit juice. J. Food Sci. *26*, No. 6, 557–563.

HULTIN, H. O., and LEVINE, A. S. 1965. Pectin methyl esterase in the ripening banana. J. Food Sci. *30*, 917–921.

ISSENBERG, P., NURSTEN, H. E., and WICK, E. L. 1964. Studies on the volatile constituents of the banana. Proc. First Intern. Congress Food Science and Technol *1*, 483–484.

ISSENBERG, P., and WICK, E. L. 1963. Volatile components of bananas. J. Agr. Food Chem. 11, 2–8; cf. Hultin and Proctor, CA 56, 3868a.

KAY, D. E. 1966. The market for mango products. Tropical Products Institute Rept. *G17*. Tropical Products Institute, London, England.

KEFFORD, J. F. 1961. Passion-fruit juice. *In* Fruit and Vegetable Juice Processing Technology, D. K. Tressler, and M. A. Joslyn (Editors). Avi Publishing Co., Westport, Conn.

KEFFORD, J. F. and VICKERY, J. R. 1961. Passion-fruit products. C.S.I.R.O. Food Preservation Quarterly *21*, No. 1, 2–12.

KINCH, D. M. 1960. A passion fruit centrifuge. C.S.I.R.O. Food Preservation Quart. *20*, No. 2, 34–39.

KINCH, D. M., and SHAW, T. N. 1954. The development of a machine to extract juice from passion-fruit. Hawaii Agr. Expt. Sta. Progr. Notes *104*.

KNOCK, G. G. 1951. Recent technical developments in the canning industry of the Union of South Africa. Intern. Congr. Canned Foods, 2 Paper No. XXV. 1–3.

LUH, B. S. 1961. Volatile reducing substances as a criterion of quality of canned apricots. Food Technol. *15*, 165–167.

LUH, B. S., and KAMBER, P. J. 1963. Chemical and color changes in canned apple sauce. Food Technol. *17*, 105–108.

LUH, B. S., LEONARD, S. J., and PATEL, D. S. 1960. Pink discoloration in canned Bartlett pears. Food Technol. *14*, 53–56.

LUH, B. S., LEONARD, S. J., PATEL, D. S., and CLAYPOOL, L. L. 1955. Volatile reducing substances in canned Bartlett pears. Food Technol. *9*, 639–642.

LUH, B. S., and SIOUD, F. B. 1966. Aseptic canning of foods. IV. Stability of pear purée, with essence recovery. Food Technol. *20*, 1590–1593.

LUH, B. S., TATE, J. N., and VILLARREAL, F. 1963. Polyphenolase activity and browning in Bartlett pears. Fruchtsaft-Ind. *8,* 274–283 (German); cf: CA *62,* No. 5, 1965, No. 5575f.

LUH, B. S., and VILLARREAL, F. 1964. Leucoanthocyanin in fresh and canned freestone peaches. Fruchtsaft-Ind. *9,* 285–293 (German); cf: CA *62,* No. 8, 1965, No. 9697g.

MARTIN, C. M., and REUTER, F. H. 1949. Isolation of a pectic substance from passion-fruit (*Passiflora edulis*). Nature (London), *164,* 407.

MCCARTHY, A. I., PALMER, J. K., SHAW, C. P., and ANDERSON, E. E. 1963. Correlation of gas chromatographic data with flavor profiles of fresh banana fruit. J. Food Sci. *28,* 379–384.

MENZIES, D. J., and KEFFORD, J. F. 1949. Apple juice blends. C.S.I.R.O. Food Preservation Quart. (Australia) *9,* No. 2, 31–32.

MILLER, C. D., and BAZORE, K. 1945. Fruits of Hawaii: Description, nutritive value and use. Hawaii Agr. Ext. Serv. Bull. *96.*

MOLLENHAUER, H. P. 1962. Fruit pulp of *Passiflora edulis.* Fruchtsaft-Ind. Verein. Confructa 7, 370–379 (German), cf: CA *62,* No. 6, 1965, No. 7036c.

MORRIS, T. N. 1935. Concentration of passion-fruit juice by freezing. Rept. Food Investigation Bd., London, p. 182.

MURATA, T., HAN-SAN KU, and OGATA, K. 1965. Postharvest ripening and storage of banana fruits. I. Respiratory and chemical changes of banana fruits during postharvest ripening. Nippon Shokuhin Kogyo Gakkaishi *12,* No. 4, 121–125 (Japan); cf: CA *64,* No. 11 1966, No. 16534h.

MURRAY, K. E., PALMER, J. K., WHITFIELD, F. B., KENNETT, B. H., and STANLEY, G. 1968. Volatile alcohols of ripe bananas. J. Food Sci. *33,* 632–634.

MUSTARD, M. J. 1945. The ascorbic acid content of some Florida-grown guavas. Florida Agr. Expt. Sta. Bull. *412.*

ORR, K. J., and MILLER, C. 1955. Description and quality of some mango varieties grown in Hawaii and their suitability for freezing. Hawaii Agric. Expt. Sta. Technical Bull. *26.*

OTAGAKI, K. K., and MATSUMOTO, H. 1958. Nutritive value and utility of passion-fruit by products. J. Agr. Food Chem. *6,* 54–57.

PALMER, J. K. 1963. Banana polyphenoloxidase preparation and properties. Plant Physiol. *38,* 508–513.

PARKER, M. E., and LITCHFIELD, J. H. 1962. Food Plant Sanitation. Reinhold Publishing Corp., New York.

POORE, H. D. 1935. Passion-fruit products. Fruit Prod. J. *14,* 264–266, 285.

PRUTHI, J. S. 1958. Organic acids in passion-fruit (*Passiflora edulis*) juice. J. Sci. Ind. Research (India) *B17,* 238.

PRUTHI, J. S. 1959A. Chemistry and technology of passion-fruit juice (*Passiflora edulis*) Sims—some observations. Food Sci. *8,* 396–397.

PRUTHI, J. S. 1959B. Preservation and storage of passion-fruit juice (*Passiflora edulis*). I. Ascorbic acid retention. Indian Food Packer *13,* No. 7, 7–12.

PRUTHI, J. S. 1959C. Preservation and storage of passion-fruit juice. II. Colour and flavor retention. Indian Food Packer *13,* No. 9. 7–12.

PRUTHI, J. S., and LAL, G. 1955. Technical aspects of manufacture of passion-fruit juice and squash. Chem. Age. India *6,* No. 2, 39–48.

PRUTHI, J. S. and LAL, G. 1958A. Carotenoids in passion-fruit juice. Food Research *23,* 505–510.

PRUTHI, J. S., and LAL, G. 1958B. Fortification of passion-fruit squash with L-ascorbic acid. Indian Food Packer *12,* No. 6, 9–14.

PRUTHI, J. S., and LAL, G. 1959A. Chemical composition of passion fruit (*P. edulis*). J. Sci. Food Agr. *10,* 188–192.

PRUTHI, J. S., and LAL, G. 1959B. Studies on passion-fruit concentrate and powder. Food Sci. *8,* 1–6.

PRUTHI, J. S., and LAI, G. 1959B. Studies on passion-fruit concentrate and (*Passiflora edulis*). Sci. Culture (Calcutta) *30,* No. 1, 48–49.

RAHMAN, A. R., ANZIANI, J., and CRUZ-CAY, J. R. 1964A. Factors affecting the stability of vitamin C in tropical fruit juices and nectars. J. Agr. Univ. Puerto Rico *48,* No. 1, 1–12.

RAHMAN, A. R., ANZIANI J., and NEGRON, E. D. 1964B. Stability of vitamin C at elevated concentrations in canned tropical fruit juices and nectars. J. Agr. Univ. Puerto Rico *48,* No. 4, 327–336.

ROGER. N. F. 1961. The recovery of methyl anthranilate in Concord grape essence. Food Technol. *15,* 309–314.

ROSS, E. 1960. Present and future of mango processing. Hawaii Farm Science *9,* No. 2, 3.

ROSS, E., and CHANG, A. T. 1958. Hydrogen-peroxide induced oxidation of ascorbic acid in passion-fruit juice. J. Agr. Food Chem. *6,* 610–615.

SANCHEZ-NIEVA, F., RODRIQUEZ, A. J., and BENERO, J. R. 1959. Processing and canning mango nectars. Univ. Puerto Rico, Agr. Expt. Sta. Bull. *158.*

SCHWARZ, H. W. 1951. Comparison of low-temperature evaporators. Food Technol. *5,* 476–479.

SCOTT, F. S. 1956. Consumer preferences for frozen passion-fruit juice. Hawaii Agr. Expt. Sta. Agr. Econ. Rept. *29.*

SEAGRAVE-SMITH, H. 1952. Passion fruit is projected for frozen concentrates. Food Eng. *24,* No. 7, 94.

SEAGRAVE-SMITH, H., and SHERMAN, G. D. 1954. How to avoid a "gel" in commercially frozen papaya purée. Hawaii Agr. Expt. Sta. Prog. Notes No. *100.*

SEALE, P. C. 1967. Processing the rarer tropical fruits. Food Technol. Aust. *19,* No. 5, 233–239.

SEALE P. E., and SHERMAN, G. D. 1960. Commercial passion-fruit processing in Hawaii. Hawaii Agr. Expt. Sta. Circ. *58.*

SEELIG, R. A. 1969. Bananas. *In* Fruit and Vegetable Facts and Pointers. United Fresh Fruit and Vegetable Association, Washington, D. C.

SGARBIERI, V. C., and FIGUEIREDO, I. B. 1967. Biochemical transformations occurring during the ripening of bananas. I. The pulp-to-peel ratio, total and soluble solids, organic acids and carbohydrates. An Assoc. Brasil. Quim. *26,* No. 1–2, 49–66 (Portuguese); cf: CA*68,* No. 12, 1968; No. 104004z.

SHAW, T. N., SAKATA, S., BOYLE, F. P., and SHERMAN, G. D. 1955. Hawaii tropical fruit flavors. Hawaii Agr. Expt. Sta. Circ. No. *49.*

SHERMAN, G. D., COOK, C. K., and NICHOLS, E. 1953. Pectin from passion-fruit rinds. Hawaii Agr. Expt. Sta. Progr. Notes *92.*

SOUTH AFRICAN BUREAU OF STANDARDS. 1949. Specifications for granadilla squash. S. Africa Bureau Standards *68.*

SREEKANTIAH, K. R., JALEEL, S. A., and RAO, T. N. R. 1968. Preparation of fruit juice by enzymic processing. J. Food Sci. Technol. *5,* No. 3, 129–132.

STAFFORD, A. E., CAVALETTO, C. G., and BREKKE, J. E. 1966. Papaya purée processing. Hawaii Agr. Expt. Sta. Technical Progress Rept. *157.*

TONAKI, K., BREKKE, J., and FRANK, H. 1967. Banana purée. University of Hawaii, Coop. Ext. Serv., Circ. *418*.

TRESSLER, D. K., and JOSLYN, M. A. 1961. Fruit and Vegetable Juice Processing Technology. Avi Publishing Co., Westport, Conn.

U. S. DEPT. AGR. 1962. Chemistry and technology of citrus, citrus products, and byproducts. Agr. Res. Serv., Agr. Handbook 98.

U. S. DEPT. AGR. 1967A. U. S. Standards for grades of frozen concentrated sweetened grape juice. Agr. Marketing Serv.

U. S. DEPT. AGR. 1967B. Fruit situation. Econ. Res. Serv., *TFS-162*.

VAL, G., SIDDAPPA, G. S., and TANDON, G. L. 1959. Fruit juices, squashes and cordials. *In*: Preservation of fruits and vegetables. Chapter VIII, 84–114. Indian Council Agr. Research, New Delhi, India.

VERMA, A. R., and SRIVASTAVA, J. C. 1966. Pectin in guava during growth and maturity. Indian J. Hort. *22*, No. 3/4, 319–321.

WALDT, L. M. and MAHONEY, R. D. 1967. Depectinizing guava juice with fungal pectinase. Food Technol. *21*, 305–307.

WALKER, L. H. 1961. Volatile flavor recovery. *In* Fruit and Vegetable Juice Processing Technology, D. K. Tressler, and M. A. Joslyn (Editors). Avi Publishing Co., Westport, Conn.

WALKER, L. H., and PATTERSON, D. C. 1955. A new improved process for pear juice concentrate. Western Canner and Packer *47*, No. 12, 22, 24, 54–55.

WANG, J. K., and ROSS, E. 1965. Spin processing for tropical fruit juices. Agr. Eng. *46*, No. 3, 154–156.

WICK, E. L., MCCARTHY, A. I., MYERS, M., MURRAY, E., NURSTEN, H., and ISSENBERG, P. 1966. Flavor and biochemistry of volatile banana components. Advan. Chem. Ser. *56*, 241–260.

WYMAN, H., and PALMER, J. K. 1964. Organic acids in the ripening banana fruit. Plant Physiol. *39*, 630–633.

YAMAMOTO, H. Y., and INOUYE, W. 1963. Sucrose as a gelation inhibitor of commercially frozen papaya purée. Hawaii Agr. Expt. Sta. Tech. Progress Rept. *137*.

YEE, W. 1963. The mango in Hawaii. Univ. Hawaii Cooperative Exten. Serv. Circ. *338*.

YEH, C. M. 1970. Guava juice beverage processing. Food Industries (Food Processing Institute, Taiwan) *2*, No. 1, 10–13.

CHAPTER 10

B. S. Luh

Nectars, Pulpy Juices and Fruit Juice Blends

INTRODUCTION

The production and preservation of fruit nectars, pulpy juices, and fruit juice blends is of great commercial importance. Many fruit juices are either too acid or too strongly flavored to be pleasant beverages without diluting or blending, or both (Pederson and Beattie 1943). Often these strong, tart juices are delicious after dilution with thin syrup or bland juice (Tressler 1961). Examples of the juices of this type are apricot, cranberry, currant, guava, and plum juice. On the other hand, some juices do not have enough flavor, and they are greatly improved if the entire fruit, with the exception of the skin and seeds, is converted into a smooth pulpy beverage.

The term "fruit nectars" is used by the industry to designate pulpy fruit juices blended with sugar syrup and citric acid to produce a ready-to-drink beverage. These beverages, although they resemble fruit juices in flavor, cannot be called fruit juices because of the presence of added water, sugar, and acid. They vary from nearly clear liquids to mixtures high in suspended solids. The commercial pack of fruit nectars consists chiefly of apricot and peach nectars with small amount of pear and plum nectars.

Nectars made from banana, guava, mango, papaya, and passion fruit have been packaged in Hawaii, Puerto Rico, and other areas. The readers are referred to Chapter 9 of this book, entitled "Tropical Fruit Beverages," for details of such products.

Many fruit nectars contain not less than 50% pure juice, either single strength, or reconstituted concentrate (Cruess 1958; Moyls 1966). Essences, vitamins, pectin, sugar, and acid may be added. Fruit juice drinks usually contain not less than 20% juice, either single strength or reconstituted from frozen or canned concentrates. Artificial flavor, color, acid, pectin, and other additives, as permitted by government regulations, may be added.

The definitions and standards of identity for canned fruit nectars have been established (Anon. 1968A).

"Canned fruit nectars are the pulpy, liquid foods prepared from one or more fruits, water, one or more sweeteners, and optional ingredients. The consistency of the finished product is such that the time of flow is not less than 30 sec by the

---

B. S. Luh is Food Technologist, Department of Food Science and Technology, University of California, Davis, Calif.

method of Lamb and Lewis (CA *53:* 14377h). The food is sealed in a container and processed by heat to prevent spoilage. The fruit ingredients are the purée, pulp, juice, or concentrate equivalent to 40% of the finished food (except where otherwise specified) as follows: apples, apricots (35%), blackberry, boysenberry, cherry, guava (25%), loganberry, mango, nectarine, papaya (33%), passion fruit, peach, pear, pineapple, and plum. Apples, cherries, passion fruit, and pineapples are used only in combination with other fruit. The sweeteners are: sugar, invert sugar syrup, dried corn syrup, glucose syrup, and dried glucose syrup. The optional ingredients are lemon juice, citric, malic, and fumaric acid as acidifiers, and ascorbic acid as an antioxidant (150 ppm) or as a vitamin (30–60 mg/4 fl oz)."

If the canned nectars are shipped in interstate commerce, the general provisions of the Food and Drug Act of 1938, sections 401 and 701, still apply.

Food processors must also comply with state and local regulations for areas in which they operate. In addition to the name of the product, name and address of the packer or distributor and the net contents in fluid measurement, the label must bear a list of all the ingredients, including water, in the order of their predominance.

Fresh or frozen fruit is preferred for making nectars. Canned fruit may be used, but it will not produce a flavor or color as acceptable as fresh or frozen fruit. Nectars afford an outlet for the more mature fruit which would not satisfactorily stand processing. Tree-ripened fruit is preferred for most fruit nectars. Fruit juice accumulated during pitting or slicing operations may be diverted to the production of nectars. Sometimes, nectar is packed during the off-season from purée originally packed in five-gal or No. 10 cans.

APRICOT PURÉE AND APRICOT BEVERAGES

In the fresh state, apricot is difficult to market because it softens quickly on ripening. Because of this, it is used principally for canning and dehydration. Apricots for nectar manufacture should be so ripe that they are soft. Purée or nectar prepared from the firm fruit, such as is used for canning, will be of inferior flavor and color. Tree-ripened fruit possesses a better flavor than that permitted to ripen after picking. Since apricots ripen unevenly, it is necessary to harvest 3 or 4 times in order to obtain the best flavored fruit.

Preparation of Sweetened Apricot Purée

Washed and pitted apricot halves are steamed until soft, and then passed through an expeller screw extractor with a 0.033-in. screen of the type commonly used for making tomato juice. One part of sugar is added to 3 of pulp. The product is filled into No. 1 plain cans, exhausted 8 to 10 min, sealed, processed at 212°F for 20 to 25 min, and cooled in water.

Courtesy of Food Processing Institute, Hsinchu, Taiwan

FIG. 95. PULPER AND FINISHER

The undiluted product prepared in this way is of purée consistency, and requires dilution with water before use as a beverage. Apricot purée diluted with sugar syrup prior to canning gives an especially attractive beverage.

Apricot Nectar

The process used for making apricot nectar may be briefly described as follows: Soft ripe apricots are thoroughly washed, and then passed over an inspection belt to eliminate damaged fruit and foreign matter. The fruit is steamed in a continuous steam cooker for approximately 5 min. The hot fruit is then run through a brush finisher equipped with 0.025 to 0.033 in. screen (Fig. 95). The resulting purée is then passed through a steam heated tubular heat exchanger where it is brought to a temperature of 190°–200°F. The purée is sweetened with approximately 1.8 times its volume of 15° to 16° Brix sugar syrup acidified with citric acid. The amount and concentration of sugar syrup and citric acid is adjusted so as to maintain a constant total solids-acid ratio throughout the season. The resulting nectar is filled into plain cans, exhausted for approximately 6 min and sealed. No. 1 tall cans are processed for 15 min at 212°F; larger cans are given a longer process.

In some canneries the purée is mixed with the acidified sugar syrup, flash heated at 205°F in a steam heated tubular heat exchanger and filled immediately; the cans are sealed, inverted and then cooled with sprays of cold water.

The apricot possesses a flavor that blends remarkably well with many other types of fruit. Replacement of all, or part of the cane sugar syrup ordinarily used, with other fruit juices such as orange or pineapple, yields very acceptable products. This is particularly true when blends of apricot pulp and the more acid fruit juices are made.

Apricot Concentrate

Apricot purées are concentrated for shipment to consuming centers where they may be combined with syrup to prepare nectars for distribution in cans.

The purées are prepared by steaming fully ripe apricot, puréeing through a pulper equipped with a 0.033-in. screen, and straining through a finisher. Steaming the fruit in a screw steamer inactivates enzymes. Ponting *et al.* (1954) demonstrated that during preparation apricot purée must be heated sufficiently to inactivate the enzyme polyphenoloxidase if a frozen product of high quality is to be obtained. Scraped-surface heat exchangers have been suggested for transferring heat to concentrated products. Some evaporator designs embody scraped surfaces. There are also available, cylindrical scraped surface heat exchangers developed from continuous ice cream freezers. This equipment is suitable for heating and cooling concentrates. It is also suitable for freezing concentrates to be distributed or stored in frozen form.

Concentrates are preserved by hot filling in small tight containers, by presterilizing, cooling and sterile-packing in tight containers, by refrigeration, by frozen storage and to some extent by solids content unfavorable for growth of spoilage organisms. Concentrated products can be sterilized by high temperature-short time procedures and aseptically filled in sterile drums and other bulk containers for storage and for shipment to population centers where fruit juice and nectars can be packed and distributed at minimum expense.

TABLE 75

CHEMICAL ANALYSES OF WHOLE APRICOTS

Product	Ash, %	Brix, 20°C	Total Solids, %	Water Insoluble Solids, %	Alcohol Insoluble Solids, %	Formol Index	Total Acidity (as Citric Acid), %	pH
Blenheim Apricots								
1	0.82	13.2	15.0	2.03	3.50	5.14	0.89	4.05
2	0.67	12.8	14.4	1.85	3.53	3.93	0.94	3.85
3	0.69	13.5	15.4	1.90	4.02	3.90	1.05	3.68
4	0.78	13.4	15.2	1.98	3.49	3.79	1.01	3.86
5	0.82	17.1	19.1	2.55	3.66	2.16	0.93	3.88
6	0.71	14.6	16.8	2.74	3.81	4.61	0.93	3.90
Tilton Apricots								
1	0.63	12.5	13.7	2.02	3.38	3.68	1.03	3.90
2	0.57	12.8	14.0	1.41	3.39	4.18	0.76	4.02
3	0.67	12.1	13.6	1.74	3.21	4.08	0.75	4.10
4	0.55	13.1	14.6	2.16	2.94	4.36	0.60	4.20
5	0.46	10.7	12.0	2.76	3.14	4.94	0.68	3.90
6	0.57	14.6	16.0	2.21	2.53	6.22	0.58	4.35

Source: Elkins and Lamb (1969).

Packages used for storing and transporting concentrates vary in size from heat-sealed, one-ounce plastic pouches to tanks with thousands of gallons capacity. Tanks may be stationary or mounted on trucks or in the holds of ships.

Packaging materials include plastic films, glass, tin plate, stainless steel, and mild steel with tin or plastic coatings.

Storage temperatures range from below zero to as high as 80°F. The rate of deterioration varies with each product, but in general is directly proportional to storage temperatures.

Products may be commercially sterile or they may depend upon composition and storage temperatures to prevent growth of microorganisms. Presterilization and cooling in scraped surface or other heat exchangers, followed by sterile filling in hermetically sealed tinned drums, or stainless steel tanks is coming into increasing use for storing fruit concentrate for subsequent use. Where concentrated products are to be held in large containers in frozen storage, slush freezing prior to packaging is used. Scraped-surface, direct-expansion freezers can congeal half the water present, speeding up the freezing process and avoiding coring and segregation of concentrates in drums or tanks.

When sterile products are to be stored in large containers, heat can be applied uniformly in scraped-surface heat exchangers and the product (under pressure) can be cooled to a noninjurious temperature for filling aseptically in presterilized storage vessels.

Fruit Content of Apricot Nectars

There is now increased concern for reliable and equitable methods for the determination of fruit content of nectars and fruit juice drinks. The possibility exists that different manufacturing procedures utilized in the

TABLE 76

CHEMICAL ANALYSES OF APRICOT PULP AND NECTARS

Pulp	Ash, %	Brix, 20°C	Total Solids, %	Water Insoluble Solids, %	Alcohol Insoluble Solids, %	Formol Index	Total Acidity (as Citric Acid), %	pH
Whole Fruit								
1	0.67	11.0	12.0	1.26	2.73	4.11	0.74	4.30
2	0.56	11.2	12.2	1.22	2.56	2.83	0.77	3.95
3	0.65	12.4	13.5	1.40	2.45	2.55	0.87	3.90
4	0.63	11.7	12.6	0.86	2.41	3.22	0.84	3.90
5	0.64	12.7	14.7	2.33	3.92	4.77	0.93	4.10
6	0.61	10.5	11.5	1.07	2.93	1.99	0.66	4.33
Nectar								
1	0.31	14.2	14.9	0.76	1.38	2.02	0.47	4.00
2	0.27	14.6	14.8	0.48	1.54	1.57	0.46	3.78
3	0.29	14.5	15.1	0.66	1.62	1.49	0.48	3.90
4	0.26	14.3	14.7	0.62	1.38	1.72	0.46	3.83
5	0.29	14.1	15.1	0.59	1.87	1.88	0.45	3.95
6	0.25	14.2	15.0	0.72	1.29	1.34	0.47	4.00

Source: Elkins and Lamb (1969).

preparation of the various fruit nectars and juice drinks may alter their composition in such a way that one or more of the elements or compounds used as indices may no longer be present in the same proportion as in the original fruit. Elkins and Lamb (1969) investigated the reliability of a variety of chemical indices of fruit content in nectars and fruit juice drinks. Authentic samples of apricot and pear nectars were prepared and analyzed.

Table 75 presents a part of their results on a number of samples of whole apricots, and Table 76 on apricot purée and nectars. Considering only the determinations which would not be affected by the pure ingredients that are added to apricot nectars (primarily sugar and acid), ash, water insoluble solids, formol index, and inorganic constituents might be usable as indices of fruit content. Calculation of standard deviation and coefficient of variability on the results obtained on raw apricots gives an estimation of the suitability of any index for enforcement of a minimum fruit content requirement. Ash, formol index and total acidity, do not change significantly as a result of screening but the total solids, water insoluble solids and alcohol insoluble solids decrease from 0.4 to 0.5%. Any index based on insoluble solids would have to take this factor into consideration. A more reliable index of fruit content may be obtained if more than a single factor were considered. For example, a combination of ash and water or alcohol insoluble solids might provide a better index than either one alone.

Beisel and Kitchel (1967) discussed factors for determining juice content by objective tests. In their opinion, only multiple regression analysis of the factors exhibiting narrowest ranges in variance will be of probative value in regulating diluted fruit juice beverages. Analytical pursuit of this problem is proceeding on an international scale. Recent work on betaine by Lewis (1966) shows some promise.

Osborn (1964) presented data on the chemical composition of fruit and fruit juices collected from principal areas of production in the United

TABLE 77

VOLATILE COMPONENTS OF APRICOT

Retention Data on Apricot Volatiles[1]

Compound	Peak	Carbowax 20M Known	Carbowax 20M Apricot	SF 96-50 Known	SF 96-50 Apricot
Myrcene	8	0.20	0.20	0.58	0.58
Limonene	10	0.27	0.27	0.71	0.71
p-Cymene	13	0.27		0.66	0.66
Terpinolene	14	0.39	0.38	0.54	0.57
Trans-2-Hexenol	17	0.54		0.29	0.29
Acetic acid	18			0.10	
Epoxydihydrolinalool(I)	20	0.72	0.72		
Epoxydihydrolinalool(II)	21	0.82	0.82		
Linalool	22	1.00	1.00	1.00	1.00
2-Methylbutyric acid	27			0.35	0.33
α-Terpineol	28	2.05	2.06	1.57	1.73
Geranial	29	2.67	2.50	2.25	2.24
Geraniol	32	3.79	3.79	2.61	2.60
γ-Octalactone	35	5.12[2]	4.94[2]	2.46	2.50
γ-Decalactone	37	10.67[2]	10.44[2]	6.45	6.26

Source: Tang and Jennings (1967).
[1] All retentions were determined on 500 ft × 0.03-in. capillary columns at 302°F except as noted. Retentions are relative to linalool.
[2] Retentions determined at 356°F.

States. Analytical determinations were concentrated on the constituents needed to estimate the fruit content of fruit juice drinks and other mixtures containing these fruits. Quantitative data were given on soluble solids, total sugars, ash, K_2O, P_2O_5, and acidity of fruits and fruit products made from apple, apricot, berries, cherry, crabapple, currant, fig, grape, guava, peach, pear, pineapple, plum, and quince. These data may be used to estimate the fruit content of fruit juice drinks and other mixtures containing these fruits.

Volatile Components of Apricots

Apricot fruit has a strong characteristic aroma which also exists in the canned apricot nectar. Tang and Jennings (1967) studied volatile components of Blenheim apricot (*Prunus armeniaca*). Through gas chromatography and infrared spectroscopic spectra of the isolated fractions, the volatile components of apricot were identified (Table 77). The typical apricot aroma appears to be due to an integrated response to the proper ratios of these compounds. Tang and Jennings (1968) subjected a charcoal adsorption essence of Blenheim apricots to repetitive gas chromatographic separations. The isolated components were characterized by infrared spectroscopy as benzyl alcohol, caproic acid, epoxydihydrolinalool IV, γ-caprolactone, γ-octalactone, δ-octalactone, δ-decalactone, γ-decalactone, δ-decalactone, and γ-dodecalactone. The aroma of apricots improved as the fruit ripened (Luh 1961).

Polyphenolic and Nitrogenous Compounds

Polyphenolic compounds in canned Blenheim apricots were investigated by El-Sayed and Luh (1965). They were extracted from the aqueous infusions of canned apricots with ethyl acetate, separated by paper chromatography, and identified by their Rf values, fluorescent behavior, absorption spectra, and degradation products. Shown to be present were three chlorogenic acid isomers, two *p*-coumaric acid derivatives, rutin, isoquercitin, quercitin, an unidentified quercitin glucoside, catechin, and epicatechin. The predominant polyphenolic compounds were chlorogenic acids and *p*-coumaric acid derivatives. Some of the phenolic compounds such as chlorogenic acid, catechin, and epicatechin are substrates of the enzyme polyphenoloxidase, and are related to enzymatic browning in apricot products.

The level of nitrogen fertilization applied in the orchard was reflected in the nitrogen content of apricots (El-Sayed and Luh 1967). Total nitrogen and amino nitrogen in the fruit increased as the nitrogen fertilizer level increased. Apricot trees fertilized with 2.5 and 5.5 lb nitrogen per tree yielded fruits of better flavor after canning than those fertilized with 0.5 lb nitrogen.

PEACH NECTAR

Freestone Peach Nectar

Yellow freestone peaches are preferred for the manufacture of peach nectar because of their delicate flavor and thinner consistency after heat processing. Tree-ripened Elberta freestone peaches are generally used for nectar manufacture. The J. H. Hale, South Haven, and Golden Jubilee varieties are also suitable. Champion is a suitable white variety. Beavens and Beattie (1942) recommend the following procedure for the preparation of peach nectar:

The peaches are thoroughly washed, halved, pitted, and passed over an inspection belt to remove damaged fruit and foreign material. Peeling is also required for most varieties, especially if the fruit is not fully ripe, otherwise a bitter flavored nectar may result. The procedure for peeling peaches was described by Postlmayr *et al.* (1956). The peaches were halved and pitted in a Filper twist pitter. The peach halves were peeled in a cup-down peeler by spraying with 1% sodium hydroxide solution at 212°F for 15 sec. They were held in the holding section for 60 sec and then spray washed with cold tap water. Fully ripe freestone peach halves can be peeled with steam at 212°F for 1 to 2 min. Immediately after scalding, the fruit should be cooled either with water sprays or by immer-

Courtesy of Fryma-Maschinen AG.

FIG. 96. VACUUM DEAERATOR

sion in cold water. After cooling, the skins are rubbed off. This method is more time consuming than the lye-peeling method.

It may be necessary, with some fruit, to treat the prepared raw fruit immediately after peeling with an ascorbic or citric acid solution prior to finishing. This will retard discoloration of the product.

The peeled peach halves should be heated in a steam jacketed kettle or a continuous steam cooker to 180°F and run through a fruit disintegrator. The resulting purée is then run through a finisher with a 0.020–0.033 in. screen. A ton of fruit yields approximately 130 gal of purée. To each 100 gal of purée 63.5 gal of 30° Brix sucrose syrup should be added. The syrup may be prepared from three parts sucrose and one part dextrose.

It may be necessary to add a small quantity of citric acid to adjust the pH of the nectar to 3.7–3.9. It is advisable to pass the finished nectars through a vacuum deaerator (Fig. 96) prior to pasteurization. This procedure will eliminate the air which has been incorporated in the product during preparation. Excess air in the nectar will lead to deterioration of color and flavor.

The high temperature-short time flash pasteurization process is the most convenient method of heat treatment for fruit nectars. If the pH of product is below 4.5, the product may be flash pasteurized for 30 sec at 230°F. Continuous flow, plate or tubular, heat exchangers are used for this purpose.

For peach nectars, cans made from plain hot dipped or differential electrolytic tin plate bodies and enameled ends are recommended. The empty cans should be protected from dampness and steam, and kept as clean as possible during storage. The can handling methods employed should be designed to prevent scratching or denting, particularly of the flange.

Immediately after pasteurization, the nectar should be filled into the cans, closed at a temperature of 190°F, inverted, and given a holding period of approximately 3 min prior to cooling. If flash pasteurization methods are not available, the nectars can be filled hot, closed, and processed for 20–30 min at 212°F when packed in cans larger than No. 1 size. No. 1 cans and smaller ones should be processed at 212°F for 15 to 20 min. Some packers practice a method of filling at 190°F, closing, holding, and cooling, but this practice may not adequately insure against spoilage caused by heat-resistant bacterial spores.

After holding or processing, the cans should be cooled immediately in water until the average temperature of the contents reaches 95°–105°F. The cooling water should contain 2 ppm available chlorine. If cooling is not thorough before the cans are cased, serious discoloration and a poor flavor may result. If the cans are cased much below 95°F they may not dry thoroughly and rusting may result.

Canned fruit nectars should be stored in a cool dry place. The warehouse must be dry at all times to prevent rusting of the cans, staining of the labels, and weakening of the fiber cases. Storage at 50°–60°F considerably increases the shelf-life of the canned nectars.

The same process may also be used to make nectarine nectar.

Improvement of Peach Nectar

Pressed peach juice, i.e., that free from pulp was found by Beavens and Beattie (1942) to be somewhat better than sugar syrup for thinning the pulpy juice; a ratio of 2 parts pulpy juice to 1 part of pressed juice was recommended.

Peach juices should be handled as rapidly as possible in order to prevent browning and oxidation. Further, direct contact with air or any treatment which incorporates air in the juice should be avoided.

Lee and Pederson (1950) suggest certain improvements in the process based upon their findings that a good yield of excellently flavored juice could be obtained by pressing fruit which had been frozen at 15°F and later thawed. A blend of the pressed juice so obtained with a puréed product resulted in a smooth textured, palatable nectar that retained the peach flavor characteristics. The fully ripened halved peaches are steam blanched for 3 min, cooled, peeled and frozen in enameled tins placing enough ascorbic acid on the surface of the peaches to obtain a level of about 40 mg per 100 gm. Later the fruit is thawed and part of the peaches are pressed in a hydraulic press and part made into a purée as described above. The clear juice and purée are then blended to give the desired consistency and sweetened to a desired flavor. Two and one-half per cent of sugar was found sufficient for well matured fruit. The proportions should be varied with different lots of fruit, but as little as 15 to 25% of purée were most pleasing. The nectar was pasteurized at 180°F, filled into bottles, capped and cooled. It was stated that the freezing process results in a more flavorous and viscous juice than can be obtained by pressing the unfrozen peaches. The same principle may also be applied to preparation of nectars from plums or apricots or similar fruits which require some puréed fruit to impart satisfactory flavor. The method is, however, more time consuming than the direct heating procedure.

Wilson *et al.* (1957) proposed an objective method for evaluating color and consistency of peach purée which should aid in obtaining uniform products commercially Luh *et al.* (1959) reported on the aseptic canning of peach and apricot nectars. The physical and chemical properties of the canned nectars were evaluated objectively.

Peach Purée as a Base for Drinks

Heaton *et al.* (1966) studied the effect of ripeness level and peeling on quality of peach purée for juice drinks made from clingstone, semi-cling and freestone peaches. They reported that several of the cling and semi-cling varieties were satisfactory for juice drink base when blended with late maturing freestone peaches. Lye peeling improved the appearance, aroma, color, and flavor of the product. The peel, if not removed, caused poor color and bitter flavor in the product. The steps in the preparation of the peach purée base were as follows:

"(1) Receive fruit within 12 hr after picking.
(2) Cool fruit to be held overnight, and ripen that which is not yet soft.
(3) Grade for ripeness and freedom from defects. Select worm-free, rot-free, soft fruit of any variety.
(4) Peel by immersing in, or spraying with, 5% lye at 210°F for 30 sec; then expose to air for 1–2 min.
(5) Wash with rotary or spray washer.
(6) Wash lightly in soft brush washer, remove rotten spots by trimming, and rewash.
(7) Heat whole fruit in a continuous thermoscrew for 2 min at 200°F to aid in pulping, prevent oxidation and stabilize cloud in purée. A jacket around the screw should maintain 20 lb steam pressure.
(8) Pulp by passing through a continuous rotary unit with $^1/_4$ in. perforated screens to remove soft flesh from seed and unripe portions.
(9) Finish the pulp by passing through rotary unit with 0.033 in. or 0.024 in. perforated, stainless steel screen. This reduces pulp to liquid and removes fiber.
(10) Accumulate in tank, add 0.14% ascorbic acid and mix, then feed uniformly to pasteurizer.

(11) Pasteurize at 190°–200°F and cool quickly to 35°F.
(12) Fill aseptically into sterile 55-gal drums or large cans for refrigerated storage. Filling hot in No. 10 or smaller size cans may also be used.
(13) Close cans using vacuum and nitrogen, or vacuumize with steam jet.
(14) Cool cans (which were not already cool) in canal or water spray.
(15) Dry cans with warm air to remove water drops and avoid rusting or staining of labels.
(16) Label containers, use code identification.
(17) Store in cool dry place."

Peach Volatiles

The attractive aroma of peach nectar is derived from the volatile components present in the fresh fruit at the optimum ripeness level. Lim and Romani (1964) used direct gas chromatography as a tool for the investigation of the relation between emanation of volatiles and the harvest maturity of peaches. The presence of detectable volatiles depend markedly on maturity at harvest. Deshpande and Salunkhe (1964) reported that volatile reducing substances and soluble solids of fresh freestone peaches increased with maturity and storage, while firmness, acidity and pectin decreased. Jennings (1967) summarized the volatile components of Red Globe peaches (Table 78). He stated that both pears and peaches contain a number of low-molecular weight volatiles that are widely and indiscriminately distributed among most fruits. Some of the components, however, would appear to be unique to the fruit investigated, e.g., the lactones and pyrone to peach (Jennings and Sevenants 1964A; Sevenants and Jennings 1966). In the process of maturation fruits produce an abundance of compounds, many of which are probably related to flavor. Broderick (1966) also studied the composition of peach volatiles with respect to their influence on flavor. The γ-lactones and decalactones were important flavor components. In addition to linalool, acetic acid, isovaleric acid, caprylic acid, acetaldehyde, furfural, isoamyl acetate, and hexylacetate were re-

TABLE 78

VOLATILE COMPONENTS OF RED GLOBE PEACHES

Acetaldehyde	Ethyl benzoate
Methyl acetate	Gamma-caprolactone
Ethyl acetate	Benzyl acetate
Ethyl alcohol	Gamma-heptalactone
Hexyl formate	Caproic acid
Hexyl acetate	Benzyl alcohol
Trans-2-hexenyl acetate	Gamma-octalactone
Hexyl alcohol	Gamma-nonalactone
Acetic acid	Hexyl benzoate
Trans-2-hexene-1-01	Gamma decalactone
Benzaldehyde	Alpha-pyrone
Iso-valeric acid	Delta-decalactone

Source: Jennings (1967).

ported. The compounds γ-dodecalactone, ethyl butyrate, ethyl isovalerate, ethyl caproate, methyl salicylate, butyric acid, caproic acid, capric acid, isoamyl, *n*-hexyl and phenyl ethyl alcohols, γ-terpineol, and methyl amyl ketone were also present in the peach.

Leucoanthocyanins and Anthocyanins

Leucoanthocyanins are shown to be present in immature Elberta freestone peaches (Hsia *et al.* 1964). The quantity of leucoanthocyanins in Red Globe freestone peaches decreased from 180 mg/100 gm in the green fruit to 58.0 mg/100 gm at the canning ripe stage (Luh and Villarreal 1964). The leucoanthocyanin in the fresh peach appears to be related to the discoloration problem in the canned product. The anthocyanin pigment in Elberta freestone peaches has been identified as cyanidin 3-monoglucoside (Hsia *et al.* 1965). It was demonstrated that varietal characteristics and ripeness level of the peach were important factors influencing the anthocyanin content which increased as the peaches ripen on the tree.

Pectin

The consistency of peach nectar may vary with the ripeness level of the fresh fruit. The pectic and cellulose materials present in the peach are important to the flow characteristics of peach nectar. The influence of maturity and processing methods on pectic changes, texture, and syrup viscosity of canned Elberta freestone peaches were investigated by Postlmayr *et al.* (1956). The protopectin in the cell wall was converted into water-soluble pectin during ripening of freestone peaches. The intrinsic viscosity of pectic materials isolated from canned clingstone peach by the versene extraction method decreased from 9.6 to 7.2 as the average pressure test of the fresh fruit decreased from 10.4 to 5.1 lb. In contrast, intrinsic viscosity of pectins from canned freestones dropped sharply from 6.8 to 1.9 as the pressure test of the fresh fruit decreased from 11.9 to 0.85 lb. The syrup viscosities of canned peaches were lower when riper fruits were used in canning. Extended processing time increased the syrup viscosity of clingstones canned at optimum maturity, but had no effect on the syrup viscosity of soft ripe freestones. Watkins (1964) studied the changes in pectic substances of stored Elberta peaches. Total and soluble pectic substances were determined in Elberta peaches harvested mature-green, stored at 30° or 34°F for 7–29 days, and when ripened for 7 days at 70°F. In fruit which ripened normally after cold storage, the level of total pectic substances was approximately half that of the green fruit. Abnormal ripening of fruit cold-stored longer than two weeks was associated with woodiness and little or no loss of total pectic substances. Treatment at 70°F with ethylene gas at 1000 ppm for 2 days prior to cold storage eliminated woodiness but caused musty breakdown in overstored fruit. Irreversible binding of pectin methylesterase to cell walls during cold storage was postulated to explain the abnormal ripening.

Hydroxymethyl Furfural (HMF)

The effect of storage temperature on HMF formation in canned peach purées was reported by Trifiro (1962). The formation of this compound in fruit purée is favored by high storage temperatures and severe processing conditions. Similar results were obtained by Luh and Kamber (1963) on formation of HMF in canned apple sauce made from Gravenstein apples and sucrose under commercial processing conditions. It was shown that undesirable chemical and color changes occurred rapidly at 86° and 98°F. Quality deterioration was related to HMF formation and sucrose inversion which was rapid at higher storage temperatures. For better quality retention and a longer storage life, the canned product should be stored at 68°F or lower. Porretta and Giannone (1963) studied the effect of storage temperature on peach and apricot purées. Storage at temperatures below 68°F are needed to preserve the organoleptic, physical, and nutritive properties of peach and apricot purées. Owing to the effect of concentration on the rate of deterioration, single strength purées keep longer than concentrated purées under the same temperature conditions.

Polyphenoloxidase

Freestone peach tends to undergo enzymatic browning if the peeled fruits are delayed in processing. Nakabayashi and Ukai (1963) studied enzymatic browning in white and yellow peaches. They were able to demonstrate the presence of strong polyphenoloxidase activity in all the eight peach varieties used in their investigation. Chlorogenic acid, *l*-epicatechin, and leucocyanidin were detected as polyphenol components by paper chromatography. The degree of browning paralleled the polyphenol content of the varieties. Sodium chloride and ascorbic acid can inhibit enzymatic browning.

Ascorbic and isoascorbic acids are equally effective in inhibiting enzymatic browning in peaches (Reyes and Luh 1962). They could inhibit polyphenolase-catalyzed oxidation of phenolic substrates, whether in model systems or in fruit tissue, but could not be used to decolorize the substrates once they were extensively oxidized. Both antioxidants can be used in canning and freezing of freestone peach products. The effectiveness of ascorbic and isoascorbic acid in inhibiting the darkening of frozen peaches thawed at 34° and 68°F was evaluated by changes in total phenolic compounds, antioxidants, and brown-colored slices. Both the control and the ascorbic-acid-treated samples lost total phenolic compounds approxi-

TABLE 79

CHEMICAL ANALYSES OF THE BEST PULPY AND PRESSED PEAR JUICES

Variety and Process[1]	pH	Total Acidity as Malic, gm/100 ml	Total Sugar as Invert, gm/100 ml	Soluble Solids by Refractive Index
	1938			
Seckel, CP (diluted 3:1 with CP crab-apple juice)	3.68	0.40	13.12	15.5
	1939			
d'Anjou, HSS 150°F (diluted 2:1 with Greening apple juice)	3.65	0.45	9.9	13.9
	1940			
d'Anjou, HSS 185°F (diluted 2:1 with Baldwin apple juice)	3.83	0.34	...	14.8
Vermont Beauty, HSS 185°F (diluted 2:1 with Cortland apple juice)	3.68	0.38	...	17.0

Source: Beavens and Beattie (1942).
[1] CP, cold-pressed; HSS, hot extraction.

mately twice as rapidly at 68° as at 34°F. No distinct difference in properties was found between the two antioxidants. The characteristics of browning enzymes in Fay Elberta freestone peaches were reported by Reyes and Luh (1960).

PEAR JUICE

Pulpy Juice Blends

Pear juice is low in acid and bland in flavor. The pulpy juice is so thick, that it does not appeal to most people. According to Beavens and Beattie (1942), a blend of pulpy pear juice with tart apple juice in the proportion of 2 to 1 is superior to a blend of the pulpy juice with either sugar syrup or pressed pear juice. The composition of some pear-apple juice blends is shown in Table 79.

Beavens and Beattie (1942) recommend the Vermont Beauty and Beurre d'Anjou varieties for making a pulpy beverage and pressed Seckel pear juice for blending with crabapple juice to obtain a clear pear-crabapple juice blend.

The procedure recommended by Beavens and Beattie for making pulpy pear juice blends involves heating to 180° to 185°F of the washed, halved pears in a steam-jacketed kettle, followed by running the hot fruit through a continuous extractor fitted with a 0.020-in. screen. Two parts of the pulpy juice thus obtained are blended with one part of a pressed tart apple juice, and the blend deaerated, flash pasteurized at 185°F and filled at this temperature. If crabapple is available, it is advisable to blend three parts of pear purée with one part of crabapple juice.

A pear juice of excellent quality may be prepared from Bartlett or Seckel pears by the same ascorbic acid method worked out for apple juice by Holgate, Moyer, and Pederson (1948).

The more stable pear juice obtained by the process may be used as it is, or blended with puréed pear or other fruits. The juice is superior to ordinary cold pressed juice in color, flavor and consistency.

Pear Nectar

The Bartlett pear is the principal variety used for making nectar. The pears were harvested at 17–20 lb pressure test, stored at 34°F for one week or longer and then ripened at 70°F under 85% relative humidity to 2 to 3 lb pressure test. This usually takes 4–5 days at 70°F (Leonard *et al.* 1954). Pears so ripened are more uniform and better in quality than those without previous cold storage. The pears at optimum ripeness level were washed and mechanically peeled and cored. The pear halves are heated to 185°F and held there for 3 min in a continuous steamer, similar to the type used for making apple sauce. This process inactivates the polyphenoloxidase and inhibits enzymatic browning. Maczynska and Rembowski (1966) steam-blanched pears at 185°F for $2^1/_2$ min to inactivate the polyphenoloxidase. Darkening of pear nectars would occur if the pears contain residual polyphenoloxidase activity caused by improper steam blanching.

The hot fruit is passed through a continuous extractor fitted with a 0.033-in. screen. The hot purée is put through a brush-type finisher fitted with a 0.020–0.030-in. screen. The smooth purée is blended with sugar, citric acid and water to the desired consistency and solids. Usually it has a Brix reading of 13°–15°, and a pH value of 3.9–4.2. The product is flash heated to 205°F in a heat exchanger, filled hot into cans, sealed at a temperature of 190°F or higher, inverted, and given a holding period of 3 min prior to water cooling. Cans made from plain hot dipped or electrolytic tin plate bodies and enameled ends are used.

The product can also be prepared from aseptically canned pear concentrate of 28% solids packed in 55 gal drums.

Clear Pear Juice

Walker and Patterson (1955) reported that the following procedure produces a juice most nearly approaching that of a fresh pear:

> "Washed whole pears are cut into $^1/_4$- to $^3/_8$-in. slices, fed directly into a screw-type blancher or thermoscrew (Fig. 97) and thence into a finisher or cyclone. The resultant purée is cooled to 100°F and depectinized at this temperature for 5 hr with 0.5% of Pectinol A or B. If desired, treatment overnight with the same amount of Pectinol at 65° to 70°F will be suitable. Four to 5%

Courtesy of Rietz Mfg. Co.

FIG. 97. THERMOSCREW

of filter aid is added and the purée is pressed in a rack-and-frame press. The pressed juice is clarified in a pressure filter with precoated plates, following addition of about 0.25% of filter aid to the juice."

Walker and Patterson (1955) have made the following additional suggestions for obtaining a flavorful juice following the procedure outlined above:

"Pears should be ripened to a pressure test of 3–5 lb before processing. Slicing is suggested to shorten the time required in the blancher. The residence time in the screw-type blancher will depend upon the particular unit used, but should lie between 2 and 4 min. The time is determined by testing purée from the finisher with catechol solution and setting the time in the blancher at a figure slightly (about 25%) longer than that needed for a negative test. The screen size in the finisher may range from 0.03 to 0.05 in. The purpose of this operation is to remove seeds and fiber and to convert the pears to a pulp or purée. Treatment with a pectic enzyme serves three purposes. Treated purée is easier to press, juice yields are appreciably higher, and the juice can be filtered to a sparkling clear product.

"Enzymatic degradation of pectins requires a certain length of time and may vary to some extent with the characteristics of various lots of fruit. The measure for completion of treatment is whether a sparkling juice can be obtained from the purée. Two simple tests can be used. A sample of purée can be filtered through filter paper, the first few drops of filtrate discarded, and the remainder examined for clarity. If a small centrifuge is available, a sample can be centrifuged and the upper layer in the tube examined for clarity.

"The amount of filter aid needed will vary with type of press, desired thickness of press cake, and variety of fruit used. Experience under conditions in a particular plant will enable the operator to arrive at a figure representing the minimum quantity that will produce a firm, dry press cake. Filter aid used here and in clarification should be both tasteless and odorless, because the juice will readily absorb odors or flavors. The presence of flavor or odor in the filter aid can be determined by smelling and tasting a water suspension of the particular type and shipment under consideration."

The Walker and Patterson method yields a clear juice of excellent flavor quite different from pear nectar. It is recommended for use in making jellies, and, after concentration, in sherbets, and, after acidification, as a beverage. Brunner (1969) studied clarification of clear pear juice concentrate with gelatin of different grades of purity. In concentrates treated with low-grade gelatin, secondary turbidity occurred within two weeks. No secondary turbidity developed in samples treated with high-grade gelatin. Chromatography on a Sephadex G-100/200 column showed a far higher content of low molecular weight components in the low grade gelatin. These low molecular-weight components are probably responsible for the secondary turbidity.

Pear Concentrate

Pear purée can be concentrated commercially for shipment to consuming areas where it can be combined with sugar, water, and citric acid to prepare pear nectars for distribution in cans. The purée is made in the same way as described in the pear nectar section, except that no acidified sugar syrup was added. Peeled and cored pears yield a better product than using the whole fruit in making the purée. The purée is concentrated in vacuum pans to 28% total solids, and then canned aseptically in 1-gal cans or 55-gal drums. The method for canning pear purée aseptically was described by Luh and Sioud (1966). Cylindrical scraped surface heat exchangers are used for heating and cooling pear concentrates and for aseptic canning.

Factors Influencing Quality of Pears

Maturity of Bartlett pears for canning has been studied by Leonard *et al.* (1954). They reported the effects of storage at 34°F and ripening at 70°F of Bartlett pears harvested at 20 pounds pressure test on their chemical and physical properties. Accompanying ripening at 70°F there was a gradual increase in soluble solids content and a decrease in pressure test and ascorbic acid and tannin content. A selected number of samples canned from fresh pears at average pressure tests ranging from 4.9 to 1.1 lb were evaluated for texture, color, aroma, and flavor. The difference in flavor among these samples due to the variation in maturity of the fresh fruit was significant at the 2% level, whereas the difference in aroma was significant at less than 1%. No significant difference in texture was observed. These results show that fresh Bartlett pears with average pressure test of 2 to 3 lb immediately before peeling were best suited for canning.

There is an interesting correlation between the maturity of fresh pears as measured by pressure test and the amount of volatile reducing substances in the canned product. As the pressure test of the fresh pears decreases, the volatile reducing substances in the canned product increase.

The influence of ripeness of fresh Bartlett pears on flavor and on the quantity of volatile reducing substances in the canned product has been reported by Luh *et al.* (1955). During ripening there was an increase in methyl alcohol, carbonyl compounds, acetyl-methyl-carbinol, diacetyl, and ester content. The rate of production of these volatile compounds was especially rapid as the pressure reading dropped below 2 lb. The presence of a large excess of total volatile reducing substances, methyl alcohol and diacetyl in the canned product might be indicative of off-flavor and overripeness. Pears canned at an average pressure test of 1.5 lb scored highest in flavor. Because of the importance of both texture and flavor to quality of the canned product, it is desirable to use fresh fruit at a pressure test range of 2 to 3 lb for canning. The gradual increase in methyl alcohol content as pears ripen may possibly be explained by the de-esterification of pectin by pectin-esterase.

Claypool *et al.* (1958) harvested Bartlett pears from three of the major pear producing districts in California at 16 to 17 lb pressure test. The fruits were refrigerated at 32°F for 6 days or longer, ripened at 68°, 77°, and 86°F under 85% relative humidity to firmnesses ranging from 3.7 to 1.1 lb. The pears were then canned in 25° Brix sucrose syrup. Bartlett pears from different growing areas differ greatly in volatile reducing substances (VRS). The VRS content in the canned product increased as the firmness of the ripened fruit decreased. Ripening at 86°F resulted in a slightly higher soluble solids content and a lower VRS content, than ripening at the two lower temperatures. Pears ripened at 68°F to a firmness of about 2 lb gave a canned product with more pear flavor than when ripening to the same firmness was conducted at a higher temperature. Firmness at canning time appeared to be as important as ripening temperature in influencing flavor of the canned product. Growing area had less influence on flavor than the other factors studied. The importance of ripening temperature and firmness at canning to flavor of the canned product is evident.

Daepp and Mayer (1964) studied the influence of raw pears on pear juice quality. They extracted juice from pears of good quality stored at 41°F and from damaged fruit stored at 77°F for one week. The juice made from low quality fruits had less total acids and malic acid, and more lactic acid, volatile acid, ethyl alcohol, glycerol, acetoin and diacetyl.

Storage Stability of Pear Purée

Bartlett pear can be processed aseptically as purée. Luh and Sioud (1966) studied stability of canned pear purée stored at 32°, 68°, 86°, and 98°F. At 86° and 98°F a distinct increase in titratable acidity and decrease in pH of the product were observed. No distinct color change was observed in the purée stored 371 days at 32° and 68°F, while darkening was distinct in the samples stored 180 days at 86° and 98°F. Hydroxymethyl-furfural (HMF) was gradually formed in the purée at 86° and 98°F, but not at 32° and 68°F. Presence of HMF in the product indicates poor quality attributable to excessive heat processing or improper post-canning storage, or both. High storage temperature caused corrosion of the tin coating and the formation of hydrogen gas in the headspace.

Pear Volatiles

Progress in the chemistry of pear volatiles has been made during the past decade. Jennings *et al.* (1960) separated essences obtained from fresh, ripe Bartlett pears into 32 fractions by gas chromatography. Each of the fractions was submitted to a trained aroma panel, and five of the fractions appeared to contribute to the desirable pear aroma, while four were classed as a typicaly and undesirable. Drawert (1962) on the basis of matching gas chromatographic retentions, tentatively identified ethyl formate, methyl acetate, ethyl acetate, ethanol, isopropanol, 2-butanol, 2-methyl propanol, *n*-butanol, pentanol, 3-methyl butanol, *n*-hexanol, and another ester in pears. In studies of the lower boiling volatiles from Bartlett pears, Lim (1963) utilized matching retentions on gas chromatography and tentatively identified ethylene, acetaldehyde, and the six normal acetates from methyl to hexyl acetate. Jennings (1961, 1965) and Jennings and Creveling (1963) established that the typical aroma of Bartlett pears was due to esters. They studied the hydrolysis products of pear essence by gas chromatographic separations and infrared and ultraviolet spectroscopy of the individual fractions. These consisted of acetic, propionic, butyric, caproic, caprylic, nonanoic, and 2,4-decadienoic acids, and ethyl, *n*-propyl, *n*-butyl, *n*-amyl, and *n*-hexyl alcohols. Jennings and Sevenants (1964B) were able to chromatograph and recover Bartlett pear essence without losing the desirable aroma characteristics. By infrared spectroscopy, they identified hexyl acetate as a "contributory flavor compound," and methyl trans:2-cis:4 decadienoate as a "character impact compound" of Bartlett pear. Heinz *et al.* (1964) and Jennings (1965) established that the level of decadienoate esters, as estimated by ultraviolet spectroscopy, correlated well with sensory evaluations of pear essence.

Table 80

VOLATILE COMPONENTS OF BARTLETT PEAR

Methyl acetate[1]	Ethyl cis:4-decenoate[2,3,6]
Ethyl acetate[1,2]	Methyl trans:2-cis:4-decadienoate[1,2,4]
Ethanol[1]	Methyl 3-hydroxy octanoate[2,3,6]
Propyl acetate[1]	Ethyl trans:2-decenoate[1,2]
Propanol[1]	Sesquiterpene, triunsaturated with moieties
Butyl acetate[1,2]	R H C=C H R R C=C $C{=}CH_2$[1,2,4] H R R
Hexanol[1,6]	
Butanol[1,2]	
Amyl acetate[1,2]	
Pentanol[1,2]	
Hexyl acetate[1,2]	
Hexanol[1,2]	
Cis-hexenyl acetate[2]	Methyl cis:2-trans:4-decadienoate[2,7]
Heptyl acetate[1,2]	Methyl trans:2-trans:4-decadienoate[2,7]
Methyl octanoate[1]	Ethyl trans:2-cis:4-decadienoate[1,2,4,7]
Methyl 4-oxy trans butenoate[2,4,5,6]	Ethyl 3-hydroxy octanoate[2,3]
n-Heptanol[1]	Ethyl dodecanoate[1]
Ethyl octanoate[1,2]	Ethyl cis:6-dodecenoate
Ethyl 4-oxy trans butenoate[2,4,6]	Ethyl trans:2-trans:4-decadienoate[2,7]
Octyl acetate[1,2]	Propyl trans:2-trans:4-decadienoate[2,7]
Methyl trans:2-octenoate[2]	Ethyl trans:2-dodecenoate[1,2]
n-Octanol[1,2]	Ethyl trans:2-cis:6-dodecadienoate[1,2]
Ethyl trans:2-octenoate[1,2]	Butyl trans:2-cis:4-decadienoate[2,7]
Methyl decanoate[1,2]	Methyl cis:8-tetradecenoate[2]
Methyl cis:4-decenoate[1,2,6,7]	Ethyl tetradecenoate[1]
Ethyl decanoate[1,2]	Ethyl cis:8-tetradecenoate[2]

Source: Jennings (1967).
[1] Retention data.
[2] Infrared spectral data.
[3] Mass spectral data.
[4] Ultraviolet spectral data.
[5] Melting points.
[6] Derivatives.
[7] Synthesis.

Components of Bartlett pear essence so far identified are listed in Table 80 (Jennings 1967). The inter-relationship among many of these compounds is immediately evident, and at least three are artifacts. The 4-oxy-trans-butenoate esters, as an example, result from hydrolytic cleavage of the cis bonds of the trans:2-cis:4-decadienoate esters. Similarly, the hexanal is produced by this same cleavage. This occurs only in the isolated essence, and requires light and oxygen. Even this essence, however, still possessed a typical desirable aroma. The decadienoate esters are of particular interest, because these have been shown to be important to the typical aroma of Bartlett pear (Heinz *et al.* 1964). Because of their triconjugate system, these possess high extinction coefficients and their concentration can be readily estimated by ultraviolet spectroscopy. Their production is closely related to the maturation of the fruit, and that the incremental increase of these esters achieves a maximum shortly after the climacteric point, when the fruit possesses optimum flavor.

Tables 78 and 80 show that both peaches and pears contain a number of low-molecular weight volatiles that are widely and indiscriminately distributed among most fruits. Some of their constituents, however, would appear to be unique to the fruit investigated, e.g., the decadienoates to pear, and the lactones and pyrone to peach.

In the process of maturation, fruits produce an abundance of compounds many of which are probably related to flavor. It is possible that these compounds do play a role in the biology and physiology of the fruit. Certain constituents, such as auxins and pigments, may be degraded as the fruit attains maturity, halting processes such as cell expansion, elongation, or photosynthesis. The resulting fragments may contribute to the formation of volatile compounds. Or, some of these volatile compounds may be produced to serve certain specific functions, such as growth regulation, color formation, softening, or some other manifestation of the ripening process (Jennings 1967).

The volatiles may be produced, at least in part, from decomposition of cellular constituents, and oxidation of unsaturated fatty acids. As the fruit attains maturity and becomes senescent, its high energy biochemical equilibria shift, the integrity of separate systems is lessened, and various reactions may occur more freely. Weakened cell walls may alloy the passage of some constituents, which may mix with other constituents once involved in vital processes. Unsaturated compounds that are now no longer protected may combine with oxygen to produce aldehydes, alcohols, and ketones. Acids and alcohols may combine to produce esters.

It is interesting to note that many of the compounds found in the Bartlett pear are the methyl and ethyl esters of reactants that can be fitted into the scheme of β-oxidation. Undoubtedly there are other reaction mechanisms that could also account for these compounds.

Romani and Ku (1966) passed water-saturated air through jars containing normal ripening pears. The vapors were then analyzed by vapor-phase chromatography. The following compounds were tentatively identified in the volatiles of normal pears: ethylene, acetaldehyde, methyl acetate, propyl acetate, butyl acetate, amyl acetate, and hexyl acetate.

Polyphenoloxidase and Phenolic Compounds in Pears

Brown discoloration occur readily in peeled pears if they were delayed in heat processing. Luh *et al.* (1963) studied polyphenolase activity and browning in Bartlett pears. Formation of brown colored pigments in canned pears was related to the level of polyphenols and polyphenoloxidase activity. Enzymatic browning can be minimized by: (a) careful handling of pears during harvest, transport, grading, and storage, so that mechanical damage to the fruit is minimized; (b) a shorter time between peeling and heat sterilization so that enzymatic browning is greatly reduced; (c) inhibition of polyphenoloxidase activity by dipping the peeled pears in 1% salt solution; and (d) rapid inactivation of polyphenoloxidase in the pears by steam blanching at 194°F or higher. Pear polyphenolase catalyzes oxidation of only ortho-dihydroxy phenolic compounds, but not meta and para dihydroxy phenolic compounds. The relative activity of the enzyme on substrates at pH 6.2 and 86°F was, in descending order; catechol, chlorogenic acid, caffeic acid, d-catechol and protocatechuic acid. Tate *et al.* (1964) studied the characteristics of polyphenoloxidase in Bartlett pears. The energy of activation, with catechol as substrate, was 4.9 kcal/mole in the temperature range 57°–86°F. Oxygen at atmospheric pressure was found to be the rate-limiting factor in the oxidation of catechol at pH 6.2. The enzyme was inhibited by ascorbic acid and isoascorbic acid.

Enzymatic browning in pear purée or nectars can be avoided by rapid heat inactivation of polyphenoloxidase during peeling, maceration, and heat processing. Ascorbic acid, isoascorbic acid, and 1% sodium chloride solutions can also be used to inhibit enzymatic browning.

Polyphenolic compounds in canned Bartlett pear purée have been identified by Sioud and Luh (1966). Leucoanthocyanins, (+)-catechin, (—)-epicatechin, chlorogenic acid, *p*-coumaryl quinic acids, and caffeic acids were found to be present in the pear purée canned by the aseptic canning process. The predominant polyphenolic compounds were chlorogenic acids, (—)-epicatechin, and leucoanthocyanidins.

Williams (1958) identified phenolic compounds in apple and perry pear juices. Chlorogenic acid was the principal phenolic compound. Also present were *p*-coumaryl quinic acid, three quercetin glucosides, phloridzin, and idaein (anthocyanin in apple skin) as well as catchins and leucoanthocyanins in varying amounts. Total phenolics may exceed 1% in apples, according to variety. Pears can contain more than 1% leucoanthocyanin which is largely responsible for clots in pear juices.

The chemistry and properties of the tannins in pears and apples were reported by Rentschler and Tanner (1956). Tannins are removed from the juices of these fruits by treatment with a fining agent. The depsides found in the juices include chlorogenic acid and quinic acid. There are indications that quinic acid is formed when fruit juices are treated with ion-exchangers.

Pink Discoloration in Pear Purée

Occasionally, pear nectars and canned pears show a pink discoloration which is considered undesirable. Factors influencing formation of pink color in canned Bartlett pears have been investigated by Luh *et al.* (1960). Growing area and soil types were found to be related to this problem. Pears from certain growing areas had low pH, high acidity, and high tannin and leucoanthocyanin content. These pears were found to develop pink color after canning especially when excessive heating and delayed cooling processes were used. The pink pigment in canned pears was shown to be identical in Rf value to that of cyanidin. An objective test for determining the amount of pink color precursor in pears was reported which involves heating a butanol extract of the pear with HCl in a boiling water bath for 10 min.

Pear Pectin

Pectins comprise the cell wall polysaccharides which consist mainly of linear α-(1,4)-glycoside bonded polygalacturonic acid members. Raunhard and Neukom (1964) compared the composition of the pulp and the protopectin during the ripening of apples and pears. Two distinct phases were evident: ripening on the tree and during post-harvest storage. There were changes in the esterification value of the pectin in the pulp and in the yield of extractable sodium pectate as well as in its viscosity. There is a decrease in protopectin content and viscosity and increase in pectate purity when pears ripen progressively. Dame *et al.* (1956) studied effect of ripening Bartlett pears at 68°F on pectin in the canned product. There was an increase in soluble solids and reducing value accompanying ripening. This was thought to be caused partly by the conversion of protopectin to soluble pectin and the hydrolysis of the water-soluble pectin to low molecular weight uronides. The intrinsic viscosity and neutral equivalent of versene-extracted pectin in pears decrease with the decrease in pressure test, indicating glycosidic hydrolysis of the polygalacturonide chain and deesterification of the methyl ester groups in the pectin molecule during ripening. The consistency of canned pear nectar may be related to the ripeness of the fresh pears, as well as to the size of screen used in the pulping and finishing processes.

Pectic enzymes are related to the changes in pectic materials in the pear during ripening. Such changes may influence the consistency of canned pear nectars. Nagel and Patterson (1967) studied the relation of pectin esterase (PE) and polygalacturonase (PG) activities to changes in total protein, firmness, size, and respiratory pattern during growth, maturation, and ripening of pear on the tree. Total PE increased during maturation and correlated with total weight, but PE activity per gram fresh weight and per mg protein decreased. The specific activity of PE decreased as the pear matured. Their results on PG activity in pears were variable. Weak PG activity was found in immature pear in two consecutive years, and none in the third year. They observed that extraction of PE by salt solution became increasingly less effective as the fruit matured and ripened. Much remains to be done to investigate the effect of ripening on cellulose which may also influence the consistency of canned pear nectars. Lamb and Lewis (1959) found large variation in consistency of commercial pear nectar samples between 41 and 347 seconds when measured with a CaLab capillary viscometer (California Laboratory Equipment Company, Berkeley, California). A majority of commercial pear nectars show capillary viscometer readings of 40–100 sec.

Organic Acids in Pears

Pears contain comparatively less organic acid than apples, peaches and other fruits. Williams and Patterson (1964) studied the changes in nonvolatile organic acids in Bartlett pears stored at 31°F for several months in five levels of CO_2. The flesh tissue of Bartlett pears stored in high levels of CO_2 accumulated succinic and citric acids. Succinic acid increased significantly while malic acid decreased in the core tissue of CO_2-stored pears. There was an indication that the succinic acid oxidase system was inhibited. The increase in succinic acid was correlated with CO_2-induced core breakdown in the fruit.

Dame *et al.* (1956) studied the effect of ripening at 68°F on organic acids in Bartlett pears. Malic and citric acids are the major acids in pears. When the pears were ripened at 68°F to pressure test below 5.5 lb, malic acid decreased rapidly, citric acid more slowly. Both acids appeared to reach a minimum value when the pressure test was 1.5 lb. Further ripening seemed to be accompanied by an increase in the two acids. A possible relation of organic acid metabolism to respiration and senescence is suggested. Chlorogenic, alpha-ketoglutaric, glycolic, pyruvic, and possibly succinic and lactic acids were present in minute concentrations.

PRUNE JUICE

Prune juice is not a fruit juice in the usual meaning of the term, but rather a water extract of dried prunes (Tressler 1961). It accounts for about 5% of the average national hot pack of all single-strength fruit and vegetable juices. The concentration of single-strength commercial prune juice ranges from 19° to 21° Brix. It is rich in mineral salts, and has a mild laxative effect. The juice is becoming one of the popular breakfast drinks. Most prune juice and prune juice concentrate are preserved by heat processing. A large quantity of prune juice concentrate (72° Brix) is shipped from California to the eastern states for reconstitution into single-strength juice. Experimental batches of frozen prune juice concentrate were shown to be superior in color, aroma, and flavor to the heat-processed juices in cans or bottles found in retail markets.

Fresh Prune Juice Processing

A procedure for preparing and preserving fresh prune or plum juice was described by Cruess *et al.* (1941, 1949) and Cruess (1950). Since most varieties of prunes do not yield a juice on crushing and pressing, it is necessary to treat fresh fruit with pectic enzyme such as "Pectinol 0" which hydrolyzes pectic substances responsible for the viscosity of crushed or puréed prunes. French, Sugar, Imperial, Italian or other varieties of prunes at optimum ripeness level should be used. The fruits are sorted to remove unfit material. The remaining procedures were as follows:

Wash and drain.

Steam 8 to 10 min to soften the prunes and prevent browning by the fruit's enzymes.

Pass the heated fruit through a pulper equipped with very coarse screen to remove pits and obtain a coarse purée containing the skins.

Cool the purée to below 120°F in a heat interchanger.

To the purée add 0.2% of Pectinol O or other pectic enzyme preparation of similar activity. Mix thoroughly to dissolve and distribute the enzyme.

Let stand until juice can be obtained readily when tested by draining a sample on cheesecloth; normally about 6 to 12 hr.

Add 2% of infusorial earth such as Hyflo Super Cel or other of like character. Mix well. It greatly aids in pressing.

Place the purée on light canvas, or heavy white muslin, which in turn lies on heavy apple press cloth. This gives double press cloths, which prevent bursting of the clothes and gives a clearer juice. Build up a "cheese" of press cloths of the purée and racks. Press as for crushed apples, using an apple juice type press.

Filter the juice. Take its Brix degree. If above 25° Brix dilute to about 23° to 22.5° Brix. Or blend with other juice to obtain the desired Brix degree.

Flash pasteurize the juice in a continuous, heat interchanger type pasteurizer to about 190°F. Fill into steamed bottles or into reenameled (double enameled) Type-L berry cans at 180° to 185°F. Seal at once. Place on sides 4 to 5 min to sterilize tops. Cool cans in cold water and bottles in tempered water.

"Or fill bottles with cold juice. Crown cap the bottles. Pasteurize by placing the bottles in cold water, bottles lying on sides, and heating the water to 180°F for 30 min for quart and smaller bottles. Cool slowly with tempered water."

Walker and Patterson (1954) have described a process for making prune juice quite similar to that outlined by Cruess *et al.* (1949). They have determined the time required for the desired action by the pectic enzyme preparation. It is dependent both on the amount of enzyme added and the temperature. When 0.2% by weight of "Pectinol A" was added to Italian prune purée, the time required for clarification was 5.0 hr at 75°F and 3.5 hr at 100°F.

Maczynska and Rembowski (1965) reported that inactivation of pectolytic enzymes in prunes improved viscosity and consistency of prune juice. The optimum conditions were 2.5 min at 185°F.

Under the Federal Food, Drug, and Cosmetic Act, vitamin C in such quantity that the total content is 30–60 mg per six fluid ounces may be added to canned prune juice (Anon. 1966A).

Coppens and de Hondt (1962) reported that the refractive index of prune juice was directly proportional to its sugar content which is related to the quality and maturity of the fresh fruit. Among the native ripe prunes they examined, fruits with sugar content of 9% were preferred over those with 13.5%.

Nectar from Fresh Prunes

Eddy and Veldhuis (1942) described a process for making nectar from fresh prunes. They recommend cooking the pitted prunes with $^1/_4$ to $^1/_3$ their weight of water for 8 to 10 min at 160° to 170°F. This cooking extracts sufficient color from the skins, reduces the viscosity of the pulp so that it easily passes through the pulper, and is not enough to cause the development of a cooked taste. The purée is diluted with sugar syrup to give it the proper sweetness (17° to 18° Brix) and consistency. The nectar is then rapidly heated to 180°F, filled into cans and processed in boiling water, 9 or 10 min for No. 1 tall cans and 12 to 13 min for No. 2 cans.

PRUNE (DRIED) JUICE

Two different methods are used commercially for making prune juice from dried prunes. One of these, the diffusion method, involves extracting the soluble components from the dried fruit by means of successive leachings with hot water. The other, sometimes called the disintegration method, consists of breaking up the dried fruit by vigorous cooking in water, followed by separation of the juice by pressing the disintegrated fruit in a hydraulic press (Hoffman 1939; Mrak 1937).

Diffusion Method

Dried prunes are thoroughly washed to free them from adhering dust. The washed fruit is placed in large wooden or stainless steel tanks, usually about 5 ft in diameter and 7 ft deep, each fitted with a perforated steam cross or a close coil in order to keep the extracting water at 185°F or slightly higher (Hoffman 1939; Kilbuck 1948). Tanks of this size hold 350 to 400 lb of prunes and 25 gal hot water per each 100 lb fruit. Steam is employed to maintain the water at 185°F or slightly higher. According to Cruess *et al.* (1941) and Kilbuck (1948), higher temperatures result in loss of prune aroma and cause a "burned taste" in the product. After 2 to 4 hr extraction, the liquor is drained and stored. Fresh hot water is placed upon the fruit in the proportion of 15 gal for each 100 lb; fruit is placed in the extractor and maintained at the extraction temperature (185°F) for the second extraction which again required 2 to 4 hr. At the end of this period the liquor is drawn off and combined with that from the first extraction. Hot water is again added to the prunes, this time in the proportion of 10 gal of water for each 100 lb of prunes used in the batch. At the end of the third extraction, the three extracts are combined, and the exhausted fruit, which is practically free of soluble matter, discarded. The extracts can either be used to extract a fresh batch of prunes and thus build up the desired concentration of soluble solids, or the liquor can be evaporated until the concentration reaches 19° to 21° Brix, the strength ordinarily desired.

If the combined extracts are used to treat a fresh lot of prunes, the resultant juice usually attains a concentration of 22° to 24° Brix and, consequently, must be diluted.

A modification of the process is to pulp the fruit prior to the third extraction, then add a quantity of water and filter the product through coarse bag filters. Infusorial earth may be used as a filter aid. This adds considerable body to the juice because of the pectin from the pulp.

Disintegration Process

The disintegration process involves thoroughly cooking the washed prunes in a wood or stainless steel tank equipped with an agitator and a heating unit of sufficient size to obtain vigorous boiling. In some instances an apple butter cooker, which can be sealed and operated under a few pounds pressure, is used. This shortens the time required for cooking.

Seven hundred gallons of hot water is placed on 1,200 lb of washed prunes in a cooker approximately 6 ft in diameter and 5 ft in depth. The water is brought to a boil and the fruit digested for 60 to 80 min, or until it is well disintegrated. The resulting prune mush is dropped from the cooker onto a cloth on a hydraulic press of the type commonly used in converting apples into juice. When a "cheese" has been built up, it is subjected to hydraulic pressure which ordinarily does not exceed 1000 lb. The juice or liquor obtained in this way is about 10° Brix. It is allowed to settle, then the clear juice is siphoned off, concentrated to about 20° Brix, and bottled. Or, it may be clarified by filtering through a filter press using about 1.0% infusorial earth (Super Cel) as a filter aid.

When the extract has attained the desired concentration (19° to 21° Brix), it is heated to 180°F prior to filling into bottles. At this point citric acid may be added to make the juice more tart. Two pounds of citric acid per 100 gal improves the flavor noticeably. If used, the presence and amount of citric acid added must be declared on the label. Quart bottles of prune juice are usually pasteurized in a water bath at 190°F for 35 min. Cans and smaller bottles require less sterilization.

The chief advantage of the diffusion process is that little equipment is required and even that is not expensive. However, more time and labor are required than is the case when the "disintegration" method is used; further the yields average only about 500 gal per ton, whereas the disintegration process yields 600 gal of 20° Brix juice per ton of prunes. According to Hoffman (1939), the flavor of the juice obtained by the latter process is superior to that made by the diffusion procedure.

Frozen Prune Juice Concentrate

The same method for extracting prune juice from dried or fresh prunes can be used to make a frozen juice concentrate. It is necessary to add $2^1/_2$ lb of pectic enzyme per 100 gal of juice. The enzyme should be mixed slowly with the juice and the mixture is allowed to stand overnight. The resulting juice is filtered, concentrated in a vacuum pan to approximately 60° Brix at a temperature of not more than 120°F, frozen, and marketed in 6 oz cans as a frozen prune juice concentrate (Anon. 1966B).

Fortified Prune Juice

A patent for fortifying fresh prune juice with volatile constituents was granted to Lang and Byer (1967A; 1967B). The prune juice is fortified with a specific fraction of volatile constituents whose boiling points are above and below that of water. The juice is separated at below 140°F and under reduced pressure in a close system into a major concentrated juice portion and a minor volatile portion. The minor portion contains the volatile flavor-producing constituents. A major portion of the volatile flavor constituents is condensed as a 1st two-phase oily-watery mixture at 30°–70°F. The minor portion of the volatile portion containing uncondensed volatile constituents is discarded. The two-phase oily-watery mixture is concentrated under reduced pressure at 50°–100°F to collect a mixture of high and low boiling constituents which is combined with a portion of nonstripped cutback juice and this later mixture is combined with juice concentrate from which the minor volatile portion has been removed in closed system.

The process may be applied to prune juice as well as to orange, grapefruit, tangerine juices and other fruit juices.

BEVERAGES PREPARED BY BLENDING FRUIT JUICES WITH SYRUP

Cherry

The juice of sour cherries, such as that of the Montmorency and the

English Morello, is too tart to appeal to most persons unless it is diluted with sugar syrup or a bland fruit juice such as that of the apple. Dilution of the juice of sour cherries with an equal volume of 15° Brix sugar syrup will keep the total solids content of the product at approximately its original level but at the same time reduce the acidity to approximately half the original value. Before dilution, Montmorency cherry juice may contain approximately 1.3% malic acid. After dilution with sugar syrup, the acidity will be approximately 0.65% acid. See Chap. 8.

Cherry juice diluted with sugar syrup, sometimes called cherry cocktail (Tressler and Pederson 1940; Tressler *et al.* 1941) is a pleasing beverage. An especially desirable product can be obtained by blending cold- and hot-pressed Montmorency and English Morello cherry juice with 15° Brix sugar syrup. A blend recommended by Tressler and Pederson (1940) is indicated below:

	%
Cold-pressed Montmorency juice	28.1
Hot-pressed Montmorency juice	9.4
Cold-pressed English Morello juice	9.4
Hot-pressed English Morello juice	3.1
15° Brix sugar syrup	50.0
	100.0

It will be noted that three-fourths of the juice used was cold-pressed, which has more of fresh cherry flavor than the hot-pressed juice. The latter was included in order to give the product an attractive bright red color. Three-fourths of the cherry juice used was from the Montmorency variety and one-fourth from English Morello cherries. The English Morello juice is somewhat more tart and flavorful than that from the Montmorency variety. If only English Morello juice was used in the blend, a somewhat larger proportion of syrup could be used.

Juice prepared from cold-pressed thawed cherries has excellent color and flavor and may be used without addition of hot-pressed juice for making an excellent cherry cocktail.

The procedures for preparing the juices used in making a cherry cocktail or similar beverage are those described for making cherry juice (Chapter 8). However, the juice should be clarified by filtration so as to obtain a brilliantly clear product (Tressler 1938).

Just before bottling or canning the "cocktail" should be flash pasteurized at 180°F, then filled at this temperature into cans or hot bottles, which are immediately closed and cooled.

CRANBERRY BEVERAGES

Cranberry beverage processing has been very limited until 1929 when the manufacture of cranberry cocktail began. This product is a diluted cranberry juice with added sugar. The making of cranberry juice is described in Chapter 8.

Cranberry Juice Cocktail

The most common commercial procedure followed in making cranberry juice cocktail is to put thawed cranberries through a tapered screw extractor. A yield of 8 to $8^1/_2$ gal of juice is obtained from each 100 lb of fruit. For cocktail, this product is diluted with twice its volume of water and sufficient sugar is added to bring the specific gravity up to 15° Brix. The pomace may be used for making strained cranberry sauce.

Cranberry juice beverages are sometimes clarified by means of Pectinol, or some similar pectic enzyme preparation. After treatment the beverage is filtered using infusorial earth (Hyflo Super Cel or Dicalite) as a filter aid. The filtrate should be heated to 185°F to inactivate the enzyme and thus prevent further action during storage. The hot product should be put into cans or bottles which are closed, then turned on their sides and cooled. Cranberry juice is very corrosive to tin plate; therefore cans lined with berry or fruit enamel should be used.

An order establishing identity standard for cranberry juice cocktail, a juice drink, has been established (Anon. 1968B). "Cranberry juice cocktail—a juice drink under the Federal Food, Drug, and Cosmetic Act, is the beverage food prepared from cranberry juice or concentrated cranberry juice or both with water and nutritive sweetener (or nonnutritive sweetened product). It contains not less than 25% of the single-strength juice. The soluble solids are 14–16° Brix as determined by refractometer. It may contain 30–60 mg vitamin C/6 fl oz. The acid content calculated as anhydrous citric acid, is not less than 0.55 gm/100 ml. It is sealed in container and processed by heat so as to prevent spoilage."

Volatiles of Cranberry Juice

Croteau and Fagerson (1968) identified the major volatile components of the juice of American cranberry. Over 95% of the aroma complex was accounted for by: (a) aromatics: Benzene, benzaldehyde (9.6% of aroma concentration), benzyl ethyl ether, acetophenone, methyl benzoate, benzyl formate, ethyl benzoate, benzyl acetate, benzyl alcohol (6.0%),

2-phenyl ethanol, 4-methoxy benzaldehyde, 2-hydroxy diphenyl, benzyl benzoate (11.9%) and dibutyl phthalate; (b) terpenes: alpha-pinene, beta-pinene, myrcene, limonene, linalool, alphata-terpineol (13.0%), and nerol; (c) aliphatic alcohols: 2-Methyl-3-buten-2-ol, 2-pentanol, pentanol, hexanol, 1 octen-3-ol, octanal, nonanol, decanol and octadecanol; (d) aliphatic aldehydes: acetaldehyde, pentanal, hexanal, octanal, nonanal and decanal; (e) other compounds: diacetyl, ethyl acetate, 2-furaldehyde and methyl heptanoate; and (f) acids: Benzoic acid (26.6%) and 2-methylbutyric acid. The remaining 5%, important to aroma, contained more than 200 components.

The aromatic compounds in the juice of lingonberries were investigated by Anjou and von Sydow (1969). Juice of lingonberries, *Vaccinium vitis-idaea*) was analyzed for volatile compounds by gas chromatography and mass spectrometry. Forty-four compounds, comprising 95% of a concentrate of the volatile were conclusively identified. Fifteen of these are aliphatic alcohols, 8 aliphatic aldehydes and ketones, 5 terpene derivatives, 7 aromatic compounds, and 9 other compounds. 2-Methylbutyric acid, amounting to 48% of the concentration and the aromatic compounds are likely to be the most important ones for lingonberry aroma.

The aromatic compounds in the juice of American cranberries (*V. macrocarpon*) were identified by Anjou and von Sydow (1968). The volatile compounds were analyzed by gas chromatography and mass spectrometry. Forty-three compounds, comprising 87% of the concentration of the volatiles, have been identified. Twelve of these are aliphatic alcohols, 11 aliphatic aldehydes and ketones, 5 terpene derivatives, 8 aromatic compounds, and 7 other compounds. Terpineol (34%) is quantitatively dominant while the amount of 2-methylbutyric acid is much smaller than in lingonberries (*V. vitis-idaea*) where it is the most important aroma compound. As the composition of the volatiles otherwise is very similar in lingonberries and American cranberries, these differences are likely to be the major cause of the aroma difference between the two berries.

FRUIT JUICE BLENDS

Many fruit juices, such as cherry, plum, fresh prune, some grape, and almost all berry juices, are so intensely flavored, that is, so tart and strong, as to make them unpalatable without dilution or blending with milder, less acid juices. After dilution or blending, a delightful beverage usually results. Juice diluted with sugar syrup or water cannot be labeled juices but should be called "nectars," "cocktails," "beverages," or "juice drinks," depending on the per cent of fruit in the formulation.

On the other hand, pear juice and several others are bland and low in acidity. They are greatly improved by blending with juices of higher acidity. Apple juice, because of its mild flavor blends well with many strong flavored juices such as cherry, raspberry, and cranberry (Beattie and Pederson 1942; Pederson *et al.* 1941; Tressler and Pederson 1940; Tressler *et al.* 1941; Anon. 1956; Hayes *et al.* 1948; and Dalrymple 1958 and 1959). Strawberry, boysenberry, plum, grape, and rhubarb can be used advantageously in many blends.

Orange juice blends well with apple, apricot, boysenberry, grape, grapefruit, lemon, lime, pineapple, prune, raspberry, and tangerine juices (Anon. 1956). Grapefruit juice blends well with apricot, boysenberry, cherry, grape, lemon, lime, orange, pineapple, prune, raspberry, and tangerine juices. Apple juice blends well with black currant, boysenberry, grape, grapefruit, lime, orange, plum, prune, and tangerine juices. Tomato juice blends well with various vegetable juices, sauerkraut juice, clam broth, lemon juice, and various spice extracts and seasonings.

Citrus Blends

Orange-grapefruit juice is a good blend of fruit juices. Considerable quantities of orange-grapefruit, tangerine-grapefruit, and other citrus juice blends are also packed commercially (see p. 12). The great bulk of the citrus juice blends are packed in Florida although smaller quantities are canned in Texas and California.

The methods employed in the production of citrus juices to be blended are the same as those used in preparing these same juices for canning (see Chapter 2, Orange and Tangerine Juices; Chapter 3, Grapefruit Juice; Chapter 4, Lemon and Lime Juices).

The proportion of orange to grapefruit juice used in preparing an orange-grapefruit blend will depend upon the color desired, the acidity and Brix of the juices to be blended, on the relative price of the fruit and other factors. As a rule, not less than 50% orange juice is used, and, if the orange juice is light in color, as much as 75% may be used. The US Standards for grades of canned blended grapefruit juice and orange juice (July 1, 1969, Par. 52.1281) are as follows (Anon. 1969):

Product Description

(a) Canned blended grapefruit juice and orange juice is the product prepared from a combination of undiluted, unconcentrated, unfermented juices obtained from mature fresh grapefruit (*Citrus paradisi*) and sweet oranges (*Citrus sinenis*). The juice of oranges from the mandarin group (*Citrus reticulata*), however, may be added in such quantities that not more than 10% by volume of the orange juice ingredient consists of juice from *Citrus reticulata.* Fruit which is clean and sound is properly washed; is packed with or without the addition of a nonliquid nutrient sweetening ingredient (*s*); and is sufficiently processed by heat to assure preservation of the product in hermetically sealed containers.

(b) It is recommended that canned blended grapefruit juice and orange juice be composed of not less than 50% orange juice; however, in oranges yielding light colored juice it is further recommended that as much as 75% orange juice be used.

Styles

(a) Style I, Unsweetened (or natural juice).

(b) Style II, Sweetened (or with added sweetening ingredient). Canned blended grapefruit juice and orange juice of this style shall have been processed with the addition of sufficient nutritive sweetening ingredient or sweetening ingredients to produce a Brix measurement of not less than 11.5°.

Grades of Canned Blended Grapefruit Juice and Orange Juice

U. S. Grade A or U. S. Fancy canned blended grapefruit juice and orange juice shows no coagulation; possesses a very good color; is practically free from defects; possesses a very good flavor; and scores not less than 85 points.

U. S. Grade C or U. S. Standard canned blended grapefruit juice and orange juice may show slight coagulation; possesses a good color; is fairly free from defects; possesses a good flavor; and scores not less than 70 points.

Substandard canned blended grapefruit juice and orange juice fails to meet the requirements of U. S. Grade C or U. S. Standard.

Explanation of Terms—Same as Grapefruit Juice.

SCORE CHART FOR CANNED BLENDED GRAPEFRUIT JUICE AND ORANGE JUICE

Factors	Points Maximum	Grade A Fancy	Grade C Standard	Grade D Substandard
Color	20	17–20	14–16	0–13
Absence of Defects	40	34–40	28–33	0–27
Flavor	40	34–40	28–33	0–27
Minimum Score		85	70	...

The lowest score of any one factor shall determine the Grade.

Scoring Factors

Color.—Grade A: Light yellow-orange color, bright and typical of freshly extracted juice free from browning oxidation, caramelization or other causes. Grade C: Fairly typical color ranging from light yellow to light amber, may be dull or show evidence of slight browning but is not off-color.

Absence of Defects.—Grade A: The juice may contain not more than 12% free and suspended pulp and not more than 0.035% by volume of recoverable oil, and no seeds or seed particles or other defects that more than slightly affect the appearance of the product. Grade C: not more than 18% free and suspended pulp nor more than 0.055% by volume recoverable oil. No seeds or seed particles or other defects that materially affect the appearance of the product.

Flavor.—Grade A: Fine, distinct, canned blended grapefruit juice and orange juice flavor, which is free from off-flavors of any kind. Grade C: good, normal canned blended grapefruit juice and orange juice flavor which is free from off-flavors of any kind. Brix not less than—Grade A unsweetened: 10°; Grade A sweetened: 11.5°; Grade C unsweetened: 9.5°; Grade C sweetened 11.5°. Acid not less than: Grade A unsweetened: 0.75 gm nor more than 1.60 gm; Grade A sweetened: 0.75 gm nor more than 1.60 gm; Grade C unsweetened: 0.60 gm nor more than 1.70 gm; Grade C sweetened: 0.60 gm nor more than 1.70 gm (calculated as anhydrous citric acid) per 100 gm of juice. Brix acid ratio not less than—Grade A unsweetened: 9.5 to 1 nor more than 18 to 1 provided that when the juice has a Brix of 11.5° or more, the ratio may not be less than 8.5 to 1. Grade A sweetened: 10.5 to 1 nor more than 18 to 1, provided that when the Brix of the juice is 15° or more the Brix acid ratio may be less than 10.5 to 1; Grade C unsweetened: 8 to 1; Grade C sweetened: 10.5 to 1; provided that when the Brix of the juice is 15° or more, the Brix acid ratio may be less than 10.5 to 1.

In order to be graded US Grade A or Fancy, the blend must contain not more than 12% free and suspended pulp and not more than 0.030% by volume of recoverable oil; it must not contain seeds or seed particles or other defects that more than slightly affect the appearance of the product (Southerland 1949).

After blending, the product should be deaerated. It is then flash pasteurized, filled immediately into cans, sealed and cooled.

A popular cocktail is unique in that in addition to orange, lemon, grapefruit and lime juices, it contains some apricot purée to give it an unusual mellow taste (Anon. 1946A and B).

Pineapple Blends

Pineapple juice blends well with many other juices, particularly apple, apricot, orange and grapefruit juices. Blends of pineapple with citrus juices were introduced very early in California (Irish and Cruess 1932). At one time, blends of pineapple and orange juice marketed as Pineora were very popular and blends of pineapple and grapefruit juice were also pleasing. These were marketed by several California packers in the 1930's but later discontinued. In the 1950's a new blend of pineapple and grapefruit juice was introduced and proved so popular that over 5,000,000 cases were marketed in the first year. This is still a popular blend. Its popularity is due to the fact that the blend is standardized as to Brix degree and total acidity by addition of water and sugar as necessary and because of this amelioration is marketed as pineapple-grapefruit drink.

The standard of identity for canned pineapple-grapefruit juice-drink has been established (Anon. 1968C). Canned pineapple-grapefruit juice-drink is the beverage food prepared from pineapple and grapefruit juice or their concentrates equivalent to 50% of the finished food, with water, a sweetener, and optional ingredients. The sweeteners are: sugar, invert sugar syrup, dextrose, corn syrup, dried corn syrup, glucose syrup, and dried glucose syrup. The optional ingredients are: citrus oil flavoring derived from orange, lemon, and (or) grapefruit; lemon juice, concentrated lemon juice, citric, malic, and fumaric acid, as acidifiers; ascorbic acid (30–60 mg/4 fl oz); and Na citrate. The viscosity of the finished food is less than 30 sec by the method of Lamb and Lewis (1959). The food is sealed in a container and processed by heat to prevent spoilage.

To make 1000 gal of drink, the following ingredients are used:

	Lb
Pineapple conc. (60° Brix)	635.8
Liquid sucrose (66.5° Brix)	728.6
Corn syrup	192.7
Grapefruit conc. (58.5° Brix)	194.2
Sodium citrate USP	11.0
Citric acid USP	38.4
Ascorbic acid USP	1.88
Orange oil emulsion	2.65

The final product should have a soluble solids of 12.5–13.5° Brix, acidity 0.8%, and ascorbic acid, 45 to 48 mg per 6 fl oz at time of packing. The quantity of sodium citrate may be varied as required to bring pH to the 3.2–3.4 range. Citric acid addition is varied in accordance with acidities of fruit ingredients.

Frozen pineapple and grapefruit concentrate in 55-gal drums should be removed from the freezer approximately 36–48 hr before usage to facilitate removal from drums. The designated quantities of pineapple concentrate, grapefruit concentrate, sugar syrup or sugar, and water are added to the blending tank and stirred to uniformity. Adjustment of the volume with water to 1,000 gal should result in the correct specification for the Brix reading. Finally, ascorbic acid is added. One gallon of orange oil emulsion is diluted with 2.73 gal of water. The diluted emulsion is dispensed to each container just prior to the filling operation (1.5 ml/46 fl oz). The filler should be equipped with a heating unit so that the specified closing temperature of 190°F is maintained at all times. The blended product is pasteurized at a temperature sufficient to give a closing temperature of 190°F filled into the containers, sealed, inverted, held for 3 min, and then water cooled to 95°F before labeling.

Blending with Apple Juice

Since apple juice is rather bland and, as a rule, is less costly than most other fruit juices, it has been recommended for blending with strong flavored juices such as cherry, plum, raspberry, strawberry, and cranberry

(Beattie and Pederson 1942; Beavens and Beattie 1942; Pederson and Beattie 1943; Tressler *et al.* 1943; Pederson 1947; Menzies and Kefford 1949; Brown *et al.* 1957; Moyls and MacGregor 1958; Tressler, 1961, Moyls 1958A and 1966).

The use of apple juice instead of sugar syrup for the dilution of strong flavored fruit juices has the advantage of maintaining the body of the blend. Further, the product may be called juice, since it is not diluted with water.

The blends recommended by the New York State Agricultural Experiment Station food technologists are indicated in Table 81.

TABLE 81

RECOMMENDED APPLE JUICE BLENDS

Fruit Blend	Other Fruit, %	Baldwin Apple Juice, %	Added Sugar, % of Blend	pH	Acidity (Malic Acid), gm per 100 ml	Brix at 17.50
Plum[1]-apple	63 Plum	37	1.5	3.40	0.98	18.50
Cherry[2]-apple	55 Cherry	45	3.0	3.22	1.14	17.75
Apple-raspberry	25 Raspberry	75	2.0	3.32	0.72	16.50
Apple-strawberry[3]	40 Strawberry	60	5.0	...	0.70	17.00
Apple-strawberry[4]	53 Strawberry	47	5.0	...	...	...
Apple-grape[5]	50 Grape	50	None	...	...	...
Apple-elderberry	20.3 Elderberry	79.7	3.3	...	...	...
Apple-cranberry	22.6 Cranberry	77.4	2.5	3.10	...	13.0

Source: Tressler, Pederson, and Beattie (1943); Beattie and Pederson (1942).
[1] Variety: Italian Prune.
[2] Varieties: blend of Montmorency and English Morello.
[3] Variety: Dresden.
[4] Variety: Premier.
[5] Variety: Concord.

The apple-raspberry blend is especially delicious (Pederson *et al.* 1941). This product is prepared by first thawing and pressing frozen pack raspberries. Approximately 60% yield is obtained from this first pressing. The pomace is heated to 145°F with equal weight of clarified apple juice and then pressed a second time. The two lots of raspberry juice are mixed together and then blended with apple juice so that the product contains 25% raspberry juice and 75% apple juice. In New York State, juice of winter apples, such as the Baldwin, Greening, and Northern Spy, is best for blending purposes although McIntosh, and Cortland juices are nearly as good. In the west, probably Winesap, Gravenstein, and Jonathan would be satisfactory varieties for this use. A 50 to 50 blend of Bristol black and Sodus purple raspberries is especially recommended. Of the red varieties tested at the New York Agricultural Experiment Station, Indian Summer, Cuthbert, and Marcy gave blends with the most intense flavor and color.

The method recommended by Pederson and Beattie (1943) for the preparation of apple-strawberry juice involves the thawing of a variety of strawberries well suited to freezing, e.g., Dresden or Culver in hot (180°F) clarified apple juice. The more intense the flavor of the frozen strawberries, the less berries and the more apple juice can be used. With strawberries of good flavor, a blend containing approximately 40% of strawberry and 60% of apple juice is best. Pederson and Beattie (1943) recommended flash pasteurization at 185°F followed by filling the hot juice into cans or bottles and immediate closure.

Beattie and Pederson (1942) recommend the use of frozen cherries for the making of cherry-apple juice. Montmorency cherries should be crushed lightly so as not to break the pits, then filled into enameled cans, frozen and stored at 0°F until apple juice is available. Then the cherries are thawed and allowed to warm up to not over 45°F and pressed in a hydraulic press. The thawed fruit presses easily and yields somewhat more juice than is obtained by either hot or cold pressing of the fresh fruit. Beattie and Pederson (1942) suggest blending 55 parts of this cherry juice with 45 parts of freshly pressed Baldwin apple juice. The blend should be clarified by holding overnight the juice to which 0.1 per cent of Pectinol M has been added, followed by filtration through a filter press using Super Cel or Dicalite as a filter aid. The filtered juice should be sweetened with sugar, about four ounces per gallon, deaerated, and flash pasteurized at 170°F and filled at this temperature into enamel-lined cans and bottles, and rapidly cooled after a three-minute holding period.

Beattie and Pederson (1942) recommend the use of fresh Italian prunes for the production of prune-apple juice. The prunes should be washed, then split and heated to 150°F in a steam-jacketed kettle with freshly pressed apple juice, using 2 gal of apple juice for each bushel of fruit. The prunes are pressed hot in a hydraulic press; double muslin cloths should be used inside the regular press cloths to prevent the flesh of the fruit from coming through. The blend should be clarified, filtered, deaerated, pasteurized, and packaged according to the procedure described above for cherry-apple juice.

Elderberry-apple juice can best be made by blending juice of thawed elderberries (Pederson and Beattie 1943) with apple juice and sweetening with about three per cent of sugar.

Menzies and Kefford (1949) prepared blends of Granny Smith apple juice (9° Brix and 0.4% acid as malic) with boysenberry, grapefruit, lime, passion fruit, pineapple, and youngberry juices. These blends were cold filled into lacquered cans, vacuum-sealed, pasteurized in steam while rotating at 100 rpm to give a center temperature of at least 190°F and then immediately cooled while rotating at the same speed under cold water sprays. All blends were rated superior to plain apple juice, the apple-passion fruit blends being especially attractive in flavor. In order of desirable flavor the blends were:

Apple-passion fruit, 5 or 10% passion-fruit juice with 1% sugar; remainder apple juice.

Apple-pineapple, 25 or 50 % pineapple juice with 1% sugar; remainder apple juice.

Apple-youngberry, 22% youngberry juice with 1% sugar, or 50% youngberry juice with 2% sugar; remainder apple juice.

Apple-boysenberry, 22% boysenberry juice with 1% sugar, or 50% boysenberry juice with 2% sugar; remainder apple juice.

Apple-grapefruit, 25% grapefruit juice with 1% sugar; remainder apple juice.

Although the two berry blends were attractive in color, it was suggested that blends based on other berries, particularly raspberries, would be more pleasing in flavor.

Moyls (1958A) studied the blending of Canadian apple juice with the juice of apricots, prunes, pineapples, and grapes and recommends the following blend:

	%
Opalescent McIntosh apple juice	47
Apricot purée (12% soluble solids)	26
Sugar	6
Water	21

Moyls (1958B) recommends blends containing from one-third to one-half opalescent McIntosh apple juice with rather small amounts of one of the following juices: apricot, prune, pineapple and grape. These later blends, when fortified with 50 mg vitamin C per 100 ml, and sweetened with sugar to bring the Brix up to 18°, are recommended for feeding infants and children.

Moyls (1966) recommended some formulas for mixed fruit nectars (Table 82) and mixed drinks (Table 83).

CITRUS PURÉES

Frozen Purées

Beavens (1949) and Bissett (1949) have shown that frozen citrus purées, if properly prepared, will not develop off-flavors. Considerable quantities of frozen purées are produced commercially in California and Florida.

The Agricultural Marketing Service (1956) has given the following description of the comparatively simple procedure used commercially for the preparation of frozen orange, lemon, lime and tangerine purées.

"Sound, fully mature fruit is first thoroughly washed, preferably with a good detergent, and rinsed well with clean cold water to reduce microbial

Table 82

FORMULATION OF SOME FRUIT JUICE NECTARS

Fruit Juice Blends	Formula	Soluble Solids, %	Acidity as Hydrous Citric Acid, %	Brix/Acid Ratio
Apple-apricot	Opalescent apple juice—47.50 gal (11.9% sol. solids) Apricot purée—26.25 gal (12% sol. solids) Sugar syrup—26.25 gal (22% sol. solids)	14.5	0.51	29
Apple-black currant	Opalescent apple juice—74 gal (14.3% sol. solids) Black currant juice—22 gal (9.6% sol. solids) Sugar—43 lb	16–17	0.68	24
Apple-cranberry	C arified Delicious apple juice—86 gal 1(12% sol. solids) Depectinized cranberry juice—14 gal (12% sol. solids) Sugar—35 lb	15	0.68	22
Apple-grape	Clarified apple juice—50 gal (12.6% sol. solids) Red or purple grape juice conc.—10 gal (50% sol. solids) Sugar—25 lb Concord grape essence—0.5 ga Water to make—100 gal	15	0.64	25
Apple-orange	Single-strength orange juice—20 gal (12% sol. solids) Opalescent apple juice—45 gal (11.9% sol. solids) Sugar syrup—35 gal (22% sol. solids) Orange oil (cold press)—4 fl oz	16.2	0.72	23
Apple-raspberry	Delicious apple juice (clarified)—75 gal (12.5% sol. solids) Raspberry juice—25 gal (7.7% sol. solids) Sugar—52 lb	16.5	0.80	20
Orange	Brazilian type concentrate—84.2 lb (63% sol. solids) Valencia type concentrate—45.3 lb (59% sol. solids) Sugar—57.8 lb Orange oil (cold press)—1.6 fl oz Water to make—100 gal	12.0–12.5	0.68	18
Opalescent apple-lime	Opalescent Delicious apple juice—97 gal (14% sol. solids) Top pulp lime juice—3 gal (8% sol. solids) Citric acid to give 0.7% total acid Sugar—14 lb	15	0.70	21.5
Pineapple-grapefruit	Pineapple concentrate—102 lb (61% sol. solids) Grapefruit concentrate—113 lb (39% sol. solids) Sugar—56.5 lb Citric acid—90 oz Sodium citrate—36 oz Water to make—100 gal	15.0	1.24	12

Source: Moyls (1966).

contamination to a minimum. With certain citrus varieties purées made from immature fruit have a tendency to be bitter. Medium to small fruit is preferred because of the better yield and quality of the juice. After the fruit is washed, the stem end may be cut off and discolored spots removed so that no dark specks will be mixed in with the bright-colored purée. If Washington Navel oranges are used, the navel end should first be removed.

"After the whole fruit has been trimmed, it is either crushed in a machine, such as an apricot pitter, or sliced by means of circular saws. The crushed or

TABLE 83

FORMULATION OF SOME FRUIT JUICE DRINKS[1]

Drink	Formula	Soluble Solids, %	Acidity as Tartaric Acid, %	Brix/Acid Ratio
Apple	Apple concentrate—36.4 lb (70% sol. solids) Sugar—91.0 lb Citric acid—2.7 lb Sodium citrate—7.2 oz Water to make—100 gal	11.5–12.0	0.41–0.44	28
Apricot-grapefruit	Apricot concentrate—8.32 gal (24% sol. solids) Grapefruit concentrate—3.25 gal (39% sol. solids) Sugar—131 lb Citric acid—1.8 lb Pectin 150 grade rapid set—1.8 lb Water to make—100 gal	14.5–15.0	0.47	31
Cherry (sweet)	Sweet cherry juice—50 gal Water—50 gal Sugar to give 14% sol. solids Citric acid to give 0.43% total acid Fruit punch flavor—5 fl oz	14.0	0.43	33
Grape	Grape concentrate—5.5 gal (50% sol. solids) Sugar Citric acid Concord grape flavoring Concord coloring Water to make—100 gal	12.0–12.5	0.45	28
Orange-apricot	Orange concentrate—1.80 ga (63% sol. solids) Apricot concentrate—5.25 gal (22% sol. solids) Sugar—90 lb Pectin 100 grade rapid set—2.75 lb Water to make—100 gal	12.5	0.65	19.3
Raspberry	Raspberry juice—33.3 gal (7.7% sol. solids) Water—66.6 gal Sugar—162 lb	16.0	0.68	23

Source: Moyls (1966).

sliced fruit is then put through a rotary or tapered screw press fitted with stainless-steel screens of appropriate mesh, so that most of the fruit is reduced to the form of a purée. Other machines may be available to accomplish the same purpose. Screen openings of 0.027- to 0.044-in. in diameter are usually employed, depending on the end use of the purée. Screen sizes of 0.027- and 0.033-in. are preferable when purées are intended for sherbets, ices, pies, and beverages, but larger sizes are better for purées intended for marmalades, jams, cake, and sundae toppings.

"Yield of purée from the whole fruit is approximately 50 to 60%, and should contain 0.40 to 0.75% of peel oil depending on the variety of fruit. With some lots of fruit and peel-oil content of the purée may be considerably higher and too strong for most uses. Then the oil content of the purée can be controlled if various proportions of the fresh fruit are passed through an abrasive machine prior to crushing to remove most of the oil sacs or flavedo. Another method of standardizing the oil content of purées is by adding different proportions of single-strength juice.

"After a purée of the required oil content is obtained, it is run into a stainless-steel tank, and dry sugar gradually added with thorough mixing in the proportion of 1 part of sugar to 5 parts of purée. Purées may be packed without addition of sugar. The sweetened or unsweetened purée is filled into enameled tin containers of 1 to $2^1/_2$ gal capacity, the cans are hermetically sealed or closed with slip tops, and the contents are frozen at subzero temperatures. The product is stored at 0° to −10°F. The time of freezing can be reduced if the purée is first frozen to a slush in a mechanically agitated heat exchanger before filling into cans."

Frozen citrus purées are used in the commercial preparation of milk sherbets and water ices. According to the Agricultural Marketing Service (1956), milk sherbets having approximately 2.5% of butterfat have a more pleasing flavor than water ices. Lemon and lime purées find use in the making of ades and other fruit drinks. Other uses for frozen citrus purées are in puddings, cakes, pies, marmalades, and jams and in making ice cream toppings.

While the preservation by freezing of beverage bases prepared from whole puréed citrus juices (particularly orange) has been successful, similar products have not lent themselves to preservation by heat. Recently citrus beverage bases have been prepared from blends of citrus juice concentrate with specially prepared purées from peel. The peel from oranges after extraction of juice may be converted into a stable smooth purée by heating with water acidified with citric acid until it is softened and the pectinesterase is inactivated. The heated mixture is then passed through a heavy duty pulper and the resulting pulp ground to a smooth paste in a colloid mill such as the Fryma. The orange oil, lost during boiling, is made up by addition of a natural oil emulsion obtained by rasping the fruit prior to extraction. This emulsion is much more stable than that prepared from cold pressed orange oil. The peel paste fortified with natural emulsion is more stable towards separation and browning than orange juice or concentrate. Similar products may be prepared from lemons and also from grapefruit. In the latter case an additional treatment is necessary to separate the excess of naringin. Comminuted fruits so prepared are used widely in England and Europe for beverage bases.

OTHER PURÉES

A recent innovation is the packing of a number of novel frozen fruit purée concentrates made from orange, lemon, and lime (Agr. Research Service 1962) a punch blend, boysenberry, Santa Rosa plum, guava, and passion fruit. When diluted with water each six-ounce can yields a quart of delicious beverage. The products are also available in a 32-oz can for institution use.

STANDARD FOR FRUIT NECTARS

Standard for Apricot, Peach and Pear Nectars

The Joint Economic Commission for Europe (ECE) and Codex Alimentarius Group of Experts on Standardization of Fruit Juices (FAO/

WHO Food Standard Programme 1969) held its Sixth Session in Geneva, Switzerland. The Standard for canned apricot, peach, and pear nectars preserved exclusively by physical means was drafted. Fruit nectar is described as an unfermented but fermentable pulpy product, intended for direct consumption, obtained by blending the total edible part of sound and ripe fruit, concentrated or unconcentrated, with water and sugars, and preserved exclusively by physical means. For the purpose of this standard and at this time, preservation by physical means does not include ionizing radiation.

Minimum Content of Fruit Ingredients.—The product shall contain not less than 40% in the case of peach and pear nectars, and not less than 35% in the case of apricot nectars, by weight of single strength fruit ingredient or the equivalent derived from any concentrated fruit ingredient.

Soluble Solids.—The soluble solids content of the product shall be not less than 13% by weight as determined by refractometer at 68°F uncorrected for acidity and read as °Brix on the International Sucrose Scales.

Apparent Viscosity.—The apparent viscosity of the product shall be such that the flow-time is not less than 30 sec according to the Lamb and Lewis method (1959).

Ethanol Content.—Ethanol content shall not exceed 3 gm/kg.

Hydroxymethyl Furfural (HMF).—The HMF content shall not be more than 10 mg/kg.

Organoleptic Properties.—The product shall have the characteristic color, aroma, and flavor of the fruit from which it is made.

Food Additives.—Citric acid and malic acid can be used as acidifying agents and l-ascorbic acid as an antioxidant.

Pesticide Residues.—The product shall comply with such requirements as may be specified by the Codex Committee on Pesticide Residues.

Contaminants.—The following provisions in respect of contaminants other than pesticide residues have, with the exception of the level for tin content, been endorsed by the Codex Committee on Food Additives:

Contaminant	Maximum Level, mg/kg
Arsenic (As)	0.2
Lead (Pb)	0.3
Copper (Cu)	5
Zinc (Zn)	5
Iron (Fe)	15
Tin (Sn)	250 provisional level (not endorsed)

There is a lack of more extensive data regarding the levels of tin found in practice on a product by product basis in a larger number of countries. The level of tin which may risk the health of the consumer is not well established at this time. The Group felt that it would be premature to do other than include a provisional limit in the standards.

On the basis of the information presently available, the Group agreed to include in the standards a figure of 250 mg/kg. This figure was to be provisional, and would be reviewed by the Group when more complete data became available. Data would need to be obtained from the industry and would also have to include medical opinion on the subject. The Group envisaged recommending to the Commission, at a later stage, a possible amendment to the standards to reduce the provisional limit for tin content.

Minimum Fill.—The nectar shall occupy not less than 90% of the water capacity of the container. The water capacity of the container is the volume of distilled water at 68°F which the sealed container will hold.

The Name of the Food.—The name of the product shall be "apricot nectar" or "pulpy apricot nectar," "peach nectar" or "pulpy peach nectar," "pear nectar" or "pulpy pear nectar," as appropriate.

List of Ingredients.—A complete list of ingredients, including added water, shall be declared on the label in descending order of proportion.

The addition of 1-ascorbic acid shall be declared on the label as "1-ascorbic acid," or "1-ascorbic acid" qualified to indicate its technological use, or "antioxidant."

Net Contents.—The net contents shall be declared by volume in either the metric ("Systeme International" units) or avoirdupois or both systems of measurement as required by the country in which the product is sold.

Name and Address.—The name and address of the manufacturer, packer, distributor, importer, exporter or vendor of the product shall be declared.

Country of Origin.—The country of origin of the product shall be declared.

When the product undergoes processing in a second country which changes its nature, the country in which the processing is performed shall be considered to be the country of origin for the purposes of labelling.

Additional Requirements.—The minimum percentage of fruit content as provided for under the standard shall be declared on the label. The pictorial representation of fruit or nectar on the label may only be that of the species of fruit present or the nectar therefrom. No claim shall be made in respect of "vitamin C" nor shall the term "vitamin C" appear on the label unless the product contains such quantity of "vitamin C" as would be accepted by national authorities as warranting such claim or the use of such term.

Bulk Packs.—In the case of fruit nectars in bulk, the information shall either be placed on the container or be given in accompanying documents

BIBLIOGRAPHY

AGRICULTURAL MARKETING SERVICE. 1956. Chemistry and technology of citrus, citrus products and by-products. U. S. Dept. Agr., Agr. Handbook *98*.

AGRICULTURAL RESEARCH SERVICE. 1962. Chemistry and technology of citrus, citrus products, and by-products. U. S. Dept. Agr., Agr. Handbook *98*.

ANJOU, K., and VON SYDOW, S. 1968. Aroma of cranberries. IV. Juice of *Vaccinium macrocarpon*. Ark. Kemi. *30*, No. 2, 9–14.

ANJOU, K., and VON SYDOW, E. 1969. Aroma of cranberries. III. Juice of *Vaccinium vities-idaea*. Acta Chem. Scand. *23*, No. 1, 109–114.

ANON. 1946A. New citrus cocktail is blend of five fruit juices. Western Canner and Packer *38*, No. 11, 61.

ANON. 1946B. California firm packs 5-juice blend. Western Canner and Packer *38*, No. 12, 70–73.

ANON. 1956. Blended fruit juices and mixed fruit drinks. Circ. Hoffmann-LaRoche, Nutley, N. J.

ANON. 1966A. Prune juice; order amending standard of identity. Federal Register *31*, 5957–5958. (April 19, 1966).

ANON. 1966B. Duffy-Mott scores first in frozen industry with frozen prune juice concentrate. Quick Frozen Foods *28*, No. 12, 82.

ANON. 1968A. Canned fruit nectars: order establishing definitions and standards of identity. Federal Register *33*, 6862–6863. (May 7, 1968).

ANON. 1968B. Cranberry juice cocktail—a juice drink; artificially sweetened cranberry juice cocktail—a juice drink; order establishing identity standard. Federal Register *33*, 5617–5618. (April 11, 1968).

ANON. 1968C. Canned pineapple-grapefruit juice-drink: order establishing definition and standard of identity. Federal Register *33*, 6863–6864. (May 7, 1968).

ANON. 1969. U. S. Standards for grades of canned blended grapefruit juice and orange juice. Consumer Marketing Service, U. S. Dept. Agr.

BEATTIE, H. G., and PEDERSON, C. S. 1942. Results of a demonstration sale of fruit juice blends. Fruit Products J. *21*, 227.

BEAVENS, E. A. 1949. New frozen purées from citrus fruits. U. S. Bur. Agr. and Indus. Chem. AIC-238.

BEAVENS, E. A., and BEATTIE, H. G. 1942. The preparation and processing of peach, pear, and plum juices. Canner *94*, No. 21, 15–18, 20.

BEISEL, C. G., and KITCHEL, R. L. 1967. Juice content-factor fallacy? Assoc. Food & Drug Officials U. S. *31*, 19–26.

BISSETT, O. W. 1949. Frozen purées from Florida citrus fruits. Fla. S. Hort. Soc. Proc. *1949*, 163–165.

BRODERICK, J. J. 1966. What is important in peach flavor? Am. Perfumer Cosmet. *81*, No. 2, 43–45.

BROWN, H. D., BARTON, R., and VAN CAMP, M. A. 1957. The utilization of apple and grape concentrate and blends. Ohio Agr. Expt. Sta. (Wooster) Research Bull. *789*.

BRUNNER, H. 1969. Gelatin quality, clarification effect, and residual turbidity in fruit juice concentrates. Schweiz. Z. Obst-Weinbau, *105*, No. 12, 277–284 (German); cf. CA *71*, No. 8, 68425a.

CLAYPOOL, L. L., LEONARD, S., LUH, B. S., and SIMONE, M. 1958. Influence of ripening temperature, ripeness level and growing area on quality of canned Bartlett pears. Food Technol. *12*, 375–380.

COPPENS, R., and DE HONDT, J. 1962. Determination of the quality and maturity of prunes by means of a refractometer. Rew. Agr. (Brussels) *15*, 399–401; cf. *CA 61*, No. 2, 2402f.

CROTEAU, R. J., and FAGERSON, I. S. 1968. Major volatile components of the juice of American cranberry. J. Food Sci. *33*, 386–389.

CRUESS, W. V. 1950. Making better prune juices. Western Canner Packer *42*, No. 3, 28.

CRUESS, W. V. 1958. Commercial Fruit and Vegetable Products, 4th Edition. McGraw-Hill Book Co., New York.

CRUESS, W. V., CHONG, G. N., RIVERA, W., and GIBSON, A. 1949. Juice of fresh prunes. Mimeo, Circ. Food Technol. Div. Univ. Calif., Berkeley.

CRUESS, W. V., LEONARD, S., PONTING, J., and LANE, A. 1941. Prune juice experiments. Fruit Products J. *20*, 196–198, 214, 233–234, 251, 253.

DAEPP, H. U., and MAYER, K. 1964. The influence of raw material on fruit juice quality. Schweiz. Z. Obst. Weinbau *73*, No. 2, 37–39.

DALRYMPLE, D. G. 1958. Marketing of fresh apple juice and cider. Univ. Conn. Storrs Agr. Expt. Sta. Progr. Rept. *27*.

DALRYMPLE, D. G. 1959. Marketing fresh apple juice and cider—some recent developments. Supplement to Prog. Rept. *27*, Storrs, Agr. Expt. Sta. Univ. of Conn.

DAME, C. JR., LEONARD, S. J., LUH, B. S., and MARSH, G. L. 1956. The influence of ripeness on the organic acids, sugars, and pectin of canned Bartlett pears. Food Technol. *10*, 28–33.

DESHPANDE, P. B., and SALUNKHE, D. K. 1964. Effects of maturity and storage on certain biochemical changes in apricots and peaches. Food Technol. *18*, 1195–1198.

DRAWERT, F. 1962. Concerning aroma and fragrant substances. Gas chromatographic investigation of aroma concentrates from apples and pears. Vitis *3*, 115–116 (German).

EDDY, C. W., and VELDHUIS, M. K. 1942. New nectar made from fresh prunes. Food Inds. *14*, No. 3, 46–47.

ELKINS, E. R., JR., and LAMB, F. C. 1969. Chemical indices of fruit content in fruit products. National Canners Assoc., Washington Research Laboratory, Research Rept. *3-69*, Washington, D. C.

EL-SAYED, A. S., and LUH, B. S. 1965. Polyphenolic compounds in canned apricots. J. Food Sci. *30*, 1016–1020.

EL-SAYED, A. S., and LUH, B. S. 1967. Amino acids and quality of canned apricots as affected by nitrogen fertilization. Food Technol. *21*, No. 3A, 98A–102A.

FAO/WHO FOOD STANDARD PROGRAMME. 1969. Draft standard for apricot, peach and pear nectars preserved by physical means. Joint FAO/WHO Food Standards Programme, Codex Alimentarius Commission. Report of the 6th Session of the Joint ECE/Codex Alimentarius Group of Experts on Standardization of Fruit Juices. ALINORM 70/14 (CX 5/55.3) Appendix II, 1–6.

FEINBERG, B. 1968. Prune juice. *In* The Freezing Preservation of Foods, Vol. 3, Chapter 4, D. K. Tressler, W. B. Van Arsdel, and M. J. Copley (Editors). Avi Publishing Co., Westport, Conn.

FELLERS, C. R., and ESSELEN, W. B. 1955. Cranberries and cranberry products. Univ. of Mass. Agr. Expt. Sta. Tech. Bull. *481*.

FITELSON, J. 1968. Detection of adulteration in dark-colored fruit juices. J. Assoc. Offic. Anal. Chem. *51*, 937–939.

HAYES, K. M., ESSELEN, W. B., and FELLERS, C. R. 1948. Applecranberry juice. Fruit Products J. *27*, 308, 329.

HEATON, E. K., BOGGESS, T. S., JR., WOODROOF, J. G., and LI, K. C. 1966. Peach purée as a base for drinks. Peach Products Conf. Rept., Georgia Expt. Sta., Experiment, Georgia.

HEINZ, D. E., CREVELING, R. K., and JENNINGS, W. G. 1965. Direct determination of aroma compounds as an index of pear maturity. J. Food Sci., *30*, 641–643.

HEINZ, D. E., PANGBORN, R. M., and JENNINGS, W. G. 1964. Pear aroma: relation of instrumental and sensory techniques. J. Food Sci. *29*, 756–761.

HOFFMAN, W. C. 1939. Manufacturing prune juice from dried prunes. Food Inds. *11*, 432–433.

HOLGATE, K. C., MOYER, J. C., and PEDERSON, C. S. 1948. The use of ascorbic acid in preventing oxidative changes in apple juice. Fruit Products J. *28*, 100–102, 112.

HSIA, C., CLAYPOOL, L. L., ABERNETHY, J. L., and ESAU, P. 1964. Leucoanthocyan material from immature peaches. J. Food Sci. *29*, 723–729.

HSIA, C. L., LUH, B. S., and CHICHESTER, C. O. 1965. Anthocyanin in freestone peaches. J. Food Sci. *30*, 5–12.

IRISH, J. H. (Revised by Cruess, W. V.) 1932. Fruit juices and fruit juice beverages. Calif. Agr. Expt. Sta. Circ. *313*.

JENNINGS, W. G. 1961. Volatile esters of Bartlett pears. J. Food Sci. *26*, 564–568.

JENNINGS, W. G. 1965. New fruit esters and the flavor of Bartlett pears. Int. Fruchtsaft-Union, Ber. Wiss. Tech. Komm. *6*, 277–287.

JENNINGS, W. G. 1967. Peaches and pears. *In* Symposium on Foods: The Chemistry and Physiology of Flavors, H. W. Schultz, E. A. Day, and L. M. Libbey (Editors). AVI Publishing Co., Westport, Conn.

JENNINGS, W. G., and CREVELING, R. K. 1963. Volatile esters of Bartlett pears. II. J. Food Sci. *28*, 91–94.

JENNINGS, W. G., LEONARD, S., and PANGBORN, R. M. 1960. Volatiles contributing to the flavor of Bartlett pears. Food Technol. *14*, 587–590.

JENNINGS, W. G., and SEVENANTS, M. R. 1964A. Volatile components of peach. J. Food Sci. *29*, 796–801.

JENNINGS, W. G., and SEVENANTS, M. R. 1964B. Volatile esters of Bartlett pear. III. J. Food Sci. *29*, 158–163.

KILBUCK, J. H. 1948. Observation on prune juice. Fruit Products J. *28*, 68–69, 91.

LAMB, F. C., and LEWIS, L. D. 1959. Consistency measurement of fruit nectars and fruit juice products. J. Assoc. Offic. Agr. Chemists *42*, 411–416.

LANG, A. A., and BYER, E. M. 1967A. Process for fortifying fruit juice. U. S. Pat. *3,310,410* (Cl. 99–205), March 21. Continuation-in-part of U. S. Pat. 3,117,877.

LANG, A. A., and BYER, E. M. 1967B. Production of flavor-enhanced apple and prune concentrates. U. S. Pat. *3,310,409* (Cl 99–205), March 21. 7 pp. Continuation-in-part of U. S. Pat. 3,118,775.

LEE, F. A., and PEDERSON, C. S. 1950. The preparation and storage of freestone peach juice and nectar. Food Technol. *4*, 466–468.

LEONARD, S., LUH, B. S., HINREINER, E., and SIMONE, M. 1954. Maturity of Bartlett pears for canning. Food Technol. *8*, 478–482.

Lewis, W. M. 1966. Chemical evaluation of orange juice in compounded soft drinks. J. Sci. Food Agr. *17,* 316–320.

Lim, L. 1963. Studies on the relationship between the production of volatiles and the maturity of peaches and pears. M. S. Thesis, University of California, Davis, Calif.

Lim, L., and Romani, R. J. 1964. Volatiles and the harvest maturity of peaches and nectarines. J. Food Sci. *29,* 246–253.

Luh, B. S. 1961. Volatile reducing substances as a criterion of quality of canned apricots. Food Technol. *15,* 165–167.

Luh, B. S., and Kamber, P. J. 1963. Chemical and color changes in canned apple sauce. Food Technol. *17,* 105–108.

Luh, B. S., Leonard, S. J., and Niketic, G. 1959. Aseptic canning of peach and apricot nectar (aseptisches eindosen von pfirsich-und Aprikosennektar). Fruchtsaft-Industrie *4,* 103–109.

Luh, B. S., Leonard, S. J., Patel, D. S., and Claypool, L. L. 1955. Volatile reducing substances in canned Bartlett pears. Food Technol. *9,* 639–642.

Luh, B. S., Leonard, S. J., and Patel, D. S. 1960. Pink discoloration in canned Bartlett pears. Food Technol. *14,* 53–56.

Luh, B. S., and Sioud, F. B. 1966. Aseptic canning of foods. IV. Stability of pear purée, with essence recovery. Food Technol. *20,* 1590–1593.

Luh, B. S., Tate, J. N., and Villarreal, F. 1963. Polyphenolase activity and browning in Bartlett pears. Fruchtsaft-Ind. *8,* 274–283 (German), cf: CA *62*(5), 1965, 5575f.

Luh, B. S., and Villarreal, F. 1964. Leucoanthocyanin in fresh and canned freestone peaches. Fruchtsaft-Ind. *9,* 285–293 (German), cf: CA *62*(8), 1965, 9697g.

Maczynska, D., and Rembowski, E. 1965. Fruit blanching for nectar processing. I. Establishment of blanching parameters for some colored fruit in processing of nectars. Prace Inst. Lab. Badawczych Przemyslu Spozywczego *15,* No. 4, 27–42, (Polish), cf: CA *64*(13), 1966, 20528d.

Maczynska, D., and Rembowski, E. 1966. Studies of fruit blanching for nectar processing. II. Effects of different blanching parameters on the quality of nectars from apples and pears. Prace Inst. Lab. Badawczych Przemyslu Spozywczego *16,* No. 1, 51–61, (Pol); cf.: CA *65*(12), 1966, 19226a.

Menzies, D. J., and Kefford, J. F. 1949. Apple juice blends. Food Preservation Quarterly (Australia) *9,* No. 2, 31–32.

Moyls, A. W. 1958A. Revised apple-apricot drink. Rept. Can. Committee on Fruit and Vegetable Preservation 1958, Can. Dept. Agr. 39–40.

Moyls, A. W. 1958B. Apple base juices for infant. Rept. Can. Committee on Fruit and Vegetable Preservation 1958, Can. Dept. Agr. 40–41.

Moyls, A. W. 1966. Fruit juice based beverages and concentrates. Canada Department of Agriculture, Research Station SP 40, Summerland, B. C., Canada.

Moyls, A. W., and MacGregon, D. R. 1958. Orange-apricot juice. Rept. Can Committee on Fruit and Vegetable Juice Preservation 1958, Can. Dept. Agr. 41–42.

Mrak, E. M. 1937. Prune juice. Fruit Products J. *16,* 230.

Nagel, C. W., and Patterson, M. E. 1967. Pectic enzymes and development of the pear (*Pyrus communis*). J. Food Sci. *32,* 294–297.

NAKABAYASHI, T., and UKAI, N. 1963. Browning of peach fruit by polyphenoloxidase. Nippon Shokuhin Kogyo Gakkaishi *10,* No. 6, 211–216 (Japan); cf: CA *63,* No. 1, 1965, 1155d.

OSBORN, R. A. 1964. Chemical composition of fruit and fruit juices. J. of A. O. A. C. *47,* 1068–1086.

PEDERSON, C. S. 1947. Apple juice with original character retained. Fruit Products J. *26,* 294–313.

PEDERSON, C. S., and BEATTIE, H. G. 1943. Preparation and preservation of juices from certain small fruits. Fruit Products J. *22,* 260–264, 281, 287.

PEDERSON, C. S., BEATTIE, H. G., and BEAVENS, E. A. 1941. Results of a demonstration sale of apple-raspberry juice. Fruit Products J. *20,* 227–228, 247.

PONTING, J. D., BEAN, R. S., NOTTER, G. K., and MAKOWER, B. 1954. Degree of heat-inactivation of polyphenol oxidase and quality of frozen apricot purée. Food Technol. *8,* 573–575.

PORRETTA, A., and GIANNONE, L. 1963. The effects of storage temperature on peach and apricot purées. Ind. Conserve (Parma) *38,* 7–20; cf: CA *62,* No. 7, 1965, 8318h.

POSTLMAYR, H. L., LUH, B. S., and LEONARD, S. J. 1956. Characterization of pectin changes in freestone and clingstone peaches during ripening and processing. Food Technol. *10,* 618–625.

RAUNHARD, O., and NEUKOM, H. 1964. Modification of the apple and pear pectins during the ripening process. Mitt. Gebiete Lebensm. Hyg. *55,* 446–454; cf: CA *63,* No. 1, 1965, 924h.

RENTSCHLER, H., and TANNER, H. 1956. The tannins of pomiferous fruit juices. Fruchtsaft-Ind. *1,* 30–35.

REYES, P., and LUH, B. S. 1960. Characteristics of browning enzymes in Fay Elberta freestone peaches. Food Technol. *14,* 570–575.

REYES, P., and LUH, B. S. 1962. Ascorbic and isoascorbic acids as antioxidants for frozen freestone peaches. Food Technol. *16,* 116–118.

RICE, C. C., FELLERS, C. R., and CLAGUE, J. A. 1939. Cranberry juice-properties and manufacture. Fruit Products J. *18,* 197–200.

ROMANI, R. J., and KU, L. L. 1966. Direct gas chromatographic analysis of volatiles produced by ripening pears. J. Food Sci. *31,* 558–560.

SEVENANTS, M. R., and JENNINGS, W. G. 1966. Volatile components of peach. II. J. Food Sci. *31,* 81–86.

SIOUD, F. B., and LUH, B. S. 1966. Polyphenolic compounds in pear purée. Food Technol. *20,* 534–538.

SOUTHERLAND, F. L. 1949. U. S. standards for grades of canned blended grapefruit juice and orange juice. Federal Register 3486 (June 28 issue).

TANG, C. S., and JENNINGS, W. G. 1967. Volatile components of apricot. J. Agr. Food Chem. *15,* 24–28.

TANG, C. S., and JENNINGS, W. G. 1968. Lactonic compounds of apricot. J. Agr. Food Chem. *16,* 252–254.

TATE, J. N., LUH, B. S., and YORK, G. K. 1964. Polyphenoloxidase in Bartlett pears. J. Food Sci. *29,* 829–836.

TRESSLER, D. K. 1938. Fruit and vegetable juices. Fruit Products J. *17,* 196–198, 210, 235–237, 249.

TRESSLER, D. K. 1961. Blended fruit juices and nectars. *In* Fruit and Vegetable Juice Processing Technology, D. K. Tressler, and M. A. Joslyn (Editors). Avi Publishing Co., Westport, Conn.

TRESSLER, D. K., and PEDERSON, C. S. 1940. Results of a demonstration sale of cherry cocktail. Fruit Products J. *19*, 195–197.

TRESSLER, D. K., PEDERSON, C. S., and BEAVENS, E. A. 1941. Cherry juice and cherry beverages. N.Y. State Agr. Expt. Sta. Circ. *180*, Rev.

TRESSLER, D. K., PEDERSON, C. S., and BEATTIE, H. G. 1943. Fruit and vegetable juice preparation and preservation. Ind. Eng. Chem. *35*, 96–100.

TRIFIRO, E. 1962. Effect of storage temperature on hydroxymethylfurfural formation in apricot and peach purée. Ind. Conserve (Parma) *37*, 113–117; cf: CA *61*, No. 6, 1964, 7617a.

WALKER, L. H., and PATTERSON, D. C. 1954. Preparation of fresh Italian prune juice concentrates. Food Technol. *8*, 208–210.

WALKER, L. H., and PATTERSON, D. C. 1955. A new improved process for pear juice concentrate. Western Canner Packer *47*, No. 12, 22, 24, 54–55.

WATKINS, J. B. 1964. Changes in the pectic substances of stored Elberta peaches. Queensland J. Agr. Sci. *21*, No. 1, 47–58.

WILLIAMS, A. H. 1958. Phenolics of fruit juices. Intern. Fed. Fruit Producers Symposium Bristol 1958, 25–63.

WILLIAMS, M. W., and PATTERSON, M. E. 1964. Nonvolatile organic acids and core breakdown of Bartlett pears. J. Agr. Food Chem. *12*, 80–83.

WILSON, D. E., MOYER, J. C., ROBINSON, W. B., and HAND, D. B. 1957. Objective evaluation of color and consistency in peach purée. Food Technol. *11*, 479–482.

CHAPTER 11

G. F. Phillips

Imitation Fruit Flavored Beverages and Fruit Juice Bases

INTRODUCTION

The imitation fruit juice beverages include a large and varied group of fruit flavors that are processed in countries throughout the world.

There are many different imitation fruit juice beverages or drinks with commercial significance as, for example orange, grape, lime, lemon, grapefruit, apple, pineapple, tangerine, cranberry, prune, blackberry, and raspberry. Within each flavor as orange and grape, there are also wide differences between the imitation fruit juice beverages. By changing the acid, sugar or juice content, different flavor characteristics can be achieved. The basic ingredients in an imitation fruit juice beverage are water (Plain or carbonated), sugar (sucrose and/or dextrose), flavor (synthetic or natural), color, acids and preservatives. All exhibit a specific characteristic to the beverage.

The present day imitation fruit juice beverages can be selected and used to add much to the pleasures of the individual. They are often referred to as beverages that can satisfy the thirst, promote mental and physical satisfaction, improve health, give refreshment, supplement nutritional requirements, promote self-efficiency, and give quick energy.

The objectives of this chapter are to provide information on the development, production, and quality control of imitation fruit juice drinks. Since the procedures for conducting research projects on product development vary from laboratory to laboratory, the data presented in this chapter on development, production and quality control must be considered only as guidelines.

In developing high quality new products as described in the succeeding pages, one must employ science and art in order to minimize problems with the products. Fruit juice beverage technology, like all other technical branches of food technology, includes chemistry, microbiology, engineering, packaging, distribution, and utilization of flavors and foods.

HISTORY

The carbonated beverage industry in the United States is recognized as having been founded in 1807 with the production of carbonated water by Joseph Hawkins in Philadelphia. During this period, Townsend Speak-

---

G. FRANK PHILLIPS is Manager, Research and Quality Control, Dr. Pepper Company, Dallas, Texas.

man, a Philadelphia druggist is said to have supplied carbonated water to the patients of Dr. Philip Sying Physick. Since plain carbonated water was not palatable to the patients, Speakman was able to improve the artificially carbonated water by flavoring it with fruit juices.

The early products came essentially as a result of experiments with natural effervescent water and their beneficial properties. After the pioneer work by Joseph Priestly 1767 and Thomas Henry 1781 on the development of artificial effervescent waters, our early physicians and scientists Dr. Benjamin Rush (1745–1813) and Dr. Valentine Seaman (1770–1817) experimented and published papers on the use of mineral waters in medicine.

During the last quarter of the 19th century, the development of Dr. Pepper (1885), Coca-Cola (1886), and ginger ales led to the development to what we know as the carbonated beverage industry today. From 1930 until today the development of imitation fruit juice beverages became significant in the market. Riley (1958) and Jacobs (1959) have presented additional information on history of the carbonated beverage industry.

The industry cannot be recognized as having gotten off to a flying start until around 1900 at the time of the development of the franchise system and the development of metal closure for the glass bottle. The franchise company holds the formula and trademark rights and does little or no bottling itself. Exceptions are cases where the company owns and operates its own plants. The franchise companies earn its profits through the sale of flavor concentrate or syrup to the franchised bottler. The franchise bottlers receive sales, advertising, technical and production aid, and information from the parent franchise company.

Another important aspect of the continuing growth of the carbonated beverage industry has been the development of high speed production equipment. With the new and advanced technological developments in beverage packaging equipment, there are increasing signs that, in the main, the growth of the industry will show a trend toward large control production facilities. This will bring about outlying sales and marketing areas from the central production plants. At the present, filling lines are operating at speeds of 800 to 1,200 containers per minute and lines are in the pilot stages of development which will package fruit juice beverages at 1,500 to 2,000 containers per minute.

As would be expected, there has been a steady increase in consumption of carbonated beverages. In 1900, the per capita consumption of carbonated beverages was 12 bottles; in 1969, the per capita consumption had reached 355. It is estimated that 15% of these are fruit flavored beverages. There is a decrease in the number of carbonated beverage plants in the United States. For example, in 1954 there were 5,626 and in 1969 there were 3,200 plants.

TABLE 84

LIQUID CONSUMPTION IN THE UNITED STATES[1]

	1968	1967	1966	1965	1964	1963	1962	1961	1960	1959
Coffee	36.6	36.8	36.9	37.8	38.8	39.6	40.5	40.5	40.2	39.9
Soft drinks	28.6	26.5	25.5	23.1	21.7	20.4	19.1	17.8	17.5	17.9
Milk	24.2	24.9	25.7	26.1	26.4	26.7	26.7	27.1	28.0	28.4
Beer	17.3	16.8	16.1	16.1	15.6	15.1	15.2	15.0	15.4	15.1
Tea	7.3	6.8	6.4	6.3	6.6	6.3	6.6	5.6	6.0	5.8
Juices	4.0	4.4	3.7	3.5	3.2	3.6	4.1	3.8	4.0	3.9
Distilled spirits	1.7	1.6	1.6	1.5	1.4	1.4	1.4	1.3	1.3	1.3
Total	119.7	117.8	115.9	114.4	113.7	113.1	113.6	111.1	112.4	112.3
Quarts per day	1.31	1.29	1.27	1.25	1.24	1.24	1.24	1.22	1.23	1.23
Imputed water consumption[2]	0.69	0.71	0.73	0.75	0.76	0.76	0.76	0.78	0.77	0.77
Total	2.00	2.00	2.00	2.00	2.00	2.00	2.00	2.00	2.00	2.00

Source: Soft Drink Journal, Jan. (1970).
[1] All figures shown in gallons per capita.
[2] Includes all others

TABLE 85

TOTAL UNITED STATES PACK—ACTUAL CASES OF FRUIT JUICES

Product	1964	1965	1966	1967
Apple juice	9,784	9,670	8,953	9,029
Grapefruit	9,741	12,215	18,377	14,063
Orange juice	13,496	14,145	17,629	12,551
Tangerine juice	151	51	124	40
Grapefruit and orange juice blended	2,084	2,384	3,050	1,809
Pineapple	12,302	13,626	13,267	13,370
Grape	7,800[1]	7,800[1]	7,600[1]	7,400[1]
Nectars	3,500[1]	3,500[1]	3,500[1]	3,500[1]
Other	6,500[1]	6,300[1]	6,200[1]	6,100[1]

Source: Data compiled by National Canners Association and Canner/Packer Magazine.
[1] Partially estimated.

The consumption of noncarbonated and carbonated fruit juice drinks in the United States has risen very rapidly in the last 15 years. The noncarbonated and the carbonated fruit juice drinks are generally available, diluted and ready to serve, in cans or bottles. Several of the first juice type drinks contain a mixture of two or more fruit juices as pineapple, grapefruit, and punch drinks.

The US liquid consumption is revealed in Table 84.

DEVELOPMENT OF FRUIT JUICE BEVERAGES

Marketing trends and packaging developments have made two main types of fruit juice beverages available to the consumer. The fruit juice beverages may be carbonated or noncarbonated. The primary difference in the carbonated and noncarbonated fruit juice beverage is the content of carbon dioxide gas. The carbonated fruit juice beverage contains carbonated water, fruit juice, sugar, acid, natural and/or artificial flavor, artificial color and sodium benzoate.

In the development and production of carbonated fruit juice drinks, there are three distinct phases or stages, namely (1) formulation of the

TABLE 86

E.O.A. STANDARD FOR OIL GRAPEFRUIT EXPRESSED[1]

	Specifications
Other general names	Oil of shaddock Oil grapefruit coldpressed
Botanical nomenclature	*Citrus Paradisi*, Macfayden *Citrus Decumana*, L
Preparation	Obtained by expression of the fresh peel of the fruit
Physical and Chemical properties	Color and appearance: A yellow oil occasionally having a reddish tinge and often showing a flocculent separation of waxy material Specific gravity at 15°C: 0.854 to 0.860 Optical rotation at 25°C: +91° to +96° Refractive index at 20°C: 1.4750 to 1.4780 Evaporation residue: 5% to 8% Method: Proceed as directed for the determination of Evaporation Residue. (See Determination E.O.A. No. 1-F) using a 5-gm sample and heating for 5 hr
Descriptive characteristics	Solubility: Benzyl benzoate: Soluble in all proportions Fixed oils: Soluble in all proportions in most fixed oils Glycerine: Insoluble Mineral oil: Soluble in all proportions, often with opalescence or cloudiness Propylene glycol: Slightly soluble Stability: Alkali: Unstable in the presence of strong alkalies Acid: Unstable in the presence of strong acids Oxidation: Adversely affected by exposure to air
Containers	Should be shipped preferably in well-filled glass or tin-lined containers. Good quality galvanized containers are also suitable.
Storage	Store in tight, full containers in a cool place protected from light.

Source: Essential Oil Association of U. S. A., New York.

[1] Oil Grapefruit Expressed is the volatile oil obtained by expression from the fresh peel of the grapefruit. Substantial quantities are produced in Florida as a by-product of the citrus canning industry. Some oil is also produced in Texas and in other regions.

flavor base or concentrate; (2) preparation of the finished bottling syrup; and (3) bottling of the finished drink. The steps in the development and production of a quality fruit juice beverage may be listed:

(1) Select the best quality raw materials available through chemical, physical, and organoleptic tests in the laboratory.

(2) Formulate the flavor base, beverage syrup, and finished beverage by mixing the constituents in a ratio that will yield a true fruit flavor.

(3) Submit the beverage to a quality control and consumer taste panel.

(4) Establish flavor ingredients cost, availability, toxicity, shelf-life characteristics, and detailed manufacturing procedures.

(5) Create a trademark or brand name and package.

(6) After the product has been market tested on a small scale, turn it over to the sales department for release to the market.

FLAVOR CLASSIFICATION

Fruit juice beverage flavors may be classified into two major groups: natural flavors and synthetic flavors.

The natural flavors are from natural products as oils, spices, and herbs. The natural flavors are obtained from fruit, flowers, leaves, buds, roots, tubers, bark, stems, and wood of various plants. For example, natural grapefruit oil flavor is derived from the fruit or grapefruit peel. See Table 86 for specifications of grapefruit oil as presented by Essential Oil Association of the United States.

TABLE 87

E.O.A. STANDARD FOR METHYL ANTHRANILATE[1]

$C_8H_9O_2N$ Mol. Wt. 151.08

(Benzene ring with $-NH_2$ and $-COOCH_3$)

Specifications		
Preparation	Esterification of anthranilic acid	
Physical and Chemical Properties	Color and appearance:	Colorless to pale yellow liquid with bluish fluorescence, having an odor of the grape type
	Specific gravity @ 15°C:	1.167 to 1.175
	Refractive index @ 20°C:	1.5820 to 1.5840
	Congealing point:	Min. 23.8°C Proceed as directed for the determination of congealing temperature. (See U.S.P. XIII, p. 629)
	Solubility in alcohol:	Soluble in 5 volumes and more of 60% alcohol
Descriptive Characteristics	Solubility:	
	Benzyl benzoate	All proportions
	Diethyl phthalate	All proportions
	Fixed oils	All proportions
	Glycerine	Insoluble
	Mineral oil	Partly soluble
	Propylene glycol	All proportions
	Volatile oils	Partly or all proportions
Stability	Acids—Fairly stable to organic acids Alkali—Stable in weak alkaline media, saponified by caustic alkali	
Containers	Should be shipped in glass, aluminum or in tin-lined containers	
Storage	Store preferably in tight, full containers in a cool place, protected from light. Prolonged storage or exposure to light may cause discoloration.	

Source: Essential Oil Association of U.S.A., New York.

[1] Methyl anthranilate occurs naturally as an ingredient of several essential oils, such as neroli oil, tuberose oil, ylang ylang oil, where it is a minor constituent. It is also found in grape juice. The commercial product is identical with the natural product, and it is made synthetically from chemicals originating from coal-tar.

The synthetic or artificial group of flavors are made from organic substances and chemically they are identical to flavors isolated from natural sources. For example, methyl anthranilate is made synthetically and it is also a flavoring material present in grapes. For standards of methyl anthranilate see Table 87. Other synthetic or artificial flavors are produced which have no known counterpart in nature.

TABLE 88

RANGES IN PPM OF DIFFERENT FLAVORS USED IN IMITATION FRUIT JUICE DRINKS

Flavor Compound	Usage Level in ppm
Lime oil	10–150
Lemon oil	10–200
Orange oil	10–150
Grapefruit oil	10–150
Allyl heptanoate	1–4
Benzaldehyde	10–30
Benzyl butyrate	1–6
Citral	5–15
Cognac	3–8
Geraniol	1–2
Isoamyl acetate	10–25
Isoamyl butyrate	10–15
Isoamyl formate	5–10
Ethyl acetate	30–50
Ethyl butyrate	10–30
Linolaol	1–3
Methyl anthranilate	5–20

HOW FLAVOR CONCENTRATES ARE MADE

The fruit juice concentrates are formulated in different forms for the beverage manufacturer. The two primary forms or physical state of the flavor bases or flavor concentrate are (1) flavor solutions or extracts and (2) flavor emulsions. The flavor extracts contain only water, or water and alcohol as solvent. Some extracts may contain propylene glycol, glycerol or surfactive agents as solvents for the flavor.

The second form, the emulsions, generally contains water, vegetable gum, flavoring components, and a preservative. The emulsions are used for preparation of a cloudy or turbid beverage, as the citrus flavors, and/or when there is an advantage for preparing a more concentrated flavor base. An emulsion is a heterogeneous system consisting of flavoring oils intimately dispersed in water in the form of globules whose diameters generally are below two microns.

The preparation of a flavor extract and flavor emulsion requires technical knowledge in the science of flavors and flavor production. It is essential to know the solubility, shelf-life characteristics, and taste threshold of synthetic flavors before they are used in product formulation.

The formulation of flavor extracts can be accomplished by blending the proper flavor components in water and alcohol. The emulsion type formulation can be a little more complicated. The first step in the formulation of an emulsion is making the oil mix. The specific quantity of flavoring oil must be determined. This can be done with a specific gravity balance, or an accurate hydrometer. Citrus oils will have a specific gravity approximately 0.84. Since citrus oils have a specific gravity below one, weighted oil is used to increase the specific gravity of the citrus oil to a level at which they can be suspended satisfactorily in a beverage. Proportions of the flavoring oils and weighted oil must be calculated. The best gravity for the oil mix depends upon the beverage formula. For example, if the beverage specific gravity is 1.04, then calculate the desired specific gravity of the oil mix. In general, a reduction of 0.02 from the desired specific gravity of the oil mix performs better than the theoretical calculation. For calculating the proportions of the oil mix, the Pearson Square Method as shown below can be employed:

Calculation

	Specific Gravity	Gravity Desired	Proportions
Orange oil	0.84		31
		1.02	
Weighted oil	1.33		18

Procedure

(1) Write the desired specific gravity in the center of a square.
(2) Write the specific gravities of the oil components in the left-hand corners of the square.
(3) Cross-subtract each corner number and the center number, the smaller number from the larger one in each case.
(4) Numbers in the right-hand corners give the proportions of ingredients by volume to use. (Since this is a ratio, the decimal point can be moved in both right-hand numbers.)

For practical purposes, specific gravity is the same as density, and it is the weight of a unit volume of a liquid. Thus, specific gravity is weight divided by volume (sp gr = wt ÷ vol). To convert the proportions in volumes into one by weight: wt in oz = vol in fl oz × sp gr × 1.04. (The factor 1.04 is needed because a weight ounce is not the same as a fluid ounce.)

Specific gravity of the oil mixture is checked by use of a good hydrometer or by weighing an accurately measured volume. Final adjustment is made if necessary by adding the required amount of weighted oil or essential oil.

The second step in the preparation of the emulsion is the mixing of the oils with the emulsifying agent or gum acacia. This involves mixing or wetting the gum with the oils. Then with high speed agitation add the water rapidly and continue to mix until a homogeneous mixture is obtained. This mixture is then pumped through a homogenizer to get proper particle or oil globule size. The emulsion should have oil globules below two microns in size. This can generally be accomplished by passing the emulsion mixture through the homogenizer at least twice under a pressure of 2,500 to 3,000 lb.

The general procedures followed in preparing carbonated or noncarbonated imitation fruit juice drinks are much the same as those used in preparing all other types of carbonated beverages. Some of the steps in product formulation, production and packaging are discussed below.

There are three phases in the development of a beverage, namely, the flavor concentrate or extract, the finished syrup and the finished beverage as drink. After the concentrate or flavor base has been developed in the laboratory, the following directions are employed for commercial preparation of the fruit juice beverage.

Imitation Orange Concentrate

(100-Gal Batch)

Primary Emulsion

Cold pressed orange oil	40 lb
Weighted oil	26 lb
Gum arabic	34 lb
Water to	20 gal

Combine the oils and mix well. After mixing the gum and oils, then with high speed agitation add water and continue to mix until all products are thoroughly blended. Then this emulsion is to be homogenized twice at 3,000 lb pressure or until oil globules are two microns or below in size.

Flavor Concentrate

Primary orange emulsion (as above)	20 gal
Benzoate soda	1/2 lb
Anhydrous citric acid	2 lb
FDC Yellow No. 6	6 lb
60° Brix orange juice	10 gal
Water to	100 gal

Bottler's Syrup

Water	21.5 gal
Sucrose	300 lb
Orange flavor concentrate	1 gal
Sodium benzoate	1/2 lb
Anhydrous citric acid	3 lb

Agitate the ingredients and water until the sugar is dissolved, then add flavor and mix thoroughly.

Finished Beverage

Employ one ounce syrup with five ounces carbonated water; that is, the syrup to water ratio is 1 to 5.

NATURAL AND ARTIFICIAL FLAVORS

Advances in organic chemistry and practical experience have harnessed the natural and artificial flavoring materials for use in the fruit juice beverages. In recent years, detailed chemical analyses and isolation of flavoring components have been made through use of vacuum distillation, gas-liquid chromatography and infrared spectroscopy. These data have contributed to improving the procedures of beverage formulation. They have established the scientific approach and the use of instrumentation in beverage formulation and quality control. New methods of analyses and techniques have raised beverage formulation from an art to a science. The use of gas-liquid chromatograms in checking flavors has been demonstrated by Teitelbaum (1957). Establishing the desired ratio of synthetic chemicals in flavors may be aided by the use of gas-chromatography. Flavor quality has been increased as a result of scientific knowledge of all flavoring ingredients. The constituents as detected in citrus oils analyses by Stanley, Ikeda, Vanvier and Rolle (1961) are typical data for testing and selection of natural flavoring oil by laboratory analyses.

The citrus oils as orange, lemon, lime, mandarin, tangerine, and grapefruit contain a high percentage of terpenes. In working with these oils it is well to keep in mind that the terpenes, which are unsaturated hydrocarbons, rapidly absorb oxygen from the air. The terpenes upon oxidation develop a terpentine taste. The oxidation shortens shelf-life and alters the delicate bouquet of fruit flavors. Antioxidants, as ascorbic acid and tocopherols (vitamin E), have been demonstrated to protect or reduce the oxidation of certain citrus oils and flavors. According to Guenther (1949) there is no variation in the physical characteristics in orange oil prepared from different varieties of Florida fruit. The method of extracting has been found to influence the physical and chemical properties of orange oil when the percentage of oil yield varies. Kesterson and Hendrickson (1959) demonstrated that the percentage of the total amount of oil that is extracted from orange peel determines the characteristics of the oil. In the selection of citrus oils, the physical constants as specific gravity, optical rotation, refractive index, alcohol solubility and color should be determined. Also, citrus oils should be judged by taste, odor, and shelf-life characteristics. These organoleptic tests are often more important than the physical tests.

Synthetic or imitation flavors used in fruit juice beverages should be of the highest grade and quality. Under controlled manufacturing and purification processes, synthetic aromatics can be purchased with a high degree of purity. The quality of the organic compounds can be maintained by laboratory analyses. The advantages of using synthetics in fruit juice beverages are (1) economy; (2) high concentration; (3) fewer storage problems; (4) greater stability; and (5) better shelf-life.

Guidelines on the formulations of fruit juice flavors are presented below.

Peach Flavor Extract Formula

	Parts
Ethyl acetate	25
Aldehyde C 14	8
Ethyl butyrate	10
Linalyl acetate	2
Iso-amyl acetate	10
Ethyl formate	10
Glyecrine	10
Ethyl alcohol as solvent	
Water to volume	

Other ingredients to employ with the flavor extract to prepare a flavor concentrate, syrup, and finished drink include water, sucrose, concentrated peach juice or purée, FDC Yellow No. 6, anhydrous citric acid, and benzoate.

Lemon-Lime Extract Formula

	Parts
Lemon oil (cold press)	6
Lime oil (distilled)	2
Terpeneless lemon oil	1
Ethyl alcohol as solvent	
Water to volume	

Other ingredients to employ with flavor extract to prepare a flavor concentrate, syrup and finished drink include water, sucrose, concentrated lemon juice, FDC Color No. 5, anhydrous citric acid, sodium citrate, and sodium benzoate.

Cherry Extract Formula

	Parts
Benzaldehyde	10
Ethyl acetate	50
Ethyl butyrate	10
Ethyl oenanthate	2

Ionone	1
Orris concrete	1
Ethyl alcohol as solvent	
Water to volume	

Other ingredients to employ with the flavor extract to prepare a flavor concentrate, syrup and finished drink include water, sucrose, concentrated cherry juice, FDC Red Color No. 2, anhydrous citric acid, and sodium benzoate.

Strawberry Extract Flavor

	Parts
Aldehyde C_{16}	10
Ethyl butyrate	20
Ionone	0.5
Vanillin	1
Orris concrete	2
Lemon oil	1
Ethyl alcohol as solvent	
Water to volume	

Other ingredients to employ with the flavor extract to prepare a flavor concentrate, syrup, and finished drink include water, sucrose, concentrated strawberry juice or purée, FDC Red No. 2, anhydrous citric acid, and sodium benzoate.

Grape Flavor Extract Formula

	Parts
Ethyl acetate	40
Methyl anthranilate	25
Ethyl butyrate	5
Amyl valerionate	5
Orange oil (fivefold)	2
Oil cognac	.5
Ethyl alcohol as solvent	
Water to volume	

Other ingredients to employ with the flavor extract, to prepare a flavor concentrate, syrup, and finished drink include water, sucrose, concentrated grape juice, FDC colors Red No. 2 and Blue No. 1, anhydrous citric acid, and sodium benzoate.

Pineapple Flavor Extract Formula

	Parts
Ethyl butyrate	60
Isoamyl butyrate	20
Allyl caprate	5
Glycerine	5
Lemon oil	1
Ethyl acetate	1
Ethyl alcohol as solvent	
Water to volume	

Other ingredients to employ with the flavor extract to prepare a concentrate, syrup, and finished drink includes water, sucrose, concentrated pineapple juice, FDC Color No. 5, anhydrous citric acid, and sodium benzoate.

Grapefruit Flavor Emulsion Formula

	Parts
Grapefruit oil (2–fold)	25
Citral	1
Weighted oil	16
Gum acacia	15
Water to desired volume	

Other ingredients to employ with emulsion to prepare flavor concentrate, syrup and finished drink include water, sucrose, concentrated juice, FDC Color No. 5, anhydrous citric acid, and sodium benzoate.

Lemon Flavor Emulsion Formula

	Parts
Lemon oil (cold press)	20
Terpeneless lemon oil	3
Citral	1
Weighted oil	16
Gum acacia	20
Water to volume	

Other ingredients to employ with emulsion to prepare flavor concentrate, syrup, and finished drink include water, sucrose, concentrated lemon juice, sodium citrate, anhydrous citric acid, FDC Color No. 5 and sodium benzoate.

Amendment published in Federal Register: * June 26, 1969; 34 F.R. 9867[1]

[1] *Effective date.* This order shall become effective 60 days from the date of its publication in the FEDERAL REGISTER, except as to any provisions that may be stayed by the filing of proper objectives. Notice of the filing of objectives or lack thereof will be announced by publication in the FEDERAL REGISTER.

§ 31.1 Soda water; identity; label statement of optional ingredients.

(a) Soda water is the class of beverages made by absorbing carbon dioxide in potable water. The amount of carbon dioxide used is not less than that which will be absorbed by the beverage at a pressure of one atmosphere and at a temperature of 60°F. It may contain buffering agents as provided in paragraph (b) (5) of this section. It either contains no alcohol or only such alcohol (not in excess of 0.5% by weight of the finished beverage) as is contributed by the flavoring ingredient used. Soda water designated by a name, including any proprietary name provided for in paragraph (c) of this section, which includes the word "cola" or a designation as a "pepper" beverage that, for years, has become well known as being made with kola nut extract and/or other natural caffeine-containing extracts, and thus as a caffeine-containing drink, shall contain caffeine in a quantity not to exceed 0.02% by weight.

(b) Soda water may contain optional ingredients, but if any such ingredient is a food additive or a color additive within the meaning of section 201 (s) or (t) of the Federal Food, Drug, and Cosmetic Act, it is used only in conformity with a regulation established pursuant to section 409 or 706 of the act. The optional ingredients that may be used in soda water in such proportions as are reasonably required to accomplish their intended effects are:

* (1) Nutritive sweeteners consisting of the dry or liquid form of sugar, invert sugar, dextrose, fructose, corn sirup, glucose sirup sorbitol, or any combination of two or more of these.

(2) One or more of the following flavoring ingredients may be added, in a carrier consisting of ethyl alcohol, glycerin, or propylene glycol:

(i) Fruit juices (including concentrated fruit juices), natural flavoring derived from fruits, vegetables, bark, buds, roots, leaves, and similar plant materials.

(ii) Artificial flavoring.

(3) Natural and artificial color additives.

* (4) One or more of the acidifying agents acetic acid, adipic acid, citric acid, fumaric acid, gluconic acid, lactic acid, malic acid, phosphoric acid, or tartaric acid.

(5) One of more of the buffering agents consisting of the acetate, bicarbonate, carbonate, chloride, citrate, gluconate, lactate, orthophosphate, or sulfate salts of calcium, magnesium, potassium, or sodium.*

(6) (i) One or more of the emulsifying, stabilizing, or viscosity-producing agents brominated vegetable oils, carob bean gum (locust bean gum), glycerol ester of wood rosin, guar gum, gum acacia, gum tragacanth, hydroxylated lecithin, lecithin, methylcellulose, mono- and diglycerides of fat-forming fatty acids, pectin, polyglycerol esters of fatty acids, propylene glycol alginate, sodium alginate, sodium carboxymethylcellulose, sodium metaphosphate (sodium hexametaphosphate).

(ii) When one or more of the optional ingredients in subdivision (i) of this subparagraph are used, dioctyl sodium sulfosuccinate complying with the requirements of § 121.1137 of this chapter may be used in a quantity not in excess of 0.5% by weight of such ingredients.

(7) One or more of the foaming agents ammoniated glycyrrhizin, gum ghatti, licorice or glycyrrhiza, yucca (Joshua-tree), yucca (Mohave), quillaia (soapbark) (Quillaja saponaria Mol.).

(8) Caffeine, in an amount not to exceed 0.02% by weight of the finished beverage.

(9) Quinine, as provided in § 121.1031 of this chapter, in an amount not to exceed 83 ppm by weight of the finished beverage.

(10) One or more of the chemical preservatives ascorbic acid, benzoic acid, BHA, BHT, calcium disodium EDTA, erythorbic acid, glucose-oxidase-catalase enzyme, methylparaben or propylparaben, —————————— propyl gallate, potassium or sodium benzoate, potassium or sodium bisulfite, potassium or sodium metabisulfite, potassium or sodium sorbate, sorbic acid, sulfur dioxide, or tocopherols; and in the case of canned soda water, stannous chloride in a quantity not to exceed 11 ppm calculated as tin (Sn), with or without one or more of the other chemical preservatives listed in this subparagraph.

(11) The defoaming agent dimethylpolysiloxane in an amount not to exceed 10 ppm.

(c) (1) The name of the beverage for which a definition and standard of identity is established by this section which is neither flavored nor sweetened, is soda water, club soda, or plain soda.

(2) The name of each beverage containing flavoring and sweetening ingredients as provided for in paragraph (b) of this section is "---------------- soda" or "---------------- soda water" or "---------------- carbonated beverage," the blank being filled in with the word or words that designate the characterizing flavor of the soda water; for example, "grape soda."

(3) If the soda water is one generally designated by a particular common name; for example, ginger ale, root beer, or sparkling water, that name may be used in lieu of the name prescribed in subparagraphs (1) and (2) of this paragraph. For the purpose of this section, a proprietary name that is commonly used by the public as the designation of a particular kind of soda water may likewise be used in lieu of the name prescribed in subparagraphs (1) and (2) of this paragraph.

SELECTION AND USE OF FRUIT JUICES

Fruit juices for use in imitation fruit drinks must meet high quality standards. The appearance, taste, odor, acidity, sugar, and shelf-life characteristics must be established on each batch of fruit juice employed in fruit drinks. All of these characteristics are most important in the selection and use of fruit juices.

The changes which occur in fruit during growth and development and during storage after harvesting markedly affect the quality and stability of the juice obtained, but information in these fields is limited and widely scattered in the botanical, physiological, and horticultural literature. With fruit juices, it is recognized that the post harvest physiological changes are markedly affected by bruising or mechanical damage and is reflected in the chemical changes, both enzymatic and nonenzymatic, which occur in the cell sap as a result of the destruction of the structural features of the intact cells and the dynamic balance between the various constituents present. Reaction between the various chemical constituents composing the sap and reaction between these constituents and the external environment (oxygen of the air, the metallic and other surfaces which the juice contact, etc.) produces undesirable changes in the expressed juice. Fruit juice is best when it is first pressed from the sound fresh tissue. Any factors which affect either the internal or external environment influence its initial quality and stability.

During all stages of handling, from the extraction to the final packaging, the juice should be protected from contamination with metals. Contamination with metal such as zinc from galvanized ware, or lead, or cadmium from plating, solder, or alloys must be strictly avoided, since the salts of these metals are extremely toxic. The sale of juice containing toxic substances is prohibited by law. Contamination with iron and copper is undesirable because of the adverse effect of these metals upon the flavor of the juice. Not only do they impart an objectionable metallic flavor, but they also hasten certain undesirable changes.

The actual concentration at which the metallic ions are detectable to taste has been investigated for but a few juices and then only under poorly controlled conditions. Metallic ions may affect the flavor, color and appearance of juices in different ways depending on the conditions, particularly oxygen tension and extent and nature of reducing conditions. In juices exposed to air, or stored under partly aerobic conditions the tolerance for metals may be high. Thus, in California Valencia orange juice, the concentration of metal detectable to taste was found to be 20 ppm for copper; 30 to 40 ppm for ferrous iron, and at about 100 ppm or over for ferric iron, aluminum, chromium, nickel, and tin. Shrader and Johnson (1934) found that copper and iron imparted off-flavor to Florida orange juice when present to the extent of 5 ppm; chromium at 30 ppm; tin over a range of 15 to 60 ppm, while aluminum and nickel did not impart any flavor.

In order to avoid the effect of metals upon color and flavor it is necessary to use equipment made of glass, or steel lined with glass or suitable enamel, or to use corrosion-resistant metals. Aluminum, nickel, certain nickel-copper alloys such as Inconel, and certain stainless steels have been found suitable. Much of the metal used for equipment in modern juice factories is stainless steel.

Other changes which occur in fruit juices may be a result of microbiological activity, or due to the presence of gases as oxygen, nitrogen and carbon dioxide. Bacteria and yeast in fruit juices can bring about fermentations which modify the physical and chemical composition of the juice. While high levels of gases as oxygen in juices can bring about oxidation reactions which can affect the shelf-life and quality of the juices.

TABLE 89

LABORATORY STANDARDS FOR WATER TO BE USED IN PREPARING FRUIT JUICE BEVERAGES

	Maximum
Alkalinity	50 ppm
Total solids	500 ppm
Iron	0.1 ppm
Manganese	0.1 ppm
Turbidity	5 ppm
Color	Colorless
Residual chlorine	None
Odor	None
Taste	No off taste
Organic matter	No objectionable content

Like all products obtained from natural sources, the fruit juices have to be carefully selected, tested, processed and stored before they are employed in a quality fruit juice beverage. Select juices from suppliers that can be purchased under specified quality on each shipment. The strength of the juice to employ in natural or imitation fruit juice beverages will depend on the type formulation.

All fruit juices purchased and used should meet the standards of identity and label statements as established by the FDA. If the quality of fruit juices falls below the standard prescribed in the federal regulations, then the packer is taking a risk in product quality and ingredient statement.

Natural fruit juices and flavors employed in fruit juice drinks are complex mixtures of chemicals, as aldehydes, esters and ketones. Their analysis is complicated and requires many different analytical techniques for detection, isolation and quantitative analyses. Instrumental methods such as gas liquid chromatography, mass spectroscopy, and examination with infrared, ultraviolet, and nuclear magnetic resonance can be used in the analysis of fruit juice flavor components. Also, the flavors can be evaluated by trained taste panels. Taste tests can determine flavor level, flavor acid ratio, flavor acid sugar ratio, effect of a process change on flavor, flavor change due to age or storage condition, effect of substituting one flavor for another, omission of a flavor and approving of the flavor for use in the beverage. The analysis, formulation and main flavor components in lemon, orange, raspberry, strawberry, and grape have been investigated by Stanley *et al.* (1961), Wolford *et al.* (1963), Winter *et al.* (1963), Mattick *et al.* (1963) Anon. (1963), Canova and Terney (1969), Eiserle and Rogers (1970) and Hall (1970).

WATER

The final diluent for each flavoring ingredient in fruit juice finished beverages is water. Since water is employed up to a level of 92% in some

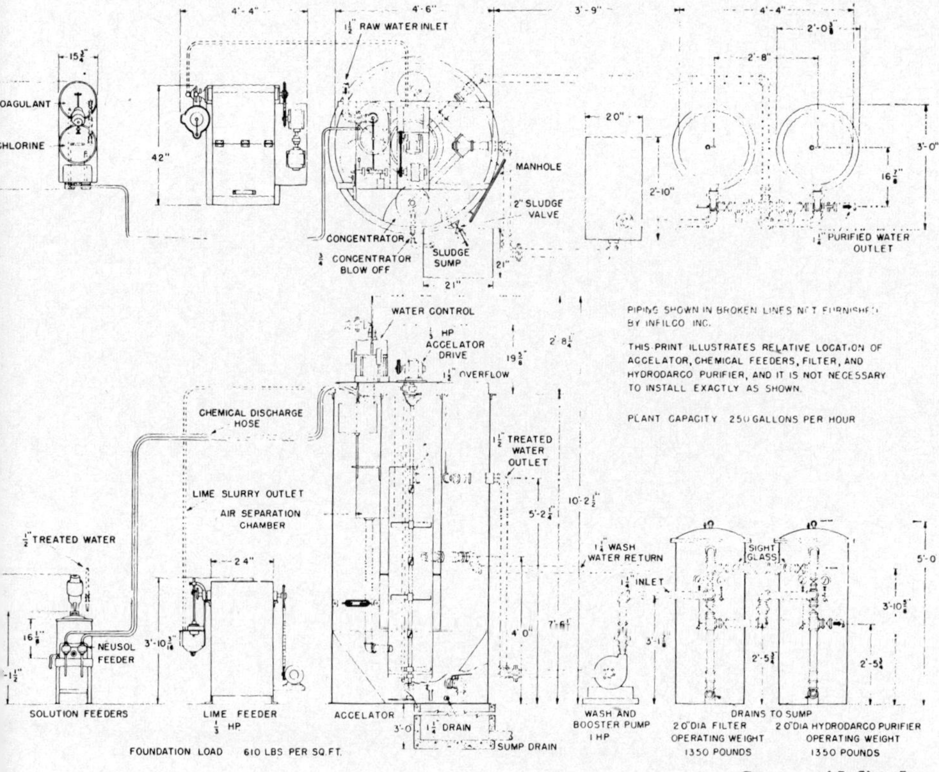

Courtesy of Inflico, Inc.

. 98. DIAGRAM OF WATER TREATMENT EQUIPMENT INCLUDING CHEMICAL FEEDERS, TREATING TANK, AND FILTERS

fruit juice beverages, it is essential that it be as near chemically pure as commercially feasible. The fruit juice beverages require a water that meets the standards as presented in Table 89.

High alkalinity is one of the most undesirable of the water impurities. If the alkalinity is high in water, it will neutralize the acid or destroy the tangy character of the beverage and thereby leave it with a taste that is too sweet or insipid. According to Braswell (1956), alkalinity in bottling water can reduce the pH of a beverage enough to lessen the effectiveness of the preservative. The alkalinity of bottling water is adjusted by chemical treatment in order that beverages may have the same reaction and be uniform in taste.

A typical arrangement of water treatment equipment is shown in Fig. 98. Properly treated water is free of objectionable levels of impurities. The methods of water conditioning or treatment for use in fruit juice bev-

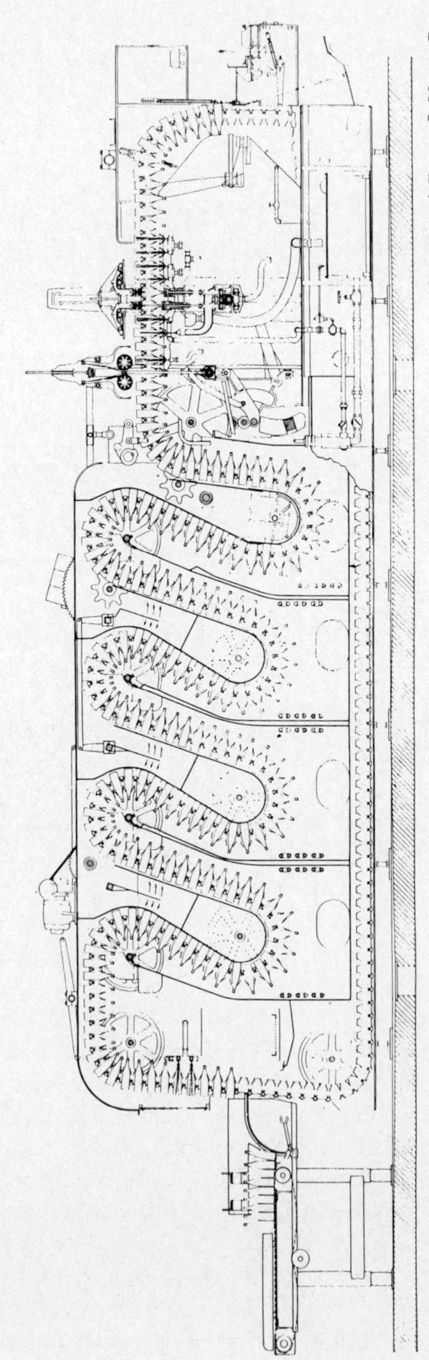

Courtesy of George J. Meyer Co.

Fig. 99. Bottle Washing Machine

In this automatic washer the fruit beverage bottle is carried by conveyor through a pre-rinse section, four tanks with proper levels of cleaning compound, and then a final rinse just prior to the discharge end.

erages may be many, btu most systems include (1) chemical treatment with ferrous sulfate or alum, soda ash, lime, and hypochlorite; (2) sand filters to clarify the water; (3) activated carbon filter to remove odors and residual chlorine; and (4) paper (polishing) filters to remove any traces or deposits not collected by the sand and carbon filters.

Water treatment by chemical process includes alkalinity reduction by use of lime. When lime is added to an alkaline water, the alkalinity is reduced by changing the soluble calcium and magnesium salts to insoluble salts. Sedimentation and/or filtration methods are then used to remove the insoluble salts. The following equations show these reactions.

$$\underset{\text{calcium bicarbonate}}{\overset{\text{(sol.)}}{Ca(HCO_3)_2}} + \underset{\text{lime}}{Ca(OH)_2} \qquad \underset{\text{calcium carbonate}}{\overset{\text{(insol.)}}{2\,CaCO_3}} + \underset{\text{water}}{2\,H_2O}$$

$$\underset{\text{magnesium carbonate}}{\overset{\text{(sol.)}}{MgCO_3}} + \underset{\text{lime}}{Ca(OH)_2} \qquad \underset{\text{magnesium hydroxide}}{\overset{\text{(insol.)}}{Mg(OH)_2}} + \underset{\text{calcium carbonate}}{\overset{\text{(insol.)}}{CaCO_3}}$$

If the alkalinity is due primarily to sodium bicarbonate and sodium carbonate rather than the calcium and/or magnesium salts, then calcium chloride or calcium sulfate may be used to form insoluble salts. The following formula shows this reaction:

$$\underset{\text{sodium carbonate}}{\overset{\text{(sol.)}}{Na_2CO_3}} + \underset{\text{calcium chloride}}{CaCl_2} \qquad \underset{\text{calcium carbonate}}{\overset{\text{(insol.)}}{CaCO_3}} + \underset{\text{sodium chloride}}{\overset{\text{(sol.)}}{2NaCl}}$$

A batch lime system may easily become a continuous process by the addition of a coagulant and chlorine in addition to the lime; the coagulant-chlorine-lime system may be operated on a batch or continuous basis. Sand and activated carbon filters are used in conjunction with, and form an integral part of, this system to remove all sediment, grit, odors, and taste from the water.

Color

Uniformity of color in imitation fruit juice beverages is very important. The processors and purchasers are aware that color variations exist in these types beverages. Uniformity of color in the imitation fruit juice beverages within a practical range is both desirable and necessary for the packer. Since color variation can be an indicator of product quality, the processor must understand the factors and conditions that are responsible for product color.

Color difference in juices and drinks occur because of such factors as fruit variety, pulp content of juice, storage conditions, microorganisms,

TABLE 90

COLOR RECOMMENDATIONS FOR IMITATION FRUIT JUICE BEVERAGES

Flavor	Color Formula	Range in Ppm
Lemon	FDC Yellow No. 5 $(C_{16}H_9N_4O_9S_2Na_3)$	10–15
Orange	FDC Yellow No. 6 $(C_{16}H_{10}N_2O_IS_2Na_2)$	30–40
Lime	95% Yellow No. 5 5% Blue No. 1	20–30
Grape	90% Red No. 2 10% Blue No. 1 $(C_{37}H_{34}N_2O_3Na_2)$	60–70
Strawberry	50% Red No. 2 50% Yellow No. 6	60–70
Raspberry	FDC Red No. 2 $(C_{20}H_{11}N_2O_{10}Na_3)$	60–70
Cherry	88% Red No. 2 10% Yellow No. 5 2% Blue No. 1	60–70
Grapefruit	FDC Yellow No. 5 Ye	5–10
Grapefruit-pineapple	FDC Yellow No. 5	5–10

metals, oxygen, and other chemicals. The juices used in the imitation beverages contain natural colors as beta carotene, lycopene, xanthophylls, lutein, and cryptoxanthin. These natural pigments are affected by fruit variety, maturity, and storage conditions.

The FDC Colors employed in imitation fruit juice beverages contribute to the attractiveness of the drink. Since color is often associated with flavor, nutritive value, and wholesomeness of the beverage, it is obvious that the correct color levels be used in all imitation fruit juice drinks. The usage level for the FDC Colors in fruit juice beverages is as presented in Table No. 90.

The FDC Colors, like the natural colors, can fade or be altered in hue. Sunlight, metals, ascorbic acid and microorganisms can affect colors. To avoid color changes, it is essential that proper grade and amount of color be employed in the beverage. The colored beverage must be handled and stored under conditions that keep them free of agents and conditions that cause color precipitation and deterioration.

CARBON DIOXIDE AND THE CARBONATION OF FRUIT JUICE BEVERAGES

One of the most important factors that relates to the taste of the bottled fruit juice beverage is carbon dioxide gas content or degree of carbonation. Carbonation is the process of dissolving carbon dioxide in a beverage so that when served it gives off the gas in fine bubbles and has the characteristic pungent taste suitable to the beverage carbonated. To get

TABLE 91

MISCELLANEOUS COMMERCIAL BEVERAGES, VARIOUS BRANDS

Sample	Flavor	Volume Carbonation	Total Soluble Solids, ° Brix	Grams Anhydrous Citric Acid per 100 Ml	pH
1	Lime	2.6	13.3	0.208	2.7
2	Lime-lemon	3.8	8.5	0.130	2.75
3	Lime-lemon	2.4	12.6	0.097	2.95
4	Lemonade	1.1	14.0	0.302	2.25
5	Tom Collins	4.0	7.4	0.365	3.2
6	Lemon-lime	3.0	13.2	0.347	3.07
7	Grape	1.3	14.5	0.124	3.1
8	Cherry	2.6	13.7	0.130	2.75
9	Blackberry	3.0	12.5	0.124	3.1
10	Blackberry	3.0	12.5	0.146	3.0
11	Strawberry	2.8	13.0	0.108	3.0
12	Raspberry	3.0	11.0	0.108	3.4
13	Raspberry	3.0	12.3	0.134	3.0
14	Orange	1.5	13.0	0.160	3.1

the gas in the solution requires a definite gas pressure on a large surface of the liquid. Once the gas is dissolved, it is held by headspace pressure.

The amounts of gas dissolved or contained in solution are spoken of as volumes. When a given volume of carbon dioxide gas (measured under standard conditions for gases) is dissolved in the same given volume of liquid, that liquid is said to contain one volume of carbon dioxide. If twice that volume of gas is dissolved, the liquid contains two volumes, etc.

Carbon dioxide dissolves in water in quantities which vary with the temperature and the pressure under which the mixture is held. The amount of gas the water will absorb increases directly with an increase in pressure or with decrease in temperature. Therefore, carbonation depends on two factors—pressure and temperatures.

At atmospheric pressure and 60°F, a given volume of water will absorb an equal volume of carbon dioxide and is said to contain one volume carbonation. The amount of gas can be measured by actually driving it off and measuring it, but the common method is to compute the volumes of carbonation by means of a special temperature pressure chart. With cold water, less gas pressure is necessary than with warm water to gain the same degree of carbonation.

At 60°F water will absorb one volume at "zero" on a gas volume tester gauge, which is really at atmospheric pressure of 15 lb. Therefore, when the gage shows 15 lb and the temperature of the water is 60°F, the water will absorb two volumes. For each additional 15 lb on the gauge, an additional volume of gas is absorbed by the water.

If we reduce the temperature to 32°F, we increase the absorption capacity of the water by 0.7 volume. Therefore, each 15 lb additional gauge pressure at 32°F (water temperature) gives an additional 1.7 volumes, not one volume as is the case at 60°F.

Suppose a bottle is filled at 32°F and a pressure of 45 lb. This would mean 1.7 × 4 volumes, or 6.8 volumes. With the crown on the bottle the

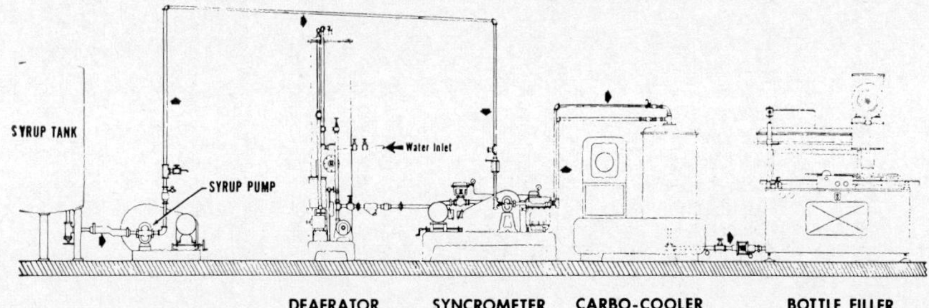

Courtesy of George J. Meyer Co.

FIG. 100. ONE FLOOR SYNCHROMIX INSTALLATION FOR CARBONATING AND BOTTLING FRUIT JUICE BEVERAGES

Water entering the deaerator passes through stainless steel baskets containing porcelain rings which disperse the incoming water and subject it to a vacuum. Experience has indicated that bottling with deaerated water reduces the tendency of foaming in the filling process. In addition, the use of deaerated water reduces the possibility of air contaminated water going to the syncrometer and carbo-cooler. Syrup and water enter the syncrometer through two separate lines. Here they are pumped to separate meters which automatically deliver the syrup and water at a constant predetermined ratio to the carbo-cooler. The syncrometer is almost continuous in its operation and only starts and stops to maintain a sufficient level of beverage in the carbo-cooler. This simple mechanical operation assures uniformity of product at all times. Water and syrup from the syncrometer enter at the top of the carbo-cooler and are combined for the first time in the distributing trough. They continue to mix as they pass down over the cooling coils in the presence of CO_2 gas. The water and syrup are mixed, cooled, and carbonated in one simultaneous operation. The finished carbonated product collects in the lower reservoir, ready for the filler. The carbonated mix flows from the carbo-cooler to the bottle filler. Bottles reaching the filler are placed on stirrups and raised into position and sealed under the filling valve. After the bottles are filled to a prescribed filling height, they are lowered and travel on to the crowner. The Meyer Dumore Crowner crimps the crown over the locking ring of the bottle tight enough to insure a leakproof seal.

gas cannot escape, and if the temperature should then be raised to 60°F, the pressure in the bottle would increase to 5.8 x 15 (atmospheric pressure), or 87 psi. This means 87 lb gauge pressure. Notice that 5.8 is multiplied by 15, although there were 6.8 volumes in the example given. This is due to the fact that one volume is shown at "0" on the gage.

In beverage manufacture, carbon dioxide not only provides the distinctive taste of carbonated drinks but also inhibits the growth of certain microorganisms. This preservative action increases in line with the number of volumes of carbonation used. However, even with highly carbonated drinks, the carbon dioxide action is just an additional safety factor and cannot be any excuse for relaxing strict sanitary controls. See Table 91 for variation for carbonation in beverages.

Carbon dioxide exists in three states—solid (Dry Ice), liquid, and gas, Temperature and pressure conditions determine the existing state.

Dry Ice is carbon dioxide gas that has been liquefied and frozen into solid form. At normal air pressure, it has a temperature of —110°F. When exposed to heat the Dry Ice vaporizes or sublimes. As long as the pressure is not increased, the vaporization acts as a self-refrigerant which maintains the 110°F temperature of the remaining solid during the vaporization process. At normal air temperature and pressure, carbon dioxide exists only as a gas.

When the Dry Ice is confined in a low pressure converter and the heat applied, the ice first sublimes, then, since gas occupies a greater volume than the solid, pressure will build up. If the pressure increases, the solid gradually warms up until it reaches a temperature of minus 70°F and a pressure of 60 psi. At this point, the Dry Ice begins to melt and liquefies rather than changes directly to the gas.

At this point, the application of additional heat does not affect the pressure and the temperature until all the solids have been liquefied. Further application of heat will cause an increase in both temperature and pressure of the carbon dioxide, and with the removal of heat, temperature and pressure both drop. A definite balance persists between pressure and temperature throughout all these changes so that for any given temperature under 87.8°F (critical temperature), a definite pressure is always found.

This change in state is reversible. Carbon dioxide gas being compressed and cooled forms a liquid which on being cooled sufficiently freezes to a solid. Conversely, the solid on being warmed forms cold gas which, if confined, creates pressure and forms a liquid. This liquid on being heated further forms compressed gas. The pressure exerted on a container is a function of the ratio of volume to weight of carbon dioxide contained.

The important physical properties which permit commercial distribution of quality carbon dioxide are the ease with which it can be liquefied and contained in economical pressure vessels, such as cylinders handled by air temperatures or insulated tank trucks holding liquid at sub-zero temperature and medium pressure; and the further property that it can be solidified and handled as Dry Ice which is either used as a refrigerant or reconverted to vapor for gas supply.

SUGARS

Chiefly significant from the nutritional standpoint, we find the sugars in the imitation fruit juice beverages to be prime source of energy. The kind and concentration of sugars in imitation fruit juice drinks vary. In general, the sugar content of these drinks has a range of 10 to 14%. Sucrose is used as the natural sweetener in most juice type beverages. Sucrose in both dry and liquid form is suitable. Assuming the quality meets the N.S.D.A. standards, the sucrose can be from cane or beets.

Liquid invert sugar, 50–50 glucose and fructose, is available and can be used in juice type beverages. Also, a blend of dextrose and sucrose liquid sugar is acceptable as a sweetener for some type beverages, that is, if the sweet taste character does not have to be predominant. Liquid sugar, produced from corn starch to yield a blend of glucose and fructose up to 90% is suitable for many fruit juice beverages.

Large users of liquid sugar install stationary storage tanks of suitable size, depending on the quantities used, with permanent piping and pumps for pumping the liquid sugar from the point of delivery to the storage tank and from the storage tank to the flavor or finished syrup mixing tanks. The storage tanks are generally provided with ultraviolet lights, fans and screened air vents to prevent growth and reproduction of yeast and other microorganisms in the liquid sugar. The storage tanks are designed to give ideal storage conditions for both the 67° Brix liquid sucrose and 76° Brix liquid invert liquid sugar, or blend of liquid sucrose and dextrose. The tanks are constructed of mild steel or other suitable materials which will not contaminate the liquid sugar with any foreign taste, odor, or mineral.

The tentative standards which follow apply to dry granulated sugar only, and are not applicable to liquid sugars. Furthermore, these standards apply to sugar as produced, immediately prior to packing.

(1) **Containers.**—For protection of the product, "Bottlers" sugar shall not be packed in cotton or fabric bags but shall be packed in multi-wall paper bags or equivalent sanitary package or bulk containers.

(2) **Container Identification.**—Each container shall be marked or coded to make it possible for the sugar producer to identify the place of production and date of packing.

(3) **Designation of Type.**—Each container shall be marked "Bottlers."

(4) **Ash.**—The ash content of "Bottlers" sugar shall not be more than 0.015%.

(5) **Color.**—The solution color of "Bottlers" sugar shall not be more than 35 reference basis units.

(6) **Sediment.**—The sediment content of "Bottlers" sugar shall not be more than shown on prepared sediment disc available from American Bot-

tlers of Carbonated Beverages, 1128 Sixteenth Street, N.W., Washington, D.C. upon request.

(7) **Taste and Odor.**—"Bottlers" sugar shall have no obviously objectionable taste or odor in either dry form or in ten per cent sugar solution prepared with tasteless, odorless water.

(8) **Bacteriological.**—"Bottlers" sugar shall not contain more than:

200	mesophilic bacteria	per 10 gm
10	yeast	per 10 gm
10	mold	per 10 gm

(9) **Sampling.**—"Bottlers" sugar shall be adequately sampled by the producer immediately prior to packing to assure compliance with these standards.

There are two other aspects of quality which are of extreme importance to the soft drink industry, namely: (1) turbidity and (2) floc-producing substances.

Universally accepted methods of testing for these factors have not yet been developed. For that reason the foregoing standards do not cover turbidity and floc-producing substances. However, as soon as accepted test methods and tolerances have been established, they will be added to this standard. Meanwhile, it is imperative that "Bottlers" sugar be as nearly free of turbidity and floc-producing substances as possible.

These sugar standards are recommended for sugars that are to be used in fruit juice beverages with two changes, namely, the sugar should be free of all mesophilic and psychrophilic microorganisms, and it should contain no flocculating substances. A quality liquid sugar or simple syrup, with similar specifications, can be used in fruit juice beverages. Generally the level of sugar in fruit juice beverages ranges from 9.5 to 14.5%.

Acids

The acids used in fruit juice beverages include citric, malic, tartaric, lactic, fumaric and in some cases phosphoric. The correct acidulant to employ in fruit juice beverage can best be determined by a taste panel. Citric acid has been more widely used in fruit beverages due to its taste, solubility, storage and handling characteristics, cost and antioxidant characteristics.

Different acid/sugar ratios and the type flavored beverage can affect the tartness of acids in fruit juice beverages. The following reveals the relative tartness or sourness of acids in beverages:

Acid	Tartness (Grams/Liter)
Citric	1.30
Tartaric	0.95

Lactic	1.60
Fumaric	0.85
Malic	1.30
Phosphoric (75%)	0.85

The proper amount of acid to use in a beverage can best be determined by an experienced taste panel. Also, the acid level should be such that permits the beverage to have a pH of 2.5 to 3.5, since the lower pH ranges increase the resistance to spoilage.

Preservative

Fruit juice beverages are an unfavorable medium for growth of many types of microorganisms. However, the composition and environment in fruit juice beverages can support growth and reproduction for some yeast and bacteria. Therefore, the carbonated fruit juice beverages generally contain sodium benzoate as a preservative. The levels of sodium benzoate employed in beverages range from 0.03 to 0.05% in most of the finished fruit juice beverages. The effectiveness of sodium benzoate as a preservative is influenced by the hydrogen ion concentration. It is a more efficient preservative in strongly acid beverages (pH 2.5) than more neutral beverages (pH 4.5) as shown in Table 92. Sodium benzoate is

TABLE 92

CONCENTRATION OF SODIUM BENZOATE REQUIRED TO INHIBIT GROWTH[1] OF INOCULATED SACCHAROMYCES CEREVISIAE F1-2A IN ORANGE JUICE CONCENTRATE FOR 72 HR INCUBATION

Initial pH	Sodium Benzoate Concentration, %				
	0.00	0.05	0.10	0.15	0.20
2.5	+	−	−	−	−
3.5	+	−	−	−	−
4.5	+	+	−	−	−
5.5	+	+	+	+	+
6.5	+	+	+	+	+

Source: Monsanto Chemical Company, St. Louis, Missouri.
[1] Growth indicated by a + sign; no growth indicated by a − sign.

permitted by the Federal Foods Laws. The noncarbonated beverage may be pasteurized to prevent spoilage. Sorbic acid and certain antibiotics have been demonstrated as effective preservatives for certain fruit juice beverages. Additional research should present other practical methods of beverage preservation as ultrasonics and radiation.

Other Ingredients

There are a number of flavors or products used in fruit juice beverages in order to improve the quality of the product. Glycerine and propylene glycol are used in some fruit juice beverages or solvents and preservatives. Glycerine is also used as a stabilizer, thickener, and humectant. Methylcellulose is used as a bodying agent for beverages. Gum arabic or gum acacia, a water soluble gum, is widely used as an emulsifying agent for flavors in fruit juice beverages. Carrageenan and other similar compounds are used in some products to improve stability. Ascorbic acid has been used in beverages as an oxygen acceptor, flavor developer and as a source of vitamin C.

PACKAGES

With fruit juice beverages, the best possible package at the most economical cost should be employed. The packages generally employed for beverages include the outer carton and the container used for the specific product. The outer carton should be developed to meet a set of specifications in regard to performance in the plant, retail and wholesale outlets, appearance and physical requirements, ease of handling on the packaging line and in the warehouse, shipping requirements, freight regulations, closures requirements, design, and structure that can be manufactured by supplier at a feasible cost.

Once the specifications for a carton have been developed, the job of keeping them current becomes most important.

The packages for the different fruit juice beverages, whether they be glass, plastic, metals, or a combination of these components, must meet specific requirements. Since fruit juice beverages contain water, sugar, flavoring oils, acids, colors, and in some cases carbonation, and the fact that some beverages are sensitive to heat, light, microorganisms, and oxidation; most beverages require a special container. The functional properties of a package—to protect adequately and preserve the product until consumed—must meet various properties of the product; that is, the package must be resistant to transmission of gas, corrosion, flavors and aroma, impermeability to microorganisms, and light. Also, the package size, shape, legal requirements, convenience features, promotional requirements, handling, and filling characteristics must be developed.

As soon as the package has been developed and proved suitable for the specific beverage, then it becomes necessary to prepare a set of quality control test procedures. Quality control testing for glass and metal containers can include tests as listed in Table 94. Each time large shipments of the product containers are purchased and received they must be inspected and tested to ensure that they meet the required specifications.

QUALITY CONTROL

Production of imitation fruit juice beverages requires the closest attention to quality control at every step of the process. This includes incoming raw materials, proper water treatment, clean and sterile packages, good manufacturing practices, and in-plant quality control tests. In these days of high volume and high speed manufacturing, the primary objective of a production manager must be to produce a high quality product.

For the purposes of discussion on the subject of quality control of imitation fruit juice beverages, let us consider three aspects of quality control (1) advantages of quality control; (2) requirements for a quality control program; and (3) guidelines on the operation of a quality control program in a fruit juice drink manufacturing plant.

Managers of fruit juice plants know and are firmly convinced that there are many advantages in establishing and maintaining an effective quality control program. They realize and have experienced the functions of a well-balanced quality control system. For instance, they know that good quality control program in the plant will: (1) protect production costs by preventing and detecting defects in products packed; (2) protect the consumer and assure that he gets a quality product with good "eye appeal"; (3) maintain plant requirements in order to meet local, state and federal good manufacturing practices; (4) protect and control the use of quality raw materials as water, sugar, acids, preservatives, flavors, and packages; (5) generate pride and increase morale of production personnel; (6) assist in product liability problems; (7) improve production efficiency; (8) assist in plant layout, design and space requirements; (9) improve waste control, (10) aid in plant safety; (11) minimize company criticism; and (12) assure sales department that products are what customers want to buy.

The requirements for a quality control program in a beverage plant involve many aspects of the entire plant operation. That is to say, to establish a practical and workable quality control program there is a need for careful planning, organizing and follow-through.

To plan and organize a quality control program, the objectives must be listed in order to accomplish or gain those desired. Future changes and emergencies in the production operation should be visualized. After a decision on what is required in the quality control program, a list of what needs to be done to accomplish the necessary program should be prepared. These requirements will include people, budget, laboratory space, policies, standard tests and specifications on products and laboratory testing equipment.

The manager of each plant must decide on the general course of action in setting up the quality control program. From the requirements on quality control, the technologists, laboratory space, standard tests and testing equipment can be determined. For example, the person(s) selected to head up the quality control section must know or be trained in function and operation of each piece of manufacturing equipment and have the knowledge to control or advise on the significant process variables, inferior product and faulty package so that he can predict the characteristics of the finished product. For example, he should know what will happen to the product if such variables as temperature, pressure and rate of water flow are detected in the filling equipment. He must know and be able to control what is occurring in the entire packaging line and be able to run all the quality control tests on raw materials, finished products and packages. Also, he should have a knowledge of the approved cleaning and sanitizing compounds. He should know the cleaning methods for the plant and equipment and be familiar with good manufacturing practices for a beverage plant.

The extent of training required for a person in quality control will depend on his experience, technical education and capacity.

The laboratory space for the quality control section should depend on the number of people to staff the laboratory, the amount of testing equipment employed (Table 93), and space to be utilized for expansion and sample storage area. The minimum space required for a small plant testing laboratory should not be less than 100 sq ft and the space could range up to 600 sq ft for the laboratory and 200 sq ft for the sample storage area in larger manufacturing plants. Planning of space and facilities for a testing laboratory in a fruit juice drink plant requires the combined skills of plant management, industrial, chemical and mechanical engineers for effective design. The laboratory space should be planned in coordination with other activities, policies and plans for future expansion. In Table 93 we have listed the laboratory testing equipment that should be used in a fruit juice drink testing laboratory to check product quality.

Since the quality control section is to protect, control and approve the use of raw materials, finished products and packages, it is an essential requirement to have a set of standard tests and specifications on these products. Tables 94 and 95 show the different quality control tests which are recommended requirements for use on different products and packages in a fruit juice beverage plant.

In order to obtain the advantages of a quality control program as listed above, the program must operate by established guidelines. (1) Appoint one person to be responsible for the quality control program. (2) Make sure the quality control personnel know their duties and responsibilities after they are properly trained. (3) Establish a testing and sampling schedule as demonstrated in Table 95. (4) Have coordination in quality control matters among people in all departments. (5) Establish a systematic method of checking the effectiveness of quality control. This can be accomplished through daily, weekly and monthly reports or by use of automatic recording systems.

TABLE 93

LABORATORY TESTING EQUIPMENT

- A. Finished Product in Bottle and Cans Testing Equipment
  - Gas volume tester
  - Dial thermometer 25°–125°F
  - Leather bottle guard, 12 oz
  - 1 Brix thermo hydrometer 5–15° Brix
  - 1 " " " 50–60°+ Brix
  - 1 Fill height gauge
  - 1 Crown crimp gauge
  - 3 100 ml beakers
  - 3 250 ml beakers
  - 1 Gas volume chart
  - 2 Hydrometer cylinders
  - 1 pH meter
  - 1 Colorimeter
  - 1 Zahn air tester
  - 1 Zahn sample bottle
  - 1 Zahn CO_2 gas purity tester
  - 1 Enamel rater
  - 1 Double beam trip scale w/weights
  - 1 Micrometer gauge
  - 1 Special gauge
  - 1 Can opener
  - 1 Nippers
  - 1 Broad face file
- B. Treated Water Testing Equipment
  - 3 250-ml Erlenmeyer flasks
  - 1 25-ml automatic burette
  - 1 100-ml Graduated glass cylinder
  - 1 Super colorimeter
  - 1 4-oz bottle ortho tolidine
  - 1 " " "T" solution
  - 1 " " phenolphthalein
  - 1 " " methyl purple
  - 1 Qt. $^1/_{50}$ N sulfuric acid
  - 1 Water hardness test kit
- C. Sugar Testing Equipment
  - 3 250-ml beakers
  - 3 100-ml beakers
  - 1 Conductivity solubridge Model No. 11
  - 1 Baumé hydrometer 29/41
  - 1 Package sediment disc
  - 1 Vacuum apparatus
  - 1 Vacuum trap
  - 1 Filter holder
- D. Additional Quality Control Testing Equipment
  - Caustic Test
    - 1 N.S.D.A. caustic test kit
    - or
    - 1 Caustic titration set
  - Pre-Mix Test
    - 1 Master premix CO_2 volume tester
    - 1 Product sampling valve
  - Additional Laboratory Equipment
    - 1 Heavy duty hand crowner
    - 1 Dead weight gauge tester
    - 1 Hand jack set (for use in repairing gauges)
    - 1 Atomic absorption unit
    - 2 Ovens
    - 1 Incubator

TABLE 94

GUIDELINE FOR TESTS ON PRODUCTS AND PACKAGES TO DETERMINE CONFORMANCE TO SPECIFICATIONS

Treated Water	Approved Sugar	Bottled Drink	Canned Drink	Empty Bottle	Empty Can
Appearance	Appearance	Appearance	Appearance	Appearance	Appearance
P-alkalinity	Color	Fill point	Total	Annealing test	Can lining
M-alkalinity	% Ash	Crown crimp	Air	Glass thickness	Litho
Taste	Taste	Sediment	Carbonation	Thermo-shock test	Seam
Odor	Odor	Carbonation	Sediment	Weight	Flange
Iron	Sediment	Taste	Taste	Capacity	Weight
Copper	Microorganism	Brix	Brix	Impact test	Enamel rater
Turbidity	pH	pH	pH	Line test	Copper sulfate
Total solids	Iron	Total acid	Total acid	Internal pressure test	Ring-pull
Color	Copper	Metals	Metals	Vertical load test	Leakage
Residual chlorine	Crystal size	Microorganisms	Microorganisms	Lubricity test	Diameter

TABLE 95

GUIDELINE SCHEDULE FOR IN-PLANT CONTROL TESTING FOR AN IMITATION FRUIT JUICE CAN PRODUCTION LINE

Tests	Frequency of Checks
Finished syrup Brix or Baumé	Each batch
Carbonation	Beginning and every hour
Syrup weight (Brix)	Beginning and every hour
Air content	Beginning and every hour Stop line when air exceeds 2.0 cc per can
Taste	Beginning and every hour
Can code	Twice in morning and twice in afternoon
Finished seam	Beginning and every 2 hr Visually every 15 min
Water treatment	Twice daily
Can fill	Beginning and every hour

Since we have no way to make sure that the quality control activities are effective, we list the following danger signals of poor quality control: (1) customer complaints on products; (2) low production efficiency; (3) inaccurate production yields; (4) no daily records on quality control tests; (5) low morale of production employees; (6) lack of good housekeeping; (7) low rating by government inspector; (8) improperly trained employees; (9) employee turnover; (10) management's lack of interest in quality control and management's lack of follow-up on the quality control program.

In summary, we have attempted to reveal the advantages, requirements and guidelines for a quality control program in a fruit drink beverage plant. We explained that a practical quality control program can be established and function effectively, if it is carefully planned, organized and followed up at frequent intervals. The program must include a budget, properly trained personnel, operating policies, lab space, standard tests and specifications on products and laboratory testing equipment.

Naarden's publication on tables tracing undesirable changes in soft drinks is typical to spoilage problems in fruit flavored beverages. Tables 96 through 99 are useful in tracing product defects and they serve as good references in quality control of fruit juice beverages.

PRODUCTION OF IMITATION FRUIT JUICE BEVERAGES

Successful manufacture of good fruit juice beverages require a combination of factors. The quality must be maintained during the manufacturing operation.

The process used in the manufacture of fruit juice syrups is similar with most all flavors. Fruit juices and flavor concentrates usually require little or no special preliminary treatment prior to the syrup mixing process. But it is essential to keep in mind the following procedures and recommendations while measuring and mixing, handling, bottling and storage of fruit juice syrup: (1) prepare the syrup according to a standard formula under clean and sanitary conditions; (2) employ approved sugar and water in the syrup; and (3) package or store prior to use under established conditions. The steps in syrup preparation by a standard formula include careful measurement of ingredients. For example, the metering of water into a mixing tank, adding the correct level of sugar and mixing until dissolved, then adding the required flavor and mixing well. Unless the product is to be pasteurized, the preservative is added at this stage.

Measurements of syrup strength are required prior to each bottling operation. Measurements for the per cent sugar in syrups may be carried out by the use of hydrometers or specific gravity spindles. According to Sharf (1940), the first adopted calibration system for hydrometers was devised by a French chemist, Antoine Baumé, late in the 18th century. This system is used today in measuring the degrees Baumé of syrup. Baumé hydrometer readings can be converted to per cent sugar as illustrated in Table 100. An Austrian chemist, Balling, developed a hydrometer scale for syrup, showing the per cent of sugar present. Brix hydrometer readings by A. F. W. Brix have practically replaced the degrees Balling readings for the per cent of pure sugar by weight in syrups. With properly calibrated hydrometers, accurate per cent sugar measurements can be made at specified temperatures.

Fruit juice syrup is sometimes produced in a separate industry, but it is so closely associated with bottling industry that it may be regarded as an essential part of the bottling plant operation.

The actual bottling or canning of a carbonated fruit juice beverage includes the preparation of a standard finished syrup under exacting conditions, then transferring the syrup and carbonated water under specified conditions into a clean and sterile package and then closing the package with minimum air content. In-plant requirements for carrying out this type of bottling process are important and essential for the production of a quality product.

Preliminary to the bottling process of the fruit juice beverage is the selection of the correct package. Let us review briefly the size and type of containers as used for packing still and carbonated fruit juice beverages. The still or noncarbonated fruit juice beverages are packed in cans, plastic or paper containers. The 46-oz can has been the most widely accepted package for the still fruit juice beverage, while the most popular size for canned carbonated beverages is the 12-oz can. Cans with special made liners are available for packing fruit juice beverages. At sporadic intervals, the market demands fruit juice beverages packed in half-gallon glass containers. The carbonated fruit juice beverages are bottled in flint, amber and green glass bottles in sizes which range from 6 to 32 oz. Consideration should be given to the type package required for each product. Studies have shown that citrus type beverages have longer shelf-life in amber glass bottles than flint bottles. According to Cole (1959) certain type green glass bottles are able to prevent light transmission and thereby extend beverage shelf-life.

Now let's review another preliminary phase to actual bottling of a carbonated fruit juice beverage. It is essential to make available a suitable package or commercially sterile bottle. The commercially sterile bottle contains no pathogenic or spoilage microorganisms. Also, it is free of any detergent or sterilizing agent, clean in appearance and is of good mechanical strength. The re-use of carbonated fruit juice beverage bottles requires a standard procedure for cleaning and sanitizing.

The procedure for cleaning and sterilizing is customarily performed by conveying the bottles through a bottle washer containing a warm alkaline solution followed by rinsing the bottles in the soaker with potable water. Completely automatic machinery for bottle washing, as shown in Fig. 99, plus the use of specialty chemical bottle washing compounds have added greatly to the efficiency of the bottle washing process.

An industry accepted procedure and conditions for bottle washing have been established. The bottle to be filled with fruit juice beverage should be first exposed to a 3% alkali solution of which not less than 60% is caustic (sodium hydroxide), for a period of not less than 5 min at a room temperature of not less than 130°F. The bottle must then be rinsed in potable water until free from alkali or washing compounds. Detailed data on factors affecting bottle washing in regards to equipment, detergents, and handling of bottles are available from bottle washer manufacturers.

All bottling and canning equipment, pipes, utensils, and surfaces that come in contact with the fruit beverage ingredients should be cleaned and properly sanitized prior to the packaging operation. The cleaning and sanitization procedure is carried out by cleaning with odor-free detergents, sanitizing with chlorine, and then rinsing. The concentration of chlorine used depends upon the contact time with the equipment to be sanitized. For example, with a concentration of 200 ppm available chlorine solution, 10 to 15 min contact time is required; with 100 ppm available chlorine solution, 20 to 40 min; and with a 50 ppm available chlorine solution 1 hr contact time.

Plant sanitation and good housekeeping are the responsibility of management. However, when directed by a properly trained person on a rigid schedule, it is easy to keep the bottling plant in good sanitary condition.

Within recent years better beverage bottling equipment has been developed through new technological designs. Many mechanical features involved in the syruping and filling operations have been modified or replaced with pre-mix filling systems similar to model in Fig. 100. The detailed beverage manufacturing equipment is presented by American Bottlers of Carbonated Beverages (1945).

After the preparation of the bottling syrup, the sequence of the actual bottling operation includes filtering of the syrup, the premixing of the bottling syrup with treated water, carbonation, washing, inspection and filling of the bottles, crowning of bottles, inspection of finished beverage, casing of the bottles, palletization of cases and warehousing of the finished beverages.

To get high quality and uniform carbonated fruit juice beverages, selected ingredients are combined in proper balance and then packaged under sanitary conditions by established technical procedures. All these steps prior to the bottling include the use of a balanced blend of high quality product, perfect adjustment of bottling equipment, correct temperature and pressure of carbonated water and the use of a suitable and attractive container.

Plant Sanitation

The new FDA laws (GMP Regulations) which became effective May 26, 1969 are federal standards covering Good Manufacturing Practices in the manufacturing, processing, packaging or holding of human foods (beverages). Some of the regulations are mandatory requirements, while others are recommended practices. The mandatory regulations are phrased in terms of "shall" and the recommended practices are presented under the word "should."

The composition of fruit juice beverages make them an unfavorable medium for growth and survival for most species of bacteria. The acid

Table 96

CHANGES IN FLAVOR

Fault	Cause	Remedy
(1) Metallic taste	(a) Tin coatings of equipment and/or storage vessels are faulty.	Renew lead-free tin coating.
	(b) Water has high iron content.	Install water purification plant.
	(c) Unsuitable storage vessels have been used.	Ensure that only acid-resistant vessels are used for preparation and storage of acids and juices.
(2) Loss of flavor	(a) Metallic traces in water.	See 1, (a), (b), and (c).
	(b) Minerals in the water destroy the flavor by chemical action.	Purify and, if necessary, soften water.
	(c) Drinks have been stored too long.	Keep stock to minimum.
(3) Musty smell or flavor	(a) Water containing chlcrine has been used.	Use dechlorination plant.
	(b) Sugar or syrup has absorbed foreign aromatic substances.	Filter syrup through activated charcoal.
	(c) Raw materials, equipment, or drinks are infected.	See: Table 98
(4) Oily or fatty taste	(a) Equipment has become greasy.	Care should be taken during lubrication; only tasteless greases to be used for pump pistons.
	(b) Gears or brushes in the washing machine have become fouled with oil or grease.	Check and clean regularly: clean brushes with fatfree detergent.
	(c) Sugar sack has stood in spilt oil.	Filter syrup through activated charcoal.
(5) Taste of turpentine	(a) Defective storage of flavor.	Store in cool dark place and use small size packing, flavors should be kept from contact with air as much as possible.
	(b) Emulsions and fruit juices have been unsuitably stored.	Store cool. Use up remainders quickly; do not allow too great a stock to accumulate.
(6) Taste of beetroot or molasses	(a) Poor quality sugar has been used.	Use only refined crystal sugar.
(7) Taste of rubber	(a) Poor quality rubber rings have been used.	Use only best quality components.
	(b) New rings have not been washed before use.	Soak in $2^3/_8$ soda solution before use and remove rubber dust.
(8) Reduced carbonation	(a) Ring in bottle is defective.	Change.
	(b) Closures are not gastight.	Change
	(c) Crowncorks not properly put on.	Bottle closing machine is worn out and should be replaced.
	(d) Plastic screw-caps do not give adequate closure.	Use correct size and thread.

Source: Naarden, Inc.

Table 97

VISIBLE CHANGES

Fault	Cause	Remedy
(1) Liquid becomes cloudy	(a) Infection.	See: Table 98
	(b) If natural mineral water has been used, impurities have been introduced with it.	Install water filtration plant.
	(c) Impurities introduced in the form of metallic traces, owing to contact of acid or fruit juice with unprotected metal.	Use properly protected vessels.
(2) Lumps and threads	(a) Syrup contains proteins.	Boil syrup and skim thoroughly.
	(b) Syrup has been inadequately filtered or not at all.	Sugar may contain impurities; it must then be filtered.
	(c) Salts in water have been chemically attacked by acids in fruit juice.	Purify and, if necessary, soften water; prepare base syrup one day previously and allow sediment to sink.
	(d) Fermentation.	See: Table 98.
	(e) Molds.	See: Table 98.
	(f) Fibers from previous batch of fruit juices have been left in equipment.	Rinse out equipment thoroughly after each mix; dismantle and clean metering pump.
(3) Opalescence	(a) Solubility of flavor too low.	Use soluble flavor.
	(b) Flavoring extract used in excess.	Reduce flavor quantity.
(4) Change in color	(a) Yellow color caused by poorly refined sugar.	Filter through activated charcoal.
	(b) Sugar slightly caramelized.	Filter through activated charcoal.
	(c) Acids and fruit juices in contact with metal: brown iron compounds.	Ensure that vessels are suitable.
(8) Loss of color	Too much oxygen in water.	Reduce air content of water; if necessary use ascorbic acid or enzyme preparation.

Source: Naarden, Inc.

TABLE 98

POOR KEEPING QUALITIES OWING TO CONTAMINATION OF RAW MATERIALS

Cause	Remedy
(1) The water is biologically contaminated.	Have water analyzed. Install sterilizing filter or chlorination plant. When chlorine has had sufficient effect on water, however, the latter should be dechlorinated, otherwise it will spoil taste. Well equipment should be cleaned out and disinfected (with chloride of lime or formalin) and then thoroughly pumped out until all trace of disinfectant has disappeared. If well is contaminated, a new one must be provided.
(2) Sugar sack has become damp and microorganisms have therefore developed that are capable of spoiling drink, for example, by fermentation.	Store sugar in dry place. Sugar that has got damp should be used without delay.
(3) Syrup containing less than 60% sugar has been kept too long and fermentation has started.	Only syrup containing more than 60% sugar can be kept for any length of time. It must be kept adequately covered, however, since microorganisms falling into it will not be killed. If syrup is diluted, they start to become active and dangerous and spoil the drink. Spoilt syrup should be thoroughly boiled; if it retains a bad taste, filter through activated charcoal.
(4) Flavor emulsion and/or fruit juice is spoilt; microbial decay has set in.	Keep cool. Containers once opened should be emptied as soon as possible. Use permitted preservatives in permitted quantities. Never use fermenting raw materials in this class. Throw them away!
(5) Sugar content of base syrup has dropped below 60% through addition of other ingredients; has then stood too long and fermentation has started.	Base syrup containing less than 60% sugar should be used within 24 hr. This will very easily go bad, and once it has done so it cannot be recovered.
(6) Acid solution in stock can also be attacked by microbes.	Do not prepare too much stock. An infected acid solution can be recovered by heating to boiling point in acid-resistant vessels. Remember that water will be lost by evaporation, so that acid concentration will increase.
(7) Molds and bacteria can also develop in liquid colors.	Ready-made color solutions usually contain preservatives when bought. When preparing own solutions, therefore, permitted preservatives should be added. A better way out of the difficulty is to prepare no more stock than is required for one or two days.

Source: Naarden, Inc.

content, carbon dioxide gas, flavors and preservatives in fruit drinks are inhibitory to many bacteria. Fruit drink flavor concentrate and syrups can be bactericidal to a large number of pathogenic microorganisms. In spite of the fruit juice beverage not being conductive to the growth and reproduction of many types of bacteria, the new and current GMP regulations

TABLE 99

POOR KEEPING QUALITIES OWING TO IN-PLANT CONTAMINATION

Cause	Remedy
Sources of Contamination in the Factory	
(1) Water sterilizing filter no longer works properly.	Employ new plates for sterilizing filter. If filter candles are used, these should be taken out, cleaned and boiled. Make sure that filters are not being overloaded.
(2) Water tank has become fouled; scum deposit on walls.	Clean and disinfect.
(3) Microbes in water have settled inside carbonator and are constantly carried along to the bottles.	Fill installation with disinfectant solution and let it stand for several hours. Rinse thoroughly afterwards.
(4) The filling machine has not been properly cleaned.	Must be dismantled more often. Clean parts thoroughly and put them in a bath of disinfectant solution. The filling cap must be removed and thoroughly cleaned.
(5) The syrup line, metering pump and valves have become dirty and consequently infected.	Supply lines must be disinfected from time to time. Keep valves clean. Rinse thoroughly after use.
Infection from Sugar-Dissolving Equipment	
(1) Equipment for dissolving sugar has not been cleaned for a long time.	Observe the very strictest cleanliness.
(2) The filter has been used too long	Wash filter cloths immediately after use. Boil them or soak them in a disinfectant solution; let them dry thoroughly. Where filters with a coating are used, the coating should be renewed at the correct times.
(3) Filtrate that was still too low in sugar content was not recycled, hence concentration was too low; or the sugar layer had become too thin, so that water seeping through it did not become saturated. Syrup could therefore ferment.	Ensure correct procedure. Boil syrup that has turned out too thin. Boil fermenting syrup and filter it through activated charcoal.
(4) Filter has become fouled and works very slowly. The water layer on top of the sugar dissolves some sugar, before seeping through, thereby allowing microorganisms to develop.	Ensure that utmost cleanliness is observed; change filters at frequent intervals.

Source: Naarden Inc.

still must be put into practice in each beverage manufacturing and storage plant. To say it another way, each beverage packer must establish and maintain good manufacturing practices.

For many years, a series of steps have been taken by most beverage manufacturers to keep their plant in compliance with good housekeeping and good plant sanitation. Through experimentation and research in many different laboratories, there have been many new cleaners and sanitizing agents developed which give excellent performance in plant sanitation practices. There have been many new methods and tools developed for cleaning and sanitizing the production areas of bottling plants. The use of hot water, good detergents, and high pressure machines (both portable and in-place type machines) have made it easier to clean and keep the equipment, floor, and other surfaces in the production department sanitary. The fruit juice beverage plants, like all food plants, must continually make changes and upgrade their operation procedures in order to improve the condition of their plant building and grounds, equipment, sanitary facilities for employees, quality control in processing, bottling and storage of beverage and beverage ingredients.

From a fruit manufacturer's point of view of GMP, it is essential to get a comprehensive concept of what the new regulations entail and avoid confusion and misunderstanding about the new law. That is, get a copy of the final regulation on Good Manufacturing Practices for the food industry which was published in the Federal Register on April 26, 1969 and become completely familiar with it.

Since Good Manufacturing Practices must be conducted and maintained constantly, it is desirable to establish a GMP program that will function effectively and efficiently throughout the daily production cycle. Sanitation changes of considerable magnitude may occur daily or even hourly with improper GMP. Thus, all production personnel should be aware of the GMP requirements and thereby prevent any significant changes in the plant that will affect your GMP standards or rating. Ideally, one person should inspect the plant daily in order to determine if the plant is in compliance with GMP.

MISCELLANEOUS DRINKS

New candidates for the soft drink market are many. Since 1960 the United States has seen new beverages as powder mixes, diet beverages, and isotonic drinks enter the market.

The powdered beverages are available as different fruit flavored beverages. The formulation of these products, in regard to flavor, is very similar to the liquid beverages. That is, the flavor portion of the product is blended and then it is spray dried, or put into a powder, or dry form by microencapsulation, or freeze-dried process. The dry flavor is then blended with the correct balance of color, acid, and sugar and packaged. The package for the powdered flavor is very important. With flavors containing a mixture of sugar, or the ready to serve powder mixes, it is essential to employ a package that is moistureproof. Powdered beverages are made available with and without sweeteners. The sweeteners in powdered flavors can be sucrose, dextrose or artificial sweeteners. Powdered beverages in present day markets are marketed as breakfast drinks and/or as drinks for children.

Diet carbonated beverage production grew from practically none to about 15–17% of the total market between 1960 and October 18, 1969.

TABLE 100

RELATIONSHIP OF DEGREES BRIX, BAUMÉ, SYRUP COMPOSITION AND WEIGHT[1,2]
(Syrup and Beverage Concentrations)

Degrees Brix° (% Sucrose by Weight)	Pounds Sugar in 1 Gal of Syrup	Weight of Syrup per Gallon (Lb)	Degrees Baumé°
6	0.51	8.52	3.35
7	0.60	8.55	3.91
8	0.69	8.59	4.46
9	0.78	8.62	5.02
10	0.87	8.66	5.67
11	0.96	8.69	6.13
12	1.05	8.72	6.68
13	1.14	8.76	7.24
14	1.23	8.80	7.79
15	1.33	8.83	8.34
36	3.47	9.64	19.81
38	3.70	9.72	20.89
40	3.92	9.81	21.97
42	4.16	9.90	23.04
44	4.39	9.98	24.10
46	4.63	10.07	25.17
48	4.88	10.16	26.23
50	5.13	10.25	27.28
52	5.38	10.35	28.33
54	5.64	10.44	29.38
56	5.90	10.53	30.42
58	6.17	10.63	31.46
60	6.44	10.73	32.49
62	6.71	10.83	33.51
64	6.99	10.93	34.53
66	7.28	11.03	35.55
68	7.57	11.13	36.55
70	7.86	11.23	37.56

[1] Computed from U.S. Bureau of Standards Circular No. 375 (Temperature 68°F).
[2] This table is adapted to typical beverages (6 to 15° Brix) and syrup (36 to 70° Brix) concentration with intermediate values not given.

That is, cyclamate and saccharin (artificial sweeteners) were used as primary sweeteners in cola and fruit-type diet beverages until the United States Food and Drug Administration removed cyclamate from the market.

The formulation, production, and quality procedures for diet beverages are similar to the regular or sugar sweetened carbonated beverages. The primary difference between the diet and sugar-type beverage is the type of sweetener. The diet beverages were formulated with a ratio of cyclamate and saccharin of approximately 90 to 10% on a weight basis. After the cyclamate was removed as an approved FDA sweetener, the carbonated beverage industry formulated diet beverages with saccharin and a low per cent of sucrose. The sucrose level in most diet drinks today ranges from 0 to 5%. All other flavoring ingredients in diet drinks are GRAS (Generally Recognized As Safe).

The so-called quick-energy, or thirst quenching drinks have been introduced for sale in the United States. These products are flavored with cola, lemon-lime, and fruit type flavors and they are sweetened with artificial sweeteners and dextrose. These beverages contain inorganic salts as potassium citrate and sodium orthophosphate. The salt mixture in this type beverage is said to reduce the quantity requirement for ingested water and the energy expenditures associated with such ingestion, when body water is lost. The beverages are said to be formulated and adjusted to approximate closely that of the body water, i.e., the intracellular water.

BIBLIOGRAPHY

American Bottlers of Carbonated Beverages. 1953. Beverage manufacturing equipment in the bottled carbonated beverage industry. Am. Bottlers Carbonated Beverages, Washington, D.C.

Anon. 1963. Fruit flavors. Givaudan Flavorist, No. 1, 1–4, 8.

Braswell, J. R. 1956. Product irregularities, their detection and correction. Tech. Publ., Royal Crown Cola Co., Columbus, Ga.

Canova, L. A., and Tierney, J. V. 1969. Man made citrus oils. Soc. Soft Drink Technol., 16th Ann. Meeting Proc.

Cole, B. C. 1959. Product protection by control of light transmission through glass. Private communication, Seven-Up Bottling Co., St. Louis, Mo.

Eiserle, R. J., and Rogers, J. 1970. Production, quality control standards, test procedures and usage of essential oils in carbonated beverages. Soc. Soft Drink Technol., 17th Ann. Meeting Proc.

Guenther, E. 1949. The Essential Oils, Vol. 3. D. Van Nostrand Co., New York.

Hall, R. 1970. Formulation of carbonated beverages. Soc. Soft Drink Technol., 17th Ann. Meeting Proc.

Jacobs, M. B. 1959. Manufacture and Analysis of Carbonated Beverages. Chemical Publishing Co., New York.

Kesterson, J. W., and Hendrickson, R. 1951. Oxidative stability of orange oil as related to method of extraction. Am. Perfumer Essential Oil Rev. 57, 441–444.

Mattick, L. R., Robinson, W. B., Weirs, L. D., and Barry, D. L. 1963. Determination of methylanthranilate in grape juice by electron affinity–gas chromatography. J. Agr. Food Chem. *11,* No. 4, 334–336.

N.S.D.A. 1953. Tentative Standards for Bottlers' Sugar, Tech. Bull.

Riley, J. J. 1958. A History of the American Soft Drink Industry. Am. Bottlers Carbonated Beverages, Washington, D.C.

Sharf, J. M. 1940. Syrup measurement and control. Fruit Products J. *20,* 81–84, 87.

Shrader, J. H., and Johnson, A. H. 1934. Freezing orange juice. Ind. Eng. Chem. *26,* 869–874.

Stanley, W. L., Ideda, R. M., Vanvier, S. H., and Rolle, L. A. 1961. Determination of relative concentrations of the major aldehydes in lemon, orange and grapefruit oils by gas chromatography. J. Food Sci. *26,* 43–48.

Teitelbaum, C. L. 1957. Gas partition chromatography. Applications to essential oils and other volatile materials. J. Soc. Cosmetic Chemists *8,* 316–327.

WINTER, M. *et al.* 1963. Food Process. Packaging *32*, No. 378, 86–88.

WOLFORD, R. W., ATTAWAY, J. A., ALBERDING, J. A., and ATKINS, C. D. 1963. Analysis of the flavor and aroma constituents of Florida orange juice by chromatography. J. Food Sci. *28*, 320–328.

CHAPTER 12

Sherman Leonard

Tomato Juice and Tomato Juice Blends

INTRODUCTION

Tomato juice has the characteristic color and mildly acid flavor of tomatoes. It is served at any meal of the day as an appetizing first course, and it also finds a variety of uses in cookery, such as preparation of jellied salads. Nutritionally it serves as an important source of vitamins A and C (see Composition and Nutritive Value) and has a firm place in both standard and special dietaries.

Commercial single-strength tomato juice has had a very remarkable development since it was introduced almost 50 years ago. This product is a refreshing beverage, as well as a good source of vitamin C (Troy and Schenck 1960). Since 1959 the production of tomato juice has been higher than that of canned peeled tomatoes.

Pack statistics for four major commodities: canned tomatoes, tomato catsup, tomato concentrate, and tomato juice are shown in Table 101. The apparent reduction in the production of tomato juice has been influenced by over-production, new varieties, and a shift in the data collection process. Up until 1967, tomato juice blends consisting of 70% or more tomato juice were reported in the pack statistics as tomato juice. Beginning in 1968, the only data available are combined data on tomato juice and tomato juice concentrate, which are reported in total actual cases (Table 102). In fact, data concerning only tomato juice blends are not available for any year.

A large proportion of the tomato juice produced continues to be packed in No. 3 cylinders (Table 103). As evidenced in this table, there has been a significant increase in the production of not only this size container, but also of individual serving can sizes which contain from 5 to 8 oz. Again, data collection systems no longer report the distribution of can sizes in 1968 and 1969.

CULTURAL PRACTICE

With mechanization, varieties and methods of planting have been changed, as having spacing, fertilization application, and irrigation procedures. These changes in cultural practices have altered acidity, flavor, color, consistency, and chemical composition.

SHERMAN LEONARD is Lecturer and Food Technologist, in the Food Science and Technology Department, University of California, Davis, California.

TABLE 101

U. S. PRODUCTION OF CANNED TOMATOES IN THOUSAND CASES OF 24 NO. 303'S (24 LB/CASE)

	1959	1960	1961	1962	1963	1964	1965	1966	1967
Canned tomatoes	29,422	30,991	34,034	35,541	33,041	36,431	36,015	32,662	39,981
Tomato catsup	22,157	28,619	28,314	36,940	28,556	32,587	34,084	35,345	37,780
Tomato concentrate	15,825	30,056	32,353	44,577	29,164	38,763	31,474	39,913	42,413
Tomato juice[1]	37,962	41,272	39,492	50,198	43,149	44,126	41,031	39,864	43,868
Total	105,366	130,938	134,193	167,256	133,910	151,907	142,604	147,784	164,042

Source: U.S. Dept. Agr., Foreign Agricultural Service, Fruit and Vegetable Division, Commodity Analysis Branch.

[1] Tomato juice here includes vegetable juice blends consisting of 70% or more tomato juice, and tomato juice concentrate.

TABLE 102

U. S. PRODUCTION OF CANNED TOMATOES AND TOMATO JUICE IN THOUSANDS OF ACTUAL CASES

Year	Canned Tomatoes	Tomato Juice
1967	30,022	33,151[1]
1968	37,491	31,359[2]
1969	24,622	36,388[2]

Source: Release of Jan. 9, 1970 by Division of Industry Statistics, National Canners Association.

[1] Includes tomato juice blends of 70% or more tomato juice and tomato juice concentrate.

[2] Does not include tomato blends (data not available).

TABLE 103

1969 TOMATO JUICE PACK[1] IN CASES OF ALL SIZES IN THOUSANDS OF ACTUAL CASES

Container Size	Units Per Case	1960	1967	1968[2]	1969[2]
Indv. 5-6-8 oz	48	3,699,290	7,049,313	...	...
211 cyl. (211 × 414)	48	1,179,787	1,421,760	...	...
No. 300 & 303	24	2,135,330	1,684,858	...	...
No. 2 (307 × 409)	24	2,237,244	1,148,019	...	...
29, 32, & 36 oz	12	891,984	804,608	...	...
No. 3 cyl. (404 × 700)	12	17,140,952	17,515,633	...	...
No. 10 (603 × 700)	6	421,122	288,633	...	...
Misc. tin		693,397	1,168,137	...	...
Misc. glass		1,537,608	2,070,247	...	...
US total:		29,936,714	33,151,208	31,358,746	26,388,142
Basis 24/2's:		33,017,987	35,094,076	N.A.	N.A.

Source: This is a summary of reports from canners packing in 1969. The figures for 1967 and previous years include vegetable juice consisting of 70% or more tomato juice and tomato juice concentrate. The figures for 1968 and 1969 include only tomato juice and tomato juice concentrate. The 1969 California pack of 13,200,535 cases is included in the above total.

[1] Releases of Dec. 23, 1960, and Jan. 9, 1970 by Division of Industry Statistics, National Canners Association.

[2] Detail by container size not available.

Variety

The attributes of quality in tomato juice (flavor, color, consistency, and nutritive value) are influenced by variety, climate, cultural practice in the field, harvest procedure, degree of ripeness at the instant of harvest, length of storage before processing, washing and sorting, and each step of the processing procedure plus packaging and warehousing.

Courtesy of California Tomato Growers Assoc.

FIG. 101. MECHANICAL HARVESTING OF TOMATOES

All of these components are important and must be properly integrated to produce a superior-quality tomato juice. Since the only permitted additive is sodium chloride, the flavor, color, consistency, and nutritive values start with the variety.

The development of a commercial mechanical harvester for the mechanical harvesting of tomatoes (Lorenzen and Hanna 1962), coupled with the rapid simultaneous development of varieties suitable for mechanical harvesting (Hanna *et al.* 1964), have put serious limits on varietal selection for tomato juice.

In California, about the only variety grown presently (UC VF-145) is an interim variety suitable for mechanical harvesting. Plant breeders are constantly seeking improved varieties for mechanical harvesting and are trying to breed into these tomatoes quality-attributes that will make them superior to the older hand-harvested varieties. Many new varieties may be expected in the next few years. Because of the economic advantages of mechanical harvesting, other tomato-growing areas in the United States are also striving to develop or to improve varieties suitable for machine harvesting. This, too, will mean a series of varietal changes. None of the varieties thus far in commercial use for mechanical harvesting has ideal quality-attributes for tomato juice.

HARVESTING, HANDLING, AND PROCESSING OF TOMATO JUICE

The changes in utilization characteristics, wholeness, serum viscosity, per cent insoluble solid and per cent soluble solid that can occur with machine harvesting, subsequent bulk handling, transportation, and storage before processing are discussed in the section on composition.

The extent of damage during harvest and storage is markedly influenced by the method of mechanization, the variety, and the degree of ripeness at the time of harvest.

It has been learned that mere mechanization of the harvest system is only the first step in changing the tomato handling systems. Additional steps and precautions are necessary. Drastic changes in handling and processing procedures are needed before the immediate long-term gains that are possible to achieve can be realized.

With mechanical harvest there has been a tendency to harvest when there is a higher percentage of well-colored tomatoes. This means that a higher percentage of soft-ripe tomatoes is obtained, than with the multiple-harvest hand-picked system.

Mechanization has resulted in bulk handling, and the consequent use of bins 48 in. × 48 in. × 24 in. that contain 600–800 lb net weight of harvested tomatoes (Fig. 101). One-ton bins are now being considered, and with new, more mechanically-resistant varieties, bulk trucks and bulk trailers are also expected to receive attention.

The harvesting of a higher percentage of soft-ripe fruits has given rise to an increased percentage of damaged fruits. This damage results in weight losses which can range from $1^1/_2$ to 4% loss in weight for firm-ripe fruit to over 30% in soft well-colored fruit.

In terms of per cent of undamaged fruit, firm-ripe fruit will have 85% undamaged tomatoes with careful transportation and no storage, whereas soft-ripe fruit with 100 miles of commercial transportation and 44 hr of storage will have only 6% undamaged fruit. These damage and storage losses result from disintegration and loss of soluble solids (Leonard and Marsh 1969), and are reflected in the serious drop in serum viscosity and by an increase in total insoluble solids. Both of these factors will have a marked influence on the viscosity and flavor of the processed tomato juice.

Washing

Because of the nature of mechanical harvesting and bulk handling of tomatoes, more care must be exercised to prevent bacterial buildups (O'Brien *et al.* 1969; York *et al.* 1964). The first or soaking-wash should contain up to 200 ppm of available chlorine and subsequent flood-washing should maintain a minimum of 5 ppm of residual chlorine.

As a measure of raw material condition and of the efficiency of washing, sorting, and trimming to eliminate defective material, it is customary to make frequent examinations of samples of juice from the line by the Howard mold-count method (Bigelow *et al.* 1950). Other contaminants which require special vigilance for their exclusion are the eggs and larvae of the ordinary fruit fly or vinegar fly, *Drosophila melanogaster* (National Canners Association 1961).

Sorting

The tomatoes receive some field-sorting on the harvester or in a central-sorting operation where loads of tomatoes can be up-graded by washing, sorting, and inspection. With field-sorting and/or central-sorting, the delivery of fresh tomatoes is more uniform, and thus cannery-sorting for the removal of tomatoes affected with mold, rot, sunburn, insect damage, off-color, etc., is minimized.

Cannery-sorting and/or trimming are critical operations; the workers require training and proper lighting. Design and operation of the belts must be such as to permit a thorough inspection. Lighting should be so arranged as to give a brilliant illumination on the tomatoes without shining into the eyes of the operators. The width of the belt should be such that no operator has to reach more than 18 or 20 in., and the speed of the belt should be in the neighborhood of 25 fpm. During a commercial operation the belts should not be loaded so heavily that the tomatoes cannot be properly inspected.

Crushing and Enzyme Treatment

There are many combinations of crushing, chopping, or even slicing which can be combined with different heat treatment for enzyme inactivation. Enzyme inactivation can be instantaneous or rapid (commonly called hot-break), or it can be slow. The treatment to induce rapid enzyme activation (commonly called activated cold-break) is also occasionally used. In addition there is the room temperature crush and extraction (commonly called cold-break). Any of these combinations of crushing and enzyme treatment can produce a desirable and wholesome tomato juice that will meet US standards and at the same time please consumers. However, the properties of the juice produced by these different methods are quite diverse, and the individual processor must consider the advantages and disadvantages of each in terms of his own production and marketing program.

The inactivation or activation of the pectic enzymes in the fresh tomato play an important role in the final consistency of the tomato juice. Luh and Daoud (1970) reported that the breakdown of pectic materials in tomato juice by enzymatic action yields a product of low consistency. The heat-stability of pectic enzymes when subjected to thermal treatment is therefore most important. Pectinesterase is less stable when subjected to heat than polygalacturonase. Pectinesterase may be completely inactivated by holding at 180°F for 15 sec, whereas polygalacturonase requires holding at 220°F for 15 sec for complete inactivation.

Since the Q_{10}°C, or the increase in the rate of reaction for an increment of 18°F is 1.45 for pectinesterase and 2.2 for polygalacturonase, when the temperature is increased from 77°F to 95°F (Garces 1970), it is critical to pass through enzyme activation temperatures (140°F) very rapidly. This point is illustrated in Fig. 102, in which the rapid heating depicts a hot-break achieving enzyme inactivation temperature in 2 sec whereas the slow heating represents a thermal treatment which passes through enzyme activation temperatures for almost 60 sec.

The fastest means of enzyme inactivation is steam injection. However, this technique is not recommended for tomato juice because it will dilute the juice with condensate, and this is prohibited by the standards of identity. Steam injection would retain at least 95% of the potential serum viscosity of the fresh tomatoes.

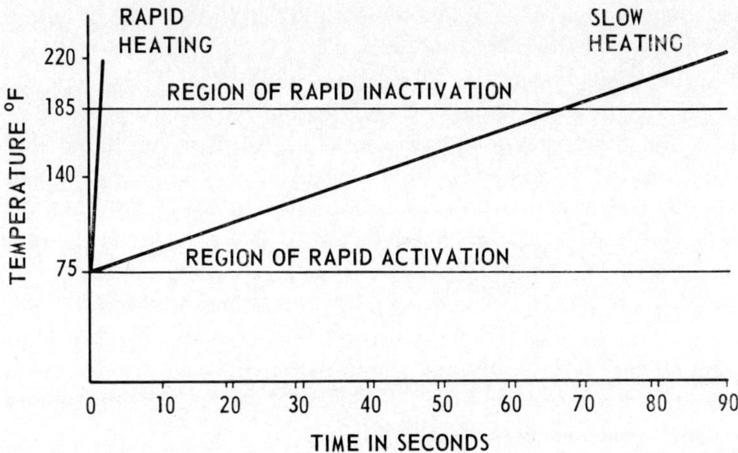

FIG. 102. INFLUENCE OF LAG TIME IN THE HEAT EXCHANGER ON ENZYME INACTIVATION

A very satisfactory enzyme inactivation can be achieved by heat treatment in a rotary coil tank (vertical or horizontal) followed by a heat exchanger and holding tube to achieve 220°F. The rotary coil tank, when run at the design heating capacity of the system, will inactivate enzymes fast enough to retain at least 90% of the potential serum viscosity in the original fresh tomato. The viscosity of the processed juice will vary in proportion to the percentage of serum viscosity retained by the treatment given.

A rotary-coil tank procedure has the added advantage that the violent boiling which occurs at the design heat-transfer capacity is an excellent means of deaeration. Air removal is important nutritionally since tomato juice containing dissolved or occluded air when processed at a high temperature will not retain the original vitamin C.

Other types of heat exchangers may be suitable for the inactivation of the pectic enzymes which are found in tomatoes. However, there is always the concern that these heat exchangers may have an extended lag-time in achieving enzyme inactivation temperature (Fig. 102). Any amount of lag-time will mean that the tomato juice will pass slowly through a range of temperature (70°–180°F) which will activate enzymes and thus degrade a high percentage of the pectin before achieving enzyme inactivation temperatures. This situation can also occur when crushed tomatoes are fed into any heat exchanger at a rate over the designed heating capacity.

Tubular heat exchangers with large tubes are commonly used in the tomato industry. This type of equipment requires a lag-time and a resulting low delta T to achieve design temperatures. In this type of equipment a major portion of the pectin is destroyed.

Many heat exchangers, including the tubular heat exchanger and the swept-surface heat exchanger, have the added disadvantage that the crushed tomatoes contain dissolved and/or excessive occluded air, and thus the ascorbic acid is markedly reduced during the heating treatment. This problem could be avoided by deaeration before heating, but this is cumbersome with fresh tomatoes and difficult with a room-temperature product.

Tomatoes can be crushed and extracted without added heat. This procedure for tomato juice would give rise to some losses in serum viscosity, but there would be no thermal degradation of color, and if properly deaerated before heating, there would be a very high retention of the original ascorbic acid of the fresh tomato.

Wagner *et al.* (1967–1970) in their series on Consistency of Tomato Products I-V inclusive, report that tomato juice consistency can be increased by the addition of acid to the tomato tissue immediately prior to or during comminution and heating. Miers *et al.* (1967) had similar finding and Becker *et al.* (1968) also reported the pH adjustment during tomato juice preparation influenced consistency also modified total pectin content and pectin characteristics.

In all of these reports, however, the authors refer to tomato juice consistency. This gives rise to a problem in semantics and definitions in accordance with the standards of identity. For the authors refer to the consistency of tomato juice while in reality they are producing and studying the consistency of tomato pulp and/or tomato purée. This comes about since the standards of identity provide for only one optional additional ingredient, salt (sodium chloride). This does not preclude the manufacture of tomato juice cocktail or mixed vegetable juices in which the major ingredient could be tomato juice. However it does prohibit the use of the acidified hot break for the production of single-strength or concentrated tomato juice.

Extraction

Juice extractors used in the tomato industry employ two basically different principles: (1) a crushing and pressing action, in contrast to (2) sieving under great agitation, such as is normally found in a pulper or finisher.

The pressing action of the juice extractor consists of an expanding helix inside a tomato juice screen, in which the tomato pulp is forced against the screen at continuing and increasing pressures. The holes in these screens may vary from as large as 0.050 in. to as small as 0.020 in. This pressing action does not churn the product, and therefore very little air is incorporated into the expressed juice.

Moyer *et al.* (1959) observed that the yield of tomato juice extracted from fresh tomatoes ranged from 29.4 to 91.5%, depending upon the type of equipment used. They found that the pressing action of a screwtype juice extractor gave an average yield of 78.9%, whereas the beating action of a paddle pulper and a paddle finisher gave an average yield of 82.4% tomato juice.

Either of these types of extractors may be pre-set to acquire a high or relatively low percentage of juice extraction. A high extraction would yield 3% skins and seeds and 97% juice. It is, however, possible to extract only 70–80% juice, a procedure which would yield a very moist residual containing useful tomato materials which could be reextracted for use in other tomato products. In some cases this low extraction yield (70%) is desirable since the extracted juice will have a high percentage of soluble solid components (which would improve flavor), and at the same time will contain a lower percentage of insoluble solids (which tend to reduce the quality of the finished juice).

Deaeration

Since heating tomato juice containing dissolved or occluded air impairs the retention of vitamin C, some canners employ deaerators in which the product is vacuum-deaerated. Ideally, this should be done as soon as possible after the tomatoes are crushed, and before they are heated at all. For practical reasons, however, vacuum deaeration is usually applied immediately after extraction of the juice. Normally a 10° flash is sufficient to remove the dissolved and occluded air. If the hot-break technique is used, deaeration at this stage loses some of its advantages; however, it is still capable of averting serious loss of vitamin C in subsequent sterilization of the juice.

Once deaeration has been accomplished, it is important to engineer the processing line so that *reaeration* will not occur. This requires the use of properly sealed pumps so that air will not be incorporated into the product by the pumping action. It would also mean filling surge tanks at the bottom instead of at the top, securing pump seals to avoid air intake, and designing the fluid flow characteristics of the entire line so as to avoid turbulence.

Salting and filling

The juice can be salted in batches at this stage or (as is more commonly the case) added to the individual cans by means of dry salt or salt tablet dispensers, a procedure which makes the accumulation of batches unnecessary. The sodium chloride added to tomato juice will range from 0.5% to 1.25% by weight. The average sodium chloride content of many commercial samples of tomato juice is 0.65% by weight.

Filling machines are adjusted to give a maximum fill, since this gives the best retention of quality and of vitamin C, as well as the best service value from metal containers. All of these factors suffer when the headspace is excessive. In No. 10 (603 $\times$ 700) and No. 3 cylinder (404 $\times$ 700) cans, the net headspace after cooling should not be over $^{7}/_{16}$ in. ($^{10}/_{16}$ in. to top of the double seam), and in shorter cans not over $^{3}/_{16}$ in. below the cover ($^{6}/_{16}$ in. gross headspace) for best results.

Containers

Tomato juice is packed in plain and enameled tin cans, and, less frequently, in glass. At the present time it is estimated that the tomato juice pack is equally divided between plain tin and enameled cans. The use of enameled cans, however, is increasing.

The U.S. Dept. Agr. has taken an interest in the amount of tin in canned tomato juice recently, and the Codex Alimentarius seems to be directed toward a tolerance of 250 ppm of tin in canned products.

While at the present time there is no official tolerance on tin in tomato products, very probably more tomato juice will be processed in enameled cans in the future. Since can manufacturers formulate rigid containers and enamels for different products, each processor should rely on his can manufacturer to furnish a type suitable for tomato juice, tomato juice cocktail, and tomato juice blends.

Homogenization

In order to retard or prevent settling and separation as much as possible, tomato juice is sometimes homogenized or viscolized in machines of the type used for milk and other dairy products. The juice is forced through narrow orifices at a pressure of 1,000–1,400 psi, thus finely breaking up the suspended solids. This step is a usual one when juice is packed in glass, and is sometimes employed for that in tin. The viscosity of the juice is increased and it is given a smoother consistency, sometimes characterized as "oily." This, however, is probably seldom noticed except in direct comparison with unhomogenized juice.

THERMAL PROCESSING OF TOMATO JUICE FOR COMMERCIAL STERILIZATION

Although tomato juice is an acid product, it has been subject to frequent outbreaks of spoilage when the conventional thermal processes for acid products have been employed.

The spoilage is caused by heat-resistant strains of *Bacillus coagulans* (*B. thermoacidurans*), as reported by Berry (1933).

Spoilage in tomato juice is of very serious economic consequence to canners. The detection of cans with *B. coagulans*-spoilage in contaminated lots is difficult because the organism does not produce appreciable gas, and therefore, swelled cans. This means that where any spoilage has been found, entire lots must be destroyed by the processor.

Tomato juice spoiled by this organism has a bitter off-flavor and a marked increase in acidity, and such spoilage is known in the trade as *flat sour spoilage.*

Many recommendations concerning intelligent sanitation, good housekeeping (Troy and Schenck 1960), and proper washing of tomatoes (Mercer and Rose 1959) have been made to keep *B. coagulans* in control. Such measures, coupled with adequate thermal processing, are the best means of preventing spoilage by this microorganism. A sterilization value equivalent of $F_0 = 0.7$ min is considered as adequate (Wessel and Benjamin 1941; Sognefest and Jackson 1947), and will minimize the chances of survival of *B. coagulans.* A table of approximately equivalent sterilizing values is given below (Troy and Schenck 1960):

Temperature of Juice, °F	Holding Time, Minutes
212	90
240	3.3
245	1.5
250	0.7 (42.0 sec)
255	0.32 (19.2 sec)
260	0.15 (9.0 sec)
265	0.07 (4.2 sec)

Blumer *et al.* (1951) indicates that "effective thermal processing is not feasible with the boiling water process, because the drastic heat treatment necessary to destroy the spores of some strains of *B. coagulans* would adversely affect the juice quality."

These workers also established that there is no color difference between samples of juice sterilized at different temperatures when equivalent sterilization values are used. They did, however, point out that sterilization values in excess of $F_0 = 0.7$ min do impair the color of flash-sterilized tomato juice.

Flash Sterilization

This procedure involves pre-heating the juice to a high temperature for a short time-interval in a continuous heat exchanger to sterilization values sufficient to destroy *B. coagulans* ($F_0 = 0.7$ min), followed by rapid cooling to 200°F, filling into cans, and closing.

Since can sterilization in this procedure is dependent upon the temperature of the cooled juice, it is critical to maintain an absolute minimum of 190°F filling and closing temperatures for No. 10 cans, and an absolute minimum filling and closing temperature of 195°F for smaller cans. These cans should be closed and inverted and then held for three min in a steam or boiling water bath to maintain the minimum closing temperature in order to insure can and lid sterilization. After the holding period the cans should be cooled in chlorinated water to a temperature of approximately 110°F.

In-Can Processing (Agitating Pressure Cookers)

In this process, the tomato juice is filled at 190°–195°F, closed, and processed in continuous-agitating pressure cookers at sterilization values equal to a thermal process that will destroy *B. coagulans* ($F_0 = 0.7$ min). It is then rapidly cooled in chlorinated water to approximately 110°F.

Boiling Water Processes

Early researchers in the processing of tomato juice (Bigelow *et al.* 1950; Cameron 1946) made suggestions for the conventional processing of tomato juice at boiling water temperatures. These include a still-cook; agitating-type cook; hot-fill (195°F) followed by air-cool; hot-fill, hold, and water cool. These procedures are described in the 1950 Ed. of Bulletin *27-L* revised 1950 National Canners Assoc. and later by Troy and Schenck (1960). These sources clearly indicate that such procedures do not "provide any significant protection against organisms such as *B. coagulans.*

Pederson and Becker (1949) suggest that if tomato juice of pH 4.15 to 4.25 could be subjected to moderate pasteurization conditions, the vegetative cells would be destroyed and the spores would be of no consequence, since they would be incapable of germinating and producing growth at these low pH values. However, Rice and Pederson (1954) indicate that while a minimum heat treatment may kill the vegetative cells, if there are significant numbers of spores present, these will tend to have an acid-tolerance comparable to the vegetative cells. A juice of pH 4.30 or even 4.25 under these conditions could not necessarily be inhibitory to the growth of *B. coagulans.*

While such procedures were used in the past, in many instances successfully, the hazard of contamination with *flat sour spoilage* organisms is so great and the consequences so disastrous that today such procedures are not being used in the commercial processing of tomato juice.

SANITATION

The purpose of processing is to design a system that will prevent spoilage. This discussion is limited to problems related to canned tomato juice.

Initial microbial counts on the raw material are critical and every effort must be made to effectively reduce these counts to a minimal level by washing in chlorinated water, as previously mentioned. Initial total bacterial counts and mold counts can be markedly reduced by thorough washing in chlorinated water (York *et al.* 1964; Mercer and Olson 1969). This chlorinated washing, which is intended to remove dirt and harmless extraneous materials which would normally accumulate in field harvesting, can reduce microbial loads to a level that will insure the safety of subsequent thermal treatment for commercial sterilization, as well as reduce the possibility of contamination later in processing.

It is in processing, subsequent to washing, that care must be exercised to insure against possible recontamination. Sorting belts, conveyors, crushers, extractors, sanitary tubing, valves, surge tanks, fillers, and can closing and conveying equipment can accumulate microorganisms and in effect inoculate a commercially-sterile product so that it will spoil.

Stainless steel tubing, sanitary connections valves, and pumps should be so engineered that they avoid dead-ends and pockets that are hard to clean. The fluid flow system should be so designed as to permit frequent in-place-cleaning. Wood or other porous materials should not be used. This design should include reservoirs where cleaning materials in solution and chlorinated water can be alternately pumped through the system at clean-up time. Mechanical equipment, crushers, extractors, etc. should be dismantled, cleaned, inspected, and reassembled.

Such a system should at all times be under the surveillance of a competent sanitarian who can monitor the system and detect microbial buildups or potential sources of contaminations.

The filled-can handling systems must also undergo rigid sanitation monitoring. Double seams should be inspected periodically. Every effort should be made to minimize empty- and full-can abuse (Troy *et al.* 1963). The empty and filled can handling equipment should be sanitized frequently.

Even when double seams are adequate and every effort has been made to avoid can-abuse, it is possible to encounter post-process leakage that will lead to spoilage (Vaughn *et al.* 1952). Cooling-water should always be chlorinated to a 5 ppm residual at the discharge end to be certain that micro-leakage during cooling will not inject viable spoilage organisms into a sterile, cool product.

In-plant chlorination for the entire food processing plant is not a panacea for sanitation, but coupled with intelligent engineering and proper sanitation control it is a necessary adjunct.

TOMATO JUICE BLENDS

Tomato juice blends came into being as a result of interest in vegetable juices, which, because of their naturally high pH, required destructive sterilization procedures.

Acidulation with organic acids would have been a logical answer, except that vegetable juices with added appropriate acids apparently did not have consumer acceptance. Tomato juice, then, became the popular natural acidulant almost 30 years ago.

Until quite recently only a nominal amount of tomato juice was seasoned with spices or blended with other vegetables to produce a tomato juice cocktail or a vegetable juice blend.

The flavorings used in addition to salt to achieve such products could include sugar, pepper, Tabasco, celery salt, Worcestershire sauce, vinegar, and lemon juice, alone or in combinations.

Among the vegetables which may be employed in such blends are celery, lettuce, carrots, onions, garlic, sauerkraut, beets, parsley, spinach, watercress, sweet pepper and/or lemon, mostly in various combinations.

Tomato juice blends are a very natural development, since single-strength tomato juice "normally elicits sweetness, sourness and saltiness" (Pangborn and Chrisp 1964). These tastes and their interrelationships can be commercially manipulated by reformulation and blending with spices and/or other vegetables to produce these blends.

From the nutritional standpoint, these tomato juice blends can yield increased nutritive values. For example, the addition of 5% red bell pepper juice to tomato juice will not only add a new flavor, but can also increase the ascorbic acid content 57% and the β-carotene 22% over that found in ordinary processed tomato juice using the materials from the same lot of tomatoes and identical methods (Yamaguchi *et al.* 1961).

As indicated in the Introduction to this chapter, reliable data concerning the commercial production of tomato juice blends are not available. However, preliminary observations on the proliferation of tomato juice blends available from different processors on the market indicate that there is activity in the production of tomato juice blends, predominantly in the individual-serving container sizes. The tomato juice blends and tomato juice cocktails are not only used as a beverage, but are also employed as mixers for alcoholic beverages.

CONCENTRATED TOMATO JUICE

The introduction of concentrated tomato juice to the civilian market in the early part of 1960 was delayed a considerable time by regulatory rather than technical obstacles.

The revised standards of identity provide that tomato purée (tomato pulp) containing not less than 20% but less than 24% of natural tomato soluble solids may be considered as "concentrated tomato juice" in lieu of the name tomato purée or tomato pulp. These limits correspond closely to the previous limits for concentrated tomato juice (not less than 21% but less than 25% expressed as salt-free tomato solids).

The regulatory problems centered around the intent, which was clouded by the fact that the armed forces had purchased tomato purée canned for beverage use (U. S. Army Quartermaster Corps 1951) which was essentially a purée used for beverage purposes. The intent was to produce in accordance with the tomato juice standards a tomato juice which was then concentrated and canned.

Methods of Manufacturing Tomato Juice Concentrate

There are many combinations of procedures used for the production of tomato juice which would be quite reasonable for the production of tomato juice concentrate if the finished product were vacuum-concentrated under reasonable conditions. Experimental work carried out at the University of California in Davis (Leonard *et al.* 1964) indicates that good-quality tomato juice can be produced by the following process.

Ripe, well-colored tomatoes were washed in chlorinated water and inspected and sorted to remove blemishes and under-colored fruit. This fruit can be cold-crushed with the addition of 0.7% salt and extracted cold in a tomato juice extractor fixed with an 0.033-in. screen, so set as to permit an 80% extraction of juice and a 20% residual of skins, seeds and reextractable tomato material.

Preferably, the cold-extracted juice should be deaerated under a high degree of vacuum. The deaerated juice should be given a presterilization treatment at a high temperature to destroy *B. coagulans* and to inactivate the pectic enzyme systems to prevent this continued activity.

This product should be evaporated in an evaporator where the total thermal treatment is minimized. A flash evaporator or a swept-surface evaporator would be ideal. In order to preserve nutrients, the processing system was designed to prevent reaeration of the product.

The tomato juice concentrate produced in this fashion and reconstituted with potable water under laboratory conditions had excellent color, flavor, and nutritive value. In fact, this product (which had initially, in the fresh tomatoes, 30 mg of ascorbic acid per 100 gm) had in the processed product almost 100% retention of the original ascorbic acid.

The important thing is that instead of producing a salted tomato purée, a tomato juice of excellent quality was produced, and every effort was made during the processing and concentrating procedure to maintain the quality attributes of tomato juice.

Since early production did not attempt to produce a top-quality tomato juice concentrate, this product has not had wide acceptance on the domestic market, but has had some use in the military feeding program.

COMPOSITION AND NUTRITIVE VALUE OF TOMATO PRODUCTS

The advent of mechanical harvesting of tomatoes only seven years ago has stimulated extensive changes in all phases of the tomato industry. Machine harvesting has meant new varieties, new systems of planting, differences in cultural practice, improved types of mechanical harvesting, and bulk handling in bins that contain 600–800 lb fruit each. The industry has experimented successfully with one-ton bins and now is considering bulk trucks for some of the newer varieties of tomatoes.

Weight losses incurred from the instant of mechanical harvest to processing 40 hr later can account for over 30% loss in weight (Leonard and Marsh 1969). These losses are influenced by variety, method of harvest, and maturity at the instant of harvest, and are the consequence of damage and storage time before processing.

When evaluated analytically to determine the types of losses occurring, these weight losses are reflected in reductions in pounds of total solids delivered, principally soluble solids. In addition, there are serious losses in serum viscosity with damage and storage.

These changes have already influenced composition and utilization characteristics, and can affect the nutritive value as well. Varieties and cultural practice are changing so rapidly that reliable research concerning composition is ancient history before it is published.

In a similar manner, new varieties not now in commercial use will influence the chemical and physical composition and the utilization characteristics of tomatoes for processing.

The standard composition of tomatoes and tomato juice is reported in Table 104 as a point of reference, in spite of the drastic changes in processing that are occurring in the transition from hand-harvested to mechanically-harvested fruit.

Bradley (1964) indicates that substantial differences in acidity exist between varieties at one location, and at the same time points out that titratable acidity, total acidity, and citric acid content differ within any one variety at different locations.

Earlier work by Bradley (1962) indicates that potassium fertilizer applications induced significant increases in titratable acidity, total acidity, citric acid content, and tomato yield, whereas neither calcium nor magnesium application produced a significant difference in acid content or in yield of fruit.

TABLE 104

COMPOSITION AND NUTRITIVE VALUE OF RAW TOMATOES AND CANNED TOMATO JUICE[1]

	Per 100 Gm	
	Tomatoes	Tomato Juice
Water, gm	94.1	93.5
Protein, gm	1.0	1.0
Fat, gm	0.3	0.2
Carbohydrate		
Total, gm	4.0	4.3
Fiber, gm	0.6	0.2
Ash, gm	0.6	1.0
Calcium, mg	11.0	7.0
Phosphorus, mg	27.0	15.0
Iron, mg	0.6	0.4
Vitamin A	1100[1]	1050[1]
Thiamine, mg	0.06	0.05
Riboflavin, mg	0.04	0.03
Niacin, mg	0.5	0.8
Ascorbic acid, mg	23.0	16.0
Food energy, cal	20.0	21.0

Source: The Heinz Handbook of Nutrition. H. J. Heinz Co., 1959.
[1] International Units.

In a study of the influence of maturity on organic acids in canned tomato juice, Villarreal *et al.* (1960) indicated that titratable acidity decreased and pH increased with maturation.

Luh and Daoud (1968) found that the relative amounts of the various amino acids in tomato juice differ somewhat with varietal characteristics. They further state that the quantitative analysis of lycopene and β-carotene indicates that lycopene will vary considerably with changes in variety, and that the content of β-carotene will have slight variation with variety. In this same study the organoleptic scores by a test panel showed significant differences in flavor between varieties.

The wide range in composition and utilization characteristics of the raw material are further influenced by variations in attention to a number of processing factors. The influence of these processing factors is summarized as follows in a memorandum of the National Canners Association-Can Manufacturers Institute Nutrition Committee.

"Tomato juice is a rich source of vitamin C provided the necessary precautions are taken in its manufacture. The following is a brief outline of the principal factors responsible for the destruction of vitamin C, together with suggestions for obtaining the maximum retention of this vitamin in tomato juice.

"1. *Excessive incorporation of air in tomato juice* is probably the most frequent cause of poor retention of vitamin C. Factors such as cyclones or finishers operated below full capacity, centrifugal pumps which suck in air, pipes discharging openly into the top of tanks, and mixers which beat air into the juice all may be responsible for the incorporation of excessive amounts of air in tomato juice. Extending or relocating pipes so as to deliver juice near the bottom of the tank, below the surface of the contents, may effect considerable improvement in vitamin retention.

2. *Holding tomato juice containing air at high temperatures* for more than a few minutes is particularly serious in causing destruction of vitamin C. If such juice must be held in storage tanks, much less destruction will occur if the juice is held at a low temperature (less than 80° to 90°F) and then brought quickly to filling or sterilizing temperature and canned without delay. In the complete absence of air very little destruction of vitamin C will occur even at high temperatures. Efficient deaeration is to be highly recommended as a means of preserving the maximum amount of vitamin C in tomato juice. Cans should be well filled, since excessive headspace will lead to entrapment of air.

"3. *Contamination of juice with certain metals.*—Small amounts of certain metals, particularly copper, from equipment with which the juice comes in contact may cause serious destruction of vitamin C, especially if the juice contains air and is held at high temperature. Copper may be dissolved into the juice from copper or brass equipment, particularly after such equipment has been idle for even a short period of time. In such cases a thin film of copper oxide forms over the surface of the metal, and this film is readily dissolved by the juice. Cleaning the equipment before each production period by a method recommended to control discoloration of certain canned foods from copper should assist in preserving ascorbic acid. For maximum retention of vitamin C, the amount of copper or brass equipment in contact with the juice should be kept to a minimum, and the time of contact of the juice with such equipment should be as brief as possible.

"Proper attention to the above factors should aid materially toward securring excellent retention of the vitamin C present in the raw tomatoes."

In common with many vegetables and fruits, tomatoes do not rank as an outstanding source of thiamine, riboflavin, or niacin, but to the extent that they are present, these nutrients are well retained in the manufacture of tomato juice. Cameron and Esty (1950) indicate an average retention of 89% for thiamine, 96% for riboflavin, and 98% for niacin.

Tomatoes contain from 0.2 to 0.6% acid calculated as citric, the amount varying according to maturity, seasonal and climatic conditions, and cultural methods. Since the pH is related to total acidity, and since low pH (other things being equal) is helpful in sterilization by heat, there has been interest in the factors connected with acidity. Tomato juice blends and tomato juice cocktail control total acidity and pH by the nature of their formulation.

Everson *et al.* (1964A) found that in tomato juice concentrate essentially 100% of the thiamine present was retained during both an experimental aseptic and a well-designed conventional processing procedure. These same workers (Everson *et al.* 1964B) further indicate that tomato juice concentrate retained a full pyridoxine activity during aseptic and conventional processing and throughout the storage period.

These two papers by Everson *et al.* (1964A and B) thus reveal little or no difference between experimental aseptic and well-designed conventional processing. However, the values reported in these papers are considerably above values reported in Table 104.

An investigation by Simandle *et al.* (1966) indicates very clearly that panel flavor scores were significantly correlated with soluble solids, pH, and soluble solids/titratable acidity ratios in the six varieties of tomatoes studied.

In studies on the effect of processing on the viscosity of tomato juice, Hand *et al.* (1955) shows the influence of insoluble structures on the consistency of tomato juice. Whittenberger and Nutting (1957) found that although insoluble structures may be building blocks for tomato juice and may be required for the development of acceptable degrees of consistency, these properties are markedly modified by the presence of pectic substances.

Colors of Tomato Juice

The characteristic reddish color of tomato juice is due to the carotenoid pigments (lycopene, carotene, and xanthophyll) in the suspended solids. The filtered serum has a pale straw color. Aesthetically and commercially, color is an important attribute to the product, a fact which is reflected in the official standards for grades.

The limitation imposed initially on the color of the juice by the character of the raw material has influenced the selection of such stock. Many processors are buying on grade specifications which limit culls and partially colored tomatoes. In some instances, processors specify varieties which have desirable utilization characteristics for both the color and the flavor of tomato juice.

Measurement of the color of tomato products, including juice, has usually been based on visual comparison. The Munsell system (Nickerson 1946) (using the Maxwell spinning-disc) is used in industry and by federal graders, the notation of this system being embodied in the US Standards for Grades of Tomato Juice. However, the desire for more objective measurement has led to the development of photoelectric instruments capable of analyzing reflected colors (Robinson *et al.* 1952; Yeatmen *et al.* 1960). The promising results obtained with a Hunter Color Difference Meter have stimulated development of simple rugged instruments for use in factory or field. Instruments such as the Agtron measure the relative redness and greenness of samples. The excellent correlation with color ratings assigned by experienced graders has already led to some use of these instruments in quality control of fresh and processed tomato products.

Blumer *et al.* (1951) have pointed out that there is no indication that conventionally-processed tomato juice is superior in color to flash-sterilized juice when the values used for the flash process are equivalent ($F_0 = 0.7$) and do not exceed the heat treatments necessary to destroy *B. coagulans.* They did, however, find evidence to indicate that sterilization values in excess of 0.7 do impair the color of flash-sterilized juice. It is important to note that their high-temperature short-time (HTST) process was followed by rapid cooling to about 200°F; filling into cans; closing, and inverting and holding for 3 min; and then water-cooling to 100°F.

In work by Davis and Gould (1955) on the effect of HTST and conventional processing techniques on hot-break and cold-break procedures for the extraction of tomato juice, little difference was found in the U.S. Dept. Agr. color scores assigned to the canned product.

STANDARDS

Under the Federal Food, Drug and Cosmetic Act enacted June 25, 1938, as corrected by amendments to May 15, 1969, tomato juice is defined in the Standard of Identity, promulgated July 27, 1939, effective January 1, 1940, as follows:

"§ **53.1 Tomato Juice: Identity.**—Tomato juice is the unconcentrated liquid extracted from mature tomatoes of red or reddish varieties, with or without scalding followed by draining. In the extraction of such liquid, heat may be applied by any method which does not add water thereto. Such liquid is strained free from skins, seeds, and other coarse or hard substances, but carries finely divided insoluble solids from the flesh of the tomato. Such liquid may be homogenized, and may be seasoned with salt. When sealed in a container it is so processed by heat, before or after sealing, as to prevent spoilage.

"§ **53.5 Yellow Tomato Juice: Identity.**—Yellow tomato juice is the unconcentrated liquid extracted from mature tomatoes of yellow varieties. It conforms, in all other respects, to the definition and standard of identity for tomato juice prescribed in § 53.1."

This definition states the nature of the product, largely in terms of the method of manufacture, and indicates the only optional additional ingredient, salt. This does not preclude the manufacture of tomato juice cocktail or mixed vegetable juices, of which the standardized product tomato juice is a major ingredient. The final reference to processing by heat embraces both flash sterilization and conventional processing.

Standards for grades of canned tomato juice are also in effect. These are promulgated by the Agricultural Marketing Service of the U. S. Department of Agriculture as a basis for buying and selling, as an aid in arriving at loan values, and to permit inspection and certification by official agencies (U. S. Dept. Agr. 1958). The Standards for Tomato Juice defined U. S. Grade A (Fancy), U. S. Grade C (Standard) and Off-Grade (Substandard) grades in terms of a scoring system in which color is given 30 points, consistency 15, absence of defects 15, and flavor 40. The method of ascertaining the rating of each factor is described in detail; color, for example, is determined by the Munsell system referred to above.

Concentrated tomato juice, has been defined for purposes of standardization under the Federal Food, Drug and Cosmetic Act, by an amendment of the standard for tomato purée, effective January 1970. The amendment states that if the product is made entirely from whole tomatoes and contains not less than 20% but less than 24% of natural tomato soluble solids the name "Concentrated tomato juice" may be applied.

Standards for grades of canned concentrated tomato juice, comparable to those for single strength juice, have also been promulgated and amended. For grading, the concentrate is reconstituted to single strength and scored for the same factors and with the same weights as those cited above for ordinary tomato juice.

BIBLIOGRAPHY

ANON. 1960. 1960 Tomato juice pack. Releases dated Dec. 22nd and 23rd Statistics Div., Natl. Canners Assoc., Washington, D. C.

ANON. 1968. New tomato varieties. VF-145. Canner/Packer *10,* B,C,E,F, 32.

ANON. 1970. 1969 Tomato juice pack. Release dated Jan. 9, 1970, Division of Industry Statistics, Natl. Canners Assoc. Washington, D. C.

BECKER, R., WAGNER, J. R. MIERS, J. C., SANSHUCK, D. W., and DIETRICH, W. C. 1968. Consistency of tomato products. 3. Effects of pH adjustment during tomato juice preparation on pectin contents and characteristics. Food Technol. *22,* 503.

BERRY, R. N. 1933. Some new heat resistant, acid tolerant organisms causing spoilage in tomato juice. J. Bacteriol. *25,* 72–73.

BIGELOW, W. D., SMITH, H. R., and GREENLEAF, C. A. 1950. Tomato products. Pulp, paste, catsup and chili sauce. With section on tomato juice by C. W. Bohrer and J. M. Reed, Natl. Canners Assoc. Res. Lab. Bull. *27-L*, Rev.

BLUMER, T. A., PARRIN, F. W., and PETERSON, G. T. 1951. Color of tomato juice. How it is affected by sterilization temperatures. Canner *112*, No. 9, 13–15, 26, 28.

BRADLEY, D. B. 1962. Fertilizer effects on plant composition. Influence of K, Ca, and Mg application on acid content, and yield of tomato fruit. J. Agr. Food Chem. *10*, 450–452.

BRADLEY, D. B. 1964. Tomato composition. Varietal and location influence on acid composition of tomato fruit. J. Agr. Food Chem. *12*, 213–216.

CAMERON, E. J. 1946. Current suggestions on processing tomato juice. Canner *102*, No. 22, 40, 42; Canning Trade *68*, No. 43, 7–8.

CAMERON, E. J., and ESTY, J. R. 1950. Canned foods in human nutrition. Natl. Canners Assoc., Washington, D. C.

DAVIS, R. B., and GOULD, W. A. 1955. Effect of processing methods on the color of tomato juice. Food Technol. *9*, 540–547.

EVERSON, G. J., CHANG, J., LEONARD, S., LUH, B. S., and SIMONE, M. 1964A. A septic canning of foods. Thiamine retention as influenced by processing method, storage time and temperature, and type of container. Food Technol. *18*, 84–86.

EVERSON, G. J., CHANG, J., LEONARD, S., LUH, B. S., and SIMONE, M. 1964B. Aseptic canning of foods. Pyridoxine retention as influenced by processing method, storage time and temperature, and type of container. Food Technol. *18*, 87–88.

GARCES, M. B. 1970. Thermal effect on pectin retention and pectin enzymes in tomato juice. Thesis. Univ. Calif., Davis, Calif.

HAND, D. B., MOYER, J. C., RANSFORD, J. R., and HENING, J. C. 1955. Effect of processing conditions on the viscosity of tomato juice. Food Technol. *9*, 228–235.

HANNA, G. C., GENTILE, A., SMITH, P. G., LIPPERT, L. F., DAVIS, G. N., and MCCOY, O. D. 1964. Recently developed vegetable varieties aid mechanization and climatic adaptability. Calif. Agr. *18*, No. 3, 8–10.

HEINZ, H. J. Co. 1959. Heinz Handbook of Nutrition. McGraw-Hill Book Co., New York.

LEONARD, S., LUH, B. S., SIMONE, M., and EVERSON, G. 1964. Aseptic canning of foods. Preparation and processing procedures. Food Technol. *18*, 81–84.

LEONARD, S., and MARSH, G. L. 1969. Consequence of damage to and the storage of tomatoes. Tomato Research Progress Rept., *T-12*.

LEONARD, S., PANGBORN, R. M., and LUH, B. S. 1959. The pH problem in canned tomatoes. Food Technol. *13*, 418–419.

LORENZEN, C., and HANNA, G. C. 1962. Mechanical harvesting of tomatoes. Agr. Eng. *43*, 16–19.

LUH, B. S., and DAOUD, H. N. 1968. Pectin, amino acids and carotenoids in tomato juices. Fruchtsaft Ind. *13*, 204–211.

LUH, B. S., and DAOUD, H. N. 1970. Pectin and pectic enzymes in VF-145 tomatoes. Tomato Research Progr. Rept. April 15, 1970.

MERCER, W. A., and ROSE, W. W. 1959. Studies on tomato washing operations. Natl. Canners Assoc. Res Lab. Rept. *59-W-54*.

MERCER, W. A., and OLSON, N. A. 1969. Tomato infield washing station study. Natl. Canners Assoc. Res. Foundation, Berkeley, Calif., Final Rept.

MIERS, J. C., WAGNER, J. R., and SANSHUCK, D. W. 1967. Consistency of tomato products. 2. Effect of pH during extraction on tomato juice consistency. Food Technol. *21,* 923–926.

MOYER, J. C., ROBINSON, W. B., RANSFORD, J. R., LOBELLE, R. L., and HAND, D. B. 1959. Processing conditions affecting the yield of tomato juice. Food Technol. *13,* 270–272.

NATIONAL CANNERS ASSOCIATION. 1961. Drosophila control. Recommendations to growers and canners. Washington, D. C.

NICKERSON, D. 1946. Color measurement and its application to the grading of agricultural products. A Handbook on the Method of Disk Colorimetry. U. S. Dept. Agr. Misc. Publ. *580.*

O'BRIEN, M., LEONARD, S. J., MARSH, G., and OLSON, N. A. 1969. Processing losses in tomatoes as affected by harvesting and handling procedures. Am. Soc. Agr. Eng. Paper *69-382.*

O'BRIEN, M., YORK, G. K., MACGILLIVRAY, J. H., and LEONARD, S. J. 1963. Bulk handling of canning tomatoes. Food Technol. *17,* No. 7, 96–101.

PANGBORN, ROSE MARIE, and CHRISP, R. B. 1964. Taste interrelationships. VI. Sucrose, sodium chloride, and citric acid in canned tomato juice. J. Food Sci. *29,* 490–498.

PEDERSON, C. S., and BECKER, M. E. 1949. Flat sour spoilage of tomato juice. N. Y. S. Agr. Expt. Sta. Tech. Bull. *287.*

RICE, A. C., and PEDERSON, C. S. 1954. Factors influencing growth of *Bacillus coagulans* in canned tomato juice. I. Size of inoculum and oxygen concentration. Food Research *19,* 115–123.

ROBINSON, W. B., WISHNETSKY, T., RANSFORD, J. R., CLARK, W. L., and HAND, D. B. 1952. A study of methods for the measurement of tomato juice color. Food Technol. *6,* 269–275.

SIMANDLE, P. A., BROGDON, J. L., SWEENEY, J. P., MOBLEY, E. O., and DAVIS, D. W. 1966. Quality of six tomato varieties as affected by some compositional factors. Proc. Am. Soc. Hort. Sci. *89,* 532–538.

SOGNEFEST, P., and JACKSON, J. M. 1947. Presterilization of canned tomato juice. Food Technol. *1,* 78–84.

TROY, V. S., and SCHENK, A. M. 1960. Flat sour spoilage of tomato juice. Continental Can Co., Chicago, Ill.

TROY, V. S., BOYD, J. M., and FOLINAZZO, J. F. 1963. Spoilage of canned foods due to leakage. Continental Can Co., Chicago, Ill.

U. S. ARMY QUARTERMASTER CORPS. 1957. Tomato purée, canned (for beverage use). Mil. Spec. *MIL-T-3529.*

U. S. DEPT. AGR. 1958. United States Standards for Grades of Canned Tomato Juice.

U. S. DEPT. AGR. 1960. United States Standards for Grades of Concentrated Tomato Juice. Amended Feb. 25, 1970.

U. S. DEPT. HEALTH, EDUCATION and WELFARE. 1970. Canned vegetables and vegetable products–definition and standards, S. R. A., F. D. C. 2, 21 *CFR 53,* Rev.

VAUGHN, R. H., KREULEVITCH, I. H., and MERCER, W. A. 1952. Spoilage of canned foods caused by the *Bacillus macerans-Polymyxa* group of bacteria. Food Research *17,* 560–570.

VILLARREAL, F., LUH, B. S., and LEONARD, S. J. 1960. Influence of ripeness level on organic acids in canned tomato juice. Food Technol. *14,* No. 3, 176–179.

WAGNER, J. R., and MIERS, J. C. 1967. Consistency of tomato products. 1. The effects of tomato enzyme inhibition by additives. Food Technol. *21,* 920–923.

WAGNER, J. R., MIERS, J. C., SANSHUCK, D. W., and BECKER, R. 1968A. Consistency of tomato products. 4. Improvement of the acidified hot break process. Food Technol. *22,* 1484.

WAGNER, J. R., MIERS, J. C., and BURR, H. K. 1968B. Production of high consistency tomato juice. U.S. Pat. 3,366,488.

WAGNER, J. R., MIERS, J. C., SANSHUCK, D. W., and BECKER, R. 1969. Consistency of tomato products. 5. Differentiation of extractive and enzyme inhibitory aspects of the acidified hot break process. Food Technol. *23,* 113.

WESSEL, D. J., and BENJAMIN, H. A. 1941. Process control of heat resistant spoilage organisms. Fruit Prod. J. *20,* No. 6, 178–80.

WHITTENBERGER, R. T., and NUTTING, G. C. 1957. Effect of tomato cell structures on consistency of tomato juice. Food Technol. *11,* 19–22.

WHITTENBERGER, R. T., and NUTTING, G. C. 1958. High viscosity of cell wall suspensions prepared from tomato juice. Food Technol. *12,* 420–424.

YAMAGUCHI, M., LUH, B. S., LEONARD, S., and SIMONE, M. 1961. Peppers add vitamins, flavor to new tomato juice cocktail. Calif. Agr. *15,* No. 11, 11.

YEATMEN, J. N., SIDWELL, A. P., and NORRIS, K. H. 1960. Derivative of a new formula for computing raw tomato juice color from objective color measurement. Food Technol. *14,* 16–20.

YORK, G. K., O'BRIEN, M., WINTER, F. H., TOMBROPOULOS, D., and LEONARD, S. J. 1964. Sanitation in mechanical harvesting and bulk handling of canning tomatoes. Food Technol. *18,* 97–100.

CHAPTER 13

C. S. Pederson

Vegetable Juices

INTRODUCTION

The nutritive value of vegetables has been generally recognized. Long before the housewife realized their nutritive value, the small amounts of vegetable juices left in preparing a meal were often used as drinks or incorporated in other foods such as soups. The supplementation of infants' milk diet with liquids from nonmilk foods is as old as civilization. The prechewing of foods by adults for the feeding of infants has been practiced for centuries and continues to be a general practice in many societies. The use of mechanical devices for grinding relatively hard foods such as cereals and legumes was one of man's earliest inventions. It was observed that the finely ground or milled products could then be removed readily by the use of water. Such water extracts might be considered the earliest form of vegetable juices. The natural fermentation of such pre-chewed and milled foods if held for any period of time is a predictable conclusion. Various types of beers resulted and were consumed by young and old. Since the lees from these fermented products were considered inferior, they were relegated to the poor, although actually the lees were superior nutritively.

The commercial production of juices extracted from low-acid vegetables and blended with tomato juice has assumed significant proportions. Of those, other than tomato juice and blends, canned at present, the greatest portion are prepared for baby food or freshly extracted for sale in health food stores at juice counters. The demand for vegetables for canning and freezing and for purées for baby foods have taxed the use of processing equipment as well as supplies of raw materials.

The flavor and aroma characteristics so desirable in fresh vegetables are difficult to retain in the processed food. The vegetables and their extracted juices are subject to considerable alteration during preparation and processing. Many juices contain materials in colloidal suspension that are precipitated at temperatures above 160°F, particularly if the inherent enzymes are not inactivated early in processing. The nature of several changes has been the subject of much study, research, and development and numerous processes have been devised or developed with many patents granted for new procedures. Because vegetables differ so much in character each presents a unique preparation problem.

CARL S. PEDERSON is Emeritus Professor, Food Science and Technology Department, New York State Agricultural Experiment Station, Cornell University, Geneva, New York.

One may group vegetables into four types based upon the part of the vegetable that is consumed. Methods of processing may be somewhat similar in each group. The first group includes those leaf or stem vegetables such as lettuce, celery, spinach, beet leaves, cabbage, watercress, dandelion, rhubarb, and others. The second group, the root vegetables, includes, carrots, beets, turnips, parsnips, singkamas, sweet potatoes, onions, and others. The third group are the seed bearing fruit in which the seeds are relatively unimportant. Of these tomatoes are the most important; however, naranjillas, peppers, cucumbers, olives, and others must be included. The fourth group is the legumes, consisting of peas, beans, lentils, soybeans and others. All are complex substances showing great diversity in characteristics. The major constituent of the vegetables of the first three groups is water. The vegetables of the fourth group are notably high in protein and possess all the essentials required for seed germination and early growth of the plant.

The root vegetables are generally higher in carbohydrates and crude fiber and possess higher calorie values than those of the first group. Many vegetables are good sources of ascorbic acid, the B vitamins, and carotene as well as minerals, lipids, proteins, and carbohydrates. The trace amounts of numerous other components have been summarized for cabbage by Pederson and Albury (1969) and it is assumed that many of these components are also present in other vegetables. With few exceptions, notably tomatoes and rhubarb, all are only slightly acid and have an alkaline ash.

Vegetable juices may be grouped into six classes. (1) The juices prepared from normally acid products, such as tomato, rhubarb, and naranjilla, may be processed at relatively low temperature. (2) Vegetable juices or their blends are acidified with such highly acid products as citrus, pineapple, tomato, sauerkraut, and rhubarb juices. Tomato juice is frequently a primary ingredient. (3) Vegetable juices are acidified with organic or mineral acids so that they can be processed at relatively low temperatures. (4) The excess juices obtained from fermented vegetables are often used in their natural state or they may be heat-processed at low temperatures. Sauerkraut juice is the important commercial product in this category. (5) Juices are freshly extracted from nonacid vegetables at health food stores immediately before consumption. They are neither heated nor acidified. (6) Vegetable juices or their blends when not acidified must be processed at relatively high temperatures to kill spores of spore-forming microorganisms.

GENERAL PRINCIPLES OF VEGETABLE JUICE PREPARATION

Juice may be obtained from any fresh vegetable by comminution followed by separation of the large, coarse particles or by pressing the comminuted juice to obtain the clear juice. Since the character of so many vegetables is resident to a considerable extent in the solid portions in suspension in the juices, the vegetables are often comminuted and handled so that the solids remain in suspension. There are a number of comminuting machines available that will express from 60 to 90% of the trimmed vegetable as a product of juice-like consistency. The selection of equipment is determined by the type of juice desired. The finer the grind, the greater will be the rupturing of the cellular structure and release of protoplasm from the cells. The vegetable may be ground so finely that it may be practically colloidal in body and result in a baby food type of purée. This has been recognized in the production of tomato catsup, purées and juices. Separation of soluble liquid components from suspended solids is difficult. Such comminution would not be feasible for producing relatively clear juice.

When a vegetable or fruit is macerated without previous heat treatment, the enzymes released from within the cells are freed to act upon the released protoplasmic substances and may catalyze chemical and physical changes. The high temperature heat processes required for sterilizing neutral or slightly acidic juices causes coagulation, flocculation, and ultimately precipitation in large agglomerates of the metabolically altered substances. The addition of acid will allow the use of lower processing temperatures, but coagulation of suspended solids will occur nevertheless. Considerable research has been conducted over a period of years to obviate the changes. The vegetables or their juices must be heated at temperatures high enough to inactivate their enzymes during early stages of preparation or the solids must be treated so that they will remain in suspension. The liquid may be separated from the precipitable solid; however, since the flavor and body of so many vegetables depends upon the suspended solids, it is often essential to retain these portions in the beverage. Since the alterations that occur are often oxidative, the development of methods has included those in which maceration and extraction are conducted in the absence of air. The use of sulfur dioxide, ascorbic acid, or the blanketing with inert gas is possible. Other methods are designed to hold the solids in suspension by macerating the tissues to a very finely-divided, purée-like consistency to yield an increased viscosity of the liquid. Thickening agents such as methyl cellulose have been used to increase stability (Tressler and Joslyn 1961; Ball 1954; Eddy 1950).

Vegetables with few exceptions are only slightly acidic; high temperature heat processes are, therefore, required to kill the spores of spore-forming bacteria that may germinate in such vegetable products. Spores of even the most acid-tolerant, spore-forming bacteria are usually unable to germinate when the pH is lower than pH 4.2. A few vegetable juices are sufficiently acid so that they are essentially sterilized by use of low temperature heat processes. Sauerkraut and other fermented juices, rhubarb, and the more acid tomato juices fall in this category. Other juices or blends must be acidified if low temperature processes are to be used. At present, acidification by the addition of organic acids, by blending, and by fermentation seems to present possibilities for retaining the more pleasing character and greater nutritive value.

Juices Prepared from Normally Acid Products

Tomato Juice and Blends.—Compared with other vegetable products, tomatoes have shown a meteoric rise in consumption. Tomato juice, discussed in the previous chapter, is a relatively new beverage. The juice, first prepared in the late 1920's consisted of the clear yellow serum comparable to that often observed in a can of tomatoes. It did not possess the body and character of present day tomato juices. Tomato juice cocktails and blends were developed later to lend variety to the juices. One of the first cocktails was acidified with citric acid and lemon juice and flavored with celery, Worcestershire sauce, sugar, and salt. Another cocktail was flavored with Tabasco sauce. Methods of preparation were similar to that used in producing tomato juice.

Several cocktail-type tomato juice blends containing appreciable amounts of juices from other vegetables have received favorable acceptance for a number of years. Some of these juices lend an almost herb-like character to the tomato juice and the beet and carrot juices added impart a deeper color than tomato juice. One such blend contains juices from tomatoes, carrots, celery, beets, parsley, lettuce, spinach and watercress to which salt and monosodium glutamate are added for flavor and ascorbic acid for fortification. The soluble solids content of about 6.8 to 7.0%, the acidity of 0.6 to 0.7% and the pH of 4.2 to 4.4 are indicative of the high tomato juice content. Spores of spore-forming bacteria, if present, are not likely to germinate in this juice.

Another blend containing juices of tomato, carrot, celery, spinach, parsley, beets, and sweet green peppers is acidified with lemon juice and citric acid, flavored with salt and spice and enriched with vitamin C. The typical tomato juice flavor of this blend is also pleasingly altered by the herb-like flavor of the other juices.

At least two companies have marketed blends of tomato juice and sauerkraut juice. The sauerkraut juice furnishes the salt for flavor and acid for acidification. One of these blends is flavored with caraway seed. The flavor of tomato juice is much more predominant than that of sauerkraut juice. Sauerkraut juice may be added to tomato juice in the home to lend zest to the juice. Care should be exercised in regulating the amount added since it is much more acid and lower in pH and may impart an excess acid flavor.

Another tomato juice blend which has been accepted is a blend with clam juice. This juice is somewhat heavier, of 12.8% soluble solids. Its higher acidity, 0.95% calculated as lactic and yet with a pH of 4.3 indicates its higher buffer content. Tomato juice, clam broth, sugar, salt, spices and artificial color are used.

Naranjilla juice is processed in Central and South America from the juice of the naranjilla fruit. Naranjilla, *Solanum quitoense,* is a close relative of the tomato. It is a native of the Andes and is grown commercially in Costa Rica, Ecuador, Panama, and Colombia. The bright orange fruit that resembles a tomato is covered with short, brittle hairs that are easily rubbed off. Robinson (1963) described the green-colored, very acid juice as heavy-bodied, delightfully flavored, refreshing and suggestive of both apricot and pineapple. Robinson reported 9.4 to 10.8% total solids, 2.0 to 2.7% acid as citric, a pH of 3.14 to 3.16, ascorbic acid of 4.5 to 9.1 mg/100 gm and carotene content of 42 to 91 mcg/gm. Because the juice is so heavy-bodied and acid, it is diluted and sweetened before consumption. This juice has possibilities for blending with other juices for variation and as an acidulant.

Rhubarb Juices and Beverages.—Rhubarb is one of the few vegetable products obtainable in quantities that is sufficiently acid to permit low temperature processing. Rhubarb juice has possibilities in blends for its acidifying ability. Rhubarb juice has been used for making wine. It has been used frequently in preparing various homemade beverages. The demand for rhubarb is seasonal. Two common varieties, Victoria and Strawberry, yield excellent, rich-flavored juices while Ruby and MacDonalds Crimson yield a highly colored juice.

In harvesting rhubarb, the leaves should be cut off as they are high in oxalic acid content. The stalks are washed, then shredded in an apple grinder made of acid-resistant metals, and the shredded rhubarb is pressed in an ordinary rack-and-cloth hydraulic press. A yield of 70 to 80% may be expected. Excess oxalic acid may be removed by the addition of 0.32% calcium carbonate to the juice heated to 180°F and held at this temperature for 30 min to facilitate the formation of large crystals. The juice is cooled, allowed to stand in a cool place to allow settling of calcium oxalate and cellular debris. The juice is racked, filtered, centrifuged if necessary, pasteurized by flashing to 165° to 170°F, canned or bottled hot, inverted for 3 min and cooled, or it may be sweetened to 18° Brix with sugar and frozen. Frozen juice retains its color and flavor better than the canned product. Juice prepared in this manner will be fairly viscous and sharp in flavor and must be sweetened to taste.

An alternate method suggested by Tressler and Pederson (1942) involves mixing the prepared rhubarb with sugar in the ratio of 10 to 1 and freezing in cans. At a later date the rhubarb is thawed and pressed immediately. The resulting juice is more viscous and has a more fruity flavor. This method usually has been successful in obtaining juice from many small fruits. A thick juice resembling tomato juice in viscosity may be made from rhubarb stalks by steam blanching 1 to 2 min and extracting the juice in a hydraulic press using a fine press-cloth with a muslin lining. The viscous juice is sweetened by the addition of sugar to 18° Brix. It may be canned or frozen. When made in this way the juice does not have such sharp flavor even though it still contains the original content of oxalic acid. Because of its viscous property, it is difficult to remove the oxalic acid. It may be removed by heating to 170° to 180°F, adding the necessary calcium carbonate, pouring hot into glass carboys and allowing it to stand until the oxalate crystals have precipitated.

Clarification.—In order to obtain juice in filterable condition regardless of the method of preparation, the juice must be treated with a commercial enzyme preparation. The juice is heated to 120°F, the enzyme preparation is added, at 20 oz to each 100 gal of juice, the juice is held for 3 hr at the above temperature to allow the enzyme to act on the pectin and thereby bring about flocculation of suspended material. The temperature of the juice is then raised to 180°F and about 0.3% calcium carbonate is added while slowly agitating the juice. The juice is cooled, refrigerated for several hours and then filtered through a plate and frame filter press with a small amount of filter aid.

Rhubarb Beverages.—Pleasing rhubarb beverages may be prepared by sweetening and diluting the juice with water in order to reduce the tartness. Depending on the variety and maturity, the juice will have a total acidity, expressed as malic acid, ranging from 1.0 to 1.7%. Such undiluted juices are too harsh to suit the average taste. In preparing a beverage, the juice should be diluted with sufficient water or other juice to reduce the total acidity of the finished beverage to 0.7 to 0.8%. Sufficient cane sugar should be added to bring the total solids content to about 14%. Such a beverage will have a pleasingly tart taste and a pronounced rhubarb flavor. The beverage may be diluted even more to suit individual tastes, and it may be carbonated for those who like the fruity, carbonated character. Rhubarb juice concentrate may be prepared by freeze concentration; when diluted with carbonated water, a pleasing beverage results. Rhubarb juice blends well with most fruit or vegetable juices; however, it must be realized that rhubarb has a pronounced flavor. Rhubarb with apple, rhubarb with cherry, and rhubarb with grape are attractive blends.

TABLE 105

COMPARATIVE BUFFER ACTION OF VEGETABLE JUICES[1]

Vegetable Juice	H-Ion Concn. pH	Cc. of 0.1 N Acid[2] Required per 100 cc. Juice to Change pH to 4.00	3.75
Celery	5.97	56.8	102.0
	6.07	60.3	180.9
	6.05	62.0	116.0
	5.90	37.2	68.0
	6.11	69.0	136.0
Carrot	...	41.6	54.0
	6.44	104.8	...
	6.21	124.1	...
	6.31	108.8	191.4
	6.48	94.0	168.0
	6.02	28.6	46.0
Beans	6.19	113.4	...
Cabbage	6.07	106.0	200.0
Onion	5.50	62.4	134.0
Beet	6.38	66.0	126.0
Beet	6.26	170.8	...
Turnip	5.80	52.0	108.0
Rutabaga	6.07	62.0	108.0
Spinach	6.18	81.6	...
Peas	6.77	177.1	...
Peas	6.65	162.7	...

1 From Tressler, Pederson, and Beattie (1943).
2 Lactic acid of sauerkraut juice expressed as 0.1 N.

Vegetable Juices Acidified by Blending

Acidification of vegetable juices should have for its purpose the offering of a variety of juices with different characters, and retention as far as possible of the typical flavor of the particular vegetable or vegetables used. In the previous section on tomato juice blends, it was stated that the blends offered a variety to the flavor of tomato juice. Although these were acid, i.e., pH 4.2 to 4.4, the acidity very nearly approximates that of average samples of tomato juice. In the practice of acidifying vegetable juices it would seem logical to use sufficient acid to avoid the use of high temperature heat processes. The lower temperature heat process, 180° to 212°F, effects less change in the character of the food and obviously is less expensive and time-consuming. High temperature heat processes are unnecessary for acid juices because the heated spores of spore-forming bacteria are unable to germinate at pH 4.2 or lower. Highly acid juices may be heat-processed at temperatures as low as 160°F, however, vegetable juice blends in the range of pH 3.8 to 4.2 would normally be processed at 180° to 212°F.

Tomato, rhubarb, sauerkraut and other fermented products and citrus, pineapple, and other fruits contain organic acids suitable for acidifying vegetables or their juices. The addition of juices from these acid products will not only lend variety to a blend but in many instances will improve the flavor of the basic vegetable juice. The amount of acid required to affect a given pH will depend upon the buffer content of the vegetables and/or fruit used (Table 105). Packers of juices must be careful to test each batch to make certain that the pH value is 4.2 or lower. If the juice is too sour, the effect can be balanced by the addition of sugar and salt with or without spice.

The processor is faced with the choice and form of acid to be used. Citrus juices, particularly lemon juices, have desirable properties. Acid juices most commonly used for blending with non-acid vegetable juices are citrus, tomato and pineapple (Graham 1940; Marsh 1942; Cruess and Chong 1941) and sauerkraut and rhubarb juices (Tressler and Pederson 1942; Beattie and Pederson 1943; Tressler, Pederson and Beattie 1943). Acidification may be accomplished by the addition of the pure acids. The highly dissociated inorganic acids are more effective than the organic acids (Fig. 103). Similarly, the more highly dissociated organic acids, such as citric and lactic acids, are more effective than acids such as acetic (Marsh 1942; Beattie and Pederson 1943).

Among the pure organic acids, citric, malic, lactic and acetic and among the inorganic acids, phosphoric and hydrochloric are available. By experience, citric and acetic, as in vinegar, are the most commonly used acidifying agents. The type of acid used will exert an influence on the character of the juice, since all acids and vegetables do not blend equally well. Marsh (1942) stated that phosphoric acid was more satisfactory than lactic acid for acidifying carrot juice. Phosphoric acid exerts a buffering effect.

The acid vegetable juices are more satisfactory acidifying agents than pure inorganic or organic acid from the flavor standpoint. Because of their buffering effect they yield a smoother, milder blend than do the pure acids.

Cruess, Thomas and Celmer (1937) carried out extensive studies with preparations of acidified vegetable juices. They concluded that acidified juices, such as carrot juice, processed at 212°F were preferable to non-acidified juices processed at 250°. Good yields of pleasantly flavored asparagus juices were obtained by steam blanching for 3 or 4 min and extracting, acidifying with citric acid and processing at 212°F for 30 min in 8 oz cans or flash heating at 200° to 212°F and filling into containers at that temperature. They concluded that celery juice, because of its pronounced and pleasing flavor had greater possibilities than any of the other vegetable juices studied. Celery blanched in live steam had a better color than fresh celery ground and pressed without blanching. Cruess and Yerman (1937) added to such celery juice 0.5% salt and 0.3% citric acid or enough deterpinated lemon concentrate to give 0.3% citric acid. The product was sufficiently acid, with pH 4.14, to permit processing at 212°F. Cruess and Celmer (1938) concluded that celery juice acidified with 0.4% citric acid was too sour. Cruess and Chong (1941) prepared a pleasing carrot juice adjusted to an acidity of pH 4.05 with orange juice. There is little need to acidify to an acidity of lower than pH 4.20.

A good sauerkraut juice is a very satisfactory acidifying agent and is inexpensive. Surprisingly it does not have an intensive flavor and is readily masked by the flavor of most vegetables. Rhubarb juice, on the other hand, has a pleasant, fruity, but intensive flavor and will mask the flavor of many vegetables. Tressler and Pederson (1942) and Beattie and Pederson (1943) prepared blends of juices from beets, onions, turnips, rutabaga, celery and carrots with sauerkraut juice. They observed that such blends could be reblended with each other and/or with tomato juice to produce pleasing vegetable beverages. Regardless of whether the juice is obtained by comminution or by pressing, following maceration, the acidifying principles are about the same. In general, it is necessary to peel root vegetables to insure removal of any earthy character. Root vegetables are usually more readily peeled after heat treatment. Beet juices are prepared commercially by acidification with organic acid. These find use in soups such borscht. Beet juices can also be produced by fermentation.

Juices from Fermented Vegetables

Fermentation is a very ancient method of preparing and storing food to retain its wholesome characteristics and nutritive values. Fermentation practices antedate recorded history. Although fermented vegetables have been prepared for centuries, it is only during the last half century that the juices of sauerkraut have been prepared commercially. Although some of the fermented vegetable products are relatively unimportant in the United States, they are significant elsewhere. The excess juices from fermented vegetables have been consumed by individuals for centuries. The pink-colored juice obtained in the fermentation of whole heads of red cabbage is used as an appetizer in some sections of Europe. Similarly, the juices from dill and sour pickles are consumed. Naturally fermented beet juices have a dextrinous consistency which could be desirable in certain foods. The vegetable blends fermented in China, Korea, Japan and other countries of the Orient are extremely important adjuncts in the diets of the peoples in these countries. In Korea, the quantity of the blend, kimchi, consumed is second only to rice. Needless to say, the excess juices produced in these fermentations are not discarded but are consumed as juices or blended with other foods. As far as is known juices from fermented vegetables other than sauerkraut have many of the characteristics of sauerkraut.

In 1930, Pederson demonstrated that the sauerkraut fermentation was initiated by the bacterial species, *Leuconostoc mesenteroides*. Since then, this species has been found to be the single important species in initiating the fermentation of many other vegetables, such as whole-head cabbage, mixed vegetables, beets, dill pickles, turnips, mustard leaves, sliced green tomatoes and many other foods (Pederson and Albury 1969). The combination of acids, alcohol, esters and other growth products imparts a unique and desirable flavor to these fermented foods.

THE MANUFACTURE OF SAUERKRAUT

The commercial production of sauerkraut is an important industry in the United States and Europe. New York, Wisconsin, and Ohio are the leading states in the production of sauerkraut. Pederson and Albury (1969) have reviewed the subject of sauerkraut manufacture, presenting a detailed account of methods of preparation, the influence of environmental factors, the nature of the fermentation, nutritive values, and other pertinent information. In their concluding remarks they emphasize that successful preservation of many foods depends upon the acids and other products produced by the lactic acid bacteria during fermentation. These acids restrict or inhibit the growth of the various undesirable organisms capable of spoiling food if allowed to develop. Although the acids and other substances are produced primarily from carbohydrates, concomitant changes occur in other constituents. Nutritive values undergo little change, since well-controlled fermentations produce only minor alterations in caloric values, minerals, and vitamins. Fermentations contribute certain desirable, flavorsome, aromatic, and physical characteristics to many food products. Although these statements were applied to sauerkraut, the same statements apply also to similar products such as the vegetable blends, (Kim and Whang 1959; Orillo *et al.* 1969).

Sauerkraut is the product of a lactic acid bacterial fermentation of cabbage under conditions favoring the production of lactic and acetic acids, alcohol, and carbon dioxide. The usual procedure is as follows: when the cabbage is mature and in condition for cutting, it is transported by conveyor to a coring machine. This machine cuts the core by means of a reversible spiral drill that allows the finely cut core to remain in the head. The cored cabbage passes to an automatic trimmer and washer and/or to a trimming table where the outer leaves and defective spots are removed. The heads then pass directly to the slicing machines where they are shredded. The shreds are conveyed to vats by belt lines or carts. As the freshly cut cabbage is distributed in the vat, 2.25% of salt is mixed with it.

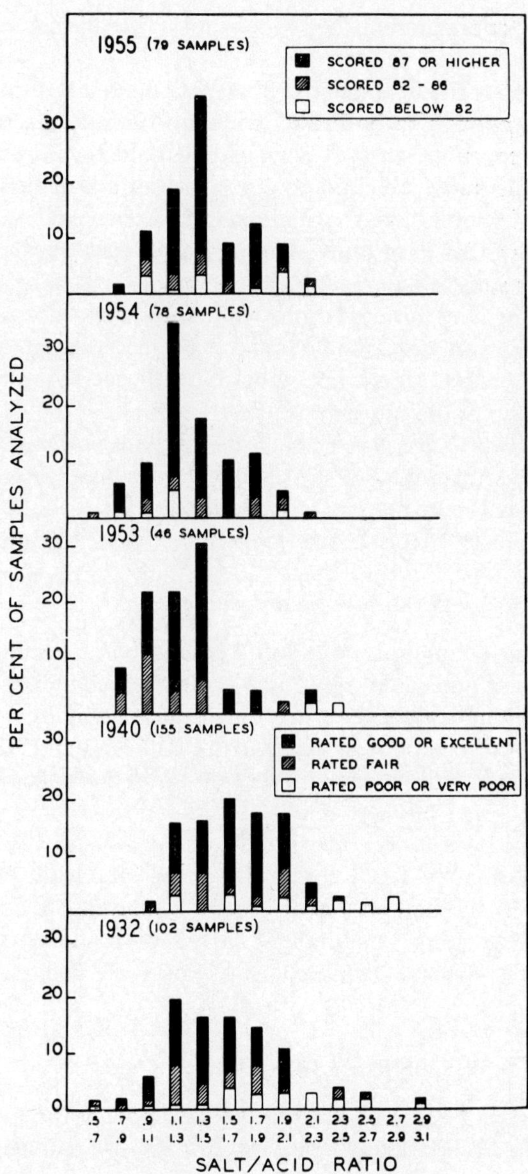

Fig. 103. Relation of Salt/Acid Ratio to the Quality of Canned Sauerkraut

The amount and distribution of salt are important factors in determining the quality of the kraut. If much more than 2.5% of salt is present, the fermentation will be retarded and undesirable changes may take place; if less than 1.7% salt is present the kraut is apt to be soft and of poor texture (Fig. 103).

When the vat is filled, the cut cabbage is covered with a plastic cover which is large enough to be brought up the sides of the vat. Water is placed in the cover to serve as a weight to hold the shredded cabbage down so that the juice will rise and cover the surface of the kraut. If the temperature of the cabbage is maintained between 60° and 75°F, the acidity will rise to 1.5% or above within 3 or 4 weeks, indicating that the fermentation is substantially complete.

During salting and fermentation, water and nutrients are withdrawn from the cabbage and unless some liquid is drained there may be an excess of 20 barrels or more sauerkraut juice that are not required in canning. This is the source of the sauerkraut juice.

Since sauerkraut juice is so acid, microorganisms are killed readily. Processing temperatures of 160° to 165°F are high enough to kill all organisms present. In fact, it is undesirable to use high temperatures since too much heat will effect the flavor and color of the juice.

Composition of Sauerkraut and Sauerkraut Juice

Aside from the content of indigestible crude fiber in kraut, the composition of sauerkraut and sauerkraut juice is approximately the same (Table 106). Cabbage and sauerkraut are much more complex. A more complete discussion of components is given by Pederson and Albury (1969).

Good sauerkraut will have an acidity of 1.5 to 2.0% in the vat. Juice containing more than 1.4% of acid is considered too sour for consumption as a beverage. Because of this, the kraut juice is usually diluted with water to approximately 1.4% acidity before it is canned. However, the balance between salt and acid is of greater importance than is the actual per cent of acid. Juice containing 1.4% acid should never have more than 2.0% salt (Pederson 1946; Pederson *et al.* 1956; Pederson and Albury 1969).

The Preservation of Sauerkraut Juice

Before sauerkraut is removed from the vat, most of the juice is drained or pumped out. When kraut is repacked in small containers for sale as fresh kraut and also when the kraut is canned, a considerable proportion of the juice may be used. Even so, much is not utilized unless it is bottled or canned for sale as a beverage. The clear brine from the bottom of the vat will invariably be lower in acid and higher in salt than the brine that is in direct contact with the solid kraut. This clear brine is less satisfactory in flavor as well as in salt-acid balance than the cloudier juice. The difference is much more marked when juice is marketed as a bottled and refrigerated product rather than a processed product.

The procedure usually followed in canning sauerkraut juice is very simple involving no processing other than exhausting or flash pasteurizing. Surplus juice from several vats is blended in a tank, ordinarily giving a blend containing from 1.5 to 1.6% lactic acid and less than 2.25% salt. The blended juice is strained through a fine screen and then run by gravity to a pasteurizer and a filler. The cans, filled to within one-half inch of the top, are slowly conveyed through a steam chamber. This exhaust heats juice packed in No. $2^1/_2$ cans in 4 min, 30 sec to 5 min, up to 165° to 170°F. As the cans are conveyed to the closing machine, they pass under streams of hot water which fill the cans almost completely. The addition

TABLE 106

COMPOSITION OF KRAUT AND KRAUT JUICE

Nutrient	Kraut, %	Kraut Juice, %
Sugar	0.78	0.69
Titrable acid	1.48	1.67
Acetic acid	0.40	0.45
Lactic acid	1.37	1.45
Ethyl alcohol	0.48	0.50
Calcium	0.042	0.043
Phosphorus	0.027	0.025

Source: Peterson *et al.* (1925).

of the hot water dilutes the juice and consequently reduces its salt and acidity. By varying the proportion of hot water added, it is a simple matter to produce a canned juice of uniform acidity. The closed cans are rolled in a continuous cooler, where the cans are cooled to 100°F with water. Sauerkraut juice is ordinarily packed in tin cans, although a small amount is packed in glass.

Unfortunately, because the carbon dioxide dissolved in the juice is not always expelled by these methods of processing, the vacuum is often reduced during storage. Deaeration methods might well be used to good advantage to remove the carbon dioxide from canned juices.

Quality of the Pasteurized Juice

Juice drawn from the kraut, shortly after fermentation is completed, is highly charged with carbon dioxide, is high in vitamin C, and has a pleasing tangy taste acceptable to many individuals. The retention of vitamin C in sauerkraut may be due to the high acidity and the fact that ascorbic acid oxidase may be destroyed in the acid product, as postulated by Schmidt-Nielson and Spilling (1942).

Juice drawn directly from the kraut vats is more pleasing to the taste than pasteurized juice, probably because the exhausting process drives off a large proportion of the carbon dioxide content of the juice, making it rather flat to the taste. Unheated juice retains its carbon dioxide and fresh flavor very well for several months if held in a refrigerator. A small amount is handled this way. In view of the fine flavor of the refrigerated product it is surprising that more sauerkraut juice is not kept under refrigeration and sold without pasteurization.

Pasteurized juice packed in tin cans keeps its flavor and appearance much better than the bottled product. Since the action of light is one cause of the rapid deterioration of the bottled product, Carpenter (1933) has suggested that the juice should be packed in green bottles.

Sauerkraut and other fermented vegetable substance have been known to provide certain mild laxative properties; both sauerkraut and its juice have been used as purgatives. The laxative effect was attributed at first to the combination of acid and salt. Sauerkraut stimulates the peptic glands. Recent studies, cited by Pederson and Albury (1969) have shown that the laxative properties of sauerkraut juice is due to its choline esters, acetylcholine and lactylcholine. Acetylcholine also known as parasympathin is of significance in nerve activity. These esters are formed during fermentation by the activity of lactic acid bacteria in several fermenting vegetables. One theory to explain sauerkraut's bactericidal activity for pathogenic bacteria was the increased peristalsis caused by acetylcholine.

Another characteristic of cabbage and sauerkraut as reviewed by Pederson and Albury may be important. European researchers have studied the goitrogenic properties of cabbage. They have noted that vegetables of the cabbage family are the chief sources of exogenous thiocyanate and noted correlation between thiocyanate content of foods and goitrogenic effect. In one study a considerably lower content of polyphenols was found in white cabbage than in winter cabbage. White cabbage is used in making sauerkraut. In another study it was found that much of the goitrogenic substance was destroyed during fermentation.

Possibilities of Other Fermented Vegetable Juices

The possibilities of producing vegetable juices from many other vegetables in a manner similar to that used for sauerkraut juice are obvious. The general methods described can be adapted readily to other vegetables. In the Orient, the excess juices obtained from fermented vegetable blends are consumed in one form or another. Excess juices from fermentation of pickles, particularly dill pickles, are often consumed as such or blended with other foods. Fermented beet juices are consumed by many Europeans as in borscht. The juices after fermentation are readily separated from the solid fibrous material by draining and pressing to yield a product quite free from suspended solids. Furthermore, except for crude fiber, the flavor and chemical composition of the juice will be approximately the same as that of the solid portions. The more or less solid vegetable offers a protective anaerobic condition toward the readily oxidizable ingredients, particularly ascorbic acid. From a nutritional standpoint therefore, the fermented product provides most of the nutritional qualities of the fresh vegetable. In addition, the bactericidal properties of fermented vegetable toward pathogenic organisms, and the increased stimulation of peristalsis due to the acetylcholine produced by the fermentation process, aids in normalizing the intestinal flora.

Hohl and Cruess (1940) have suggested the preparation of a fermented product from lettuce. Hsio-Hui Chao (1949) described the fermentation of paw-tsay prepared from a mixture of vegetables, usually turnip, red pepper, cowpea, and others. When properly prepared, sliced and salted beets, turnips, chard, celery, tomatoes and other vegetables will undergo fermentation. Mixtures of these and other vegetables may provide that ideal balance of sugars, proteins, minerals and other ingredients so common to cabbage and which make cabbage such an ideal vegetable in providing a good fermentation. Since the product will naturally be highly acidic it can be useful in acidifying juices prepared from fresh vegetables and therefore will need only a low temperature process.

Further exploration is needed concerning possible preparation and sale of vegetable juices prepared from mixtures of fresh and fermented material and which offer a highly nutritious attractive beverage.

NONACID VEGETABLE JUICES

Nonacid vegetable juices are difficult to extract from vegetable tissue and to preserve without undesirable changes occurring in flavor and appearance. The flavor characteristics so desirable in fresh vegetables are difficult to retain in the processed product. Flavor characteristics are resident to a considerable degree in the suspended solids. Most vegetable juices contain materials in colloidal suspension that are precipitated at temperatures of 160°F or above. Often the addition of acid promotes the coagulation of suspended materials. The high temperature process of 250°F required for sterilizing neutral or slightly acidic juices causes coagulation, flocculation, and ultimately precipitation in large agglomerates. Unless preheated to inactivate enzymes when the vegetable is macerated, the enzymes released act upon the protoplasmic liquid, causing rapid metabolic changes that are unnatural to undamaged tissue.

The neutral or slightly acidic vegetable juices must be heated at high temperatures in order to inactivate enzymes and to kill the microorganisms, thereby eliminating any danger of spoilage. Pure canned or bottled carrot, spinach, lettuce, celery, asparagus, turnip, and other vegetable juices of only slight acidity must be heated in a pressure sterilizer at 240° to 250°F, in order to destroy the spores of the more heat-resistant organisms. When heated at this temperature, they sometimes acquire to some extent the typical, disagreeable taste of scorched or overcooked vegetables. Several suggestions have been presented in the past to overcome these undesirable changes. The manufacturers of baby foods, have been successful in processing a number of vegetable purées without imparting the typical, disagreeable taste of scorched or overcooked vegetables.

Carrot, Celery, Spinach, Asparagus, Beet and Cabbage Juices

In the late thirties and early forties, considerable interest was developed in the possibilities of preparation of vegetable juices. This may have been due to the general acceptance of tomato juice and to the acceptance of raw vegetable juices. Beginning in the early forties, the studies of Cheney and coworkers on the influence of cabbage juice on peptic ulcers, the several studies that demonstrated the bactericidal activity of fresh vegetable juice, and the general observations that the vegetables were valuable nutritionally, all may have influenced the acceptance of raw vegetable juices. Raw vegetable juices may be prepared by macerating the tissues in one of the standard-type mills. The coarse materials may be separated from the juice by screening or pressing; the juices, however, undergo undesirable changes in flavor and appearance unless they are chilled or frozen immediately after extraction. Rapid freezing techniques permit the latter, and when so frozen, the juices retain their desirable raw vegetable characteristics. Heat processing inactivates enzymes and kills microorganisms; however, changes in character occur.

Certain substances present in cabbage contain certain chemical identities that are valuable because they inhibit growth and even cause death of certain undesirable gram-negative bacteria (Pederson and Albury 1969). Such substances are present in other raw vegetables. Some excellent vegetable blends have been prepared with tomato juice as the base. Only a few juices have been processed commercially.

One pleasing, neutral carrot juice is being marketed and contains approximately 10% soluble solids, with a titrable acidity of about 0.15% and a pH of 6.1. The studies of Cruess *et al.* (1937), Lachele (1938), Turner (1939), Graham (1949), Cruess and Chong (1941), Marsh (1942), Tressler and Pederson (1942), Beattie and Pederson (1943), Tressler *et al.* (1943), Cruess (1944), Lee *et al.* (1948), Joslyn and Sano (1956), Ball

(1954) and others may have markedly affected the development of this industry (Tressler and Joslyn 1961).

A carrot juice resembling orange juice in color and consistency has been prepared by the following procedure: The washed and trimmed vegetables are comminuted in a mill. The juice is given a preliminary heat treatment at 180°F to coagulate all materials unstable to heat. The mixture is then homogenized to prevent coagulation of the insoluble material during any further heat treatment. The juice is preheated to 160°F, filled into cans and processed at 250°F for 30 min. The addition of 0.33% of salt will bring out the carrot flavor. An acceptable carrot juice may also be prepared by pressing in a hydraulic press carrots which have been blanched 15 min in boiling water. The product is deep orange in color. During blanching some soluble solids are dissolved in the blanch water. A juice may also be obtained from carrots by milling and pressing in a hydraulic press, but the yield and flavor are unsatisfactory. A better-flavored juice is obtained from mature carrots rather than from young carrots. The bitter character associated with stem and skin is lessened by peeling before milling or heating.

Excellent cabbage juice also may be obtained by milling, followed by pressing in a hydraulic press but the juice obtained must then be chilled or frozen immediately to avoid changes in flavor and color and loss of ascorbic acid. This is the type of juice that Cheney used in the fifties for vitamin U therapy of peptic ulcer (Pederson and Albury 1969).

Celery juices have a pleasing, almost herb-like flavor. Good yields of juice may be obtained by steam-blanching for 3 min, prior to crushing and pressing the vegetables in a hydraulic press. After straining the juice, it is filled into cans, exhausted for 6 min and processed at 240°F for 21 min or 250°F. To prevent the coagulation of suspended solids, it has been recommended that the juice be centrifuged prior to filling into cans. The necessity of rapid processing to prevent development of bitter flavors is obvious for a juice so delicately flavored as that from celery.

Juice prepared from spinach has been described as unattractive in appearance but possessing a pleasing flavor. The spinach after trimming and washing is steam-blanched for 3 min, then passed through a juicer to prepare a purée. Since the green color, the chlorophyll, is not soluble in water or in the juice, the leaves must be ground to a fine purée. Since the purée is fairly thick, it may be diluted with a suitable amount of clear juice obtained by pressing the milled product in a hydraulic press. The purée and juice should be put through a tomato finisher. Salt, at the level of 0.5 to 1.0% will improve the flavor. Spinach juice coagulates quickly at 250°F as do juices from many other vegetables. The color turns to the usual gray-green of retorted spinach. Less change in character is obtained when the juices are acidified to pH 4.2 and then flash-heated and bottled at 200° to 212°F.

The same principles may be applied to other vegetables. Pleasing juices may be obtained from root vegetables in a manner similar to that used for carrot juices and juices from the leafy vegetables by methods similar to those used for celery and spinach. Pleasing juices have been prepared from both beets and turnips; however, the turnips are prone to develop very strong flavors. Juices from either beets or turnips must be processed at 250°F for 30 min or at 200° to 212°F if acidified.

Asparagus juice may be used as an ingredient of mixed vegetables. Although it has a pleasant flavor, it possesses the well known odor of asparagus. A recommended procedure is to steam-blanch the washed stalks on a wire screen for 3 or 4 min and extract the juice using a mill. The canned juice should be flavored with 0.75% salt and processed at 240°F for 20 min. Asparagus, like turnips and rutabagas, develops a bitter flavor if the product is not handled rapidly, it is, therefore, essential to express the juice soon after the asparagus is gathered. Juice from the tips is richer in flavor and less bitter than that from the butts.

Juices from the highly flavored vegetables, such as onions and garlic, find an outlet in small amounts in other food preparations. Cruess (1944) described methods for preparing onion and garlic juice extracts and preserving them in high vinegar and salt concentrations. Lee *et al.* (1948) concentrated onion juice by freezing concentration, obtaining a satisfactory, stable concentrate.

Joslyn and Sano (1956) ascribed the source of the flavoring constituent of garlic to its flavorless precursor, alliin, an unsaturated sulfur-containing amino acid, resulting from the action of the enzyme, alliinase. The characteristic flavor of cabbage and closely related vegetables is usually associated with the sulfur-containing constituents. Pederson and Albury (1969) briefly reviewed the work of Masters and McCance, Masters and Garbutt, McRorie *et al.*, Dateo *et al.* and others who have identified the sulfur glucoside, its hydrolysis products, and the activity of the enzymes that cause the alterations.

Soybean Milk

The first recorded history of the soybean plant in China, according to Lo (1964) was written in Sheng Nan's "Materia Medica" in 2838 B.C. Piper and Morse (1923) stated that Whai Nain Tse introduced soymilk to China more than 2,000 years ago. Soybean milk is consumed in substantial amounts in China, Hongkong, Singapore, Thailand, and Taiwan. In Taiwan, the farmers' cooperative associations prepare soymilk for their members.

In China, soybeans are soaked in cold water until hydrated, then they are ground with water in a stone mill to a fine slurry. This is filtered to remove the large insoluble particles and the milk is then boiled to stabilize the flavor. The product has been an important source of protein in the diet of millions of Orientals for centuries. The dispersion in water also contains other nutritive substances in solution or suspension.

The utilization of soybean milk is still so new that there are many unsolved problems involved in its production and use. These concern inhibiting the development of the so-called "beany" flavor and obtaining a milk with the maximum nutritive value. Hackler *et al.* (1963) reported that the ingredients extracted in the soak water failed to support the growth of rats and that the insoluble residue contained the highest quality of protein. This suggested the development of methods for extracting more of the nutritionally valuable protein. Hand *et al.* (1964) described a method for manufacturing soymilk that involved dehulling and grinding steam-dried soybeans and slurrying to produce a soymilk. The resulting suspension contained 90% of the soybean. Mustakas and Mayberry (1964) developed another process by which soybean flakes are fed into an extruder and forced through an orifice under high-pressure, high-temperature conditions. The bean mixture emerges puffed and dried and can be ground to a fine powder which is slurried to yield soymilk. It was reported in Lo *et al.* (1968A) that soymilk could be prepared from dry soybeans by grinding them in boiling water. By elimination of the hydration step, during which enzymatic changes resulted in the development of oxidative changes, a milk of superior flavor characteristics was obtained.

Development of off-flavors was attributed to the enzymatic oxidation of fat. Wilkins, Mattick and Hand (1967) reported that a grinding temperature of 176°F was required to produce a soymilk relatively free of oxidized and rancid flavors. Lo *et al.* (1968B) observed that extraction temperatures above 185°F resulted in substantial decreases in solids. The highest yields were obtained at 131° to 149°F with nonsoaked beans, but there was little difference in extraction yields from presoaked beans at temperatures from 131° to 174°F. Lo *et al.* (1968B) noted that as the soaking time for soybeans was increased, larger quantities of water-soluble solids leached into the soak water where they were lost. Hackler *et al.* (1965) in studying the nutritive value of soymilk protein, observed that cooking at 199.4°F for 1 to 6 hr had no adverse effect on protein efficiency, growth, or available lysine. A definite decline in protein efficiency occurred when the soymilk was heated for 32 min at 249.8°F.

A basic improved process designed to inactivate enzymes consists of washing the beans, soaking for 4 to 6 hr in a 0.1% sodium hydroxide solution, draining, rinsing, grinding in 10 times the weight of water heated to

170° to 212°F, filtering the slurry and sterilizing at 250°F for 12 min. Using soymilks prepared in this way, Steinkraus *et al.* (1968) developed flavor blends with sugar, coconut milk, vanilla and chocolate that were acceptable to Filipino school children. Flavorings used by processors in the Orient are industrial secrets but include among others, malt flavors, cow's milk and those mentioned above. Studies are underway to utilize other legumes such as ming beans in preparation of similar types of beverages.

BIBLIOGRAPHY

BALL, C. O. 1954. Preparation of a juice product from fruit and vegetables containing insoluble solids in suspension. U.S. Pat. 2,696,440. Dec. 7.

BEATTIE, H. G., and PEDERSON, C. S. 1943. Acidified vegetable juice blends. Food Research *8*, 45–53.

CARPENTER, D. C. 1933. Effect of light on bottled juices. Apple and kraut juices. Ind. Eng. Chem. *25*, 932–934.

CHAO, H. H. 1949. Microbiology of Paw Tsay. I. Lactobacilli and lactic acid fermentation. Food Research *14*, 405–412.

CRUESS, W. V. 1944. Experiments in garlic and onion extracts. Fruit Products J. *23*, 305–313.

CRUESS, W. V., and CELMER, R. 1938. Experiments on canning vegetable juices. Western Canner Packer *30*, No. 5, 43.

CRUESS, W. V., and CHONG, G. N. 1941. Orange-carrot juice, a new canned beverage. Canner *93*, No. 26, 11.

CRUESS, W. V., THOMAS, W. B., and CELMER, R. 1937. Experiments in canning vegetable juices. Canner *85*, No. 3, 9–10.

CRUESS, W. V., and YERMAN, F. 1937. Notes on celery juice. Fruit Products J. *17*, 9.

EDDY, C. W. 1950. Drying fruit and vegetable materials containing added methyl cellulose. U.S. Pat. 2,496,278. Feb. 7.

GRAHAM, W. E. 1940. Canning of the newer vegetable juices. Canning Age *21*, No. 12, 522–523.

HACKLER, L. R., HAND, D. B., STEINKRAUS, K. H., and VAN BUREN, J. P. 1963. A comparison of the nutritional value of protein from several soybean fractions. J. Nutr. *80*, No. 2, 205–210.

HACKLER, L. R., VAN BUREN, J. P., STEINKRAUS, K. H., EL RAWI, I., and HAND, D. B. 1965. Effect of heat treatment on nutritive value of soymilk protein fed to weanling rats. J. Food Sci. *30*, No. 4, 723–728.

HAND, D. B., STEINKRAUS, K. H., VAN BUREN, J. P., HACKLER, L. R., EL RAWI, I., and PALLESON, H. R. 1964. Pilot-plant studies on soymilk. Food Technol. *18*, No. 12, 139–142.

HOHL, L. A., and CRUESS, W. V. 1940. Lettuce kraut, an investigation of changes occurring in fermentation of lettuce. Proc. Inst. Food Technologists *1940*, 159–166.

JOSLYN, M. A., and SANO, T. 1956. Green pigment in garlic tissue. Food Research *21*, 170–183.

KIM, HO-SIK, and WHANG, KYN-CHAN. 1959. Microbiological studies of kimchis. Part 1. Isolation and identification of anaerobic bacteria. Bull. Scientific Research Inst. Korea *4*, 56.

LACHELE, C. E. 1938. Problems in canning fruit and vegetable juices. Canner *86*, No. 12, Part II, 87–88.

LEE, F. A., BEATTIE, H. G., and PEDERSON, C. S. 1948. Onion juice concentrate prepared by freezing concentration. Fruit Products J. *27*, 141, 153.

LEE, C. Y., and DOWNING, D. L. 1970. The production of beet juice, 1970. Unpublished manuscript.

LO, K. S. 1964. Pioneering soymilk in Southeast Asia. Soybean Dig. *24*, No. 7, 18–20.

LO, W. Y., STEINKRAUS, K. H., HAND, D. B., WILKINS, W. F., and HACKLER, L. L. 1968A. Yields of extracted solids as affected by temperature of water of various pretreatments of beans. Food Technol. *22*, No. 10, 1322 ff.

LO, W. Y., STEINKRAUS, K. H., HAND, D. B., HACKLER, L. R., and WILKINS, W. F. 1968B. Soaking soybeans before extraction as it affects chemical composition and yield of soymilk. Food Technol. *22*, No. 9, 1188–1190.

MARSH, G. L. 1942. Vegetable juices—1942 model. Canner *95*, No. 9, 7–8, 12–13, 95, No. 10, Part II, 15–16.

MUSTAKAS, G. C., and MAYBERRY, D. H. 1964. Simplified full-fat soy-flour process. Food Eng. *36*, No. 10, 52.

ORILLO, C. A., SISON, E. C., LUIS, M., and PEDERSON, C. S. 1969. The fermentation of vegetable blends. Appl. Microbiol. *17*, No. 1, 10–13.

PEDERSON, C. S. 1946. Improving methods for salting sauerkraut. Food Packer *27*, No. 10, 53–57.

PEDERSON, C. S., and ALBURY, M. N. 1969. The sauerkraut fermentation. N. Y. State Agr. Expt. Sta. Bull. *824*.

PEDERSON, C. S., ALBURY, M. N., and ROBINSON, W. B. 1956. Effect of salt-acid ratio on quality of sauerkraut. Food Packer *37*, No. 7, 28, 39; No. 8, 26.

PETERSON, W. H., FRED, E. B., and VILJOEN, J. A. 1925. Variations in the chemical composition of cabbage and sauerkraut. Canner *61*, No. 4, 19–21.

PIPER, C. V., and MORSE, W. S. 1923. The Soybean. McGraw-Hill Book Co., New York.

ROBINSON, W. B. 1963. Juice from the tomato's Latin American cousin, *Solanum quitoense*. N.Y. State Agr. Expt. Sta. Farm Research.

SCHMIDT-NIELSON, S., and SPILLING, G. 1942. Ascorbinase action of certain root vegetables. Kgl. Norske Viderskaab Selskab Forh. *15*, 49–52.

STEINKRAUS, K. H., DAVID, L. T., RAMOS, L. J., and BANZON, J. 1968. Development of flavored soymilks and soy-coconut milks for the Philippine market. Philippine Agriculturist. *52*, No. 5, 268–276.

TRESSLER, D. K., and JOSLYN, M. A. (Editors). 1961. Fruit and Vegetable Juice Processing Technology, 1st Edition. Avi Publishing Co., Westport, Conn.

TRESSLER, D. K., and PEDERSON, C. S. 1942. Home preparation and preservation of fruit and vegetable juices. N.Y. State Agr. Sta. Circ. *194*.

TRESSLER, D. K., PEDERSON, C. S., and BEATTIE, H. G. 1943. Fruit and vegetable juice preparation and preservation. Ind. Eng. Chem. *35*, 96–100.

TURNER, E. L. 1939. Vegetable juices winning place in modern diet. Canner *88*, No. 5, 39–40.

WILKINS, W. F., MATTICK, L. R., and HAND, D. B. 1967. Effect of processing method on oxidation of flavors of soybean milk. Food Technol. *21*, 86–89.

Index